BEYOND HUMAN RIGHTS

A paradigm change is occurring in the course of which human beings are becoming the primary international legal persons. In numerous areas of public international law, substantive rights and obligations of individuals arguably flow directly from international law. The novel legal status of humans in international law is now captured with a concept borrowed from constitutional doctrine: international rights of the person, as opposed to international law protecting persons. Combining doctrinal analysis with current practice, this book is the most comprehensive contemporary analysis of the legal status of the individual. *Beyond Human Rights*, previously published in German and now revised by the author in this English edition, not only deals with the individual in international humanitarian law, international criminal law, and international investment law, but it also covers fields such as consular law, environmental law, protection of individuals against acts of violence and natural disasters, refugee law, and labour law.

ANNE PETERS is Director at the Max Planck Institute for Comparative Public Law and International Law Heidelberg (Germany), and a professor at the Universities of Heidelberg, Freie Universität Berlin, and Basel (Switzerland). She has been a member of the European Commission for Democracy through Law (Venice Commission) in respect of Germany (2011–2015) and served as the President of the European Society of International Law (2010–2012). Her current research interests relate to public international law, including its history, global animal law, global governance and global constitutionalism, and the status of humans in international law.

CAMBRIDGE STUDIES IN INTERNATIONAL AND COMPARATIVE LAW

Established in 1946, this series produces high-quality, reflective, and innovative scholarship in the field of public international law. It publishes works on international law that are of a theoretical, historical, cross-disciplinary, or doctrinal nature. The series also welcomes books providing insights into private international law, comparative law, and transnational studies which inform international legal thought and practice more generally.

The series seeks to publish views from diverse legal traditions and perspectives, as well as of any geographical origin. In this respect, it invites studies offering regional perspectives on core problématiques of international law, and in the same vein, it appreciates contrasts and debates between diverging approaches. Accordingly, books offering new or less orthodox perspectives are very much welcome. Works of a generalist character are greatly valued, and the series is also open to studies on specific areas, institutions, or problems. Translations of the most outstanding works published in other languages are also considered.

After 70 years, Cambridge Studies in International and Comparative Law remains the standard-setter for international legal scholarship and will continue to define the discipline as it evolves in the years to come.

A list of books in the series can be found at the end of this volume.

BEYOND HUMAN RIGHTS

The Legal Status of the Individual in International Law

ANNE PETERS

Max Planck Institute for Comparative Public Law and International Law Heidelberg, Germany

TRANSLATED BY JONATHAN HUSTON

Revised and updated by the author

CAMBRIDGE
UNIVERSITY PRESS

CAMBRIDGE
UNIVERSITY PRESS

University Printing House, Cambridge CB2 8BS, United Kingdom

Cambridge University Press is part of the University of Cambridge.

It furthers the University's mission by disseminating knowledge in the pursuit of education, learning, and research at the highest international levels of excellence.

www.cambridge.org
Information on this title: www.cambridge.org/9781107164307

Previously published in German by Mohr Siebeck, 2014.

First published in English 2016

A catalogue record for this publication is available from the British Library.

Library of Congress Cataloging-in-Publication Data
Peters, Anne, 1964– author.
Beyond human rights : the legal status of the individual in international law / Anne Peters.
Cambridge [UK] ; New York : Cambridge University Press, 2016. |
Series: Cambridge studies in international and comparative law ; 126
LCCN 2016028961 | ISBN 9781107164307 (hardback)
LCSH: Human rights. | Civil rights. | BISAC: LAW / International.
LCC K3240 .P48 2016 | DDC 341.4/8–dc23
LC record available at https://lccn.loc.gov/2016028961

ISBN 978-1-107-16430-7 Hardback

CONTENTS

PREFACE TO THE GERMAN EDITION OF 2014

The topic of this book has concerned me for more than ten years. In December 2000, I held my trial lecture in Basel on the *LaGrand* case, which had not yet been decided by the International Court of Justice. I delivered my inaugural lecture – entitled "The Rise of the Individual in International Law" – in November 2002, which was attended by friends, colleagues, and supporters (not least of all Jost Delbrück and his wife Gesa). I have learned quite a bit more since then. But this is not the only reason I am happy that I never published that inaugural lecture. Far more important is that over the course of the past decade, the international legal position of the individual has become dramatically stronger. Intensive judicial and codification activity has set out and determined more and more individual rights and duties. This phenomenon has not only quantitative but also qualitative significance. A paradigm shift, which has been called the humanization of international law, has taken place. The basic thesis of this book – namely that the individual is an original (and not only a derivative) subject of international law and the owner of international individual rights – aims to give this topos of humanization a doctrinal and empirical legal foundation.

Chapters 1–3 and 17 began with the study "Das subjektive internationale Recht", which was published in *Jahrbuch des öffentlichen Rechts der Gegenwart* (59 (2011), 411–456); however, I have substantially further developed and modified my findings. I would like to thank the publisher for the kind permission to reuse these parts. Shorter remarks on the international legal position of the individual as the most important member of the international constitutional community can be found in my Chapter 5 of *The Constitutionalization of International Law* (Oxford: Oxford University Press 2009 (rev. ed. 2011), 157–179), the book being co-authored with Jan Klabbers and Geir Ulfstein. Sections from a preliminary version of Chapter 11 have been included in an article I wrote together with my Basel colleague, Sabine Gless

(Verwertungsverbot bei Verletzung der Pflicht zur Belehrung nach Art. 36 WÜK? *Der Strafverteidiger* 31 (2011), 369–377).

Generations of research assistants, first and foremost Liliane Probst, retrieved the literature and documents for this study. For special research and constructive criticism of my drafts, I would like to thank Thore Neumann and Simone Peter. Ralf Alleweldt, Sigrid Boysen, Tillmann Rudolf Braun, Oliver Dörr, Sabine Gless, Tatjana Hörnle, Markus Krajewski, Christoph Schreuer, and Antje von Ungern-Sternberg critically reviewed parts of the manuscript and provided valuable feedback. Birgit Bürgy, Henriette Beisel-Welti, and Margit Dagli helped proofread. Jannika Jahn compiled the Index and Table of Cases. The intellectual and elegant surroundings of the Berlin Institute for Advanced Study offered the perfect home for finalizing the book. Only thanks to the freedom it offered from all everyday concerns, teaching, and university administration – and not least of all with the help of the phenomenal library service – was I at last able to complete this manuscript. Finally, I would like to thank the publishers of *Jus Internationale et Europaeum*, Thilo Marauhn and Christian Walter, for including me in their publication series. The help I received from my assistant Claudia Jeker is so wide-ranging and important that a simple thank you does not suffice.

I dedicate this book to Heiner, Charlotte, and Johannes.

PREFACE TO THE ENGLISH EDITION

Since the finalization of the German edition in 2013, the international political and legal system has been changing. The trend of "humanization" of international law (Chapter 1) may have slowed down or stopped, while State sovereignty may have become more important again. This may have to do with the recognition that strong and well-functioning States are needed to protect human rights, that the basic "Westphalian" principles such as territorial integrity and the prohibition on the use of force have been violated and thus need to be re-emphasized, and that non-Western States and cultures which have their own views on the meaning of human rights are in economic and political terms on the rise.

For the English edition, I tried to accommodate these changes and challenges, notably in Chapters 1 and 17. At other places, I clarified some passages and inserted new literature and case law. In particular, I thoroughly revised Chapter 8 on the responsibility to protect, and on protection of persons in the event of disaster in order to accommodate the final articles of the ILC on the latter topic, and a certain sobering about R2P. I also quite intensely revised Chapter 10 on rights and duties of investors so as to reflect the rising concern about the imbalance of the regime. In Chapter 14 on human rights and other rights, I was able to refine my thoughts on refugee rights and on labour rights. I added a section on the postmodern critique of rights in Chapter 17. These revisions not only seek to incorporate the current evolution of the relevant law, but are also owed to reviewers' comments on my English draft manuscript, to important comments by Giulio Bartolini and Tommaso Natoli on Chapter 8, and to lucid observations by Evelyne Lagrange, Julie Maupin, Dalia Palombo, and the participants of my Max Planck research seminar on Chapter 10. I have further benefited from comments by Alessandro Bufalini on reparations in Chapter 6, by John Quigley on consular protection in Chapter 11, by Franz Ebert on labour rights in Chapter 14, and by James Hathaway on refugee rights in the same Chapter.

Thanks to generous funding of the Max Planck Society I was able to recruit a brilliant translator, Dr Jonathan Huston. It proved to be a challenge to find the adequate expressions for doctrinal constructs originating from German legal doctrine and theory. Most of them have to some extent been used in international law, but often mainly by international lawyers with a German basic legal education. Of course, this made me reconsider the usefulness of such concepts for international law. And although the German origins of my legal training will probably remain visible to readers, I am confident that – in a joint enterprise with the translator – I have managed to communicate the ideas to an international audience. This endeavour then is, hopefully, an example for the potential enrichment of international legal scholarship through the hybridization of national background traditions and understandings. In this context, I would like to thank my student research assistants for their diligent work, notably for checking the English translations or English original versions of books quoted.

ABBREVIATIONS

ABGB	General Civil Code (Austria)
ACHR	American Convention on Human Rights
AIDI	*Annuaire de l'Institut de Droit International*
AJIL	*American Journal of International Law*
AöR	*Archiv des öffentlichen Rechts*
AP	Additional Protocol
ArbGG	Labour Court Act (Arbeitsgerichtsgesetz, Germany)
ARIEL	*Austrian Review of International and European Law*
ATCA	Alien Tort Claims Act
AVR	*Archiv des Völkerrechts*
BBl.	Federal Gazette (Bundesblatt, Switzerland)
BGB	Civil Code (Bürgerliches Gesetzbuch, Germany)
BGE	Decisions of the Federal Supreme Court (Bundesgerichtsentscheide, Switzerland)
BGH	Federal Court of Justice (Bundesgerichtshof, Germany)
BGHSt	Decisions of the Federal Court of Justice in Criminal Matters (Entscheidungen des Bundesgerichtshofs in Strafsachen, Germany)
BGHZ	Decisions of the Federal Court of Justice in Civil Matters (Entscheidungen des Bundesgerichtshofs in Zivilsachen, Germany)
BIT	Bilateral Investment Treaty
BRICS	Brazil, Russia, India, China, South Africa
BVerfG	Federal Constitutional Court (Bundesverfassungsgericht, Germany)
BVerfGE	Decisions of the Federal Constitutional Court (Entscheidungen des Bundesverfasssungsgerichts, Germany)
BVerfGK	Chamber Decisions of the Federal Constitutional Court (Kammerentscheidungen des Bundesverfasssungsgerichts, Germany)
BVerwG	Federal Administrative Court (Bundesverwaltungsgericht, Germany)

BVerwGE	Decisions of the Federal Administrative Court (Entscheidungen des Bundesverwaltungsgerichts, Germany)
BYIL	*British Yearbook of International Law*
CAT	Committee Against Torture/Convention Against Torture
CEDAW	Committee on the Elimination of Discrimination Against Women/Convention on the Elimination of Discrimination Against Women
CEDEAO	Communauté Economique des Etats de l'Afrique de l'Ouest
CERD	Committee on the Elimination of Racial Discrimination
CERN	European Organization for Nuclear Research
CESCR	Committee on Economic, Social and Cultural Rights
CFI	Court of First Instance of the European Communities
CFSP	Common Foreign and Security Policy
CST	European Union Civil Service Tribunal
CTS	Consolidated Treaty Series
DÖV	*Die öffentliche Verwaltung*
DSU	Understanding on Rules and Procedures Governing the Settlement of Disputes
ECCC	Extraordinary Chambers in the Courts of Cambodia
ECE	Economic Commission for Europe
ECHR	European Convention on Human Rights
ECJ	Court of Justice of the European Union
ECOWAS	Economic Community of West African States
ECT	Energy Charter Treaty
ECtHR	European Court of Human Rights
EEC	European Economic Community
EJIL	*European Journal of International Law*
EPIL	*Max Planck Encyclopedia of Public International Law*
ETS	European Treaty Series
EU	European Union
EuGRZ	*Europäische Grundrechte-Zeitschrift*
EULEX	European Union Rule of Law Mission in Kosovo
FES	Fair and equitable treatment standard
FGO	Code of Procedure for Fiscal Courts (Finanzgerichtsordnung, Germany)
FTA	Free Trade Agreement
GA	General Assembly
GA res.	General Assembly resolution
GAOR	General Assembly Official Reports

GATT	General Agreement on Tariffs and Trade
GC	Geneva Convention
GDR	German Democratic Republic
GG	Basic Law of the Federal Republic of Germany (*Grundgesetz*)
GYIL	*German Yearbook of International Law*
HNS Convention	International Convention on Liability and Compensation for Damage in Connection with the Carriage of Hazardous and Noxious Substances by Sea
HRAP	Human Rights Advisory Panel (Kosovo)
HRQ	*Human Rights Quarterly*
HRRP	Human Rights Review Panel (Kosovo)
IAEA	International Atomic Energy Agency
IACOmHR	Inter-American Commission on Human Rights
IACtHR	Inter-American Court of Human Rights
IBRD	International Bank for Reconstruction and Development
ICC	International Chamber of Commerce *or* International Criminal Court
ICCPR	International Covenant on Civil and Political Rights
ICERD	International Convention on the Elimination of Racial Discrimination
ICESCR	International Covenant on Economic, Social and Cultural Rights
ICISS	International Commission on Intervention and State Sovereignty
ICJ	International Court of Justice
ICLQ	*International and Comparative Law Quarterly*
I•CON	*International Journal of Constitutional Law*
ICRC	International Committee of the Red Cross
ICSID	International Centre for Settlement of Investment Disputes
ICTR	International Criminal Tribunal for Rwanda
ICTY	International Criminal Tribunal for the former Yugoslavia
IDI	Institut de Droit International
IHL	International Humanitarian Law
IIA	International Investment Agreement
ILA	International Law Association
ILC	International Law Commission
ILDC	International Law in Domestic Courts
ILM	*International Legal Materials*
ILO	International Labour Organization

ILR	*International Law Review*
IRRC	*International Review of the Red Cross*
JZ	*JuristenZeitung*
LQR	*Law Quarterly Review*
LTTE	Liberation Tigers of Tamil Eelam
NAFTA	North American Free Trade Agreement
NATO	North Atlantic Treaty Organization
NGO(s)	Non-Governmental Organization(s)
NJW	*Neue Juristische Wochenschrift*
OECD	Organisation for Economic Co-operation and Development
OJ	Official Journal of the European Union
OLG	Higher Regional Court (Oberlandesgericht, Germany)
OVG	Higher Administrative Court (Oberverwaltungsgericht, Germany)
ÖZÖR	*Österreichische Zeitschrift für öffentliches Recht*
PCIJ	Permanent Court of International Justice
PCIJ Ser. A or B or A/B	Permanent Court of International Justice, Collection of Judgments and Advisory Opinions
R2P	Responsibility to Protect
RdC	Recueil des Cours: Collected Courses of The Hague Academy of International Law
RFDA	*Revue Française de Droit Administratif*
RGDIP	*Revue Générale de Droit International Public*
RGZ	Decisions of the Imperial Court in Civil Matters (Entscheidungen des Reichsgerichts in Zivilsachen, Germany)
RS	Federal Gazette (Recueil Systématique, Switzerland)
SC res.	Security Council resolution
SCC	Stockholm Chamber of Commerce
SGG	Social Courts Act (Sozialgerichtsgesetz, Germany)
SPS	WTO Agreement on the Application of Sanitary and Phytosanitary Measures
StPO	Code of Criminal Procedure (Strafprozeßordnung, Germany)
TAM	Tribunaux arbitraux mixtes
TEU	Treaty on European Union
TFEU	Treaty on the Functioning of the European Union
TRIPS	Trade-Related Aspects of Intellectual Property Rights
UDHR	Universal Declaration of Human Rights
UK	United Kingdom
UKHL	United Kingdom House of Lords

UN	United Nations
UNCITRAL	United Nations Commission on International Trade Law
UNCLOS	United Nations Convention on the Law of the Sea
UNCTAD	United Nations Conference on Trade and Development
UNECE	United Nations Economic Commission for Europe
UNESCO	United Nations Educational, Scientific and Cultural Organization
UNFPA	United Nations Population Fund
UNICEF	United Nations Children's Fund
UNITA	União Nacional para a Independência Total de Angola (National Union for the Total Independence of Angola)
UNMIK	United Nations Interim Administration Mission in Kosovo
UNOCI	United Nations Operation in Côte d'Ivoire
UNSC	UN Security Council
UNTS	United Nations Treaty Series
USSR	Union of Soviet Socialist Republics
VCCR	Vienna Convention on Consular Relations
VCDR	Vienna Convention on Diplomatic Relations
VCLT	Vienna Convention on the Law of Treaties
VPB	Federal Collection of Administrative Decisions (Verwaltungspraxis der Bundesbehörden, Switzerland)
VwGO	Code of Administrative Court Procedure (Verwaltungsgerichtsordnung, Germany)
WHO	World Health Organization
WTO	World Trade Organization
YB	Yearbook
ZaöRV	*Zeitschrift für ausländisches öffentliches Recht und Völkerrecht*
ZGB	Civil Code (Zivilgesetzbuch, Switzerland)
ZISG	Federal Act on Cooperation with the International Criminal Court (Bundesgesetz über die Zusammenarbeit mit dem Internationalen Strafgerichtshof, Switzerland)
ZÖR	*Zeitschrift für öffentliches Recht*
ZPO	Code of Civil Procedure (Zivilprozeßordnung, Germany)

TABLE OF CASES

International Courts and Bodies

Permanent Court of Justice (PCIJ)

PCIJ, *Mavrommatis Palestine Concessions Case*, Judgment of 30 August 1924, PCIJ Ser. B, No. 3 (1924), 12 pp. 306, 389–391

PCIJ, *Jurisdiction of the Courts of Danzig*, Advisory Opinion of 3 March 1928, PCIJ Ser. B, No. 15 (1928) pp. 7, 29–32, 77, 316, 499, 501, 505, 519

PCIJ, *Case Concerning the Factory at Chorzów (Claim for Indemnity - Merits)*, Judgment of 13 September 1928, PCIJ Ser. A No. 17 (1928) pp. 170, 337

PCIJ, *Case Concerning the Payment of Various Serbian Loans Issued in France*, Judgment of 12 July 1929, PCIJ Ser. A, No. 20/21 (1929) p. 173, 294

PCIJ, *Peter Pàzmàny University Case*, Judgment of 15 December 1933, PCIJ Ser. A/B, No. 61 (1933) p. 48

PCIJ, *League of Nations, Advisory Committee of Jurists*, Procès-Verbaux of the Proceedings of the Committee (16 June–24 July 2010) with annexes (The Hague: van Langenhuisen Brothers 1920) pp. 428

International Court of Justice (ICJ)

ICJ, *Reparation for Injuries Suffered in the Service of the United Nations*, Advisory Opinion of 11 April 1949, ICJ Reports 1949, 174 pp. 36, 414, 433

ICJ, *South West Africa Cases (Ethiopia/South Africa; Liberia/South Africa) (Second Phase)*, Judgment of 18 July 1966, Dissenting Opinion of Judge Tanaka, ICJ Reports 1966, 6 p. 428

ICJ, *Barcelona Traction, Light and Power Company (New Application 1962) (Second Phase)*, Judgment of 5 February 1970, ICJ Reports 1970, 4 pp. 391–396

ICJ, *Case concerning the Gabčíkovo-Nagymaros Project* (Hungary *v.* Slovakia), Judgment of 25 September 1997, ICJ Reports 1997, 7 p. 520

ICJ, *La Grand Case* (Germany *v.* United States of America), Judgment of 27 June 2001, ICJ Reports 2001, 466 pp. 32, 48, 77, 316, 350–359, 369–372, 391, 416, 486, 526

ICJ, *La Grand Case*, Judgment, 27 June 2001, Separate Opinion of Vice-President Shi, ICJ Reports 2001, 466 p. 351

International and Regional Criminal Courts and Tribunals

International Criminal Court (ICC)

International Criminal Tribunal for Rwanda (ICTR)

International Criminal Tribunal for the former Yugoslavia (ICTY)

Special Tribunal for Lebanon

Human Rights Institutions

UN Human Rights Committee

Apirana Mahuika et al. *v.* New Zealand, No. 547/1992, Communication of 10 December 1992, UN-Doc. CCPR/C/70/D/547/1993 (2000) p. 547

Kennedy *v.* Trinidad and Tobago, Communication No. 845/1998, Decision declaring a decision admissible of 31 December 1999, UN-Doc. CCPR/C/67/D/845/1999 p. 542

Jiménez Vaca *v.* Columbia, No. 859/1999, Communication of 15 April 2002, UN-Doc. CCPR/C/74/D/859/1999 pp. 182–183

Albert Wilson *v.* Philippines, No. 868/1999, Communication of 11 November 2003, UN-Doc. CCPR/C/79/D/868/1999 (2003) p. 183

Messaouda Kimouché *v.* Algeria, No. 1327/2004, Communication of 10 July 2007, UN-Doc. CCPR/C/90/D/1327/2004 p. 262

Sathasivam *v.* Sri Lanka, No. 1436/2005, Communication of 8 July 2008, UN-Doc. CCPR/C/93/D/1436/2005 pp. 183, 262

Amirov *v.* Russian Federation, No. 1447/2006, Communication of 2 April 2009, UN-Doc. CCPR/C/95/D/1447/2006 pp. 183, 262

Felipe und Evelyne Pestaño *v.* Philippines, No. 1619/2007, Communication of 23 March 2010, UN-Doc. CCPR/C/98/D/1619/2007 pp. 183, 262

European Court of Human Rights (ECtHR)

ECtHR, Handyside *v.* United Kingdom, No. 5493/72, Judgment of 7 December 1976 p. 484

ECtHR, Ireland *v.* United Kingdom, No. 5310/71, Judgment of 18 January 1978, 82 p. 319

ECtHR, Sunday Times *v.* United Kingdom, No. 6538/74, Judgment of 26 April 1979 p. 83

ECtHR, Airey *v.* Ireland, No. 6289/73, Judgment of 9 October 1979 p. 476

ECtHR, Case of Guzzardi *v.* Italy, No. 7367/76, Judgment of 6 November 1980 p. 540

ECtHR, X. und Y. *v.* Netherlands, No. 8978/80, Judgment of 26 March 1985 p. 259

ECtHR, C. R. *v.* United Kingdom, No. 20190/92, Judgment of 22 November 1995 p. 130

ECtHR, Petra *v.* Romania, No. 27273/95, Judgment of 23 September 1998 p. 65

ECtHR, Osman *v.* United Kingdom, No. 87/1997/871/1083, Judgment of 28 October 1998 pp. 238, 248

ECtHR, Matthews *v.* United Kingdom, No. 24833/94, Judgment of 18 February 1999 pp. 276, 478

ECtHR, Rekvényi *v.* Hungary, No. 25390/94, Judgment of 20 May 1999 p. 84

ECtHR, Oğur *v.* Turkey, No. 21594/93, Judgment of 20 May 1999 pp. 259, 260

ECtHR, Selmouni *v.* France, No. 25803/94, Judgment of 28 July 1999 p. 540

European Commission on Human Rights (EComHR)

Inter-American Court of Human Rights (IACtHR)

Inter-American Commission on Human Rights (IAComHR)

African Commission on Human and People's Rights (ACHPR)

International Arbitral Tribunals

International Centre for the Settlement of Investment Disputes (ICSID)

Other Arbitral Tribunals

Other International and Regional Courts

European Courts

European Court of Justice (ECJ)

European Court of First Instance (EuC)

European Union Civil Service Tribunal (EuCST)

Domestic Courts

Germany

Bundesverfassungsgericht (BVerfG) (Federal Constitutional Court)

Bundesgerichtshof (BGH) (Federal Court of Justice)

In civil matters

In criminal matters

Bundesverwaltungsgericht (BVerwG) (Federal Administrative Court)

Lower Courts and Appeal Courts

Reichsgericht (RG) (Imperial Court)

France

Japan

Supreme Court of Japan

Tokyo District and High Court

Switzerland

Bundesgericht (BGer) (Federal Tribunal)

United States of America

US Supreme Court

Other US Courts

United Kingdom

Other Domestic Courts

1

Definition of the Question

1.1 Individualization of International Law?

The starting point for this study is the observation that with increasing frequency international legal norms directly address and engage individuals. For instance, individual rights under international law appear to arise from extradition treaties, treaties of friendship and establishment, double taxation agreements, transport treaties, intellectual property treaties, investment protection treaties, treaties on the legal status of foreigners, and the Vienna Convention on Consular Relations. On the side of duties, the criminal responsibility of individuals under international law has in recent decades been fleshed out by the work of the ad hoc criminal tribunals and the International Criminal Court.[1]

Accordingly, scholars of international law have around the turn of the millennium noted a transformation of the international system. The inclusion of individuals under international law was claimed to have become a "fundamental axiom" of the international legal order.[2] A "paradigm shift" consisting in the increasing significance of the individual in international law,[3] a shift "from international law to world law",[4] "from international law to global law",[5] to the "new *jus*

[1] See Chapter 5.

[2] See Oliver Dörr, Privatisierung des Völkerrechts, *JuristenZeitung* 60 (2005), 905–916 (905); see also P. K. Menon, The Legal Personality of Individuals, *Sri Lanka Journal of International Law* 6 (1994), 127–156 (148).

[3] Wolfgang Benedek, Das Individuum als Völkerrechtsubjekt, in: August Reinisch (ed.), *Österreichisches Handbuch des Völkerrechts*, Band I: Textteil (5th ed., Wien: Manzsche Verlags- und Universitätsbuchhandlung 2013), 291, paragraph 1238.

[4] Angelika Emmerich-Fritsche, *Vom Völkerrecht zum Weltrecht* (Berlin: Duncker & Humblot 2007).

[5] Rafael Domingo, *The New Global Law* (Cambridge: Cambridge University Press 2010), 133.

gentium of humanity"[6] and to "humanity's law"[7] has been proclaimed, and a "humanization of international law" has been diagnosed.[8]

These views have not gone unchallenged. In a fairly recent Hague course entitled "The Emancipation of the Individual from the State under International Law", Gerhard Hafner reached the conclusion that this "emancipation" is incomplete and that "the status of individuals in international law is restricted".[9] Others have warned against an overstretched individualization of international law: In a case note on a German Constitutional Court decision rejecting an international-law-based individual right on compensation for violations of international humanitarian law (IHL), a scholar held that

> "the increasing recognition of the individual ... is limited to certain, rather narrow, fields of law, which are still based on (and therefore tightly circumscribed by) state consent; their embrace of individual rights *does not erode the general structure of international law,* where, in principle, the individual remains an object of protection ... The Court's decision might even be a useful portent that *the overstretched concept of the individualization of international law has reached its useful limits.*"[10]

The controversy about any potential "individualization" of international law is at the same time a debate about the basic structure of the system and must be seen in that context. The diagnosis of the German scholar Christian Tomuschat, lecturer of the 1999 General Course on Public International Law at the Hague Academy of International Law, was that the international community had been "progressively moving from a sovereignty-centred to a ... individual-oriented system. ... The international legal order cannot be understood any more as being

[6] Antônio Augusto Cançado Trindade, International Law for Humankind: Towards a New Jus Gentium, *Recueil des Cours* 316 (2005), 9–444.

[7] Ruti Teitel, *Humanity's Law* (Oxford: Oxford University Press 2011). *Ibid.*, 31: "Humanity offers a distinctive subjectivity: the status of the human is a basis for new and diverse claims, on the part of diverse voices that are new to international law and politics."

[8] Theodor Meron, *The Humanization of International Law* (Leiden: Martinus Nijhoff 2006). See also Antonio Cassese, *The Human Dimension of International Law: Selected Papers*, ed. Paola Gaeta and Salvator Zappalà (Oxford: Oxford University Press 2008).

[9] Gerhard Hafner, The Emancipation of the Individual from the State under International Law, *Recueil des Cours* 358 (2011), 263–453 (437). Hafner sought to apply "an anthropocentric approach to international law instead of a State-centric approach, without, however, losing sight to the present dynamic and contradictory structure of international law" (*Ibid.*, 287), and reached quite different conclusions from this study.

[10] Klaus Ferdinand Gärditz, Bridge of Varvarin, *American Journal of International Law* 108 (2014), 86–93 (91; italics mine).

based exclusively on State sovereignty. . . . States are no more than instruments whose inherent function it is to serve the interests of their citizens as legally expressed in human rights. At the present time, it is by no means clear which one of the two rivalling Grundnorms will or should prevail in case of conflict. Over the last decades, a crawling process has taken place through which human rights have steadily increased their weight, gaining momentum in comparison with State sovereignty as a somewhat formal principle". Importantly, Tomuschat continued that "*[t]he transformation from international law as a State-centred system to an individual-centred system has not yet found a definitive new equilibrium*".[11]

1.2 Backlash in the Age of BRICSs?

In the new millennium, the global political and economic constellation has changed with the rise of the BRICS States (Brazil, Russia, India, China, and South Africa) and a concomitant decline of the United States and Europe. The question is whether and how this power shift affects the international legal system, and with this, the status of the individual in it. Was the phenomenon of "humanization" or "individualization" of international law only "a hallmark of the period of U. S. leadership"[12] which spread an ostensibly typically US-American "narcissistic rights culture"?[13] If this were the case, a reversal of the "individualization" of international law would seem likely, because the voices of non-Western States which have traditionally been more sceptical of the purported "individualization" have gained more salience.

In post-Soviet Russian international law scholarship, the "debate between the statist and the pro-individual school" had been initially spearheaded by pro-individualists.[14] In 1990, then President Yeltsin

[11] Christian Tomuschat, International Law: Ensuring the Survival of Mankind on the Eve of a New Century: General Course on Public International Law, *Recueil des Cours* 281 (1999), 11–438 (237 and 161–62; italics mine). See for the view that the current international legal order is based on *three* pillars, namely peace, development, and human rights, Emmanuelle Tourme-Jouannet, *Le droit international* (Paris: PUF Que sais-je 2013), 70–122.

[12] William W. Burke-White, Power Shifts in International Law: Structural Realignment and Substantive Pluralism, *Harvard International Law Journal* 56 (2015), 1–80 (77).

[13] Georg Nolte/Helmut Philipp Aust, European Exceptionalism?, *Global Constitutionalism* 2 (2013), 407–436 (424).

[14] Lauri Mälksoo, *Russian Approaches to International Law* (Oxford: Oxford University Press 2015), 98.

had declared at the first assembly of national deputies of the Russian Federation "that from then onwards the 'first sovereignty in Russia will be the human being'".[15] But since then, the pro-individual school has not gained ground in Russia. On the contrary, the Russian Statist school seems to be dominant in the intellectual centres, and this fits to the political climate under President Putin.[16]

Also the Chinese scholar and judge at the International Court of Justice (ICJ), Hanquin Xue, insists on the centrality of the State for the protection of human rights: "There are increasing communal interests shared by all states, such as ... human rights promotion and protection ..., but to realize these goals, States are the crucial actors at both national and international level ... Any weakening of the status and role of the State, as demonstrated in many a case, could only mean more misery and sufferings for individuals."[17] She also explains Chinese insistence on non-intervention as a reaction to double standards applied by the West.[18]

The insistence of China and Russia on State sovereignty, even at the expense of human security, was manifest in the two States' representatives' statements in the Security Council when vetoing, at two occasions, draft resolutions which sought robust action against Syria, in 2011 and 2012. The proposals tabled in the Security Council reacted to documented war crimes and crimes against humanity committed by Syrian armed forces and the State's manifest failure to protect its population.[19] Although the draft resolutions did not foresee a military

[15] *Ibid.*, quoting the Russian author M.V.Ill'in. [16] *Ibid.*, 99.

[17] Hanquin Xue, Comments on Hurrell, in: James Crawford/Sarah Nouwen (eds), *Select Proceedings of the European Society of International Law* 3 (Oxford: Hart 2012), 27–29 (28).

[18] Hanquin Xue, Chinese Contemporary Perspectives on International Law: History, Culture and International Law, *Recueil des Cours* 355 (2011), 41–233 (153), speaking of "China-bashing": "[E]ven Western scholars admit that China has been subjected to double standards in the assessment of its human rights performance. Such bias became even more evident when human rights issues were driven by strategic interests and economic benefits against China. Under such circumstances, it is not surprising that China would invoke the principles of sovereignty and non-interference to defend its socio-political system and reject double-standards in the human rights dialogue."

[19] See Francis Deng and Edward Luck, Special advisers of the UN Secretary General on the Prevention of Genocide and on R2P. On the situation in Syria, Press Release 21 July 2011. See on human rights violations, war crimes, crimes against humanity committed by government forces notably the various reports of the Independent International Commission of Inquiry on the Syrian Arab Republic, inter alia, UN Documents A/HRC/19/69 of 22 February 2012, paragraph 126; A/HRC/21/50 of 16 August 2012, paragraph 145; A/HRC/30/48 of 13 August 2015, paragraphs 165–167.

intervention but only demanded, inter alia, that the Syrian government immediately put an end to all human rights violations and attacks against persons exercising their rights to freedom of expression, peaceful assembly, and association,[20] they were vetoed by China and Russia with the argument that such measures would interfere unduly with Syrian sovereignty.[21]

Against the background of the current "power shifts in international law", William Burke-White has recently found that the "reassertion of the centrality of the State conflicts with the individualization of international law" and has predicted that "[f]or legal rules and regimes that seek to advance this individualization or draw their effectiveness from it ... the return of the state will likely have pronounced negative consequences. Over time these regimes may be ratcheted back as international law returns closer to its Westphalian origins as a system of sovereignty, among sovereigns".[22]

The re-insistence on the legitimate role of the State in the entire system, and the potential "re-Vattelisation" of international law going with it, has a number of reasons and motivations which are only in part linked to the ongoing power shift. Steven Ratner has usefully summarized the three main moral justifications for the position that "the interests and claims of states ... deserve serious consideration alongside with the interests and claims of individuals":[23] First, States have (some) "moral standing" *when* they express the interests of their population (in a Kantian paradigm

[20] Draft resolutions of 4 October 2011 (UN SCOR 66th sess., UN Doc. S/2011/612) and 4 February 2012 (UN Doc. S/2012/77). The draft texts also called for access for humanitarian aid, and the 2011 draft resolution in addition called for "vigilance and restraint" over the transfer of arms (paragraph 9).

[21] In 2011, the Russian delegate insisted on a "logic of respect for the national sovereignty and territorial integrity of Syria as well as the principle of non-intervention, including military, in its affairs" (UN Doc. S/PV.6627, 6627th meeting of 4 October 2011, 6 p.m., p. 3). The Chinese delegate asked that any Security Council resolution "should fully respect Syria's sovereignty, independence and territorial integrity. Most important, it should depend upon whether it complies with the Charter of the United Nations and the principle of non-interference in the internal affairs of States" (*Ibid.*). In 2012, the Russian delegate deplored that the draft on humanitarian assistance was in reality "calling for regime change" (UN Doc. S/PV.6711, 6711th meeting of 4 February 2014, 10 a.m., at p. 9). The Chinese delegate vetoed the resolution because "the sovereignty, independence and territorial integrity of Syria should be fully respected" (*Ibid.*).

[22] Burke-White, Power Shifts, 2015, 77.

[23] Steven Ratner, *The Thin Justice of International Law* (Oxford: Oxford University Press 2015), 85–87.

which is valid only for some States); second, States are vessels for the creation of individual identity (in the communitarian paradigm). Third – in my view most importantly – from a consequentalist perspective, the State system "is in fact the best available structure to advance individual welfare".[24] This claim has recently, not the least due to political experience and empirical research, gained more salience. We have come to realize that consolidated and well-functioning States are an important factor for complying with human rights norms.[25] My own view is distinct from the three views just mentioned; I would say that State sovereignty is being recognized by positive international law as instrumental for securing the well-being of humans.[26] But whatever view on the State's moral standing one takes, we must pragmatically acknowledge that "[t]he state system appears to be a fixed attribute of the international order . . . as a practical matter, states remain the primary and indispensable agents of individuals".[27]

The ongoing re-emphasis on the importance of States, accompanied by a certain backlash against "over-individualization", might have been triggered by the recognition that basic "Westphalian" principles such as territorial integrity and the prohibition on the use of force have been violated by leading powers (e.g., in 2003 by the United States with the intervention in Iraq, and in 2014 by Russia with the annexation of Crimea). Concomitantly, it is often perceived that these principles deserve re-emphasis. Related reflections are that the so-called humanitarian intervention in Kosovo in 1999 is widely seen to have overstretched international law and that the application of the doctrine of the responsibility to protect in Libya in 2011 has not improved the situation of the population.

[24] *Ibid.*, 86.

[25] Constructivist authors have identified the degree of Statehood as the most important condition influencing the ability of States to comply, but the authors also encourage the search for alternatives (Thomas Risse/Kathryn Sikkink, Conclusions, in: Thomas Risse/Stephen C. Ropp/Kathryn Sikkink (eds), *The Persistent Power of Human Rights: From Commitment to Compliance* (Cambridge: Cambridge University Press 2013), 275–295 (291–292)). Steven Pinker, *The Better Angels of Our Nature: Why Violence Has Declined* (New York: Viking 2011) identifies as the single most important factor for the improvement of human security the emergence of stable States (see *ibid.*, 822, also 63, 66, and *passim*).

[26] Anne Peters, Humanity as the A and Ω of Sovereignty, *European Journal of International Law* 20 (2009), 513–544.

[27] Ratner, *The Thin Justice*, 86.

1.3 *The Legal* Acquis Individuel*: Structure of the Book*

However, political disappointment about the "failure" or "abuse" of Western interventions in the Middle East and mere assertions of a novel Statism are not able as such to destroy the global legal *acquis individuel*. That acquis is the topic of this book. My overarching question is how the phenomenon of the growth of individual rights and duties under international law can be described, systematized, and evaluated in a legally meaningful way.

To answer this question, the study will draw three lines. Firstly, I will briefly recapitulate the *history of ideas and the doctrine* of the status of individuals under international law, i.e., their international legal personality (international legal subjectivity). This international legal personality – provisionally understood here as the ability to have international rights and duties[28] – depends on the ideational background understanding, on the observer's doctrinal conceptualization, and of course on the state of positive international law. For these reasons, the historical paradigms, the varying terminology, and the legal practice will be traced briefly (Chapter 2), so that I can subsequently (in Chapter 3) propose a definition of international legal personality I believe to be useful.

Secondly, the study will take up a comment by the International Law Commission: "Individual rights under international law may also arise *outside the framework of human rights*."[29] Even just a few decades ago, the Federal Constitutional Court of Germany found this to be unusual: "*Outside the domain of the minimum standard for human rights*, current general international law only rarely contains norms establishing (individual) 'subjective' rights or duties of private individuals directly at the level of international law; its scope essentially covers the sovereign international relations between States and associations of States; individual rights or duties of private individuals are, as a general rule, established or affected only indirectly via domestic law."[30] My survey of current legal practice aims to show the extent to which international legal rights (and duties) of individuals not relating to human rights actually exist in current law – deviating from the legal situation

[28] On the terms "international legal person/personality" and "international legal subject/subjectivity" (used synonymously here), see Chapter 3.

[29] ILC Commentary on Article 33 of the ILC Draft Articles on State Responsibility (*Yearbook of the International Law Commission* (2001) Vol. II, Part 2, 94–95 (95, paragraph 3; referring to PCIJ, *Danzig*, and ICJ, *LaGrand*; italics mine).

[30] BVerfGE 46, 342 et seq., 362, Ruling of 13 December 1977 – *philippinische Botschaftskonten* (italics mine).

determined by the German Constitutional Court thirty-five years ago. Individual rights under international law that are not human rights – as well as individual duties under international law – will be clearly identified and named.[31] By bracketing human rights, the survey aims to show how rich and differentiated the legal status beyond human rights is (Chapters 4–12). We shall see that international-law-based rights and obligations of individuals are widespread and refined – which suggests, I submit, that they would be difficult to dismantle. Incidentally, by analysing in detail the legal position of the individual in international law as it stands, this study also suggests that the two-pillar image of the international legal order (resting on States and individuals), as evoked above, is somewhat simplistic.

Thirdly, a sound concept of international legal personality and the empirical survey of the accumulated individual rights and duties under international law will be used as a basis to work out a key factor: the independence of this new international legal status of the individual from the State. The individual has become a primary subject (person) of international law.[32] Individuals not only have numerous "subjective" international rights (in the plural) but also are further entitled to international legal subjectivity (international legal personality) in virtue of their personhood on the basis of customary international law and general principles of law and as an aspect of their human right to legal personality. Put differently, the international legal personality of human beings is rooted in Art. 16 ICCPR and already forms a general principle of law (Chapter 13).

The crystallization of this primary international legal personality of the individual will be encapsulated by introducing the term of the international individual right. This legal institution will be explained in terms of legal doctrine and theory and also justified ethically in Chapter 17.

Overall, this legal development (the crystallization of "simple" rights and duties and the underlying institution of the subjective international right) is compatible with the structures and fundamental values of

[31] For the parallel, already more advanced crystallization of subjective rights protected by European law, see fundamentally Johannes Saurer, *Der Einzelne im europäischen Verwaltungsrecht: Die institutionelle Ausdifferenzierung der Verwaltungsorganisation der Europäischen Union in individueller Perspektive* (Tübingen: Mohr Siebeck 2013). See already Stefan Kadelbach, *Allgemeines Verwaltungsrecht unter europäischem Einfluss* (Tübingen: Mohr Siebeck 1996), 410–441.

[32] I use the term "subject of international law" as a synonym with "international legal person"; and "(legal) subjectivity" synonymously with "(legal) personality". See in detail Chapter 3.

international law. The distinction between simple rights and duties of individuals (in contrast to human rights; see Chapter 14) suggests that different legal layers of law may exist *within* international law. Such a distinction would fit to the theory of global constitutionalism. Global constitutionalists believe that within the international legal order a body of especially important rules, principles, and structures exists which deserves the label of international constitutional law. In principle, only human rights would appear to form part of this body of international constitutional law, while the simple individual rights and duties would rank below the constitutional level.

1.4 Scope of Investigation: "The Individual"

The term "individual" ("individu") is not a technical term usually found in international treaties or other hard or soft legal texts.[33] It is common in international legal literature, however. First and foremost, individuals in this study are natural persons.

Especially in the chapter on investment protection (Chapter 10), I also include legal persons under national private law engaged in *business* (undertakings). Their status under international law is independent of their national legal form. From the perspective of international law, it is irrelevant whether these collective business actors are constituted under national law as legal persons or as entities without legal personality.

Whether and when a group of individuals forms an entity to which legal responsibility can be attributed is determined by the legal order whose rights and duties are at stake. So, for the purposes of imposing duties under international law, it is international law that determines which groups will constitute persons under international law (international legal subjects). Put differently, international law governs the preconditions under which collectives other than States, for example international organizations, armed groups, NGOs, and business

[33] In international legal texts, especially relating to counterterrorism, individuals are sometimes distinguished from "entities". For instance, UN Security Council resolution 1989 (2011) to combat al-Qaida refers throughout to "individuals, groups, undertakings and entities". Article 53, paragraph 1 of the Geneva Convention (I) for the Amelioration of the Condition of the Wounded in Armies in the Field (First Geneva Convention) of 12 August 1949 refers to "individuals, . . . firms or companies either public or private". In principle, the various actors are subject to identical legal consequences in the aforementioned texts.

enterprises, are able as such to be bearers of international legal rights and duties.

Human rights are considered in this study only at two places: First, for carving out a distinct category of individual rights that are *not* human rights (Chapter 14). Second, human rights may generate duties of individuals or business actors (Chapter 4). Such potential obligations of political, economic, and private actors to respect the human rights of others are an important manifestation of their so-called passive status as subjects bound by international law, beyond the requirement to refrain from international criminal acts.

What is bracketed in this study is the legal status of ethnically, linguistically, culturally, or politically defined groups that – as a collective or through coordination of their members – assert the right of self-determination under international law or rights as minorities. Finally, transnationally active organizations of civil society (NGOs) are not considered. These can be distinguished at least as a matter of degree from private economic actors due to their pursuit of the common good. This goal might potentially justify the conferral of specific international legal positions (e.g., rights to participate in international law-making processes) that are not granted to natural, so-called private persons, irrespective of their formal legal status under national law. The specific status of NGOs under international law is a separate topic.

2

Historical Theory and Practice of the International Legal Status of the Individual

2.1 History of Ideas

2.1.1 The Individual as Addressee of Natural Law and International Law

The rights of individuals were present in the discipline of *jus naturae et gentium*, which was examined in a scholarly fashion starting in the sixteenth century. This discipline was concerned not with legal relationships between independent communities (States) but rather with the universal validity of certain norms for communities and persons.[1] As all law was ultimately derived from nature, international law was not clearly separated from domestic law. Neither were the respective actors clearly distinguished. This means that the individual remained embedded in the natural and international legal order. According to William Blackstone still, individuals were considered participants in the affairs of international law. In his *Commentaries*, which appeared for the first time in 1753, he defined international law as follows: "The law of nations is a system of rules, deducible by natural reason, and established by universal consent among the civilized inhabitants of the world; in order to decide all disputes, to regulate all ceremonies and civilities, and to insure the observance of justice and good faith in that intercourse which must frequently occur between two or more independent states, *and the individuals belonging to each*."[2]

Not coincidentally, it was in this context that the seed of the natural law idea that human beings have legal capacity in virtue of being human was planted. In his *Relectiones*, published posthumously in 1557, Francisco de Vitoria argued that the Native Americans in the territories conquered by Spain and Portugal had rights and claims under both public law and private

[1] See Ulrich Scheuner, Die großen Friedensschlüsse als Grundlage der europäischen Staatenordnung zwischen 1648 und 1815, reprinted in: Scheuner, *Schriften zum Völkerrecht* (ed. Christian Tomuschat (Berlin: Duncker & Humblot 1984)), 352–354.

[2] William Blackstone, *The Commentaries on the Laws of England*, Vol. 4 (London: John Murray 1876) (orig. 1753), 55 (italics mine).

law, just like Christians, because nobody was a slave by nature.[3] He apparently considered the legal relations between Spaniards and Native Americans to be international relations in today's sense, given that he discussed the law of warfare and titles of government. But Vitoria did not distinguish between "private" war and the war of a prince or ruler.[4] The State was still defined without reference to sovereignty.[5] Hugo's *De jure belli ac pacis* of 1625 is considered the first construction of a legal system (founded on a rationalized conception of natural law) that was based on individual rights instead of objective law.[6]

The natural law tradition never vanished entirely. According to Johann Caspar Bluntschli, international law "as the universal law of humanity" united "Christians and Muslims, Brahmanists and Buddhists, the followers of Confucius and the worshipers of stars, the believers and the unbelievers".[7] Especially after the Second World War, individual-centric international legal theory again drew inspiration from natural law.[8]

2.1.2 *The Displacement of the Individual by Statism and Legal Positivism*

As sovereign States consolidated beginning in the eighteenth century, the concepts of the legal personality of the State, the basic rights and duties of the State, and, not least of all, sovereignty itself were developed by scholars.[9]

[3] See Francisco de Vitoria, Relectiones Theologicae, De Indis (orig. 1532, publ. 1557), Sec. I, paragraph 24 (in: *The Classics of International Law*, ed. Ernest Nys (Washington: Carnegie Institution 1917), 128 (engl.) and 232 (lat.)).

[4] See *ibid.*, 167–169.

[5] See *ibid.*, 169. See, generally, Felix Hafner/Adrian Loretan/Christoph Spenlé, Naturrecht und Menschenrecht: Der Beitrag der Spanischen Spätscholastik zur Entwicklung der Menschenrechte, in: Frank Grunert/Kurt Seelmann (eds), *Die Ordnung der Praxis: Neue Studien zur Spanischen Spätscholastik* (Tübingen: Niemeyer 2001), 123–153.

[6] On Grotius's term "jus", see p. 528, Chapter 17 with n. 13. For a famous, but maybe distorted, reading of Grotius's natural law approach and his significance to international law, see Hersch Lauterpacht, The Grotian Tradition of International Law, *British Yearbook of International Law* 23 (1946), 1–53.

[7] Johann Caspar Bluntschli, *Das moderne Völkerrecht der civilisirten Staten: als Rechtsbuch dargestellt* (3rd ed., Nördlingen: Verlag der C. H. Beck'schen Buchhandlung 1878), § 6 paragraph 3 (61). On the international legal subjectivity of the individual founded on natural law, see also Pasquale Fiore, *Le droit international codifié et sa sanction juridique* (3rd ed., Paris: Pedone 1911; translated from Italian), § 61 (108–110).

[8] See below p. 23–25.

[9] It is worth noting that, in a seeming paradox, the rise of the sovereign State itself had arguably been triggered and promoted exactly by new ideas about individual rights (against the feudal regimes of unequal entitlements). See Christian Reus-Smit,

Concomitantly, emphasis was increasingly placed on States as political actors and subjects of international law. And with the ascent of the methods of legal positivism, international law was gradually detached from natural law and, in parallel, clearly distinguished from domestic law. Both movements led to a concentration of international law on rules governing relationships between States, and individuals were largely crowded out of this legal order.[10] Human beings, in their capacity as citizens, took part in relationships governed by international law only through the mediation of their home State. In the eighth edition of his textbook of 1888, for instance, August Wilhelm Heffter discussed "the international legal relations of private individuals",[11] but he noted that "This entire discussion of human rights is not a part of international law, but rather a part of politics and legal philosophy, given that . . . individuals participate in affairs governed by law only as citizens of States."[12] According to Felix Stoerk, "citizenship is the point of passage that the individual must have reached in order to enter the light of international legal consideration."[13]

Towards the end of the nineteenth century, however, the statist evolution of international law increasingly conflicted with the proliferation of individual protection through international treaties. For instance, Article 29 of the General Act of Brussels of 1890, relative to the African slave trade, began with the sentence that "Any slave detained against his will on board of a native vessel shall have *the right* to demand his liberty."[14] Contrary to the wording, which explicitly referred to the rights of the individual, this and similar international agreements were construed by legal positivism and dualist theory as mutual obligations existing solely

Individual Rights and the Making of the International System (Cambridge: Cambridge University Press 2013).

[10] See, e.g., Albert Zorn, *Grundzüge des Völkerrechts* (2nd. ed., Leipzig: Verlagsbuchhandlung von J. J. Weber 1903), 3: "Holders of international relationships are therefore never private individuals but rather only States" (translation mine; here and for subsequent translations from German to English, "translation mine" denotes translation by Jonathan Huston as reviewed and revised by Anne Peters). See also *ibid.*, 26 et seq.

[11] August Wilhelm Heffter, *Das europäische Völkerrecht der Gegenwart auf den bisherigen Grundlagen* (8th ed., Berlin: Verlag von H. E. Müller 1888), 130 et seq. (title of the first book, first chapter, third section; translation mine).

[12] *Ibid.*, 132 n. 1 (translation mine).

[13] Felix Stoerk, Staatsunterthanen und Fremde, in: Franz von Holtzendorff (ed.), *Handbuch des Völkerrechts auf Grundlage Europäischer Staatspraxis, Vol. 2: Die völkerrechtliche Verfassung und Grundordnung der auswärtigen Staatsbeziehungen* (Hamburg: Verlag von J. F. Richter 1887), 583–655 (589; translation mine).

[14] General Act of Brussels for the Repression of the African Slave Trade of 2 July 1890, *American Journal of International Law* 3 (1909), Supplement p. 29 on p. 41 (italics mine).

between States, from which individuals were unable to derive any international claims.[15] As Heinrich Triepel, a proponent of the dualist theory, argued: "If international law exists, it can only apply to the mutual relations among coordinated States. The legal proposition ... decides the type of status accorded to the individual. This status cannot be that of a legal subject. From the perspective of a legal community bringing States as such together, the individual is not capable of being the holder of autonomous rights and duties emanating from the legal order of that community. It is irrelevant that what the international legal propositions aim to protect are largely the interests of the individual ... Agreements between States for the benefit of African Negroes do not elevate Blacks, whose welfare they are intended to promote, to subjects of the legal community whose propositions refer to them. The individual under ... international law can be considered only an *object* of international legal rights and obligations."[16] According to this "object theory", international law – and especially international treaty law – entitled and obligated only the contracting parties, i.e., States.[17] In international treaties, individuals were not accorded a right, but rather they enjoyed only a legal reflex. They were beneficiaries but not rights-holders, objects not subjects of international law.

Object theory is strictly based on the legal positivist method[18] that denied a necessary connection between law and morality.[19] According

[15] On the slavery conventions, see Emanuel Ullmann, *Völkerrecht* (2nd ed., Tübingen: J. C. B. Mohr (P. Siebeck) 1908), § 133 (402–406).

[16] Heinrich Triepel, *Völkerrecht und Landesrecht* (Leipzig: Verlag von C. L. Hirschfeld 1899), 20–21; see also *ibid.*, 13–18, 259–262 (translation and italics mine).

[17] See, fundamentally, Paul Heilborn, *Das System des Völkerrechts aus den völkerrechtlichen Begriffen* (Berlin: Springer 1896), 58–138 (esp. 68, 70–73, 79–80, 82–83, 110) and 372, 374, 382, 417. For an extensive critical discussion of object theory, see George Manner, The Object Theory of the Individual in International Law, *American Journal of International Law* 46 (1952), 428–449.

[18] For a critical view, see Antônio Augusto Cançado Trindade: "The old monopoly of the State of the condition of being subject of rights is no longer sustainable, nor are the *excesses of a degenerated legal positivism*, which excluded from the international legal order the final addressee of juridical norms: the human being. The need is acknowledged nowadays to restore to this latter the central position – as subject of domestic as well as international law – from where he was unduly replaced, with disastrous consequences, evidenced in the successive atrocities committed against him in the last decades. All this occurred with the indulgence of *legal positivism, in its typical subservience to State authoritarianism.*" Inter-American Court of Human Rights, 1 October 1999, Advisory Opinion OC-16/99, Concurring Opinion, paragraph 12 (italics mine).

[19] International law was likewise defined immanently, without reference to values external to the law: International norms were considered to be only, but also all, texts generated by

to this approach, international law was to be divorced from politics, comity, Roman and Canon law, and theology, and (international) jurisprudence was to be purged of all political, philosophical, "dialectic", and "metaphysical" speculations.[20] Positivist object theory was thus thought to be a reaction to the confused treatment of individuals under prior natural and international laws – i.e., treatment that was allegedly speculative, utopian, and non-juridical. In legal positivism, any legal personality of the individual was consequently seen as the mere product of legislated law. The legal order of the State was the authority conferring legal personality to individuals. For want of international treaties granting individuals true rights, the individual could not be a person (subject) of international law. Franz von Liszt got to the heart of the matter but also opened up an alternative perspective: "International law entitles and obligates only the States themselves, not their citizens. The national authority of the State stands between citizens and the international community of States ... One thing should not be overlooked in this regard, however; the regulations of the 'international commissions' ... contain the first hints of an international law that binds the citizens of the various states directly. But precisely these hesitant beginnings cast the rule that is still valid into even sharper relief."[21] This "rule" that the individual is not a subject of international law was argued in leading textbooks until after the Second World War,[22] but it was never beyond dispute, as will be shown in the following.

a certain procedure, regardless of their content. No law was recognized beyond the (positive) international law created in this way. See the founder of object theory, Heilborn, *System des Völkerrechts*, 1896, 370: "International law is the embodiment of the legal norms recognized by States as rules for their coexistence" (translation mine).

20 See Zorn, *Grundzüge des Völkerrechts*, 1903, 10: "The legal sources of international law therefore do not include natural law or legal and moral philosophy, politics, or the results of historical developments" (translation mine).

21 Franz von Liszt, *Das Völkerrecht systematisch dargestellt* (4th ed., Berlin: Verlag von O. Häring 1906), 41 with n. 2 (translation mine).

22 For views *against* the international legal status of the individual as a subject, see, e.g., Lassa Francis Lawrence Oppenheim, *International Law: A Treatise*, Vol. I (London: Longmans Green 1905), § 1 (3), § 14 (19–20); Rolf Knubben, *Die Subjekte des Völkerrechts* (Stuttgart: Kohlhammer 1928), 487 et seq.; Dionisio Anzilotti, *Corso di Diritto Internazionale* (3rd ed., Rome: Athenaeum 1928), 113, 121 et seq.; Karl Strupp, *Grundzüge des positiven Völkerrechts* (5th ed., Bonn: Röhrscheid 1932), 1 et seq., 32 et seq., 95 et seq., 102 et seq.; Georg Schwarzenberger, *A Manual of International Law* (London: Stevens 1947), 35, 53–54. For numerous additional references, see Manner, Object Theory, 1952, 429 n. 2.

2.1.3 *Individualistic International Legal Theories from the Nineteenth Century until after the Second World War*

Already in 1860, Robert von Mohl found fault with international jurisprudence's fixation on sovereignty and believed the (academic) "promotion" of States should be only a "last resort for achieving the purposes of human life".[23] "Legal propositions must be found that govern connections among individuals at their most potent, namely beyond the life of the individual State, for the achievement of their life purposes . . . First, all *subjects of an international connection* must be taken into account; not only the States themselves, but also social circles and *individual human beings*."[24] Other authors of the time pointed out the obligations of individuals arising from the legal acts of the early international organizations (international river commissions) and customary international law (law of piracy, blockade, and smuggling). In 1899, Wilhelm Kaufmann concluded from the existence of offences against international law (piracy, slave trade, etc.) that direct international legal obligations existed for individuals.[25] By virtue of international treaties or other international law, Kaufmann claimed that "direct, autonomous international legal obligations can be derived for subjects of the State".[26] He further stated that "these are *individual rights and legal obligations* governed and determined by international law, some of which are referred to as private, some of which as public rights and obligations".[27] Kaufmann did not justify these in terms of natural law, but rather voluntaristically: He claimed the validity of international law was based on the "joint act of will" in consequence of the *assentio mentium*. This meant that international law applied "to individual States *and possibly to individuals* and to organs of the State, because they are encompassed by the international

[23] According to Mohl, it was erroneous to "examine the entire subject matter generally only from the perspective of the sovereignty of States . . . On this view, the effort naturally aims to give up as little autonomy as possible; instead, the right view is rather that, once autonomy is secured (which must, however, come first as the basis of all thriving), the community of the largest organic connections among human beings – called States – should be promoted to the extent possible as a last resort for achieving the purposes of human life. The usual treatment of international law thus breaks off right in the middle" (Robert von Mohl, *Staatsrecht, Völkerrecht und Politik*, Vol. 1 (Tübingen: Laupp & Siebeck 1860), 585; translation mine).

[24] *Ibid.*, 586 (translation and italics mine). See also *ibid.*, 599 and 626–636 (on the "promotion of the purposes of individuals" through international law).

[25] See Wilhelm Kaufmann, *Die Rechtskraft des internationalen Rechtes und das Verhältnis der Staatengesetzgebung und der Staatsorgane zu derselben* (Stuttgart: F. Enke 1899), 27.

[26] *Ibid.*, 25 (translation mine). [27] *Ibid.*, 3 (translation and italics mine).

community of peoples".[28] "It should rather be traced back to the introduction of new objective legal norms brought about by the international treaty – a *jus supra partes* – that these individual rights and duties arise or can arise."[29]

In a discussion of the "Chinese question" in 1901, Albert de Lapradelle drew attention to the global "interdependence" of States and postulated a (moral or international legal) cooperation obligation between States. He justified his call for the primacy of the protection of (international) human rights over State sovereignty in *democratic* terms: "It is not in respect of the sovereignties, but in the defence of the rights of man against them, that international law summons up its principle and finds its end. *The new public law, which has placed the will of humans as the basis of governments, needs a new law of nations which sets as the programme and the objective of international law the protection of human rights.*" More speculatively than on the basis of the law applicable in 1901, de Lapradelle saw the human being as the rationale and purpose of a "new" manifestation of international law: "Thereby, replacing the old law of nations which did not look further than to the sovereign states, a new law of nations which sees man as over and above the states has found itself."[30]

According to Hermann Rehm, individuals were "subjected to" but not "members of" the international legal community. They were "international legal subjects", but they did not have the same legal status as States, i.e., they were second-class subjects. Rehm based his arguments on the different categories of States recognized at that time; from the fact that the individual obligations for individuals in the different categories of States were identical, he concluded that those obligations were directly subject to international law. According to Rehm, the legal status of individuals was manifested by the fact that they had the international legal obligation not to break blockades or supply war contraband. Rehm claimed that these obligations were, as a matter of logic, directly subject to international law because they were also imposed on the citizens of neutral States (which themselves were not bound by the blockade). Moreover, the obligation not to engage in piracy was not mediated by the State, because it also applied to citizens of "civilized States".[31]

[28] *Ibid.*, 77 (translation and italics mine). [29] *Ibid.*, 30 (translation mine).

[30] Albert Geouffre de Lapradelle, La Question Chinoise, *Revue Générale de Droit International Public* 8 (1901), 272–340, 339 (italics and translation by the author, here and in the following, translations from French by Anne Peters).

[31] *Hermann Rehm*, Untertanen als Subjekte völkerrechtlicher Pflichten, *Zeitschrift für Völkerrecht und Bundesstaatsrecht* 1 (1906), 53–55.

After the adoption of the Convention (XII) Relative to the Creation of an International Prize Court at The Hague of 1907 – which never entered into force – Walther Schücking was one of the theorists affirming a partial international legal subjectivity of the individual on the basis of the individual power to bring claims afforded by that convention. Schücking pointed out that international obligations for individuals had "always" existed and – in exceptional cases – so had rights.[32] According to John Westlake, "The society of states … is the most comprehensive form of society among men, but it is among men that it exists. States are its immediate, men are its *ultimate members*. The duties and rights of States are only the duties and rights of men who compose them."[33]

After the First World War and as a reaction to rampant nationalism, individualistic points of view gained considerable momentum. Starting in the 1920s, a sociological school emerged. It was based on a radical French constitutional theory that was opposed to the idea of the State as a sovereign collective personality with its own "will of the State" and instead reduced the State to "social reality" alone, i.e., to the individuals performing functions of the State.[34] This individualistic conception was transferred to international law by Georges Scelle. He argued that legal relationships were social relationships. Social relationships could only exist among individuals. Consequently, "sociabilité internationale" was also based on interindividual relationships. According to Scelle, the international legal order determines all domestic law, which must be compatible with international law. For this reason, every individual was also directly subject to international law. International law acted merely in different roles:[35] "An international society, just like any national society, is a society of individuals, and nothing but individuals."[36]

32 See Walther Schücking, *Der Staatenverband der Haager Konferenzen* (Munich and Leipzig: Duncker & Humblot 1912), 141–148.

33 John Westlake, Chapter VI: The Principles of International Law, in: Lassa Oppenheim (ed.), *The Collected Papers of John Westlake on Public International Law* (Cambridge: Cambridge University Press 1914), 78–85, 78 (italics mine).

34 See Léon Duguit, *Traité de droit constitutionnel*, Vol. I (2nd ed., Paris: E. de Boccard 1921), § 38 (324–335), on international legal subjectivity in § 62 (560–565); Vol. II, 1923, *passim*, e.g., 2, 404, 417, 428–429. However, Duguit argued throughout his life against the possibility of individual rights (in contrast to solely objective law).

35 Georges Scelle, Règles générales du droit de la paix, *Recueil des Cours* 46 (1933/IV), 327–703, 342–343; Scelle, *Droit International Public* (Paris: Les Ed. Domat-Montchrestien 1944), 410–411; Scelle, Some Reflections on Juridical Personality in International Law, in: George A. Lipsky (ed.), *Law and Politics in the World Community* (Berkeley: University of California Press 1953), 49–58.

36 Scelle, Règles générales, 1933, 343 (translation by the author).

"Only individuals are subject of public international law."[37] Similarly, Louis Le Fur claimed, "The legal personality must be the simple translation of natural personality, so that it must be accorded to every individual."[38]

Hans Kelsen reached the same conclusion, albeit with a different justification: "The idea that there could exist, among States and between States and individuals, relationships which would not be relationships between individuals, is a simple illusion which can be explained only by the inadmissible hypostasis of the State as a superman."[39] According to Nicolas Politis, international law since the Great War has been undergoing a phase of transformation from the international law of States into a genuinely universal law of human beings. Because States are only fictions and consist of human beings, and because ultimately all law must serve human beings, international law as a social product does not have any other structure than that of domestic law.[40] Maurice Bourquin diagnosed "a thrust, every day more visible, in favour of what could be called the international emancipation of the individual".[41] And James Brierly claimed, "In the final analysis, only individuals are able to be subjects of this law" (i.e., of international law).[42]

The authors of that era referred back to various theoretical justifications: While Kelsen emphasized the legal status of the individual as a normative-logical abstraction, Scelle referred to the socio-biological awareness of human solidarity. All of these approaches "represented an effort to preserve the interwar legal order against the destructive powers of European nationalism by way of the medium of the law".[43] The literature thus contained an overlapping consensus in favour of the international legal subjectivity of the individual.

[37] Georges Scelle, Précis de droit des gens: Principes et systématique, Vol. I, *Introduction, le milieu intersocial* (Paris: Sirey 1932), 42 (translation by the author).

[38] Louis Le Fur, La Théorie du Droit Naturel Depuis le XVIIe Siècle et la Doctrine Moderne, *Recueil des Cours* 19 (1927/III), 259–442 (404; translation by the author).

[39] Hans Kelsen, Les Rapports de Système entre le Droit Interne et le Droit International Public, *Recueil des Cours* 14 (1926/IV), 231–329 (281; translation by the author).

[40] See Nicolas Politis, *Les nouvelles tendances du droit international* (Paris: Hachette 1927), 55–93, esp. 76–77.

[41] Maurice Bourquin, Règles Générales du Droit de la Paix, *Recueil des Cours* 35 (1931/I), 5–229 (46; translation by the author).

[42] James Leslie Brierly, Règles Générales du Droit de la Paix, *Recueil des Cours* 58 (1936/IV), 5–237 (47).

[43] Jochen von Bernstorff, *The Public International Law Theory of Hans Kelsen: Believing in Universal Law* (Cambridge: Cambridge University Press 2014), 150.

In summary, *international individualism* was the thesis advocated by international legal scholars, especially during the interwar period. This was not only a reaction to the horrors of the First World War; the thesis was also strongly supported by democratic thought and fear of the emergence of mass society. The international lawyers of the 1920s and 1930s who had an individualistic orientation felt the rise of totalitarianism and tried to protect the individual from it with the help of international law.[44] Although at the political level, this intellectual current appeared unsuccessful at first – as the outbreak of the Second World War soon thereafter showed – it did create a breeding ground for the later general recognition and codification of international human rights.

Out of the catastrophe of the Second World War arose the second pillar of the readjustment and centring of the international system around the individual – in the form of the Nuremberg trials of 1946. These war crimes trials postulated the criminal responsibility of individuals under international law and removed the perpetrators from the protective shield of the State, behind which they tried to hide (see Chapter 5).

The plurality of justifications of the international legal personality of the individual continued after the Second World War. Still under the impression of the war and the nuclear threat, Philip C. Jessup performed a thought experiment on the "assumption that progress must and can be made in the social sciences to come abreast of the new advances in the physical sciences". Among the "keystones of a revised international legal order" (his model order), he included "the point that international law, like national law, must be directly applicable to the individual". His method was hypothetical: "[T]ake as a *hypothesis* the general acceptance of the thesis that international law does apply directly to the individual, that it does bind him as well as states directly, and in the light of that hypothesis re-examine the existing law as it has developed through the centuries to see what changes, what modifications would need to be made to fit the law to the new basis."[45]

In contrast, the academic trailblazer of the Nuremberg trials and the codification of human rights, Hersch Lauterpacht, argued in terms of natural law. According to Lauterpacht, "in relation to both rights and

[44] See Janne Elisabeth Nijman, *The Concept of International Legal Personality: An Inquiry into the History and Theory of International Law* (The Hague: TMC Asser Press 2004), 87, 126–127, 130, 147–148, 171, 187, 225 and *passim*.

[45] Philip C. Jessup, *A Modern Law of Nations* (New York: Macmillan 1950), pp. 2 and 10 (italics mine), see also pp. 9 and 17.

duties, the individual is the final subject of all law",[46] "the ultimate unit of all law, international and municipal".[47] The necessity of the status of the individual as a subject was justified by Lauterpacht with reference to the prevention of general irresponsibility due to the establishment of a protective screen by the State. Only in that way, he opined, generally accepted standards of ethics among civilized communities could be realized.[48]

2.1.4 The International Legal Status of the Individual in Contemporary Paradigms

Since the 1950s and 1960s, sociological "policy-oriented" jurisprudence (New Haven School) has started from the premise that law and policy cannot be sharply separated. The representatives of the New Haven School define international law as a specific decision-making process and as a communication flow with political content and the intention to exercise control.[49] In this model, the dichotomy of "subjects" and "objects" is rejected. There are only "participants". From this perspective, individuals are "participants in the world power process" alongside States and international institutions.[50]

Participants include both holders of rights and duties and creators of law; an actor who holds rights without the power to make law is not given any special conceptual designation. The term "participant" also tends to negate any distinction between objective law and subjective rights. Usage of the term "participant" thus omits two distinctions that would be helpful for analytical purposes; thus, the term is under-differentiated.

The next paradigm, critical legal studies, has an anti-individualistic orientation. While critical theory finds fault with the traditional ("liberal") legal methodology for wrongly ignoring the subject and subjectivity in its

[46] Hersch Lauterpacht, *International Law and Human Rights* (London: Stevens 1950), 69.

[47] Lauterpacht, Grotian Tradition, 1946, 1–53 (27).

[48] See Hersch Lauterpacht, Chapter 5: The Subjects of International Law, in: Elihu Lauterpacht (ed.), *International Law: Being the Collected Papers of Hersch Lauterpacht (1970–1978), Vol. I: The General Works* (Cambridge: Cambridge University Press 1970), 279–307 (280–281).

[49] See Siegfried Wiessner/Andrew Willard, Policy-Oriented Jurisprudence, *German Yearbook of International Law* 44 (2001), 96–112 (101–102).

[50] Myres McDougal, International Law, Power, and Policy: A Contemporary Conception, *Recueil des Cours* 82 (1953/I), 133–260 (173–174); Rosalyn Higgins, *Problems and Process: International Law and How We Use It* (Oxford: Clarendon 1995), 50.

analysis of the application and interpretation of the law,[51] its premise is that the individual is not an essential subject but rather socially constituted by multiple factors. According to the postmodernists, the individual is transformed into a psychological system – the minimum copy of a plural society – whose design is similarly complex to the wider world of the complicated nucleus of an atom. According to this view, the individual has entered the facelessness of networked system connections and perceives itself within that network as a divisible and divided being whose connection even with itself is doubtful.[52] Under the topic "The disappearance of the subject", it is established from this point of view that "the subject has become suspect"; the subject as a central category of modernity is dead.[53] In postmodern legal writings, identity is seen as "political", not "essential". Because social relationships determine the positions of every social actor, every actor is the locus of many "subject positions" and cannot be reduced to a single one. Moreover, every social position is in turn the locus of "multiple possible constructions", depending on the discourses that "construct" this position.[54] Every statement about status as a subject is therefore linked to a political commitment.

And then there is the postmodern criticism of individual rights as such: The rhetoric of rights is said to be so open and indeterminate that both parties to a dispute can instrumentalize them. The right that appears so progressive in one case can be used in the next case against the pretender. Rights are a component of the narrative of legitimacy and thus a masquerade that serves to perpetuate power structures.

This postmodern deconstruction of the individual and the individual's rights may be appealing within the field of literary studies, but it cannot be reconciled with the existence of law as a social fact and an instrument of control. Law views the person as a legal, indivisible unit of attribution with an identity across time. This view of the person is necessary to demand compliance with contractual obligations and to justify civil

[51] See Pierre Schlag, The Problem of the Subject, *Texas Law Review* 69 (1991), 1627–1743; Jack M. Balkin, Understanding Legal Understanding: The Legal Subject and the Problem of Legal Coherence, *Yale Law Journal* 103 (1993), 105–175.

[52] In the domain of literary history, see Wolfgang Frühwald, *Der Zerfall des Individuums: Über szientifisches Erschrecken in der Literatur* (Heidelberg: C. F. Müller 1993), 15–17.

[53] Peter Bürger, *Das Verschwinden des Subjekts: eine Geschichte der Subjektivität von Montaigne bis Barthes* (Frankfurt a. M.: Suhrkamp 1998), 9 and 12 (translation mine).

[54] Robert S. Chang, The End of Innocence or Politics after the Fall of the Essential Subject, *American University Law Review* 45 (1996), 687–694 (688, 690–691, 694), quoting, amongst others, Chantal Mouffe.

liability and criminal responsibility. Abandoning the person or the legal subject would render order through law impossible. The specific critique of rights will be addressed in the final chapter (pp. 530–36).

Unlike critical studies, the economic analysis of law ("law and economics") is based on methodological individualism. Its representatives accept that the individual is the actual source of rights (including international rights). "Consumer sovereignty" holds sway.[55] The emergence of the international legal order is explained in individualistic terms. It is claimed to have arisen spontaneously as an unintended product of individual, preference-maximizing behaviour.[56] States are recognized as collective entities without their own rationality. Viewed in this light, States act only as imperfect mediators for individuals. From the rational choice perspective, the choices of the State are in reality choices of individuals participating in the decision-making process.[57] However, the economic analysis of international law is predominately focused on the State. The significant works adopting this approach do not even include individuals.[58] The approach is thus unable to explain the bulk of current developments in international law.

The communitarian critique in the 1980s and 1990s of "liberal" individualism and its – according to the communitarian view – empirically faulty and morally questionable focus on the "unencumbered self" (Michael Sandel) had practically no impact on international legal scholarship.[59] Instead, the present era – which is often perceived as a period of crisis in positive international law – has seen a renaissance of *natural law*, in which the individual is celebrated as the "true subject" of international law. In his general Hague lecture in 2005,

[55] Jeffrey L. Dunoff/Joel P. Trachtman, The Law and Economics of Humanitarian Law Violations in Internal Conflict, *American Journal of Internatinal Law* 93 (1999), 394–409 (397).

[56] See Joel P. Trachtman, *The Economic Structure of International Law* (Cambridge, MA: Harvard University Press 2008), 10.

[57] See *ibid.*, 18.

[58] See, e.g., Andrew Guzman, *How International Law Works* (Oxford: Oxford University Press 2008). In Jack L. Goldsmith/Eric A. Posner, *The Limits of International Law* (Oxford: Oxford University Press 2005), human rights are mentioned only from the perspective that the ratification of human rights treaties is in States' own interests because doing so enhances prestige and does not entail any true disadvantages if the treaties are not complied with. The economic approach is thus part of the political scientific tradition of realism, even though it sometimes sees itself differently.

[59] See, generally, Shlomo Avineri/Avner De-Shalt (eds), *Communitarianism and Individualism* (Oxford: Oxford University Press 1992).

Antônio Augusto Cançado Trindade elaborated on this idea: "the consolidation of the legal personality and capacity of the individual as subject of International Law constitutes the most precious legacy of the international legal thinking of the second half of the twentieth century. Such thinking overcame the exclusion of the individual from the international legal order by State legal positivism, and achieved the rescue of the individual as subject of International Law. ... Individuals appear nowadays as true subjects – rather than simply 'actors' – of International Law."[60] "The recognition of the individual as subject of both domestic law and International Law represents a true juridical revolution – to which we have the duty to contribute in the search for the prevalence of superior values – which comes at last to give an ethical content to the norms of both public domestic law and International Law."[61] Along these lines, Janne Elisabeth Nijman writes, "[T]he right to legal personality is part of man's human identity and humanity is under an obligation to defend it if the 'primary' political community fails to provide the necessary conditions. It therefore follows *that the individual is the legal personality par excellence of international law, i.e., the law of mankind.* Yes, states are international legal persons, but they are secondary persons; individual human beings are the universal human society."[62] Similarly, Rafael Domingo asked to "recover the centrality of the person for global law, abandonned as it was in international law". According to Domingo, States are (merely) legal persons consisting ultimately of human beings; all law is created by people for people and not by States, which are meant to serve people. The person (not as a holder of rights, but as a human being) is the protagonist of law. According to Domingo, the golden rule of "the new global law" is "*ex persona ius oritur*" (law arises from humans). Human beings are the "authentic" holders of rights, at all times and everywhere.[63]

60 Antônio Augusto Cançado Trindade, International Law for Humankind: Towards a New *Jus Gentium, Recueil des Cours* 316 (2005), 9–444 (252) (footnotes omitted; see also *ibid.*, 34, 58).

61 *Ibid.*, 274. For Cançado Trindade's approach, which clearly follows the natural law paradigm, see *ibid.*, 33–34, 57, 147, 265–267. The author understands the "historical process of humanization of International Law" as a process of focusing on "fundamental values" and the "realization of superior common goals" (*ibid.*, 282).

62 Nijman, *International Legal Personality*, 2004, 473 (italics mine). See in this sense also Sinthiou Estelle Buszewski, Das Individuum als Völkerrechtssubjekt, Ad Legendum (2014) no. 3, 178–183.

63 Rafael Domingo, *The New Global Law* (Cambridge: Cambridge University Press 2010), 124–126.

A neo-natural law paradigm is best suited for justifying an "original" international legal personality of the individual that is not dependent on the State. However, such a paradigm hardly satisfies today's scientific standards of intersubjective comprehensibility. It must therefore be supplemented by doctrinal considerations on the basis of public law. I will furnish such considerations in Chapter 13 after giving an overview of the law as it stands.

2.2 Historical Legal Practice

Have these ideas on the international legal status of the individual been reflected in legal practice, and have they correctly analysed the actual legal situation and inspired their further development? Only a very brief overview will be provided here.[64] I will enter into the details on the development of various legal institutions in the subsequent chapters.

2.2.1 From 1900

The procedural status of individuals was strengthened by Mixed Arbitral Tribunals at the beginning of the twentieth century. According to the *Hague Convention of 1907 Relative to the Creation of an International Prize Court*, which never entered into force, an individual ("neutral individual" or "an individual subject or citizen of an enemy Power") would have been able to appeal to the International Prize Court as an appellate court against decisions of the national prize courts. Individuals would have been able to contest the lawfulness of a "prize", i.e., the capture of a merchant ship or its cargo in a naval war where such capture encroached on the individual's property.[65]

Between 1907 and 1918, a *Central American Court of Justice* existed, which from the outset was established for a limited period of ten years after the last ratification of the convention establishing it.[66] It also had

[64] The history of the international legal practice on the status of the individual is discussed by Kate Parlett, *The Individual in the International Legal System* (Cambridge: Cambridge University Press 2011).

[65] Articles 4 and 5 of the Convention (XII) relative to the Creation of an International Prize Court of 18 October 1907, available at http://worldcourts.com.

[66] Convención para el Establecimiento de una Corte de Justicia Centroamericana/ Convention for the Establishment of a Central American Court of Justice (Costa Rica, El Salvador, Guatemala, Honduras, Nicaragua) of 20 December 1907 (*American Journal of International Law* 2 (1908), Supp. 231–243). On the limitation in time, see Article XXVII.

jurisdiction to hear complaints of individuals.[67] The court dealt with a total of ten cases, seven of which were brought by individuals. Only one of the individual complaints resulted in court proceedings, and that complaint of arbitrary and illegal expulsion by Costa Rica was unsuccessful on its merits.[68] The right of individuals to bring proceedings against States granted here, without depending on support from the home State, was seen as a "revolutionary measure" in international law.[69]

2.2.2 *After the First World War*

The rise of the individual in international legal practice continued after the First World War. The *Versailles minority protection system* (on the basis of bilateral treaties, provisions in the peace treaties, and unilateral declarations to the League of Nations) granted members of minority groups substantive rights or privileges: the right of option; special rules governing child-rearing, schooling, and religion; financial support; and political autonomy. The substantive provisions were secured procedurally by the "dual guarantee", namely by national and international legal protection. The international component of this guarantee included rights of petition and complaint by individual members of minority groups. The most important bilateral treaty that served as a model was the *Upper Silesia Agreement* of 15 May 1922 between Germany and Poland; this was operational from 1922 to 1937.[70] The agreement provided two mechanisms of interest here. Firstly, it allowed individuals to bring proceedings for compensation before an international arbitral tribunal on grounds of "revocation of or interference with vested rights".[71] In a groundbreaking award, the arbitral tribunal decided that

[67] Article III of the Convention (*ibid.*): "It shall also take cognizance of the cases which by common accord the contracting Governments may submit to it, no matter whether they arise between two or more of them or between one of said Governments and individuals. It shall also have jurisdiction over cases arising between any of the Contracting Governments and individuals, when by common accord they are submitted to it."

[68] See Rosa Riquelme Cortado, Central American Court of Justice (1907–18), in: Rüdiger Wolfrum (ed.), *The Max Planck Encyclopedia of Public International Law* (Oxford: Oxford University Press 2012), paragraph 16 and other references.

[69] *Ibid.*, paragraph 21.

[70] German-Polish Agreement on Upper Silesia (Upper Silesia Agreement) of 15 May 1922, X LNTS 38.

[71] Article 5 of the Upper Silesia Agreement (n. 70): "Concerning the question of whether and to what extent the State must provide compensation for the revocation of or interference with vested rights, the arbitral tribunal shall decide directly on the complaint of the entitled person."

such proceedings were also permissible against the home State, thus clarifying that the "rights" were those of individuals, not their States.[72] The arbitral tribunal dealt with a total of approximately 4,000 such individual complaints, of which most were ultimately found to be unjustified, however.[73]

Secondly, the Upper Silesia Agreement granted members of minority groups the right to individual and collective petitions regarding violations of the minority protection provisions of the agreement. A petition had to be addressed to the applicable "State minority office" (defined by the agreement) and was then forwarded to the chairman of the Mixed Commission for comments; if the author of the petition was not satisfied, the author could call upon the Council of the League of Nations.[74] The Mixed Commission dealt with a total of 2,300 petitions submitted by individuals.[75]

Georges Kaeckenbeeck, who served as president of the arbitral tribunal for the duration of its existence, i.e., from 1922 to 1937, called the experience of the Upper Silesia arbitral tribunal a "vital lesson".[76] Kaeckenbeeck assumed that these bilateral agreements granted individual rights and did not only stipulate obligations between States: "The Arbitral Tribunal's activity relating to the protection of vested rights assumed a pioneering character for the international protection of *individual rights* after a cession of territory."[77] The granting of these international individual rights was a means to an end for the purpose of ensuring peace and prosperity in the region: The Upper Silesia Agreement "characteristically assumed the necessity of guaranteeing a number of individual rights in order to ensure peace and the maintenance of economic prosperity in the partitioned area".[78] This (also) instrumental understanding of international individual rights is typical for international law, but I do not believe that it devalues those rights (see Chapter 15, p. 472–74).

Kaeckenbeeck furthermore believed that "the peculiarity of the direct access of individuals to the Arbitral Tribunal" under international law,

[72] See the landmark decision of the Upper Silesian Arbitral Tribunal, Case No. 188, *Steiner and Gross* v. *Poland* of 30 March 1928, Annual Digest of Public International Law Cases Vol. 4 (London: Longman 1931), 291–292, note by Georges Kaeckenbeeck, *The International Experiment of Upper Silesia* (Oxford: Oxford University Press 1942), 47–54.

[73] See Kaeckenbeeck, *Upper Silesia*, 1942, 482.

[74] Chapter III of the Upper Silesia Agreement (n. 70), esp. Article 149.

[75] According to Hans Kelsen, *Principles of International Law* (2nd ed., New York: Holt Rinehart and Winston 1966), 225.

[76] Kaeckenbeeck, *Upper Silesia*, 1942, 482. [77] *Ibid.*, 523 (italics mine). [78] *Ibid.*, 528.

which was new at the time, was necessary to ensure effective legal protection of individuals: "[O]ne thing remained absolutely beyond doubt: the protection of the population of territories subjected to changes of sovereignty is not and cannot be satisfactorily ensured by international organs which only the Governments themselves can set in motion."[79]

After the First World War, the institution of international mixed arbitration was also employed beyond the realm of minority rights to deal with the consequences of the war. Under the Treaty of Versailles,[80] where the property, rights, or interests of nationals of allied or associated powers were affected by certain exceptional war measures or measures of transfer in German territory, those individuals were able to assert their claims for compensation directly against Germany and on their own behalf without intervention by their own governments. From these procedural powers stipulated by the treaty, the competent Mixed Arbitral Tribunals themselves derived a substantive and personal right to compensation grounded in the treaty.[81]

The granting of direct international rights to individuals after the First World War did not, however, constitute a conscious attempt to transform the structures of international law. According to Kate Parlett, "the engagement of individuals as rights-holders was the by-product of particular forces, not an end in itself."[82] In other legal arrangements of the interwar period, in refugee law, and within the framework of the International Labour Organization founded in 1922, individuals were protected in two different ways: either only as beneficiaries of State obligations or as direct holders of rights. "These structural devices do not appear to have been applied in accordance with any overarching sense that one or the other was more appropriate in a given situation."[83] Parlett sees "no discernible pattern or distinction" as to whether

[79] *Ibid.*, 482.

[80] Article 297(e) (on property, rights and interests in enemy territory) in conjunction with Article 304(b) (on the Mixed Arbitral Tribunal) of the Treaty of Versailles of 28 June 1919, 225 CTS 188.

[81] See, e.g., the German-French arbitral tribunal in the case *Sigwald c. Etat allemand* (1926), Recueil des décisions des tribunaux arbitraux mixtes, institúes par les traités de paix (TAM) 6, 888, in regard to Article 297(e) of the Treaty of Versailles (n. 80): "Ce droit à réparation constitue un droit individuel de chaque ressortissant allié, droit que celui-ci peut exercer directement contre l'Etat allemand sans intervention du gouvernement français." Similarly, see the German–British arbitral tribunal in the case *Lederer v. German Government* (1923), TAM 3, 762. In regard to proceedings brought by individuals against their home State, the arbitral tribunals declared they did not have jurisdiction (see, e.g., TAM 1, 606, 740, 916; TAM 2, 600; TAM 3, 415–416; TAM 6, 978).

[82] Parlett, *Individual*, 2011, 348. [83] *Ibid.*

individuals were to be seen as beneficiaries due to a legal reflex or to be endowed with their own international rights: "there seems to have been no consideration given to the question of which normative framework was better suited to the type of benefit or protection."[84]

2.2.3 *The* Danzig *Advisory Opinion of the PCIJ*

A milestone of international case law in the interwar period was the 1928 advisory opinion of the Permanent Court of International Justice (PCIJ), *Jurisdiction of the Courts of Danzig*. In that groundbreaking opinion, the PCIJ recognized that international treaties may grant individual rights and that their violation is actionable before domestic courts. At issue was the agreement between Poland and what was then the Free City of Danzig (the *Beamtenabkommen*, or Agreement concerning Officials, of 1921). However, the opinion is (probably intentionally) formulated in an ambiguous manner so that diametrically opposed conclusions can be drawn from it.[85] A crucial passage is as follows: "[B]eing an international agreement, [it] *cannot, as such*, create direct rights and obligations for private individuals. But it cannot be disputed that the very object of an international agreement, according to the *intention* of the contracting parties, may be *the adoption by the Parties of some definite rules creating individual rights and obligations* and enforceable by national courts."[86]

The first and second sentences of the key passage mentioned above are in tension with each other. The *first* sentence claims that, as the normal case, an international agreement *cannot* create rights and duties for individuals. In the following second sentence, this legal presumption is relativized (only) in the event that the treaty parties have specially intended to grant individual rights.

[84] *Ibid.*, 349.

[85] On the intentional ambiguity, see Hersch Lauterpacht, The Subjects of International Law (reprinted. in: Lauterpacht, *International Law, Being the Collected Papers of Hersch Lauterpacht* (Cambridge: Cambridge University Press 1970), chapter 5, 279–307 (289)): "And yet the Court was so ingeniously restrained in the manner in which it gave the decision that some have regarded it not as a far-reaching modification, but as an affirmation, of the established doctrine."

[86] PCIJ, *Jurisdiction of the Courts of Danzig*, PCIJ Ser. B, No. 15 (1928), pp. 17–18 (italics mine). The question for the Advisory Opinion was whether the railway employees who passed from the railway service of the City of Danzig (which had previously belonged to the German Empire) to Polish service were entitled to bring actions against the Polish railways administration in respect of pecuniary claims before Danzig courts based on an agreement between Poland and the Free City of Danzig.

In *Danzig*, the PCIJ then interpreted the *Beamtenabkommen* – taking the intention of the treaty parties into account – as a "part" of the employment relationship between the railway officials and the Polish Railway Administration: "That there is such an intention in the present case can be established by reference to the terms of the *Beamtenabkommen*."[87] Consequently, the railway employees were able to base their pecuniary claims against the railways administration on the provisions of the agreement before Danzig courts.[88]

It is important to note that the passage "*the adoption by the Parties of some definite rules creating individual rights and obligations* and enforceable by national courts"[89] is unclear. What is meant by "*some definite rules*"? The dualist reading[90] of this passage is that these must be rules of domestic law. According to this reading, which was advocated most prominently by the president of the PCIJ at the time, Dionisio Anzilotti, the court had indeed *not* determined that an international agreement could itself contain individual rights, but rather it had only drawn attention to the fact that the treaty parties could create such individual rights *in their implementing legislation*. According to the dualist interpretation, it was crucial that a treaty party (in the case of the *Beamtenabkommen*, Poland) failing to implement the treaty into its domestic law could not in turn rely on its inaction to justify the treaty breach under international law *vis-à-vis the other State party to the treaty*.[91]

87 *Ibid.*, p. 18.

88 *Ibid.*, p. 21: "that, consequently, the Danzig officials have, in accordance with the first part of the Decision, a right of action against the Polish Railways Administration for the recovery of pecuniary claims based on the *Beamtenabkommen*".

89 *Ibid.*, pp. 17–18 (italics mine).

90 For a distinction between the question of direct application from the issue of the inclusion of international law in the domestic legal sphere (monism/dualism), see Chapter 16, pp. 499–501.

91 See Dionisio Anzilotti, *Corso di Diritto Internazionale, Volume primo, Introduzione – Teorie Generali* (Padova: Cedam 1955), 339–340: The Advisory Opinion "certainly does not say that a treaty as such can create rights and duties of individuals without the provisions necessary for this purpose having been transposed into domestic law". According to Anzilotti, the court believed "that a treaty party undertaking to adopt its own *domestic legal* provisions could in no case assert the non-fulfilment of that obligation in order to avoid the duties imposed by the agreement *vis-à-vis the other treaty party*" (translation and italics mine). For a view similar to Anzilotti in the contemporary literature, see James Crawford, Continuity and Discontinuity in International Dispute Settlement: An Inaugural Lecture, *Journal of International Dispute Settlement* 1 (2010), 3–24 (8–9). From today's perspective, see also Article 27 of the Vienna Convention on the Law of Treaties (VCLT): "A party may not invoke the provisions of its internal law as justification for its failure to perform a treaty."

The opposite understanding of the advisory opinion was advocated by Hersch Lauterpacht. According to Lauterpacht, the first sentence of the cited key passage merely pays lip service to the established doctrine at the time. The court "receded *pour mieux sauter*".[92] According to this view, "some definite rules" referred to the provisions of international treaties themselves. If the treaty parties so intended and if the treaty provisions are definite enough, those provisions can create individual rights that are also directly applicable (i.e., can be invoked before a domestic court).[93] In this view, the advisory opinion is "in effect a revolutionary pronouncement", and "[i]t is difficult to exaggerate the bearing of the Opinion on the subject".[94]

This reading of the key passage does in fact fit better with the conclusions of the advisory opinion, in which the court found:

> "that, in the intention of the contracting Parties, the relations between the Polish Railways Administration and the Danzig officials should be governed by the *Beamtenabkommen*, the provisions of which constitute part of what the High Commissioner calls the 'contract of service', and that consequently, the Danzig officials have, ... *a right of action* against the Polish Railways Administration for the recovery of pecuniary claims *based on* the *Beamtenabkommen*".[95]

The monist reading of the advisory opinion has prevailed.[96] But even according to the *Danzig* opinion interpreted in this way, the direct application of a treaty provision is still the exception that has to be specially proven. According to the advisory opinion, the criteria are the intention of the treaty parties and the definiteness of the rules.

2.2.4 *After the Second World War*

Only after 1945 was the full potential of the *Danzig* opinion developed. This happened through the punishment of individuals for serious

[92] Hersch Lauterpacht, *The Development of International Law by the International Court* (2nd ed., London: Stevens 1958), 174.

[93] See Lauterpacht, *Subjects of International Law*, 1970, 288: "The decision amounts to a clear denial of the view that individuals can acquire rights only through the instrumentality of municipal legislation; it denies the exclusiveness of States as beneficiaries of international rights."

[94] Lauterpacht, *Development of International Law*, 1958, 174 and 175.

[95] PCIJ, *Jurisdiction of the Courts of Danzig* (n. 86), p. 21 (italics added).

[96] For a very detailed and convincing justification of this understanding, see the impressive analysis by Kate Parlett, The PCIJ's Opinion in *Jurisdiction of the Courts of Danzig*: Individual Rights under Treaties, *Journal of the History of International Law* 10 (2008), 119–145, with the refutation of Anzilotti's reading, especially at 142–144.

violations of international law and with the acknowledgement of international human rights as a matter for the international community. The key phrase in the Nuremburg Judgment of 1946 against the major war criminals was as follows: "That International Law imposes duties and liabilities upon individuals as well as upon States has long been recognized. . . . Crimes against International Law are committed by men, not by abstract entities, and only by punishing individuals who commit such crimes can the provisions of International Law be enforced."[97] Nevertheless, the legal justification of this criminal liability was still long in dispute.[98] Moreover, "an international military tribunal was a political solution to a practical problem, and individual responsibility under international law was a by-product of that solution".[99]

The international protection of human rights received an enormous boost by the establishment of the United Nations, the adoption of the Universal Declaration of Human Rights of 10 December 1948, decolonization, and the adoption (1966) and entry into force (1976) of the two general human rights covenants as well as other human rights agreements. From today's perspective, international human rights are the central and entirely undisputed element of the international legal status of the individual. For exactly this reason, they are not an object of this study.

The most recent milestone in the consolidation of the legal practice relating to the international legal status of the individual is the 2001 judgment of the International Court of Justice (ICJ) in the *LaGrand* case. Here, the court derived international individual rights from the Vienna Convention on Consular Relations and placed them next to the rights of the State.[100] Unlike the PCIJ, which in *Danzig* relied substantially on the intention of the treaty parties when deriving individual rights from an international treaty, the ICJ overrode the historical intention of the contracting parties. This can be seen as a further step in the individualization of legal practice. Several years later, an arbitral tribunal found "[t]he rule according to which the dispositions of a treaty can confer subjective rights on individuals . . . . This rule forms part of contemporary international law."[101]

[97] International Military Tribunal, judgment of 1 October 1946, in: The Trial of German Major War Criminals, Proceedings of the International Military Tribunal sitting at Nuremberg, Germany, Part 22 (22 August 1946–1 October 1946), 446–447.

[98] For details, see Chapter 5. [99] Parlett, *Individual*, 2011, 352.

[100] ICJ, *LaGrand* Case (*Germany* v. *United States of America*), ICJ Reports 2001, 466. The individual rights within consular law are discussed in Chapter 11.

[101] Arbitral Tribunal, *France* v. *UNESCO*, Question of the tax regime governing pensions paid to retired UNESCO officials residing in France, Decision of 14 January 2003, *Revue*

2.3 Conclusion

In the final analysis, "[t]he idea that international law rules not only the intercourse of independent states but also that its provisions are directly binding on individuals without the intermediary of their state, is at least as old as the science of international law".[102] This established scholarly thesis was based on certain foundations in the actual practice of international law and in turn has inspired the further development of those foundations. However, the idea of the international legal personality of the individual has hardly been single and uniform. Over the course of the development phases of international law and its "science", this personality has been justified in various ways (through natural law, sociologically, psychologically, or in terms of legal logic).[103] In other words, the evaluation of the international legal subjectivity (international legal personality) of the individual has always been influenced by trends. It is the function of the scientific paradigm prevailing in each era.

Hersch Lauterpacht can be considered the most influential representative of an "individualistic" view because his conception has influenced the reality of the protection of human rights and international criminal law most clearly.[104] Summarizing the ideational and practical legal development, Antônio Augusto Cançado Trindade – judge at the Inter-American Court of Human Rights at the time and now judge at the ICJ – argued that "there is nothing intrinsic to International Law that impedes or renders it impossible to non-State actors to enjoy international legal personality. No one in sane conscience would today dare to deny that the individuals effectively possess rights and obligations which emanate directly from International Law, with which they find themselves, therefore, in direct contact".[105]

So is it even useful nowadays to specially explain or justify the international legal personality of individuals? Three considerations indicate that it is. Firstly, there has so far been no bottom-up explication of that

générale du droit international public 107 (2003), 221–256, paragraph 82 (p. 261; translation by the author).

102 Marek St. Korowicz, The Problem of the International Personality of Individuals, *American Journal of International Law* 50 (1956), 534–562 (534).

103 See the excellent study by Roland Portmann, *Legal Personality in International Law* (Cambridge: Cambridge University Press 2010), 126–172 on the "individualistic conception" of international legal personality.

104 *Ibid.*, 127.

105 IACtHR, *Juridical Status and Human Rights of the Child*, Advisory Opinion OC-17/02 of 28 August 2001, Concurring Opinion Antônio Cançado Trindade, paragraph 28.

international legal status from the rapidly changing body of positive international law since the 1990s. Secondly, the *original, objective international legal personality* of the individual – already entertained by Lauterpacht but almost unanimously rejected so far – must be justified in more detail and defended (Chapter 13). Thirdly, a new label – that of the international individual right – will be proposed for this legal finding (Chapter 17).

3

The Doctrine of the International Legal Personality of the Human Being

3.1 Basic Terminology: International Legal Subject and International Legal Person

There is no *numerus clausus* for the subjects (persons) of international law.[1] Moreover, international law has no general codified norm governing the definition and attribution of international legal personality (subjectivity).[2] This means that unlike its historical structural model – domestic civil law – international law includes no general "law on persons". Neither relevant treaties nor generally accepted principles of customary international law exist that would determine and attribute international legal personality.[3] International law is therefore an open system in a twofold sense.

Nevertheless, the following questions must be answered in international law as well: What is a legal subject? Who is included? Which participant in the legal process is entitled to apply the law to the facts in this regard? Is there even a specific procedure for attributing or granting the quality of a subject?

According to the terminology taken as a basis here, international legal personality (international legal subjectivity) refers to legal capacity:[4] Just as legal personality in general (in any given legal order) refers to the capacity to have an individual right or duty (arising from that legal order) and to not merely be at the mercy of objective

[1] See, fundamentally, Hermann Mosler, Die Erweiterung des Kreises der Völkerrechtssubjekte, *Zeitschrift für ausländisches öffentliches Recht und Völkerrecht* 22 (1962), 1–48.

[2] See Roland Portmann, *Legal Personality in International Law* (Cambridge: Cambridge University Press 2010), 271.

[3] On the legal basis for the international legal personality of human beings, see in detail Chapter 13.

[4] This terminology is widespread. See, e.g., Christian Walter, Subjects of International Law, in: Rüdiger Wolfrum (ed.), *The Max Planck Encyclopedia of Public International Law* (Oxford: Oxford University Press 2012), paragraph 1: "entities which are capable of possessing international rights and duties".

law,[5] international legal subjectivity means the *capacity to have an international individual right or duty* and not merely to be at the mercy of objective international law. All other "capacities", notably transactional ones, are discussed further in the following (see pp. 44–54).

In line with the case law of the ICJ and current literature,[6] the terms "international legal subject" and "subject of international law" are used synonymously and interchangeably with "international (legal) person". In its *Reparation for Injuries* advisory opinion, the ICJ equated the terms "international person" and "subject of international law".[7]

In contrast, older literature frequently distinguished between international legal subject and international legal personality (legal person). "Legal person" was often used to designate a broader group of entities, while the quality of being an international legal subject was defined more narrowly and was limited to States.[8] In its broader sense, the term "legal person" would (merely) do the work of designating social actors that the legal order takes into account or includes in some way. Other actors or entities that are not legal persons are thus excluded from the legal order, i.e., they are simply not relevant to the law.

A different restrictive view of the term "international legal subject" is held by authors who load up the term with content and in that way limit it to a narrow group of rights-holders. The term "international legal subject" is then used to designate only entities that enjoy a minimum "abundance" or "density" of rights, a certain freedom of action, or a certain generality of entitlements.[9] An entity that has only selective, particular rights is, according

[5] "Personality or person is the capacity to be a holder of rights, in other words: legal capacity" (Georg Jellinek, *System der subjektiven öffentlichen Rechte* (Tübingen: Mohr 1905), 28; translation mine).

[6] On the synonymous usage, see explicitly Kate Parlett, *The Individual in the International Legal System* (Cambridge: Cambridge University Press 2011), 29–30; Robert McCorquodale, The Individual in the International Legal System, in: Malcolm Evans (ed.), *International Law* (3rd ed., Oxford: Oxford University Press 2010), 284–310 (286).

[7] ICJ, *Reparation for Injuries Suffered in the Service of the United Nations*, Advisory Opinion, ICJ Reports 1949, 174 (179).

[8] Parlett, *Individual*, 2011, 29–30 and 356–357, and other references.

[9] See Karl Zemanek, Internationale Organisationen als Handlungseinheiten in der Völkerrechtsgemeinschaft, *Österreichische Zeitschrift für öffentliches Recht* 7 (1956), 335–372 (349–350 and 357–358); Christian Tomuschat, International Law: Ensuring the Survival of Mankind on the Eve of a New Century: General Course on Public International Law, *Recueil des Cours* 281 (1999), 11 et seq. (160): "identifying a special category of subjects of international law makes sense only with regard to entities which have a certain freedom of action on the international level and which engage in international transactions beyond a framework rigidly fixed once and for all in their constitutive instrument".

to this view, not an international legal subject. Expert bodies of human rights treaties and international courts are then not considered international legal subjects, even though they have individual powers such as those arising from human rights treaties and host State agreements. Any qualification of individuals under this system would require a precise examination of all the international rights and duties potentially held by individuals. This examination would show that individuals are situated in a grey area: Individuals have selective rights and duties, but the scope of those rights and duties is on the rise.

According to what may be called a "substantive approach", certain typical substantive rights or capacities can be derived from international legal personality,[10] especially the right to conclude treaties, the right to establish diplomatic missions, legal liability, and the right to participate in international organizations.

The same result emerges from the analytically converse strategy of other authors, which qualifies only those entities as international legal subjects that have certain capacities, e.g., the capacity to be held liable, the capacity to enjoy international privileges and immunities, and especially the capacity to conclude treaties.[11] This focus on the capacity to conclude treaties overlaps with the view that international legal subjectivity is limited to those who also create law (see pp. 50–54). The quality of being a person is then equated with capacity or capacities.[12] In discussions of this sort, it sometimes

[10] See, e.g., Manuel Rama-Montaldo, International Legal Personality and Implied Powers of International Organizations, *British Yearbook of International Law* 44 (1970), 111–155 (116 und 139–144). See esp. 139: "From the personality of an organization, as from that of a State, arise only those rights and duties which find their source in personality itself . . .: the rights to bring a claim, to negotiate, to conclude a special agreement, protest, request for an inquiry, etc. The *rights arising from personality* constitute in their totality, 'capacity to operate upon an international plane'" (italics mine).

[11] Christian Dominicé, for instance, requires this bundle of capacities. The individual is not a subject of international law because the three core capacities are missing: the capacity to conclude treaties, the capacity to maintain diplomatic relations, and the capacity to be held liable under international law (Christian Dominicé, L'émergence de l'individu en droit international public, in: Christian Dominicé, *L'ordre juridique international entre tradition et innovation* (Paris: PUF 1997) (original 1987), 109–123, 122). According to Tomuschat, Survival of Mankind, 1999, 160: "Then, the capacity to conclude international treaties would stand out as the main element permitting identification as a subject of international law."

[12] For this interchangeable usage, see Walter, Subjects of International Law, 2012, paragraph 21. For an inclusion of the *capacité à agir* in the concept of a subject of international criminal law, see Anne Laure Vaurs-Chaumette, *Les sujets du droit international pénal: Vers une nouvelle définition de la personalité juridique internationale?* (Paris: Pedone 2009).

remains unclear what capacity is at issue: the capacity to have rights and duties, the capacity to create law, the capacity to enforce law (by way of legal proceedings or otherwise), or the capacity to be held legally responsible?[13]

Independently of whether international legal personality defined in this way is considered as a precondition or as a consequence of the enumerated capacities or substantive rights, both approaches associate international legal personality with a minimum set of rights/capacities. Using that terminology, individuals would not be considered international legal subjects, because they have no right to conclude treaties and no right to establish and maintain diplomatic missions.

According to the approach taken here, the status as a person or subject is identified only with the first-mentioned capacity, namely the capacity to have rights and duties (as will be discussed in the following). I will also call "subjects" those actors who do not possess any capacity to create law (see pp. 50–54).[14]

It is sometimes argued that international legal subjects must have not only rights but also duties.[15] This would include individuals whose direct criminal responsibility under international law has meanwhile been established. Another widespread view is that international legal subjectivity is linked to the ability to assert substantive rights before an international dispute settlement body.[16] According to this conception, the individual is only a very limited international legal subject.

Finally, international legal theory, especially in the Soviet Union, once aimed to limit international legal subjectivity to sovereign entities and thus ultimately to States.[17] The view that only entities endowed with

[13] This reflects the ambiguity of "legal capacity" (which I use here as "being able to *hold* rights or duties") in Anglo-American law. Most UK and US readers think of "legal capacity" in a transactional sense. I thank my translator Jonathan Huston for clarifying this point.

[14] For an approach similar to the one taken here – with a clear distinction between "juridical personality" in the sense of "aptitude to be titulaire of rights and duties" and "capacity" in the sense of "aptitude to exercise", see IAGMR, *Juridical Status and Human Rights of the Child*, Advisory Opinion OC-17/02 of 28 August 2001, Concurring Opinion Cançado Trindade, paragraph 8.

[15] See Peter James Nkambo Mugerwa, Subjects of International Law, in: Max Sørensen (ed.), *Manual of Public International Law* (London: Macmillan 1968), 247–310 (249); David Feldman, International Personality, *Recueil des Cours* 191 (1985/II), 343–413 (359).

[16] See below p. 45.

[17] On the gradual recognition of the limited international legal personality of some (not all) international organizations in Soviet doctrine, see Chris Osakwe, Contemporary Soviet Doctrine and the Juridical Nature of Universal International Organizations, *American Journal of International Law* 65 (1971), 502–521. On the recognition of the international legal subjectivity of the individual only in the final phase of Soviet doctrine, see Rein

general political power can be international legal subjects appears to be an echo of the sovereignty-focused approach: "Ultimately, only those are subjects who participate and who have weight in international political life."[18] All other rights-holders are said to have merely *capacité internationale* but are not considered international legal subjects. According to this power-oriented template, individuals would not be international legal subjects.

Christian Walter has suggested getting rid of the term "international legal subject" and instead introducing "international law relationship" as the basic term. "The question would not be who acts, but rather whether the action in question is governed by international law or not. The focus consequently shifts from the international legal personality to what could be called an international law relationship." The hope would be that this conception "would contribute to a re-conceptualization of international law which takes into account the proliferation of its subjects".[19] This proposal is reminiscent of the advocacy within (German) administrative law doctrine of an "administrative law relationship" as the basic term to replace subjective-public rights.[20] It remains unclear what is gained by this shift. Relationships ordered by law contain one or several rights. I believe it is irrelevant whether the relationship constitutes the right or vice versa, since in either case a holder must be identified.

The best new clarification of the term "international legal personality" has been proposed by Roland Portmann.[21] Under the "concept" of international legal personality, he identifies five "conceptions" advocated throughout international legal history, some of which are still competing with each other today.[22] Portmann convincingly shows that some of these conceptions do not (or no longer) correspond to the contemporary premises of the international legal order.[23] According to him, only a combination of the "formal"

A. Mullerson, Human Rights and the Individual as Subject of International Law: A Soviet View, *European Journal of International Law* 1 (1990), 33–43 (esp. 35).

18 Robert Kolb, Nouvelle observation sur la détermination de la personalité juridique internationale, *Zeitschrift für öffentliches Recht* 57 (2002), 229–241 (236, further elaborated at 236–237; translation by the author).

19 Walter, Subjects of International Law, 2012, paragraphs 30–31.

20 See Anne Peters, Nebenpflichten im Verwaltungsrechtsverhältnis?, *Die Verwaltung* 35 (2002), 177–221.

21 See Portmann, *Legal Personality*, 2010.

22 Portmann refers to these as the States-only conception, the recognition conception, the individualistic conception, the formal conception, and the actor conception of international legal personality.

23 Portmann mentions the following basic premises: "State" is a legal status; the freedom and welfare of individuals is a concern of the international community; there are peremptory

and "individualistic" positions makes sense in the current framework.[24] The legal concept proposed here of an "international individual right" is easily compatible with Portmann's "combination theory" (see also Chapter 17).

But is the question of the international legal personality of an actor simply a theoretical game? For Theodor Schweisfurth, the qualification of the individual as an international legal subject is merely *l'art pour l'art*. According to Schweisfurth, placing individuals next to States as the main subjects of international law is even "ludicrous".[25]

So is the question of the status of the subject irrelevant, because *practically speaking, what matters are the individual rights and duties*, and these in turn can be verified in legal-empirical terms? "The identifier 'subject' has no objective and meaningful content, since it denotes no particular capacities: hence it fails to provide any revealing description of the relationship of the entity to the international legal system."[26] According to the pragmatic point of view, the set of rights and duties constitutes the real and effective legal status of an entity, including the individual.[27]

From this perspective, one might – along with Hans Kelsen – consider the concept of the international legal subject or person to be an artificial aid to thought or an auxiliary term: "'Person' is merely a personified unitary expression referring to a bundle of legal obligations and entitlements."[28] This would mean that "personality" is an "empty notion"[29] and that international legal

rules of international law; law cannot be derived immediately from facts (Portmann, *Legal Personality*, 2010, 268–269).

24 *Ibid.*, 243, 268–270 and *passim*.

25 Theodor Schweisfurth, *Völkerrecht* (Tübingen: Mohr Siebeck 2006), 42 (paragraph 147). This is consistent with his own definition, according to which international legal subjects are only entities with the capacity to create international law.

26 Parlett, *Individual*, 2011, 38, also 354.

27 See Portmann, *Legal Personality*, 2010, 3: "Personality is acquired whenever an international norm is addressed at a particular entity." See also Thilo Marauhn, Vorwort, in: Thilo Marauhn (ed.), *Die Rechtsstellung des Menschen im Völkerrecht* (Tübingen: Mohr Siebeck 2003), V: "But does it suffice ... to attest that the individual has international legal subjectivity? Should the question rather be asked what the concrete effects are of this 'change in status'?" (translation mine).

28 Hans Kelsen, *Reine Rechtslehre* (Leipzig: Franz Deuticke 1934), 177–178 (translation mine). Kelsen took a critical stance towards the "ideological" concept of the individual right (*ibid.*, 42–44) and believed legal obligations, not rights (entitlements), were primary (*ibid.*, 51).

29 Anna Mejknecht, *Towards International Personality: The Position of Minorities and Indigenous People in International Law* (Antwerpen: Intersentia 2011), 31.

personality is a "useless concept".[30] According to that critique, the search for "personhood" constitutes a "top-down approach" that gives no sustainable support for determining the rights, duties, and responsibilities actually attributable to an actor.[31] If the objection is formulated more strongly, the search for legal personality is even misleading: The labelling of an actor as a legal subject might suggest that the actor has rights and obligations to which he is not entitled. The shared generic term might also conceal the more important fact in practice that these so-called international legal subjects have very different sets of rights and duties.[32]

Kelsen and the cited international legal scholars correctly assume that no basic set of rights (e.g., the capacity to conclude treaties) can be derived from international legal personality, as discussed above. Once again, international legal subjectivity (personality) means international legal *capacity*, not the status of actually being an international rights-holder. In this sense, international legal subjectivity is purely a "formal term".[33] But a special term designating legal capacity is still not superfluous. Flagging out separately the international legal personality of the individual helps organizing the law. The determination of who in a given legal order is capable of possessing rights and obligations should be made beforehand, because this will help to answer upcoming questions – on whether a concrete legal text contains rights or obligations or not – easily and more consistently. Besides, only an explicit conceptualization of legal capacity makes it possible to confer *new* rights on an actor, irrespective of whether those rights are granted by a treaty. The equation (rejected here) of legal personality with the existing set of rights would mean that the status of the legal subject would be trapped in the current state of positive law.

30 Riccardo Pisillo Mazzeschi, Impact on the Law of Diplomatic Protection, in: Menno T. Kamminga/Martin Scheinin (eds), *The Impact of Human Rights Law on General International Law* (Oxford: Oxford University Press 2009), 211–233 (214–215).

31 José Alvarez, Are Corporations Subjects of International Law? *Santa Clara Journal of International Law* 9 (2011), 1–36 (26).

32 See, e.g., James Crawford, *Brownlie's Principles of Public International Law* (8th ed., Oxford: Oxford University Press 2012), 121: "to classify the individual as a 'subject' of international law is unhelpful".

33 Georg Dahm/Jost Delbrück/Rüdiger Wolfrum, *Völkerrecht*, Vol. I/2 (2nd ed., Berlin: De Gruyter 2002), 267.

3.2 Traditional Classification of International Legal Subjects: The State and Everyone Else

Customarily, the individual is referred to as a derivative, artificial, agreed, selected, partial, limited, passive, potential, or *sui generis* subject of international law. All of these designations begin with the normal case of the State as international legal subject or the State as the "natural person" of international law.[34] They manifest a mentality fixated on "the disenfranchisement of anything which is not a state" and on accepting "the consequence of the disenfranchisement of the natural person".[35] This will be shown in the following discussion by using the usual categorizations of international legal personality.[36]

In regard to the *material scope* of international legal personality, a distinction is made between "full"/"universal"/"general" subjects on the one hand and "partial"/"functionally limited" international legal subjects on the other hand. Only the State is claimed to be a "full legal subject". This view holds that only the State is potentially able to have all kinds of international legal rights and obligations. In this way, the State has full international legal personality. In contrast – under this classification – all other actors have only partial legal personality in international relations. They have only the capacity to hold certain types of rights or selective rights, depending on the norm that explicitly or implicitly concedes their legal personality. For instance, according to the predominant view, the international legal subjectivity of an international organization extends only as far as the tasks of the organization require pursuant to the founding charter or statute. The principle of *compétence d'attribution* applies. Because the international legal subjectivity of international organizations depends on their founding charters, it remains – according to this view – "derived" from States.

The idea of limited legal personality makes sense. For instance, no one would claim that individuals can declare war or acquire territory with international legal effect. But then, for the sake of consistency, the State should also be considered merely a limited legal subject: States do not – even potentially – possess the totality of all legal positions possible

[34] Along these lines, see also Hélène Ruiz Fabri, Les catégories de sujet du droit international, in: Société française pour le droit international (ed.), *Colloque de Mans: Le sujet en droit international* (Paris: Pedone 2005), 55–71 (66).

[35] Christopher Barbara, International Legal Personality: Panacea or Pandemonium? Theorizing About the Individual and the State in the Era of Globalization, *Austrian Review of International and European Law* 12 (2007), 17–58 (22).

[36] See, paradigmatically, Mosler, Völkerrechtssubjekte, 1962.

in international law. For instance, they are unable to enjoy human rights. In the final analysis, only partial international legal subjects exist, with a wide range of different rights and duties and very different levels of compactness.

A different classification arises from the following question: *In relation to whom* is international legal subjectivity effective? In other words, who has to recognize or treat the entity as an international legal subject? At this level, the "objective"/*erga omnes* international legal subjects are juxtaposed with the merely "particular" subjects. According to this approach, objective international legal personality means it is effective in relation to all actors, and any recognition by other subjects has a merely declaratory effect. It is sometimes claimed that important international organizations have "objective" international legal personality.[37] Transferring the considerations made regarding organizations to individuals, one could argue that individuals are merely particular international legal subjects.[38] Then a human being would, for instance, be a holder of the human rights guaranteed by the UN covenants only in relation to the States parties to those Covenants.

Yet another classification divides the "original"/"native"/"primary"/"necessary"/"natural"/"direct" international legal subjects from the "derivative"/"derived"/"secondary"/"conferred" subjects. Original (or similarly designated) international legal subjects are said to be only States: "The state is the original and at the same time necessary subject of the law of nations. It is it which *historically* has established a legal order of which, *logically*, its own personality is a presupposed necessity."[39] According to this view, States are not products of the law, but rather they are the creators of the law themselves; they are a fact presupposed by the legal order; they themselves are the basis of

[37] See, fundamentally, Finn Seyersted, *Objective International Personality of Intergovernmental Organizations: Do Their Capacities Really Depend upon the Conventions Establishing Them?* (Copenhagen: Krohns Boy Trykkeri 1963).

[38] See, e.g., Peter Malanczuk, *Akehurst's Modern Introduction to International Law* (London: Routledge 1997), 104: "if states of the first group confer international rights on individuals, then individuals are subjects of international law *as far as those states are concerned*" (italics mine); see also Riccardo Pisillo Mazzeschi, International Obligations for Reparation Claims?, in: Albrecht Randelzhofer/Christian Tomuschat (eds), *State Responsibility and the Individual: Reparation in Instances of Grave Violations of Human Rights* (The Hague: Martinus Nijhoff 1999), 149–172 (172): "relative" or "*inter-partes*" international legal personality of the individuals.

[39] Joe Verhoeven, *Droit International Public* (Bruxelles: Larcier 2000), 50 (italics and translation by the author).

international law. Derivative (or the like) means the international legal subject is constituted only within the already pre-existing legal order; the status as a subject is conferred upon the entity (by States) via an international treaty. That status can therefore also be withdrawn again. The premise here is that only States can generate international law (see also Chapter 17, pp. 544–48). Under this assumption, the distinction between States and all other political entities is precisely reflected in the distinction between original and derivative international legal subjects, as well as in the associated view that only those entities that create international law can also be full subjects of international law. Doctrinal objections will be made in the following against the coupling of legal capacity with the capacity to create law that gives rise to the categorizations of "native versus conferred" and "original versus derivative" (see pp. 50–54). In Chapter 13, I will return to the fundamental objection by traditionalists that the legal personality of the individual is necessarily "created" by the State, that it can always be revoked, and that it ultimately always is precarious (p. 409). In that chapter, I will argue that the dichotomy between States and all other international legal subjects is no longer fully tenable and, moreover, that the individual – not the State – is the "natural" person under international law.

3.3 Decoupling Substantive and Procedural Individual Rights under International Law

According to the traditional view, human beings are international legal subjects only to the extent they are able to avail themselves of proceedings before international courts and similar forums in order to enforce their rights autonomously without relying on diplomatic protection by their home State.[40] Otherwise, according to the traditionalists, individuals can at most be "potential" subjects of international law.[41] Along these lines,

[40] See Hans Kelsen, *Principles of International Law* (2nd ed., edited by Robert W. Tucker, New York: Holt, Rinehart & Winston 1966), 234, and the predominant view until a few years ago. See, e.g., Alfred Verdross/Bruno Simma, *Universelles Völkerrecht* (Berlin: Duncker & Humblot 1984), 256; Brownlie, Principles of International Law, 2008, 57.

[41] See Marek St Korowicz, The Problem of the International Personality of Individuals, *American Journal of International Law* 50 (1956), 534–562 (535): "But if we do not endow the individual with even a partial, limited capacity for action before international judicial or political bodies, we may speak of him as of a potential subject of international law, because the protection of his international rights, directly conferred upon him, still rests with the state."

Bruno Simma writes that when procedural enforcement possibilities are lacking, people are not international legal subjects in a "traditional" (formal) sense.[42] In contrast, this section argues that the international legal personality of the individual does not depend on individualized international enforcement possibilities.

3.3.1 Separation of Individual Rights and Remedies in Domestic Law

The classic view mentioned above links the substantive legal status to the procedural legal status. The intuitive starting point of that view is that the content of individual rights typically is defined in detail only in the event of conflicts. If rights are to give rise to true claims and not merely be programmatic appeals, they must also be enforceable in the event of conflict.[43] This idea is the basis of the legal adage of "no right without a remedy".

This traditional view, namely that rights must be actionable, originates in the Roman theory of action. According to that theory, what mattered was *actio*, i.e., the definition of the cause of action; any separate concept of a substantive legal claim was still underdeveloped. Recognition of a substantive claim as the basis of legal action began only in the twelfth and thirteenth centuries. This recognition emerged from the commentaries of the *Decretum Gratiani* and the *Corpus juris civilis* and the resulting canon and common law as it encountered natural law theory in the late scholastic period.[44]

For a long time, common law limited itself to this fixation on the writ and the associated formula "remedies precede rights". In the words of Frederic William Maitland, "[t]he forms of action we have buried, but they still rule us from the graves."[45]

42 Bruno Simma, Der Einfluss der Menschenrechte auf das Völkerrecht: Ein Entwurf, in: Isabelle Buffard/James Crawford/Alain Pellet/Stephan Wittich (eds), *International Law between Universalism and Fragmentation: Festschrift in Honour of Gerhard Hafner* (Leiden und Boston: Martinus Nijhoff 2008), 729–745 (734). Simma adds that this formal criterion is not decisive from a "pragmatic" perspective.

43 See Michael Ignatieff, The Attack on Human Rights, *Foreign Affairs* 80 (2001), 102–116 (108–109).

44 See Marietta Auer, Subjektive Rechte bei Pufendorf und Kant, *Archiv der civilistischen Praxis* 208 (2008), 584–634 (593–598) (589 and other references).

45 Frederic William Maitland, *Equity, also the Forms of Action at Common Law: Two Courses of Lectures*, edited by Alfred Henry Chaytor/William Joseph Whittaker (Cambridge: Cambridge University Press 1910), Lecture 1, 296 (http://archive.org/stream/equityalsoformso00mait#page/n5/mode/2up).

Also in German legal discourse, the substantive and procedural aspects of a (public) individual right were often conflated. Jellinek's classic definition of a public individual right as the "capacity to *actuate* legal norms in the individual interest"[46] has contributed to this conflation. By "actuating", however, Jellinek only meant the invocability of a norm by the citizen, such as before administrative authorities, and not actionability as a precondition for the existence of an individual right. For Jellinek, the existence of a public individual right was independent of the actual procedural ability of the rights-holder to enforce the right *in court*. It should not be inferred from the lack of developed legal protection that individual rights as such are also lacking.[47]

In fact, probably all legal systems of States now distinguish between substantive and procedural rights. Contemporary domestic law is based on an ideal-typical distinction between rights and legal protection.[48] The German Basic Law clearly distinguishes the two. According to Article 19(4), "Should any person's rights be violated by public authority, he may have recourse to the courts." This constitutional clause would be superfluous if one were to assume a definition that already includes the power of the individual to bring proceedings as part of the concept of an (individual) right.[49]

According to this clause, enforceability in court is a legal consequence of the substantive right, not a precondition thereof.[50] The Pandectist Bernhard Windscheid formulated this as follows: "For today's perception of the law, rights are primary and legal actions are secondary; rights are what create and legal actions are what is created."[51] With a slight delay, this also became the rule in English law. According to Holdsworth's History of English Law, " 'Ubi remedium ibi jus' had been the point of

[46] Jellinek, *System der subjektiven öffentlichen Rechte* 1905, 51 (translation and italics mine). See also Ottmar Bühler, *Die subjektiven öffentlichen Rechte und ihr Schutz in der deutschen Verwaltungsrechtsprechung* (Berlin: Kohlhammer 1914), 224: "Public individual rights are the legal position of the subject vis-à-vis the State in which the individual can demand something from the State or do something in relation to the State on the basis of a legal transaction or a compulsory legal proposition enacted for the protection of the individual's interests which the subject may invoke vis-à-vis the administration" (translation and italics mine). As distinguished from actionability, see ibid., 12–13.

[47] See Jellinek, *System der subjektiven öffentlichen Rechte*, 1905, 349–361, esp. 351.

[48] See Johannes Saurer, *Der Einzelne im europäischen Verwaltungsrecht: Die institutionelle Ausdifferenzierung der Verwaltungsorganisation der Europäischen Union in individueller Perspektive* (Tübingen: Mohr Siebeck 2013), 138.

[49] See *ibid.* [50] See *ibid.*, 68 et seq.

[51] Bernhard Windscheid, *Die Actio des römischen Zivilrechts vom Standpunkte des heutigen Rechts* (Düsseldorf 1857; reprint Aalen: Scientia 1969), 3 (translation mine).

view of the older law: it is beginning to give place to the modern point of view: 'ubi jus ibi remedium'."[52] This statement must be qualified even further today: Actionability is not a necessary but rather only a *possible* consequence. "Jus" can exist without "action" (or "remedium").

Alongside the theory of action, legal positivism is a further (outdated) inspiration for the coupling thesis. The "command" legal positivism of the nineteenth century viewed penalties and compulsory enforceability as conceptually necessary elements of the law. This conception of the law is, however, very narrow and not generally recognized. Even rights that are not actionable still play an important ordering and legitimating function. Accordingly, numerous legal norms are not enforceable *in courts* even in domestic law. Especially clauses found in national constitutions are often not fully justiciable.[53]

3.3.2 *Is the Separation of Substantive Law and Procedural Enforceability in International Law Useful?*

But is the conceptual distinction between substantive rights and judicial actionability, as has evolved in domestic law, also appropriate in international law? International law has been strongly influenced by Anglo-Saxon law. This provides a genetic explanation for the persistence of the coupling thesis. Schooled in the English system, Rosalyn Higgins did not yet dare in 1995 to throw the link between substantive law and the power to bring proceedings entirely overboard, but rather she merely asked the question: "Is . . . a right without a remedy . . . virtually no legal right at all? Or is that something that international lawyers, operating in a decentralized system, are not allowed to think? . . . Is the statement that international law is about inter-state obligations only, the consequence of a procedural disability under which the individual labours, or is it the cause of that procedural disability?"[54]

52 William Searle Holdsworth, *A History of English Law*, Vol. 3 (3rd ed., London: Methuen 1923), 456–457.

53 In the German Basic Law, see the objectives of the State (Article 3(2) sentence 2; Article 20(1); Article 20a; Article 23(1) sentence 1 of the Basic Law). In the Swiss Constitution, see the social objectives set out in Article 41.

54 Rosalyn Higgins, *Problems and Process: International Law and How We Use It* (Oxford: Clarendon Press 1995), 52–53. She tended towards decoupling the two, however: "[W]e are not unaccustomed to separating our definition of a right from our appraisal of a remedy." "My own view is that the individual does have certain rights owed to him under international law (and not just to his state)."

The ICJ posed the question of the potential international legal personality of the United Nations as follows: "whether the Charter has given the Organization such a position that it possesses, in regard to its Members, *rights which it is entitled to ask them to respect*. In other words, does the Organization possess international personality?"[55] Here, the ICJ saw the power to assert own rights as a necessary component of legal personality. This conceptualization is tantamount to the "actuation" of Jellinek's formulation.

In contrast, other international judgments clearly distinguish between substantive rights and actionability. Already the Permanent Court of International Justice held: "It is scarcely necessary to point out that the capacity to *possess* civil rights does not necessarily imply the capacity to *exercise* those rights oneself."[56] Also in the *LaGrand* case, the ICJ assumed without further ado that the VCCR "creates individual rights" that can (only) be asserted by the home State before the court.[57]

The uncertainty in the literature and case law has a deeper reason. Irrespective of historic remains of obsolete domestic legal patterns, the demand in international law for a coupling of rights and enforceability is mainly a manifestation of the *principle of effectiveness* in international law. According to this principle, many international legal institutions are defined by reference to real, factual, circumstances.[58] Along this line, while effectiveness is not a sufficient condition of an international legal right, it is a necessary condition thereof. The purpose of the principle of effectiveness is to prevent a divergence of the legal right from legal reality. Because international rights would be devalued if they are not realized – so the thinking goes – it is better not to recognize non-enforceable, i.e., non-effective, assertions as rights in the first place. The principle of effectiveness plays a greater role in international law than in domestic law because international law is more

[55] ICJ, *Reparation for Injuries Suffered* (n. 7), 178 (italics mine).

[56] PCIJ, *Peter Pàzmàny University Case*, Ser. A/B, No. 61 (1935), 231 (italics mine). See also IACtHR, *Judicial Condition and Human Rights of the Child*, Advisory Opinion No. 17, 28 August 2002, holding 1 of the opinion (p. 79) and concurring opinion of Cançado Trindade, paragraphs 6 and 8: The child is a holder of (human) rights irrespective of the child's capacity to act, i.e., the capacity to exercise those rights.

[57] ICJ, *LaGrand Case* (*Germany* v. *United States of America*), ICJ Reports 2001, 466, paragraph 77.

[58] The existence of a rule of customary international law requires corresponding practice, and the existence of a State as an international legal subject requires an effective government, etc.

vulnerable. As there is no central power endowed with the monopoly on the use of force that backs up the rights and that guarantees the effectiveness of international law in a general way, effective management at the micro level is important. An international individual right that cannot be asserted per se at the international level by the individual himself or herself does not appear to be automatically effective. The objection is therefore that the creation (by treaties and courts) and academic justification of individual rights that cannot be enforced internationally threaten to diminish the effectiveness of international law in general.[59]

The reality of international law conflicts with the demands of the principle of effectiveness, however: States are not subject to any compulsory international jurisdiction (even against other States that bring claims). This finding makes it even more inappropriate to link substantive rights and the legal personality of the individual with the availability of options to bring claims against States. While such "naked" rights may not be very effective, States themselves also suffer from the lack of effectiveness entailed by non-actionability. Despite this, we still assume that States have international powers and rights.

Moreover, the possibility of remedy that is properly envisaged by the advocates of a narrow, procedural concept of international legal personality may take on different forms. It does not necessarily require determination by the courts, as was implied by the procedural concept of international legal personality. This is even more true given that in international law the boundaries between the political-diplomatic and the legal-judicial resolution of disputes, i.e., of power-based and rights-based approaches, are fluid. Throughout history, various diplomatic conflict resolution mechanisms have gradually been incorporated into law, and the universal human rights mechanisms have also become more court-like.

Finally and especially, the procedural conception of the international legal personality of the individual ignores that the enforcement of rights can occur at different levels, i.e., at both the domestic and international levels. Thanks to the decentralized enforcement of individual rights through domestic institutions on the basis of a more generous recognition of the direct effect of international legal norms protecting the individual (see Chapter 16), the effectiveness of

[59] See Bernd Grzeszick, Rechte des Einzelnen im Völkerrecht, *Archiv des Völkerrechts* 43 (2005), 312–344 (342).

international individual rights can be enhanced. The coupling thesis underestimates the important role of domestic institutions in the decentralized enforcement of international law. This systemic function of domestic courts is not only a stopgap where a fully elaborated, international, court-like system for the protection of individual rights is lacking. On the contrary, the action of domestic courts is desirable on normative grounds because domestic courts are well placed to take care of the protection of international rights, as implied by the the legal principle of subsidiarity (on the enforcement of international individual rights, especially before domestic courts, see Chapter 15).

For all these reasons, but especially because of the important systemic function of domestic courts, it appears inconsistent from a doctrinal standpoint to elevate the proceedings available to the individual before international enforcement bodies to the defining characteristic of the international legal personality of the individual. In the ultimate analysis, therefore, the traditional coupling of legal personality with the individual power to bring claims should finally be dissolved.[60] Hence, the "procedural" conception of international legal personality is not convincing.

3.4 Legal Capacity and the Power to Create Law

Although individuals have rights and duties in contemporary international law, they do not have full capacity to create hard international law. As a general rule, they cannot conclude international treaties, and in the current scheme, their conduct does not constitute relevant practice that might lead to the creation of customary international law.

[60] Along these lines, see already Hersch Lauterpacht, The Subjects of the Law of Nations (Part I), *Law Quarterly Review* 63 (1947), 428–460 (455), repr. in: Elihu Lauterpacht (ed.), *International Law: Being the Collected Papers of Hersch Lauterpacht, Vol. 2: The Law of Peace Part I: International Law in General* (Cambridge: Cambridge University Press 1975), chapter 18. In more recent literature, see Karl Doehring, *Völkerrecht* (2nd ed., Heidelberg: C. F. Müller 2004), paragraphs 246–250; McCorquodale, The Individual and the International Legal System, 2010, 293; Walter, Subjects of International Law, 2012, paragraph 22. For a decoupling of the power to bring claims from international legal personality (but with the opposite conclusion), see also Dominicé, L'émergence de l'individu, 1997, 123: While States have granted individuals the power to bring claims, the individual is still not a subject of international law (mainly because the individual does not have the power to create law).

3.4.1 *Individuals as "Passive" Subjects of International Law at Best, Due to Lack of Power to Create Law?*

Several authors refer especially to the (supposed) lack of power by individuals to create international law in order to deny them the status of full subjects of international law. The lack of individuals' power to create law not only means that individuals cannot produce whatever international legal norms without further ado (as States can, for instance) but it also automatically means that they cannot enact any norms *on their own behalf*. Rights (and the legal personality that precedes rights) have been granted to them by States and can be taken away from them again by States as well. This consideration is the core of the references to "derivative" or "passive" international legal subjects.[61] Stricter authors using a narrower concept of the international legal subject even deny international legal subjectivity to individuals entirely, given their lack of power to create international law.[62] From that perspective, individuals must still be regarded "as an object on which to bestow or recognize rights, not as agents from whom emanates the power to do such bestowing . . . as an object or, at best, a consumer of outcomes, but not as an agent of process".[63] The problem of the *third-party conferral* of international legal status will be taken up again in Chapter 13. Here, only the coupling of the status as a subject with the actor's power to create law will be discussed. Neither does this coupling appear theoretically persuasive, nor is it based on accurate legal empirical premises, as will be shown in the following analysis.

3.4.2 *Technical Objections to the Coupling of International Legal Capacity with the Power to Create Law*

The coupling of international legal subjectivity with the power to create law contradicts the usual legal doctrine that distinguishes between the

[61] For details, see Chapter 17 (pp. 544–551).

[62] See Prosper Weil, Le droit international en quête de son identité: Cours général de droit international public, *Recueil des Cours* 237 (1992/VI), 9–370 (122): Individuals are merely objects of international law, because they cannot create international law themselves, but rather they have only been granted certain rights and duties by States. With detailed justification, see also Schweisfurth, *Völkerrecht* 2006, paragraphs 9–14 and 137–147. See also Alexander Orakhelashvili, The Position of the Individual in International Law, *California Western International Law Journal* 31 (2001), 241–276 (276).

[63] Joseph H. H. Weiler, The Geology of International Law – Governance, Democracy and Legitimacy, *Zeitschrift für ausländisches öffentliches Recht und Völkerrecht* 64 (2004), 547–562 (558).

capacity to hold rights and the power to create rights. In private law, legal personality and the capacity to contract are different concepts. Public law makes a distinction between the capacity to hold rights (e.g., the capacity to hold fundamental rights) and the right to vote (entitlement to participate in the creation of law).

From the perspective of public law, it goes without saying that individuals are not autonomous creators of law but rather are merely co-legislators exercising their democratic right to elect representatives and their direct-democratic right to vote. The idea of "self-legislation" within the framework of democracy is a legal fiction that reconciles the antagonistic principles of individual self-determination with subordination to the collective.

Again, the question arises whether the distinction that is obvious in domestic law between the capacity to hold rights and the capacity to create law is not applicable in international law because of special characteristics of the international legal order. It must be determined whether a specific structure of international law requires a stricter concept of the subject than in domestic law. Is it true that, because of the peculiarities of international law, only actors that are simultaneously creators of law can be subjects in that legal order? The special characteristic of international law is that it lacks a central legislative power. Does this fact justify acknowledging only creators of law as legal subjects? From a traditional perspective, this question must be answered in the affirmative, since international law is a mutually agreed ("*genossenschaftlich*") order characterized by the fact that subjects bind *themselves*. This (in visual terms) "horizontality" has been seen as analogous to private law: international law as "private law writ large".[64] States are seen as analogous to natural private persons who pursue their own interests; sovereignty is seen as the basic principle analogous to private autonomy. But this kind of quasi-"private" law is not embedded in a meta-order which would set the frame within which actors (the States) are allowed to carry out their transactions. Therefore the private law analogy is imperfect.

On the premise of autonomy/sovereignty, any rights and duties can only accrue to those actors who have agreed to them. This is obvious in the case of rights and duties arising from international treaties. And according to the traditional view, this is also true of rights and duties arising from customary law: "The essence of a customary rule lies in the fact that it arises from the

[64] Thomas Holland, *Studies in International Law* (Oxford: Clarendon 1898), 152.

conduct of those whom it binds."[65] The legitimacy – or in the old-fashioned terminology, the "grounds of validity" – of international law would consist in State consent. According to this scheme, legal subjects would in fact only be those who are simultaneously the creators of law.[66] Only on the basis of this premise can a particular strictness (or narrowness) of the concept of the subject be explained and justified with reference to the fact that the "principle of mediation of the individual in international law follows from the character of international treaty law as a consensual legal order between States".[67]

This premise is obsolete, however. The construction of international law that is purely analogous to private law does not fully match the reality of the law. Normal customary international legal norms are to some extent independent of the consent of individual States, since they arise already from general (not necessarily uniform) practice and *opinio juris*, in which international legal subjects other than States may also be involved. The analogy to private law is, moreover, obsolete in the light of many legal developments, ranging from the recognition of *erga omnes* norms and *jus cogens* to the practice of majority decisions for the adoption of secondary law in international regimes. In the new configuration of contemporary international law, which to a large extent is international *public* law,[68] there is no reason in

[65] Michel Virally, The Sources of International Law, in: Max Sørensen (ed.), *Manual of Public International Law* (London: Macmillan 1968), 116–174 (130). A somewhat more modern explanation of "self-legislation" consists in the idea of democracy between States. If international law is "a law of, by, and for nations" (Anthony D'Amato, *International Law: Process and Prospect* (2nd ed., Irvington NY: Transnational Publishers 1995), 148), then it is legitimized by that mechanism, and a divergence between creators of the law and those subject to the law would not be desirable. This democratic allusion is misleading, however. Subjects of a democracy are individuals, not States.

[66] See, e.g., Alexander Hold-Ferneck, *Lehrbuch des Völkerrechts, erster Teil* (Leipzig: Felix Meiner 1930), 247: "The question discussed for a long time and answered in the affirmative by so many writers as to whether individuals are or at least can be subjects of international law is in principle settled by the observation that the rules of international law are directed only to communities that govern themselves; international obligations can exist only when such a community creates or refrains from creating an act of legislation, adjudication, or administration; an international right is the claim of another self-governing community to have such an obligation fulfilled. *Individuals are not subjects of international law, nor can they be under any circumstances*" (translation and italics mine).

[67] Grzeszick, Rechte des Einzelnen 2005, 312–344 (335).

[68] See Anne Peters, Transnational Law Comprises Constitutional, Administrative, Criminal, and Quasi-private Law, in: Pieter Bekker/Rudolf Dolzer/Michael Waibel (eds), *Making Transnational Law Work: Liber Amicorum Detlev Vagts* (Cambridge: Cambridge University Press 2010), 154–173; Armin von Bogdandy/Rüdiger Wolfrum/Jochen von

terms of legal construction that would permit a limitation of the capacity to hold rights to only those actors with the capacity to create law.

Even if, deviating from the above considerations, individuals' lack of power to create law would lead to an international legal status of a lesser sort, this gradation would have to be measured by the actual practice of the formation of international law with the participation of non-State actors.[69] The characterization of individuals as mere consumers of international law does not do justice to the actual range of their possibilities for generating international law – irrespective of the fact that individuals cannot conclude international treaties. The question of the actual extent of the participation of individuals and other non-State actors in the creation of international law will be taken up in Chapter 17 at pp. 544–51. Here, it need only be noted that international legal personality should not be equated with the power to create international law. The thesis that only creators of international law can be (full) subjects of international law is not (or no longer) plausible.[70] The merely partially developed power of individuals to create law is therefore no obstacle to their international legal subjectivity.

3.5 Individualism, Monism, and Dualism

But doesn't the international legal personality of the individual stand and fall with the answer to the more general question of the relationship between international law and domestic law? The following discussion will show that these two questions can and should be evaluated separately. Unlike the view advocated here, however, the key concept of "mediation" of individuals by their States combines both aspects. Accordingly, the acquisition of the individual's own international rights is referred to as "immediation" of the individual's relationship to international law.[71] The widespread understanding of international legal subjectivity as a direct relationship to international law[72] excludes by

Bernstorff/Philipp Dann/Matthias Goldmann (eds), *The Exercise of Public Authority by International Institutions* (Heidelberg: Springer 2010).

69 See McCorquodale, The Individual and the International Legal System, 2010, 299, 306, and *passim*: Individuals have participation rights in the law-creation process and are therefore also subjects of international law.

70 See IACtHR, *Juridical Status* (n. 14), paragraph 26.

71 See Andreas Fischer-Lescano, Subjektivierung völkerrechtlicher Sekundärregeln, *Archiv des Völkerrechts* 45 (2007), 299–381 (306).

72 See, e.g., Albert Bleckmann, *Völkerrecht* (Baden-Baden: Nomos 2001), 46.

definition that individuals can be international legal subjects as long as State law and international law are seen as different legal orders.

Along these lines, Gaetano Arangio-Ruiz has classified contemporary international legal science into two major schools of thought: those who regard international law as an "inter-state" system and those who understand international law as an "interindividual system". According to Arangio-Ruiz, these two camps correspond to the earlier schools of dualism and monism.[73]

In fact, within the traditional conceptual framework (monism versus dualism), the international legal subjectivity of the individual appeared possible only according to the monist perspective. For instance, in his Hague lecture on the systemic relationships between national law and international law, the monist Hans Kelsen argued vehemently that individuals are the actual subjects of international law.[74] In contrast, the great dualists denied the international legal subjectivity of the individual. Dionisio Anzilotti spoke of an "evident confusion of the international legal order with a supposed general law of humanity," i.e., with a "non-existent legal order of humanity".[75]

> "The customary legal norms or treaties that appear to impose obligations on individuals in reality oblige the State to prohibit individuals from engaging in certain acts and to punish them, or they authorize the State to do so when it otherwise would be forbidden. The obligations exist for the individual only if the State has enacted the requisite legal order; *nullum crimen sine lege* (no crime without law). And the norms that seemingly grant rights to individuals in reality oblige or authorize the State to grant these rights."[76]

A similar view is supported by Lassa Oppenheim: "If we look more closely into these rights, it becomes quite obvious that they are not given

[73] Gaetano Arangio-Ruiz, Dualism Revisited: International and Interindividual Law, *Rivista di diritto internazionale* 96 (2003), 909–999 (914–915).

[74] See Hans Kelsen, Les rapports de système entre le droit interne et le droit international public, *Recueil des Cours* 14 (1926/IV), 231–329. See also another great monist, Georges Scelle, Règles générales du droit de la paix, *Recueil des Cours* 46 (1933/IV), 327–703, 342–343; *idem*, *Droit International Public* (Paris: Les Ed. Domat-Montchrestien 1944), 410–411; Scelle, Some Reflections on Juridical Personality in International Law, in: George A. Lipsky (ed.), *Law and Politics in the World Community* (Berkeley: University of California Press 1953), 49–58; Scelle, *Précis de droit des gens: Principes et systématique, Vol. I, Introduction: Le milieu intersocial* (Paris: Sirey 1932).

[75] Dionisio Anzilotti, *Corso di Diritto Internazionale, Volume primo, Introduzione – Teorie Generali* (Padova: Cedam 1955), 120–121 (English translation mine).

[76] *Ibid.*, 121 (English translation mine).

to the favoured individuals by the Law of Nations directly. For how could International Law, which is a law between States, give rights to individuals concerning their relations to a State? ... [T]hese rights are, therefore, not international rights, but rights derived from Municipal Laws. ... [I]nternational treaties between two or more Powers ... do not create these rights, but they impose the duty upon the contracting States to call these rights into existence by their Municipal Laws."[77]

According to Heinrich Triepel, it was "first of all impossible that a proposition of one legal order might come into conflict with a proposition of the other legal order. This is of the utmost importance under different aspects. Firstly, for everyone subject to the laws of a State. They are ... in no way governed by international legal norms. International law does not grant them any rights, and it does not address any commands or prohibitions to them. And what is most important: Their obligations toward their State or their fellow citizens can never conflict with their international obligations, since they do not have any such obligations".[78] According to this template, it is logically consistent that – after implementation of the international treaty by the State party – the individual can have an internal, i.e., purely *domestic legal* right vis-à-vis the State, but never an international right. Consequently, the individual could therefore never contest the non-fulfilment or violation of an international treaty before an international body. Only domestic remedies would be at the individual's disposal. At the inter-State level, the home State of the adversely affected individual can exercise the individual's rights as the State's own rights and invoke diplomatic protection for the benefit of the State's citizen. Finally, according to Triepel, what was at issue was the loyalty of "those subject to the State" (*Unterthanen*), thus giving his theory at least a latently anti-democratic impulse: "For this reason, the duty of those subject to the State to obey the laws of the State – irrespective of the relationship thereof to international law – is entirely unconditional."[79]

However, the monist construction of the relationship between international law and domestic law is only then a precondition of the international legal subjectivity of the individual if international legal subjectivity is understood as a direct relationship to international law in a specific sense, namely

[77] Lassa Francis Lawrence Oppenheim, *International Law: A Treatise*, Vol. I (London: Longmans Green 1905), § 289 (pp. 342–343).

[78] Heinrich Triepel, *Völkerrecht und Landesrecht* (Leipzig: Verlag von C. L. Hirschfeld 1899), 254 (translation mine).

[79] *Ibid.*, 261 (translation mine).

in the sense of direct determination of the legal status of the individual by international law. Only from a monist perspective is the legal status of the individual governed directly by international law. In a dualist world, in contrast, the legal status of the individual is necessarily mediated by the State.

It appears preferable, however, not to mix up the international legal personality of the individual with the question of the relationship between international law and national law. International legal subjectivity concerns a legal quality of actors, while the question of the relationship is a structural problem.[80] The distinction of both problem areas is compatible with the usual talk of the mediation of the individual. In international legal discourse, this mediation is often – in contrast to what was described here – used in the sense of a procedural mediation activity of the State. Using this (likewise common) terminology, the individual is not mediated if he or she is himself or herself able to enter into direct contact with international institutions (independently of the theoretical determination of the relationship between international and domestic law).

In this light, the individual can simultaneously be a subject of several legal orders. In a pluralistic world in which domestic law can be supplemented not only by European and international law but also by a multitude of private and hybrid regimes, such multiple subjection is nothing special.

However, the concern of the historical opponents of the international legal subjectivity of the individual regarding the weakening of State sovereignty associated with the "relaxing of the absolute subjection of the individual to the State" becomes relevant. Sovereignty is affected not only if the individual asserts rights vis-à-vis the State but also already by the fact that the individual is subject to several legal regimes.[81] Already in such cases, a concern arises which also shone through the reflections of Heinrich Triepel which I quoted earlier. The concern is that the

80 The amalgamation of both aspects here is similarly confusing as in the context of the problem of direct effect. Here again (especially in Anglo-American theory and practice), the question of direct effect (or of the self-executing character) of an international legal norm is mixed up with that of incorporation into national law. For details, see Chapter 16.

81 A typical situation giving rise to this concern was the law of armed conflict. In the past, States objected especially to the status of individuals as subjects in civil wars because the States feared that individuals would (given their status as "belligerents") thus be removed from the application of the domestic legal order. This would then mean that States could no longer punish them under the domestic criminal law – a consequence which States did not like (see Chapter 7, p. 221).

individual might be caught in a conflict between contradictory normative requirements that might result from the rules of different legal orders.[82] Nowadays, such conflicts appear to be less and less resolvable by invoking a simple hierarchy of norms,[83] but that is a different problem.

In view of what has been said above, the (originally international) rights of the individual (and the underlying legal proposition that the individual can in principle have such rights) can therefore be incorporated by States into their legal order in either a monist or dualist way. To achieve practical effect, this legal personality and the specific rights must in any event be respected by States. But it is irrelevant whether they are seen as "transformed" or not.

3.6 Conclusion

The evaluation of the international status of the individual depends in part on the underlying concept of international legal subjectivity (international legal personality). All underlying limitations and classifications of international legal subjectivity reflect and perpetuate the distinction between States and all other entities. States appear as the prototypical international legal subjects, and all other international subjects – measured according to this benchmark – have deficits.

After a review of the multiple historical concepts of the international legal subject, the following conceptualisation appears to be useful: International legal personality (or subjectivity) is international legal *capacity* in the sense of the entitlement to be a holder of international rights and duties. International legal subjectivity does not require that an actor be able to generate international law himself or herself, and it does not require that the actor himself or herself be able to assert his or her rights before international monitoring bodies. International legal personality precedes the ownership of rights. It is filled by specific rights and/or duties but is not constituted by them. Instead, the attribution of a concrete right (e.g., arising from a human rights covenant) or obligation to an actor implies that this actor is a legal subject in the first place. The recognition of legal personality

[82] See Dahm/Delbrück/Wolfrum, *Völkerrecht*, 2002, 267: "In that case, there is a danger that the individual would experience unresolvable conflicts and would follow the rules of the national power of the State, which is often perceived as closer to the individual than the international community" (translation mine).

[83] See Anne Peters, Rechtsordnungen und Konstitutionalisierung: Zur Neubestimmung der Verhältnisse, *Zeitschrift für öffentliches Recht* 65 (2010), 3–63 (42–49).

(subjectivity; capacity) does not automatically imply specific, concrete rights or entitlements. Legal personality can in theory be entirely empty or without function if no specific rights are granted. International legal personality thus does not say anything about the real legal position of a concrete entity. The international legal personality would therefore be a *potential* – but one that is essential to the emancipation of the human being. The international legal personality of the individual understood in this way is analytically independent of the correctness of a monist, dualist, or pluralist theory.

4

International Individual Obligations

4.1 Definition of the Problem

International law may impose duties on individuals directly without any interposition of national law.[1] Although the International Law Commission stated this principle already during one of its first sessions – dedicated to the formulation of the Nuremberg Principles on the criminal responsibility of natural persons – this legal statement remained controversial until recently. As late as 1999, the following assessment could be found in the literature: "After all, it remains doubtful whether individuals are bearers of obligations under public international law."[2] These doubts have likely been eliminated entirely over the course of the last decade: "It seems unquestionable that in recent times a number of international rules have come into being that directly impose obligations upon individuals."[3] Antonio Cassese expresses this as follows: "Thus individuals are at present under many international obligations ... incumbent upon *all individuals of the world*: they are all obliged to refrain from breaching the ... rules ... regardless of whether the national legal system within which individuals live contains a similar or the same obligation (translated into national legislation)."[4] According to Daillier and Pellet, "The individual is also ... the immediate subject of a 'sanctioning' international law. This quality is not a privilege. Instead of conferring him rights, this quality only attributes to him obligations

[1] Formulation of the Nuremberg Principles, Report of the International Law Commission covering its second session, 5 June–29 July 1950 (GAOR, 5th sess. Suppl. No. 12 (A/1316), YB ILC 1950 II, 374–378 (paragraph 99).

[2] Albrecht Randelzhofer, The Legal Position of the Individual under Present International Law, in: Albrecht Randelzhofer/Christian Tomuschat (eds), *State Responsibility and the Individual: Reparation in Instances of Grave Violations of Human Rights* (The Hague: Martinus Nijhoff 1999), 231–242 (241).

[3] Antonio Cassese, *International Law* (2nd ed., Oxford: Oxford University Press 2005), 144. "These general rules first crystallized in the area of armed conflict" (*ibid.*).

[4] *Ibid.*, 144–145.

whose disregard will engage its responsibility. It is no less true that from a legal point of view, this individualization makes significant inroads into the interstate structure of international law."[5] So Daillier and Pellet emphasize that imposing obligations on individuals represents a "significant attack" on the inter-State structure of international law. Moreover, intensifying the imposition of obligations on individuals justifies speaking of a "regulatory turn" in international law, as Jacob Katz Cogan does. As used here, regulation is understood to be the imposition of public authoritative obligations on private parties to act or to refrain from acting in certain ways, without mediation[6] by the traditional intermediary, namely the State.[7] "[R]egulatory authority over individuals, a common characteristic of government, is now within the mainstream of international law."[8]

The legal possibility of imposing primary and secondary obligations on individuals directly under international law is an aspect of the latter's international legal subjectivity, understood as their international legal capacity. This legal capacity includes the "passive" capacity to be bound by obligations. According to the view argued here, this legal capacity of the individual is rooted in customary international law and a general principle of law akin to an empirically grounded natural right (on the legal foundation of international legal personality, see Chapter 13). Today, the focus of the discussion and controversial assessment is less on the status of being bound by obligations in principle than on the possible legal sources of specific obligations and on individual *responsibility as a legal consequence* of a breach of individual obligations: Where a primary international obligation is not fulfilled, the international responsibility of individuals may take effect, which in turn generates secondary obligations. These are discussed in Chapter 5.

[5] Patrick Daillier/Alain Pellet, *Droit International Public* (7th ed., Paris: LGDJ 2002), 650 (translation by the author).

[6] The term "mediation" is unusual though not unknown in English international law literature and is therefore used here for want of a better term. The German-language literature uses "*Mediatisierung*" frequently to express the function of domestic law to act as a bridge or an intermediary between the natural person and international law.

[7] Jacob Katz Cogan, The Regulatory Turn in International Law, *Harvard International Law Journal* 52 (2011), 321–372 (324). The regulatory turn consists in three developments: Firstly, in the imposition of direct international duties and their enforcement; secondly, in the expansion of the substantive scope of international law and the increasing specificity of the legal provisions; and thirdly, in the extension and the particularizing of facilitative law and processes (*ibid.*, 346).

[8] *Ibid.*, 370.

In this context, a distinction should be made between the substantive legal status of being bound by obligations at the primary level and the criminal or non-criminal responsibility of individuals directly under international law. Only obligations at the level of primary law are discussed in this chapter. The basic problems of primary obligations of individuals directly under international law will be discussed using examples from various domains of the law. The specific obligations, in light of their thematic relevance, of groups and individuals in the law of *armed conflict* are the subject of Chapter 7; specific obligations of *investors* are dealt with in Chapter 10.

4.2 Basic Categories

The individual obligations at the level of primary law and the obligors and obligees of these obligations may be categorized according to the *types of obligations*: International individual obligations are essentially *duties of omission*, such as the obligation to refrain from genocide, war crimes, or certain military activities. Since a general presumption of freedom applies to individuals, the prohibition to do something (such as to enslave another person) is identical to the obligation to refrain from that conduct. Not only obligations to refrain from action but also *positive obligations on individuals to act* have been formulated, especially by the UN Security Council, such as obligations to participate in suppressing the trade in blood diamonds and drug smuggling. Positive obligations grounded in international treaties, such as the duty of an investor to undertake development measures, are also conceivable. Another group is constituted by *obligations to tolerate*. For instance, recent practice appears to support that self-defence under Article 51 of the UN Charter is permissible and lawful also against armed attacks by non-State actors such as terrorist groups.[9] The legal option available according to this view of making individuals a permissible target of self-defence measures implies a direct international obligation to tolerate on the part of the individual attackers. The most important obligation to tolerate is that of tolerating interference with one's own freedom in the form of limitation of a human right (typically effected by organs of the State). For instance, Article 105 of the UN Convention on the Law of the Sea authorizes every

[9] Rejecting this view, see ICJ, *Legal Consequences of the Construction of a Wall in the Occupied Palestinian Territory*, Advisory Opinion of 9 July 2004, ICJ Reports 2004, 136, paragraph 139. Supporting this view, see Declaration of Judge Buergenthal, *ibid.*, 240–245, paragraphs 5–6.

State party to seize a suspected pirate ship on the high seas and to arrest the persons on board, thereby obligating the persons concerned to tolerate this limitation of their freedom.[10] I specifically mention this obligation to tolerate because it opens up a new perspective on the requirement of legality (requirement of a legal basis), which is developed in this chapter as a crucial prerequisite for imposing international obligations on individuals (in detail in the following).

The types of obligors: As in the domain of international individual rights, both natural and legal persons (under domestic private law) may be holders of potential individual duties. Legal persons play a role primarily in the domain of international investment protection law (see Chapter 10) and in the overlapping discussion on the potential obligation of (transnationally operating) companies to respect international human rights (see pp. 99–110). The status of legal persons as obligors becomes especially problematic in the case of obligations enforced by criminal penalties. Under the rule of law, culpability is a precondition for punishment, and it is difficult to make sense of the culpability of non-human actors. For these reasons, many legal orders reject the criminal responsibility of legal persons, e.g., of companies. In contrast, liability of legal persons under civil law is unproblematic.

This chapter does not discuss the obligations of *State-like collectives*. Traditionally, the binding nature of international law (especially rules of armed conflict and human rights) on certain collective actors has been affirmed with reference to territorial control and quasi-sovereignty. For instance, the Pictet commentary states that armed groups are bound by Common Article 3 because they constitute a "responsible authority" and exercise "effective sovereignty".[11] The established practice of the

[10] Article 105 UNCLOS: "Seizure of a pirate ship or aircraft: On the high seas, or in any other place outside the jurisdiction of any State, every State may seize a pirate ship or aircraft, or a ship or aircraft taken by piracy and under the control of pirates, and *arrest the persons* and seize the property on board. The courts of the State which carried out the seizure may decide upon the penalties to be imposed, and may also determine the action to be taken with regard to the ships, aircraft or property, subject to the rights of third parties acting in good faith" (italics mine). See also Article 73(1) UNCLOS for the authorization granted to a coastal State to take coercive measures against individuals.

[11] Jean Pictet (ed.), Commentary on the Geneva Conventions of 12 August 1949, Vol. I, Geneva Convention I for the Amelioration of the Condition of the Wounded and Sick in Armed Forces in the Field (Geneva: ICRC 1952), 51. In regard to the binding nature of human rights on armed opposition groups in non-international armed conflicts, see the

Commission on Human Rights, its successor the Human Rights Council, and of the missions and special rapporteurs appointed by those institutions assume that non-State actors, especially political groups that carry out State-like functions and control a territory, are bound by international human rights not only morally but also legally. Relevant reports and resolutions have called upon armed political groups such as the Palestinian Sunni Islamist organization Hamas,[12] the Lebanese Shi'a Islamist Hezbollah,[13] and the Sri Lankan separatist organization Liberation Tigers of Tamil Eelam (LTTE)[14] to respect human rights – regardless of the fact that these actors are not parties to the human rights conventions and are not permitted to ratify them. These and similar collectives and entities that carry out quasi-State functions and accordingly exercise political and military power should therefore – analogously to States – be bound by relevant international law. The underlying consideration is the analogy to the State, thus ultimately operating within the statist paradigm.[15] In contrast, the goal of this chapter is to substantiate the status of individuals as being bound by obligations independently of this analogy to the State.

Obligees/beneficiaries of international individual obligations: This already touches upon a further question: To whom are the postulated individual obligations directly under international law owed – the home State, all other States and subjects of international law, or other (private) individuals? All these actors could be considered obligees, depending on the relevant obligation. For instance, the purported "basic" international obligations of the individual would be owed to the home State. Any

restrictive practice of States to date (Liesbeth Zegveld, *The Accountability of Armed Opposition Groups in International Law* (Cambridge: Cambridge University Press 2002), 38–55 and other references).

12 Human Rights Council, Human Rights Situation in Palestine and Other Occupied Arab Territories, Combined Report, UN Doc. A/HRC/10/22, 29 May 2009, paragraph 22; Human Rights Council, Human Rights in Palestine and Other Occupied Arab Territories: Report of the United Nations Fact Finding Mission on the Gaza Conflict, UN Doc. A/HRC/12/48, 15 September 2009, paragraphs 305 and 1370.

13 Human Rights Council, Report of the Special Rapporteur on extrajudicial, summary or arbitrary executions: Mission to Lebanon and Israel, UN Doc. A/HRC/2/7, 2 October 2006, paragraph 19.

14 Commission on Human Rights, Report of the Special Rapporteur on extrajudicial, summary or arbitrary executions: Mission to Sri Lanka, UN Doc. E/CN.4/2006/53/Add.5, 27 March 2006, paragraph 25.

15 As a further legal justification of the legally binding nature postulated here, some of the texts cited above refer to the Preamble of the Universal Declaration of Human Rights and the legitimate expectations of the international community expressed therein.

existing obligation of transnational corporations to respect human rights would be owed to the holders of human rights themselves (see below at pp. 66–67 on corresponding claims).

International obligations are potentially obligations *erga omnes* in a twofold sense: They may potentially be directed at anyone as an obligor and also generate obligations towards any obligee. Judge Antônio Cançado Trindade emphasizes the obligor side: "In a vertical dimension, the obligations erga omnes of protection bind both the organs and agents of (state) public power, *and the individuals themselves* in the inter-individual relations."[16] Antonio Cassese writes, "Clearly, the international legal status of individuals is unique: they have a lopsided position in the international community. As far as their *obligations* are concerned, *they are associated with all the other members of the international community*; in contrast, they do not possess rights in relation to all members of that community."[17]

Substantive and procedural status as an obligor: As in the context of individual rights, the existence of individual obligations (substantive legal level) should be distinguished from their enforceability (procedural level). An individual may be subject to an international obligation independently of the possibility and form of enforcement (with respect to criminal responsibility, see Chapter 5, pp. 122–23). International individual obligations may be asserted and enforced by both national and international bodies. Despite the existence of a direct international individual obligation that is analytically independent of enforcement, the actual practice of enforcement plays a major role in regard to its legitimation and acceptance. As long as international individual obligations were more or less virtual and were barely enforced, their intrinsic justification was hardly discussed. The more operational and effective bodies for enforcing international law become (e.g., the international criminal tribunals and courts), the more probable the real enforcement of international individual obligations becomes, and the more important observation of the principle of legality appears.

In the context of enforcing obligations, the existence of a substantive legal obligation should moreover be distinguished from two aspects of its realization: firstly, from the *direct application* of a (potentially obligation-generating) international legal norm by State authorities and courts, and

[16] IACtHR, *Juridical Condition and Rights of the Undocumented Migrants*, Advisory Opinion OC-18/03 of 17 September 2003, Concurring Opinion of Cançado Trindade, paragraph 77 (italics mine).

[17] Cassese, *International Law*, 2005, 150 (italics mine).

secondly, from the general question of *inclusion* of the (potentially obligation-generating) international legal norm in the legal order of the State.

4.3 Partially Corresponding Individual Claims

Where individuals are beneficiaries of a potentially direct international obligation of another person, a direct international claim (right) of the affected individual against the private obligor to perform or (more frequently) to refrain from the act – such as refraining from war crimes or human rights violations – *may* correspond to that obligation of the other individual. But an obligation of the latter individual may also exist (only) *erga omnes* without a specific other person having a claim (right) for the obligation's fulfilment.[18] The beneficiaries of the international status of individuals as obligors may therefore be either only reflexive beneficiaries or genuine rights holders.

The discussion obscures the question of the status of the individual as an obligor if the problem is analysed only from the reverse perspective, i.e., from the perspective of the potential beneficiary. Antonio Cassese argues, for instance, that – "consistent from the viewpoint of legal logic but also in keeping with new trends emerging in the world community" – rights under customary international law have arisen that are vested directly in individuals. "They are entitled to respect for their life and limbs, and for their dignity, hence they have a right not to become a victim of war crimes, crimes against humanity, aggression, torture, terrorism."[19] Christian Tomuschat has likewise identified a "personal right [of the individual] not to be subjected to genocide".[20] The assertion of a right is clothed here in the vocabulary of an international individual claim. While the postulated individual claim has something to do with key human rights (the right to life, etc.), it is more

[18] While as a matter of principle, one may only speak of a right if someone else's obligation corresponds to it (principle of the "attendant obligations" of the right), this correspondence relationship is not reversible. See Marietta Auer, Subjektive Rechte bei Pufendorf und Kant, *Archiv der civilistischen Praxis* 208 (2008), 584–634 (591 and 598).

[19] Cassese, *International Law*, 2005, 145.

[20] Christian Tomuschat, Individual Reparation Claims in Instances of Grave Human Rights Violations: The Position under General International Law, in: Albrecht Randelzhofer/ Christian Tomuschat (eds), *State Responsibility and the Individual: Reparation in Instances of Grave Violations of Human Rights* (The Hague: Martinus Nijhoff 1999), 1–25 (13).

specific by being directed against certain forms of attack. This means it is a claim beyond human rights.

It remains an open question, however, against whom this claim is directed. Is it a form of injunctive claim, directly addressed to potential perpetrators and containing a mirror-image individual obligation to refrain from such crimes? Or is it a claim directed against the State for protection from such crimes committed by private individuals or the State itself (acting through its officials)?

As discussed above, the respondent in the normal case is the State, not another individual. However, State duties of protection do not in all cases generate individual claims for fulfilment, as the example of the State duty to investigate and punish shows (for details, see Chapter 9, pp. 255–69).

On systematic and teleological grounds, the possibility of a twofold thrust of the claim should be recognized in principle. Because the normative conditions of a direct international obligation on private parties are met (importance of the legal good, foreseeability of the obligation, and increased risk of inadequate fulfilment of the State's duty of protection – see on these conditions in detail p. 88), the claim arising from customary international law – derived from general international rules – not to become a victim of an international crime should be interpreted not only as a claim for protection against the State but *also* as an injunctive claim against individuals. Only a twofold interpretation of this kind provides comprehensive and effective protection for the victim.

4.4 The Normal Case of Merely Indirect Imposition of Obligations upon Individuals through State Duties of Protection

The discussion of the obligations of individuals raises the basic question of the tasks and modes of operation of international law in contrast to those of domestic law. A fundamental objection to direct international obligations of individuals is that they entail a *superfluous legal duplication*. From this sceptical perspective, there is a place for obligations of the individual in national administrative law but not in international law, which is essentially different. According to this view, the purpose of international law is "merely to serve as a sort of second line of defence and to set field markers . . . that should be considered indispensable in the light of contemporary values".[21]

[21] Christian Tomuschat, Grundpflichten des Individuums nach Völkerrecht, *Archiv des Völkerrechts* 21 (1983), 289–315 (312 and 315, translation mine).

The scheme of merely indirect imposition of obligations upon individuals through State duties of protection takes account of the structural difference between international law and domestic law and their relationship as complementary lines of defence. This scheme is most evident in the field of international protection of human rights, but it also applies in respect of other individual legal positions under international law. It will be illustrated here using the example of human rights.

Under Article 2(2) ICCPR, the State parties undertake "to adopt such laws or other measures as may be necessary to give effect to the rights recognized in the present Covenant". According to Article 1 ECHR, the States parties "secure to everyone within their jurisdiction" the rights of the Convention. Article 1(1) ACHR states: "The States Parties to this Convention undertake to *respect* the rights and freedoms recognized herein and to *ensure* to all persons subject to their jurisdiction the free and full exercise of those rights and freedoms" (italics mine). According to Common Article 1 of the Geneva Conventions of 1949, the States parties "undertake to respect and to ensure respect for the present Convention in all circumstances". In its General Comment 31, the UN Human Rights Committee held that the ICCPR obligations are binding on States parties and "do *not*, as such, have direct horizontal effect as a matter of international law",[22] i.e., do not constitute direct obligations on other actors as well. Instead, the ICCPR imposes positive duties on States parties as spelled out by the Human Rights Committee as follows: "[T]he positive obligations on States Parties to ensure Covenant rights will only be fully discharged if individuals are *protected* by the State, not just against violations of Covenant rights by its agents, but also against acts committed by private persons or entities that would impair the enjoyment of Covenant rights in so far as they are amenable to application between private persons or entities. There may be circumstances in which a failure to ensure Covenant rights as required by article 2 would give rise to violations by States Parties of those rights, as a result of States Parties' *permitting or failing to take appropriate measures or to exercise due diligence to prevent, punish, investigate or redress* the harm caused by such acts by private persons or entities."[23]

[22] UN Human Rights Committee, General Comment No. 31 [80], Nature of the General Legal Obligations Imposed on States Parties to the Covenant (CCPR/C/21/Rev.1/Add. 13 (26 May 2004), paragraph 8 (italics mine).

[23] *Ibid.* (italics mine).

The positive obligations of States thus encompass the duty to *protect* the enjoyment of human rights by private persons and entities from interference. States are not required to guarantee an outcome, but they must exercise sufficient due diligence to prevent, investigate, and repair infringements of rights by third parties, especially by private individuals. The obligations imposed by the ICCPR and other human rights conventions on States are hence in regard to conduct, not outcome. In this way, third parties are obligated indirectly.

Combined, this means that there are two links for the international responsibility of the State: its active conduct through its bodies and its failure to exercise protection and due diligence. State due diligence in turn requires the State not only to enact sufficient national legislation (in the abstract) to prohibit violations of individual rights and where applicable to punish such violations but also to intervene in individual cases to prevent specific infringements of rights. Due diligence is accordingly, from the perspective of the victims, also a comprehensive duty of protection incumbent upon the State. This duty must be met by the State by imposing a duty of omission upon its legal subjects under national law and furthermore by adopting actively protective State measures.

Apart from the general duties of protection that are entailed by all human rights, numerous human rights treaties lay down *specific* State duties of protection. These again only indirectly obligate individuals. An example is the Convention against Torture (CAT) of 1984. In its General Comment on the general duty to implement Article 2 CAT, the Committee against Torture emphasized that *"[t]he Convention imposes obligations on States parties and not on individuals"*.[24] The acts of officials, agents, private contractors, and all persons acting on behalf of the State, in conjunction with the State, or under its direction or control, or otherwise under colour of law are attributed to the States parties.[25] The State party also bears responsibility where its failure to intervene enhances the danger of privately inflicted harm akin to torture.[26] All State bodies and other actors attributable to the State must exercise due diligence to prevent, stop, and punish torture (and private acts akin to torture). Since the failure of the State to exercise due diligence facilitates and enables non-State actors to commit acts akin to

[24] CAT, General Comment No. 2, Implementation of article 2 by States parties (UN Doc. CAT/C/GC/2/CRP.1/Rev. 4 of 24 January 2008, paragraph 15, italics mine).

[25] *Ibid.*, paragraph 15. [26] *Ibid.*, paragraph 15.

torture, the State's indifference or inaction is considered a form of commission that likewise triggers State responsibility.[27]

Specific duties of protection are also laid down for *prohibitions of discrimination under human rights law*. These are suited especially for being (indirectly) applied to some types of relationship between "private" individuals. It is also especially warranted that the prohibitions on discrimination are brought to bear in these constellations.. They would be largely ineffective if their scope did not extend – via State duties of protection – to the social, private sphere, especially the workplace. Under Article 2(1)(d) of the International Convention on the Elimination of All Forms of Racial Discrimination (ICERD),[28] "[e]ach State Party shall prohibit and bring to an end, by all appropriate means, including legislation as required by the circumstances, racial discrimination by any *persons, group or organization*" (italics mine). Article 2(1)(d) ICERD also requires the States parties to guarantee the right to equal treatment by securing equal enjoyment of rights and freedoms when they are threatened especially by private persons. Article 5(b) ICERD requires State protection against violence and bodily harm, even if inflicted by private parties. ICERD also requires State guarantees of non-discrimination with regard to the "right to housing" (Article 5(e)(iii)) and of equal access to services intended (normally by private persons) for use by the general public, such as hotels, restaurants, and cafés (Article 5 (f)). Article 2(e) of the Convention on the Elimination of All Forms of Discrimination against Women (CEDAW)[29] requires States parties to "take all appropriate measures to eliminate discrimination against women by any *person, organization or enterprise*" (italics mine). Finally, the UN Guiding Principles on Business and Human Rights of 2011 (Ruggie Principles) first and foremost mention the *duty of States to protect* persons under their jurisdiction from human rights abuse by business enterprises.[30] Another area includes duties of protection in the

[27] *Ibid.*: "[T]he State's indifference or inaction provides a form of encouragement and/or de facto permission" (paragraph 18).

[28] International Convention on the Elimination of All Forms of Discrimination of 7 March 1966, UNTS vol. 660, p. 195.

[29] Convention on the Elimination of All Forms of Discrimination against Women of 18 December 1979, UNTS vol. 1249, p. 13.

[30] Report of the Special Representative of the Secretary-General on the issue of human rights and transnational corporations and other business enterprises, with Guiding Principles in the Annex (UN Doc. A/HRC/17/31) of 21 March 2011, Principle 1, adopted by the Human Rights Council, UN Doc. A/HRC/RES/17/4.

event of natural disasters and in situations covered by the "responsibility to protect", as discussed in Chapter 8.

In the context of the model of protection and mediation as just scetched out, the direct imposition of obligations on individuals should be seen as the exception. It is an exception to the basic principle of the indirect imposition of obligations on individuals via State duties of protection, which primarily are met by the enactment and enforcement of national legal provisions. Reaching through to individuals requires special justification. In other words, direct international individual obligations need to be justified, based on the need for global ordering and limited by the principle of legality. Both aspects will be discussed in detail in the following sections.

4.5 Direct International Individual Obligations as an Exceptional Case

The model of indirect imposition of obligations on individuals via State duties of protection and due diligence was discussed above. As a system that continues to operate primarily between States, international law requires States to transpose into their national law the precepts and prohibitions contained in treaties, customary international law, and general principles of law. States meet their positive obligations primarily by enacting and enforcing their national law. The paradigm of the duty of protection thus overlaps with the paradigm of mediation.

In light of the comprehensive and gapless responsibility of States, are parallel prohibitions and precepts directly addressed to individuals even needed? It must be conceded to sceptics that the international rules are indeed not intended "to be a precise reflection of the status of rights and duties of the individual in the constitutional structure of the home State".[31] Additionally, there is the danger that States might weasel out of their regulatory obligations by referring to the international imposition of obligations on individuals. There are also the *practical* difficulties of imposing obligations on seven billion actors. And finally, direct international individual obligations raise specific problems of *legitimation* (as will be discussed immediately below). For all these reasons, it must be emphasized in line with the Human Rights Council that international law should "not be viewed as a substitute for domestic criminal or civil law".[32] As a first step, two

[31] Tomuschat, Grundpflichten des Individuums, 1983, 315 (translation mine).
[32] UN Human Rights Council, General Comment No. 31 [80] (n. 22).

common doctrinal constructions will be discussed in the context of direct international individual obligations and exposed as irrelevant. It will be shown that in principle no reason exists in the nature and structure of international law that would prevent it from addressing individuals and imposing legal obligations on them.

4.5.1 *Not Prevented by the* pacta tertiis *Rule*

The *pacta tertiis* rule might make direct individual obligations under international treaties legally impossible from the outset. In the view defended here, however, that rule does not apply. According to my argument, the problem of legitimation in regard to direct international individual obligations is not due to the fact that States themselves (rather than individuals) are the creators of the international obligations, so that State obligations might be understood as a form of self-commitment while individual obligations would constitute a form of third-party commitment. Anyone supporting the old view that international law (by analogy with private law) is a "mutually agreed" (*genossenschaftliches*) law of self-legislation[33] would then have to demand that potential obligors – i.e., the actors limited in their freedom by the legal obligation – would have to have a *right of participation* in the creation of that legal obligation. In the traditional paradigm analogous to private law, the limitation of freedom by international individual obligations would appear to be an impermissible contract at the expense of third parties. According to that view, the basic idea contained in Article 35 of the Vienna Convention on the Law of Treaties (VCLT) appears to be relevant. But that provision cannot be applied directly, because it governs treaties at the expense of third States: An obligation arises for a third State from the provision of a treaty only "if the parties to the treaty intend the provision to be the means of establishing the obligation and the third State expressly accepts that obligation in writing".[34] Individuals and groups of individuals are not States and hence not third parties for purposes of the *pacta tertiis* rule established in Article 35 VCLT.

Should the provision be applied *mutatis mutandis* to non-State actors? Then the obligated actors, such as business enterprises, would have to consent separately to their obligation under international law. According to this view, enterprises should not be burdened with direct obligations

[33] On the antiquatedness of this view, see Chapter 3, pp. 52–54.
[34] Article 35, Treaties providing for obligations for third States.

arising from human rights treaties, because they are not parties themselves and were not involved in the elaboration of the treaties. From this perspective, the lack of participation or the merely indirect participation of individuals in the creation of law at the international level would be a grave legitimacy deficit.

But according to the view defended here, it is not appropriate to apply the *pacta tertiis* principle to non-State actors. The non-State actors whose obligations are at issue – i.e., transnational corporations, armed opposition groups, and individuals – are usually private persons. They are not State bodies or officials acting within their mandate. These actors are accordingly not in a position comparable to that of third States. Unlike States, they are not public actors. They are entirely unable to become treaty parties at the same level as the States concluding the treaty. The rationale of the provision in Article 35 VCLT and the underlying *pacta tertiis* rule is to protect the sovereignty and independence of States. This rationale does not fit in the case of non-State actors.

Additionally, the deeper reason for the legal obligation of States does not actually lie in their voluntary and "autonomous" consent, but rather it lies in the international rule of law. This consideration is based on a change of perspective away from international law constructed by analogy with private law towards international law as international public law. This perspective emphasizes that States as political constructs are not means in themselves and that their existence is justified only by performing useful tasks for the coexistence of human beings. Therefore, they do not possess any "rights" comparable to those of natural persons, only powers. There is no presumption of freedom; on the contrary, the basic principle under the rule of law is that States may act only within the boundaries of law. The analogy between individuals and States popular in the international legal literature of the eighteenth and nineteenth centuries and the corresponding analogy between human freedom and State sovereignty as a "fundamental right" appear misleading.[35] Consequently, the imposition of obligations on States is the normal case, founded ultimately not on State consent to a limitation of sovereignty but on the international rule of law.[36]

[35] See p. 52.

[36] Jeremy Waldron, The Rule of International Law, *Harvard Journal of Law and Public Policy* 30 (2006), 15–30 (25–26): "Essentially, the rule of law in the international realm constrains the administration not in the way that domestic law constrains an individual, but in the way that domestic law constrains a lawmaker."

In stark contrast, the imposition of obligations on individuals must be specially justified separately. The traditional argument in favour of the imposition of obligations on individuals by analogy with private law does not take account of the categorical difference between States and private persons. In the private law paradigm discussed above, legal obligations are justified as voluntary self-limitation, i.e., as an expression of the personal freedom to bind *oneself*. Self-legislation or "auto-nomy" is the basic idea behind both contract law and democracy. However, no inappropriate analogy between State sovereignty and the private autonomy of natural persons should be constructed to take account of this basic concern. The obligations imposed on individuals are not generated by other private persons – against whom private autonomy would have to be taken into account – but rather by a public authority. The *pacta tertiis* principle is thus not useful in this context.

Nevertheless, the basic concern of the *pacta tertiis* rule, namely to *secure the consent of those on whom obligations are imposed*, remains relevant.[37] This concern must be taken into account in ways other than recourse to the *pacta tertiis* principle. The legal requirements for imposing international precepts and prohibitions on individuals must therefore be sought in the reservoir of public law and global constitutionalism.

4.5.2 No Principle of Legislative Competence

Attempts have been made to explain and justify direct international individual obligations with reference to a pseudo-democratic principle. From this perspective, no individual burden is permissible without representation. But can States be viewed as representing seven billion individuals who might potentially be bound by international obligations? If so, it should suffice for the States to create obligations through treaties or customary international law without having the potential holders of obligations participate *directly*.

In traditional international law, representation as required by the argument above is not demanded in the form of democratic representation. Rather, the "principle of legislative competence" is said to apply.[38] When a State ratifies a treaty, it does so for all individuals in

[37] This is apparently why Christine Chinkin wants to apply the *pacta tertiis* rule to individuals (Christine Chinkin, *Third Parties in International Law* (Oxford: Clarendon 1993), 14 and 120–122).

[38] Sandesh Sivakumaran, Binding Armed Opposition Groups, *International and Comparative Law Quarterly* 55 (2006), 369–394 (381).

its territory, according to this approach.[39] Even if the State is not organized democratically and thus does not represent its people in a democratic sense, it is considered – from the perspective of international law – not just as the representative of the State's people but also as the representative of the entire population, i.e., of all individuals in its territory irrespective of nationality and of any internal chain of legitimacy according to national law and politics. In this sense, during a codification conference on Additional Protocol (I) to the Geneva Conventions in regard to international humanitarian law, the representative of the USSR stated: "Any international instrument signed by a Government was binding on all those within its territory ... There must therefore be a clear understanding of the nature of the legal document which would be adopted and would become national law, imposing an obligation on both the Government concerned and the institutions *and citizens within its territory* ... That was the normal situation when a Government accepted a legal instrument."[40]

The problem with this perspective, as the statement quoted above shows, is that it does not clearly separate the question of the personal scope of application of a treaty text from that of its transposition into national law (and the resulting validity as the law of the State). But these are two aspects that must be evaluated separately.

Another problem is that this construction is "constitutionally blind" and does not pay attention to whether the contracting States really transport the views of their citizens to the international level or not, i.e., whether they represent individuals not only in a formal sense but also in a substantive sense. Moreover, this construction cannot explain how and why international obligations can ideally bind not only the citizens of States parties but also others "within its territory." And finally, potential individual obligations under *customary* international law go beyond the boundaries of consent conveyed through representation.

39 *Ibid.*, 381–382: "The individuals that are bound by ratification of a treaty on the part of the state are private individuals and collectivities of individuals" (quote on p. 382).

40 Summary of the Statement by Mr. Blishenko (Union of Soviet Socialist Republics), Official Records of the Diplomatic Conference on the Reaffirmation and Development on International Humanitarian Law Applicable in Armed Conflicts, Geneva (1974–1977) Vol. XIV, p. 314, CDH/III/SR.32, paragraphs 22–25 (p. 314, italics mine).

4.6 The Need to Close Regulatory Gaps as a Reason for and Limit to Direct International Individual Obligations

It is evident nowadays that a merely indirect subjection of individuals to international law (via transposition into national law) does not suffice in all cases to achieve the regulatory goals of international law. Just as in the domain of individual rights, there is a need for the possibility of international law to address individuals directly, especially because *there is the general risk that individual States are unable or unwilling to transpose international legal provisions properly and hence that global goods are not adequately protected.* Global interdependence, the increasing power of non-State actors, and the weakness of some States have enhanced the risk of insufficient State measures. These new challenges are the background for the "regulatory turn" of international law. The regulatory turn is based on the acknowledgement of the fact that private actors and groups (from terrorists and organized criminals to transnational corporations) may now threaten the global public order and that States are no longer able to maintain that order using the instruments of State law. "International law and international organizations are not replacing the state; rather, the idea behind the regulatory turn is to use those techniques to shore up and back up states that are thought to be failing in their regulatory responsibilities in critical sectors and to enhance, as well, the capacities of other, more capable states in this regard."[41] On the basis of this new and newly perceived need for regulation, a direct subjection of the individual to international law can and should join subjection to national law as a matter of principle. This principle will be referred to in the following as *the global need for regulation.*

International individual obligations are therefore necessary as a matter of principle for closing regulatory gaps. But are they also legitimate? In the preceding section (pp. 72–74), it was shown that direct international individual obligations are not illegitimate a priori and not per se due to any violation of the *pacta tertiis* rule. The key question is therefore not *whether* direct international individual obligations are possible in principle, but rather *when, i.e., under what circumstances and within what limits.*

The starting point is that due to both the practical problems and the problems of legitimacy, the direct imposition of obligations on

[41] Katz Cogan, Regulatory Turn, 2011, 330. In this direction, see also Heiner Geldermann, *Völkerrechtliche Pflichten multinationaler Unternehmen* (Baden-Baden: Nomos 2009), 237–238 and other references.

individuals must remain the *exception*, requiring special justification.[42] "Horizontal" international individual obligations are, in other words, in special need of legitimation. They must also be explained and justified *differently* from international obligations imposed on States (as the protracted and meandering debate on the "correct" and appropriate legal basis for the criminal responsibility of individuals for crimes proscribed under international law shows). However, the principle of legislative competence or democratic representation, as shown above (pp. 74–75), is not plausible as a justification of such obligations.

Also, the principle of conferring individual rights through treaties (in the sense of the *Danzig* and *LaGrand* case law) cannot be transferred analogously to obligations without further ado. Unlike in the case of granting individual rights under international law – which may even be presumed if the wording of the treaty is open – stricter requirements apply to the imposition of obligations.

The first condition for legitimating direct international individual obligations is, as mentioned above, a regulatory gap. It must be shown that in a specific area of the law, the indirect imposition of obligations on individuals via State duties of protection is not sufficient, so that it must be complemented by direct international "horizontal" obligations of individuals. The question is therefore under what conditions and in what contexts the protection of legal goods is not adequately realized, even when national laws are adopted so as to correspond to the international prescriptions and which of course also must be interpreted and applied in conformity with international law.

The threshold of necessity is reached when the practical benefit of a direct international individual obligation outweighs the legitimacy concerns. This practical benefit consists in the creation and continued existence of a direct international individual obligation that may even be enforceable by international bodies or third States if a State fails to enact adequate domestic law prohibitions or even adopts domestic law plainly contrary to international law. This practical benefit outweighs the countervailing considerations (only) if the obligation in question *is so important in terms of content* that an enhanced interest in gapless and reliable compliance with that obligation arises. Individual obligations should therefore (only) be acknowledged if these appear necessary to enforce

42 As is the case for the imposition of obligations in the form of Security Council resolutions: Matthias Herdegen, *Die Befugnisse des UN-Sicherheitsrates: Aufgeklärter Absolutismus im Völkerrecht?* (Heidelberg: C.F. Müller 1998), 32–33.

important concerns of the international community. John Knox has operationalized this idea by positing two conditions for the recognition of direct international individual obligations: Firstly, the obligation in question must be extraordinarily significant; secondly, it must be extraordinarily ill-suited for pure State enforcement using instruments of national law.[43]

Prototypical examples of significant international concerns are the prohibition of the use of military force, the punishment of international crimes, and the international protection of key human rights, the violation of which often simultaneously constitutes a crime. There is, in particular, agreement that the aforementioned normative conditions are met in the case of the commission of core crimes. In other words, as long as violation of the norms protecting certain legal goods is sanctioned by international law with criminal punishment, the individual thrust of the norm in the form of a duty of omission addressed to individuals is uncontroversial. State practice in international criminal law shows this: The principle of individual international criminal responsibility for acts contrary to international law is recognized even if domestic law shields (allows or even mandates) such crimes. In this sense, Article 33 of the Statute of the International Criminal Court (ICC) makes clear that the order of a government or of a superior, whether military or civilian, does not relieve the perpetrator of his international criminal responsibility in principle.[44] Individual obligations under international criminal law, with the special legal consequence of direct international criminal responsibility, are discussed in detail in Chapter 5.

The interesting question now is as follows: To what extent do direct international individual obligations beyond criminal law already exist as part of current international law as it stands, or to what extent should they be developed? The protection of legal goods with which the international community is concerned – which constitutes the starting point for potential individual obligations and effective enforcement of the associated obligations – must operate within the framework of the rule of law. This principle sets additional limits on the imposition of individual obligations by international law; these limits are discussed immediately below.

[43] John H. Knox, Horizontal Human Rights Law, *American Journal of International Law* 102 (2008), 1–47 (30).

[44] Along these lines, see already Principles II and IV of the Nuremberg Principles (n. 1), 374–378.

4.7 Further Limitation of Individual Rights by the Transnationalized Principle of Legality

International law may impose obligations on individuals only in accordance with the principle of legality.

4.7.1 *Definition, Legal Nature, and Rationale of the Principle of Legality*

For our purposes, the principle of legality is understood to mean that interferences with human freedom require a legal basis. The principle of legality's classic expression is found in Article 4 of the French Declaration of the Rights of Man and of the Citizen and is here formulated from the human rights perspective of limitation of freedom: The limits of freedom "can only be determined by law".[45] In this tradition, the general law appears as an expression of the *volonté générale* and as a guarantor for the equal treatment of citizens. The principle of legality is a public law principle. It is a key achievement of liberal constitutionalism, arising from the idea that the citizen owes obedience to the State only on the basis of clearly established rules and otherwise is free. This public law perspective indicates a way to deal with the fundamental problem of legitimating international individual obligations, in contrast to the traditional paradigm of analogy with private law, which leads to a dead end.

A transnationalized principle of legality as an international legal norm: The principle of legality originates from the national (public) law of liberal constitutional States. I share Kenneth Gallant's view that it is now a general principle of law as referred to in Article 38(1)(c) of the ICJ Statute and hence also an international legal norm.[46] A principle of law is general if it is widespread in representative legal orders and is structurally suited for insertion into international law.[47] The principle of

[45] "La liberté consiste à pouvoir faire tout ce qui ne nuit pas à autrui: ainsi l'exercice des droits naturels de chaque homme n'a de bornes que celles qui assurent aux autres Membres de la Société, la jouissance de ces mêmes droits. Ces bornes ne peuvent être déterminées que par la Loi" (Declaration des Droits de l'Homme et du Citoyen of 26 August 1789).

[46] Kenneth S. Gallant, *The Principle of Legality in International and Comparative Criminal Law* (Cambridge: Cambridge University Press 2009), 241.

[47] Alain Pellet, Article 38, in: Andreas Zimmermann et al. (eds), *The Statute of the International Court of Justice: A Commentary* (2nd ed., Oxford: Oxford University Press 2012), 832–840 (paragraphs 250–269, esp. paragraph 254 (p. 834)).

legality meets both conditions. Legal comparison shows that it is known in most legal orders.[48] As a public law principle, it can also be transferred to international law understood as "inter-public law".[49] The content of the principle of legality must be determined through an evaluative comparison of law. The principle has been shaped differently in different national legal traditions. Since the principle of legality in various States does not make exactly identical demands on the form and content of the legal basis for limitations of freedom, a common denominator must be found. That common denominator should be based not on the minimum standard but rather on the overarching rationale of the principle. Moreover, the international or transnational principle of legality must take account of the special features of international sources of law and of the processes for generating international law. An international legal basis cannot meet exactly the same demands as a national legal basis.

National authorities and courts tasked with verifying the existence of a direct international individual obligation must, purely formally speaking, apply the principle of legality of their own legal order. Due to the functional exchangeability of national and international law-applying institutions, the benchmark in both situations should, however, be substantively equivalent in order to prevent contradictory evaluations. The evaluation of the formal and substantive demands that an international norm must meet so as to legitimately impose obligations is a question not of its incorporation into national law (which would follow the rules of that national law) but rather of its interpretation. The interpretation of international legal norms is not a purely domestic matter; instead, it must satisfy international requirements and principles of international legal interpretation. Adjustment of the principle of legality within the applicable national legal system to the international standard can therefore be achieved by way of an interpretation of national law that is in conformity with international law (for details, see Chapter 5, on interpretation of the *nullum crimen* principle in conformity with international law).

[48] See fundamentally Gallant, *Principle of Legality* 2009, synopsis of the legal provisions of all States in the world in Appendix C, 438 et seq.

[49] Benedict Kingsbury/Megan Donaldson, From Bilateralism to Publicness in International Law, in: Ulrich Fastenrath et al. (eds), *From Bilateralism to Community Interest: Essays in Honour of Judge Bruno Simma* (Oxford: Oxford University Press 2011), 79–89 (83, 80, and 84).

The principle of legality as a component of international law – as a general principle of law as referred to in Article 38(1)(c) of the ICJ Statute – requires an abstract, normally written legal basis for interventions in human freedom. This principle (as in national law) serves a *dual protective purpose*, which is slightly modified at the level of international law.

In national law, the principle of legality secures the legitimation of limitations of freedom, firstly in terms of the rule of law and secondly in terms of democracy. (Any imposition of an international obligation to refrain from an act, to perform an act, or also to tolerate a limitation of a fundamental right on the part of the State constitutes a limitation of individual freedom – for purposes of applying the principle of legality.) The principle of legality guarantees the separation of powers and functions between the body adopting the law (in a democratic State, normally the parliament) and those bodies applying the law, i.e., the courts. The separation of powers is central to the rule of law because it prevents concentrations of power, thus limiting power and preserving spheres of freedom. The interest in the separation of powers overlaps with the concern for democratic legitimation – the second protective purpose of the principle of legality.

Within the scope of international law, preventing concentration of power is likewise a concern. The international principle of legality is – just as in national law – an element of the rule of law. As in the national domain, the purpose of the "rule of *international* law" is to secure freedom, namely by stabilizing expectations. Referring to international law, Jeremy Waldron puts it this way:

> "[T]he whole point of the rule of law is to secure individual freedom by providing a predictable environment in which individuals can act freely, plan their affairs, and make decisions. To eliminate uncertainty in the interests of freedom and to furnish an environment conducive to the exercise of individual autonomy constitutes the raison d'être of the rule of law."[50]

Securing freedom through the distribution of power within the multi-level system of international and national law is achieved less through the "horizontal" separation of powers than through a "vertical" separation between international bodies for the enforcement of individual obligations (such as through monitoring bodies, compliance committees, and the like) and national authorities.

[50] Waldron, The Rule of International Law, 2006, 15–30 (17).

(In principle, international norms generating individual obligations can be applied at both levels and by both kinds of institutions.[51]) With respect to the international legal bases, the second, democratic concern of the principle of legality can be taken into account in a limited way. For instance, an international treaty might – on democratic grounds – be given preference to customary international law as a legal basis. Treaties enjoy a stronger democratic legitimation than customary international law, because in many cases national parliaments must consent to their entry into force. Overall, however, international legal norms generally enjoy less democratic legitimation than national laws, and on structural grounds the ideal of a democratically legitimated international law – which, for instance, would have to be adopted by a world parliament with representatives of seven billion people – is very difficult to realize. A key demand of legitimacy which international law must fulfil, however, is that international actors be accountable. This principle has a similar containing function as the democratic principle, and therefore one of the well-known rationales of the principle of legality (namely to secure accountability) plays in international law, too.

4.7.2 *International Norms Are Formally Suitable as a Legal Basis*

From a continental European constitutional perspective, the type of norm with the best legitimation in terms of democracy and the rule of law is an act of parliament. In democratic States, laws are enacted by citizens themselves or by democratically elected representatives in a formalized, public, and deliberative process. The legal form of an act of parliament available in national legal systems is not an option in international law. But this does not prevent fulfilment of the principle of legality in principle. The progressive globalization and Europeanization of governance forbids to continue focusing on acts of parliament. Other types of legal bases, including non-State legal bases, have become customary and necessary. It has been observed that "the principle that the exercise of public power must ultimately rest on an act of parliament has in a variety of sectors receded into the background due to the demands of European law and the integration of

[51] On the question of direct application of international legal norms imposing obligations on individuals, see Chapter 16.

legal orders. Legality has waned, and one can say that at least the foundational function of legality has been eclipsed".[52] As the legal basis for the restriction of individual rights, any (abstract-general) norm with an external effect may in principle be considered nowadays. With regard to the domestic domain, for instance, the ECtHR recognizes that common law norms – even if they have not been codified – may constitute a suitable legal basis for State measures burdening individuals.[53] Accordingly, international law cannot be ruled out as a legal basis on grounds of principle. The Statute of the International Criminal Court also assumes in principle that all classical international sources of law may serve as the basis not only for individual obligations but also for individual criminal responsibility (see Article 21 of the ICC Statute with regard to the law to be applied by the ICC[54]). Finally, the ECtHR (in regard to the fulfilment of the requirements set out in Article 5 ECHR, according to which deprivation of liberty must be "in accordance with a procedure proscribed by law" and "lawful") has regarded an *international legal* basis for deprivation of liberty (and accordingly for imposition of the obligation to tolerate such deprivation) to be sufficient.[55] In the final analysis, the international principle of legality does not per se prohibit the imposition of a legal obligation (limiting freedom) by way of an international legal norm.

52 Leonard F. M. Besselink/Frans Pennings/Sacha Prechal (eds), *The Eclipse of the Legality Principle in the European Union* (Alphen aan den Rijn: Kluwer 2011), 301.

53 ECtHR, *Sunday Times* v. *UK*, No. 6538/74, 26 April 1979, paragraphs 46–53.

54 Article 21 of the Rome Statute: "1. The Court shall apply: (a) In the first place, *this Statute*, the Elements of Crime and its Rules of Procedure and Evidence; (b) In the second place, where appropriate, applicable treaties and the *principles and rules of international law*, including the established principles of the international law of armed conflict; (c) Failing that, *general principles of law* derived by the Court from national laws of legal systems of the world . . ." (italics mine).

55 ECtHR (Grand Chamber), 29 March 2010, *Medvedyev* v. *France*, No. 3394/03, paragraph 79: "The Court further reiterates that where the 'lawfulness' of detention is in issue, including the question whether 'a procedure prescribed by law' has been followed, the Convention refers essentially to national law but also, where appropriate, to other applicable legal standards, including those which have their *source in international law* . . ." (italics mine). *Ibid.*, paragraph 80: "The Court stresses that where deprivation of liberty is concerned it is particularly important that *the general principle of legal certainty* be satisfied. It is therefore essential that the conditions for deprivation of liberty *under domestic and/or international law* be *clearly defined and that the law itself be foreseeable in its application*, so that it meets the standard of 'lawfulness' set by the Convention, a standard which requires that all law be sufficiently precise to avoid all risk of arbitrariness and to allow the citizen – if need be, with appropriate advice – to foresee, to a degree that is reasonable in the circumstances of the case, the consequences which a given action may entail . . ." (italics mine).

4.7.3 Substantive Demands on the Legal Basis

What substantive demands does the international principle of legality make on the imposition of legal obligations? A *European* principle of legality has been defined in the case law of the ECtHR. While the Court has spelled out the principle of legality only under the perspective of the limitation of fundamental rights contained in the ECHR, the principle developed there can be generalized to the imposition of other obligations (including obligations to tolerate limitations of fundamental rights). They are also a relevant indicator for the demands of a universal principle of legality because they have been freed from the purely national context of a specific legal order and reflect the consensus of liberal constitutional States. According to this case law, the principle of legality requires the existence of a legal basis for the imposition of a legal obligation and the concomitant limitation of freedom. The imposed obligations must be covered by this legal basis. In a qualitative sense, the legal basis must be accessible. The individual must have the possibility of gaining knowledge of the legal norms applicable to the case.[56] Furthermore, the legal basis must be specified in such a way that citizens can align their behaviour accordingly. The legal basis must therefore ensure that the obligation (as well as the legal consequences that may be ordered if that obligation is breached) is foreseeable.[57]

The requirement of foreseeability does not demand of the legal basis that it govern all details. The legal basis must, however, offer minimum protection against arbitrariness. The degree of the required specificity depends on the context in this regard: Among other factors, it depends on the legal matters governed, the range of addressees, and the legal consequences ordered.[58] This contextual evaluation makes sense, because depending on the legal matter, a prohibition or precept and the legal consequences of a breach may be foreseeable for a specific addressee but not for another, even if the wording of the provision in question is identical. Where the violation of an individual obligation is punishable by a criminal penalty, the principle of legality applies in its strictest form (see Chapter 5).

In the final analysis – along with the requirement that direct international individual obligations may be derived from an international legal norm only if this appears necessary to protect important legal goods – the

[56] *Ibid.*, paragraph 49.

[57] See, e.g., ECtHR, *Petra* v. *Romania*, No. 27273/95, 23 September 1998, paragraph 37.

[58] ECtHR, *Rekvényi* v. *Hungary*, No. 25390/94, 20 May 1999, paragraph 34.

demands of the principle of legality, i.e., the specificity and accessibility of the norm and accordingly the foreseeability of the individual obligations derived from that norm, set a clear limit to the recognition of direct international obligations. One could argue that the democratic legitimacy deficit inherent in an international legal basis constitutes a handicap that must be compensated through *enhanced requirements on specificity and, accordingly, foreseeability.*

4.8 Legal Bases of Specific Individual Obligations

Now that the preliminary question of whether international law can satisfy the principle of legality in general has been answered in the affirmative, the legal bases of a *specific* individual obligation must be examined. The question arises as to which international legal form is best suited to satisfy the principle of legality. For want of international legislation, under what conditions do the international legal forms – i.e., treaties, customary law, general principles of law, and case law – meet the requirements of the principle of legality? The answer to this question can be found only if the twofold rationale of the principle of legality, namely ensuring the rule of law and accountability, is observed.

4.8.1 Treaty

The current legal situation can be described as follows: Normally, treaty practice entails mediation of the obligations of the individual. As a general rule, international law does not impose obligations on individuals directly, but rather only indirectly via national law. It is controversial whether international treaties are sufficient as a legal basis for international individual obligations. The debate focuses on the question of criminal responsibility (see Chapter 5), thus masking the prior fundamental question of whether such obligations can be justified at all.

4.8.1.1 General Adherence to the Principle of Legality

Advocates of the justifiability of individual obligations under international treaty law refer to the well-known passage in the judgment of the Nuremburg Military Tribunal: States may do together what any one of them might have done singly. Indeed, this passage refers (inter alia) to the legal basis of the punishable acts: "The signatory Powers created this Tribunal, *defined the law* it was to administer, and made regulations for the proper conduct of the Trial. In doing so, *they have done together what any one of them might have done singly*; for it is not to be doubted that any nation has the right thus to set up special courts to administer law."[59] Marko Milanovic elaborates: "The direct imposition of obligations by states acting collectively merely dispenses with the further step of states doing so singly by implementing domestic legislation."[60]

Dispensing with this "further step", namely enacting domestic legislation, represents a crucial legitimacy deficit in the view of critics, however. In fact, the question of individual obligations pursuant to treaties should be evaluated primarily from the perspective of legitimation, which means (according to what was said above) on the basis of the following criteria: the risk of a regulatory and enforcement gap, foreseeability, and accessibility of the legal basis.

As mentioned above, the *democratic* legitimation of treaties is weaker than that of the laws of a democratically organized State, given that the treaty text is set out by government representatives and not by parliaments. Their legitimation in terms of the *rule of law* is also weaker with respect to legal clarity and transparency because they (traditionally) are negotiated without significant public participation. Nevertheless, the ECtHR has deemed treaties – not only multilateral treaties, but also bilateral treaties – to be a sufficient legal basis for limiting fundamental rights. It accordingly considers such treaty norms to be "law" for purposes of the ECHR.[61] As a general matter, the suitability of international law to form a legal basis for intrusive State action is explicitly forseen in Art. 7(1) ECHR, which mentions "a criminal offence under national *or international law* ". This approach will be followed here also in regard to the imposition of other obligations (beyond obligations to tolerate limitations of fundamental rights, and beyond the obligation to accept the imposition of a criminal penalty). Classifying an international treaty as an *accessible* and *foreseeable* legal basis is defensible because nowadays – due to increased demands on transparency – parliaments and even the general public are informed at least selectively and during certain phases about the content of treaty negotiations, because treaties must be ratified by the parliaments of the democratic States concerned and are

[59] International Military Tribunal, judgment of 1 October 1946, in: The Trial of German Major War Criminals. Proceedings of the International Military Tribunal sitting at Nuremberg, Germany, Part 22 (22 August 1946 to 1 October 1946), 444 (italics mine).

[60] Marko Milanovic, Is the Rome Statute Binding on Individuals? (And Why We Should Care), *Journal of International Criminal Law* 9 (2011), 25–52 (45).

[61] ECtHR (Grand Chamber), *Slivenko* v. *Latvia*, No. 48321/99, 9 October 2003, paragraphs 100 et seq. (international treaty concerning the withdrawal of Russian troops).

published in the end. Ultimately, the question is no longer *whether* an international treaty can in principle impose obligations on individuals (a question that must be affirmed), but rather *when* it does so and *in regard to whom*.

4.8.1.2 Specific Conditions: Risk of Regulatory Gap, Significance, Specificity, Accessibility, and Foreseeability

Under what conditions does a treaty norm impose direct international obligations on individuals? The starting point for answering this question must in all cases be the wording of the treaty itself.

From a normative perspective, the mediation common today (i.e., the forgoing of any direct imposition of individual obligations by the treaty) is welcome, given the practical problems and problems of legitimacy associated with direct individual obligations. While *rights* of individuals can readily be assumed to arise from international treaties with open wording (and possibly even a presumption in favour of individual rights exists, Chapter 13, pp. 414–16), this is not the case in regard to the imposition of obligations. Where the wording of the treaty is open, it cannot be presumed that individuals are being addressed directly. The direct imposition of international obligations on individuals is the exception and must be justified specially. Hence, there is a presumption *against the existence of individual obligations.* International treaties must therefore be interpreted regularly as generating purely State obligations, unless there are clear indicators for the creation of individual obligations.

Following this line, the Federal Constitutional Court of Germany has several times already refused to derive individual obligations from international treaties. In its judgment on the German–Czechoslovak treaty, which found the Munich Agreement to be void, the Court stated, "Direct duties of action or conduct by individual citizens may be derived from international treaties . . . only if and to the extent this is expressed unambiguously by the wording of the treaty."[62] It also refused to derive individual obligations from the treaties between the Federal Republic of Germany on the one side and the Soviet Union, Poland, and the German Democratic Republic (*Ostverträge*). Here, the Court held "that a corresponding will of the

[62] BVerfGE 43, 203, 209 (1977; translation mine). The Federal Constitutional Court considered possible violations of fundamental rights. No obligation by individuals can be derived from Article IV of the Treaty on the Inviolability of Borders and Mutual Respect for Territorial Integrity. Since no duties of conduct were established, no limitation of fundamental rights (such as a violation of the freedom of opinion of individuals) is conceivable.

contracting parties to create specific legal *duties* of action and conduct may be presumed only if and to the extent this is *expressed unambiguously* by the wording of the treaty. If this is true already of the obligations of the contracting parties themselves, it must be especially true of direct duties of action and conduct of *individual citizens*; it is already generally *the exception* for international treaties to define *legal obligations for private persons*, and such an exception *may not be considered to have been agreed without a clear indication in the wording*".[63] The presumption manifest here that obligations should not be interpreted into the wording of treaties if they do not – explicitly or obviously implicitly – address individuals is consistent with the principle of legality: Only if the wording is clear, or at least if the individual thrust is obvious, is the requirement satisfied that the obligor be able to foresee the obligation.

For the interpretation of international treaties, this means that individual obligations may be derived from them only if (1) their wording clearly expresses this, or such an interpretation is foreseeable for potential obligors and if the further normative conditions, namely (2) the importance of the legal good and (3) a special risk of inadequate implementation and enforcement by State law, are also met.

The first condition of the foreseeability of individual obligations is currently *not* met by international *human rights treaties*. Their wording does not indicate who the addressees of the obligation to respect, observe, and promote human rights are. The historical intention of the contracting parties was to obligate only the States parties. While the obligations in question are very important and their enforcement would be improved by addressing private obligations directly, no dynamic interpretation of the human rights treaties so as to address private actors as obligors is currently foreseeable. This means that the agreements should not abruptly be interpreted as having a direct effect on third parties, because such a re-interpretation would go beyond the open wording and violate the principle of legality (for details, see pp. 100–102).

Another example is the provision in Article 22(2) of the Vienna Convention on Diplomatic Relations (VCDR), which imposes the "special duty" on receiving States to protect foreign embassies.[64] According to

[63] BVerfGE 40, 141, 164–165 (1975; translation and italics mine).

[64] Vienna Convention on Diplomatic Relations of 18 April 1961, Article 22(2): "The receiving State is under a special duty to take all appropriate steps to protect the premises of the mission against any intrusion or damage and to prevent any disturbance of the peace of the mission or impairment of its dignity."

the principles just mentioned above, *no* individual obligations can be derived from this provision, because according to its wording and meaning, only the States parties to the VCDR are addressed. This means the treaty norm cannot supply a sufficient basis for burdensome (administrative) measures against private persons.[65] But this is not because the provision is found "merely" in an international treaty. Even if an identically formulated duty of protection were set out in national law, such as in a police act, it would not suffice as a basis for authorizing burdensome administrative acts. From the perspective of the principle of legality, what matters is not the formal source of the norm, but rather its specificity and the foreseeability of the resulting duty of conduct for the individual.

In contrast, the conditions of unambiguous wording addressing individuals and the further normative conditions are met by the *Rome Statute of the International Criminal Court*: While the treaty does not explicitly impose obligations on individuals, the individual thrust of the obligations is foreseeable. The obligations to refrain from the enumerated crimes are important, and their enforcement through State law alone does not suffice to prevent impunity. (On the punishments for breaches of individual obligations, see Chapter 5).

The wordings of some treaties in international humanitarian law also meet the conditions of foreseeability, importance, and enforcement risk. This is why individual obligations can be derived from international humanitarian law "when it is clear from a *plain reading* that this is the effect of the relevant treaty".[66]

4.8.1.3 Determining the Addressees of the Obligation

The follow-up question is which addressees may be covered by a treaty obligation that is addressed to individuals in principle. Every human being in the entire world? Or can an international treaty obligate only persons belonging to the contracting parties?

In the case of the Rome Statute of the International Criminal Court, for instance, obligations are assumed to be created in principle only for persons affiliated with States parties. Where the Rome Statute gives rise to substantive obligations, these obligations are to be addressed only to persons who themselves or through their acts are linked to a State party

[65] Christian Tomuschat, Article 25 of the Basic Law, in: Wolfgang Kahl/Christian Waldhoff/Christian Walter (eds), *Bonner Kommentar* (140th Update June 2009), paragraph 105.

[66] See Kate Parlett, *The Individual in the International Legal System* (Cambridge: Cambridge University Press 2011), 219 (italics mine).

either personally or territorially, by analogy to the jurisdiction rule set out in Article 12 of the Rome Statute.[67] If an international treaty were to claim a worldwide power to bind any given person, this would be "exorbitant". But one could assume that an individual would then be bound by the treaty obligations exactly in the same way as by exorbitant national laws, even where such laws violate the sovereignty of other States.[68]

Since, as was discussed above, the internal legitimacy of the treaty-based obligations is not the principle of legislative competence for the inhabitants of a State territory, but rather the global need for regulation (pp. 76–78), the possibility in principle for a treaty to bind all human beings – irrespective of their affiliation with a contracting party – appears consistent. However, binding persons affiliated with non-States parties is *foreseeable* only if they know or should know that the treaty giving rise to the obligation is to be applied universally in principle. This is the case only if it protects global legal goods. The considerations would have to be similar to those justifying the universal legislative jurisdiction of the State to prescribe, which extends the scope of national laws beyond the territory of the State and its citizens. One could then argue that if all States are allowed to enact laws for subject matters worldwide, then they should also be able to do so by treaty, as long as the treaty is sufficiently specific. Accordingly, obligations arising from international treaties that bind individuals who are not affiliated with a contracting party can arise only if the universal jurisdiction of the State to prescribe is respected.

Ultimately, the recognition of treaty-based individual obligations should remain the exception, requiring special justification. This justification is given if the obligations are foreseeable, if they serve to protect important legal goods, and if they appear necessary to prevent or close a regulatory gap at the level of State law.

4.8.2 *Customary International Law and General Principles of Law*

Customary law and general principles of law are by nature even less specific than treaty law. Nevertheless, the ECtHR has found customary norms of the law of armed conflict to be sufficient not only as the legal basis of a duty of omission but also as a basis for criminal responsibility. The controlling judgment of the ECtHR on the compatibility of imposing

[67] Milanovic, Rome Statute Binding, 2011, 48 and 51. [68] *Ibid.*, 50.

a criminal punishment on the basis of customary international law with the *nulla poena* principle set out in Article 7 ECHR is *Kononov* v. *Latvia* (2010).[69] This judgment was based on the following fact pattern: The applicant commanded a group of partisans of the Red Army during a punitive expedition in 1944 against the inhabitants of a Latvian village who were suspected of collaborating with the German Wehrmacht. Nine unarmed villagers were killed. The applicant was found guilty of war crimes by the Latvian Supreme Court in 2004. In 1944, neither the USSR nor Latvia were parties to the Hague Convention of 1907. The question was therefore whether already at the time of commission (1944) there was a sufficient legal basis for a war crimes conviction. In the view of the court, fundamental provisions of international humanitarian law – including those set out in the Hague Convention of 1907 respecting the Laws and Customs of War on Land for the protection of the civilian population – were already applicable as customary international law in 1944 and were also subject to punishment according to customary law. This means that the conduct against the villagers was punishable as a war crime already in 1944.[70] In particular, the ECtHR held the criminality of the acts based exclusively on international law to be sufficiently accessible and foreseeable.[71] Consequently, customary law and general principles of law may constitute a legal basis for direct international obligations of the individual if the norms are sufficiently foreseeable for the individual, which must be examined in each specific case.

4.8.3 Case Law

Does mere case law also meet the requirements of the principle of legality? The democratic legitimation of the judgments of international courts is comparatively weak. Nevertheless, one can argue that in terms of legal clarity and appropriateness to the subject matter, the legitimacy of case law is stronger than that of international treaty law. As discussed above, international treaties are not equivalent to democratic law: They are the outcome of a negotiating process rather than a deliberative process – bargaining instead of arguing. They traditionally are created without the involvement of the public – diplomacy instead of democracy.

[69] ECtHR (Grand Chamber), 17 May 2010, *Kononov* v. *Latvia*, No. 36376/04. In this connection, see Thomas Kleinlein, Der EGMR und das Völkerrecht im Rahmen von Art. 7 EMRK, *Europäische Grundrechte-Zeitschrift* 37 (2010), 544–560.

[70] On criminal responsibility, see Chapter 5.

[71] ECtHR (Grand Chamber), 17 May 2010, *Kononov* v. *Latvia*, No. 36376/04, paragraph 236.

The element of power politics is not filtered out at the international level: Treaties are typically the product of a political compromise. For the wording of the treaty – whose *specificity* is a key factor in the legitimation of the legal obligation (especially, but not only, if breaches are subject to criminal sanction) – the political character has dire consequences. The wording is sometimes deliberately ambiguous, often contrived, and difficult to manage. Elies van Sliedregt concludes that "[u]nder such circumstances, judicial lawmaking is essential and compensates for a flawed process of lawmaking".[72]

A follow-up question is whether the case law of national courts can offer a legitimate legal basis equal to the case law of international courts and whether a distinction between civil and criminal case law must be made. For instance, the secondary obligations of individuals (i.e., at the level of international responsibility) are currently developed by civil courts at the national level. In the final analysis, case law as the legal basis of individual obligations is ambivalent.

4.8.4 *Secondary International Law*

Secondary international law might also be considered a legal basis for individual obligations. For instance, the ECtHR allows secondary law of the European Union to serve as a legal basis for the obligation to tolerate a restriction of fundamental rights.[73]

Numerous international legal provisions are enacted by international territorial administrations.[74] After the end of the East–West conflict, for instance, comprehensive international administrations were established in Mostar (Bosnia and Herzegovina, 1994–1996), Eastern Slavonia (Croatia, 1996–1998), East Timor (1999–2002), and Kosovo (since 1999), run by the UN, NATO, or the EU.[75] The international territorial administration regimes pursue governance policies such as regulation of the legal status

[72] Elies van Sliedregt, *Individual Criminal Responsibility in International Law* (Oxford: Oxford University Press 2012), 14.

[73] ECtHR, *Bosphorus Airways* v. *Ireland*, No. 45036/98, 30 May 2005, paragraphs 143–148 (EU regulation concerning the seizure of means of transportation from the former Yugoslavia).

[74] See Ralph Wilde, *International Territorial Administration: How Trusteeship and the Civilizing Mission Never Went Away* (Oxford: Oxford University Press 2008); Mariano J. Aznar Gomez, *La administración internacionalizada del territorio* (Barcelona: Atelier 2008).

[75] See the table in Wilde, *International Territorial Administration*, 2008, 94–95. Wilde distinguishes between the establishment of plenary administrative authority and projects granting partial international administrative prerogatives.

of a territory; promotion of democracy, rule of law, and the free market; channelling of migrants; and exploitation of natural resources. In the case of plenary administrative authority, the international actors do not limit themselves to influencing the State; rather, they replace the State: "[T]hey are acting as that State."[76] Because of the very high "level of intrusiveness"[77] of administrative activity, an international territorial administration has a much stronger impact on the local population than other forms of international politics. Accordingly, international territorial administration imposes obligations (at least obligations to tolerate) on individuals, for instance in the course of privatizations and the detention of migrants in camps. This secondary rulemaking will not be discussed any further here. The following discussion analyses the extensive practice of addressing individuals as developed by the UN Security Council.

4.8.4.1 The Practice of Security Council Resolutions

Firstly, several Security Council resolutions state that terrorist acts (which normally are committed by natural persons) represent threats to the peace for purposes of Article 39 of the UN Charter.[78] But these resolutions do not impose any obligations on terrorists as such; they address States. For instance, Resolution 1624 (2005) "calls upon all States to adopt ... measures ...", and the Member States are in particular called upon to "[p]rohibit by law incitement to commit a terrorist act or acts".[79] Resolution 1540 (2004) on weapons of mass destruction has the explicit objective of minimizing the risk should non-State actors acquire such weapons.[80] But this resolution still only specifies obligations of States. The same is true of basically all UN Security Council resolutions on piracy.[81]

The aforementioned resolutions resemble international treaties imposing the obligation on contracting parties to prohibit individual forms of conduct in their national law and, where applicable, to criminalize and punish them (suppression conventions). Because the wording of these resolutions does not address individuals directly, they should not – following the principles above – be interpreted in that expanded sense, since that would not be foreseeable for the individuals.

[76] *Ibid.*, 280. [77] *Ibid.*, 279.

[78] See, e.g., UNSC res. 1368 (2001); 1377 (2001); 1735 (2006); 1757 (2007).

[79] UNSC res. 1624 (2005), paragraph 1(a).

[80] UNSC res. 1540 (2004), preambular paragraph 8.

[81] Ranging from UNSC res. 1838 (2008) to UNSC res. 2039 (2012). Res. 2020 (2011) condemns the practice of hostage-taking by privates and calls for the release of hostages in its preamble and in paragraph 1.

A so far unique deviation from this pattern is the resolution on foreign terrorist fighters (Res. 2178). Most of its operative parts address Member States and obliges them to take preventive and suppressive action against terrorist activities, recruitment, financing, transit of suspect individuals, and so on. But in addition, the resolution directly and upfront addresses individuals: The Council "demands that all foreign terrorist fighters disarm and cease all terrorist acts and participation in the conflict".[82]

A second group of Security Council resolutions governs *sanctions*. These resolutions likewise aim at influencing the conduct of individuals. The first subgroup consists of *comprehensive* regimes of economic sanctions against an entire country. These aim to interrupt economic relations that normally exist between private exporters and importers. Their typical consequence is to prevent the performance of private contracts that have already been concluded, and hence they affect private rights.

The new resolutions imposing *targeted* sanctions are directed against specific individuals often referred to by name, especially political office-holders or terrorist suspects. The goal of these resolutions is to make individuals bring their personal conduct into conformity with international law and previous Security Council resolutions.

However, both types of sanctions directly first of all oblige States to take measures under their national law, especially to prohibit private individuals within their jurisdiction from engaging in trade, to prohibit them from leaving or transiting through the country, and to freeze their accounts.[83] The typical formulation of the Security Council is that it "*calls upon all States to take appropriate measures to ensure* that individuals and companies in their jurisdiction . . . act in conformity with United Nations embargoes, . . . and, as appropriate, take the necessary judicial and administrative action to end any illegal activities by those individuals and companies".[84] Technically speaking, the individuals here are still mediated through their States (or, in the case of the EU, through the EU). Unlike EU directives and regulations on sanctions,[85] the Security

[82] Res 2178 (2014), paragraph 1. See on the question of the direct effect of the resolution below Chapter 16, pp. 508–09.

[83] See, e.g., UNSC Res. 1267 (1999) against the Taliban; res. 1390 (2002) against the Taliban and al-Qaida; res. 1591 (2005) against belligerents in Darfur; res. 1672 (2006) against Sudanese officeholders.

[84] Paragraph 21 of UNSC res. 1343 (2001) on Sierra Leone (italics mine). See also paragraph 18 of UNSC res. 1408 (2002).

[85] See, e.g., Council Decision 2011/782/CFSP of 1 December 2011 concerning restrictive measures against Syria and repealing Decision 2011/273/CFSP (OJ 2011/L 319/56). This decision inter alia prohibits the sale of weapons and arms to Syria by "nationals of

Council resolutions do not impose direct obligations on natural and legal persons. This is true of traders exporting weapons or other goods to crisis areas and also of named individuals on whom travel restrictions are to be imposed (by UN Member States).

Only a few Security Council resolutions explicitly impose sanction decisions directly on non-State actors. For example, Resolution 1474 (2003) "stresses the *obligation* of all States and *other actors*" to comply with a previous resolution imposing an arms embargo in respect of Somalia.[86] In a sanction resolution concerning the Democratic Republic of the Congo, the Security Council seems to have directly imposed financial and travel sanctions on individuals, e.g., on persons who recruit child soldiers, or who attack peacekeepers.[87]

Moreover, the more recent *sanctions committees* (subsidiary organs of the Security Council as referred to in Article 29 of the UN Charter) make decisions that are binding on individuals. For instance, the al-Qaida and Taliban Sanctions Committee designates individuals.[88] It is mandated to consider requests for the listing and delisting of persons.[89] The committee makes these decisions itself; for instance, it decides to delist a person on the recommendation of the ombudsperson.[90]

A third type of Security Council resolution and presidential statement expressly directs *recommendations* to individuals and groups. Several times, the Security Council has called upon private persons, NGOs, and companies to support UN sanctions policy. In regard to Sierra Leone, the Security Council asked the diamond industry to cooperate with the

Member States" (Article 1) and freezes all funds "belonging to, or owned, held or controlled by persons responsible for the violent repression against the civilian population in Syria" (Article 19). In this spirit, see also Articles 2 and 4 of Council Regulation (EU) No 442/2011 of 9 May 2011 concerning restrictive measures in view of the situation in Syria (OJ 2011/L 121/1).

86 Res. 1474 (2003) of 8 April 2003, paragraph 1 (italics mine); identical in res. 1519 (2003) of 16 December 2003, paragraph 1. The arms embargo was introduced with resolution 733 (1992).

87 Res. 2136 (2014), paragraph 4: "4. Decides that the measures referred to in paragraph 3 above [financial and travel measures] *shall apply to the following individuals*, and, as appropriate, entities, as designated by the Committee: .... (d) Individuals or entities operating in the DRC and recruiting or using children in armed conflict in violation of applicable international law; (i) Individuals or entities who plan, direct, sponsor or participate in attacks against MONUSCO peacekeepers."

88 Res. 1333 (2000), paragraph 8(c).

89 See, e.g., Guidelines of the 1267 Committee of 7 November 2002, most recently amended on 15 April 2013, paragraph 4(c).

90 See, e.g., SC/10282, Press release of 15 June 2011, decision of the al-Qaida and Taliban Sanctions Committee following review of the delisting requests on 14 June 2011.

official government.[91] In regard to Liberia, the Security Council called upon "civil society" to contribute to peace in the region.[92] A recent example is a resolution on the crisis after the presidential elections in Côte d'Ivoire (extension of the UNOCI mandate (United Nations Operation in Côte d'Ivoire)): The Security Council "calls upon the government and all international partners, *including private companies*, involved in assisting the Government in the reform of the security sector, to comply with the provisions of resolution 1980 (2011)".[93]

The President of the Security Council has characterized drug trafficking and the associated cross-border criminal activity as a threat to the peace, calling upon civil society and stakeholders to combat it.[94] What is important, however, is that these resolutions do not impose strict obligations on individuals but rather only "encourage" or "invite" them to take steps.

So far, decisions of the Security Council appear to unambiguously impose strict legal obligations on private actors in situations of *non-international armed conflict*.[95] In this connection, several resolutions have called upon not only the involved States but also other political groups and individuals to immediately cease hostilities, to comply with previously agreed ceasefire agreements, and the like.[96]

[91] See UNSC res. 1306 (2000) of 5 July 2000, paragraph 10: "*Encourages* the International Diamond Manufacturers Association, the World Federation of Diamond Bourses, the Diamond High Council and all other representatives of the diamond industry to work with the Government of Sierra Leone." Paragraph 11: "*Invites* States, international organizations, *members of the diamond industry and other relevant entities in a position to do so* to offer assistance to the Government of Sierra Leone." Paragraph 13: "*Welcomes the commitments* made by certain members of the diamond industry not to trade in diamonds originating from conflict zones, including in Sierra Leone, *urges all other companies and individuals* involved in trading in rough diamonds to make similar declarations in respect of Sierra Leone diamonds, and underlines the importance of relevant financial institutions encouraging such companies to do so" (italics mine). See also UNSC res. 1343 (2001) of 7 March 2001, paragraph B.16.

[92] UNSC res. 1408 (2002) of 6 May 2002, preambular paragraph 8: "*Encouraging civil society initiatives* in the region ... to continue their contribution towards regional peace."

[93] UNSC res. 2000 (2011) of 27 July 2011, paragraph 16 (italics mine). See also UNSC res. 2020 (2012), paragraph 25 on piracy.

[94] UN Doc. S/PRST/2009/32 of 8 December 2009.

[95] See ICJ, *Accordance with International Law of the Unilateral Declaration of Independence in Respect of Kosovo*, Advisory Opinion of 22 July 2010, paragraph 115.

[96] The Security Council did this several times during the Kosovo conflict and also in the context of other non-international armed conflicts. Res. 1160 (1998) of 31 March 1998, paragraph 2, "calls also upon the Kosovar Albanian leadership to condemn all terrorist action." Res. 1199 (1998) of 23 September 1998, paragraph 1, "demands that all parties, groups, and individuals immediately cease hostilities and maintain a ceasefire." Res. 1203

4.8.4.2 Real Individual Obligations via Resolutions?

The question is whether the resolutions mentioned above are able to impose legally binding international obligations on the individuals addressed here. According to the wording of Article 25 of the UN Charter, the resolutions of the Security Council appear to oblige only the UN Member States: "The *Members* of the United Nations agree to accept and carry out the decisions of the Security Council in accordance with the present Charter" (italics mine). In its *Kosovo* advisory opinion, however, the ICJ finds that it can "establish, on a case-by-case basis, . . . for whom the Security Council intended to create binding legal obligations".[97] The ICJ did not rule out a binding effect of Security Council resolutions on individuals in principle. It did not even limit the potential binding effect to non-State actors that enjoy international legal personality. In the *Kosovo* proceedings, the ICJ merely found that Resolution 1244 was directed not at the authors of the declaration of independence but rather at the UN Member States, the UN itself, and its organs. According to the ICJ, "There is no indication, in the text of Security Council resolution 1244 (1999), that the Security Council intended to impose, beyond that, a specific obligation to act or a prohibition from acting, addressed to such other actors."[98] From the absence of such an "indication", the ICJ concluded that no individual obligations existed. The focus on a mere "indication" suggests that it would be possible to impose obligations on non-State actors where such obligations can be inferred by the circumstances, even if they are not explicit. According to the principles discussed above, such implicitly expressed obligations must be viewed critically because they risk violating the principle of legality.

This overview of practice has shown that the Security Council has imposed unambiguous individual obligations only in non-international armed conflicts so far; this includes the Kosovo situation. The functional justification for addressing armed groups and individuals directly in this

(1998) of 24 October 1998, paragraph 4, "demands that the Kosovo Albanian leadership and all other elements of the Kosovo Albanian community comply" with earlier resolutions. Res. 814 (1993) of 26 March 1993, paragraph 8 "demands that all Somali parties, *including movements and factions*" comply with their earlier obligations arising from a ceasefire and disarmament agreement. Res. 1010 (1995) of 10 August 1995, paragraphs 1 and 2, demands that the Bosnian Serb party give access to UN and ICRC personnel and respect their rights. Res. 1127 (1997) of 28 August 1997, paragraphs 2 and 3, "demands" that UNITA (the Angolan independence movement) meet its demilitarization obligations and supply information on disarmament.

[97] ICJ, *Independence in Respect of Kosovo* (n. 95), paragraph 117.

[98] *Ibid.*, paragraph 115.

context is that in the situation of a civil war, the lack of State control over these groups is obvious, because otherwise there would be no armed conflict. If a Security Council resolution aims to have a peacemaking effect, it must directly address the armed non-State groups. It would not be sufficient and would even be counterproductive if the Security Council were to call upon only the States involved to suppress the military activities of the opposition and to punish them using the resources of national criminal law. It is precisely such measures of central power and the resistance met by such actions that constitute the military conflict. The risk of a regulatory gap and especially of an enforcement gap is evident here, so that the first normative condition for imposing direct international individual obligations is met.

The basic objection that obligations are redundant duplications under national law and international law thus specifically does not apply in this context. The international, State-directed prohibition of force (see Article 2(4) of the UN Charter) must be supplemented here by an individually effective obligation to refrain from military force. It is not sufficient to require States – through the prohibition of force – to qualify military activities of private parties as criminal acts under national law and accordingly to punish them using the resources of domestic criminal law.[99] The resolutions referred to above show that the Security Council itself apparently did not deem it sufficient to rely on implementation by nation-States. In fact, States involved in military conflicts during which the force of arms is used by non-State actors often do not have the possibility of enforcing their domestic law. In this context, addressing individuals directly under international law as a flanking measure appears especially important.

The doctrinal explanation for the hard formulations of these resolutions might be that in an armed conflict, individuals and armed groups are in any event bound directly by applicable international law.[100] As a consequence, the Security Council resolutions do not impose entirely new legal obligations on these actors, but rather in essence they merely enforce the obligations that already arise from treaties and customary law.[101] Nevertheless, the legal specification of pre-existing obligations constitutes an independent legal effect on individuals, beyond the declaratory effect of the resolutions.

[99] But for a sceptical view, cf. Tomuschat, *Bonner Kommentar*, 2009, Article 25, paragraph 99.

[100] See Chapter 7. [101] Herdegen, *Befugnisse des UN-Sicherheitsrates* 1998, 32.

The second group of individual obligations in this context arises, as mentioned, from the decisions of the sanctions committees. Because the powers of the sanctions committees are considered to be delegated powers of the Security Council, the sanctions committees must act within the scope of recognized principles of delegation.[102] A key precondition for delegation is that the Security Council cannot delegate more powers than it may exercise itself. The Security Council itself must therefore be entitled to impose obligations on individuals if the committees are expected to do so with legal effect.

It follows from this that the doctrinal explanation for this binding effect of resolutions on the individuals addressed does not consist in the consent of the individuals subject to the law or in the principle of legislative competence of the Member States in regard to all actors on their territory but rather in the principle of the need for global regulation (see pp. 76–78). Like international treaties, resolutions of the Security Council or its subsidiary bodies may impose obligations on individuals because the UN Charter, which enjoys a special legal quality (in the view of some, as a world constitution), endows the Security Council with a special authority that – within the boundaries of the principle of legality – also is effective *erga omnes* vis-à-vis individuals.

It follows that the resolutions are in principle suitable as a legal basis for international obligations, in accordance with the principle of legality. That principle states that the resolutions may give rise to real individual legal obligations only if those obligations are foreseeable for the individuals addressed. This is the case only if the obligations and their addressees can be derived from the wording of the resolutions with sufficient contextual determinacy.

4.9 Individual Obligation to Observe International Human Rights?

Private (economic) actors as potential addressees of international individual obligations have been considered especially in terms of their respect for human rights.[103] The legal form of a business enterprise

[102] Dan Sarooshi, *The United Nations and the Development of Collective Security: The Delegation by the UN Security Council of Its Chapter VII Powers* (Oxford: Oxford University Press 1999), 106–107.

[103] See, fundamentally, Steven Ratner, Corporations and Human Rights: A Theory of Legal Responsibility, *Yale Law Journal* 111 (2001), 443–545; Philip Alston (ed.), *Non-State Actors and Human Rights* (Oxford: Oxford University Press 2005), 315–350; Andrew Clapham, *Human Rights Obligations of Non-State Actors* (Oxford: Oxford

under national law does not play a role in regard to the imposition of such obligations under international law, because every legal order defines the capacity of actors to assume rights and duties in accordance with its own rules (see Chapter 3, p. 35). The background for the debate on the binding nature of human rights is the expansion of the freedom of action of transnational corporations as a consequence of globalization. The extremely improved and lower-cost communication and transport possibilities in conjunction with the opening up of new production locations, employee pools, and sales markets have given globally operating companies substantial potential to interfere with certain human rights, such as health at the workplace, social security, as well as the freedom of association and opinion. This new potential for abuse motivates the efforts to read binding human rights obligations into existing international law and/or to provide a new basis for that purpose. The basic considerations can be applied to the question of corporate obligations to respect other international individual rights, some of which can be derived from International Labour Organization (ILO) conventions.

4.9.1 *Direct International Obligations Are Possible and Permissible while Respecting the Principle of Legality*

The norm according enterprises international legal personality and hence also a ("passive") capacity to be bound by international obligations vis-à-vis other individuals has already emerged as a principle of customary international law.[104] This international legal capacity permits non-State

University Press 2006); Knox, Horizontal Human Rights Law, 2008. More recently, see Radu Mares (ed.), *The UN Guiding Principles on Business and Human Rights: Foundations and Implementation* (Leiden: Martinus Nijhoff 2012). See also Anne Peters, Sind transnationale Unternehmen verpflichtet, (internationale) Menschenrechte zu respektieren und zu fördern?, in: Peter Kirchschläger/Thomas Kirchschläger/Andréa Belliger/David Krieger (eds), *Menschenrechte und Wirtschaft im Spannungsfeld zwischen State und Nonstate Actors* (Bern: Stämpfli 2005), 127–135.

[104] On the international legal personality and international treaty-making power of transnational corporations, see Georg Dahm/Jost Delbrück/Rüdiger Wolfrum, *Völkerrecht*, Vol. I/3 (2nd ed., Berlin: De Gruyter 2002), 531; Matthias Herdegen, *Internationales Wirtschaftsrecht* (3rd ed., Munich: Beck 2002), 234; Waldemar Hummer, Internationale und transnationale Akteure an oder unter der Schwelle der Völkerrechtssubjektivität, in: Hans-Peter Neuhold/Waldemar Hummer/Christoph Schreuer (eds), *Österreichisches Handbuch des Völkerrechts*, Vol. 1 (4th ed., Vienna: Manz 2004), 233–243 (238); Pierre-Marie Dupuy, *Droit International Public* (7th ed., Paris: Dalloz 2004), 263;

economic actors to become holders of (new) international rights and duties. Whether or not such duties already exist in concrete terms is another question.

According to current law, enterprises are not obliged *directly* by human rights treaties to respect and protect the rights set out therein, because those treaties do not explicitly address them as obligors. The same is true of customary law as it stands: The obligation to observe human rights under customary law is, according to current practice and accepted legal doctrine, not directed at private enterprises. An exception currently applies only in regard to those human rights belonging to mandatory international law, such as the prohibition of torture. Because *jus cogens* applies unconditionally, it also binds non-State actors such as individuals and collective actors, including armed groups and business enterprises.[105]

Beyond *jus cogens*, the imposition of (new) international obligations on enterprises could in principle occur by way of new international treaties or a dynamic interpretation of existing treaties, beyond their wording and the original intent of the contracting States, in the sense of an expansion of the addressees of the obligations, or finally as new customary international law. New international obligations would, however, need to have a sufficiently foreseeable and accessible legal foundation (*requirement of legality*; see above pp. 79–85). A dynamic interpretation of the human rights treaties such that they bind enterprises directly would, in light of their open wording, be possible in principle. This would, however, have to occur gradually, in order to be sufficiently foreseeable for the new addressees. An abrupt paradigm shift would not be foreseeable for the new obligors and would violate the principle of legality.

The principle of legality would be better respected if new legal instruments were enacted that unambiguously and directly impose obligations

Karsten Nowrot, *Normative Ordnungsstruktur und private Wirkungsmacht: Konsequenzen der Beteiligung transnationaler Unternehmen an den Rechtssetzungsprozessen im internationalen Wirtschaftssystem* (Berlin: Berliner Wissenschaftsverlag 2006), 562–595.

105 See Report of the Independent International Commission of Inquiry on the Syrian Arab Republic (UN Doc. A/HRC/19/69, 22 February 2012), paragraph 106 "[A]t a minimum, human rights obligations constituting peremptory international law (*ius cogens*) bind States, individuals and non-State collective entities, including armed groups. Acts violating *ius cogens* – for instance, torture or enforced disappearances – can never be justified". But see for a denial of the bindingness of international customary law (including *ius cogens*) on companies US Court of Appeals, *Kiobel* v. *Royal Dutch Petroleum Company*, 621 F.3d 111 (2d Cir. 2010). See in detail Chapter 5, pp. 162–63.

on enterprises. In terms of content, such treaties could require the contracting States to adopt implementing legislation that binds the enterprises. But beyond this, they could also formulate direct obligations for enterprises. This is in principle legitimate in order to protect global goods, given the increased risk in this domain of a regulatory gap. The principle of legality would be respected if the treaty obligations are formulated with sufficient precision. If specificity is lacking, not only the principle of legality but also the underlying principle of democracy would be violated. However, there is currently no political prospect for "hard", legally binding treaties in this sense.

4.9.2 Current "Soft" Regulation and Case Law

International organizations such as the OECD and the UN have so far pursued mainly soft regulatory approaches.[106] The OECD Guidelines for Multinational Enterprises (updated in 2011)[107] include labour conditions, environmental standards, human rights, corruption, and taxation. The OECD Guidelines also envisage a dispute settlement procedure using National Contact Points. In the first fifteen years of the existence of this system (2000–2015), approximately 250 proceedings have been instituted at the National Contact Points.[108] In the *Afrimex* case, for instance, the UK National Contact Point found that the Afrimex corporation had violated the OECD Guidelines by paying bribes to rebel groups in the Democratic Republic of the Congo and buying raw materials from Congolese mines that employed child labourers and forced labourers.[109]

[106] See, e.g., ILO Tripartite Declaration of Principles Concerning Multinational Enterprises and Social Policy of 17 November 2000 (ILM 41 (2002), 186 et seq.). For the UN, see the following documents: Norms of the Responsibilities of Transnational Corporations and Other Business Enterprises of the UN Sub-Commission on the Promotion and Protection of Human Rights (UN Doc. E/CN.4/Sub.2/2003//12/Rev.2 (2003) of 13 August 2003); Report of the United Nations High Commissioner on Human Rights on the Responsibilities of Transnational Corporations and Related Business Enterprises with Regard to Human Rights (UN Doc. E/CN.4/2005/91 of 15 February 2005).

[107] OECD Guidelines for Multinational Enterprises (2011), OECD Publishing. http://dx.doi.org/10.1787/9789264115415-en.

[108] OECD Watch (Caitlin Daniel, Joseph Wilde-Ramsing, Kris Genovese, Virginia Sandjojo), Remedy Remains Rare: Analysis of 15 Years of NCP Cases and their Contribution to Improve Access to Remedy for Victims of Corporate Misconduct (Amsterdam 2015), 13.

[109] UK National Contact Point, *Global Witness* v. *Afrimex Ltd.*, Final Statement of 28 August 2008. A Contact Point may not deliver a judgment, but rather only issue a recommendation.

The UN Special Rapporteur on Human Rights and Transnational Corporations and other Business Enterprises, John Ruggie, in 2011 presented thirty-one Guiding Principles on Business and Human Rights ("Ruggie Principles").[110] These Guiding Principles were adopted by Resolution 17/4 of the Human Rights Council on human rights and transnational corporations and other business enterprises of 6 July 2011.[111] The principles are divided into three pillars: Firstly, they require that States meet their duty to protect; secondly, they define corporate responsibility; and thirdly, they require States to provide effective remedies, i.e., complaint mechanisms.

With Resolution 17/4 (2011), the Human Rights Council also established a "Working Group on the issue of human rights and transnational corporations and other business enterprises" (UNWG) and an annual "Forum on Business and Human Rights".[112] One of the mandates of the ongoing Working Group is the comprehensive dissemination and implementation of the Ruggie Principles. It may also make recommendations to improve access to effective remedies (at the national, regional, and international levels) for human rights abuses by economic actors. But the Working Group is not empowered to receive and deal with complaints in concrete cases.[113]

The corporate responsibility set out in the Ruggie Principles (Principles 11–24) means that business enterprises – irrespective of positive law – must "respect" the core internationally recognized human rights and the ILO workers' rights and also carry out due diligence in this regard. The corporate responsibility to respect human rights requires not only that enterprises refrain from having negative impacts on human rights but also that they prevent or mitigate abuses directly linked to their operations, even if they have not contributed to those impacts.[114] Relevant human rights encompass at least the International Bill of Human Rights and the ILO Declaration of Fundamental Principles and Rights at Work of 1998.[115]

110 Special Representative of the Secretary-General on Human Rights and Transnational Corporations and Other Business Enterprises, Report with Guiding Principles in the Annex (n. 30). See John H. Knox, The Human Rights Council Endorses "Guiding Principles" for Corporations, *ASIL* Insights 15 (2011), No. 15 of 1 August 2011.

111 Human Rights Council, UN Doc. A/HRC/RES/17/4, paragraph 1.

112 *Ibid.*, paragraphs 6 and 12. The mandate of the Working Group was extended until 2017 by HRC Resolution 26/22 "Human rights and transnational corporations and other business enterprises" of 15 July 2014, paragraph 11. So far, the Working Group has guided several annual Forums. Cf. *ibid.*, paragraph 9.

113 HRC Res. 17/4, paragraph 6.

114 Guiding Principles (n. 30), Principle 13(b).

115 *Ibid.*, Principle 12.

To implement their responsibility, enterprises should carry out human rights due diligence. This includes assessing human rights impacts, integrating and acting upon the findings, and communicating externally how impacts are addressed by the enterprise.[116] Finally, enterprises should provide for remediation for human rights violations that they have caused or to which they have contributed, or they should contribute to the search for such remediation.[117]

The source and legal nature of this corporate responsibility are not expressly discussed. Clearly, corporate responsibility here does not mean responsibility in the sense of the law of international responsibility, i.e., the secondary obligations arising from a violation of international law. Rather, the concept of responsibility here is linked to the term "corporate social responsibility". It appears to be a code for attenuated standards of conduct that have a political/moral/social basis rather than a legal basis. In this sense, the Ruggie Principles themselves do not claim to generate new international obligations: "The Guiding Principles' normative contribution lies not in the creation of new international law obligations."[118] As the basis for "embedding" their responsibility to respect human rights, the Guiding Principles also call upon enterprises to express their commitment to meet this responsibility through a "statement of policy".[119] It is thus relatively clear that these are not real legal obligations of the business enterprises but are politically morally binding standards. The term "responsibility" in this sense is incidentally also used in other institutions, such as the "responsibility to protect" and in relation to the Security Council (responsibility for the maintenance of international peace and security pursuant to Article 24 of the UN Charter) and also in human rights practice. The UN Economic and Social Committee, for instance, states that "all members of society – individuals, including health professionals, families, local communities, intergovernmental and non-governmental organizations, civil society organizations, as well as the private business sector – have *responsibilities* regarding the realization of the right to health".[120] It follows that current human rights norms do not impose hard legal obligations

[116] *Ibid.*, Principles 17–21. [117] *Ibid.*, Principle 22 ("remediation").
[118] *Ibid.*, introductory paragraph 14. [119] *Ibid.*, Principle 16.
[120] UN Committee on Economic, Social, and Cultural Rights, General Comment No. 14 "The right to the highest attainable standard of health", 14 August 2000 (UN Doc. E/C.12/2000/4, paragraph 42; italics mine).

on private economic actors directly under international law to respect, promote, or comply with international human rights.[121]

4.9.3 De lege ferenda: *For and against Direct International Obligations for Private Actors to Respect International Human Rights*

Since 2013, a number of African, Arab, Latin American, and other mainly capital-importing States have lobbied for an internationally legally binding instrument. In 2014, the Human Rights Council first decided "to establish an open-ended intergovernmental working group on transnational corporations and other business enterprises with respect to human rights; whose mandate shall be to elaborate an international legally binding instrument to regulate, in international human rights law, the activities of transnational corporations and other business enterprises".[122] Most Western States voted against this resolution, and both the US and the EU officially declared not to support such a treaty. One day after, HRC Resolution 26/22, adopted without a vote, requested the Working Group to launch a consultative process with States in which "the benefits and limitations of a legally binding instrument" shall be explored.[123] So what doctrinal, legal theoretical, and moral arguments can be invoked in favour of making individual rights based on international law, and especially human rights, directly binding on transnationally operating enterprises and other private actors under international law – *de lege ferenda*, either by interpreting existing treaties dynamically or by adopting a new one?

Human rights in particular and, in their wake, other individual public rights were invented as rights against the State because the State was endowed with sovereignty. The State is authorized to enact laws unilaterally that massively restrict the liberty of the individuals subject to its sovereignty, and the State has a special power apparatus to enforce those laws, especially in virtue of the monopoly on the legitimate use of force through the police and military. Individual public rights constitute

[121] But affirming this trend, cf. Clapham, Human Rights Obligations 2006, 268: "[I]nternational law already applies to corporations and *is developing* the scope of their obligations not to commit or assist in human rights abuses" (italics mine).

[122] HRC Resolution 26/9 "Elaboration of an international legally binding instrument on transnational corporations and other business enterprises with respect to human rights" of 14 July 2014, paragraph 1.

[123] HRC Resolution 26/22 "Human rights and transnational corporations and other business enterprises" of 15 July 2014, paragraph 28. A report is due to the HRC for the 32d session (in the fall of 2016).

the necessary corrective here to contain the one-sided danger and abuse potential of the State.

In a liberal society and legal order, economic actors are in a fundamentally different starting position. They are not authorized to enact provisions *unilaterally*, such as by law, that all persons must respect, and they do not have a power apparatus similar to that of the State. But business enterprises may abuse individual rights and especially human rights in many different ways. This may occur in virtue of the labour conditions offered by enterprises, or in connection with the extraction of commodities, or in the context of the manufacture of primary products purchased by enterprises, or finally through the exploitation of location conditions offered in totalitarian States through practices that violate human rights. As a rule, the abuse occurs in the context of contractual relationships that become effective only with the consent of employees. But because of the structural inferiority of job seekers and workers, especially in light of the geographic mobility of enterprises, their subjection to inhuman conditions is not necessarily an expression of their true consent to the working and living conditions to which they are exposed. To that extent, enterprises have the possibility – de facto unilaterally and in the final analysis similarly to that of States – to interfere with the freedom and well-being of individuals de facto subjected to them. Along these lines, authors affirming that economic actors are bound directly by international human rights or by constitutionally supported basic national rights regularly assume that the potential power of these actors ultimately poses just as much a threat to human rights and basic rights as that of States, i.e., that economic power and political power should be equated in this regard.[124]

From the market economic perspective taken here, however, such a sweeping equation is not sufficiently differentiated. The economic power of private capital is not structurally comparable to the political

[124] In German law along these lines, see the classic opinion of Hans Carl Nipperdey, *Grundrechte und Privatrecht* (Krefeld: Scherpe Verlag 1961), who spoke in favour of an "absolute effect" of basic rights vis-à-vis private "and in some cases anonymous powers" that individuals face in a merely "fictitious situation of equality". For France, see Jean Rivero, La protection des droits de l'homme dans les rapports entre personnes privées, in: Institut International des Droits de l'Homme (ed.), *René Cassin Amicorum Disciplorumque Liber*, Vol. 3 (Paris: Pedone 1971), 311–322, especially with reference to the indivisibility of human rights and the unity of the system of values. More recently, see Andrew Clapham, *Human Rights in the Private Sphere* (Oxford: Clarendon 1993); Gavin W. Anderson, *Constitutional Rights after Globalization* (Oxford and Portland: Hart 2005).

apparatus of the State responsible for public welfare. Corresponding to this, private enterprises do not bear any primary political responsibility for the common good, but rather they mainly promote overall welfare (and thereby also respect for all rights of the individual) by producing goods and providing jobs. In the words of Milton Friedman, in "a free economy . . . there is one and only one social responsibility of business – to use its resources and engage in activities designed to increase its profits as long as it stays within the rules of the game, which is to say, engages in open and free competition, without deception or fraud".[125]

However, Friedman's strict free-market separation of spheres of responsibility is no longer tenable in the era of globalization. Rightly so, a social expectation has developed in recent decades that enterprises bear a more extensive, moral responsibility for the welfare of their employees and, alongside the state, for the common good (corporate social responsibility) that is also well justified by moral philosophy.[126]

Based on these considerations in conjunction with the principle of the need for global regulation discussed at the outset, it is natural to make individual rights – and especially human rights – directly binding on enterprises under international law, but only when those rights are not sufficiently protected by the much more precise provisions of civil law, labour law, and criminal law (which are normally at the level of the State). These provisions of ordinary (national) law in turn implement the basic idea of human dignity within the entire legal order and serve to prohibit enterprises from engaging in inhuman practices. As long as these regulatory goals are met, it is not necessary to impose additional human rights obligations on enterprises.[127] And despite the individual thrust of the prohibitions found in the law of armed conflict identified in Chapter 7, it is not a contradiction of values to maintain that human rights guarantees are *addressed to the State in principle*.[128] In armed conflict, individuals with weapons do in fact face each other, so the

[125] Milton Friedman, *Capitalism and Freedom* (Chicago: University of Chicago Press 1962), 133.

[126] See Christian Neuhäuser, *Unternehmen als moralische Akteure* (Berlin: Suhrkamp 2011).

[127] See in favour of holding corporations responsible for human rights violations on the basis of domestic tort law rather than on the basis of international (customary) law, e.g., Dalia Palombo, Chandler v. Cape: An Alternative to Piercing the Corporate Veil beyond Kiobel v. Royal Dutch Shell, *British Journal of American Legal Studies* 4 (2015), 453–471.

[128] See René Provost, *International Human Rights and Humanitarian Law* (Cambridge: Cambridge University Press 2002), 99.

preponderant real danger is actually posed by individuals. This tends not to be the case for human rights violations in times of peace.

An additional layer of norms with direct international obligations on private business enterprises becomes necessary, however, when the civil and criminal law tailored to "horizontal" situations among private actors no longer offers sufficient protection (on the normative condition of the need for global regulation, see pp. 76–78 above). It is decisive in this regard that in the age of globalization, such gaps in protection actually do exist at the level of national law, so there is a specific and increased risk of under-regulation of the protection of global goods. The national law of many host countries – especially those offering cheap conditions of production – is often not effective enough. Their national standards are low and/or are not enforced. Moreover, the enterprises operate globally and are able to escape from undesired strict requirements under national law by changing locations. For this reason, an additional, globally applicable regulation of business activity appears to make sense, in order to protect the individuals who are de facto subjected to such enterprises.

On the other hand, it is relevant that the private persons in turn are also holders of basic rights. An international regulation of an enterprise should not amount to an inhibiting restriction of entrepreneurial freedoms that are in turn protected by fundamental rights (economic freedom and property rights). The abstract weighing of legal positions and interests involved on both sides should be undertaken primarily by democratically legitimized institutions on the basis of a transparent process and in accordance with formal procedures (i.e., by concluding a formal treaty ratified by national parliaments), not by way of academic or judicial production of law.[129] Such procedures would also satisfy the principle of legality.[130] Nevertheless, fine-tuning of antagonistic interests by those who decide on individual cases always appears necessary in the case of "private" relationships in addition to the assignment of legal positions by general norms. Such (possibly judicial) decisions must in turn enjoy sufficient legitimacy.

In the context of this study, it is important to note that human rights – which are principle-based, programmatic, and formulated very generally – are not especially suited to bind private actors legally. The complex

[129] For a proposal of a sensible international regulation strategy, see Surya Diva, *Regulating Corporate Human Rights Violations: Humanizing Business* (New York: Routledge 2012), esp. 214–220.

[130] See above pp. 79–85.

system of balancing rights and interests established by civil and criminal law is disrupted by the sweeping imposition of obligations to respect human rights. More appropriate would be the fine-tuning of labour relationships using stricter norms of a (new) international law that would include elements of civil, labour, and criminal law and contain corresponding individual rights and duties (on international labour law, see Chapter 14, pp. 457–68). Finally, the imposition of human rights obligations on enterprises should not be sweeping, but rather it should be specific to particular human rights. Not all human rights are affected by economic activities, and not all are suited to be effective in the private sphere. Especially relevant, for example, would be the rights to non-discrimination, to freedom of opinion, of assembly, and of association, and to physical integrity.

Even if a formal international treaty were concluded that imposes new binding obligations on transnationally operating enterprises, substantial problems of enforcement would remain. It can hardly be expected that a weak host State would be better able to implement an international norm than its own domestic laws. For this reason, the international rules would have to be enforceable by international bodies. But the existing bodies for the protection of human rights are not suited to this purpose. Effective international labour rights institutions would have to be created, possibly by expanding the existing ILO.

Finally, the danger already discussed above exists also in the economic context, namely the danger that States might shirk their responsibility. If reformed international human rights bodies were to deal with human rights violations by enterprises as well, some States would presumably seize the opportunity to divert attention away from themselves. It follows that expanding the binding nature of human rights into the sphere of transnational business is neither normatively desirable without reservations nor does it have good prospects as a practical matter.[131] It would be more promising, and more tailored to the qualitative difference between States and enterprises, to strengthen only the *indirect* imposition of the obligation to respect human rights on enterprises by intensifying the duties of the State to protect, as demanded by the Ruggie Principles.

[131] In the literature, more far-reaching normative conditions are discussed under which the imposition of direct international obligations on enterprises to respect human rights might make sense. Steven Ratner, for instance, relies on four factors: the relationship between the enterprise and a State, the nexus with the affected population, the human rights concerned, and the position of individuals within the company structure (Ratner, Corporations and Human Rights, 2001).

So far, States are bound to discharge their duty to protect through national action plans (NAPs) which aim to translate the UN principles into practical action *at the national level.* The mentioned UN Working Group has issued a "Guidance" which provides recommendations on the development, implementation, and update of these NAPs.[132] For the EU, the European Commission has requested that EU Member States develop plans, and at the time of writing, nine Member States have done so.

Besides, on the level of international law, *international labour law* – which is actually the appropriate vehicle for provisions governing relationships between economic actors – would have to be supplemented by norms directly imposing obligations on enterprises, which in turn would be enforced by national and international bodies.

4.10 No "Fundamental Duties" of Individuals under International Law

An old question is whether there are or should be fundamental duties as a corollary to international fundamental rights (human rights).[133] This question is important for the international legal status of the individual as a whole, because the non-Western human rights discourses emphasize such duties, and to some extent that emphasis undermines the claim of human rights to universality. The non-European regional human rights texts, especially, assume such fundamental duties. For instance, Chapter 2 (Articles 29–38) of the American Declaration of the Rights and Duties of Man of 2 May 1948 entitled "Duties" governs the duty to obey the law, the duty to render civil and military service, the duty to cooperate with the State, and the duty to pay taxes. The Universal

[132] UN Working Group on Business and Human Rights, Guidance on National Action Plans on Business and Human Rights, version 1.0 of December 2014. The Guidance states: "As an instrument to implement the UNGPs, NAPs need to adequately reflect a State's duties under international human rights law to protect against adverse corporate human rights impacts and provide effective access to remedy. A NAP further needs to promote business respect for human rights including through due diligence processes" (at p. ii).

[133] See Tomuschat, Grundpflichten des Individuums, 1983, 289–315; Erica-Irene Daes, *Freedom of the Individual under Law: A Study on the Individual's Duties to the Community and the Limitations on Human Rights and Freedoms under Article 29 of the Universal Declaration of Human Rights* (New York: United Nations 1990), 41–63; Eva Brems, *Human Rights: Universality and Diversity* (The Hague: Martinus Nijhoff 2001), 424–441.

Declaration of Human Rights of the United Nations was adopted by the General Assembly several months after the American Declaration, on 10 December 1948. Their authors deliberately rejected any specification of fundamental duties for fear of abuse by the State.[134] In contrast, Article 32(1) of the American Convention on Human Rights of 22 November 1969 states: "Every person has responsibilities to his family, his community, and mankind." The fundamental duties in the African Charter on Human and Peoples' Rights of 27 June 1981 are especially comprehensive, as contained in Chapter 2 on "Duties".[135]

The first question is who would be the obligee of such duties. Fundamental duties – understood as the legal converse of fundamental rights, which are also directed against the State – would be owed to the State. If international fundamental duties were the converse of international *human rights*, then they would not in all cases be owed to the home State, but rather to the State against which the affected individuals could also assert human rights, i.e., the State under whose jurisdiction the person is found. If they were to be seen as the converse of *civil rights* (e.g., the right to participate in general elections under Article 25 ICCPR), then they would apply only in relation to the home State. Fundamental duties as such are not merely the obligations to tolerate limitations of human rights by the State. One example of the specification of the latter duty is Article 29(1) of the Universal Declaration of Human Rights. The provision states: "Everyone has duties to the community in which alone the free and full development of his personality is possible." Article 29(2) specifies the preconditions for limiting human rights (legal basis and legitimate purpose of limitation, especially the purpose of respecting the rights and freedoms of others). The structure and the wording indicate that the duties referred to in Article 29(1) mean particularly the duty to respect the human rights of others, i.e., the (inherent) limit of any exercise of human rights; they do not mean additional, isolated duties towards the State.

134 On the historical discussion during the drafting of the Universal Declaration of Human Rights, see Knox, Horizontal Human Rights Law, 2008, 4–10.

135 Article 27(1) of the African Charter on Human and Peoples' Rights states: "Every individual shall have duties towards his family and society, the State and other legally recognised communities and the international community." Article 28 concerns respect towards fellow beings. Article 29 governs a whole series of concrete duties towards family, State, and society. These include respect for parents, service to the national community, preserving and strengthening national solidarity, defence of the country, payment of taxes, promotion of the moral well-being of society.

The idea of fundamental duties owed to the State encounters misgivings. A first problem results from the fact that in real life, both processes (the imposition of an obligation to tolerate the limitation of one's own (fundamental) right and the imposition of additional duties) are often interrelated. For instance, the obligations to serve in the military or pay taxes simultaneously constitute a limitation of personal freedom or property. Because of this interrelationship, the assumption of fundamental duties in reality often constitutes a pretext for the State to limit fundamental rights. Secondly, there is a risk of circumvention: According to current law, limitations of international human rights must satisfy the requirements set out in treaties in accordance with the rule of law, and they must especially be based on a sufficient legal foundation and be proportionate. An undifferentiated invocation of "fundamental duties" risks circumventing precisely these limits on limitations of human rights set out in positive international law.

Thirdly and generally speaking, the assertion of fundamental duties vis-à-vis the State constitutes an attempt to provide additional legitimation of State power. It is no coincidence that fundamental obligations are mentioned prominently in those human rights documents formulated during a time and in regions in which the State power of newly founded States was still fragile, namely in South America in the 1940s and Africa in the 1980s.

Finally, the conception of fundamental duties owed to the State as a corollary to fundamental rights is misleading at a basic level. It suggests that the State in turn has "fundamental rights" and "claims" vis-à-vis individuals. This is misguided, because the State is in a superior position in light of its instruments of power. It is not in need of protection like the individual. It is not an end in itself and does not enjoy any rights, only powers.

Another important idea is that of a *moral* and *political* responsibility towards *fellow human beings and society*. This idea is reflected in the identical preambular sentence of the two human rights covenants of 1966: "Realizing that the individual, having duties to other individuals and to the community to which he belongs, is under a responsibility to strive for the promotion and observance of the rights recognized in the present Covenants." This is also how the Preamble of the Universal Declaration of Human Rights of 10 December 1948 should be understood: "to the end that *every individual and every organ of society*, keeping this Declaration constantly in mind, shall strive by teaching and education to promote respect for these rights and freedoms and by progressive measures, national and international, to secure their universal and effective recognition and observance, both among the peoples of Member States themselves and among the peoples of territories under their jurisdiction."[136]

Classifying the responsibility set out here and the call to promote respect for human rights as fundamental duties would be misleading. Fundamental duties in the sense of hard legal obligations legally owed to the State are not a component of universal international law, nor should they be.

4.11 Conclusion

A "twofold individualization" of international law,[137] both on the side of entitlement and on the side of obligation, can be observed here. Current international law imposes obligations on individuals in numerous sub-domains, to an extent Jacob Katz Cogan referred to as the *regulatory turn* in international law. Alongside these obligations, however, the normal international legal regulatory scheme persists. This scheme consists in the merely indirect imposition of obligations on individuals by way of the international obligations of States to enact national precepts and prohibitions, which in turn are addressed to private actors so that other private actors can be protected from their interference as envisaged by the international regulatory objective in question. Because of the practical and normative difficulties associated with these obligations, the development of further individual obligations directly under international law should be recognized only under two conditions: There must in fact be a need for global regulation in that regard, and the principle of legality must be respected. In situations where these conditions are properly met, individual obligations may be established through treaties, customary international law, general principles of law, case law, and secondary international law, especially resolutions of the Security Council. According to current international law, economic actors are not subject to any hard legal obligation to observe international human rights, but they do bear a political responsibility (driven by international law), which also appears morally justified in

136 Italics mine.
137 Andreas Fischer-Lescano, Subjektivierung völkerrechtlicher Sekundärregeln, *Archiv des Völkerrechts* 45 (2007), 299–381 (366; translation mine).

principle because of the risk of regulatory gaps arising from globalization. Individuals do not have fundamental duties as a corollary to human rights, and the recognition of such duties is not advisable, given their inherent potential of abuse as a pretext for disproportionate limitations of human rights.

5

The International Responsibility of the Individual

5.1 Foundations

This chapter deals with the secondary obligations of individuals that may be triggered by violations of the primary obligations discussed in Chapter 4. The level of secondary law is referred to as the law of international responsibility. While the international responsibility of States and international organizations is recognized, the crystallization of an international responsibility of individuals is currently in flux.

So far, only the category of international criminal law, which imposes obligations on individuals and punishes the violation thereof, is well established. In a strict sense, the label "international criminal law" refers – from the perspective of the law of international responsibility – to both the level of primary obligations and the level of secondary obligations. The specific characteristic of this area of the law is seen mainly at the level of secondary law, however, in that a special legal consequence – namely a criminal penalty – is triggered. In the terminology of the law of international responsibility, this is referred to as the international criminal responsibility of individuals.

It is argued here that the international responsibility of individuals is not limited to the field of international criminal law, but it rather goes beyond it. The reason for assuming a comprehensive capacity of the individual to be held responsible under international law – beyond international criminal law – is that the imposition of international individual obligations would be largely pointless if their violation did not entail any international responsibility of the obligor. In systematic and functional terms, the possibility of individual international responsibility is legally inescapable: Without the possibility of triggering secondary consequences, fulfilment of the primary obligations by the individuals addressed would be a question of good will, and this would already call into question the legal character of such obligations. So if the international legal order is to be consistent, it must allow that the international legal personality of an actor – in the sense of the actor's capacity to have international obligations – necessarily is accompanied by the actor's capacity for international responsibility. By actually recognizing primary obligations directed at individuals as real legal obligations, legal practice simultaneously implies the capacity of the individual to assume international responsibility.[1] The individual is thus capable of being not only the direct addressee of a primary obligation but also the subject of a relationship of secondary responsibility and therefore, e.g., potentially liable for damages under international law.

In the literature, individual obligations are sometimes divided into "criminal law" and "civil law" obligations, with a view to the type of secondary obligation triggered.[2] In this study, however, a public law perspective is preferred. The obligations imposed on individuals by international law result from provisions enacted in the global public interest; this type of international law is *public* international law in the true sense of the word. This means that individuals are subject to global regulation.[3] Non-criminal individual obligations at the level of primary and secondary law should therefore – deviating from the civil law analogy mentioned earlier – be referred to as individual obligations under international administrative law or international constitutional law, possibly depending on the obligee or owner of the claim.[4] The most important example of the administrative obligations of individuals, which are also punishable with penalties (fines) similar to administrative law, can be found in the competition law of the EU under Articles 101–103 TFEU and the relevant EU regulations. Beyond EU law, the responsibility assumed by individuals when they violate regulatory provisions of international law should not be understood by analogy with civil law, but

1 For the crystallization of the capacity of individuals to be held responsible, see Oliver Dörr, Privatisierung des Völkerrechts, *JuristenZeitung* 60 (2005), 905–916 (913–914).

2 See, e.g., Andrew Clapham, The Role of the Individual in International Law, *European Journal of International Law* 21 (2010), 25–30; James Crawford, The System of International Responsibility, in: James Crawford/Alain Pellet/Simone Olleson (eds), *The Law of International Responsibility* (Oxford: Oxford University Press 2010), 17–25 (19).

3 See Jacob Katz Cogan, The Regulatory Turn in International Law, *Harvard International Law Journal* 52 (2011), 321–372 (324).

4 See Anne Peters, Transnational Law Comprises Constitutional, Administrative, Criminal, and Quasi-Private Law, in: Pieter Bekker/Rudolf Dolzer/Michael Waibel (eds), *Making Transnational Law Work: Liber Amicorum Detlev Vagts* (Cambridge: Cambridge University Press 2010), 154–173.

rather either as "simply 'international' "[5] or as an administrative penalty – also at the level of the general international *secondary* law.

Because of the still largely uncertain structure of the non-criminal responsibility of individuals, this chapter will first examine the already recognized criminal responsibility of individuals.

5.2 The International Criminal Responsibility of Individuals

5.2.1 Historical Overview

International criminal law prohibits certain conduct and imposes the special punishment of a criminal penalty when the prohibitions are violated. The prohibitions (or the obligations to refrain from conduct contained therein) are all directed at individuals, and even in their personal capacity. Neither is it necessary to be an officeholder of a State[6] nor does such a position protect the perpetrator from punishment. This last aspect represents the historical achievement of international criminal law since the Nuremberg trials: It breaks with the traditional immunity of organs of the State.

International criminal law as discussed earlier (in the strict sense) is a product of the twentieth century. The Treaty of Versailles, which ended the First World War, contained criminal provisions for the German Emperor and other individuals.[7] Article 227 provided: "The Allied and Associated Powers publicly arraign William II of Hohenzollern, formerly German Emperor, *for a supreme offence against international morality and the sanctity of treaties*. A special tribunal will be constituted to try the accused, thereby assuring him the guarantees essential to the right of

5 Alain Pellet, Can a State Commit a Crime? Definitely, *Yes! European Journal of International Law* 10 (1999), 425–434 (433).

6 The obligations to refrain from conduct subject to penalties are defined only *ratione materiae*: The perpetrator may be an organ of the State or a private person (see Anne Laure Vaurs-Chaumette, *Les sujets du droit international pénal: Vers une nouvelle définition de la personalité juridique internationale?* (Paris: Pedone 2009), 333). In fact, international criminal proceedings have been instituted not only against officeholders and State employees acting in their official capacity as military personnel or politicians, but also against private persons, e.g., industrialists (US Military Tribunal at Nuremberg, *US* v. *Alfred Krupp et al., The United Nations War Crimes Commission, Law Reports of Trials of War Criminals*, Vol. X (1949), 130–159; ICTR, *Prosecutor* v. *Kayishema and Rutaganda*, Judgement, Case No. ICTR-95-1-T, of 21 May 1999). However, international crimes are typically committed by organs of the State and in the context of a State policy as political crimes, not by private individuals acting for personal motives.

7 Articles 227–230 of the Treaty of Versailles of 28 June 1919, 225 CTS 188.

defence ..." (italics mine). This provision and others in the Treaty of Versailles implied that individuals could be held directly responsible for the violation of the law of armed conflict or for treaty violations.[8] But they did not mention the actual source or legal basis of the criminal responsibility of the Emperor. The provisions were indeed not applied; since the Netherlands failed to extradite the Emperor, there were no proceedings before the special tribunal planned for that purpose.

After the Second World War, Article 6 of the Nuremberg Charter provided: "The Tribunal established by the Agreement referred to in Article 1 hereof for the trial and punishment of the major war criminals of the European Axis countries shall have the power to try and punish persons who, acting in the interests of the European Axis countries, whether as individuals or as members of organizations, committed any of the following crimes. *The following acts, or any of them, are crimes coming within the jurisdiction of the Tribunal for which there shall be individual responsibility: ....*"[9] Crimes against peace, war crimes, and crimes against humanity are enumerated here.

The Nuremberg judgment against the major war criminals of 1946 assumed the direct imposition of obligations on individuals under international law: "It was submitted that International Law is concerned with the actions of sovereign States and provides no punishment for individuals; and further, that where the act in question is an act of State, those who carry it out *are not personally responsible*, but are protected by the doctrine of the sovereignty of the State. In the opinion of the Tribunal, both these submissions *must be rejected. That International Law imposes duties and liabilities upon individuals* as well as upon States *has long been recognized*. ... Crimes against International Law are committed by men, not by abstract entities, and only by *punishing individuals* who commit such crimes can the provisions of International Law be enforced. ... He who violates the laws of war cannot obtain immunity while acting in pursuance of the authority

[8] See Kate Parlett, *The Individual in the International Legal System* (Cambridge: Cambridge University Press 2011), 274.

[9] Article 6 of the London Agreement for the Prosecution and Punishment of the Major War Criminals of the European Axis of 8 August 1945 (concluded by the United Kingdom, the United States of America, France, and the Soviet Union), with the Charter of the International Military Tribunals ("Nuremberg Charter") in the Annex to the Agreement (*AJIL* 39 (1945), suppl. p. 257 et seq.; italics mine).

of the State if the State in authorizing action moves outside its competence under International Law."[10]

Already the prosecutor for the United Kingdom had emphasized that the individual criminal responsibility of individuals on the basis of international law was an old principle of international law: "Nor is the principle of individual international responsibility for offences against the law of nations altogether new. It has been applied not only to pirates. *The entire law relating to war crimes, as distinct from the crime of war, is based upon the principle of individual responsibility.*"[11]

The Tribunal sought to present the principle of individual international criminal responsibility as a pre-existing practice, in order to avoid the accusation that the prohibition on retroactivity (*nullum crimen sine lege*) had been violated. It is still disputed whether the Nuremberg judgment was really able to draw on principles already recognized at the time or whether it was the first to identify the criminal responsibility of individuals directly under international law and to impose a penalty. In any event, the legal doctrine thereafter quickly became entrenched that individuals can – directly in virtue of international law – be held criminally responsible for violations of internationally defined crimes. In 1950, the International Law Commission (ILC) formulated the Nuremberg Principles. Principle I states: "Any person who commits an act which constitutes a crime under international law is responsible therefor and liable to punishment."[12] The ILC commentary on Principle I of the Nuremberg Principles states that there is a "general rule" underlying Principle I according to which international law may impose duties on individuals directly without any interposition of internal law.[13] According to Principle II of the Nuremberg Principles, the fact that internal law does not impose a penalty for an act which constitutes a crime under international law does not relieve the person who committed the act from responsibility under international law.

[10] International Military Tribunal, judgment of 1 October 1946, in: The Trial of German Major War Criminals. Proceedings of the International Military Tribunal sitting at Nuremberg, Germany, Part 22 (22 August 1946–1 October 1946), 446–447 (italics mine).

[11] Sir Hartley Shawcross, in: The Trial of German Major War Criminals. Proceedings of the International Military Tribunal, Sitting at Nuremberg Germany, Transcript Twelfth Day, Tuesday, 4 December 1945, 56 (italics mine).

[12] ILC, Formulation of the Nuremberg Principles, Report of the International Law Commission on its Second Session, 5 June to 29 July 1950 (GAOR, 5th sess. Suppl. No. 12 (A/1316), YB ILC 1950 II, 374–378 (374).

[13] *Ibid.*, paragraph 99; see already Chapter 4.

By way of explanation, the ILC commentary cites the judgment of the Nuremberg Military Tribunal. The Tribunal had stated: "[T]he very essence of the Charter is that *individuals have international duties* which transcend the national obligations of obedience imposed by the individual State."[14] The ILC interpreted this passage as follows: "The Tribunal considered that international law can bind individuals even if national law does not direct them to observe the rules of international law."[15] The UN General Assembly took note of the Nuremberg Principles already in 1950.[16] After the Nuremberg judgment of 1946, criminal sentences were imposed again only after 1990 by the ad hoc criminal tribunals and by the International Criminal Court established in 1998.

5.2.2 *Definition of the Problem and Perspectives*

The legal basis of individual criminal responsibility has not been fully clarified in State practice. Two aspects should be distinguished in this regard: The first aspect is the (abstract) capacity of the individual to be subject to an obligation grounded in international law and to be subject to the legal consequence of a criminal penalty if the obligation is breached, or in other words, the individual's international criminal responsibility. The second aspect is the legal basis of a concrete criminal offence. Even if the individual is in principle directly criminally responsible under international law, it must be clarified for every potential criminal offence whether it exists in virtue of international law, and if so, on precisely which legal basis.

Alongside the perspective of the law of international legal personality, there is another perspective, namely that of the global rule of law (including human rights). This second perspective is concerned with the principle of legality in its strict form of the *nullum crimen* principle. With reference to the principle of legality, it was sometimes claimed in the past that international law could never be the sole legal basis of a criminal offence – a claim that simultaneously denied the direct international criminal responsibility of the individual. Today, this basic objection has been overcome, but the question of

[14] International Military Tribunal, judgment of 1 October 1946 (n. 10), 447.

[15] ILC, Formulation of the Nuremberg Principles, Report of the International Law Commission (n. 12), 375, paragraph 102.

[16] UNGA res. 488(V) of 12 December 1950.

the precise legal basis for concrete offences arises from the perspective of the principle of legality.

Finally, the activity of domestic criminal courts raises the more general problem of the direct effect (self-execution) of international law (see Chapter 16). Direct recourse to international law as the legal basis of a concrete criminal offence and the imposition of a penalty must satisfy not only the principle of legality but also the principles of direct effect; the rationale of these principles and the resulting requirements overlap. In this context, the Special Tribunal for Lebanon held that the normal case is the non-self-executing nature of the norms of international criminal law: "As a general rule, international norms criminalising conduct are non-self-executing, for their implementation requires national legislation defining the crime and the relevant penalty."[17] From this perspective, the question arises whether – or under what conditions – national courts may (on an exceptional basis) apply international criminal law and use it as a basis for a criminal penalty.[18] Also on the side of obligations (as on the side of rights), this systematic aspect of direct effect should be distinguished from the substantive legal status of the individual. In the context of criminal law, the invocability of the international legal norm does not play a role as part of direct effect, because the courts must in principle apply the international legal provision *ex officio*.

National practice is not at all uniform. For centuries, domestic courts have applied criminal norms found in international treaties and customary law (on piracy, war crimes, and offences against consuls) without any major awareness of difficulties. Recently, more restraint has become common. While some domestic criminal courts do still apply international law directly, other courts refuse to do so, with a variety of justifications. Many judgments derive substantive criminal responsibility from a mix of international and national provisions that is difficult to untangle.[19] Especially, the actual legal basis of the criminal responsibility for core crimes is "more often than not shrouded in uncertainty".[20]

[17] Special Tribunal for Lebanon, Appeals Chamber, Case No. STL-11-01/I, Interlocutory Decision on the Applicable Law, 16 February 2011, paragraph 76.

[18] See fundamentally Ward N. Ferdinandusse, *Direct Application of International Criminal Law in National Courts* (The Hague: TMC Asser Press 2006).

[19] See *ibid.*, 85. [20] *Ibid.*, 86.

5.2.3 *Direct International Criminal Responsibility Independent of the Enforcement Body*

The preventive and repressive implementation of the prohibitions of international criminal law is in principle the responsibility of both domestic and international bodies. The potential status of the individual as bound by obligations must be distinguished from the procedural question of the enforceability of those obligations. In particular, the existence of direct international individual obligations is not coupled to the availability of international enforcement mechanisms. It is immaterial for the genuinely international character of an individual obligation (and its criminality) whether the international provisions are enforced by international criminal tribunals or by domestic courts applying the international norms either directly or indirectly.[21] In contrast, it is sometimes assumed that individuals are subject to a direct international obligation and can be held responsible directly under international law only if the criminal prosecution is carried out by an *international criminal tribunal*.[22] According to this view, international criminal responsibility flows only from the statutes of the competent criminal tribunal; these statutes would then have not only organizational and jurisdictional content but would also be the (sole) substantive basis of criminal responsibility.[23] Ultimately, this narrow standpoint is the mirror image of the view that the international legal personality of the individual is coupled to the independent procedural right to assert rights before an international body. As argued above, the coupling of the status of the individual as bearing rights and obligations to the available enforcement options is not persuasive on grounds of principle, however, because this coupling would mix up the substantive and procedural legal dimensions.[24]

In the domain of international criminal law, this view is even less persuasive, since according to the explicitly stipulated principles of subsidiarity and complementarity (e.g., Article 9 of the ICTY Statute;[25]

21 See Gerhard/Florian Jessberger, *Principles of International Criminal Law* (3rd ed. Oxford: Oxford University Press 2014), paragraph 91.

22 See Albert Bleckmann, *Völkerrecht* (Baden-Baden: Nomos Verlagsgesellschaft 2001), 46; Bernhard Kempen/Christian Hillgruber, *Völkerrecht* (Munich: Beck 2007), 334 ("international criminal law in a narrow sense").

23 Along these lines, see ICTR, *Prosecutor* v. *Kanyabashi*, Case No. ICTR-96-15-T, Decision on the Defence Motion on Jurisdiction, 18 June 1997, paragraph 35, see also text below at p. 143 with n. 82).

24 See Chapter 3, pp. 44–50.

25 Article 9 of the Statute of the International Criminal Tribunal for the Former Yugoslavia of 25 May 1993, Annex to UNSC res. 827: "1. The International Tribunal and national

Articles 1[26] and 17[27] of the Rome Statute of the International Criminal Court), national courts have at least concurrent jurisdiction for enforcing criminal law. Even if one were to assume that the statutes also have a substantive legal content, they do not in all cases constitute the sole basis of criminal responsibility, but rather overlay – for some crimes – the pre-existing criminal responsibility flowing from other agreements or customary international law. If the contrary view is thought through to the end, it would imply that an offence is not criminal if no international tribunal is competent to punish it. This would directly contradict the values inherent in the principle of the primacy of national jurisdiction to prosecute. It would also mix up questions of the applicable substantive law with questions of jurisdiction and admissibility.

Additionally, the parallel problem in regard to obligations of the State should be noted: There is no doubt that States can be obligated under international law, even though the international enforceability of such State obligations is only fragmentary given the lack of compulsory jurisdiction. Appraisal of the status of being bound by obligations should be no different for individuals than it is for States.[28] It follows from this that individual obligations (including obligations enforced by criminal penalties) exist independently of any international enforcement body, even if in that case they might not be very effective.

5.2.4 *The Suitability of International Law in Principle as a Legal Basis for Individual Criminal Responsibility*

The problem of the possibility of direct international criminal responsibility can also be formulated as a problem of mediation of the individual: Can individual obligations to refrain from acts and the imposition of penalties flow directly from international law, or does the individual remain mediated by national law? In other words, can international

courts shall have concurrent jurisdiction to prosecute persons for serious violations of international humanitarian law committed in the territory of the former Yugoslavia since 1 January 1991. 2. The International Tribunal shall have primacy over national courts. At any stage of the procedure, the International Tribunal may formally request national courts to defer to the competence of the International Tribunal in accordance with the present Statute and the Rules of Procedure and Evidence of the International Tribunal."

26 Article 1: "[The Court] shall be complementary to national criminal jurisdictions . . ."

27 Article 17: "1. . . . the Court shall determine that a case is inadmissible where: (a) The case is being investigated or prosecuted by a State which has jurisdiction over it, unless the State is unwilling or unable genuinely to carry out the investigation or prosecution . . ."

28 See Parlett, *Individual*, 2011, 267.

norms, firstly, obligate individuals directly, i.e., without the interposition of national law? And, secondly, can those norms attach a specifically criminal consequence to the violation of that obligation?

Older literature often assumed that international norms such as the Geneva Conventions are not applied as such by national courts and especially cannot be used in and of themselves as the basis for a criminal sentence imposed by a national court. According to this view, the individual's duty of omission arises only through the national implementing (criminal) law; in all cases, a complementary or more detailed national criminal norm would have to be enacted, forming the actual basis for the individual obligation and the criminal sentence.[29]

Deviating from that old view, the possibility of direct international criminal responsibility should be affirmed today. The principle that individuals can be held criminally responsible for their non-compliance with international prohibitions – i.e., that they are in principle criminally responsible directly under international law and not necessarily by way of mediation – has now been established by practice (see p. 119). The international criminal courts and tribunals do actually and exclusively apply international law. The practice of these bodies has therefore already answered the basic question of the possibility of the direct international criminal responsibility of individuals in the affirmative. This practice, meanwhile, has also been accepted in principle by States and other international actors, including the affected individuals; it does not appear contrary to international law per se and as a whole, but rather as an expression of accepted legal doctrine.

At the same time, this means that international law in principle can be considered a legal basis for individual criminal responsibility and is not categorically ruled out as a legal basis. There is no strict mediation paradigm according to which international law would merely obligate States to enact domestic criminal norms that define conduct as crimes in their national law, i.e., to make their commission punishable and to sentence perpetrators in domestic criminal proceedings.

[29] See Friedrich Josef Berber, *Lehrbuch des Völkerrechts: Zweiter Bd.: Kriegsrecht* (2nd ed., Munich: Beck 1969), 242–244; Michael Bothe, The Role of National Law in the Implementation of International Humanitarian Law, in: Christophe Swinarski (ed.), *Studies and Essays on International Humanitarian Law and Red Cross Principles in Honour of Jean Pictet* (Dordrecht: Martinus Nijhoff 1984), 301–312 (302). For a sceptical view, cf. Albrecht Randelzhofer, The Legal Position of the Individual under Present International Law, in: Albrecht Randelzhofer/Christian Tomuschat (eds), *State Responsibility and the Individual: Reparation in Instances of Grave Violations of Human Rights* (The Hague: Martinus Nijhoff 1999), 231–242 (241).

This entails that only the following questions remain unanswered: (1) What is the legal source of this *capacity* of individuals in principle to be held criminally responsible directly under international law? (2) What is the precise legal basis for specific international crimes, and how is it determined? (3) Do all findings apply equally to international and to national criminal courts? May domestic criminal courts also use international law directly as a basis for their criminal sentences?

The first question regarding the precise legal source of direct international criminal responsibility might be answered by referring to the applicable treaties, customary international law, or a general principle of law. The legal presumption proposed by Roland Portmann is helpful: "[T]here is a rebuttable presumption that individuals possess personality in international law when international crimes and basic human rights are concerned ... It follows that there is no need to separately establish whether international crimes *bind* individual human beings: they automatically do so *on the basis of legal principle* without a statutory provision or customary practice necessarily indicating so." This is "just a matter of them being individual human beings and as such under an obligation to respect fundamental international norms."[30] The "legal principle" assumed here can, in my view, be understood best as a principle of customary international law: The development outlined earlier testifies to the *opinio juris* that individuals can be held criminally responsible in virtue of international law, and it thus constitutes the subjective element of a rule of customary international law to that effect.[31]

The important consequence of grounding the (general) criminal responsibility of the individual in general international law is that individual States cannot suspend, reverse, or limit this criminal responsibility.[32] Anyone who agrees with Roland Portmann that a general principle (not only in customary international law) constitutes the basis of criminal responsibility must also assume that criminal responsibility cannot fall into desuetude through contrary State practice. In this view, individuals are actually "as a matter of fundamental legal principle ... a priori international persons in this limited context".[33]

[30] Roland Portmann, *Legal Personality in International Law* (Cambridge: Cambridge University Press 2010), 273 (italics mine).

[31] See also Parlett, *Individual*, 2011, 258.

[32] See Robert McCorquodale, The Individual in the International Legal System, in: Malcolm Evans (ed.), *International Law* (3rd ed., Oxford: Oxford University Press 2010), 284–310 (292).

[33] Portmann, *Legal Personality*, 2010, 273.

The second question, to be dealt with separately, is that of the criminality of specific acts. What categories of international legal norms (treaty law, customary international law, general principles of law, others?) can be considered as the legal basis of the offence? Should some legal sources be eliminated from the outset? And, what conditions must a provision fulfil in concrete terms in order to justify the legal consequence of criminality? The demands of the principle of legality in its strict form must be taken into account in this regard. It must be considered here whether the answers would be different depending on whether an international or a national criminal court decides, or whether (in my view correctly) basically the same principles should apply.

As soon as *national* criminal courts have jurisdiction, the problem presents itself as a variant of the more general question concerning the direct effect of international law. Where the issue is individual rights arising from international law, the direct effect of international law means that contrary national law steps back. This would be similar in regard to criminal law: Any justifications or excuses under national law would not be considered, and deviating definitions of crimes under national law would likewise be immaterial. For this reason, the third question arises for the national judiciary concerning the possibility of direct international criminal responsibility of the individual before national courts as well. Can direct international criminal responsibility also be realized by national criminal courts? The question whether the criminal responsibility of the individual – where invoked by a national criminal court – results directly from international law or whether it arises only via mediation by national law is of practical significance for two reasons. Firstly, there must be clarity about whether national criminal courts are entitled to identify lacking or faulty implementation of the international criminal norms in their national criminal law and hence may invoke international criminal law directly in such cases. Secondly, the interest of the international community in combating impunity for international crimes may give rise not only to the entitlement, but in certain constellations even the *obligation* of national courts to apply international criminal law directly. For all these reasons, the basic question of the possibility of direct international individual criminal responsibility *before national criminal courts* must be answered. This question is in turn determined by considerations of the principle of legality/*nullum crimen*. This principle will therefore be discussed first.

5.2.5 Nullum crimen sine lege

5.2.5.1 Definition of the Problem

The requirement of legality, which was already discussed in Chapter 4, applies in the field of criminal law in a strict form expressed by the maxim *nullum crimen, nulla poena sine lege*. This maxim, like the general principle of legality, requires that legal burdens be foreseeable by those affected. But here, the demands are slightly stricter. In the context of international individual obligations whose breach is *not* criminal, we have seen that international treaties and even customary law in principle may constitute a sufficient legal basis for an individual obligation that satisfies the requirement of legality (Chapter 4, pp. 85–91). In contrast, it is still in doubt whether international law may be considered a direct legal basis for *criminality* – at least when national criminal courts have jurisdiction. The following remarks are relevant primarily in regard to punishment by national criminal courts, and additionally for the work of international criminal tribunals that must likewise observe the *nullum crimen* principle (see below, pp. 131–34).

Advocates of a strict principle of *nullum crimen, nulla poena sine lege* assume that international law cannot be considered a sufficient legal basis for a criminal sentence imposed by a national court. This means, in other words, that international criminal law would not be directly applicable (self-executing).[34] Does this entail that – in order for a national court to pass a sentence – it would still be necessary for the international criminal norms to be implemented as national criminal law?[35] This question is relevant in practice. While direct recourse to norms of international law and hence their direct application is not (or no longer) necessary as soon as the international criminal norms have been implemented effectively into national criminal law, this recourse to international law by national criminal courts remains useful in States whose national criminal legislation is deficient in this regard. The question then arises whether the courts may directly punish serious violations even without a national legal basis, and solely with reference to international law. In national criminal law, definitions of offences may be entirely lacking or unclear, full of loopholes, or more restrictive than in international law.

[34] See Georg Dahm/Jost Delbrück/Rüdiger Wolfrum, *Völkerrecht*, Vol. I/3 (2nd ed. Berlin: De Gruyter 2002), 994.

[35] On the principle of legality as a "key legal obstacle" for the direct application of international criminal norms by national criminal courts, see Ferdinandusse, *Direct Application*, 2006, chapter VI.

The second constellation of national criminal law that is simply too "weak", as opposed to missing entirely, appears even more problematic than the first constellation. Where norms exist but are weak, there additionally is a clear conflict of norms between national and international criminal law, raising the question of the hierarchy of norms (primacy of international law?) in order to resolve the conflict. Furthermore, an accused person may in principle rely on existing provisions in national criminal law. In this situation, faith in the national provisions may be more worthy of protection than where the offence has not been defined at all under national law.

5.2.5.2 Rationale of the Principle

The answer to the question of the direct effect of international criminal norms must be guided by the rationale of the *nullum crimen* principle. This principle was developed during the European Enlightenment. In criminal law scholarship of the nineteenth century it was formulated, for instance, as follows by Franz von Liszt: "Nullum crimen sine lege, nulla poena sine lege. These two phrases are the citizen's bastion against the omnipotence of the State; they protect the individual against the ruthless power of the majority, against the Leviathan."[36] The principle thus embodies a key concern of constitutionalism. The reason for the strictness of the principle of legality in criminal law is that the individuals affected by it are not merely being burdened with obligations but are even being punished, which entails a more intensive limitation of freedom.

Kenneth Gallant identifies four overlapping sets of purposes of the principle of legality in criminal law: protection of the (human) rights of the individual, ensuring of the legitimacy of governance, separation of powers and functions of the institutions, and promotion of the purposes of criminalization (individual and general prevention due to foreseeability of the precept and the resulting duties of conduct).[37] The connection with the penal objectives (deterrence) entails that the principle of legality is important especially for the special parts of criminal law (definitions of the crimes) and less so for the general parts.

The fourfold rationale of the *nullum crimen* requirement entails the need for parliamentary approval (*Parlamentsvorbehalt*), as is the case within the scope of the general principle of legality. In both cases, parliamentary

[36] Franz von Liszt, *Die deterministischen Gegner der Zweckstrafe, Zeitschrift für die gesamte Strafrechtswissenschaft* 13 (1893), 325–370 (357, translation mine).

[37] Kenneth S. Gallant, *The Principle of Legality in International and Comparative Criminal Law* (Cambridge: Cambridge University Press 2009), 19–31.

approval is thought to – inter alia – safeguard legitimacy in terms of democracy and the rule of law: Securing the freedom of the citizen is at stake, along with political accountability and legal certainty. All of this is guaranteed to a greater extent when criminal offences are defined by the parliament, not by the executive or the courts. These concerns were formulated as follows by an English jurist and taken up approvingly by the House of Lords: "[I]nternational law could not create a crime triable directly, without the intervention of *Parliament*, in an English court. ... it would be odd if the Executive could, by means of that kind, acting in concert with other States, amend or modify specifically the criminal law, with all the consequences that flow for the *liberty* of the individual and rights of personal property. There are, besides, powerful reasons of *political accountability, regularity and legal certainty* for saying that the power to create crimes should now be regarded as reserved exclusively to Parliament, by Statute."[38]

5.2.5.3 Legal Bases in National and International Law

The principle of *nullum crimen, nulla poena sine lege* is first of all a principle of national law. It is specified not only in ordinary national (criminal) law but also in four-fifths of all States at the level of the constitution. The prohibition of retroactive offences and penalties is thus considered a higher-ranking constitutional principle in the vast majority of States.[39]

At the same time, the principle is a requirement under international law that national courts must observe. The provisions found in the international human rights covenants (Article 15(1) ICCPR; Article 7 ECHR) are addressed to national criminal courts. They even enshrine the principle as a non-derogable human right (Article 4 ICCPR; Article 15 ECHR). Finally, *nullum crimen, nulla poena sine lege* also applies beyond codified international treaty law as part of customary international law and as a general principle of law as referred to in Article 38(1)(c) of the ICJ Statute. The development of the *nullum crimen* principle into a rule *of international law* simultaneously represents the crystallization of

[38] Sir Franklin Berman, Jurisdiction: The State, in: Patrick Capps/Malcolm Evans/Stratos Konstantinidis (eds), *Asserting Jurisdiction: International and European Legal Perspectives* (Oxford: Hart 2003), 3–15 (11; italics mine). This passage was quoted approvingly by Lord Bingham in the UK House of Lords, *R.* v. *Jones et al.*, Judgement of 29 March 2006 [2006] UKHL 16, paragraphs 28–29.

[39] See Gallant, *Principle of Legality*, 2009, 243–251 and other references. Gallant mentions 162 of 192 States. See also the synopsis of the law of all States in the world with a reproduction of the provisions on p. 438 et seq. One example is Article 103(2) of the German Basic Law.

a substantive human rights standard, a limitation on a court's jurisdiction to define criminal offences, and finally a limitation of sovereignty.[40] As a preliminary conclusion, it should be noted that the prohibition of retroactivity (the prohibition of retroactive definitions of crimes and penalties) is a general principle of law that applies in all States of the world in virtue of international law and national law (as a constitutional principle, additionally as a legal provision, and pursuant to ratification of the relevant international treaties): "Non-retroactivity is a world-wide standard."[41]

5.2.5.4 Requirements in Various National Legal Orders

Nullum crimen sine lege, nulla poena sine lege places demands on the *form* and *content* of the criminal norm. In terms of content, it requires criminal law to be formulated with sufficient specificity and to contain an unambiguous and clear description of the penalty. The required legal form is normally an act of parliament. The maxim "no crime and no penalty without a law" simultaneously implies a prohibition of retroactivity and of analogy in the field of criminal law.

A comparison of laws shows that within the various national legal orders, the principle of *nullum crimen* is interpreted in different ways. Especially in civil law legal orders, there is generally a strict requirement of a *lex scripta*. In common law, punishment on the basis of an existing common law rule as well as settled case law and prosecution practice have traditionally been permitted.[42] This has been seen as compatible with the *nullum crimen* requirement also by the ECtHR, as long as the dispensation of justice is compatible with the "essence" of the offence and has developed gradually and hence foreseeably.[43]

A few years ago, however, the House of Lords tightened the requirements and no longer recognized international law as a legal basis for "new crimes". In the case of boycott actions against British participation in the Iraq military campaign of 2003, the court had to decide as an interlocutory matter whether a war of aggression constituted a domestic offence under English law.[44] If this were the case, then the objective of preventing that crime might have legitimated the actions of some of the protesters. Some of these actions were unlawful, and the accused invoked the justification of self-defence. In its judgment, the court applied a strict

[40] See *ibid.*, 356. [41] *Ibid.*, 241 and 353. [42] See *ibid.*, 393 and 405–406.

[43] ECtHR, *C. R.* v. *UK*, No. 20190/92 (1995), paragraph 34 (on recognizing rape within marriage as a criminal offence in the United Kingdom).

[44] UK House of Lords, *R.* v. *Jones et al.* (n. 38), paragraph 59.

principle of legality, which Lord Hoffmann formulated as an expression of the democratic principle: "[A]ggression is not a crime in English domestic law. The first is the democratic principle that it is nowadays for Parliament and Parliament alone to decide whether conduct not previously regarded as criminal should be made an offence ... The same reasoning applies to the incorporation into domestic law of new crimes under international law. The law concerning safe conducts, ambassadors and piracy is very old. But new domestic offences should in my opinion be debated in Parliament, defined in a statute and come into force on a prescribed date. *They should not creep into existence as a result of an international consensus to which only the executive of this country is a party.*"[45]

This case was only about reaching a judgment in a national court and the question of whether English courts may apply international law directly and use it as a basis for a criminal sentence. This question intersects with that of the transposition of international law into national (English) law by enacting national legislation. The aspect of transposition must be assessed differently for treaty law and for customary law.

5.2.5.5 Application also to International Criminal Tribunals

The *nullum crimen* principle and the prohibition of retroactivity contained therein have gradually evolved from a (moral) requirement of justice into a binding legal principle, one that must also be observed by international courts. The retroactive application of (international) criminal law by an international tribunal may have been acceptable in the era of Nuremberg, but it is no longer today.[46] Now, the principle is binding on all international criminal tribunals and the International Criminal Court. Articles 22–24 of the Rome Statute expressly specify *nullum crimen sine lege, nulla poena sine lege* and a prohibition of retroactivity as principles to be observed by the International Criminal Court. These provisions say nothing about the exact legal bases for the crimes defined in the Statute, however. They accordingly say nothing about which sources of international law can be considered "lex" for purposes of the principle of *nullum crimen sine lege*.[47]

[45] *Ibid.*, Lord Hoffmann, paragraphs 60 and 62 (italics mine).
[46] See Gallant, *Principle of Legality*, 2009, 405.
[47] See for a detailed examination with a view to Art. 22 ICC-Statute Leena Grover, *Interpreting Crimes in the Rome Statute of the International Criminal Court* (Cambridge: Cambridge University Press 2014), 134–219.

5.2.5.6 Special Formal and Substantive Features of International Norms as "lex" and the Necessity and Permissibility of Modifying the Principle

The demands of foreseeability and accessibility as well as legal clarity are not fulfilled as well by international norms as they are by national laws. Firstly, it is striking that substantive international criminal law (both customary law and general principles of law as well as treaty law) generally does not specify the penalties to be imposed. Thus it appears – even where the international norms define the criminal offence (*crimen*) precisely – that international law in any event does not preserve the principle of *nulla poena* (with respect to penalties).

In general, negotiators (diplomats and government officials) do not enjoy the same democratic legitimacy and accountability as members of national parliaments; I have already pointed this out in the discussion of the general principle of legality (outside criminal law, Chapter 4, pp. 81–82). The international process for generating law is fundamentally different from the democratic legislative process. Unwritten law in the form of customary international law continues to be an important form of law. Because of the global pluralism of political and moral values and (compared with domestic legislative processes) the stronger politicization of law-making processes, international provisions are often vague and full of compromises.

But the question is whether the requirements of the *nullum crimen* principle applicable to norms of international criminal law must be identical to and as high as those applicable to provisions of national criminal law. Already in light of the heterogeneity of national criminal law, this must be answered in the negative. A schematic transfer of the *nullum crimen* principle from national criminal law already fails because the requirements of the national legal orders – as just mentioned – are not identical. This means that in any event, only the lowest common denominator could be used for the application of international criminal norms. It appears more appropriate to carve out a transnational or transnationalized *nullum crimen* principle that, first of all, relies on an evaluative comparison of law[48] and, secondly, takes account of the special

[48] To determine a general principle of law, it is not necessary to undertake a systematic comparison of law, which would be impossible to do in practice, but rather only an evaluative summary overview of national legal orders: See ICTY, *Prosecutor* v. *Erdemovic*, Case No. IT-96-22-A, Judgment, Appeals Chamber, 7 October 1997, paragraph 57: "[O]ur approach will necessarily not involve a direct comparison of the specific rules of each of the world's legal systems, but will instead involve a survey of those jurisdictions whose jurisprudence is, as a practical matter, accessible to us in an effort to discern

features of international law, in particular the special legal sources of the international legal order and the absence of international "laws".

It would be unrealistic to demand that treaty negotiations would simply result in a clear code of criminal norms. Along these lines, a Canadian Supreme Court justice stated in a case involving Nazi war crimes and crimes against humanity: "The nature of a decentralized international system is such that international law *cannot be conveniently codified in some sort of transnational code*. Its differing sources may alarm some strict legal positivists, but almost all international lawyers now recognize that such a crude analogy to the requirements of a domestic law system is simplistic."[49]

The conclusion is: *Nullum crimen sine lege* "must be complied with also at the international level, albeit subject to a number of significant qualifications".[50] For instance, it is sometimes still assumed (in regard to penalties) that the *nulla poena* principle is not applicable at all (and hence cannot be violated) "at the international level" (i.e., by international criminal tribunals).[51] But Article 23 of the Rome Statute specifies: "A person convicted by the Court may be *punished* only in accordance with this Statute" (italics mine). The transnational *nullum crimen* standard relevant to the prosecution of international criminal offences does not make demands identical to those of the prohibitions of retroactivity found in individual legal orders, but it must be sufficiently strict to respect the basic concerns.[52]

The transnational standard is preserved when the criminal norms are specific and accessible and thus are *foreseeable* for individuals in terms of both the concrete legal obligations and the associated penalties. In its discussion of the principle of *nullum crimen sine lege*, the Nuremberg Military Tribunal focused on the foreseeability of the violation of international law and the criminality of aggression by holding that the accused must have known that their acts were contrary to international law: "[T]he defendants, or at least some of them, must have known of the

a general trend, policy or principle . . ." (in the concrete case, regarding the justification of duress).

49 Canada, Supreme Court, *Her Majesty the Queen* v. *Imre Finta et al.*, Judgment of 24 March 1994 [1994] 1 S.C.R. 701; La Forest, J. (dissenting), 95.

50 Antonio Cassese, *International Criminal Law* (2nd ed., Oxford: Oxford University Press 2008), 41.

51 See *ibid.*, 51–52.

52 This transnationalization and the modification of the *nullum crimen* principle entailed thereby is similarly necessary and permissible as within the scope of the general principle of legality (see Chapter 4., pp. 79–80).

treaties signed by Germany, outlawing recourse to war for the settlement of international disputes; *they must have known* that they were acting in defiance of all International Law when in complete deliberation they carried out their designs of invasion and aggression."[53] Kenneth Gallant also summarized the discussion with a focus on foreseeability: "Once it is understood, however, that common or customary law creation can meet the goals of the principle of legality as well as statutory enactments (or nearly as well), then there is no a priori problem with the notion of an international criminal law binding individuals in the current world situation. This is why some have suggested the slogan might be changed to '*nullum crimen, nulla poena sine iure*' ... The claim that *unpredictable* expansion of criminal law has been greater in this system than in national systems because there is no general international legislative body is becoming less sustainable."[54] Foreseeability is thus the relevant benchmark, because punishment requires culpability (accusation of a wrong), and such an accusation of culpability can only be levelled if a person knew or should have known that he or she was violating a legal norm and did it anyway. When international law is sufficiently foreseeable, its application by international courts does not violate the prohibition of retroactivity.

5.2.5.7 Modification in the Application of International Criminal Law also by National Courts

The follow-up question is whether the *transnationalized nullum crimen* principle outlined above applies only to international criminal bodies or also to *national* courts when they are confronted with international crimes. Thought through to the end, the democratic objection formulated by Lord Hoffmann would rule out entirely that international law might constitute the legal basis for punishing individuals. This view has – with respect to international criminal sentences – become obsolete due to the practice of the international criminal tribunals. Evidently, these bodies do not interpret the *nullum crimen* principle as requiring approval of criminal norms by parliament. This would indeed be impossible because the international courts must apply international treaties and customary law and are not able to avail themselves of legislation.

What is decisive for the question of the benchmark to be applied by national criminal courts is the *functional exchangeability* of international

[53] International Military Tribunal, judgment of 1 October 1946 (n. 10), 444 (italics mine).

[54] Gallant, *Principle of Legality*, 2009, 374 (italics mine).

and national criminal jurisdiction envisaged by the existing court statutes. This functional exchangeability requires that the demands of the *nullum crimen* principle that must be observed by the two "branches" of criminal jurisdiction should not deviate significantly from each other, because such deviations would represent a contradiction of values. Formally speaking, the *national* criminal courts faced with the question of applying international criminal law have to start with their national *nullum crimen* principle because they have to operate within their own legal order. The applicable national principle must, however, be interpreted in line with international law (more on this in the following section).

The result is that international law permits and requires international *and also national criminal courts* to apply international criminal law directly, both in the form of treaty law and in the form of customary international law. In other words, both international treaty law and customary law can and should in principle be the direct legal basis for determining guilt and passing sentences, by both international and national criminal courts. This is indeed recognized explicitly by the ICCPR and the ECHR, which address only national criminal courts: According to Article 7(2) ECHR and Article 15(2) ICCPR, the prohibitions against retroactivity set out in the conventions in Article 7(1) ECHR and Article 15(1) ICCPR "shall not prejudice the trial and punishment of any person for any act or omission which, at the time when it was committed, was criminal *according to the general principles of law recognised by civilised nations*".[55] According to the basic idea of the *nullum crimen* principle, however, the conditions of specificity and hence of foreseeability and accessibility of the international prohibitions enforceable by penalties must be fulfilled in all cases.

5.2.5.8 Harmonization of the International Penal Requirement with National Law

The constitutionalist rationale of the *nullum crimen* principle and its constitutional guarantee in some States entail that the national criminal courts must observe this principle as a matter of priority. The conflict of goals between the punishment of individuals envisaged by international law and the observation of the *nullum crimen* principle – which is grounded in the rule of law, required by human rights, and often also constitutionally guaranteed – is, viewed in this light, at the same time a conflict between international law and national constitutional law.

[55] This is the wording of Article 7 ECHR; Article 15(2) ICCPR is equivalent.

German criminal courts encountered such a conflict after the fall of the Berlin Wall in the border guard trials. Article 103(2) of the Basic Law contains a strict requirement of a parliamentary basis: "An act may be punished only if it was defined by a law as a criminal offence before the act was committed." Within the scope of application of the German Basic Law, it is thus always a question whether this constitutional provision is opposed to direct punishment of the individual under international law. In this conflict between the international principle of the direct international criminal responsibility of the individual and the constitutional norm, does the provision of the Basic Law always take precedence, or should there rather be a balancing between the international requirement and the constitutional requirement by harmonizing interpretations? The case law of the Federal Constitutional Court of Germany ultimately undertook such an internationally compatible interpretation of the prohibition of retroactivity set out in the Basic Law. In the border guard trials, the Court limited the protection of legitimate expectations granted by the strict requirement of legality set out in the Basic Law in the case of an "evident, intolerable violation of elementary precepts of justice and internationally protected human rights".[56] This means that also according to German constitutional law, direct international criminal responsibility, without the existence of a formal act of parliament, is permissible under certain circumstances – it does not constitute a violation of Article 103(2) of the Basic Law.

This strategy should be welcomed. If the conflict of goals cannot be resolved in other ways, i.e., if only the direct application of an international provision makes criminal prosecution possible, then the national court must apply international law directly. In other words, if, in a concrete case, direct application of the international criminal norm is the only possible way to realize that international norm effectively, then the principle of legality in the form of the *nullum crimen* principle (which

[56] BVerfGE 95, 96 (135) (1996; translation mine). This case law did not refer directly to punishment without a legal basis, but rather to the situation that the justification recognized by the East German law (the order to shoot) was not recognized by the criminal courts of the Federal Republic in the criminal trials after the change of regime. In other words, the legally provided justification was subsequently (and hence retroactively) seen as immaterial and ineffective. The principle of the limitation of protection of legitimate expectations expressed in the judgment of the Federal Constitutional Court, and the affirmation of the foreseeability of criminal responsibility despite the East German justification, can be transferred to our question. Cf. also the different reasoning of the ECtHR (Grand Chamber), 22 March 2001, *Streletz, Keßler and Krenz* v. *Germany*, No. 34044/96 notably from the perspective of Article 7 ECHR.

starts out as being national but which is being transnationalized because of the need for harmonization) must be read and applied in accordance with international law, too. And this means that the principle of legality must here be interpreted generously in the light of the international obligation to punish. In any case, the *nullum crimen* principle cannot be employed as an absolute barrier against the direct application of the international criminal norm.[57] Conversely, however, this duty of application is not absolute: It can apply only if the international norms in question meet the minimum requirements of specificity and foreseeability. This must be checked separately for each criminal offence. For instance, foreseeability is given in the case of the core crimes. The wrong of such offences is evident, and so their punishment is foreseeable for every perpetrator. The *nullum crimen* principle may be dealt with generously here, and this has been the case in practice so far.

5.2.6 *The Legal Bases of Concrete Criminal Responsibility*

Now that it has been shown that international law in principle can be considered a legal basis for prohibitions enforced by penalties that are directed at individuals, also in accordance with a transnationalized *nullum crimen* requirement, possible concrete legal bases will be examined. The following discussion of these legal bases will include examples of relevant offences.

5.2.6.1 International Treaty Law

There is now agreement that crimes directly under international law on the basis of treaties alone (without underlying customary law) are conceptually possible and that the application of international treaties does not violate the principle of legality. This was held, for example, by the ICTY in *Kordić and Čerkez*: "The maxim of *nullum crimen sine lege* is also satisfied where a State is already treaty-bound by a specific convention, and the International Tribunal applies a provision of that convention irrespective of whether it is part of customary international law."[58] In the literature, however, it is sometimes pointed out that the international criminal bodies assumed such treaty-based crimes "too hastily".[59]

[57] See Ferdinandusse, *Direct Application*, 2006, 270–272.

[58] ICTY, *Kordić and Čerkez*, Case No. IT-95-14/2-A, Appeals Chamber, 17 December 2004, paragraph 44.

[59] Claus Kreß, International Criminal Law, in: Rüdiger Wolfrum (ed.), *The Max Planck Encyclopedia of International Law* (Oxford: Oxford University Press 2012), paragraph 12.

Against this backdrop, a differentiated conception is proposed, according to which treaty law – especially in the field of international humanitarian law – often does not constitute the actual basis of criminal responsibility, but rather only the "context" for individual criminal responsibility under customary international law, which has evolved "on top" of the prohibitions directed at States.[60]

As the treaty basis of criminal responsibility for concrete offences, various international agreements may be considered, especially the statutes of the criminal tribunals and the International Criminal Court itself. *Which* norms give rise to which duties (of omission) enforced by penalties and in this sense constitute genuine "international" crimes? Whether a treaty directly criminalizes human behaviour must be determined through interpretation. The wording alone does not play the determinative role, given that the wording is often self-contradictory. The overall context of the progressive development of the overlapping areas of international humanitarian law and international criminal law must be taken into account. In the following discussion, various types of international treaty norms are distinguished.

5.2.6.2 Suppression Conventions

The suppression conventions do not direct prohibitions at individuals. They contain obligations to act directed at States, and they require the contracting parties to issue national criminal provisions. In these regimes, national law mediates between the international norms and individuals.[61] Classic examples include the Slavery Convention of 1956, Article 6 of which states: "The act of enslaving another person . . . shall be

[60] See, e.g., Dapo Akande on some IHL treaties: "[T]he treaty provisions themselves do not create individual criminal responsibility. The transformation of the rule establishing violations of international humanitarian law by states into one which imposes individual criminal responsibility on individuals takes place under customary international law. Thus, although reference is made to treaties creating rules of international humanitarian law, those provisions are not applied qua treaty but rather as the context for a rule of customary law which has developed on top of the treaty rule and which criminalizes the same conduct" (Dapo Akande, Sources of International Criminal Law, in: Antonio Cassese et al. (eds), *The Oxford Companion to International Criminal Justice* (Oxford: Oxford University Press 2009), 41–53 (48; italics mine)).

[61] Only a few of the suppression conventions could also be interpreted as a direct basis for criminal responsibility in light of their wording. For instance, Article 3(1) of the SUA Convention states: "Any person commits an offense if that person unlawfully and intentionally . . .", followed by an enumeration of criminal offences against ships. Convention for the Suppression of Unlawful Acts Against the Safety of Maritime Navigation of 10 March 1988.

a criminal offence *under the laws of the States Parties* to this Convention and persons convicted thereof shall be liable to punishment."[62] Article 113 of the Convention on the Law of the Sea of 1982 requires States parties to regulate and criminalize the destruction of submarine cables.[63] Article 4 of the UN Convention against Torture of 1984 requires, "Each State Party shall ensure that all acts of torture are offences *under its criminal law*."[64] The central obligation set out in the OECD Anti-Bribery Convention of 1999 is: "*Each Party shall take any measures necessary to establish* that complicity in, including incitement, aiding and abetting, or authorisation of an act of bribery of a foreign public official *shall be a criminal offence . . .*"[65]

A new generation of agreements defines very detailed State obligations relating to punishment, cooperation, information exchange, mutual legal assistance, confiscation of proceeds of crime, sanctions, etc. This includes the UN Convention against Transnational Organized Crime of 2000 and its three protocols;[66] the UN Convention against Corruption of 2003;[67] the renewed Convention for the Suppression of Unlawful Seizure of

[62] Article 6 of the Supplementary Convention on the Abolition of Slavery, the Slave Trade, and Institutions and Practices Similar to Slavery of 7 September 1956 (italics mine).

[63] Article 113 UNCLOS: "Breaking or injury of a submarine cable or pipeline: *Every State shall adopt the laws and regulations necessary* to provide that the breaking or injury by a ship flying its flag or by a person subject to its jurisdiction of a submarine cable beneath the high seas done wilfully or through culpable negligence, in such a manner as to be liable to interrupt or obstruct telegraphic or telephonic communications, and similarly the breaking or injury of a submarine pipeline or high-voltage power cable, shall be a punishable offence. This provision shall apply also to conduct calculated or likely to result in such breaking or injury. However, it shall not apply to any break or injury caused by persons who acted merely with the legitimate object of saving their lives or their ships, after having taken all necessary precautions to avoid such break or injury" (italics mine).

[64] Italics mine. Convention against Torture and Other Cruel, Inhuman or Degrading Treatment or Punishment of 10 December 1984 (GAOR, 39th sess., resolutions, Suppl. No. 51, UN Doc. A/39/51, 197).

[65] OECD Convention on Combating Bribery of Foreign Public Officials in International Business Transactions of 17 December 1997, in force since 15 February 1999, Article 1 ("The Offence of Bribery of Foreign Public Officials"), paragraph 2 (italics mine).

[66] Convention against Transnational Organized Crime of 15 November 2000 with protocols. See Article 5 of the Convention; Article 5 of the Protocol to Prevent, Suppress and Punish Trafficking in Persons, Especially Women and Children of 15 November 2000; Article 6 of the Protocol Against the Smuggling of Migrants by Land, Sea and Air of 15 November 2000; Article 5 of the Protocol Against the Illicit Manufacturing of and Trafficking in Firearms, Their Parts and Components and Ammunition, UNGA res. 55/255 of 31 May 2001.

[67] United Nations Convention against Corruption of 31 October 2003 (UNTS 2349, No. 41; UN Doc. A/58/422), duties to punish set out in chapter III, "Criminalization and law

Aircraft of 2010;[68] and the Anti-Counterfeiting Trade Agreement of 2011.[69] But even these modern conventions do not themselves constitute the criminal law basis of individual obligations to refrain from certain acts, and they are not themselves legal foundations of criminal responsibility. A draft protocol to the WHO Framework Convention on Tobacco Control is formulated unambiguously in this regard: "Each Party shall adopt, subject to the basic principles of its domestic law, such legislative and other measures as may be necessary to establish all of the following conduct as unlawful *under its domestic law*: . . ."[70]

Jakob Katz Cogan describes the new structure of the suppression conventions as follows: "While still mediated, the obligations of states established by many of these treaties are much more detailed – the individual duties are more elaborately stated, their elements are more specific, the forms of liability (aiding and abetting, attempt, conspiracy, and so on) are broader, the sanctions to be imposed by states are more precise and harsher, and the obligations of states to elaborate and apply the law are clearer."[71] Despite the new level of detail, however, it is still the case that the suppression conventions establish only an "indirect control scheme"[72] – they do *not* address individuals directly.

A duty to punish directed at UN Member States is also contained in Security Council resolution 1373 against the financing of terrorism of 2001. In this resolution, the Security Council decided "*that all States shall*: . . . (e) *Ensure that* any person who participates in the financing, planning, preparation or perpetration of terrorist acts or in supporting terrorist acts is brought to justice and ensure that, in addition to any

enforcement." Article 15 states: "Each State Party shall adopt such legislative and other measures as may be necessary to establish as criminal offences . . . ."

[68] The Convention of 16 September 1970 was amended by the Protocol of 10 September 2010 (Protocol Supplementary to the Convention for the Suppression of Unlawful Seizure of Aircraft). Article 2 in the 2010 version states: "Each State Party undertakes to make the offences set forth in Article 12 punishable by severe penalties."

[69] Anti-Counterfeiting Trade Agreement between the European Union and its Member States, Australia, Canada, Japan, the Republic of Korea, the United Mexican States, the Kingdom of Morocco, New Zealand, the Republic of Singapore, the Swiss Confederation, and the United States of America of 23 August 2011, punishment obligations in Articles 23–26. According to Article 23, "Each Party shall provide for criminal procedures and penalties to be applied at least in cases of wilful trademark counterfeiting or copyright or related rights piracy on a commercial scale . . ."

[70] Draft Protocol to Eliminate Illicit Trade in Tobacco Products of 11 May 2012 (FCTC/COP/5/6), Article 14 (in Part IV: "Offences"; italics mine). See also *ibid.*, Article 16.

[71] Katz Cogan, Regulatory Turn, 2011, 351.

[72] M. Cherif Bassiouni, An Appraisal of the Growth and Developing Trends of International Criminal Law, *Revue internationale de droit pénal* 45 (1974), 405–433 (429).

other measures against them, *such terrorist acts are established as serious criminal offences in domestic laws* and regulations and that the punishment duly reflects the seriousness of such terrorist acts; . . ."[73] Similarly, the anti-piracy resolution 1918 (2010) "[c]alls on all States, including States in the region, to criminalize piracy *under their domestic law*".[74] The interpretation that resolution 1373 asserts that "terrorist action per se gives rise to individual responsibility", according to Robert McCorquodale,[75] is not covered by the wording of the resolution and appears to go too far.

In many treaties, it is open and unclear whether they are only suppression conventions or are themselves the treaty basis of criminal responsibility. One example is Article 3 of the Convention for the Suppression of Unlawful Acts against the Safety of Maritime Navigation.[76] This provision states: "1. Any person commits an offence if that person unlawfully and intentionally . . .," followed by a detailed enumeration of offences. Article 5 states: "Each State Party shall make the *offences set forth in article 3* punishable by appropriate penalties which take into account the grave nature of those offences." The provision in Article 3 is clear and specific enough to be applied directly as the definition of a criminal offence. According to its wording, the requirement of punishment directed at States in Article 5 concerns the legal consequences that must be governed by domestic law. Against the background of the interest of the international community as a whole expressed in the Preamble to the Convention,[77] Article 3 should be recognized as a source of the criminalization of acts of terrorism against ships.

[73] UNSC res. 1373 of 28 September 2001, paragraph 2(e) (italics mine).

[74] UNSC res. 1918 of 27 April 2010. See also *ibid.*, preambular paragraph 13: "Commending those States that have amended their domestic laws in order to criminalize piracy . . ." (italics mine).

[75] McCorquodale, Individual in the Legal System, 2010, 292.

[76] Convention for the Suppression of Unlawful Acts against the Safety of Maritime Navigation of 10 March 1988 (UNTS Vol. 1678, I-29004, 201).

[77] Relevant passages in the Preamble are: ". . . Considering that unlawful acts against the safety of maritime navigation . . . undermine the confidence of the peoples of the world in the safety of maritime navigation, Considering that the occurrence of such acts is a matter of grave concern *to the international community as a whole*, Being Convinced of the urgent need to develop international co-operation between States in devising and adopting effective and practical measures for the prevention of all unlawful acts against the safety of maritime navigation, and the prosecution and punishment of their perpetrators . . ." (italics mine).

5.2.6.3 The Statutes of the International Criminal Courts and Tribunals

The statutes of the criminal tribunals and the ICC are first and foremost the organizational basis of the institutions, defining their jurisdiction. Apart from this jurisdictional content, the statutes might at the same time constitute the substantive basis for criminal offences. However, neither the statutes of the criminal tribunals and the International Criminal Court nor the case law of these international bodies provides unambiguous information on the precise legal basis of the individual criminal responsibility for the offences referred to in the statutes. The texts thus do not say whether the statutes have the aforementioned substantive content. For instance, Article 7(1) of the Statute of the ICTY states, "A person who planned, instigated, ordered, committed or otherwise aided and abetted in the planning, preparation or execution of a crime referred to in articles 2 to 5 of the present Statute, *shall be individually responsible for the crime.*"[78] The statutes mention the principle of individual criminal responsibility, but they do not state the basis establishing the criminality of the statutory crimes.

In addition to the treaty basis (contained in the statute or other agreement), the criminality of an offence might arise from customary international law; this could underpin the treaty law, so to speak. But this triggers the follow-up question of whether both legal bases are congruent. For instance, it is generally assumed that the provisions of the Rome Statute of the International Criminal Court go beyond pre-existing customary law in some respects. Looking at the Rome Statute from a purely "jurisdictional" perspective, there would be no legal basis for the criminality of the parts overshooting customary law,[79] and this would in any event violate the *nullum crimen* requirement.

The case law of the ad hoc criminal tribunals is not uniform on this point. In its *Tadić* appeal decision, the Appeals Chamber of the Yugoslavia Tribunal assumed that the criminality of violations of Common Article 3 of the Geneva Conventions is derived from customary international law: "*[C]ustomary law* imposes criminal

[78] ICTY Statute of 25 May 1993, Annex to UNSC res. 827 (1993) (italics mine). Article 6 of the ICTR Statute is identical.

[79] Marko Milanovic, Is the Rome Statute Binding on Individuals? (And Why We Should Care), *Journal of International Criminal Law* 9 (2011), 25–52 (30).

liability for serious violations of common Article 3."[80] According to this view, criminal responsibility would exist irrespective of the international instrument that established the tribunal, in this case Security Council resolution 827 (1993) with its Annex, the ICTY Statute.[81]

In contrast, the Rwanda Tribunal assumed that the criminality of offences under its jurisdiction was based only on the statutes of the tribunals: "[B]y establishing [the ICTY and the ICTR] the Security Council explicitly *extended* the international legal obligations and criminal responsibilities directly to individuals for violations of international humanitarian law. In doing so, the Security Council provided an important innovation of international law . . ."[82]

Article 25 of the Rome Statute has the following to say about criminal responsibility: "1. The Court shall have jurisdiction over natural persons pursuant to this Statute. 2. A person who commits a crime within the jurisdiction of the Court shall be *individually responsible and liable for punishment in accordance with this Statute.* 3. *In accordance with this Statute, a person shall be criminally responsible and liable for punishment for a crime within the jurisdiction of the Court* if that person . . ."[83] This formulation is ambiguous in regard to the legal source of individual criminal responsibility. It says only that criminal responsibility is derived "in accordance with" the Statute but not that the Statute is the source. Article 24(1) of the Rome Statute points in that direction, however: "No person shall be criminally responsible *under this Statute* for conduct prior to the entry into force of the Statute" (italics mine). It follows that the Rome Statute is itself likely to be a treaty basis for the criminality of the crimes mentioned in the Statute and thus likely to bind individuals directly.[84] This view is covered by the existing case law of national criminal courts. For instance, the military tribunals of the Democratic

[80] ICTY, *Prosecutor* v. *Duško Tadić*, Decision on the Defence Motion for Interlocutory Appeal on Jurisdiction, Case No. IT-94-1-AR72, Appeals Chamber of 2 October 1995, paragraph 134.

[81] The ICTY Statute accordingly has only jurisdictional significance, not the significance of a substantive legal basis for the criminality of offences that are under the jurisdiction of the ICTY. At the same time, this means that the Statute does not bind individuals, i.e., does not impose obligations on them.

[82] ICTR, *Prosecutor* v. *Kanyabashi*, Decision on the Defence Motion on Jurisdiction, Case No. ICTR-96-15-T, 18 June 1997, paragraph 35 (italics mine). Marko Milanovic, in contrast, is of the view that the ICTR Statute, like the ICTY Statute, has only jurisdictional effect (Milanovic, Rome Statute Binding, 2011, 28).

[83] Italics mine.

[84] See Milanovic, Rome Statute Binding, 2011, passim, esp. 32.

Republic of the Congo applied the Rome Statute directly, because the definitions of war crimes and crimes against humanity in national criminal law deviated from the Rome Statute or were full of gaps.[85] The criminal responsibility of the accused individuals under the Rome Statute does not rule out that most of the offences are criminal already on the basis of the underlying customary international law.[86]

5.2.6.4 Grave Breaches of the Geneva Conventions

The Geneva Conventions on international humanitarian law do not give a clear answer whether the breach of their provisions (or other provisions of the law of armed conflict) entails the direct international criminal liability of the individual offender. The fundamental provision governing war crime trials, Article 85 of Geneva Convention (III), reads: "Prisoners of war prosecuted *under the laws of the Detaining Power* for acts committed prior to capture shall retain, even if convicted, the benefits of the present Convention."[87] This norm thus implies that prisoners are prosecuted under national law. But the provision refers primarily to the criminal proceedings, not to the substantive legal basis of criminal responsibility. As a result, the provision does not rule out that the "prosecution" might be carried out by State bodies in criminal proceedings governed by national law, but for criminal offences directly under international law. This interpretation of Article 85 of the Geneva Convention (III) does not contradict the wording of Article 99 of the same Convention: "No prisoner of war may be tried or sentenced for an act which is not forbidden by the law of the Detaining Power *or by international law*, in force at the time the said act was committed ..." (italics mine). This norm assumes that international law may impose direct prohibitions. However, it does not necessarily have to be interpreted such that these prohibitions are also addressed directly to the combatants. Neither can it be inferred from the wording of Article 99 of

[85] See Democratic Republic of the Congo, Tribunal Militaire de Garnison de l'Ituri, *L'auditeur Militaire* v. *Bongo Massaba*, 24 March 2006, paragraphs 61–74 on war crimes (ILDC 387 (CD 2006)); Democratic Republic of the Congo, *L'auditeur Militaire* v. *Kahwa Panga Mandro*, Ituri District Military Court, 2 August 2006, paragraphs 65–70 on war crimes and crimes against humanity (ILDC 524 (CD 2006)). The tribunals refer to the primacy of international treaties over national laws according to the Congolese constitution.

[86] Article 22(3) of the Rome Statute refers to this: "This article shall not affect the characterization of any conduct as criminal under international law independently of this Statute."

[87] Italics mine.

Geneva Convention (III) whether the criminality of breaches of the prohibitions set out in the treaty arises directly in virtue of international law.

Important potential treaty crimes are contained in the provisions of the Geneva Conventions on grave breaches.[88] The breach of certain precisely designated norms, which in turn prohibit wilful killing, torture or inhuman treatment, wanton destruction of property, unlawful deportation, taking of hostages, or rape and the like, is considered a grave breach. The contracting parties are required to enact penal sanctions for grave breaches, to investigate in cases of suspicion, or to hand suspects over to another contracting party. According to their wording, these norms are directed only at States. They do not address any direct command to individuals to refrain from committing grave breaches. The provisions themselves also do not specify the legal consequence of criminal responsibility, but rather oblige the contracting parties to "enact any legislation necessary to provide effective penal sanctions" in their national law.[89] On the whole, the provisions are thus formulated in a way that addresses States. At the diplomatic conference adopting the Geneva Conventions of 1949, the US delegate argued that the provisions governing grave breaches would become crimes only when national implementing legislation had been adopted,[90] and this view was apparently not contradicted at the conference.[91] Along these lines, there is a widespread view today that the provisions of the Geneva Conventions are *not* able to

[88] Article 49 of GC I; Article 50 of GC II; Article 129 of GC III; Article 146 and 147 of GC IV; Article 85(1) of AP I.

[89] See, e.g., Article 49 of Convention (I) for the Amelioration of the Condition of the Wounded and Sick in Armed Forces in the Field of 12 August 1949: "The High Contracting Parties *undertake to enact any legislation* necessary to provide effective penal sanctions for persons committing, or ordering to be committed, any of the grave breaches of the present Convention defined in the following Article.

"Each High Contracting Party shall be under the obligation to search for persons alleged to have committed, or to have ordered to be committed, such grave breaches, and shall bring such persons, regardless of their nationality, before its own courts. It may also, if it prefers, and *in accordance with the provisions of its own legislation*, hand such persons over for trial to another High Contracting Party concerned, provided such High Contracting Party has made out a 'prima facie' case" (italics mine).

[90] According to US delegate Yingling: "The term 'crimes' is clearly inappropriate to express violations of this Convention, which will not be crimes until they are made so by domestic penal legislation" (Final Records of the Diplomatic Conference of Geneva of 1949, Vol. II Section B, 21st Plenary Meeting, 30 July 1949, 353 et seq. (357)).

[91] Richard R. Baxter believes this view cannot be reconciled with the earlier practice of national courts in sentencing war criminals (Richard R. Baxter, The Municipal and International Law Basis of Jurisdiction over War Crimes, in: M. Cherif Bassiouni/ Ved

constitute the legal basis for the criminality of the breach of their norms in virtue of treaty law (also not in regard to grave breaches). This view is supported, firstly, by the argument that the Geneva Conventions are not able to generate individual obligations: "Those instruments were never meant to and cannot do so conceptually as they are not binding qua treaty upon individuals, but only upon signatory states."[92] This statement does not appear to be accurate, however. In Chapter 7, it will be shown that the Geneva Conventions can obligate individuals directly, in addition to the contracting parties. A better argument is the distinction between two levels of legal consequences: unlawfulness and criminality. Even if the Conventions – as assumed by this study – prohibit individuals from certain acts and qualify them as contrary to international law, this does not automatically mean that such breaches are actually criminal.

But the second level may have been reached through the further development of the law. Article 85 of Protocol I to the Geneva Conventions of 1977 refers to the "grave breaches" explicitly as "war crimes". This formulation either clarifies the original meaning of the Geneva Conventions or it expresses a change of meaning that may have occurred over the course of the thirty intervening years. The term "war crime" indicates that the Geneva Conventions themselves constitute the basis for the criminality of a grave breach.[93]

P. Nanda (eds), *A Treatise on International Criminal Law*, Vol. II (Charles Thomas Publisher: Springfield, Illinois 1973), 65–86 (71)).

[92] Guénaël Mettraux, *International Crimes and the ad hoc Tribunals* (Oxford: Oxford University Press 2005), 9. Along these lines, see also Parlett, *Individual*, 2011, 188: "In these circumstances, it seems clear that the conventions themselves do not impose direct obligations on individuals not to commit grave breaches."

[93] See Kai Ambos, *Treatise on International Criminal Law*, Vol. 1 (Oxford: Oxford University Press 2013), 14. For the direct international criminal responsibility of perpetrators of a "grave breach" of the Geneva Conventions, see already Otto Triffterer, *Dogmatische Untersuchungen zur Entwicklung des Völkerstrafrechts seit Nürnberg* (Freiburg: Albert 1966), 181 and 190; George H. Aldrich, Individuals as Subjects of International Humanitarian Law, in: Jerzy Makarczyk (ed.), *Theory of International Law at the Threshold of the 21st Century: Essays in Honour of Krysztof Skubiszewski* (The Hague: Kluwer Law International 1996), 851–858 (853). Hans Heinrich Jescheck, Verbrechen gegen das Völkerrecht, in: *Deutsche Landesreferate zum IV. Internationalen Kongress für Rechtsvergleichung in Paris 1954* (Düsseldorf: Michael Triltsch Verlag 1955), 351–400 (371–372) held that direct international criminal responsibility for grave breaches existed in principle, but that it could not be enforced in Germany, because of the constitutional requirement of the existence of a formal law as the basis for punishment (Article 103(2) of the Basic Law). On the restrictive interpretation of Article 103(2) of the Basic Law in conformity with international law, see p. 136).

Along these lines, the Security Council held in two resolutions in 1992 on the massive breaches of international humanitarian law in Bosnia during the Yugoslav civil war that "all parties [to the conflict] are bound to comply with the obligations under international humanitarian law and in particular the Geneva Conventions of 12 August 1949, and that *persons who commit or order the commission of grave breaches of the Conventions are individually responsible* in respect of such breaches".[94]

In the final analysis, criminal responsibility for the commission of grave breaches is derived from the Geneva Conventions. This is also foreseeable for persons subject to them on the basis of the wording of Article 85 of Protocol I and the later practice of the Security Council. Punishment directly under international law for the commission of a grave breach is thus compatible with the principle of legality.

5.2.6.5 Customary International Law and General Principles of Law

Customary international law and general principles of law are a direct source of individual criminal responsibility. This is presupposed by the provisions already mentioned above, Article 15(2) ICCPR and Article 7(2) ECHR.[95] Both kinds of legal sources are often summarized as "general rules" by international criminal lawyers.[96] It is now no longer called into question that there are crimes rooted in customary international law and general principles of law (as opposed to mere treaty crimes). The question is solely which offences should be considered as such. For instance, it is disputed whether apartheid[97] and terrorist acts are criminal in virtue of customary law (irrespective of or supplementary to their penalization in treaties).

[94] UNSC res. 764 of 13 July 1992, paragraph 10; identically, UNSC res. 771 of 13 August 1992, paragraph 1 (italics mine).

[95] See p. 135.

[96] The formulation in Article 21(1) of the Rome Statute is misleading, according to which the ICC applies "the principles and rules of international law" according to (b) and "general principles of law derived by the Court from national laws of legal systems of the world . . ., provided that those principles are not inconsistent with this Statute and with internationally recognized norms and standards" according to (c).

[97] Article 3 of the Apartheid Convention of 1973 states: "International criminal responsibility shall apply, irrespective of the motive involved, to individuals, members of organizations and institutions of the State . . ." International Convention on the Suppression and Punishment of the Crime of Apartheid, UNGA res 3068 (XXVIIII) of 30 November 1973 (italics mine).

From the perspective of the "principle of justice" invoked in the Nuremberg judgment,[98] which traditionally dominated international criminal law in the view of some,[99] the general rules (i.e., customary international law and general principles of law) are even the more legitimate legal foundation for direct international criminal responsibility because they reflect the fundamental values of the international community.[100] From the perspective of the principle of legality, in contrast, the general rules are less legitimate legal foundations than rules codified in treaties because the obligations and penalties imposed by them are more difficult for legal subjects to identify and foresee than written and published treaty provisions.

Formulations in the judgment of the Nuremberg Tribunal show that in the view of the Tribunal, it was applying *international* substantive law, not national law, even though that law had not been codified in an international treaty at the time of the judgment.[101] According to the judgment, the Nuremberg Charter is "the expression of *international law* existing at the time of its creation; and to that extent is itself a contribution to international law".[102] The relevant "international law existing at the time" can only be customary international law or a general principle of law.

On the occasion of the establishment of the Yugoslavia Tribunal, the UN Secretary-General dealt with the principle of legality in his report on Security Council resolution 808. To avoid a violation of the *nullum crimen* principle, and especially in the criminal prosecution of grave breaches, the Tribunal – according to the Secretary-General – should apply customary international law only where that law is beyond any doubt. This would address the problem that not all States were parties to the treaties in question.[103] The Secretary-General thus assumed that customary

[98] International Military Tribunal, judgment of 1 October 1946 (n. 10), 52.

[99] See Cassese, *International Criminal Law*, 2008, 38–39.

[100] See Kreß, International Criminal Law, 2012, paragraph 11: "[I]nternational law stricto sensu may be articulated in international treaties to correspond with the principle of legality in its most stringent form. Ultimately, however, it must be rooted in general international law because of its inextricable connection with fundamental values of the international legal community as a whole."

[101] See Baxter, Municipal and International Law Basis, 1973, 70.

[102] Judgment of the International Military Tribunal sitting at Nuremberg (n. 10), 444: "The Charter [of the Nuremberg Tribunal] is not an arbitrary exercise of power on the part of the victorious nations, but in the view of the Tribunal, as will be shown, it is the expression of international law existing at the time of its creation; and to that extent is itself a contribution to international law" (italics mine).

[103] See Report of the Secretary-General Pursuant to Paragraph 2 of Security Council Resolution 808, UN Doc. S/25407 of 3 May 1993, paragraph 34: "In the view of the

international law, where it existed "beyond any doubt", constituted a sufficient legal basis for criminal responsibility and that its application was also compatible with the *nullum crimen* requirement. The Yugoslavia Tribunal itself likewise believes that direct international criminal responsibility of the individual is possible on the basis of treaty law or customary law: "[T]he violation of the rule must entail, *under customary or conventional law*, the individual criminal responsibility of the person breaching the rule."[104]

According to the Yugoslavia Tribunal, the criminality of an offence under customary international law can be assumed when the two elements of customary international law, namely accepted legal doctrine and practice, are clearly established: "the clear and *unequivocal recognition* of the rules of warfare in international law and State practice indicating an intention to criminalize the prohibition, including statements by government officials and international organizations, as well as *punishment* of violations by national courts and military tribunals".[105] The objective element of customary international law, namely State practice, is thus established when State courts have prosecuted violations under criminal law.

The core crimes, i.e., genocide, crimes against humanity, war crimes, and aggression, are recognized as being criminal directly in virtue of international law. The remaining question is only whether the legal basis of criminality consists in the various treaties that deal with these offences or in underlying customary international law. In my view, the criminality of these crimes can be derived already from customary international law. The relevant treaties can plausibly be read as references to already existing criminality: For instance, the Preamble of the Rome Statute refers to the core crimes as "the most serious crimes of concern to the international community as a whole" and as "international crimes". Article I of the Genocide Convention of 1948 states, "The Contracting Parties *confirm* that genocide, whether committed in time of peace or in time of war, is

Secretary-General, the application of the principle nullum crimen sine lege requires that the international tribunal should apply rules of international humanitarian law which are beyond any doubt part of customary law so that the problem of adherence of some but not all States to the specific convention does not arise. This would appear to be particularly important in the context of an international tribunal prosecuting persons responsible for serious violations of international humanitarian law."

[104] ICTY Appeals Chamber, *Tadić* (n. 80), paragraph 94 (italics mine).

[105] *Ibid.*, paragraph 128, with reference to the Nuremberg judgment (italics mine).

a crime under international law which they undertake to prevent and to punish."[106]

The Yugoslavia Tribunal has further assumed that violations of Common Article 3 of the Geneva Conventions are criminal in both types of armed conflict. This provision itself says nothing about criminality; the criminality of the violations is derived not from the Convention itself, but rather from customary international law.[107]

New decisions of international courts have not always held criminal convictions by national criminal courts on the basis of unwritten general rules to be admissible. For instance, the Community Court of Justice of the Economic Community of West African States (ECOWAS) was called upon by the former President of Chad, Hissein Habré, after he had been prosecuted by national courts in Senegal for aiding and abetting crimes against humanity, even though that offence had been incorporated into national law only after the fact. The accused asserted a violation of the prohibition of retroactivity. The ECOWAS Court referred to Article 15(2) ICCPR (permissibility of criminal prosecution on the basis of general principles of law recognized by the community of nations). However, it noted that the mandate of the African Union demanded the establishment of a "competent court" and hence that an *ad hoc* court would have to be created. According to the Court, prosecution of crimes against humanity by Senegalese courts without a criminal offence set out in legislation violated the prohibition of retroactivity.[108] Implicitly, the ECOWAS Court thus found that the Senegalese courts should not make the general principle of law governing the offence of a crime against humanity the basis for punishing Hissein Habré.

A counterexample approving of the derivation of criminality from customary international law can be found in the *Kononov* v. *Latvia* judgment of the ECtHR of 2010 already mentioned at p. 91 (in Chapter 4).[109] In the view of the Strasbourg Court, fundamental provisions of international humanitarian law, including under the Hague Convention respecting the Laws and Customs of War on Land of 1907 for the protection of the civilian population, were not only applicable as customary international law already in 1944 but also were enforceable by criminal penalties under customary

[106] Convention on the Prevention and Punishment of the Crime of Genocide of 9 December 1948, UNTS Vol. 78, 277 (italics mine).

[107] See ICTY Appeals Chamber, Tadić (n. 80), paragraphs 128–129.

[108] Community Court of Justice of the Economic Community of West African States (CEDEAO/ECOWAS), *Hissein Habré* v. *Senegal*, 18 November 2010, paragraphs 57–58.

[109] ECtHR (Grand Chamber), 17 May 2010, *Kononov* v. *Latvia*, No. 36376/04.

international law.[110] Ill-treatment of prisoners of war and summary executions were therefore punishable as war crimes already in 1944.[111]

5.2.6.6 Interim Conclusion

In the final analysis, the dividing line between a mere duty to punish (through incorporation into national criminal law), treaty-based criminality, and criminality based on customary international law is still unclear with respect to certain offences.[112] This is because conduct covered by treaties such as the Rome Statute or even just the suppression conventions may be punishable directly under international law already in virtue of customary international law. In that case, the individual is addressed only by the underlying customary international law, while the treaty is directed only at the contracting States. For instance, the implementation clause of the Genocide Convention (Article V) does not preclude that genocide can at the same time be punished directly under the Convention (and under parallel customary international law).[113] Unlike in the case of genocide, (additional) criminality directly under international law is disputed in the case of terrorist acts. The Terrorist Bombings Convention of 1997,[114] for instance, addresses States parties directly with a duty to punish (Article 4). The Preamble of the Convention refers to substantive criminality of the offence directly in virtue of international law: The States parties formulate an "unequivocal condemnation of all acts, methods and practices of terrorism *as criminal* and unjustifiable .... Considering that the occurrence of such acts is a matter of *grave concern to the international community as a whole* ..."[115] In the light of this formulation and State practice, it is sometimes assumed that at least certain terrorist acts are punishable already in virtue of customary international law. However, especially with respect to offences that are referred to (only) in suppression conventions, the wording of the provisions addressed only to States appears to make it more difficult for potential perpetrators to foresee criminality directly under international law. For

[110] For an explicit statement of this view, see the judgment of the lower instance, ECtHR (Chamber), 24 July 2008, *Kononov* v. *Latvia*, No. 36376/04, paragraph 120. This is disputed by Judges Costa and others in their dissenting opinion, paragraph 11.

[111] See ECtHR (Grand Chamber), *Kononov* (n. 109), paragraphs 202–204.

[112] See Ferdinandusse, *Direct Application*, 2006, 260. [113] See *ibid.*, 257.

[114] International Convention for the Suppression of Terrorist Bombings of 15 December 1997, in effect since 23 May 2001.

[115] Preamble (italics mine).

this reason, one might easily level the accusation that the principle of legality would be violated if those provisions were applied as a direct legal basis for punishment.

5.3 The International Non-criminal Responsibility of the Individual

Considerable legal uncertainty prevails beyond the criminal responsibility of the individual directly under international law. This section shows that even outside criminal law, the responsibility of the individual directly under international law is possible and already exists in certain respects.

5.3.1 The Saving Clause of Article 58 of the ILC Articles on State Responsibility

Article 58 of the ILC Articles on State Responsibility states: "These articles are without prejudice to any question of the *individual responsibility* under international law of any person acting on behalf of a State."[116] While this provision mentions only individual responsibility for individual acts "on behalf of the State", it does not prohibit individual responsibility under international law for purely private conduct without direction by the State. The provision is found in a text that otherwise deals only with State responsibility. Its purpose is merely to cut off the argument that the codified articles might rule out the individual responsibility of officeholders in addition to State responsibility. Individual liability is otherwise not the object of these ILC Articles on State Responsibility, and the clause thus should not be deemed exhaustive. Independent individual liability did not have to be referred to in the Articles on State Responsibility, since in that situation, there would be no question of danger that a State might shirk liability or conversely that the individual might hide behind the protective shield of the State. The provision in Article 58 of the ILC Articles on State Responsibility thus cannot be used to derive any statement against the possibility of international responsibility of private persons.

Instead, the opposite conclusion imposes itself. The provision was conceived as a saving clause in the direction of the possibility of individual responsibility. The ILC commentary on its Articles on State

[116] UNGA res. 56/83 of 12 December 2001, Annex.

Responsibility points out that the principle of individual international responsibility has so far become operational only in the sense of international criminal responsibility. "[B]ut it is not excluded that developments may occur in the field of individual civil responsibility."[117] The misleading term "civil responsibility" means non-criminal responsibility on the basis of international law, i.e., international responsibility that, as discussed above, could be understood just as well as international administrative responsibility, or responsibility arising from international *public* law (see above p. 116). The saving clause of Article 58 of the ILC Articles should not stand in the way of such a development of the law, and it therefore uses the term "individual responsibility *under international law*" according to the Special Rapporteur of the ILC, James Crawford.[118]

5.3.2 *Mediated or Direct International Responsibility of Individuals? The Example of the Nuclear and Environmental Liability Conventions*

Under existing law, is non-criminal responsibility triggered directly under international law when international individual duties are violated, even if those duties are not enforced by criminal penalties? Or is that responsibility implemented only through national (civil) law, in accordance with the principle of mediation? In the environmental field, reaching non-State actors – i.e., primarily business enterprises operating facilities that are potentially damaging to the environment – is especially important, because environmental threats emanate primarily from these operators, not from States themselves. For this reason, attempts to further develop international environmental law have also targeted these entities.

In international nuclear and environmental law, several "civil"[119] liability conventions exist. "Civil liability" in this context is not

[117] ILC YB 2001 Vol. II, Part Two, Report of the International Law Commission on the work of its fifty-third session (23 April–1 June and 2 July–10 August 2001), UN Doc. A/56/10, Draft Articles on Responsibility of States for Internationally Wrongful Acts, Text of the draft articles with commentaries thereto, 30–143 (142 paragraph 2). Similarly, see the Special Rapporteur of the ILC, James Crawford, *The International Law Commission's Articles on State Responsibility: Introduction, Text, and Commentaries* (Cambridge: Cambridge University Press 2002), 312.

[118] Crawford, *International Law Commission's Articles*, 2002, 312.

[119] See the official titles of these conventions, e.g., Lugano Convention on Civil Liability for Damage Resulting from Activities Dangerous to the Environment of 21 June 1993 (ETS No. 150), not yet in force.

necessarily understood as a contrast to criminal responsibility of the operators, but rather especially as a contrast to *State* responsibility. "Civil" according to this usage therefore means the responsibility of private persons which – as mentioned earlier – should preferably be understood as a kind of public law responsibility of these private persons.

So far, liability conventions of this kind have been drafted in regard to maritime oil pollution, nuclear damage, and transboundary movement of hazardous wastes; not all of them are in force. The only cross-sectoral international liability instrument is the Lugano Convention on Civil Liability for Damage Resulting from Activities Dangerous to the Environment, which likewise has not yet entered into force.[120]

The conventions concern the *secondary obligations* of enterprises. In the environmental context, these obligations are often referred to as *liability* in order to differentiate them from State responsibility; but in the view put forward here, they are obligations of economic actors directly under international law, arising from a relationship of secondary *responsibility* under international law.[121] When the secondary obligations are understood as being directly under international law, this would imply at the same time that the economic actors are under a *prior primary obligation* to refrain from environmental damage. "Plainly stated, the treaties place duties on businesses not to cause pollution," Steven Ratner writes.[122] If the wording of the conventions allows it and when the direction of the obligations and their content are foreseeable for the legal subjects, these primary obligations could be read into the conventions as well. But such an interpretation is legitimate only under very strict conditions. The primary obligations of individuals directly under international law are discussed in detail in Chapter 4.

[120] See *ibid.*

[121] In older treaty texts, the term "liability" is used in the sense of the international responsibility of States for breaches of international law. An example is Article 235 of the Convention on the Law of the Sea (UNCLOS): "Responsibility and liability: 1. States are responsible for the fulfilment of their international obligations concerning the protection and preservation of the marine environment. They shall be liable in accordance with international law" (italics mine).

[122] Steven Ratner, Business, in: Daniel Bodansky/Jutta Brunnée/Ellen Hey (eds), *The Oxford Handbook of International Environmental Law* (Oxford: Oxford University Press 2007), 807–828 (814).

5.3.2.1 The Wording of the Provisions Giving Rise to the Obligations

The starting point for answering the question of whether the secondary obligations (liability or responsibility) stipulated in the environmental liability conventions are directed at States or individuals is their wording. For instance, Article III(1) of the Oil Pollution Convention in the version of 1992 states: "[T]he owner of a ship at the time of an incident . . . *shall be liable* for any pollution damage caused by the ship as a result of the incident."[123] Article 4 of the Basel Protocol of 1999 on Liability and Compensation for Damage Resulting from Transboundary Movements of Hazardous Wastes and Their Disposal provides strict liability for waste generators or exporters: "The person who notifies in accordance with Article 6 of the Convention [the Basel Convention on the Control of Transboundary Movements of Hazardous Wastes and Their Disposal of 22 March 1989] *shall be liable for damage* until the disposer has taken possession of the hazardous wastes and other wastes."[124] Additionally, Article 5 of the Protocol stipulates fault-based liability of "any person" for damage resulting from lack of compliance with the provisions implementing the Basel Convention. This liability is expressly independent of the domestic law of the contracting parties.[125]

Article II(1) of the Vienna Convention on Civil Liability for Nuclear Damage as amended by the Protocol of 29 September 1997 states:

[123] International Convention for Oil Pollution Damage (CLC) of 29 November 1969, superseded by the Protocol of 27 November 1992, in force since 30 May 1996, with the Fund Convention (International Convention on the Establishment of an International Fund for Compensation for Oil Pollution Damage (FUND) of 18 December 1971, superseded by the Protocol of 27 November 1992 (in force since 30 May 1996).

[124] Basel Protocol on Liability and Compensation for Damage Resulting from Transboundary Movements of Hazardous Wastes and Their Disposal of 10 December 1999, not yet in force. Article 6 of the Basel Convention of 22 March 1989 provides for notification of the planned export by the waste generator or exporter. Similarly, see the Kiev Protocol on Civil Liability and Compensation for Damage Caused by the Transboundary Effects of Industrial Accidents on Transboundary Waters to the 1992 Convention on the Protection and Use of Transboundary Watercourses and International Lakes and to the 1992 Convention on the Transboundary Effects of Industrial Accidents of 21 May 2003, not in force, Article 4, "strict liability": "1. The operator shall be liable for the damage caused by an industrial accident."

[125] Basel Protocol (n. 124), Article 5, "Fault-based liability": "Without prejudice to Article 4, any person *shall be liable for damage* caused or contributed to by his lack of compliance with the provisions implementing the Convention or by his wrongful intentional, reckless or negligent acts or omissions. This Article *shall not affect the domestic law* of the Contracting Parties governing liability of servants and agents" (italics mine).

"The operator of a nuclear installation *shall be liable* . . ."[126] Similarly, Article 3(1) of the OECD Paris Convention on Nuclear Third Party Liability of 1962 in the version of 1982 states: "The operator of a nuclear installation shall be liable, in accordance with this Convention, for . . ."[127]

The cross-sectoral Lugano Convention on environmental liability has the following goal, according to Article 1: "This Convention aims at ensuring adequate compensation for damage resulting from activities dangerous to the environment and also provides for means of prevention and reinstatement." According to Article 6 on "[l]iability in respect of substances, organisms and certain waste installations or sites", "(1) The operator in respect of a dangerous activity mentioned under Article 2, paragraph 1, sub-paragraphs a to c *shall be liable* for the damage caused by the activity as a result of incidents at the time or during the period when he was exercising the control of that activity."[128] This convention is not yet in force, however.[129]

Article 7(1) of the HNS Convention on Liability and Compensation for Damage in Connection with the Carriage of Hazardous and Noxious Substances by Sea in the version of 2010 states: "[T]he owner at the time of an incident shall be liable for damage caused by any hazardous and noxious substances in connection with their carriage by sea on board the ship . . ."[130] At the same time, Article 6 stipulates "Duties of State Parties": "Each State Party shall ensure that any obligation *arising under this Convention* is fulfilled and shall take appropriate measures under its law including the imposing of sanctions as it may deem necessary, with a view to the effective execution of such obligation."[131] So in order to effectively meet their obligations arising from the convention, States are required to impose sanctions to help enforce the obligations of ship owners. Again, the traditional understanding of the Convention is that

[126] IAEA Vienna Convention on Civil Liability for Nuclear Damage of 21 May 1963, as amended by the Protocol of 29 September 1997, in force since 4 October 2003 (italics mine).

[127] OECD Paris Convention on Third Party Liability in the Field of Nuclear Energy of 29 July 1960, as amended by the Additional Protocol of 28 January 1964 and by the Protocol of 16 November 1982, in force since 7 October 1988.

[128] Lugano Convention (n. 119; italics mine).

[129] The Lugano Convention needs only three ratifications to enter into force and has so far not been ratified by a single State; so far, there are nine signatories.

[130] International Convention on Liability and Compensation for Damage in Connection with the Carriage of Hazardous and Noxious Substances by Sea of 3 May 1996 and the Protocol of 2010 (HNS Convention), not yet in force.

[131] Italics mine.

it does not give rise to liability of ship owners directly under international law: "[T]he relationship between the person causing the damage and the victims of the damage are essentially placed under the domain of national laws of one of the contracting parties, save for the specific rules established under the convention which have become an integral part of national laws."[132] This traditional view is, however, in no way mandated by the wording of the cited provisions. The clear formulation of Articles 6 and 7 of the HNS Convention could certainly be read so that the obligations of the ship owners are derived directly from the Convention itself, not only from the flanking legislation. The fact that these liability conventions directly address operators becomes even clearer when they are compared with the indirect approach to maritime polluters taken by the UN Convention on the Law of the Sea (Article 230 UNCLOS),[133] which allows States parties to impose monetary penalties for the violation of international environmental standards.

5.3.2.2 Direct Secondary Obligations of Operators under International Law?

The traditional reading is that these conventions obligate the States parties to ensure the liability of business enterprises and to guarantee their obligation to pay compensation. According to this view, individual responsibility is mediated completely and is not directly under international law: "Although regulated by an international agreement, responsibility for ... damage does not result from international law. The sole function of these ... Conventions is to establish certain minimal rules for the responsibility of the operator ..., rules which must be transposed in the internal legal order by the States parties to them ... All things considered, the obligations of the operator remain essentially subject to

[132] Christian Tomuschat, The Responsibility of Other Individuals: Private Individuals, in: James Crawford/Alain Pellet/Simone Olleson (eds), *The Law of International Responsibility* (Oxford: Oxford University Press 2010), 317–329 (325).

[133] Article 230 UNCLOS: "Monetary penalties and the observance of recognized rights of the accused: 1. Monetary penalties only may be imposed with respect to violations of *national laws and regulations* or applicable international rules and standards for the prevention, reduction and control of pollution of the marine environment, committed by foreign vessels beyond the territorial sea. 2. Monetary penalties only may be imposed with respect to violations of *national laws and regulations* or applicable international rules and standards for the prevention, reduction and control of pollution of the marine environment, committed by foreign vessels in the territorial sea, except in the case of a wilful and serious act of pollution in the territorial sea. 3. In the conduct of proceedings in respect of such violations committed by a foreign vessel which may result in the imposition of penalties, recognized rights of the accused shall be observed" (italics mine).

the civil law of a State."[134] This means that the conventions make use of the classical method of harmonization of (civil) law by creating uniform law.

The text of most of the conventions mentioned above tends to speak against the traditional reading of addressing the State, and it would permit a direct international liability of individuals. According to their wording, all these conventions (with the exception of the Convention on the Law of the Sea) obligate the operators directly. The cited provisions would furthermore have to be sufficiently specific and complete in the sense that no further national provisions would be needed to specify them and make the obligations perfect. To do this, the conventions would have to contain unambiguous substantive standards – i.e., general principles of liability, provisions on the form of the liability (such as determining fault-based or strict liability), and rules on the scope of liability and the temporal and financial limits of liability. The conventions would also have to contain clearly specified minimum standards governing the forum, standing, the applicable law, and the recognition and enforcement of judgments.[135] Such specifications are in any event contained in some of the conventions mentioned. The conventions that are "perfect" in this sense would then be suitable for application by State authorities and courts from the perspective of direct effect, and they would also be sufficiently foreseeable for the obligors from the perspective of the principle of legality.[136]

But is direct international responsibility of private economic actors sensible and called for in light of the object and purpose of the treaties? A regime of "civil liability" has a threefold objective: Firstly, it is intended to protect the environment by means of a preventive effect, and secondly, it is intended to give victims of environmental pollution the retrospective possibility of compensation. Thirdly, the liability regimes are part of a transnational risk management: The operators are to be protected from incalculable financial risks. Along with liability, the conventions mentioned above also establish upper limits to liability[137] and – together with the residual responsibility of the State by establishing funds, etc. – make operator risk insurable to begin with.[138]

[134] Tomuschat, Responsibility, 2010, 323–324.
[135] I would like to thank Sigrid Boysen for this point.
[136] For more details, see Chapter 4 and the previous sections in this chapter.
[137] See, e.g., Article 9 of the Kiev Protocol (n. 124) on "financial limits".
[138] For instance, the background of the Vienna Convention on Civil Liability for Nuclear Damage (n. 126) included economic and security policy interests of European States that

In regard to the first-mentioned goal of environmental protection, which has become the focus since the 1990s, three advantages of a liability regime are usually mentioned: The polluter is brought to internalize the costs of pollution, the threat of liability creates an economic incentive to comply with environmental standards, and the regime creates a catch-all system if environmental damage occurs nonetheless.[139] But Jutta Brunnée is sceptical in regard to the actual benefit for protection of the environment: "Based on international and domestic experience, it seems unlikely that liability regimes will play a significant role as a tool for environmental protection."[140]

The lack of effectiveness of the liability conventions for environmental protection so far would be improved if a direct international responsibility of the operators were assumed. If the source of the responsibility is international law, irrespective of whether it is implemented or paralleled by national norms, it is a subordinate question of how and with what legal technique the States parties implement the convention into their national law (i.e., by enacting parallel laws or simply by referencing the text of the convention, for example). In this reading, in any event, the non-implementation or deficient implementation of the regime by a State party would not relieve the operators of their direct international responsibility.

In contrast, the third objective of the environmental liability conventions, namely the discharge of operators of installations, would not be promoted by their interpretation as conventions addressing the individual. The motive of some conventions, especially in the field of nuclear damage, is not (primarily) to impose obligations on the operators of installations, let alone environmental protection, but – quite to the contrary – to *exonerate* the entire supplying industry. So the conventions are not really about liability, but rather about limiting liability by specifying maximum amounts and State support measures (funds, etc.).[141] The interpretation of the conventions as addressing individuals contributes nothing to this objective.

Other considerations speak against the interpretation of the environmental liability conventions as a legal basis for direct international

also wanted to be independent of the United States in terms of energy supply. I would like to thank Sigrid Boysen for this point.

[139] Jutta Brunnée, Of Sense and Sensibility: Reflections on International Liability Regimes as Tools for Environmental Protection, *International and Comparative Law Quarterly* 53 (2004), 351–368 (365).

[140] *Ibid.*, 367. [141] I would like to thank Sigrid Boysen for this point.

obligations of private operators. Such environmental obligations of operators derived from international or supranational law are not even accepted in the strongly developed law of the EU. For instance, the EU Environmental Liability Directive of 2004 governs extensive primary and secondary obligations of operators: obligations to prevent and remedy damage and bear the costs for those measures.[142] But this does not give rise to *direct* obligations of operators under EU law. EU directives are in principle directed at Member States, which must implement the requirements into their national law. If the directive is not implemented, the general principles developed in case law indicate that while rights may under certain circumstances be derived for private persons, no private *obligations* can be derived in principle.[143] Accordingly, the direct effect of the key provisions of the Environmental Liability Directive on the environmental obligations of operators is denied in the literature.[144]

The ILC "Draft Principles on the Allocation of Loss in the Case of Loss from Transboundary Harm Arising out of Hazardous Activities", which concern the liability of private operators, persons, or entities operating highly risky enterprises, such as nuclear power plants, likewise do not provide for direct international responsibility of those private actors. Principle 4 of these Draft Principles obligates States to take all necessary measures to ensure compensation for victims, including the introduction of a liability regime *in national law*,

[142] EU Directive 2004/35/EC of 21 April 2004 on environmental liability with regard to the prevention and remedying of environmental damage (OJ 2004 L 143/56), esp. Articles 5–8. The directive covers only "environmental damage" (Article 2), not "private" damage incurred by individuals.

[143] See ECJ, Case 152/84, *Marshall I* [1986] ECR 723, paragraph 48. More recently, however, the ECJ has allowed certain exceptions to the prohibition of third-party effects burdening individuals. See ECJ, Case C-201/02, *The Queen, on the Application of Delena Wells* v. *Secretary of State for Transport, Local Government and the Regions* [2004] ECR I-748, paragraphs 56–57 on triangular relationships (contesting State licences, etc.). See also case C-194/94, *CIA Security International SA* v. *Signalson SA and Securitel SPRL* [1996] ECR I-2230, paragraphs 32–55 and C-443/98, *Unilever Italia* v. *Central Food*, [2000] ECR I-7535, paragraphs 35 and 50–52, on the application of national provisions and product standards in civil disputes where these provisions came about in violation of the notification and standstill requirements of Directive 83/189. In both groups of cases, the ECJ held that the effect burdening the individual did not defeat application of the directive. But this does not mean that the ECJ has given up its fundamental position of *Marshall*. I would like to thank Sebastian von Kielmansegg for this point.

[144] See Gerd Winter/Jan H. Jans/Richard Macrory/Ludwig Krämer, Weighing up the EC Environmental Liability Directive, *Journal of Environmental Law* 20 (2008), 163–191 (186–188).

which in turn must meet international legal requirements (no proof of fault, etc.).[145]

Ultimately, the "individualistic" reading of the conventions cannot help overcome other fundamental obstacles to effectiveness. The first problem for any liability rule is posed by the diffuseness of global environmental problems. This diffuseness makes it more difficult to attribute damage to specific polluters. But the requirement of an identifiable polluter and a causal connection of some definable kind is a precondition for any liability rule. If damage cannot be attributed, the regime may prove futile. The second problem depends solely on the States; they may fail to accept the liability conventions. If the conventions do not enter into force due to an insufficient number of ratifications, they also cannot establish any responsibility of the operators. The individualized reading is in any event not likely to further diminish the political willingness to ratify, and so it is not likely to be counterproductive.

5.3.3 *Enforcement of International Individual Obligations with the Help of National Civil Jurisdiction*

Direct international obligations of individuals may in part be enforced with the help of national civil jurisdiction. This fact is likely partially responsible for inspiring the civil law analogy (rejected here) on which the potential non-criminal international responsibility of individuals usually relies. The focus is on the US Alien Tort Claims Act (ATCA).[146]

[145] ILC, Draft Principles on the Allocation of Loss in the Case of Loss from Transboundary Harm Arising out of Hazardous Activities 2006 ("International liability for injurious consequences arising out of acts not prohibited by international law", Report of the ILC, 58th sess., GAOR 61st sess. Supp. No. 10 (A/61/10), 101–182: Text with commentaries; Commentary on Principle 4 on pp. 151–166). This "liability" is not international responsibility for acts in violation of international law, but rather for lawful but risky acts. The responsibility thus does not arise from a breach. ILC, Draft Principles on the Allocation of Loss 2006, Commentary on p. 118. But see for a different reading of the Draft Principles Julie-Anne Richards/Keely Boom, *Big Oil, Coal and Gas Producers Paying for their Climate Damage* (Heinrich Böll Foundation, Series Ecology vol. 39, Berlin 2014), 28–29, who see "growing support for the notion that these political statements should be translated into the direct legal regulation and responsibility of transnational corporations … Clearly, the main emphasis of Draft Principle 4 is upon operator liability."

[146] Alien Tort Claims Act (1789), US Code, Title 28, § 1350: "The district courts shall have original jurisdiction of any civil action by an alien for a tort only, committed in violation of the law of nations or a treaty of the United States."

The ATCA permits claims for damages before US courts for torts committed abroad against aliens in violation of international law – independently of the nationality of the perpetrator.[147] In practice, private persons and (transnational) corporations are often sued. To some extent, US civil case law assumes direct primary international obligations of individuals. These usually involve criminal offences, but only in regard to their (from the US perspective) dimension of "civil" liability, which is handled by civil courts. In an early case under the ATCA, the Serbian leader Karadžić was sentenced to compensation in the amount of USD 745 million to be paid to Bosnian claimants for international crimes committed in Bosnia. The US Court of Appeals held "that certain forms of conduct violate the law of nations whether undertaken by those acting under the auspices of the state *or only as private individuals*".[148] In other words, the court assumed that private individuals are directly bound by certain norms of international law or – expressed differently again – that international law imposes duties of conduct and omission on individuals. The secondary legal consequences of the violation of these obligations would normally also have to be guided by international law, so in this sense they involve the international responsibility of individuals. As mentioned at the outset, this might be interpreted as "public law" responsibility (see above p. 116).

In contrast, a US Court of Appeals rejected the responsibility of *legal* persons (corporations) for human rights violations in the *Kiobel* judgment of 2010.[149] In *Kiobel*, the issue was the extraction of petroleum by Shell Oil (Royal Dutch Petroleum) in the Niger Delta, during which Shell was involved in destroying the living environment of the Ogoni people. The affected persons sued Shell and its subsidies in US courts for complicity with the Nigerian government in the commission of torture, inhuman and cruel treatment, summary executions, arbitrary arrests, and crimes against humanity. The question was whether the oil company was responsible under customary international law for aiding and abetting serious human rights violations by the dictatorial regime. The Court

[147] In its landmark decision *Sosa* v. *Alvarez Machain*, the Supreme Court imposed two limiting conditions on the jurisdiction of US courts. The asserted, allegedly violated norm of international law must, firstly, be specific and, secondly, be universally recognized (US Supreme Court, *Sosa* v. *Alvarez Machain*, 542 US 692). Illegal detention lasting less than a day did not meet these criteria, so that the US courts were not permitted to grant compensation to the Mexican citizen Alvarez Machain on the basis of the ATCA.

[148] US Court of Appeals, *Kadić* v. *Karadžić*, 70 Fd 3d 232, 239 (2d Cir. 1995; italics mine).

[149] US Court of Appeals, *Kiobel* v. *Royal Dutch Petroleum Company*, 621 F.3d 111 (2d Cir. 2010).

of Appeals determined that in the previous case law of international tribunals, the issue was always the responsibility of *natural*, but not legal, persons. Where business enterprises were accused of crimes and human rights violations, courts found a responsibility of the leaders of the business enterprise, but not the enterprise itself, for instance in the *I.G. Farben* case before the Nuremberg war crimes tribunal, in which Carl Krauch and 22 other members of the management were accused.[150] In *Kiobel*, the Court of Appeals concluded: "No corporation has ever been subject to any form of liability (whether civil, criminal, or otherwise) under the customary international law of human rights ... Acknowledging the absence of corporate liability ... is ... a recognition that the States of the world, in their relations with one another, have determined that moral and legal responsibility for heinous crimes should rest *on the individual* whose conduct makes him or her, *hostis humani generis*, an enemy of all mankind."[151] After this judgment, lawsuits under the ATCA for business activities may be lodged only against employees, managers, or members of the board of directors of a business enterprise set up as a legal person. For lawsuits against legal persons themselves, the Court of Appeals found that the federal courts do not have subject-matter jurisdiction pursuant to the ATCA special legislation. The US Supreme Court did not rule on the question of human rights responsibility, but rather dismissed Kiobel's claim as inadmissible on grounds of extraterritoriality.[152]

National civil or administrative courts may create a corpus of case law on international responsibility, i.e., on the direct secondary international obligations of natural and legal persons. Explicitly or implicitly, this also helps give shape to primary international obligations whose violation triggers international individual responsibility. Generally speaking, case law (i.e., the case law of international and national courts) plays an important role in regard to the international responsibility of individuals because it provides sharper contours to the very indefinite primary and secondary obligations and thus can make them foreseeable for the

[150] Law Reports of Trials of War Criminals, Vol. X: The I.G. Farben and Krupp Trials (London: Published for the United Nations War Crimes Commission by His Majesty's Stationery Office 1949): Trial of Carl Krauch and twenty-two others.

[151] US Court of Appeals, 2nd Circ., *Kiobel*, Conclusions (internal citations omitted, some italics mine).

[152] US Supreme Court, *Kiobel* v. *Royal Dutch Petroleum*, Judgment of 17 April 2013, 569 US (2013). For details, see Ingrid Wuerth, The Supreme Court and the Alien Tort Statute: *Kiobel* v. *Royal Dutch Petroleum Co.*, *American Journal of International Law* 107 (2013), 601–621.

affected obligors. The judgments of national courts are also a primary form of enforcement of international individual obligations in accordance with the principle of subsidiarity.

5.4 Conclusion

Individuals can be held responsible under international law, they may be subject to secondary obligations in accordance with the law of international responsibility. It must be said that the international responsibility of individuals follows a different logic from State responsibility. The breach of a State obligation toward another State happens at the level of equals. Both actors, the offender and the injured State, are and remain sovereign. As a matter of principle, individuals are subject to the power of a State and do not enjoy State sovereignty.[153] Christian Tomuschat concludes from this that there is a "fundamental difference" between the international responsibility of States and that of individuals: "The responsibility of individuals has a different tone from that of States."[154] But the differences should not be overemphasized. In my view, it is hardly relevant for the question of responsibility that an individual does not have the same "ceremonial dignity" as a State.[155]

The international responsibility of the individual appears in two forms: as criminal and as non-criminal responsibility, the latter of which is best interpreted as being held to account under public law. The capacity of individuals to be held criminally responsible under international law has been established as a principle of customary international law. A concrete criminal responsibility of individuals directly under international law may result from customary international law, general principles of law, and international treaty law, taking account of a transnationalized *nullum crimen* requirement; the further specification of criminal offences through case law plays a major practical role that is also relevant to legitimacy.

International law is far enough advanced that in addition to the firmly established direct international criminal responsibility of individuals, the non-criminal responsibility of individuals can be established as well. "The advanced process of 'humanization' of international law would surely suggest such a liability. However, so far States have not been ready to agree on it," Bardo Fassbender claims.[156]

[153] See Tomuschat, *Responsibility*, 2010, 320. [154] *Ibid.* [155] But cf. *ibid.*

[156] Bardo Fassbender, Can Victims Sue State Officials for Torture? *Journal of International Criminal Justice* 6 (2008), 347–369 (369). Fassbender speaks of "state officials". This is because only actors that can be attributed to a State are able to commit torture within the

An explicit agreement or stipulation in this sense would not be necessary if the principle of individual responsibility were to arise already from existing practice, accompanied by accepted legal doctrine, as a norm of customary international law. But only a few steps have been made in this direction so far, which have been developed especially in case law. The existing "civil" liability conventions might, as shown, be interpreted as a basis for the direct international responsibility of individuals with regard to the environmental damage covered by the conventions. However, neither the proposals by the ILC nor the much more differentiated law of the EU has taken it this far.

The legal possibility of imposing secondary international legal obligations on individuals as well as primary obligations should be welcomed from an abstract perspective in principle. Such a development on the side of obligations represents a fair corollary to the progressive unfolding of individual rights and would consolidate the legal status of the individual as a primary subject of international law. The concrete and practical utility of such a development is questionable, however. The legal consequence would be that individuals in principle could be made subject to the obligation to compensate victims of violations of international law. While injured parties already have the possibility of claiming damages from (cross-border) environmental pollution caused by other private persons and enterprises before national courts in accordance with the principles of private international law and the applicable national law, a direct imposition of international obligations on the operators and the assumption of a secondary relationship of responsibility under international law between the injured party and the (private) injuring party would only make sense if doing so would improve the possibilities of liquidation. But the conditions for realizing this would in turn (due to the lack of an international legal arrangement) primarily or even exclusively have to be created using the means of national law, albeit also in accordance with the requirements of international law. The practical advantages of a direct international responsibility of operators thus appear modest for the injured parties.

First and foremost, attention must be paid that the international responsibility of individuals does not relieve States of their responsibility, since otherwise there is a risk that injured parties will not obtain any

meaning of the Convention against Torture (special offence). Fassbender's formulation does not permit the conclusion that the author intended to limit his discussion to state officials as potential holders of secondary international obligations.

remedy for breaches of international law.[157] In this connection, it is significant that States parties do not currently appear willing to actually take on the obligations stipulated in the environmental liability conventions. This is seen in the fact that several of these conventions are not (yet) in force due to an insufficient number of ratifications. One might ask whether the willingness to ratify would be higher if these conventions were interpreted as addressing individuals. In principle, ratifications would be positive if they were to allow the conventions to enter into force. But if the individualistic reading were to contribute to relieving the States of their guarantee responsibility, this would not be a recommended strategy in terms of legal policy.

A direct international responsibility of individuals should not lead to their exclusive responsibility to the exclusion of State responsibility, but rather to a parallel responsibility. How to deal with the duality of the simultaneously existing responsibility of individuals and of States for violations of international law has not been defined at all in current international law, however.[158] Both any ranking of liability and the internal legal relationship among the multiple holders of secondary obligations are still unclear and require further consideration.

[157] See Christine Evans, *The Right to Reparation in International Law for Victims of Armed Conflict* (Cambridge: Cambridge University Press 2012), 236. For a sceptical view on whether direct international (environmental and human rights) responsibility of enterprises makes sense, cf. also André Nollkaemper, Responsibility of Transnational Corporations in International Environmental Law: Three Perspectives, in: Gerd Winter (ed.), *Multilevel Governance of Global Environmental Change* (Cambridge: Cambridge University Press 2006), 179–199 (191–199).

[158] See, e.g., for the (theoretical) possibility of "joint and several responsibility" of a business actor and a State in the field of seabed exploitation: "Joint and several liability arises where different entities have contributed to the same damage so that full reparation can be claimed from all or any of them." The Chamber did not consider this to be the scheme of responsibility envisaged by UNCLOS Annex III, Article 22 (ITLOS (Seabed Chamber), Responsibilities and Obligations of States Sponsoring Persons and Entities with Respect to Activities in the Area, Advisory Opinion No. 17 of 1 February 2011, paragraph 201).

6

Individual Rights Arising from International Responsibility

6.1 Definition of the Problem

Rights arising from international responsibility are usually referred to as secondary rights or secondary claims.[1] The typical holders of international secondary rights are States; the typical respondents are also States. In this chapter, in contrast, possible international secondary rights *of individuals* against States (their home State or third States) are considered. As a minimum requirement, claims of this kind would require that the individual concerned had a primary right under international law that has been violated.[2] In contrast, the violation of a State obligation that is owed only among States and that benefits individuals only reflexively (without a corresponding primary right of that individual against the State) cannot trigger State responsibility vis-à-vis that individual, but it might trigger international responsibility vis-à-vis the individual's home State.

In the development of international law, two steps had to be climbed in order to grant international secondary claims to the individual: Firstly, primary claims of the individual (and not only of the individual's home State) had to be recognized. Secondly, a convergence of the holders of primary and secondary claims had to be accepted, i.e., it had to be recognized that the violation of an individual primary claim would trigger a secondary claim in the personal capacity of *the injured party*, not only of the injured party's home State.

The interpreters of "classical" international law did not even take the first step. State interference on the part of third States with the legal position of individuals was traditionally construed as a violation of the rights only of the home State of the person concerned ("Vattelian

[1] I use these terms interchangeably in this book.

[2] The thesis that the violation of a primary right of the individual also gives rise to a secondary claim *in the individual's personal capacity* is still controversial and will be justified in more detail in this chapter.

fiction"). This fiction has in any event been abandoned in some areas of international law. This means that in some areas of the law, international primary claims of the individual are conceivable. The best-known international primary claims (with corresponding obligations of the States to respect, protect, and fulfil) are derived from international human rights, which are not the subject of this book. International primary claims of individuals against States, the violation of which triggers secondary claims, are often injunctive claims (rights against interference) – this is the classical situation of the liberal human rights guarantees. The primary claims of individuals against States might also be claims for positive action by the State, including protection by organs of the State from attacks by private persons or forces of nature.[3]

Other than that, the most common and densest legal relationships between a State and an individual are those of national administrative, criminal, and private law, not those of international law. Theoretically, however, these *prima facie* domestic relationships of rights and duties can be "internationalized", such as in international investment protection law.[4]

But international legal doctrine has clearly not taken the second hurdle yet. There still is no agreement on the convergence of the holders of primary and secondary claims. This means that – even if the violated primary norm is of an international legal nature, protects the individual, and gives rise to a primary claim of the individual – it is not automatically concluded that an individual international *secondary* claim also exists. Quite to the contrary, the orthodox distinction between primary and secondary rules, a cornerstone of the ILC work on State responsibility, and the concomitant wisdom that a breach of an international rule brings into being a new and distinct legal relationship of responsibility ("une ambiance nouvelle juridique") lend themselves to allowing a *change* of the *titulaire* of the relevant legal positions.[5] So the question remains as to

[3] These primary claims to protection from violence and forces of nature are dealt with in Chapter 8.

[4] In the chapter on investment protection, an internationalization of both the substantive legal *investor–State contracts* and the procedural *investor–State* agreements to arbitrate will be discussed. A consequence of complete internationalization would have to be that the secondary claims are also of an international legal nature when the obligations arising from the contract are violated. But this consequence is not yet being drawn (see Chapter 10).

[5] *Cf.* Emmanuel Roucounas, Facteurs privés et droit international public, *Recueil des Cours* 299 (2002), 9–419 (346–348) on "l'individu et les règles primaires et secondaires: le cas ou les partenaires changent".

between whom the relationship of responsibility exists. A primary claim of the individual is, from the traditional perspective, a necessary but not sufficient condition for the emergence of an individual secondary claim.

When the violator of the right is not the home State of the injured individual, but rather a third State, additional questions arise. By recognizing primary and possibly secondary claims of individuals, it is not yet clear what happens with the (originally exclusive) primary and secondary claims of the home State of the injured party. Do they exist parallel to the claims of the individual, or do they expire?

Current international law leaves the claims of States on the table. It is assumed that even in situations where an injured individual is himself or herself a holder of claims (against a third State) for compliance with the primary norms of conduct under international law, the individual's State likewise has such claims against the injuring State. The modern view is accordingly that of a dual ownership of claims and a dual violation of the individual and the individual's home State.[6]

Those who assume a dual claim (of the individual and the individual's home State) at the primary level must assume a triangular relationship at that level (i.e., in relation to the claims for compliance with precepts and prohibitions) among the injuring State, the victim, and the victim's home State. Logically speaking, this trilateral relationship would have to continue at the level of secondary law.[7] Then the question arises as to which secondary claim against the third State takes precedence: that of the individual or that of the individual's home State?

Only in some areas of international law are potential secondary claims of individuals being discussed. The first area is the protection of human rights. The second area is international humanitarian law (IHL). Secondary claims arising from violations of international humanitarian law will be considered in Chapter 7. Thirdly, secondary claims arising from the violation of transnational investment protection agreements are important (see Chapter 10). In this chapter – independently of the special questions in those specific areas of the law – basic questions regarding individual claims arising from international responsibility will be

[6] Roughly along these lines, see Karl Doehring, *Die allgemeinen Regeln des völkerrechtlichen Fremdenrechts und das deutsche Verfassungsrecht* (Cologne: Carl Heymann 1963), 110; Riccardo Pisillo Mazzeschi, Impact on the Law of Diplomatic Protection, in: Menno T. Kamminga/Martin Scheinin (eds), *The Impact of Human Rights Law on General International Law* (Oxford: Oxford University Press 2009), 211–233 (217). For details, see Chapter 12.

[7] See Pisillo Mazzeschi, Diplomatic Protection, 2009, 219.

analysed. The legal answers must be gained from an overall view of the law of international responsibility using principles of human rights law, because no other set of legal instruments for evaluating individual secondary claims is available yet.

6.2 Law of International (State) Responsibility

Recently, it has been argued that individuals may be holders not only of certain primary rights to fulfilment of international obligations but also of the correlative secondary claims arising from international (State) responsibility.[8] This view will be defended and justified in the following remarks. It deviates from the State-fixated perspective, which will first briefly be called to mind.

6.2.1 The Classical View: States as Holders of the Secondary Rights

Already in the *Chorzów* case in 1928, the PCIJ recognized that one and the same act by a State might injure another State *and* that State's citizens. The injurious act may trigger parallel secondary legal relationships: between the injuring State and the private person, and between the injuring State and the home State of the affected individual.[9] The PCIJ strictly separated the two levels (and the two legal relationships): "Rights or interests of an individual the violation of which rights causes damage are always in a different plane to rights belonging to a State, which rights may also be infringed by the same act."[10] The court did not make any

[8] Along these lines, see Christian Dominicé, La prétention de la personne privée dans le système de la responsabilité internationale des Etats, in: *Studi di diritto internazionale in onore di Gaetano Arangio-Ruiz*, Vol. 2 (Naples: Editoriale Scientifica 2004), 729–745 (esp. 735 and 744): State responsibility with the usual content may also arise vis-à-vis private persons. The relationship of secondary rights exists between the State and the individual. See also Oliver Dörr, Privatisierung des Völkerrechts, *JuristenZeitung* 60 (2005), 905–916, (909): The injured private person acquires his or her own individual right to reparation. See also Pisillo Mazzeschi, Diplomatic Protection, 2009, 218: Individuals are the "holders of true rights deriving from secondary norms of international law". See also Roland Portmann, *Legal Personality in International Law* (Cambridge: Cambridge University Press 2010), 3 and 275; Oliver Dörr, Völkerrechtliche Deliktsansprüche Privater – auf der Grundlage und in den Grenzen einer völkerrechtlichen Schutznormlehre, in: Martin Breuer/Astrid Epiney/Andreas Haratsch/Stefanie Schmahl/Norman Weiß (eds), *Der Staat im Recht: Festschrift Eckart Klein zum 70. Geburtstag* (Berlin: Duncker & Humblot 2013), 765–782.

[9] See PCIJ, Case Concerning the Factory at Chorzów (Claim for Indemnity – Merits), PCIJ Series A No. 17 (1928), 27–28.

[10] *Ibid.*, 28.

explicit statement regarding the legal nature of the individual claims. The strict separation of a "plane" cited above indicates that the court qualified the individual rights as non-international. On the other hand, the PCIJ mentioned the special international forums made available to individuals to deal with the damage arising from the First World War.[11] It mentioned the Upper Silesian Arbitral Tribunal and the German-Polish Mixed Arbitral Tribunal, to which private persons had access and before which they could assert their claims. From this individual power to bring claims, one might infer a substantive entitlement under international law – but this conclusion was not drawn by the PCIJ.

According to the PCIJ in *Chorzów*, the home State asserts its *own* secondary claim. The amount of the reparation in the form of an indemnity can be measured by the damage suffered by the home State's citizens. This basis of calculation changes nothing about the inter-State nature of the reparation claim: "The reparation due by one State to another does not however change its character by reason of the fact that it takes the form of an indemnity for the calculation of which the damage suffered by a private person is taken as the measure."[12]

After the Second World War, no arbitral tribunals were made available to individuals as they had been after the First World War. The basic rule applied that in any event the international secondary legal relationship – even where an international primary right was recognized for the individual – arises only between the injuring State and the home State of the injured individual. Only the home State of the victim was considered the holder of secondary claims. This view was still represented just a few years ago by the Federal Constitutional Court of Germany and the Federal Court of Justice in regard to claims arising from international humanitarian law. In a ruling on the land reform of 2004, the Federal Constitutional Court held: "This right to damages under secondary law, however, exists only in the international legal relationship between the States involved and is subject to their disposition. In this respect, the claim to damages differs from the involved persons' entitlement under primary law that the prohibitions of humanitarian public international law be observed; this [primary] claim exists in the international legal relationship between the State occupying a territory and the population living in this territory."[13] This construal will be referred to here as the

[11] See Chapter 2, pp. 26–29 [12] PCIJ, *Chorzów* 1928 (n. 9), 28.

[13] BVerfGE 112, 1 (2004), Ruling of the 1st Chamber of the Second Senate of 28 June 2004, 2 BvR 1379/01, *Neue Juristische Wochenschrift* 57 (2004), 3257 et seq. – *Bodenreform III*, paragraphs 32–33 (translation mine). Along these lines, see also BGH (III ZR 190/05),

"separation approach" because it distributes the ownership of the claim at the levels of primary and secondary law between two different subjects: the victim, on the one hand, and the victim's home State, on the other.

6.2.2 *Provisions in the ILC Articles on State Responsibility*

In principle, State responsibility may arise in relation not only to other States but also to other subjects of international law.[14] According to Article 33(1) of the ILC Articles on State Responsibility, Part 2 of the ILC Articles (content of State responsibility) is applicable as such only to secondary obligations owed to other States or to the international community as a whole. But according to Article 33(2) of the ILC Articles, secondary claims arising from State responsibility against non-State actors remain unaffected: The provisions are "without prejudice to any right, arising from the international responsibility of a State, which may accrue directly to any person or entity other than a State".[15] According to the ILC's own commentary, the ILC Articles "do not exclude the possibility that an internationally wrongful act may involve legal consequences in the relations between the State responsible for that act and persons or entities other than States".[16] Elsewhere, the ILC makes a clear statement regarding the possible holders of secondary claims arising from State responsibility: "For instance, a State's responsibility for the breach of an obligation under a treaty concerning the protection of human rights may exist towards all the other parties to the treaty, but the individuals concerned should be regarded as the ultimate beneficiaries and *in that*

Judgment of 2 November 2006 – *Varvarin,* paragraph 11: "In particular, the rule continues to apply that – independently of any primary legal claim by the affected persons for compliance with international law – claims for damages under secondary law arising from acts of State in violation of international law against citizens of foreign States continue to be due only to the home State as a matter of principle" (translation mine).

[14] ILC Commentary on Article 1, Articles on the Responsibility of States for International Wrongful Acts (hereinafter: "ILC Articles on State Responsibility"), YB ILC (2001) Vol. II, Part 2, p. 33, paragraph 5.

[15] Article 33(2) of the ILC Articles on State Responsibility (UN Doc. A/CN.4/L.602, Rev.1 (2001)).

[16] The commentary on the article governing legal consequences continues: "This follows from article 1, which covers all international obligations of the State and not only those owed to other States" (ILC-Commentary (n. 14) on Art. 28, YB ILC (2001) Vol. II, Part 2, p. 87, paragraph 3).

sense as the holders of the relevant rights."[17] So the ILC Articles and the commentary hold that it is possible in principle for individuals to participate in the secondary legal relationship arising from the breach of a primary international norm that protects individuals.

The assumption of a (secondary) legal relationship between the injuring State and the individual does not entail that the identical rules apply here as in the relationship of responsibility between States, especially in regard to the content of State responsibility. However, the ILC commentary in turn does not mention any compulsory deviations from the principles of responsibility between States. This means that the principles of the ILC Articles represent at least a useful starting point for the analysis of international State responsibility towards individuals.

6.2.3 *Modifications of the Law of International Responsibility and Follow-Up Questions*

Does this mean the rules of State responsibility towards individuals are identical to those towards States? An argument in favour of this view is that traditional responsibility between States also included infringements of rights that concerned individuals in substance but that were asserted by way of State diplomatic protection and treated as if they were claims of the State (see Chapter 12). This means that these de facto individual claims were covered already by traditional international law. The dispute between a State and a foreign (private) claimant is – in the words of the Permanent Court of International Justice – "fundamentally identical"[18] to the related dispute between the former State and the individual's home State, which exercises diplomatic protection. A judge of the German Federal Constitutional Court referred to this as the "necessary identity of the substantive basis of the claim".[19]

It makes no sense to modify the relevant principles of State responsibility only because individuals themselves are now seen as holders of rights themselves and can, under certain circumstances, assert their claims themselves, such as before an ICSID arbitral tribunal. Using this argument, an ICSID arbitral tribunal assumed that the principles of State

[17] ILC Commentary on Article 33, YB ILC (2001) Vol. II, Part 2, pp. 94–95 (95, paragraph 3; italics mine).

[18] PCIJ, *Case Concerning the Payment of Various Serbian Loans Issued in France*, PCIJ, Series A, No. 20/21 (1929), 18.

[19] BVerfG, 2 BvM 1/03, Ruling of the Second Senate of 8 May 2007, dissenting opinion of Judge Gertrude Lübbe-Wolff, paragraph 90.

responsibility for the benefit of individuals must in principle be identical to those applicable to the claims of States.[20]

What now are the contents of international State responsibility towards individuals? The ILC Articles on State Responsibility govern these contents in their Part 2. But that part is explicitly *not* applicable to secondary claims of individuals (Article 33(2) ILC Articles[21]). Nevertheless, the customary law underlying the ILC Articles appears to recognize claims for cessation, non-repetition, and reparation also in regard to individuals in principle (as envisaged also by Articles 30 and 31 of the ILC Articles). According to Article 34 of the ILC Articles, reparation may in principle take the form of restitution, compensation, or satisfaction. However, the fact that individuals present themselves as claimants appears to make modifications necessary. In the field of human rights and international humanitarian law, for instance, the individual claim to compensation is especially controversial (see Section 6.3, pp. 175–89). Conversely, in investment protection law, monetary compensation is the usual or possibly even the only legal consequence that an arbitral tribunal may award to an injured investor. Restitution for foreign investors is not available as a matter of principle. For this reason, some observers no longer want to attribute the secondary obligations of the host State in regard to foreign investments to the international law of State responsibility, but rather to qualify them as a *sui generis* regime of legal consequences.[22]

Deviations of the content of State responsibility towards individuals (compared with responsibility toward States) should, however, be specially justified and not sweepingly assumed. A relevant difference

[20] See ICSID, *MTD* v. *Chile*, decision on the application for annulment of 21 March 2007, paragraph 99: "Part II of the ILC Articles . . . is concerned with claims between States, though it includes claims brought on behalf of individuals, for example, within the framework of diplomatic protection. There is no reason not to apply the same principle . . . to claims for breach of treaty brought by individuals" (footnotes omitted).

[21] See n. 15 with upper text.

[22] See Zachary Douglas, Investment Treaty Arbitration and ICSID, in: James Crawford/Alain Pellet/Simone Olleson (eds), *The Law of Responsibility* (Oxford: Oxford University Press 2010), 815–842 (829); Tillmann Rudolf Braun, Globalization-Driven Innovation: The Investor as a Partial Subject in Public International Law: An Inquiry into the Nature and Limits of Investor Rights, *The Journal of World Investment and Trade* 15 (2014), 73–116 (115–116). But see for the right of the investor to choose between reparation in kind and monetary compensation, based on the general international law of State responsibility, ICSID, *Franck Charles Arif* v. *Moldova*, Case ARB/11/23, Award of 8 April 2013, paragraphs 559–572.

between individuals and States in the role of claimant is likely to be the quantitative dimension: Natural persons appear in much larger numbers (compared to States asserting claims, see Section 6.4, p. 191).

Follow-up questions concern the existence of *additional* secondary claims of the home State due to the violation of norms that refer to and entitle the individual, as well as the enforcement options for both claims. It cannot be ruled out in principle that, in addition to the individual claim, a secondary claim of the home State continues to exist, as was assumed in the traditional view when norms governing the international law relating to aliens were breached. To make international responsibility for mass breaches manageable in the first place, the secondary claims of the State could be treated preferentially in terms of procedure. Then the individual claims arising from State responsibility could only be activated if the involved States have not agreed any or sufficient compensation arrangements or if the affected persons do not fall within the scope of such arrangements (see Chapter 7, pp. 212–13). In terms of the legal cause, however, the State claims should be seen as ancillary to the individual claim, so that they cannot be asserted by the State at the international level if the affected individual objects.[23]

Finally, individual secondary claims cannot be enforced in all cases by the individual alone. Because Part 3 of the ILC Articles of States Responsibility explicitly governs invocation of State responsibility only by States,[24] that part (like Part 2 of the ILC Articles) is not applicable to individual claims. For this reason, it is up to the applicable rule of primary law to determine whether and to what extent individuals may themselves *invoke* State responsibility.[25]

6.3 Human Rights and International Humanitarian Law: Remedy and Reparation

In the context of human rights and international humanitarian law, the problem of an individual secondary claim is discussed under the heading

[23] See Dominicé, La prétention de la personne privée, 2004, 744: The secondary claim of the State remains latent as long as the individual has his or her own enforcement options at his or her disposal.

[24] The heading of Part 3, Chapter 1 is: "Invocation of the responsibility of a State." All provisions in that chapter govern only the invocation of the responsibility of a State by other States.

[25] See James Crawford, *The International Law Commission's Articles on State Responsibility: Introduction, Text, and Commentaries* (Cambridge: Cambridge University Press 2002), 210.

"right to remedy and reparation".[26] So far, this discussion is linked relatively seldomly to the basic rules of the law of State responsibility as outlined earlier. In the terminology of that area of the law, reparation is the content of a secondary claim arising from international responsibility.

Although human rights are not an object of this study, the possible secondary claims from breaches of human rights will be mentioned here because the secondary claims themselves do not necessarily have the character of human rights, and in the discussion they often are not separated from claims due to the breach of international humanitarian law. Because of the interrelationship with the primary rights and duties in the law of armed conflict, the details of the claims to compensation due to breaches of international humanitarian law will be discussed in Chapter 7. This chapter will outline the foundations. Two claims must be distinguished at the outset. The first claim, namely to remedy, is primarily a procedural claim to legal protection or effective remedy. The second is a substantive claim to reparation.[27] Within the scope of the possible forms of reparation (according to general international law: restitution, compensation, and satisfaction), compensation in turn is especially problematic.

[26] See, e.g., George Ulrich/Louise Krabbe Boserup (eds), *Reparations: Redressing Past Wrongs, Human Rights in Development Yearbook 2001* (Dordrecht: Kluwer 2003); Pablo de Greiff (ed.), *The Handbook of Reparations* (Oxford: Oxford University Press 2006), with case studies; Koen de Feyter/Stephan Parmentier/Marc Bossuyt/Paul Lemmens (eds), *Out of the Ashes: Reparations for the Victims of Gross and Systematic Human Rights Violations* (Antwerp: Intersentia 2005); REDRESS, *Implementing Victims' Rights: A Handbook on Basic Principles and Guidelines on the Right to a Remedy and Reparation* (London: The Redress Trust 2006); Carla Ferstman/Mariana Goetz/Alan Stephens (eds), *Reparations for Victims of Genocide, War Crimes and Crimes against Humanity: Systems in Place and Systems in the Making* (Dordrecht: Martinus Nijhoff 2009).

[27] The terminology is not consistent. Often, the legal consequence of reparation is counted as a "remedy", so that "remedy" is split into a procedural and a substantive aspect (as in Principle 11 of the Basic Principles and Guidelines on the Right to a Remedy and Reparation for Victims of Gross Violations of International Human Rights Law and Serious Violations of International Humanitarian Law, UN Doc. A/Res/60/147 (21 March 2006)). Logically speaking, this terminology does not fit with the title of the GA resolution, which speaks of "remedy *and* reparation". Some authors in turn include the procedural claim as part of "reparation" and distinguish "procedural" and "material" reparation. For yet another classification, see M. Cherif Bassiouni, International Recognition of Victims' Rights, *Human Rights Law Review* 6 (2006), 203–279 (260). Bassiouni refers to three basic rights of the victim: access to justice (Principle 12 of the Basic Principles and Guidelines on the Right to a Remedy of 2006), reparation (Principle 15), and the "right to truth" (Principle 11; in more detail Principle 24).

6.3.1 *The 2006 Basic Principles of the General Assembly*

After decades of preparatory work by the Commission on Human Rights and its Sub-Commission on Prevention of Discrimination and Protection of Minorities, the UN General Assembly adopted the resolution entitled "Basic Principles and Guidelines on the Right to a Remedy and Reparation for Victims of Gross Violations of International Human Rights Law and Serious Violations of International Humanitarian Law" by consensus in 2006 (hereinafter the "2006 Basic Principles of the General Assembly on Remedy").[28]

The second aspect – reparation – is especially controversial, most of all due to its lack of an unambiguous treaty basis. Principle 18 of the 2006 Basic Principles of the General Assembly on Remedy enumerates various forms of reparation, according to which reparation may encompass restitution (in kind),[29] (monetary) compensation,[30] rehabilitation,[31] or satisfaction.[32] These types of reparation should, as appropriate and proportionate to the gravity of the violation, be awarded alternatively or cumulatively.[33]

Cherif Bassiouni described the 2006 Basic Principles of the General Assembly on Remedy as a "monumental milestone in the history of human rights as well as international criminal justice".[34] The resolution as such does not constitute binding international law and also does not claim to be a progressive development of international law. It implies that the two aforementioned rights to a remedy and reparation can be derived from existing international law in connection with national law in the case of serious violations of rights representing an attack against human dignity.[35]

[28] Basic Principles and Guidelines on the Right to a Remedy and Reparation for Victims of Gross Violations (n. 27). See the detailed commentary on the 2006 text by Cherif Bassiouni, who was involved in their drafting (Bassiouni, Victims' Rights, 2006, 247–279). The work was initiated by UNGA res. 40/34, Declaration of Basic Principles of Justice for Victims of Crime and Abuse of Power of 29 November 1985. Other texts were Theo van Boven's Draft Basic Principles of 1997, the Draft Principles of 2000, and a revised version of 2003. The final resolution was first adopted in 2005 by the Commission on Human Rights, with forty States in favour, none against, and thirteen abstentions, and then confirmed by the GA in consensus.

[29] For more details, see Principle 19 of the 2006 Basic Principles of the General Assembly on Remedy (n. 27). Restitution may, for example, be in the form of restoration of liberty, return to one's place of residence, return of property.

[30] For more details, see *ibid.*, Principle 20.

[31] For more details, see *ibid.*, Principle 21.

[32] For more details, see *ibid.*, Principle 22.

[33] See *ibid.*, Principle 18.

[34] Bassiouni, Victims' Rights, 2006, 278.

[35] Along these lines, see also numerous voices in the literature, such as Carla Ferstman/Mariana Goetz/Alan Stephens, Introduction, in: Ferstman et al., *Reparations for Victims*

6.3.2 Reparation through International *Courts*

The question is, what are the exact legal bases of the claim to remedy and reparation postulated in the 2006 Basic Principles of the General Assembly on Remedy? The provisions in Article 41 ECHR, Article 63 ACHR, and Article 75 of the Rome Statute are special in this regard, since they authorize *international* courts to award reparations.[36] These provisions do not obligate the States parties to make reparations under national law, but rather reparations are determined and awarded by the international bodies themselves at their own discretion; the legal basis of the duty to award reparations is in the treaty itself, directly or indirectly.[37]

According to Article 75 of the Rome Statute, victims have a claim to reparation.[38] (On the other rights of victims under the Rome Statute, see Chapter 9). According to this provision, the court must establish principles relating to reparations. These principles may also be developed

2009, 7–16 (16). The rapporteur for the UN guidelines speaks more cautiously of emerging customary international law that does not yet have a firm place in the *acquis* (Theo van Boven, Victims' Rights to a Remedy and Reparation: The New United Nations Principles and Guidelines, in: Ferstman et al., *Reparations for Victims 2009*, 19–40 (26–27)). See also Manfred Nowak, The Right to Reparation of Victims of Gross Human Rights Violations, in: George Ulrich/Louise Krabbe Boserup (eds), *Reparations: Redressing Past Wrongs, Human Rights in Development Yearbook 2001* (Dordrecht: Kluwer 2003), 277–308 (308).

36 See Article 75 of the Rome Statute below in note 38. Article 41 ECHR: "If the Court finds that there has been a violation of the Convention or the protocols thereto, and if the internal law of the High Contracting Party concerned allows only partial reparation to be made, the Court shall, if necessary, afford just satisfaction to the injured party." In practice, despite the term "satisfaction", monetary compensation is awarded. According to the wording of the provision, it is awarded as a substitute for reparation. For this reason, we will only speak of reparation from now on. The formulation of Article 63 ACHR is similar to Article 41 ECHR. On the pioneering role of the IACtHR in this regard, see Elisabeth Lambert Abdelgawad/Kathia Martin-Chenut (eds), *Réparer les violations graves et massives des droits de l'homme: la Cour interaméricaine, pionnière et modèle?* (Paris: Société de législation comparé 2010).

37 Article 41 ECHR and Article 63 ACHR do not themselves grant the claim to reparation, but rather authorize the international courts to find a claim to reparation under international law.

38 According to Article 75(2) of the Rome Statute, the International Criminal Court may "make an order directly against a convicted person specifying appropriate reparations to, or in respect of, victims, including restitution, compensation and rehabilitation". Contrasted with this, at the time of adoption of the statutes of the ad hoc criminal tribunals, the attempt to set out a claim of victims to compensation still met with great resistance and failed. See the ICTY report on "Victims' compensation and participation", with the proposal to appoint an international "claims commission" to award compensation to victims (UN Doc. S/2000/1063 (2000)).

through case law as applied to individual cases, and the ICC appears to be taking this path. Reparation includes restitution, compensation, or rehabilitation. The Rules of Procedure and Evidence (hereinafter "Rules"[39]) provide further details on the award.[40] The reparation procedure may be initiated on the written application of the victim (Rule 94) or on the motion of the court (Rule 95). The ICC may address the order for reparation only to the convicted person, but not to the State to which the perpetrator belongs.[41] A trust fund was established to make reparation payments (Article 79 of the Rome Statute). The court may order money and other property collected through fines or forfeiture to be transferred to the trust fund (Article 79(2) of the Rome Statute).[42] Article 75(5) in conjunction with Article 109(1) of the Rome Statute provides that the States parties must implement and enforce the ICC's reparation orders. For this reason, the States parties' domestic laws on the Rome Statute contain provisions implementing the victims' right to reparation into national law.[43]

One reason international criminal jurisdiction has been tasked with reparations to victims lies in the specific structure of the international enforcement bodies. Within States, reparation for the current victim is a responsibility of civil law, while national criminal law deals only with what the perpetrator owes society.[44] At the national level, the usual division of labour between civil and criminal law in the nation State does not apply, so reparation must also fall within the domain of (international) criminal jurisdiction.[45]

Moreover, the ICC can act only if the State that would have jurisdiction (typically the State where the crime is committed) is unwilling or

[39] Rules of Procedure and Evidence of the ICC (UN Doc. PCNICC/2000/1/Add.1 (2000)).

[40] Rules, Chapter 4, Section III, Subsection 4: "Reparations to victims", Rules 94–99. See also Article 85 of the Rome Statute: "Compensation to an arrested or convicted person." See also ICC, TC I, Situation in the Democratic Republic of the Congo in the Case of the Prosecutor *v.* Thomas Lubanga Dyilo, Public Decision Establishing the Principles and Procedures to be applied to Reparations, Case No. ICC-01/04-01/06, of 7 August 2012.

[41] This limitation was necessary to overcome the resistance of some negotiating States to the reparation obligation.

[42] See Article 77(2) of the Rome Statute on fines and forfeiture of proceeds, property and assets derived from the crime.

[43] For Switzerland, see Article 41 on "Handing over for forfeiture, transfer to the Trust Fund, or restitution" of the Federal Law on Cooperation with the International Criminal Court (CICCL) of 22 June 2001 (RS 352.6).

[44] See Kurt Seelmann, Paradoxien der Opferorientierung im Strafrecht, *JuristenZeitung* 44 (1989), 670–676 (671).

[45] On the legal nature of reparation under Article 75 of the Rome Statute, see Chapter 9, p. 276.

unable genuinely to carry out the investigation or prosecution (Article 17(1)(a) of the Rome Statute). In this situation, reparation according to national legal provisions cannot be obtained in national proceedings. It is thus justified to transfer the power to award reparations directly to the ICC.

In conclusion, the possibility specifically provided in the ECHR, ACHR, and the Rome Statute of the ICC for those international courts to award reparations is subsidiary to possible reparations under domestic law. Most importantly, reparation remains coupled to the specific case before the international court. Finally, reparation is placed within the discretion of the court. All these characteristics tend to speak more against than in favour of the ability to extrapolate a general individual claim to reparation from these provisions.[46]

6.3.3 *Measures of* National *Bodies Provided in Human Rights Treaties*

Already Article 8 of the 1948 Universal Declaration of Human Rights contains a human right to legal protection. According to this provision, "[e]veryone has the right to an effective remedy by the competent national tribunals for acts violating the fundamental rights granted him by the constitution or by law". This norm – which meanwhile has likely attained the status of customary law – refers to violations of basic rights granted under national law, but not to violations of the international human rights guaranteed in the Declaration itself.

6.3.3.1 Remedy

In contrast, human rights treaties typically provide that the States parties must create effective remedies in their national legal order for cases of violation of the rights enumerated in the treaty in question. The best-known examples of such provisions are Article 2(3) ICCPR,[47]

46 See Christian Tomuschat, *Human Rights between Idealism and Realism* (2nd ed. Oxford: Oxford University Press 2008), 364: "Given this strong discretionary element, it is hard to speak of a true right to financial compensation of aggrieved individuals . . .". But see ICC, TC I, Lubanga, Public Decision of 7 August 2012 (n. 40), para. 185: "The Chamber accepts that the right to reparations is a well-established and basic human right, . . .".

47 Article 2(3)(a) ICCPR: "Each State Party to the present Covenant undertakes to ensure that any person whose rights or freedoms as herein recognized are violated shall have an effective remedy . . ." The right to remedy under the ICCPR is a key guarantee of the treaty that is non-derogable even during states of emergency (UN Human Rights Committee, General Comment No. 29, States of Emergency (Article 4) of 31 August 2001, paragraph 14 (CCPR/C/21/Rev.1/Add.11).

Article 13 ECHR,[48] Article 25 ACHR,[49] Articles 12–14 of the UN Convention against Torture,[50] and Article 47 of the EU Charter of Fundamental Rights.[51] These provisions constitute *obligations directed at the States parties*. The States parties are called upon to enact adequate legal provisions in their national legal order. States are thus obligated under international law to provide for a remedy, first of all in a procedural sense by establishing (or modifying) supervisory mechanisms that receive complaints. Some, but not all, of the provisions require the States to institute judicial review; an independent complaints body with its own power to review and decide is sufficient under Article 13 ECHR. With respect to domestic remedies, some questions are still open. For instance, there is probably no general right under international conventions to have a national judgment revoked or annulled where that judgment solidified a human rights violation. Such a claim for annulment has, however, been introduced step-by-step as a claim under national law in many ECHR Member

[48] Article 13 ECHR: "Everyone whose rights and freedoms as set forth in this Convention are violated shall have an effective remedy before a national authority . . ." Article 13 ECHR is breached if the State investigation is seriously deficient or biased, if it is delayed, or if only a bogus prosecution takes place. See especially for unlawful detention as a violation of the human right to personal liberty, Article 5(5) ECHR; Article 9(5) ICCPR. Especially for the situation of miscarriage of justice, see Article 14(6) ICCPR; Article 10 ACHR. See also Article XX of the Agreement on Government Procurement of 15 April 1994, which requires an effective challenge procedure for suppliers who have not been awarded a contract (1915 UNTS 103).

[49] Article 25 ACHR, Right to Judicial Protection: "1. Everyone has the right to simple and prompt *recourse*, or any other effective recourse, to a competent court or tribunal for protection against acts that violate his fundamental rights *recognized by the constitution or laws of the state concerned or by this Convention*, even though such violation may have been committed by persons acting in the course of their official duties. 2. The States Parties undertake: a. to ensure that any person claiming such remedy shall have his rights determined by the competent authority provided for by the legal system of the state; b. to develop the possibilities of judicial remedy; and c. to ensure that the competent authorities shall enforce such remedies when granted." (italics mine). The obligation to make an effective remedy available is derived from Article 25 in conjunction with the general convention obligation to respect and ensure rights (Article 1(1) ACHR; see below n. 57).

[50] Articles 12–14 CAT (right to "impartial investigation", "right to complain to, and to have his case promptly and impartially examined" by the competent authorities, "enforceable right to fair and adequate compensation").

[51] Article 47 of the Charter of Fundamental Rights of the European Union of 7 December 2000: "Everyone whose rights and freedoms guaranteed by the law of the Union are violated has the right to an effective remedy before a tribunal in compliance with the conditions laid down in this Article . . .".

States through revisions of national codes of procedure.[52] Despite uncertainties at the level of detail, it is indisputable that the obligation to make a remedy available is one of the basic pillars of the rule of law.[53]

6.3.3.2 Reparation

Beyond this, some treaty norms stipulate not only a right to (procedural) remedy or complaint but also a right to (substantive) reparation or compensation. Examples of such provisions can be found in Article 6 of the UN Convention of the Elimination of Racial Discrimination[54] and Article 14 of the 1984 Convention against Torture.[55] More precisely, these provisions require the States parties to create (or modify) a secondary claim to reparation or compensation under national law.

With respect to treaties whose wording does not mention reparation, this second, substantive aspect (the obligation of reparation) has been partially developed by case law and read into the treaty provisions on remedy. According to the case law of the UN Human Rights Committee, for instance, the Convention guarantee of effective remedy under Article 2(3) ICCPR also entails the obligation to make reparations, including appropriate compensation.[56] The Inter-American Court of Human

[52] In Germany, § 359(6) of the Code of Criminal Procedure (StPO) provides that reopening of the criminal proceedings is admissible if the ECtHR has held that there has been a violation of the ECHR and of its protocols and when the judgment was based on that violation. Beyond this, the ECHR-related restitution action under § 580(8) of the Code of Civil Procedure (ZPO) was introduced effective 1 January 2007. This provision is referenced in paragraphs 79 of the Labour Court Act (ArbGG); 179 of the Social Court Act (SGG); 153 of the Code of Administrative Court Procedure (VwGO); 134 of the Code of Fiscal Court Procedure (FGO). According to these provisions, the restitution action takes place if the ECtHR has held that there has been a violation of the ECHR and the judgment was based on that violation.

[53] See Antônio Augusto Cançado Trindade, *The Access of Individuals to International Justice* (Oxford: Oxford University Press 2011), 56: "The relevance of the duty of States to provide adequate and effective domestic remedies should never be understated ... The right to a simple, prompt and effective remedy before the competent national tribunals or judges, enshrined in Article 25 of the ACHR, is a fundamental provision: it constitutes, ultimately, one of the basic pillars not only of the ACHR, but of the rule of law (État de droit) itself in a democratic society."

[54] Article 6 CERD: "the right to seek from such tribunals just and adequate reparation or satisfaction for any damage suffered as a result of such discrimination".

[55] Article 14(1) CAT: "an enforceable right to fair and adequate compensation".

[56] UN Human Rights Committee, General Recommendation No. 31 [80], Nature of the Obligations imposed on States Parties to the Covenant, of 26 May 2004, paragraph 16. See the following individual decisions of the UN Human Rights Committee: *José Vincente et al.* v. *Colombia*, No. 612/1995, Views of 19 August 1997, paragraph 10; *Jiménez Vaca*

Rights has derived a (conditional) obligation of reparation, including compensation, from the general "respect and ensure" treaty norm (Article 1(1) ACHR).[57] The ECtHR likewise interprets Article 13 ECHR such that when fundamental rights are violated – such as the right to life and protection from mistreatment (Articles 2 and 3 ECHR), especially in cases of deadly use of force by the police or a suspicious death in State custody – the provision set out in Article 13 requires the establishment of a remedy that in appropriate cases must lead to fair compensation (also for non-pecuniary damage).[58]

6.3.3.3 Preliminary Conclusion

As a result, remedies for victims of human rights violations are granted under international treaty law only if expressly provided for in the treaty or developed through judicial interpretation or expansion of the treaty. However, the principle of procedural remedy (in the sense of legal protection) does not clearly constitute an *individual claim* for access to a judicial or other effective review body, but rather prima facie an

v. *Colombia*, No. 859/1999, Views of 15 April 2002, paragraph 9; *Sathasivam* v. *Sri Lanka*, No. 1436/2005, Views of 8 July 2008, paragraph 8; *Amirov* v. *Russian Federation*, No. 1447/2006, Views of 2 April 2009, paragraph 13; *Felipe und Evelyne Pestaño* v. *The Philippines*, No. 1619/2007, Views of 23 March 2010, paragraph 9. See also UN Human Rights Committee, *Albert Wilson* v. *The Philippines*, No. 868/1999, Views of 11 November 2003, UN Doc. CCPR/C/79/D/868/1999 (2003), paragraph 9. The compensation awarded by the Committee in *Wilson* is based on part on the provision in Article 9 ICCPR, which expressly imposes a duty of compensation for unlawful detention. But the Committee appears to base the compensation on the breach of other violations of the Convention as well (Articles 7 and 10).

[57] Article 1(1) ACHR: "The States Parties to this Convention undertake to *respect* the rights and freedoms recognized herein and to *ensure* to all persons subject to their jurisdiction the free and full exercise of those rights and freedoms . . ." (italics mine). IACtHR, *Velásquez Rodriguez* v. *Honduras*, Ser. C No. 4 (1988), paragraph 166: "The second obligation of the States Parties is to 'ensure' the free and full exercise of the rights recognized by the Convention to every person subject to its jurisdiction. This obligation implies the duty of the States Parties to organize the governmental apparatus and, in general, all the structures through which public power is exercised, so that they are capable of juridically ensuring the free and full enjoyment of human rights. As a consequence of this obligation, the States must prevent, investigate and punish any violation of the rights recognized by the Convention and, moreover, if possible attempt to restore the right violated and *provide compensation as warranted for damages* resulting from the violation" (italics mine).

[58] See ECtHR, *Hugh Jordan* v. *UK*, No. 24746/94, 4 May 2001, paragraph 160 (case of a victim shot by the police). On compensation for non-pecuniary damage, see ECtHR, *McGlinchey* v. *UK*, No. 50390/99, Judgment of 29 April 2003, paragraph 63 (fatal collapse of a drug addict in custody).

obligation directed at States to implement the human rights treaties in question.

The treaty provisions mentioned above accordingly refer to *national* courts (or their functional equivalent) – not to international bodies – as monitoring bodies. (The exceptions found in Article 75 of the Rome Statute, Article 41 ECHR, and Article 63 ACHR have already been mentioned.) Because of the systemic role played by State courts in the decentralized international order when implementing international law, this can nevertheless be considered an international mechanism in functional terms. From the perspective of the duty of protection generated by human rights law, the obligation to assume responsibility for human rights violations (including by granting reparations) can also be seen as a special form of the positive duty of protection.[59]

6.3.4 Obligation *under Customary International Law to Provide Remedy and Reparation to Individuals?*

As a second legal basis for remedy and reparation (to be granted under national law), one might consider customary international law. In fact, more recent international case law and "soft" case law assume that States are *obligated* to grant remedy and reparation to individuals under certain circumstances. In some instances, but not always, this legal finding is clothed in the language of personal *claims* of the individual, so that the individuals themselves appear as holders of rights to reparation and compensation. In this section, that State practice will be recapitulated briefly. The question of whether the obligation assumed in that practice corresponds to an individual right to the provision of remedy and reparation – to be realized primarily by *national* institutions – will be discussed in the next section.

The International Commission of Inquiry on Darfur held that serious violations of human rights and international humanitarian law trigger State responsibility, which includes obligations not only towards other States parties but also towards victims. Victims in turn would have a corresponding international individual right to reparation (including compensation) against the injuring State for those crimes.[60]

[59] See Christine Evans, *The Right to Reparation in International Law for Victims of Armed Conflict* (Cambridge: Cambridge University Press 2012), 237.

[60] See Report of the International Commission of Inquiry on Darfur to the United Nations Secretary-General, pursuant to Security Council resolution 1564 of 18 September 2004, Report of 25 January 2005, paragraphs 593, 597, see also paragraph 601. "[T]here has now

A report issued by the judges of the Yugoslav Tribunal on the topic of "Victims' compensation and participation"[61] states: "The integration of human rights into State responsibility has removed the procedural limitation that victims of war could seek compensation only through their own Governments, and has extended the right to compensation to both nationals and aliens. There is a strong tendency towards providing compensation not only to States but also to individuals based on State responsibility."[62] The ICTY judges continue: "[T]here is a clear trend in international law to recognize a right of compensation in the victim to recover from the individual who caused his or her injury ... Although there is an *emerging* right of compensation, the law is much less developed on the mechanism by which the right can be exercised ... The question then is not so much is there a right to compensation but how can that right be implemented."[63]

In its 2006 report, the Commission of Inquiry on Lebanon established by the Human Rights Council recommended that the Human Rights Council "redress violations of humanitarian law and human rights". The Commission diagnosed the "serious lacunae" as regards the individual enforcement of claims to reparations and compensation. It recommended that the Human Rights Council create a commission competent to examine individual claims.[64] The report thus assumed that the affected individuals are entitled to secondary rights in a substantive sense.

In his 2004 report on transnational justice, the UN Secretary-General held: "States have an obligation to act not only against perpetrators, but also on behalf of victims, including through the provision of reparations."[65] And most importantly, the ICJ found in its advisory

emerged in international law a right of victims of serious human rights abuses (in particular, war crimes, crimes against humanity and genocide) to reparation (including compensation) for damage resulting from those crimes" (paragraph 597).

61 The report was prepared by the ICTY Rules Committee and adopted by the judges on 13 September 2000. See Victims' Compensation and Participation, Appendix to the Letter dated 2 November 2000 from the Secretary-General addressed to the President of the Security Council (UN Doc. S/2000/1063 (2000)).

62 *Ibid.*, Appendix 11–12, paragraphs 20–22.

63 *Ibid.*, paragraphs 20–22 (italics mine). The judges refer to the Declaration of Basic Principles of Justice for Victims of Crime adopted by the General Assembly in 1985, the 2006 Basic Principles of the General Assembly on Remedy (n. 27), and the Rome Statute.

64 Report of the Commission of Inquiry on Lebanon Pursuant to Human Rights Council Resolution S-2/1 (UN Doc. A/HRC/3/2) of 23 November 2006, paragraph 349(m)–(n).

65 Report of the Secretary-General on the Rule of Law and Transitional Justice in Conflict and Post Conflict Societies, S/2004/616, 23 August 2004, paragraph 54.

opinion on the Israeli wall that "Israel has the obligation to make reparation for the damage caused to all the natural or legal persons concerned".[66] Unfortunately, the Court did not give further reasons for this finding.

In any event, the obligation to grant procedural remedy can plausibly be construed as the correlate to the traditional requirement of "local remedies" under the international law governing aliens. An obligation of the state under customary international law to make local remedies available in the event of human rights violations is functionally necessary for the following reason: If human rights were not enforceable in the courts of the injuring State, then the desirable effect of discharging international bodies would not be achieved, and the individual would loose one judicial level. The requirement that the injured individual exhaust domestic legal remedies in the injuring State should thus be an obligation on the State to make such legal remedies available, because otherwise the "local remedies" principle would be devoid of function (for details, see Chapter 15, pp. 480–83). As a result, an obligation under customary law to provide procedural remedies appears to emerge.

A different question, however, is the substantive obligation of reparation, such as in the form of monetary compensation. It is currently an open question whether a general obligation under customary international law to provide compensation to individuals for serious violations of human rights and international humanitarian law can be assumed.[67] Moreover, the possible claim to procedural remedy under customary law, derived from the principle of local remedies, cannot be enforced by the individual himself or herself using international mechanisms.

6.3.5 *Towards a Direct International Individual Right to Remedy and Reparation?*

The norms on remedy mentioned in the preceding section would resemble the usual domestic (sometimes constitutional) norms on

[66] ICJ, *Legal Consequences of the Construction of a Wall in the Occupied Palestinian Territory*, Advisory Opinion of 9 July 2004, ICJ Reports 2004, paragraph 152.

[67] For arguments against the existence of customary international law in this regard, see Tomuschat, *Human Rights* 2008, 358. For a different opinion, cf. Ferstman/Goetz/Stephens, Introduction, in: Ferstman/Goetz/Stephens et al., *Reparations for Victims* 2009, 7: "It is recognised that there is already a sound legal basis for the right to reparation . . ." *Ibid.*, 8: "reparation is understood as a right of victims, not only as an inter-state prerogative or an act of compassion or charity."

access to a court only if they embodied not only an "objective" *obligation* of States to grant a remedy but also a personal ("subjective") *right* under international law to receive it. The putative right to a remedy would have to be implemented by the national courts. The question whether such a right exists in international law is not made entirely clear in the practice of the human rights bodies discussed earlier, but the pertinent decisions do not seem to negate it either.[68]

I submit that the provisions mentioned above to provide remedy and make reparation (e.g., Article 2(3) ICCPR, Article 13 ECHR, Article 25 ACHR, Articles 12–14 of the UN CAT, and Article 47 of the EU Charter of Fundamental Rights) can indeed be interpreted as *international rights* of the victims against the injuring States. In terms of their wording and structure, they are suitable for interpretation as personal claims and not only as principles of objective law. They are suitable for direct application (i.e., for being invoked before national courts and authorities). This understanding also makes sense in terms of their protective purpose. It would be largely meaningless to require States to provide monitoring bodies and the possibility of reparation if individuals were unable to invoke those guarantees before national courts.[69]

A different question is whether the individual claim for remedy can be read more strongly as an individual right of punishment. This has to be answered in the negative, given that modern criminal law is characterized by the movement of the national and international right of punishment into the domain of objective law (see Chapter 9).

The intrinsic justification for a genuine international (i.e., based on treaties and perhaps even customary law) *individual right* to a remedy (and even reparation) is the status of the individual as a normative point of reference for international law. This argument is accepted within the framework of EU law. In EU law, which is further developed than general international law, no individual secondary right to compensation under

[68] See also the General Comment of the Committee against Torture on the general obligation to implement Article 2 CAT: In the view of the Committee, Article 2 CAT obligates every State party to ensure within its legal system that victims of torture are provided with remedies (Committee against Torture, General Comment No. 2: Implementation of article 2 by States Parties (UN Doc. CAT/C/GC/2/CRP.1/Rev. 4 of 24 January 2008, paragraph 18)).

[69] See Riccardo Pisillo Mazzeschi, International Obligations for Reparation Claims?, in: Albrecht Randelzhofer/Christian Tomuschat (eds), *State Responsibility and the Individual: Reparation in Instances of Grave Violations of Human Rights* (The Hague: Martinus Nijhoff 1999), 149–172 (163 and 165).

Union law has been set out in treaties in the event of violation of Union law by a Member State. Such a right has been created by case law, however.[70] The main argument for recognizing such a genuine claim for compensation under Union law was the finding that not only Member States but also individuals are subjects of the EU's "own legal system".[71] Realization of the right to compensation under Union law requires to involve domestic law. Under Union law, the Member States are obliged to modify their domestic liability in such a way that individuals can be compensated.

In general international law, the individual is principally recognized as a subject of international law, albeit – according to the traditional view – not on equal terms with the State.[72] In contrast, this study supports the thesis that the overall development of recent international law suggests that the individual should be recognized as the primary subject of international law in normative terms (see Chapter 13). While this thesis cannot be used to "derive" an individual claim for remedy and reparation in a strict sense without circular reasoning, the overall development in other areas of international law must be taken into account when interpreting treaty provisions on remedy in accordance with Article 31(3)(c) VCLT as part of the applicable "relevant rules of international law". This speaks in favour of an "individualized" interpretation of these norms.

Another question concerns the legal quality of the claims for remedy and reparation. Are they *human rights* guarantees or claims under ordinary law? Many consider remedy and reparation to be correlates of the human rights concerned.[73] Others deem the invocation of reparation to be a "radical affirmation of human rights" because they extend the universality claim of human rights backwards in time.[74] From this perspective, it would make sense to grant the quality of human rights

[70] See ECJ, Cases C-6/90 and C-9/90, *Francovich* [1991] ECR I-5357, paragraphs 31–46; ECJ, Cases C-46/93 and C-48/93, *Brasserie du Pêcheur* [1996] ECR I-1029, paragraphs 20–23.

[71] See the argument for the existence of a claim for compensation under Union law in ECJ, *Francovic* (n. 70), paragraph 31. On the legal personality of the individual in the EU legal order, see the standing case law of the ECJ since *Van Gend & Loos*. Article I-1 of the Treaty establishing a Constitution for Europe of 29 October 2004, which never entered into force, clearly expressed the position of citizens as subjects alongside States: "Reflecting the will of the citizens and States of Europe to build a common future, this Constitution establishes the European Union . . ." (OJ 2004 C 310/1).

[72] See Chapter 3. [73] See, e.g., Evans, *Right to Reparation* 2012, 42 and 126.

[74] See George Ulrich, Introduction: Human Rights with a View to History, in: George Ulrich/Louise Krabbe Boserup (eds), *Reparations: Redressing Past Wrongs, Human Rights in Development Yearbook 2001* (Dordrecht: Kluwer 2003), 1–10 (5).

to claims for remedy and reparation. But at the same time, reparation is a substantive secondary obligation from the perspective of the law of international responsibility, belonging to the content of State responsibility (see the provision in Article 31 of the ILC Articles, which is not directly applicable to individual claims).

The individual claim to remedy (and even reparation) postulated here may in part be based on international treaties and possibly even customary law, but it is intended to be realized using the resources of national law. This claim is implemented within the national justice system. When States refuse to provide remedy and reparation by creating a new basis for the rights and new procedures in national law, they violate the relevant human rights treaties and possibly customary international law as well. Individuals may contest that refusal by using the complaints mechanisms afforded by the regime in question. Such complaints may aim to remedy systemic deficits in the domestic legal order.

6.4 Rationale and Necessity of Individual Rights Arising from International Responsibility

Historical, systematic, and teleological arguments can be cited to support the view of the ILC, the ICTY judges, the ICJ, and the UN General Assembly that individuals can be holders of international rights arising from State responsibility, especially the claims for remedy and reparation (which would be realized primarily by the national bodies). Because the secondary legal claims are a direct consequence of the violation of a primary obligation of conduct, they should normally be assigned to the same actor to whom the primary duty was owed. In purely formal terms, this pattern should also apply where the holder of the infringed right is an individual.[75]

Any deviation from the parallelism of the holders of primary rights and secondary rights, which should reasonably be expected, would have to be specially justified. In the situation where the holder of the primary right is not a State but an individual, the deviation can be justified only historically. The separation of the ownership of claims (between the individual as the holder of the primary right and the home State as the holder of the secondary right) is a relict from the historical period when the individual was mediated completely by the State. Anyone denying

[75] Oliver Dörr speaks of an "immanent parallelism *ratione personae* of both legal relationships" (Dörr, Völkerrechtliche Deliktsansprüche Privater 2013, 780; translation mine).

individual ownership of claims at the secondary level is adhering to the mediation of the individual (only) at the secondary level.

The assumption of exclusive ownership of the claim by the State when norms protecting individuals are violated (under the law governing aliens) was the basis of diplomatic protection. In an era before human rights, violations of the law on aliens could be construed as a breach of international law only by way of the fiction of State rights deemed violated in the person of the State's national.[76] By separating the owners of the primary and the secondary claim, a doctrinal concept from the law on aliens and diplomatic protection is now being preserved, even if only at the level of secondary law. What is crucial, however, is that in the context of the law on aliens, the individual is injured by a *foreign* State. The same is true of the classic situation of the violation of international humanitarian norms. Also in international armed conflict, States are opposing each other, and the breaches of the law are typically committed by a foreign State, i.e., the enemy. Only in this situation is it conceivable to assign the secondary claim to the home State of the injured individual, i.e., to separate ownership of the primary and the secondary right.

In the field of human rights and non-international armed conflict, in contrast, the individual is typically injured by his or her *own* State. This means that mediation must be ruled out at the level of both primary law and secondary law. If the home State were seen simultaneously as the violator of the right and as the holder of the secondary claim, the secondary claim would be meaningless.[77] This means the separation approach is not practicable at least in this situation, unless the secondary claim is de facto destroyed. But preserving the separation approach only for individual claims against *other* international legal subjects (not for claims against the home State) in turn leads to a discontinuity in the system. It is precisely the essence of human rights that they are independent of citizenship and in principle can be asserted against both foreign States and the home State. What should determine the individual ownership of the secondary claims should therefore not be the addressee (the foreign State or the home State), but rather primarily the quality and ownership of the primary claims.

[76] On diplomatic protection, see Chapter 12.

[77] See Moritz von Unger, *Menschenrechte als transnationales Privatrecht* (Berlin: Duncker & Humblot 2008), 101: "Situating the mediation of the individual under secondary law – as it arises from the international law on aliens – within a human rights framework distorts the rationale of both systems of protection" (translation mine).

In addition to this systematic argument, teleological considerations are crucial. As an argument against convergence and in favour of preserving the purely inter-State character of international responsibility, it has been said that recognizing individuals as holders of secondary rights would trigger a flood of legal action. The resources lacking in many countries for dealing with mass claims would destabilize the respondent States and thus pose a threat to international peace. This would mean that the admissibility of individual international secondary claims would be inadvisable from the standpoint of legal policy.[78] This argument presupposes that such complaints would be mass phenomena involving weak States. But this is often the case for violations of individual rights. The special case of violations of international humanitarian law will be treated separately (see Chapter 7).

Full convergence of primary and secondary ownership of claims arising from norms protecting individuals, in contrast, is supported by the fact that referring to the home State for the purpose of realizing secondary claims incapacitates individuals and subjects them to political considerations. The individual protection intended by a primary norm would be weakened if the secondary norm were not also construed as generating an individual right, i.e., as a claim. In other words, the emancipation of the individual would be incomplete if it did not continue at the level of secondary law. When an international norm makes the individual the addressee (beneficiary) of the primary obligation, the individual must as a matter of consistency be recognized as the owner of the secondary claims. This convergence arises from the principles of autonomy and human dignity as the relevant normative points of reference for contemporary international law. The current system of international law essentially not only aims to *protect* an individual (in a paternalistic way) as an object of such protection but rather recognizes the human being as an *agent* or subject.[79]

[78] See Christian Tomuschat, Individual Reparation Claims in Instances of Grave Human Rights Violations: The Position under General International Law, in: Randelzhofer/ Tomuschat, *State Responsibility* 1999, 1–25 (25).

[79] In support of convergence, see Dörr, Völkerrechtliche Deliktsansprüche Privater 2013, 774: "The legal core of human rights protection is constituted by the normative orientation of international rules toward the individuals they cover as addressees of their fulfilment, and by the consequences of that orientation in the event of breach: Individual secondary claims are thus the touchstone in terms of the international law of responsibility for how seriously and consistently the international community is pursuing the idea of international human rights protection and is realizing that idea in its legal order" (translation mine).

As a German court held in a case involving a violation of international humanitarian law, "the fundamental denial of an individual's own claim for suspension of the relevant detention norm and the referral to the channel of diplomatic protection . . . would often render the individual's claim for compliance with international humanitarian law meaningless, since the breach would remain without penalty. The defeated State, especially, will often not have any real possibility and will also not be willing to effectively claim violations of international humanitarian law perpetrated against its nationals vis-à-vis the victorious State by way of diplomatic protection."[80] The same is true of weak or failed States, i.e., especially for a typical constellation in armed conflict. These States are likewise often unable or unwilling to assert secondary claims for the benefit of individuals at the international level. Finally, an extreme case is the special situation where there is no State, a situation in which individuals are entirely without protection when they are not accorded their own secondary claims. This is presumably why the ICJ advisory opinion concerning the Israeli wall referred to individuals as holders of the claims,[81] because – given Palestine's lack of statehood – there was no State to act on behalf of the victims.

These historical, systematic, and teleological considerations can be used to justify that international State responsibility can and should go beyond mere *inter-State* responsibility. When primary norms granting individuals international rights (i.e., human rights and all other individual rights) are breached, a relationship of responsibility arises between the injuring State and the individual. This would also mean that individuals own the secondary rights independently of their citizenship, against both third States and their home State.

6.5 Conclusion

In conclusion, current general international law permits individual secondary rights held by individuals arising from State responsibility. This legal possibility results from the interplay between the international law

[80] As found by the appellate court in the *Varvarin* case, Higher Regional Court of Cologne, *Neue Juristische Wochenschrift* 58 (2005), 2860 et seq. (translation mine). However, the Federal Court of Justice did not follow this argument in BGH (III ZR 190/05), Judgment of 2 November 2006) (see above n. 13).

[81] See above n. 66.

of international responsibility, on the one side, and human rights protection and the law of armed conflict, on the other.[82]

In principle, a convergence of ownership of primary and secondary rights should be assumed. It is an open question, however, whether beyond the minimum requirement of individual entitlement at the primary level, other procedural or substantive conditions must be met in order to trigger a secondary claim of an individual. Oliver Dörr believes it is "conceivable that the law of international responsibility will develop further conditions for asserting secondary claims of individuals, not only of a procedural but indeed also of a substantive legal nature". For instance, a "sufficiently qualified" breach of protective norms might be demanded.[83]

This chapter has also supported the view that the content of this secondary claim is directed at procedural remedies that must be provided primarily by national bodies. The State obligation to provide remedies can be seen as a correlate of the local remedies principle. International individual claims for damages or compensation may arise from special treaty provisions, some of which have been further developed in a dynamic way by international bodies. It is currently an open question whether beyond this a claim for compensation under customary international law exists in the event of gross violations of human rights and international humanitarian norms.

Beyond the core of gross violations, the legal status of the individual is even weaker. Under current international law, there is (still) no international individual right to compensation in the event of violations of other norms of international humanitarian law that protect and entitle individuals, but such claims would be advisable *de lege ferenda* (see Chapter 7). An international individual claim for the prosecution or even punishment of perpetrators does not exist, but the general ensure-and-respect clauses of the human rights treaties and the Geneva Conventions on international humanitarian law do give rise to obligations of conduct, which may in extreme cases amount to an obligation to prosecute without guaranteeing punishment (see Chapter 9).

[82] See for an analysis of this interplay Giulio Bartolini, *Riparazione per violazione dei diritti umani e ordinamento* internazionale (Napoli: Jovene Editore 2009), arguing that the interplay of both bodies of law results in creating a "binary" relationship between the violator State and the victims, so that these enjoy an "autonomous right to reparation" (translation mine).

[83] Dörr, Völkerrechtliche Deliktsansprüche Privater, 2013, 780–781 (translation mine).

7

Individual Rights and Duties in the Law of Armed Conflict

International individual rights in the law of armed conflict (used here synonymously: international humanitarian law, IHL) may arise at various levels of the law. Firstly, there are potential claims for compliance with precepts and prohibitions (level of primary law). Secondly, claims may exist that arise from the relationship of responsibility in the event of a breach of a primary norm (level of secondary law). Finally, individuals have an obligation to observe the norms of international humanitarian law.

7.1 Individual Rights at the Primary Level

The first question concerns potential individual rights to compliance with the law of armed conflict at the level of primary law. Numerous precepts and prohibitions in the four Geneva Conventions, their two Additional Protocols, and parallel customary international law require the protection of individuals. Already, the term used to describe this area of the law or significant parts thereof, "international humanitarian law", draws attention to its main purpose: The provisions are intended to protect human beings. According to the traditional view, individuals were beneficiaries but not holders of claims; they were objects of protection but not subjects. The relevant treaty provisions were interpreted as giving rise to obligations *between States*, the fulfilment of which was owed only to the other contracting States.

In fact, most of the provisions in the Geneva Conventions and Additional Protocol I (AP I) expressly stipulate State obligations and do not clothe them in the language of rights. The provisions are generally formulated as prohibitions addressed to the State or as State duties of protection without a reference to the "rights" of protected persons. Customary international law as included in the ICRC compilation also appears *prima facie* to define prohibitions and precepts or standards of treatment but not individual rights. An example of a norm formulated as objective law is Common Article 3 of the Geneva Conventions: "Persons taking no active part in the hostilities ... *shall in all circumstances be treated humanely*, without any adverse distinction founded on race, colour, religion or faith, sex, birth or wealth, or any other similar criteria. To this end, the following acts are and shall remain *prohibited* at any time and in any place whatsoever with respect to the above-mentioned persons: ..." Even the important list of fundamental guarantees set out in Article 75 of AP I is formulated as protection requirements and prohibitions, not as rights.

In recent literature, René Provost and Kate Parlett represent the view that the law of armed conflict merely provides standards for the treatment of individuals and consists solely of obligations between States but does not assign claims to individuals.[1] This purely objective conception of the law of armed conflict appears implausible, however, in light of the wording, genesis, and context of the provisions. Some of the norms in the existing treaties expressly refer to the "rights", "claims", "entitlements", "liberty", or "guarantees" in regard to the individual. This is true of the Hague Regulations respecting the Laws and Customs of War on Land,[2] the Third Geneva Convention relative to the Treatment of Prisoners of War (GC III),[3] the Fourth Geneva Convention relative to the Protection of Civilian Persons in Time of War (GC IV),[4] the Protocol Additional to the Geneva Conventions relating to the Protection of Victims of International Armed Conflicts

[1] See René Provost, *International Human Rights and Humanitarian Law* (Cambridge: Cambridge University Press 2002), 27–34 (116). *Ibid.*, 33: "Protection given to individuals thus would not be in the nature of rights, either for the state or the individual, but more in the nature of standards of treatment." Kate Parlett, *The Individual in the International Legal System* (Cambridge: Cambridge University Press 2011), 176–228. *Ibid.*, 224: "[T]he normative framework of international law applicable in international armed conflict is one which establishes standards of treatment for individuals rather than creating direct rights for individuals."

[2] Article 3, Article 12, Article 13, Article 18, Article 23(1)(h), Article 32, and Article 46(1) of the Annex to Hague Convention (IV) respecting the Law and Customs of War on Land of 1907 (205 CTS 277). The Annex consists of the regulations respecting the laws and customs of war on land.

[3] Article 6(1), Article 7, Article 14(1), Article 50(2), Article 54(2), Article 78(1) and (2), Article 84(2), Article 96(4), Article 105(1), Article 106, Article 113(1), Article 129(4), and Article 130 of GC III.

[4] Article 5(3), Article 7(1), Article 8, Article 27(1), Article 35(1) and (2), Article 38, Article 40(4), Article 43(1), Article 48, Article 52(1), Article 72(1), Article 73, Article 75(1), Article 76(3), (6), and (7), Article 78(2), Article 80, Article 101(1) and (2), Article 146(4) and Article 147 of GC IV.

(AP I of 1977),[5] and the Protocol Additional to the Geneva Conventions relating to the Protection of Victims of Non-International Armed Conflicts (AP II of 1977).[6]

7.1.1 Non-renunciation Clauses and Saving Clauses as Indicators of Individual Rights

An important indicator of the contracting parties' intention to lay down individual rights in these texts is provided by two types of non-disposal clauses. Firstly, each of the four Geneva Conventions contains a non-renunciation clause.[7] Convention (III) relative to the Treatment of Prisoners of War states, for example: "Prisoners of war may in no circumstances renounce ... *the rights secured to them* by the present Convention ...".[8] According to Article 11 of AP I, no scientific experiments may be conducted or organs removed or similar acts performed even with the consent of the person concerned. The wording of these non-renunciation clauses indicates that rights are granted to or conferred on the individual directly by the conventions themselves, not only once domestic law has been enacted by the contracting parties.[9] It has been pointed out that, normally, the power to renounce legal positions shows that these legal positions belong to the person holding that power,

[5] Article 11(5) ("right" to refuse surgical operation), Article 32 ("right" of families), Article 44(2), (5), and (6) ("rights" of combatants and prisoners of war), Article 45 ("claim" to the status of prisoner of war), Article 56(3) ("entitlement" of the civilian population to protection), Article 79(2) ("right" of journalists), and Article 85(4)(e) ("rights" of fair and regular trial) of AP I.

[6] Article 4(1), Article 5(1)(e), Article 6(2)(a) and (e), and Article 6(3) of AP II.

[7] On the parallel question in international investment protection law whether an investor's waiver of ICSID proceedings is permissible, see Chapter 10, pp. 324–28.

[8] Article 7 of GC III (italics mine). According to Article 8 of Convention (IV) relative to the Protection of Civilian Persons in Time of War, "Protected persons may in no circumstances renounce in part or in entirety the *rights secured to them* by the present Convention, and by the special agreements referred to in the foregoing Article, if such there be" (italics mine). Similarly, see Article 7 of GC I, Article 7 of GC II.

[9] Kate Parlett, in contrast, assumes that the wording of the non-renunciation clause ("the rights secured to them by the present Convention") leaves open the possibility that these rights are to be conferred only by national law (Parlett, *Individual*, 2011, 184). This reading is not compatible with the official German translation: "Die geschützten Personen können in keinem Falle, weder teilweise noch vollständig, auf die Rechte verzichten, die ihnen das vorliegende Abkommen und gegebenenfalls die im vorhergehenden Artikel genannten besonderen Vereinbarungen *einräumen*" (italics mine). Also, Jean Pictet (ed.), *Commentary of the Geneva Conventions of 12 August 1949*, Vol. I Geneva Convention I for the Amelioration of the Condition of the Wounded and Sick in Armed Forces in the Field (Geneva: ICRC 1952), 82 refers to "secure" as the "still stronger term" than "confer".

belonging in the form of rights.[10] This apt observation does not permit the converse argument, however. The non-renunciation defined in the conventions does not mean that individual rights are not at stake here. The purpose of granting protected persons their own rights was to remove those persons from the interference and sovereignty of their home States but not to let the affected persons decide themselves whether the provisions should be applied or not.[11] Typically, the affected persons – such as prisoners of war – are put under pressure by the custodial States to renounce their rights. The non-disposal rule was intended precisely to prevent this type of extortion and to take any incentive away from the States to exercise coercion. In light of the typical plight of protected persons (as injured persons or prisoners in the hands of the enemy), in which free decision-making is unlikely, the recognition of the affected persons' power of disposal over their rights would create only a "pseudo-liberté".[12] Pictet says of the non-renunciation clause in Convention (IV) relative to the Protection of Civilian Persons that it is "of the greatest assistance to all protected persons. It allows them to claim the protection of the Convention, not as a privilege, but as a right . . .".[13]

Moreover, the non-renunciation clauses signal that these rights are of the utmost importance. The legal construction is similar to that of human rights. In that context, the talk of "inalienable" human rights underscores precisely this importance and by no means implies that human rights do not belong to individuals as the holders of those rights. The non-disposability of the protective norms can thus be read as an indication of the high rank of the protected rights. This reading is best suited to the intention of the treaty makers to "safeguard the dignity of the human person".[14]

The second indicator of individual rights is found in the prohibitions of all special agreements (saving clauses) that are contained in each of the

[10] See Parlett, *Individual*, 2011, 185.

[11] See René-Jean Wilhelm, Le caractère des droits accordés à l'individu dans les Conventions de Genève, *Revue international de la Croix-Rouge* 32 (1950), 561–590 (587).

[12] Wilhelm, Le caractère des droits accordés 1950, 587.

[13] Jean Pictet (ed.), *Commentary on the Geneva Conventions of 12 August 1949*, Vol. IV, Geneva Convention IV Relative to the Protection of Civilian Persons (Geneva: ICRC 1958), 79. Similarly, see Pictet, *Commentary Geneva Conventions* Vol. I 1952, 84 on GC I on wounded and sick persons.

[14] Pictet, *Commentary on the Geneva Conventions* Vol. I 1952, 82, also 81: "The initiators of the 1864 and following Conventions wished to safeguard the dignity of the human person, in the profound conviction that imprescriptible and inviolable rights were attached to it even when hostilities were at their height."

conventions. (On the question of derogation by States, see pp. 213–16). Article 6 of Convention (I) for the Amelioration of the Condition of the Wounded and Sick in Armed Forces in the Field states: "No special agreement shall adversely affect the situation of the wounded and sick, of members of the medical personnel or of chaplains, as defined by the present Convention, nor restrict the rights which it confers upon them."[15] According to Article 6 of Convention (III) relative to the Treatment of Prisoners of War, "No special agreement [by the High Contracting Parties] shall adversely affect the situation of prisoners of war . . . nor restrict the *rights* which it confers upon them." The provision in Article 7 of Convention (IV) relative to the Protection of Civilian Persons in Time of War states: "No special agreement shall adversely affect the situation of protected persons, as defined by the present Convention, nor restrict the *rights* which *it* confers upon them."[16] The wording of the latter saving clause again indicates that rights are conferred on individuals, and again directly by the international agreement itself.

7.1.2 Negotiating History

The negotiating history of the Geneva Conventions suggests that their provisions should not be thought of solely as objective norms of protection. Rather, it indicates that certain provisions should be interpreted so as to generate individual rights.[17] At the Diplomatic Conference in 1949, the early proposal in regard to the non-renunciation clause – "the rights which it stipulates on their behalf" – was abandoned in favour of the formulation "the rights which it confers upon them".[18] This change can be read as a weak indication of the intention to provide individual ownership of the claim: These are not simply norms "on behalf of" or in the interest of the protected persons, but rather they are rights that are "conferred". The Conference was of the view that the phrase "on their behalf" would have implied only "an 'indirect' benefit resulting from the attitude prescribed to the States". For this reason, the Diplomatic Conference preferred the formulation previously proposed by the

15 Article 6, sentence 2 of GC I. Similarly, see Article 6 of GC II.

16 Italics mine.

17 But cf. Parlett, *Individual*, 2011, 185 and other references, believing that the negotiating history is not very fruitful.

18 Final Record of the Diplomatic Conference of Geneva of 1949 (New York: William S. Hein & Co. 2004), Vol. II, Sec. B, 76 (Special Committee, Joint Committee, 23rd meeting).

ICRC ("confers upon them"), according to the authoritative Pictet commentary on the Geneva Conventions.[19]

At the same time, Pictet shows that this "individualization" of the law of armed conflict, i.e., the charging of precepts and prohibitions with individual claims, represented a novelty after the Second World War. In regard to Convention (III) Relative to the Treatment of Prisoners of War, Pictet notes: "At the outset, however, the treatment which belligerents were required to accord to persons referred to in the Convention was not presented, nor indeed clearly conceived as constituting a body of 'rights' to which they were automatically entitled . . .: It was not . . . until the Convention of 1949 (in particular in Articles 6 and 7[20]) that the existence of 'rights' conferred on prisoners of war was affirmed."[21]

Pictet attributes the conscious and deliberate focus on individual rights to the influence of the recognition of international human rights.[22] This recognition manifests the view that people are protected better by the conferral of individual rights than by the mere stipulation of objective duties of protection.

7.1.3 *Objections*

Kate Parlett presents three arguments against the rights-based ("subjectivist") view and in favour of an understanding of the law of armed conflict based purely on duties based on "objective" law (as opposed to "subjective" rights): Firstly, the "objective" interpretation is easier to reconcile with the non-renunciation clauses and the prohibition of special agreements because these types of clauses prohibit both individuals and States from deviating from the standards. Secondly, the "objective" interpretation is compatible with a legal framework in which the individuals do not have any legal or even any factual possibility to enforce their rights.[23] And finally, according to Parlett, the purely objective legal construction is not necessarily less effective for the protection of the individual.[24] All three considerations are comprehensible but not

[19] Pictet, *Commentary on the Geneva Conventions* Vol. I 1952, 82–83.

[20] The non-renunciation clause and the prohibition of special agreements.

[21] Jean Pictet (ed.), *Commentary on the Geneva Conventions of 12 August 1949*, Vol. III, Geneva Convention III Relative to the Treatment of Prisoners of War (Geneva: ICRC 1960), 91 (footnote added).

[22] Pictet, *Commentary on the Geneva Conventions* Vol. I 1952, 83, stating the formulation was influenced by "the concomitant trends of doctrine, which also led to the universal proclamation of Human Rights".

[23] Parlett, *Individual*, 2011, 187. [24] See *ibid.*, 224, 225, and 228.

compelling. As already discussed, the non-renunciation clauses are intended to move the guarantees into the vicinity of human rights, i.e., the individual rights *par excellence*. The prohibitions of deviations by way of agreements between States are ambivalent: On the one hand, they imply that certain guarantees are subject to State disposition; but they also withdraw other guarantees from the power of the States. If the States are not the obligees of the owed duties of protection, then individuals must be the obligees. The problem of the lack of international procedural mechanisms available to the individuals for the purpose of enforcing their rights does not diminish the substantive legal content of these rights (on the distinction between the substantive and procedural dimensions, see Chapter 3, pp. 44–50). Moreover, individuals can avail themselves of the national legal process to enforce their rights (see pp. 217–20).

Finally, Parlett's thesis – that protection purely under objective law (treaty obligations owed solely to other States parties) would be just as effective as the conferral of rights – touches on the rationale for granting individual rights. Individual rights may be asserted by the individual *irrespective of the view the individual's home State takes on this point.* Precisely that point had been addressed by the ICRC at the Preliminary Conference convened in 1946 to prepare a revision of the Geneva Conventions: "[T]he Commission unanimously recommended that the rights conferred by the Convention on prisoners of war should have a personal and intangible character, allowing the latter to claim them irrespective of the attitude adopted by their home country."[25] In principle, we assume that individual rights have an *emancipatory potential* that is best suited to the moral status of the individual and also is able to provide argumentative support for efforts to improve their practical enforceability (see pp. 536–41). Treating the human being as an object in the law of armed conflict – a relict of the nineteenth century – would be counterproductive here.

7.1.4 Interim Conclusion

While the wording and negotiating history of the current provisions of the law of international armed conflict permit both conceptions (the

[25] International Committee of the Red Cross, *Report on the Work of the Preliminary Conference of National Red Cross Societies for the Study of the Conventions and of Various Problems Relative to the Red Cross* (Geneva, July 26–August 3, 1946) (Geneva 1947), 71. The "Commission" was one of the three Conference committees; in this context, it gave its opinion on the planned revised agreement on prisoners of war.

conception of purely objective law and the individualistic conception), they tend to speak in favour of an individualistic reading. There are many reasons for interpreting (some) provisions of the war of armed conflict such that the obligations set out therein are owed not (only) to other States, but (also) *directly to individuals* and correspondingly contain individual rights for their fulfilment.[26] "Thereby, all happens as if the 'protected persons' were themselves 'subjects' of international law."[27] "The conventions of 1949, once more, reinforce the position and the rights of the 'protected persons', in short, of the individual."[28] A more recent case law of national courts appears to assume virtually unanimously that numerous provisions of the Geneva Conventions and their Additional Protocols stipulate individual rights. For instance, the Federal Constitutional Court of Germany speaks of the "primary legal claim of the affected person to compliance with the prohibitions of international humanitarian law".[29]

Whether a specific precept or prohibition in the law of armed conflict actually generates individual rights must be determined in each case by interpreting the provisions (or clarifying the content of the underlying norm of customary law). With respect to these provisions, individuals have a corresponding individual right to protection and accordingly to compliance with these primary norms of international humanitarian law that protect individuals. In other words, there is a primary legal relationship between the obligor and the entitled individual. The State claim for compliance with international humanitarian law can, theoretically, persist alongside the individual claim. The side of the addressee – i.e., the question of whether obligors under international humanitarian law may be (in addition to States) individuals or armed groups – will be discussed at pp. 220–31. The individual entitlement at the primary level does not,

[26] In lieu of many others, see Marco Sassòli, State Responsibility for Violations of International Humanitarian Law, *International Review of the Red Cross* 84 (2002), 401–434 (419); Oliver Dörr, Völkerrechtliche Deliktsansprüche Privater – auf der Grundlage und in den Grenzen einer völkerrechtlichen Schutznormlehre, in: Martin Breuer/Astrid Epiney/Andreas Haratsch/Stefanie Schmahl/Norman Weiß (eds), *Der Staat im Recht: Festschrift Eckart Klein zum 70. Geburtstag* (Berlin: Duncker & Humblot 2013), 765–782 (779).

[27] Wilhelm, Le caractère des droits accordés 1950, 562 (translation by the author).

[28] *Ibid.*, 585 (translation by the author).

[29] BVerfGE 112, 1 et seq., paragraph 38 (2004; translation mine) – *italienische Militärinternierte.* Leaving the question open, see BGHZ 169, 348 ff. (III ZR 190/05), Judgment of 2 November 2006 – *Varvarin*, paragraph 15. For more details on the case law, see pp. 204–07.

however, prejudice the ownership of the claim at the secondary level. This is the subject of the following section.

7.2 Secondary Rights of Individuals *de lege lata*

The main discussion regarding the status of the individual in international humanitarian law is concerned with secondary claims. At issue is the content of State responsibility triggered by the violation of primary norms of international humanitarian law. The basic problem of the possibility of individual secondary claims in the context of the ILC Articles on State Responsibility and the discussion of remedy and reparation are dealt with in Chapter 6. Because of the thematic link, secondary claims arising specifically from violations of international humanitarian law and their enforcement will be discussed in this chapter. Also, in this area of the law, the aspect we are most interested in is the obligation to grant (monetary) compensation.[30] If the individual were recognized as the holder of a secondary claim to compensation, this would entail an "'individualization' of the financial settlement of armed hostilities".[31]

It is now recognized that an international individual claim to compensation under secondary law would not be ruled out already by the exclusivity of State claims to reparation. The international principle of the "exclusivity of peace treaty provisions" on war reparations (and perhaps other settlement claims not subject to reparation law), which was still often assumed in the wake of the Second World War, does not exist (or no longer exists). A parallelism of claims, i.e., an international entitlement of individuals *alongside* States, is also possible at the secondary level.[32]

The 2006 Resolution of the General Assembly on the Right to a Remedy and Reparation[33] refers to "gross violations of international

[30] See, e.g., Philipp Stammler, *Der Anspruch von Kriegsopfern auf Schadensersatz* (Berlin: Duncker & Humblot 2009).

[31] Niclas von Woedtke, *Die Verantwortlichkeit Deutschlands für seine Streitkräfte im Auslandseinsatz und die sich daraus ergebenden Schadensersatzansprüche von Einzelpersonen als Opfer deutscher Militärhandlungen* (Berlin: Duncker & Humblot 2010), 300.

[32] See BVerfGE 94, 315 et seq. (1996) – *jüdische Zwangsarbeiter*. This decision concerns only individual claims for payment under German *national* law. The Federal Constitutional Court assumed that international law does not forbid a parallelism with the claims between States under international law.

[33] Basic Principles and Guidelines on the Right to a Remedy and Reparation for Victims of Gross Violations of International Human Rights Law and Serious Violations of International Humanitarian Law, UN Doc. A/RES/60/147 of 21 March 2006. For details, see Chapter 6.

human rights law and serious violations of international humanitarian law". The conflation of these two areas of the law in regard to the question of compensation was, however, many States' main point of criticism of the General Assembly resolution.[34] Moreover, as already discussed in Chapter 6, the aspect of monetary compensation is especially controversial. Because that General Assembly resolution as such cannot constitute an actual legal basis, the basis for a claim for compensation arising from violations of international humanitarian law would have to be found in treaty law or customary law.

7.2.1 *No Treaty Basis for Claims*

The general treaty norms on the obligation to pay compensation for violations of provisions of international humanitarian law, i.e., Article 3 of the Hague Convention (IV) of 1907[35] and Article 91 of AP I of 1977,[36] are now predominantly interpreted so that they mean only compensation *between States.*[37] The contrary view argued by Frits Kalshoven, namely that those provisions grant individual claims,[38] has not prevailed so far.

34 For instance, when the resolution was adopted in 2005 in the body preceding the GA, the Commission on Human Rights, Germany abstained with the justification that the resolution did not differentiate sufficiently between human rights and international humanitarian law. The GA subsequently adopted the resolution by consensus, i.e., without a formal vote.

35 Article 3, sentence 1: "A belligerent party which violates the provisions of the said Regulations shall, if the case demands, be liable to pay compensation." (Convention respecting the Laws and Customs of War on Land (Hague Convention (IV)) of 18 October 1907, 205 CTS 277).

36 Article 91, sentence 1: "A Party to the conflict which violates the provisions of the Conventions or of this Protocol shall, if the case demands, be liable to pay compensation" (Protocol Additional to the Geneva Conventions of 12 August 1949 relating to the Protection of Victims of Armed Conflicts (Protocol I) of 8 June 1977, UNTS Vol. 125, 3).

37 See, representatively, Wolff Heintschel von Heinegg, Entschädigung für Verletzungen des humanitären Völkerrechts, *Berichte der Deutschen Gesellschaft für Völkerrecht* 40 (2003), 1–61 (25, 31): International humanitarian law prescribes only performances between States; the sole claimant is the State.

38 Fundamentally, see Frits Kalshoven, State Responsibility for Warlike Acts of the Armed Forces, *International and Comparative Law Quarterly* 40 (1991), 827–858 (835–6): "[T]he Article [Article 3 of the Hague Convention of 1907] is unmistakably designed to enable these people to present their bills directly to the State, i.e. to its competent (military or other) authorities, either during or after the war." Kalshoven also argues that Article 91 of AP I grants individual victims direct claims (*ibid.*, 646–647). See also, more recent, Eric David, *Principes de droit des conflits armés* (3rd ed. Brussels: Bruylant 2002), 633–634.

The predominant judicial practice concerns compensation claims against Japan and Germany for war crimes committed in the Second World War. Between the 1960s and now, Japanese courts have – in numerous judgments in connection with the atomic bombings,[39] internments of Korean[40] and Dutch nationals,[41] the use of "comfort women",[42] and bacteriological warfare against China – repeatedly denied compensation claims, usually with the reasoning that individuals are not owners of the claims.[43]

Representative of German case law[44] are the decisions on the attacks on the bridge of *Varvarin*. The case involved the killing and wounding of civilians by a NATO bombing of a bridge in Serbia during the Kosovo War of 1999.[45] In its decision on the compensation claims of the victims, the

[39] Residents of Hiroshima and Nagasaki sued the Japanese government for damages because they had failed to assert all compensation claims against the United States in connection with the US atomic bombings. In *Shimoda et al.* v. *State of Japan*, Tokyo District Court of 7 December 1963, the claims were rejected with the argument that the affected individuals could only be granted international compensation claims by a special treaty, but that no such treaty existed. Claims under national law had effectively been waived (English translation in *The Japanese Annual of International Law* 8 (1964), 231 et seq., Part 4).

[40] *X. et al.* v. *State of Japan*, Tokyo High Court, Judgment of 27 July 1995, rejected claims arising from Article 3 of the Hague Convention (IV) and customary international law. The Court held: "[N]either the general practice nor the conviction (*opinio juris*) that the State has a duty to pay damages to each individual when that state infringes its obligations under international human rights or international humanitarian law can be said to exist." (English translation in *The Japanese Annual of International Law* 39 (1996), 265). Confirmed by the appeal in *X. et al.* v. *State of Japan*, Tokyo High Court, Judgment of 7 August 1996 (English translation in *The Japanese Annual of International Law* 40 (1997), 116).

[41] *X. et al.* v. *State of Japan*, Tokyo District Court, Judgment of 30 November 1998, rejected individual compensation claims arising from Article 3 of the Hague Convention (IV) (English translation in *The Japanese Annual of International Law* 42 (1999), 143).

[42] *Henson et al.* v. *State of Japan*, Tokyo District Court, Judgment of 9 October 1998, rejected individual compensation claims arising from Article 3 of the Hague Convention (IV) (English translation in *The Japanese Annual of International Law* 42 (1999), 170).

[43] For other references to Japanese case law, see, e.g., Roland Bank/Elke Schwager, Is There a Substantive Right to Compensation for Individual Victims of Armed Conflicts against a State under International Law?, *German Yearbook of International Law* 49 (2006), 367–412 (373).

[44] In addition to the decisions referred to in the following text, see, e.g., BGHZ 52, 371 (1969): The claimant, a limited company, had had its property in the form of machines confiscated by the French army for reparation purposes immediately after the end of the Second World War. It demanded compensation from the Federal Republic of Germany. The Federal Court of Justice found: "There is no general principle of international law according to which a party affected by war damage would be able to derive a direct claim to compensation against the party's home State independently of any applicable domestic basis for the claim" (384).

[45] BGHZ 169, 348 et seq. – *Varvarin* (n. 29).

Federal Court of Justice found that individuals were unable to derive direct international claims (for damages) from violations of international humanitarian law.[46] The Federal Court of Justice stated that not every "rule relating to human rights" in treaties actually assigned individual *rights*. The Court constructed an opposition between an "individual right" or (understood synonymously) an "independent privilege" of the individual on the one hand and the mere "factual privilege" of the individual or a "*legal reflex*" to the individual's benefit.[47] According to the Court, the holder of the secondary claim for damages arising from Article 3 of the Hague Convention (IV) and Article 91 of AP I continued to be the home State.[48] The wording, history, and existing treatment especially of Article 91 of AP I did not give rise in practice to any individual (secondary) claim for reparation.[49]

In its ensuing inadmissibility decision, the German Federal Constitutional Court endorsed this reasoning. It held: "Despite the – continuously progressing – developments in the area of human rights which has led to a recognition of a partial legal personality of the individual and to the establishment of treaty-based complaint mechanisms, a similar development on the level of secondary claims cannot be ascertained. *Rights to reparation for breaches of international law by a State towards aliens still belong, as a matter of principle, only the individual's State of nationality.*"[50]

In the *Distomo* case, involving massacres in a Greek village by the German Wehrmacht in the Second World War, the Federal Constitutional Court of Germany held similarly: "Article 3 of Hague Convention (IV) does not give rise to any direct individual claim for damages when the international law of war is breached . . . The history of the norm does show that it is intended to protect the individual and thus has a nature that directly protects human rights . . . But it does not follow from this that the provision could be considered a basis for a direct,

[46] The Federal Court of Justice (paragraphs 25 et seq.) left open, however, whether claims for damages might arise from State liability under German domestic law (§ 839 of the German Civil Code in conjunction with Article 34 of the Basic Law). In the *Varvarin* case, no official duty had been breached, because the injurious acts were not attributable to Germany. The German military had not participated directly in the NATO attack on the bridge and knew nothing of the specific operation.

[47] BGHZ 169, 348 et seq. – *Varvarin* (n. 29), paragraph 11 (translation and italics mine).

[48] *Ibid.*, paragraphs 12–21.

[49] *Ibid.*, paragraphs 15–20 with references from the materials in paragraph 17.

[50] BVerfG, 2 BvR 2660/06, inadmissibility decision of 13 August 2013 – *Bridge of Varvarin*, esp. paragraphs 43–47, quotation paragraph 46 (translation and italics mine).

original claim for damages under international law by the affected individual against the State."[51] "Irrespective of developments at the level of the protection of human rights, which have led to recognition of a partial international legal subjectivity of the individual and to the establishment of individual complaints procedures set out in treaties, secondary claims for damages arising from acts of a State in violation of international law against foreign nationals continue to be assigned only to the home State in principle."[52]

The same stance was taken in 2013 by a first instance civil court on individual claims for monetary compensation for the loss of family members due to the German attack in 2009 on two gasoline trucks near Kunduz, Afghanistan.[53] It deserves to be noted that this line of cases operates on the idea that the ownership of the claims on the primary level and on the secondary level of State responsibility are split: While the owner of the claim in substance may be the individual, the ownership of the secondary claim to reparation is assigned to the State. While this split is not untenable in terms of legal logic, it is at least complicated.[54]

This front of rejection is opposed by only a few court decisions that have awarded war victims damages on the basis of Article 3 of Hague Convention (IV).[55] For instance, the Court of First Instance of Levadia affirmed claims for compensation under Article 3 of Hague Convention (IV) due to breach of Article 46 of the Regulations of Hague Convention (IV) (obligations of the military authority) arising from killings and destructions in the village of Distomo on 10 June 1944 by German troops. The Court qualified Article 46 of the Regulations as *jus cogens* and assumed an exception from State immunity.[56] The appellate court (Areopagos) did not consider the basis for the claim under Article 3 of Hague Convention (IV), but rather only State immunity.

[51] BVerfG, 2 BvR 1476/03, Non-admissability Order of the 1st Chamber of 15 February 2006, *Neue Juristische Wochenschrift* 59 (2006), 2542 et seq., paragraph 20 (translation mine). *Distomo.* Along these lines, see also the lower court decision in BGH, III ZR 245/98, Judgment of 26 June 2003 – *Distomo = Neue Juristische Wochenschrift* 56 (2003), 3488 et seq.

[52] BVerfG, *Distomo* 2006 (n. 51), paragraph 21 (translation mine).

[53] Landgericht (LG) Bonn, judgment of 11 December 2013, 1 O 460/11, paragraphs 41–43.

[54] See pp. 167–69.

[55] Higher Administrative Court (OVG) of Münster, Judgment of 9 April 1952, *Neue Juristische Wochenschrift* 5 (1952), 1030 et seq.; English translation in *International Law Reports* 19 (1957), 632 et seq. (civilian victim of a traffic accident caused by a vehicle of an occupying power).

[56] Court of First Instance of Levadia, *Prefecture of Voiotia* v. *Federal Republic of Germany*, Case No. 137/1997, Judgment of 30 October 1997, English summary and annotations by Ilias Bantekas, *American Journal of International Law* 92 (1998), 765–768.

In summary, the traditional reading preferred by the courts is that individuals do not have any general treaty claim to compensation arising from Article 3 of Hague Convention (IV) or Article 91 of AP I due to violations of international humanitarian law.

7.2.2 Other International and National Bases for Claims

Occasionally, *special international treaties* have been used after armed conflicts to recognize compensation claims in the specific situation. Under the Treaty of Versailles, for example, citizens of the Allied and Associated Powers were able to lodge compensation claims directly against Germany, in their own name and without the involvement of their own governments, in connection with certain exceptional war measures during the First World War and measures of transfer in German territory that affected their property, rights, and interests.[57] The competent mixed arbitral tribunals themselves derived a substantive, personal claim to reparation from the procedural power stipulated by the treaty: "[C]e droit à réparation constitue un droit individuel de chacque ressortissant allié, droit que celui-ci peut exercer directement contre l'Etat allemand sans intervention du gouvernement français."[58]

A more recent example of individual claims grounded in special treaties is the 2000 Agreement between Ethiopia and Eritrea. Here, the evaluation of war-related compensation claims by individuals is assigned to a Claims Commission.[59] While only the involved States may assert these claims, they may do so "on behalf of" affected persons (Article 5(8)

[57] Article 297(e) (on "property, rights, and interests in enemy territory") in conjunction with Article 304(b) (on the "Mixed Arbitral Tribunals") of the Treaty of Versailles of 28 June 1919 (225 CTS 188).

[58] German–French Arbitral Tribunal, *Sigwald* v. *Etat allemand* (Award of 27 August 1926), Tribunaux Abritraux Mixtes (TAM), Vol. VI (1926–1927), 888 et seq. (890), in regard to Article 297(e) of the Treaty of Versailles. See also the German–British Arbitral Tribunal in re *Lederer* v. *German Government* (28 February, 14 May, and 13 December 1923), TAM Vol. III (1924), 762–766.

[59] See Article 5(1) and (8), (9) of the Agreement between the Government of the Federal Democratic Republic of Ethiopia and the Government of the State of Eritrea of 12 December 2000, reprinted in ILM 50 (2001), 260 et seq. The relevant passage in Article 5(1) reads: "The mandate of the Commission is to decide through binding arbitration all claims for loss, damage or injury … by nationals (including both natural and juridical persons) of one party against the Government of the other party or entities owned or controlled by the other party that are (a) related to the conflict …, and (b) result from violations of international humanitarian law, including the 1949 Geneva Conventions, or other violations of international law."

and (9) of the Agreement). In terms of substantive law, the claims are thus individual claims. "The wording 'on behalf' indicates that *the claim remains the property of the individual* and that any eventual recovery of damages should accrue to that person", the Claims Commission held.[60] Furthermore, the Security Council derived an individual claim for compensation in the event of breaches of Article 27 of Geneva Convention (IV) (civilians entitled to respect for their persons, their honour, their family rights, and their religious convictions).[61]

Other bases for individual claims involving compensation for the consequences of war will not be discussed here; they may arise under the *national law* of the injuring State or even the home State of the injured person. They may involve State liability, claims arising directly from (national) fundamental rights, and civil law claims. Numerous claims of this sort have been brought before the national courts of the injuring States as well as those of the victims' home States – generally without success. The most important problem under international law for claims against the injuring States before the court of another State is State immunity. In recent years, Italian courts especially have granted compensation claims under civil law brought against the Federal Republic of Germany for crimes committed during the Second World War, assuming an exception to State immunity in the case of *jus cogens* breaches and war crimes such as deportation for forced labour.[62] Responding to a complaint brought by Germany, the ICJ found in *Jurisdictional Immunities* that these court judgments violated Germany's State immunity.[63] The question of immunity is not an object of this study.

7.2.3 Basis for Claims under Customary International Law? Preliminary Conclusion

In addition to claims based on treaty law, one might also consider an unwritten basis under customary international law for individual compensation claims. However, there have hardly been any court decisions so far

[60] Eritrea-Ethiopia Claims Commission, Partial Award – Civilian Claims – Eritrea's Claims 15, 16, 23, 27–32, 17 December 2004, paragraph 19 (italics mine).

[61] UNSC res. 471 (1980), paragraphs 2 and 3 (on Israel).

[62] See, especially, Supreme Court of Cassation of Italy (Corte Suprema di Cassazione), *Ferrini*, Appellate Judgement of 11 March 2004, No. 5044/4; ILDC 19 (IT 2004).

[63] See ICJ, *Case Concerning Jurisdictional Immunities* (*Federal Republic of Germany* v. *Italian Republic*), Judgment of 3 February 2012. See Markus Krajewski/Christopher Singer, Should Judges be Front-Runners? The ICJ, State Immunity and the Protection of Fundamental Human Rights, *Max Planck Yearbook of United Nations Law* 16 (2012), 1–34.

recognizing war victims' claims for damages.[64] There is likewise hardly any practice of international courts or arbitral tribunals that would have awarded compensation. In contrast, the more recent practice of truth and reconciliation commissions points in the direction of State espousal of responsibility, including the award of reparations. Accordingly, a study of the cases of Guatemala, Sierra Leone, East Timor, and Cambodia reaches the conclusion that "state responsibility for reparations in favour of individuals has acquired certain customary standing".[65] Recognition of State responsibility and the compensation awarded in these cases do not clearly entail recognition of a corresponding legal claim of individuals, however. In its judgment in the *Jurisdictional Immunities* case, the ICJ denied the existence of a *jus cogens* norm for individual compensation: "Moreover, against the background of a century of practice in which almost every peace treaty or post-war settlement has involved either a decision not to require the payment of reparations or the use of lump sum settlements and set-offs, it is difficult to see that international law contains a rule requiring the payment of full compensation to each and every individual victim as a rule accepted by the international community of States as a whole as one from which no derogation is permitted."[66] This statement does not concern the existence or non-existence of an "ordinary" obligation under international law to pay compensation, but it does suggest that the ICJ would likewise deny such an obligation. It would, however, be possible to develop a basis for claims under customary international law to this effect through further positive practice, especially court practice.[67]

In conclusion, the legal situation is relatively clear. Under current international law, international individual compensation claims for violations of international humanitarian norms are in some cases governed specially; however, there is no general claim of war victims under treaty law or customary law for damages arising from the violation of

[64] See the judgments cited in notes 39–56.

[65] Christine Evans, *The Right to Reparation in International Law for Victims of Armed Conflict* (Cambridge: Cambridge University Press 2012), 43; also 127. For the existence of such a norm under customary international law on the basis of detailed analysis of court practice, see Andreas Fischer-Lescano, Subjektivierung völkerrechtlicher Sekundärregeln, *Archiv des Völkerrechts* 45 (2007), 299–381.

[66] ICJ, *Jurisdictional Immunities* (n. 63), paragraph 94.

[67] See, e.g., Pierre D'Argent, *Les réparations de guerre en droit international public: La responsabilité internationale des États à l'épreuve de la guerre* (Brussels: Bruyant 2002), 788.

provisions of international humanitarian law. It makes sense to continue the discussion of individual claims at the secondary level only *de lege ferenda*.

7.3 Secondary Claims of Individuals *de lege ferenda*

A strong current in the literature is favourable to recognizing individual compensation claims for violations of international humanitarian law.[68] In its Declaration of International Law Principles on Reparation for Victims of Armed Conflict, the International Law Association (ILA) also stated in 2010: "Victims of armed conflict have a right to reparation from the responsible parties" (Article 6).[69] The ILA appears to have intended this principle not as a finding of international law already in existence, but rather as a progressive development of the law, especially when the Declaration appeals to States as follows: "States are encouraged to confirm expressly, supplement, extend, and amplify the principles contained in the present declaration" (Article 14(2)).

Courts might award compensation without the need for a formal treaty amendment. The individualized reading of the provisions in Article 3 of Hague Convention (IV) and Article 91 of AP I would not, for the reasons mentioned immediately below, represent an illegitimate further development of the law by judges, but rather a legitimate dynamic interpretation of the relevant provisions. Their wording does not contradict their understanding as a basis for individual claims. It is true that according to Article 2 of Hague Convention (IV), the treaty applies "between Contracting powers", and Article 3 refers to the "belligerent party" as obligor. But the provisions leave the identity of the *claimants* entirely open. These provisions must be interpreted in the light of other relevant norms of international law. The sensitivity to the relevance of human rights in armed conflict that has grown substantially since 1907 (and even since 1977) and the intense discussion on a right to remedy

[68] Along these lines (*de lege ferenda*), see, e.g., Liesbeth Zegveld, Remedies for Victims of Violations of International Humanitarian Law, *International Review of the Red Cross* 85 (2003), 497–527; Rainer Hofmann, Victims of Violations of International Humanitarian Law: Do They Have an Individual Right to Reparation Against States under International Law?, in: Pierre-Marie Dupuy/Bardo Fassbender/Malcolm N. Shaw/Karl-Peter Sommermann (eds), *Völkerrecht als Wertordnung/Common Values in International Law* (Kehl: Norbert Paul Engel Verlag 2006), 341–359; Bank/Schwager, Substantive Right 2006, 410–411.

[69] Resolution No. 2/2010 of the International Law Association, 74th Biennial Conference of the ILA, The Hague, 15–20 August 2013.

play a role in this regard (see Chapter 6). This development of the law suggests an "individualized" interpretation of the compensation provisions.

Additionally, the human rights principle of the equal treatment of conflict victims is relevant. This principle demands that, with the help of legal safeguards, compensation become independent of the political constellation between States. Experience throughout history has shown that conflicting parties with the political means generally absolve themselves of the obligation to compensate war victims.[70] One of the advantages of recognizing individual claims for damages would be to break open this kind of victors' justice.[71]

To ensure the logic of legal solutions, it should also be considered that many violations of the law of armed conflict simultaneously constitute grave breaches of human rights. The most important human rights treaties grant a treaty claim to effective remedy and even a claim to monetary compensation.[72] For instance, provided that the ECtHR has jurisdiction, the ECtHR may interpret Article 2 ECHR (right to life) systemically, i.e., taking account of "any other relevant rules of international law applicable in the relations between the parties" (Article 31(3)(c) VCLT). The legal rules to be taken into account also include the rules of armed conflict. The breach of provisions of international humanitarian law makes a deprivation of life "arbitrary", thus breaching Article 2 ECHR. The ECtHR may award damages for breaches of the ECHR.[73] While formally correct, it would still be a contradiction of values for a deprivation of life that "merely" constitutes a violation of Article 51 of AP I (protection of the civilian population) to not generate individual secondary claims – for instance, because no human rights body has jurisdiction – while the same act would give rise to a compensation claim when it can be qualified as a violation of Article 2 ECHR as well.

Considerations of principle also call for the recognition of individual compensation claims. This recognition would do justice to the existential importance of the provisions violated here, would take appropriate account of the "humanization" of the law of armed conflict, and would constitute extremely effective leverage for compliance with the rules of the law of armed conflict.

70 On the waivers typical of peace treaties, see p. 214.

71 See Stammler, *Anspruch von Kriegsopfern* 2009, 334–335.

72 See pp. 180–83.

73 See ECtHR, *Isayeva, Yusopova and Bazayeva* v. *Russia*, No. 57947–9/00 (2005), paragraphs 168–200. The ECtHR did not explicitly use the method of systemic interpretation.

Ultimately, however, the discussion about the compensation claims of war victims also manifests the limits of the power of law. In the case of hundreds of thousands or even millions of victims, equal enforcement of the fundamental individual right appears utopian. Against the recognition of individual claims for damages, it is thus argued that this would open the floodgates for legal action. It is argued that payment of compensation to individuals especially in post-conflict States is not practicable on financial and logistical grounds. An international rule should, in fact, be valid both for victims of wars in poor countries with weak rule of law and for victims in wealthy regions. However, it does not make sense that the extreme situation should determine the solution.[74] Some of the more recent armed conflicts, such as NATO's Kosovo intervention, have triggered a manageable number of compensation claims. The typical practical difficulties arising from compensation claims – namely that individual claims after armed conflicts are asserted *en masse* – could be managed with the help of reasonable procedures and international support. The capacity of the State obligor to pay can be taken into account when determining the amount of compensation.

All these considerations argue in favour of a dynamic interpretation of Article 3 of Hague Convention (IV) and Article 91 of AP I as a basis for individual compensation claims. The minimum requirement for an individual compensation claim would be, however, that the primary norm violated contain an individual right to compliance with the prohibition contained in that norm. An individual claim to reparation for the violation of protective norms that are merely "objective" (not rights-generating) would be strange from a legally systematic point of view.

First and foremost, the important objection of practicability must be taken into account. This can be done with the help of a sensible definition of the relationship between individual secondary claims and State secondary claims (in relation to citizens) that may also arise from the violation of norms establishing individual rights. For instance, the individual right to compensation might be interpreted as procedurally *subsidiary* to any State claims on behalf of the citizens of that State. The individual claim should be assertable only if the involved States have not concluded any (or any sufficient) compensation arrangement or if the affected persons do not fall within their scope.[75] Precisely, this situation appears to have been the case in the dispute between Italy and Germany over compensation to forced labourers during the Second

[74] See Stammler, *Anspruch von Kriegsopfern* 2009, 335. [75] See *ibid.*, 339.

World War: Neither did the Italian government vigorously represent the interests of the victims nor did it seriously defend the decisions of the Italian civil courts denying Germany's State immunity due to violations of *jus cogens* in the proceedings before the ICJ.[76]

However, the individual should also have ultimate control over secondary claims to the extent that he or she should be able to contradict assertion of those claims by the State. In this dialectical relationship, secondary claims of the home States would take precedence over individual claims in regard to the violation of individual rights of its citizens, but those claims would not be assertable against the will of the affected individuals if they want to assert their secondary claims themselves, and if upon reasonable consideration the State route is likely to be insufficient. The contents of the two groups of secondary claims could and should also be reconciled with each other, so as not to overwhelm the respondent.[77]

Additionally, there is a statute of limitations on breaches of international law except for the most serious crimes such as genocide. This statute of limitations helps ensure legal certainty. Finally, compensation claims before foreign courts are opposed by State immunity as a matter of principle. All these counter-principles and limitations mean that a recognition of an international individual claim to compensation for violations of international humanitarian law under Article 3 of Hague Convention (IV) and Article 91 of AP I would not lead to a flood of legal actions, but rather would take appropriate account of the status of the individual under international law, with due consideration of countervailing interests of States.

7.4 Ownership of Claims and Waiver

The ownership of the claims has legal consequences for the possibility of waiving those claims.[78] Waiver of the primary claims of protected persons is expressly ruled out by the saving clauses in the Geneva

[76] See Krajewski/Singer, Should Judges be Front-Runners? 2012, 31–32. The authors propose a procedural solution for this situation: Individuals could be authorized to represent their interests in arbitration proceedings between States by means of *amicus curiae* briefs.

[77] See Dörr, Völkerrechtliche Deliktsansprüche Privater 2013, 781.

[78] On the question of waivers in connection with the ownership of claims, see also the discussion in international investment protection law: The problem there is different, in that it is about (often implicit) waivers of investors to ICSID proceedings, not waivers of States. Also in that discussion, the ownership of the claim does not fully prejudice the question of admissibility of the waiver (see pp. 324–28).

Conventions (prohibition of special agreements) already mentioned (see pp. 197–98).

These prohibitions of depriving individuals of rights conferred on them by way of agreements between States are a novelty of the 1949 Geneva Conventions, with which the authors of the conventions were responding to the practice of special agreements to the detriment of prisoners of war during the Second World War. Jean Pictet refers to this novelty as being "of paramount importance" for the purpose of ensuring the comprehensive application of the conventions without exception as the standard regime under all circumstances.[79] Because of the explicit rule, it is pointless to speculate whether State waiver of the individual rights contained in the Geneva Conventions would be ineffective even without explicit prohibitions.

The question of waiver is, however, relevant to practice in regard to the *secondary claims* arising from violations of the law of armed conflict. There are no provisions in the Geneva Conventions and the Additional Protocols governing that kind of waiver. In peace treaties, States often reciprocally waive their claims to reparations.[80] For instance, the Allied States in the Second World War waived all reparation claims, other State claims, and all claims of their citizens that might have arisen from the conduct of Japan or of Japanese citizens during the war.[81]

Legally speaking, such a waiver is possible only if the claims are construed as rights of the States themselves (in relation to their citizens) over which the States have power of disposal. Also, under current international law, such waiver agreements continue to be permissible in principle – within the limits of peremptory international law: States merely cannot waive reparation claims for the violation of *jus cogens*.[82] While the Geneva Conventions prohibit disclaimers of responsibility for grave breaches (Article 51 GC I; Article 52 GC II; Article 131 GC III,

[79] Pictet, *Commentary on the Geneva Conventions* Vol. I 1952, 71–72.

[80] See the numerous references to such waiver clauses in peace treaties in BVerfGE 94, 315, paragraphs 55 et seq. (1996) – *jüdische Zwangsarbeiter*.

[81] Article 14(b) of the Treaty of Peace between the Allied Powers and Japan of 8 May 1951 (Treaty of San Francisco). See also Heintschel von Heinegg, Entschädigung für Verletzungen 2003, 33 in regard to the Second World War: States were free to defer fulfilment of the compensation obligation until the end of the war and beyond, and to waive them fully or in part by way of a treaty.

[82] See Marco Sassòli, Reparation, in: Vincent Chétail (ed.), *Post-Conflict Peacebuilding: A Lexicon* (Oxford: Oxford University Press 2009), 279–290 (284–285).

Article 148 GC IV),[83] according to the historical view, these provisions referred only to the punishment of war criminals, from which the contracting parties were not allowed to desist. They might, however, be interpreted dynamically as a prohibition of the waiver of reparations by States for grave breaches.

In two judgments in 2007, the Supreme Court of Japan found the waiver clauses in the Treaty of San Francisco to be valid and accordingly dismissed a group of compensation claims relating to forced labour and sexual slavery lodged by Chinese citizens.[84] The claimants had argued that the individual rights of citizens attributable to them in a personal capacity could not be limited by an agreement between States. The Supreme Court rejected this legal assertion with the argument that, in virtue of its sovereignty, the State is able to dispose of the international claims of its citizens.[85] The Court drew attention to the legitimate goals of reciprocal waivers conferred by treaties. But it interpreted treaty waivers as a procedural clause, not in a substantive sense: The treaty arrangement was able solely to defeat the power to bring claims. Because this did not affect the substantive claims, the obligors were at liberty to satisfy the claims on a voluntary basis.

This pragmatic argumentation should be considered critically. On the one side, it appears to be a requirement of legal logic to deny the possibility of State waiver entirely when individuals are the owners of the claim: As soon as it is recognized that compensation claims belong to the individuals themselves (possibly alongside State claims for compensation), a waiver by the home State of these individual claims does not appear possible, because the State does not own the claim. A radical argument would be that States do not have power of disposal over these third-party claims. An alternative and probably preferable approach

[83] See, e.g., Article 51 GC I: "No High Contracting Party shall be allowed to absolve itself or any other High Contracting Party of any liability incurred by itself or by another High Contracting Party in respect of breaches referred to in the preceding Article."

[84] See *Nishimatsu Construction Co* v. *Song Jixiao*, 61 Minshu 1188, 1969 Hanrei Jiho 31, 2004 (Ju) No. 1658 (Supreme Court of Japan, 2nd Petty Bench), Judgment of 27 April 2007 (judgment concerning paragraph 5 of the Joint Communiqué of the Government of Japan and the Government of the People's Republic of China). *Ko Hanakao et al.* v. *Japan*, 1969 Hanrei Jiho 38, Supreme Court of Japan (1st Petty Bench), Judgment of 27 April 2007. Annotations of both judgments by Mark A. Levin in *American Journal of International Law* 102 (2008), 148–154.

[85] 2004 (Ju) No. 1658, Section II (3): "However, upon entering into a peace treaty to end a war, each nation has the power to dispose all relevant claims including claims held by individuals based on its sovereignty over citizens."

would be to qualify the State waiver as a conceivable limitation of individual rights in principle. But a mere reference to State sovereignty would not suffice for that purpose. The limitation of rights would have to pursue legitimate public interests and be proportionate. In fact, waivers relating to compensation claims after armed conflicts can in principle be motivated by legitimate public interests: They serve to bring about lasting peace in society, they create legal certainty, and they prevent the involved States from being overwhelmed by numerous unforeseeable claims. But are the waiver clauses also proportionate? An argument against appears to be that the waiver does not merely limit the right in question, but defeats it entirely. The core and essence of that right is not affected only if an adequate substitute (not necessarily in the form of a right) is offered. In the final analysis, the ownership of the claim by the individual shows the direction of a solution to the waiver problem by ruling out an unconditional and limitless power of disposal by the State.

Like none other, the current controversy about whether the victims of breaches of international humanitarian law have a direct, personal claim to reparation including monetary compensation *de lege lata* or whether such a claim should be recognized *de lege ferenda* reflects the entire structural development of international law. The academic and political pressure in the direction especially of allowing claims for financial compensation under civil law before national courts for breaches of international humanitarian law appears to be growing. It is a manifestation of the trend towards "individualization" of international law in both a procedural and a substantive sense, combined with a strengthening of the role of national courts as enforcers of international law.

7.5 Individual Enforcement of Secondary Claims in the Law of Armed Conflict

7.5.1 Individual Enforcement at the International Level

The substantive ownership of the rights must be distinguished from the enforcement of the postulated secondary individual claims under international humanitarian law. An individual claim for reparation under substantive law may exist independent of the individual's power to bring the claim under procedural law.[86] The Eritrean–Ethiopian

[86] On the decoupling of the substantive status of the individual under international law from the individual's procedural possibilities of enforcement before international bodies, see pp. 44–50.

agreement mentioned earlier is an example in which individual rights are granted that can be asserted only by States before the Claims Commission "on behalf of" the individuals.[87] However, it normally contributes to the realization of such claims if they can also be enforced by the affected individual who is interested in having them satisfied.

Under general international humanitarian law, protected persons – i.e., civilians, prisoners of war, wounded persons, etc. – are by the treaties merely entitled to "apply to" the national authorities, to the representatives of the Protecting Powers, the ICRC, or national Red Cross Societies (e.g., Article 78 of Geneva Convention (III); Articles 30 and 101 of Geneva Convention (IV)). Individuals do not, however, have standing before international courts or other international bodies to claim violations of the primary norms of international humanitarian law that protect individuals and to assert the contents of the international relationship of responsibility (reparation, etc.). The provision in Article 90 of AP I to the Geneva Conventions establishing an International Fact-Finding Commission does not provide for any inclusion of victims in the fact-finding procedure. However, the Rules of the Commission do provide for enquiries *in loco* and the hearing of witnesses (which presumably includes victims).[88] Due to lack of consent by the States in question, however, this Fact-Finding Commission has never become active. Academics and NGOs are proposing new international mechanisms for monitoring compliance with norms of international humanitarian law that protect individuals. A State reporting system or an individual complaints procedure could be established.[89] But these proposals have not yet been taken up by the political actors.

7.5.2 *Individual Enforcement at the National Level*

Because individuals do not have an international forum at their disposal, the only option remaining is that of national jurisdiction. However, international humanitarian law treaties do not require contracting parties to make a national legal process available. There is also no special requirement under customary international law to this effect.[90] As late as

[87] See above pp. 207–08.

[88] Rule 27 of the Rules of the International Humanitarian Fact-Finding Commission of 8 July 1992, amended on 11 March 2003.

[89] See von Woedtke, *Verantwortlichkeit Deutschlands* 2010, 303–304 and other references.

[90] But on the obligations of contracting States based on human rights conventions to provide remedies and in part also reparations within the national legal system, see Chapter 6. For a conceivable general obligation under customary international law to

2004, the Federal Constitutional Court of Germany held in its ruling on the Italian military internees that there is "no rule or presumption ... that a State breaching international law must grant claims to the injured persons based on its own national law. Rather, the specific design of the domestic legal order is determinative in that regard."[91] Since then, however, national legal systems have moved in that direction. The authoritative compilation of international humanitarian law diagnosed "an increasing trend of enabling victims ... to seek reparation directly from the responsible State".[92] This means that the possibility of victims themselves enforcing any existing individual claims to reparation, including compensation, is still in the hands of national legislators and judges.

The precondition for the success of such individual claims is that national courts recognize individual ownership of the claims at both the primary and the secondary levels. National courts, however, have so far seldom done this (on the relevant case law, see pp. 204–07). Moreover, the courts would have to recognize the direct effect (self-executing character) of the relevant provisions of international humanitarian law. But also on this third point, the predominant case law is negative, both in terms of the primary norms and in terms of the secondary norms for reparation, especially in the form of monetary compensation. For instance, US courts have recently rejected the self-executing character of the Geneva Conventions in decisions regarding Guantánamo Bay. The Supreme Court held: "We may assume that 'the obvious scheme' of the 1949 Conventions is identical in all relevant respects to that of the 1929 Convention, and even that that scheme would, absent some other provision of law, *preclude* Hamdan's *invocation of the Convention's provisions as an independent source of law* binding the Government's actions and furnishing petitioner with any enforceable right."[93] A Court of Appeals stated: "[T]he Geneva Convention is not self-executing. 'Courts will only find a treaty to be self-executing if the document, as a whole, evidences an intent to provide a private right of action' ...

provide procedural remedies as a correlate of the local remedies principle, see Chapter 15, pp. 480–83.

[91] BVerfGE 112, 1 (2004; translation mine), Ruling of 28 June 2004 – *italienische Militärinternierte*, paragraph 39.

[92] Jean-Marie Henckaerts/Louise Doswald-Beck, *Customary International Humanitarian Law, Vol. I, Rules* (Cambridge: Cambridge University Press 2005), 541.

[93] US Supreme Court, *Hamdan* v. *Rumsfeld*, Judgment of 29 June 2006, 548 US 557, 627 (2006) (italics mine).

The Geneva Convention evinces no such intent. . . . We therefore agree with other courts of appeals that the language in the Geneva Convention is not 'self-executing' and does not 'create private rights of action in the domestic courts of signatory countries.'"[94]

Concerning the self-execution of secondary norms (i.e., the treaty bases for a claim to reparation, especially in the form of monetary compensation), the Federal Constitutional Court of Germany deemed the provision in Article 3 of Hague Convention (IV) to be "non-self-executing": "Arguments against this already include the wording, according to which a belligerent party which violates the provisions of the Regulations shall, 'if the case demands,' be liable to pay compensation. Since in light of the restrictive clause, Article 3 of Hague Convention (IV) is not self-executing in this respect, the understanding of the norm as a basis for individual claims is defeated already by the lack of self-executing character."[95]

This rejection of the direct effect of the treaty norms governing compensation is not persuasive, however. Article 80(1) of AP I requires the contracting parties and the parties to the conflict to execute the Geneva Conventions and the Protocol.[96] According to the interpretive principle of *effet utile*, the "execution of their obligations under the Conventions", as provided here by the treaty itself, must be effective. This suggests that the execution requirement should be interpreted as an obligation of the State Parties to recognize the direct effect/self-execution of those provisions suitable for that purpose in accordance with the generally accepted criteria (see Chapter 16 on direct effect). Article 91 of AP I, in particular, is sufficiently specific and unconditional to constitute a basis for a court decision even without implementing legislation.

This means that no problem of insufficient specificity of the treaty norms stands in the way of a dynamic judicial reading of the Geneva Conventions and their Additional Protocols in the direction of embodying a procedural obligation of the contracting parties to create *the possibility of remedies under civil law* for treaty violations by States,

[94] US Court of Appeals for the Fourth Circuit, *Hamdi* v. *Rumsfeld*, Judgment of 8 January 2003, 316 F. 3d 450 (4th Circ. 2003); reprinted in ILM 42 (2003), 197 et seq. (208) (internal citations omitted). The final Supreme Court judgment in *Hamdi* in 2004 did not discuss the question of self-execution.

[95] BVerfG, *Distomo* 2006 (n. 51), paragraph 21 (translation mine).

[96] Article 80(1) of AP 1: "The High Contracting Parties and the Parties to the conflict shall without delay take all necessary measures for the execution of their obligations under the Conventions and this Protocol."

officeholders, and private perpetrators. Such a procedural treaty obligation – derived from Article 80 of AP I and the underlying general principle of good faith performance of the treaty – would constitute a parallel to the explicit obligations of the Contracting Parties to punish grave breaches. Relevant court practice could also develop it as an obligation under customary international law. This treaty obligation to grant direct effect, arising from the Geneva Conventions, would be – specifically in international humanitarian law – a stronger version of the so-called right to a remedy arising from human rights treaties and under customary international law.[97]

Overall, most domestic courts have so far shied away from enforcing any individual rights arising from IHL. This corresponds to the "avoiding role" of national courts when applying IHL more generally. Such avoidance has recently been identified as one of various roles espoused by national courts towards IHL, besides other, even contradictory attitudes such as legitimizing illegal state policies (some forms of detention) or – inversely – actively developing the law (e.g., when allowing human rights-based exceptions of immunity in law suits concerning war crimes).[98] The insight that national courts are apparently in a process of "defining their own role as enforcing organs of international law"[99] makes it likely that in the future at least some national courts will acknowledge individual rights on the level of primary law (IHL) and secondary law (State responsibility), and will apply those norms directly.

7.6 Individual Obligations in the Law of Armed Conflict

7.6.1 Foundations

Apart from individual claims, the law of armed conflict may also give rise to individual obligations directly under international law. In Chapter 4, we have shown that international individual obligations are an exception in need of justification, given the associated problems of practicability and legitimation. Such individual obligations should (alongside the State obligations to protect global legal goods by enacting national implementing legislation, which in turn contains individual obligations) be recognized only if they are necessary for the effective protection of global legal

[97] See Chapter 6, pp. 175–89.
[98] Sharon Weill, *The Role of National Courts in Applying International Humanitarian Law* (Oxford: Oxford University Press 2014).
[99] *Ibid.*, 198.

goods (risk of regulatory deficit) and if they rest on a legal basis that defines the obligations so unambiguously that they are foreseeable for the obligors (principle of legality).[100]

7.6.1.1 In Non-International Armed Conflict

Especially in non-international armed conflict, there is evidently a gap in protection, so the first-mentioned normative condition for the acceptance of individual obligations directly under international law is met. In this situation, non-State actors are involved whose military actions cannot sensibly be attributed to the State they are fighting. Given the lack of attribution to the State, there is a special need here to admit individuals or groups as holders of the primary obligations under international humanitarian law and to hold them responsible under international law (by imposing secondary obligations).

In the past, however, States have rejected the status of individuals and armed opposition groups (formerly referred to as insurgents or rebels) as subjects under international law with respect to non-international armed conflict because they feared that those actors might (by being recognized as "belligerent parties") be withdrawn from the scope of the national legal order. States affected by civil war are interested in discrediting the armed opposition as criminals and prosecuting them under their domestic criminal law. But this intention and desire is not obstructed by granting a status to opposition groups (also) under international law. The two legal roles are not mutually exclusive; this is not a question of either–or. Subjecting groups and individuals to the international norms of armed conflict does not as such remove them from national law. "Immunity" from criminal prosecution under domestic law granted only to combatants applies in international (as opposed to non-international) armed conflicts. In non-international conflicts, individuals simultaneously remain subject to the national criminal law of the territorial State. It remains possible to punish members of opposition groups under national criminal law, whatever additional international legal status we grant to them.[101]

[100] For details, see Chapter 4, pp. 76–85.

[101] See Constitutional Court of Colombia (Judgment No. C-225/95), paragraph 14 (reprinted in Marco Sassòli/Antoine A. Bouvier, *How Does Law Protect in War?* (3rd ed. Geneva: ICRC 2011), 2240 et seq.).

7.6.1.2 In International Armed Conflict

In international armed conflict, the primary actors are members of the State armed forces, whose conduct is attributed to the involved State parties to the conflict. For this reason, the question of individual and direct imposition of obligations on these persons (combatants for purposes of international humanitarian law) has hardly been posed. But also in international armed conflict, there is a certain need to reach individuals directly under international law in order to prevent impunity and to protect the especially important legal goods at stake (life, physical integrity, etc.) more effectively.

In regard to legal obligations *enforced by criminal penalties*, it is generally recognized that it would not be sufficient for international law to address only States. Especially in armed conflict, experience has shown that national norms purported to prohibit violations of international humanitarian law are often too weak or are not strictly enforced, or national law even contradicts international requirements and permits or covers conduct of individuals that is contrary to international law. This means that in international armed conflict as well, there is a specific risk of a regulatory gap. Precisely for this reason, Article 25(4) of the Rome Statute makes clear that parallel international responsibility of States and individuals can and should exist: "No provision in this Statute relating to individual criminal responsibility shall affect the responsibility of States under international law." Going beyond this provision, i.e., also in regard to precepts and prohibitions of international humanitarian law that are not considered international crimes, the normative conditions referred to in Chapter 4 for direct international imposition of obligations on individuals are likely to be met in international armed conflicts.

7.6.2 International Obligations of Armed Opposition Groups ("Insurgents") in Non-International Armed Conflict

The subjection of armed opposition groups in non-international armed conflict to the relevant provisions of international humanitarian law (i.e., to common Article 3 of the Geneva Conventions, Additional Protocol II (AP II), and customary international law) is largely recognized in practice.[102] In this context, two questions arise: Who exactly is being

[102] For evidence from practice and case law to this effect, see Liesbeth Zegveld, *The Accountability of Armed Opposition Groups in International Law* (Cambridge: Cambridge University Press 2002), 10–12.

addressed (the armed group as an autonomous entity or its individual members)? And how can the binding nature of these provisions under international law be justified in regard to these groups of persons or individuals?[103]

Traditionally, recognized insurgents are granted limited international legal personality in the domain of international humanitarian law, i.e., they have international legal capacity. This means the individuals who have come together as an opposition group *can* in principle be holders of international obligations under international humanitarian law.[104] But this does not yet indicate which obligations actually apply to a group in a specific case and how these obligations arise.

7.6.2.1 Obligations through International Treaties

The first path is the imposition of obligations by treaty. But armed groups are not themselves contracting parties to the international humanitarian law conventions (Geneva Conventions and AP II). They are thus not bound by these conventions in virtue of any status as parties. Common Article 3(2) of the Geneva Conventions, however, provides the possibility of concluding additional agreements: "The *Parties* to the conflict should further endeavour to bring into force, *by means of special agreements*, all or part of the other provisions of the present Convention" (italics mine). The question is, who are the "Parties" addressed here. Because Article 3 contains minimum rules for non-international armed conflicts, i.e., for wars in which a non-State armed group is involved on at least one side, "Parties" must mean the parties to the armed conflict, including the *non-State party or parties*, and not the (necessarily State) parties to the Geneva Conventions themselves.

According to common Article 3(2), the opposition groups may therefore conclude "agreements" with the State or with each other in which they commit themselves to observing international humanitarian law. In terms of content, the scope of these agreements may differ. They may stipulate or confirm the application of the minimum norms of common Article 3, the norms of AP II, or all norms of international humanitarian law. In terms of their object and purpose and in light of their mention in common Article 3, these agreements are to be qualified not only as

[103] See, fundamentally, Antonio Cassese, The Status of Rebels under the 1977 Geneva Protocol in Non-International Armed Conflict, *International and Comparative Law Quarterly* 30 (1981), 416–439; Sandesh Sivakumaran, Binding Armed Opposition Groups, *International and Comparative Law Quarterly* 55 (2006), 369–394.

[104] See Sivakumaran, Armed Opposition Groups 2006, 374.

contracts under national law but as international treaties. The opposition groups may also conclude additional agreements, for instance ceasefire agreements, whose content goes beyond the application of international humanitarian law. Whether these agreements are also considered international treaties must be determined depending on the context, content, and intention of the parties.[105] In all such agreements, the subjection of the group to international humanitarian law may be agreed explicitly between the parties to the conflict or may be derived through interpretation of the agreements.[106]

7.6.2.2 International Obligations through Unilateral Declarations

The second type of international obligation results from unilateral declarations made by numerous armed opposition groups, in which they declare that they will respect the relevant rules of international humanitarian law.[107] Article 96(3) of AP I to the Geneva Conventions specifically permits representatives of armed self-determination fighters to make such a declaration.[108] Unilateral declarations made by international legal subjects (i.e., entities with legal capacity) may create legal obligations.

7.6.2.3 International Obligations Directly from the Geneva Conventions?

A third way to impose legal obligations – and the most difficult to justify – results from the treaties that *only* the State where the civil war takes place has ratified, i.e., from the Geneva Conventions and AP II themselves. The chapeau of common Article 3 of the Geneva Conventions stipulates: "In the case of armed conflict not of an international character occurring in the territory of one of the High Contracting Parties, each Party to the conflict shall be bound to apply, as a minimum, the following [minimum]

[105] See Anne Peters, Treaty Making Power, in: Rüdiger Wolfrum (ed.), *The Max Planck Encyclopedia of Public International Law* (Oxford: Oxford University Press 2009), paragraphs 61–62.

[106] See Sivakumaran, Armed Opposition Groups 2006, 389–392 with examples.

[107] For examples from practice, see *ibid.*, 387–388.

[108] Article 96(3) of AP I: "The authority representing a people engaged against a High Contracting Party in an armed conflict of the type referred to in Article 1, paragraph 4, may undertake to apply the Conventions and this Protocol in relation to that conflict by means of a unilateral declaration addressed to the depositary. . . .". For example, the Polisario made such a declaration in 2015 on behalf of the people of Western Sahara.

provisions [enumerated below]." This provision is first of all addressed to the State Parties. The Additional Protocol II poses the similar problem, because it has been (and can be) ratified only by States, not by armed groups. The same is true of other special treaties in international humanitarian law, such as the Optional Protocol on the Involvement of Children in Armed Conflict.[109] Article 4(1) of this Optional Protocol specifically addresses "[a]rmed groups that are distinct from the armed forces of a State" and prohibits those groups from using child soldiers. However, insurgent groups are not even able to ratify these treaties. These treaties can be joined only by States; requests by non-State groups to accede have always been rejected by the contracting parties and by Switzerland, the depositary State of the Geneva Conventions.

It is disputed whether these treaty provisions legally bind opposition groups. That thesis is *rejected* by the restrictive view of mediation represented by several States at the Diplomatic Conference that prepared the AP II. According to that view, the AP II, especially, only creates legal obligations among the contracting parties.[110] These obligations are owed only to the other contracting parties (not to the opposition groups). The States parties have an obligation to enact national laws in which they require opposition groups to respect the provisions of AP II. According to this view, the mediation of opposition groups is complete. Their rights and duties arise only from the national law that the States parties must enact to implement their obligations set out in AP II.

According to the second view, rebels are "third parties" under treaty law, to whom the binding nature of a treaty may be extended only by way of an exception to the *pacta tertiis* principle (by analogy to Articles 34–36 VCLT).[111] For this purpose, the contracting parties would have to intend to impose legal obligations on third parties, and the third parties would have to consent to being bound in that way. Finally, they would become contracting parties only by way of their consent. This construal was already criticized above because of its misleading analogy with private law: Natural persons are not "third parties" within the meaning of the *pacta tertiis* rule (see Chapter 4, pp. 72–74).

In contrast, this study espouses the view that the legal obligations of the groups are derived directly under international law from common Article 3 of the Geneva Conventions, irrespective of the groups' consent

109 Optional Protocol to the Convention on the Rights of the Child on the Involvement of Children in Armed Conflict of 25 May 2000, UN Doc. A/RES/54/263, Annex I.

110 For references to the positions held by the States, see Cassese, Status of Rebels 1981, 420–422.

111 See *ibid.*, 423–429.

and irrespective of the enactment of domestic implementing norms. In the early literature on the Geneva Conventions, this way of binding the groups was affirmed as follows: "Who are the 'Parties to the conflict' and to whom do they owe the obligations imposed in Article 3? It would seem that these obligations are international and not municipal. Does the article have the effect of attributing a functional semi-personality upon an association of individuals operating as . . . rebel groups? . . . A possible solution . . . is to consider that *the obligations imposed by the article devolve upon the whole of the population* of the State concerned, at any time, so that any person taking part in an internal conflict on either side is exposed to the risk of being in breach of an international obligation if he acts in violation of article 3. This would, if correct, be an instance of *obligations, international in nature, inhering directly in individuals.*"[112] But in the case of that author, it still remains unclear why the obligations arising from common Article 3 should extend to all natural persons participating in the armed conflict.

A possible explanation already discussed in Chapter 4, pp. 74–75, is the "principle of legislative competence". When a State ratifies a treaty, it does this for all individuals (or for all actors that are deemed to have international legal capacity in principle) in its territory; it represents them in an international legal sense.[113] A similar explanation can be found in the reference to a rule of customary international law, according to which the consequences of ratification carried out by a State are extended to every new subject of international law coming into being in its territory.[114] The obligations of the members of the armed group are then not themselves based on customary law, but rather they are obligations arising from Article 3, whose circle of addressees is expanded in virtue of customary law.

The objections to the principle of legislative competence have already been discussed in Chapter 4, p. 75. The principle is "constitutionally blind" and does not take account of the substantive representation of the views of the population by the governments concluding the treaty. This paradigm also often confuses obligations arising from international law with obligations under national law (which may exist in parallel).[115]

[112] Gerald Irving Anthony Dare Draper, The Geneva Conventions of 1949, *Recueil des Cours* 114 (1965/I), 59–165 (96).

[113] See, especially, Sivakumaran, Armed Opposition Groups 2006, 381–382.

[114] See Michael Bothe, Conflits armés et droit international humanitaire, *Revue Générale de Droit International Public* 82 (1978), 82–102 (92). On the practice underlying this view, see Zegveld, *Accountability* 2002, 14–18.

[115] But Sivakumaran, Armed Opposition Groups 2006, 385, separates them clearly.

In contrast, it is better to view the question whether a treaty directly imposes obligations on a non-state group (as opposed to on the State) as entirely independent from the question of whether and how the treaty in question has been incorporated into the domestic legal order. Especially in the context of non-international armed conflict, any "mandate" of the government to act on behalf of, or with a legal effect for, the rebels is implausible. Such conflicts are defined by the fact that the rebels deny the legitimacy of the government and its very entitlement to represent them. On the contrary, they fight the government by military means. It would be a contradiction of values to bind the armed opposition groups by norms that their enemy had consented to "for them". Finally, the representation thesis is unable to explain how groups are bound by relevant customary (as opposed to treaty-based) international humanitarian law. Potential direct international obligations of armed opposition groups arising directly from common Article 3 can therefore not easily be explained with reference to the principle of legislative competence.

The better view is that individual obligations arise from Article 3 because that provision protects important legal goods, and because without imposing obligations directly on individuals, a regulatory deficit emerges. The obligations set out here must apply *erga omnes* in order to be effective. As mentioned at the outset, there is a specific risk in non-international armed conflict of under-regulation by national law. The extension of the direction of the obligations to include individuals is easily reconcilable with the open wording of Article 3 ("parties to the conflict"). An interpretation of the provision according to which not only State obligations but also individual obligations are derived therefrom is easily foreseeable given the long legal and political debate on the topic for sixty years now. This means these direct international obligations are also covered by the principle of legality. In parallel, armed groups are also bound by norms that emerge primarily from *opinio juris* and State practice. The follow-up question of whether their own practice may contribute to the formation of customary law, i.e., whether non-State groups also have the capacity to *generate* law in addition to their capacity to assume rights and obligations, probably must be answered in the affirmative.[116]

But who exactly are the addressees of the obligations postulated here? In practice and in the accompanying legal discussion of the obligations arising from the law of non-international armed conflict, no clear conceptual distinction has crystallized so far between armed groups and their

[116] See p. 547.

members. On the basis of an analysis of treaty texts, relevant declaration, and soft law documents, Kate Parlett concludes: "Whether the relevantly bound entity is the armed opposition group as such or the individuals constituting the group cannot be determined on the basis of these texts; rather, it seems there is no clear conceptual division between the group and its membership and individual members of the group are in practice treated as though they are directly and personally bound."[117]

Because the obligations of the group usually cannot be distinguished from the obligations of the group members, reference points can be derived from the usual practice for the more general question of how individuals (rebels and combatants) can be bound by the law of non-international and international armed conflict. This aspect will be examined in more detail in the following discussion.

7.6.3 Towards Individual Obligations in All Types of Armed Conflict

A traditional characterization of the treaty regime of armed conflict is as follows: "The Geneva Conventions and their Additional Protocols are international treaties and as such, in principle, are binding on states only. Even if it were accepted that some of their provisions might be self-executing and would therefore apply to individuals qua treaty, none of those provisions, not even their grave breaches sections, were ever meant to be regarded per se as an international criminal code the breach of which could entail international criminal responsibility directly under the treaty regime."[118] This statement – as is typical of this debate – confuses three aspects: the question of substantive individual obligations, the question of direct effect (self-executingness), and the question of criminal responsibility. While the contents of these three aspects are interlinked, they can be separated analytically. In this section, we are only interested in the first aspect, namely the substantive status of being bound by obligations.

Direct international obligations from the corpus of international humanitarian law – and in principle from both treaty law and customary international law – may be imposed on the individual participants in an armed conflict. In principle, the possibility of subjecting individuals directly under international law to the norms of international humanitarian law is now recognized. It remains an open question *when* such individual obligations

[117] Parlett, *Individual* 2011, 227, see also 197.

[118] Guénaël Mettraux, *International Crimes and the Ad hoc Tribunals* (Oxford: Oxford University Press 2005), 8.

arise from international humanitarian law and how they can be explained legally. The starting point of the analysis should be the wording of the codified law of armed conflict. Only in very scattered provisions do the Geneva Conventions explicitly mention obligations of individuals, and then only in relation to less fundamental aspects. Article 17 of Geneva Convention (III) prescribes: "Every prisoner of war, when questioned on the subject, is bound to give only his surname, first names and rank, date of birth, and army, regimental, personal or serial number, or failing this, equivalent information." Article 39(2) of the same Convention says: "Prisoners of war, with the exception of officers, must salute and show to all officers of the Detaining Power the external marks of respect provided for by the regulations applying in their own forces." Nevertheless, it is assumed in principle that individual obligations may arise also from other rules that do not explicitly address individuals. As Jean Pictet writes, "Rights entail obligations. With reference to the individual, ... the rules of the Conventions, or certain of them, can also be considered as obligations directly incumbent on the persons protected. It is an indisputable fact that certain *obligations*, such as the respect due to the wounded and sick under Article 16, are also laid upon *persons* who can claim protection under the Convention."[119]

Very relevant to practice in armed conflict is the obligation of individuals to tolerate internment, which at the same time constitutes deprivation of liberty relevant to fundamental rights. Internment in international armed conflicts is governed by the Geneva Conventions and customary international law for prisoners of war and civilian persons. The measure is ordered by a party to the conflict. The legal basis is, however, found in international law, which represents the source of the obligation to tolerate.[120] There is no international legal basis for internment in non-international armed conflict.[121]

[119] Pictet, *Commentary on the Geneva Conventions* Vol. IV 1958, 79 (italics mine).

[120] Article 21 of GC III (prisoners of war): "The detaining power may subject prisoners of war to internment." Article 118 of GC III: "Prisoners of war shall be released and repatriated without delay after the cessation of active hostilities." Article 42(1) of GC IV (civilian population): "The internment or placing in assigned residence of protected persons may be ordered only if the security of the Detaining Power makes it absolutely necessary." See also Article 42 of GC IV on voluntary internment. Article 78 of GC IV: "If the occupying Power considers it necessary, for imperative reasons of security, to take safety measures concerning protected persons, it may, at the most, subject them to assigned residence or to internment."

[121] See, generally, Els Debuf, *Captured in War: Lawful Internment in Armed Conflict* (Oxford: Hart 2013).

The possibility of legally binding individuals exists both in international and in non-international armed conflicts. "International humanitarian law creates obligations for all individuals in times of armed conflicts. The relationship between an individual and his or her state is irrelevant to that fact."[122] "[I]ndividuals clearly have an active role to play as bearers of individual rights and obligations under international humanitarian law."[123]

The explanation for this can be found in the *erga omnes* character of international law, the highest ranking of the legal goods in question (right to life, etc.), and the experience that imposing obligations only on States in all types of armed conflict typically does not suffice to protect these legal goods in an effective way (for details, see Chapter 4). For this reason, every individual combatant and every civilian is a direct addressee of the norms of international humanitarian law *relevant to his or her situation*, where permitted by the wording of the norms and if the imposition of obligations is sufficiently foreseeable for the person concerned (the condition of the principle of legality). Numerous prohibitions of international humanitarian law are sufficiently specific and unconditional to satisfy the principle of legality. This is why international humanitarian law prohibits every combatant from employing methods of warfare that cause unnecessary suffering (Article 35(2) of AP I), carrying out indiscriminate attacks (Article 48 of AP I), or attacking civilian objects (Article 52 of AP I). International humanitarian law also prohibits every civilian from taking part directly in hostilities, sanctioning breaches with the loss of civilian immunity (Article 51(3) of AP I). According to the view put forward here, these obligations are addressed directly to individuals, not only to their home States or supreme commanders of the troops in question. Provided the condition of specificity and foreseeability is met, individuals are likewise bound by the obligations under customary international law that almost always exist in parallel with the treaty norms.

In regard to the norms of international humanitarian law *enforced by criminal penalties*, the status of the individual as being bound by obligations arises already from the fact that the violation of these norms entails individual criminal responsibility. While the status as a subject of obligations and the status as a subject of responsibility (in regard to sanctioning the obligations with the legal consequence of a penalty) are two different

[122] Provost, *International Human Rights* 2002, 98.

[123] Dieter Fleck, The Role of Individuals in International Humanitarian Law and Challenges for States in its Development, in: Michael Schmitt/Leslie Green (eds), *The Law of Armed Conflict: Into the Next Millennium* (Newport: Naval War College 1998), 119–139 (136).

legal statuses, the imposition of a punishment on the person allows one to draw the conclusion that that person was obligated from the outset not to commit certain acts.[124]

In the final analysis, the understanding of the key prohibitions of the law of armed conflict as directed at individuals and therefore as generating individual obligations ensures their full effectiveness. The status of the individual as being subject directly to international obligations under international humanitarian law safeguards actual compliance with the prohibitions and thus satisfies a legal policy desideratum of the greatest importance. It is still an open question, however, which norms obligate individuals and under what conditions they may do so. The subjection of individuals to norms of international humanitarian law "calls for some limiting principle", otherwise that body of law would displace all other (including national) criminal norms applicable in an armed conflict. But such a limiting principle is difficult to formulate. It could, for instance, rely on the motives or nature of the violation or a nexus to the conflict.[125] The observation and systematization of future practice must still clarify these triggering conditions for individual obligations based on concrete norms of the law of armed conflict.

7.7 Conclusions

International individual rights in international humanitarian law may arise on two levels. Firstly, individual claims for compliance with the precepts and prohibitions of IHL (level of primary law) exist, as the non-renunciation clauses and savings clauses testify. Whether a specific precept or prohibition in the law of armed conflict actually generates individual rights must be determined in each case.

Secondly – and this is in practical terms most relevant and thus controversial – claims may arise from the relationship of responsibility at the secondary level in the event of a breach of a primary norm. The traditional reading preferred by the courts is that individuals do not have any general treaty claim to compensation arising from Article 3 of Hague Convention (IV) or Article 91 of AP I due to violations of international humanitarian law. An unwritten basis under customary international law for individual

[124] See Provost, *International Human Rights* 2002, 75: "Although the distinction between a subject of responsibility and a subject of obligations has been clearly stated, there is a tendency to accept the notion that a person punished for an offence has been under a duty all along not to commit that offence."

[125] See *ibid.*, 98–99.

compensation claims is not recognized by courts either. But occasionally, special international treaties have been used after armed conflicts to recognize compensation claims in the specific situation. *De lege ferenda,* a strong current in the literature is in favour of recognizing individual compensation claims for violations of international humanitarian law.

However, no international mechanisms for an individualized enforcement of such claims exist. The only option remaining is that of national jurisdiction. However, international humanitarian law does not require contracting parties of the conventions to make a national legal process available. Individual claims for compensation can succeed only if national courts not only recognize individual ownership of the rights but also recognize the direct effect of the relevant provisions of international humanitarian law. However, most domestic courts have so far shied away from enforcing any individual rights arising from IHL.

Finally, every individual combatant and every civilian is a direct addressee of the norms of international humanitarian law *relevant to his or her situation*, where permitted by the wording of the norms and if the imposition of obligations is sufficiently foreseeable for the person concerned (the limiting condition of the principle of legality).

The legal situation differs in international and non-international armed conflict. In the latter case, obligations can be imposed through treaties, through unilateral declarations, and might flow directly from the Geneva Conventions in conjunction with AP II. Arguably, individual obligations arise from common Article 3 because that provision protects important legal goods, and because without imposing obligations directly on individuals, a regulatory deficit emerges. However, so far no clear conceptual distinction between armed groups and their members has crystallized.

8

Protection against Acts of Violence and Forces of Nature

8.1 Definition of the Problem

This chapter is about potential trans-boundary international legal claims of the individual, notably against third states, to protection and assistance in acute emergencies that threaten the elementary legal goods of human beings such as life and physical integrity, food, and shelter.

Expressed in terms of the traditional categories of international law, this concerns the international protection of human rights, the law of armed conflict, international criminal law, international environmental law, and the law of State responsibility, with some overlap among these areas. The special aspect of this problem area is the absence of a comprehensive international legal codification of extraterritorial State obligations to protect and provide assistance. Unlike the clearly defined duties of omission in the law of armed conflict, the preliminary question is whether transboundary legal obligations of States even exist in this area (unless arrangements have been made in special treaties). Only once this question is answered in the affirmative does the follow-up question arise concerning the obligees of these duties: Do the obligations exist only vis-à-vis other States, or do they also exist vis-à-vis the persons concerned?

But does it make sense to look at the situations of natural disasters, war, and mass crimes in parallel when considering the possibility of individual rights? At first glance, there are considerable differences among these domains. The causes of humanitarian emergencies are either natural or human. Assistance by third parties to victims of natural disasters is generally attributed to the domain of morality. Such assistance appears to arise from a (merely) moral, not legal, requirement, not least of all because the emergency is not caused by human action. In contrast, both war and crimes by definition fall within the domain of law, i.e., they are legally constructed and circumscribed and require a legal response. Here again, the starting point for differentiating between the moral and legal evaluation of human acts of violence is whether these acts occur in times of war or peace. While attacks against the physical integrity and life of others are normally considered crimes, such acts are in principle allowed among combatants during armed conflict.

But there are several reasons for analysing the situations of natural disasters, war, and mass crimes in a comparative fashion. The law of armed conflict prohibits numerous patterns of behaviour in war and qualifies them as crimes. Also the offences of genocide and crimes against humanity are often accompanied by armed conflict. Finally, war of aggression is itself an international crime. This means that the domains of war and crime are not strictly separate.

Moreover, many emergencies are complex emergencies, resulting from an interplay between natural and political-military factors. Resource questions sometimes trigger armed conflicts (struggle for water, raw materials, climate wars). Conversely, some so-called natural disasters are due to human intervention. The humanitarian emergency then arises from the concurrence of a natural disaster and armed conflict. Finally, the behaviour of State authorities in the event of natural disasters may in turn constitute a violation of international law such as a crime against humanity. This means that public, private, and so-called natural threats often coincide in the cases of armed conflicts, mass crimes, and natural disasters.

A further consideration speaks in favour of a comparative analysis of individual rights in humanitarian emergencies; the legal assessment of emergencies should look to the persons concerned as the starting point. From that perspective, the causes of the emergency are less important than their effects on life, physical integrity, food, and shelter. It should therefore be welcomed that recent international law has experienced a reorientation in this regard. A flood of new literature deals with the status of the victim in international humanitarian law and international criminal law.[1] A reconfiguration of these areas of the law according to

[1] See, e.g., Ilaria Bottigliero, *Redress for Victims of Crimes under International Law* (Leiden: Martinus Nijhoff 2004); Raquel Aldana-Pindell, An Emerging Universality of Justiciable Victims' Rights in the Criminal Process to Curtail Impunity for State-Sponsored Crimes, *Human Rights Quarterly* 26 (2004), 605–685; M. Cherif Bassiouni, International Recognition of Victims' Rights, *Human Rights Law Review* 6 (2006), 203–279; Gioia Greco, Victims' Rights Overview under the ICC Legal Framework: A Jurisprudential Analysis, *International Criminal Law Review* 7 (2007), 531–547.

a "victim-centric" approach is being demanded.[2] The victim-centric perspective is meant to replace the traditional conflict-centric perspective. For instance, it is irrelevant according to the victim-centric view whether an act of torture is committed during an international or a national armed conflict or in times of peace. In parallel, a "rights-based approach" is being advocated in the law of disaster relief.[3] For instance, Article 2 of the International Law Commission (ILC) Draft Articles on the Protection of Persons in the Event of Disasters (in the following, Draft Articles on Disaster Protection), as adopted by the ILC on second reading in 2016,[4] describes the purpose of the legal framework as follows: "to facilitate the adequate and effective response to disasters, and reduction of the risk of disasters, so as to meet the essential needs of the persons concerned, with full respect for their rights."[5]

Together, the amalgamation of natural and human threats mentioned at the outset and the postulate that the perspective of the persons concerned is relevant lead to the insight that a *juridification* of the obligation to provide assistance[6] is similarly appropriate (or inappropriate) in the various situations of humanitarian emergency and should be assessed in a parallel fashion. The more the focus shifts from the causes to the consequences of all forms of humanitarian emergency (natural disaster, war, mass crimes), i.e., to human needs and human security, the less

[2] See, fundamentally, Bassiouni, Victims' Rights, 2006.

[3] For instance, the ILC Special Rapporteur on the Protection of Persons in the Event of Disasters, Eduardo Valencia-Ospina (see ILC, Report of the International Law Commission on its 60th session (2008) (n. 26), paragraphs 227–229).

[4] In this Chapter, I will refer to the draft articles as quoted in ILC, Sixty-eighth session (Geneva, 2 May–10 June and 4 July–12 August 2016), Protection of Persons in the Event of Disasters: Titles and texts of the preamble and draft articles 1 to 18 of the draft articles on the Protection of persons in the event of disasters adopted, on second reading, by the Drafting Committee UN doc A/CN.4/L.871) of 26 May 2016.

[5] Ibid.

[6] We might note that the locus classicus on disaster relief, a passage by Vattel, mentions an inter-State duty to aid as an "office of humanity", founded on "the eternal and immutable law of Nature": "[W]hen the occasion arises, *every Nation should give its aid* to further the advancement of other Nations and save them from disaster and ruin, so far as it can do so without running too great a risk . . . if a Nation is suffering from famine, all those who have provisions to spare should assist in its need, without, however, exposing themselves to scarcity . . . To give assistance in such dire straits is so instinctive an *act of humanity* that hardly any civilized Nation is to be found which would refuse absolutely to do so . . . Whatever be the calamity affecting a Nation, the same help *is due* to it." Emer de Vattel, *Le droit des gens ou Principes de la loi naturelle* (London 1758, Classics of International Law, Carnegie Institution 1916, Vol. I, engl. transl. The Law of Nations or the Principles of Natural Law Applied to the Conduct and to the Affairs of Nations and of Sovereigns, Vol. III, book II, chap. I, 1758, pp. 114–115 (§§ 4-5); italics mine).

plausible becomes the strict legal differentiation in regard to the possible obligations of third parties to provide assistance.[7]

Conceivable contents of individual rights are rights to prevention of threats, protection from threats, and elimination of threats. These are not primarily rights to omission but rather rights to action (e.g., to humanitarian assistance). Procedural rights are also conceivable, such as a right to effective investigation and criminal prosecution of perpetrators and participation in criminal proceedings (see Chapter 9).

The potential rights of individuals may be addressed to States (firstly to the State of residence and secondly to third States) and also against private individuals. This chapter is concerned only with potential rights addressed to States and the corresponding obligations of States towards the persons concerned. Conceivable international individual rights addressed directly to private individuals and the corresponding international obligations of private parties are discussed only in Chapter 4.

Moreover, rights and duties may arise not only at the primary level but also at the secondary level (of State responsibility). Individual claims against States at the level of secondary law (to *in rem* restitution, damages, etc.) are discussed in Chapter 6. They require the recognition of a relationship of responsibility at the level of secondary law between the injuring State and the victim. Within that framework, a claim under secondary law for reparation might exist, for instance.

8.2 Obligations Arising from the Responsibility to Protect (R2P)

In hardly any other subdomain of international law has the paradigm shift from the powers of the State towards the needs, and possibly even the *rights* of the individual become as apparent as in the law of the prohibition of force and intervention. The debate emerging in the wake

[7] It is therefore consistent that modern international human rights instruments address the multiple situations of emergencies in one stroke. See, e.g., Art. 11 of the Convention on the Rights of Persons with Disabilities of 30 March 2007: "States Parties shall take … all necessary measures to ensure the protection and safety of persons with disabilities *in situations of risk, including situations of armed conflict, humanitarian emergencies and the occurrence of natural disasters*" (italics mine). See for the emergence of a *common* standard on the question of State consent to external humanitarian assistance both in the law of disaster response and in the law of armed conflict Sandesh Sivakumaran, Arbitrary Withholding of Consent to Humanitarian Assistance in Situations of Disaster, *International and Comparative Law Quarterly* 64 (2015), 501–531, for the convergence, "because the underlying issue is the same", esp. pp. 514 and 531.

of NATO's Kosovo intervention about the permissibility of humanitarian intervention focused on the human rights of the persons concerned. But only the concept of the responsibility to protect (R2P) invented by an independent commission of experts[8] and recognized by heads of State and government in the World Summit Outcome Document of 2005[9] brought about a fundamental shift in perspective, namely from a State right to intervene towards a possible obligation to intervene, from non-intervention towards non-indifference to mass crimes.

The ideational starting point of R2P is the insight that the individual and the individual's rights and interests are the normative ground line of the international legal system. Consequently, State sovereignty can no longer supply any ultimate justification for that system.[10] Sovereignty can and must be justified in turn, namely as an instrument to protect human beings. The core content of the principle of State sovereignty is then no longer considered to be the control of territory but rather responsibility towards the inhabitants of that territory.

If a territorial State is unable or unwilling to honour this responsibility, it temporarily forfeits its territorial integrity and thus its protection against third-party intervention. Under the premise of a multilevel system in which the governance tasks should be assigned to the level that can accomplish them most effectively, and under the assumption that an

[8] International Commission on Intervention and State Sovereignty (ICISS), The Responsibility to Protect (2001). The ICISS report is inspired by Francis Mading Deng/Donald Rothchild/I. William Zartman, *Sovereignty as Responsibility: Conflict Management in Africa* (Washington DC: Brookings Institution Press 1996).

[9] Resolution of the General Assembly, World Summit Outcome Document, UN Doc. A/RES/60/1 of 24 October 2005, paragraphs 138–139: "138. Each individual State has the responsibility to protect its populations from genocide, war crimes, ethnic cleansing and crimes against humanity. This responsibility entails the prevention of such crimes, including their incitement, through appropriate and necessary means. We accept that responsibility and will act in accordance with it. The international community should, as appropriate, encourage and help States to exercise this responsibility and support the United Nations in establishing an early warning capability. 139. The international community, through the United Nations, also has the responsibility to use appropriate diplomatic, humanitarian and other peaceful means, in accordance with Chapters VI and VIII of the Charter, to help to protect populations from genocide, war crimes, ethnic cleansing and crimes against humanity. In this context, we are prepared to take collective action, in a timely and decisive manner, *through the Security Council*, in accordance with the Charter, including Chapter VII, on a case-by-case basis and in cooperation with relevant regional organizations as appropriate, should peaceful means be inadequate and national authorities are manifestly failing to protect their populations from genocide, war crimes, ethnic cleansing and crimes against humanity . . ." (italics mine).

[10] Anne Peters, Humanity as the A and Ω of Sovereignty, *European Journal of International Law* 20 (2009), 513–544.

international principle of solidarity exists, the responsibility to protect shifts from the territorial State to the international community. However – at least according to the view of States manifested in the Outcome Document – military intervention must be authorized by the Security Council.[11] According to the Outcome Document, the only triggers of R2P are genocide, war crimes, and crimes against humanity ("atrocity crimes").

To that extent, there is agreement concerning the shape of R2P.[12] However, there is controversy concerning any international legal quality of the concept that goes beyond moral and political responsibility. What is recognized is solely the legal obligation of the *territorial State* (and any State effectively exercising jurisdiction over a territory or persons[13]) to protect the persons *de facto* subject to that jurisdiction from human rights violations, which often simultaneously are considered crimes. This obligation to protect arises firstly from the provision in Article I of the Genocide Convention in which the Contracting Parties undertake "to prevent and to punish" genocide[14] and additionally from the human rights to life and physical integrity.[15] The two sources together give rise to an international individual right not to become a victim of international crimes: According to Antonio Cassese, individuals "are entitled to respect for their life and limb, and for their dignity; hence they have a right not to become a victim of war crimes, crimes against humanity,

[11] See n. 9.

[12] Seven reports of the UN Secretary-General have been published as of the spring of 2016, beginning with "Implementing the Responsibility to Protect" (UN Doc. A/63/677 of 12 January 2009) to "A Vital and Enduring Commitment: Implementing the Responsibility to Protect" (UN Doc. A/69/981-S/2015/500 of 13 July 2015).

[13] The precise demands on such "extraterritorial" responsibility are in flux and depend in part on the human rights in question and the applicable treaty regime.

[14] For a derivation of R2P as a legal principle from existing treaty law, see Edward C. Luck, Special Adviser to the Secretary-General, Remarks to the General Assembly on the Responsibility to Protect, New York, 23 July 2009, 3; Louise Arbour, The Responsibility to Protect as a Duty of Care in International Law and Practice, *Review of International Studies* 34 (2008), 445–458 (447–448 and 450).

[15] On the positive dimension of the obligation to protect arising from the civil and political rights contained in the ICCPR, see UN Human Rights Committee, General Comment No. 31 [80], Nature of the General Legal Obligations Imposed on States Parties to the Covenant (CCPR/C/21/Rev.1/Add.13 (26 May 2004)), paragraph 8. For the ACHR, see fundamentally the Inter-American Court of Human Rights (IACtHR), *Velásquez Rodríguez* v. *Honduras*, Judgment of 29 July 1988, Ser. C No. 4 (1988), paragraphs 172–177. For the ECHR, see fundamentally ECtHR, *Osman* v. *UK*, No. 87/1997/871/1083, Judgment of 28 October 1998, Reports 1998-VII, 3124, paragraphs 115–122.

aggression, torture, terrorism".[16] The "right" postulated here is a right to protection addressed to the territorial State or State of jurisdiction, and beyond this possibly a procedural right addressed to the international prosecution authorities.

The situation is different in regard to a potential obligation to protect on the part of *third States* that do not have effective control over the persons or territory concerned. Such an obligation cannot necessarily be derived from human rights (see also pp. 245–46). So far, no "hard" legal obligation to protect has emerged directly from R2P. In the negotiations on the Outcome Document of 2005, the US delegate expressly rejected a legal obligation of the United Nations, the Security Council, or individual States to intervene.[17] In a General Assembly debate in July 2009, during which forty-nine States took the floor,[18] five States (including China and Brazil)[19] spoke out explicitly against a legal character of the responsibility to protect, and only Canada expressly affirmed the quality of R2P as a legal norm.[20]

The subsequent legal development, especially the responses of the international community in the Libya and Syria situations, does not manifest any trend towards a juridification of the concept of R2P.[21] The Security Council did justify its authorization of military intervention in Libya to protect the civilian population with reference to the territorial State's failure to fulfil its obligation to protect.[22] And before the operation, the UN Secretary-General spoke of an "obligation of the international community" to protect the

[16] Antonio Cassese, *International Law* (2nd ed. Oxford: Oxford University Press 2005), 145. According to Christian Tomuschat, "the individual enjoys a personal right not to be subjected to genocide" (Christian Tomuschat, Individual Reparation Claims in Instances of Grave Human Rights Violations: The Position under General International Law, in: Albrecht Randelzhofer/Christian Tomuschat (eds), *State Responsibility and the Individual: Reparation in Instances of Grave Violations of Human Rights* (The Hague: Martinus Nijhoff 1999), 1-25 (13)).

[17] Letter of the US representative to the United Nations (John Bolton) dated 30 August 2005: "We do not accept that either the United Nations as a whole, or the Security Council, or individual states, have an obligation to intervene under international law."

[18] GAOR (A/63/PV.97–100) of 23, 24, and 28 July 2009.

[19] Brazil (A/63/PV.97, p. 13); Guatemala (A/63/PV.97, p. 14); Morocco (A/63/PV.98, p. 13); China (A/63/PV.98, p. 24); Venezuela (A/63/PV.99, p. 9); Monaco (A/63/PV.99, p. 12).

[20] A/63/PV.98, p. 26: "We have at our disposal a sophisticated normative legal framework based on international law."

[21] See the analysis of the legal quality of R2P, taking account of the State responses to the Libya situation, in Stephan Hobe, The Responsibility to Protect and Security Council Action in Libya, *Indian Journal of International Law* 51 (2011), 502–512 (506–9).

[22] UNSC resolutions 1970 and 1973 (2011).

civilian population.[23] Individual statements by UN Member States after the vote on the Libya resolution also indicate a legal conception supporting an obligation to intervene.[24] However, neither the abstentions by Russia, China, and several non-permanent members of the Security Council in the Libya situation nor the prevention of military measures against the Syrian government through vetos since 2012 were characterized as *violations of international law* through omission in the context of intergovernmental relations. This means that the "responsibility to protect" does not offer a "hard" legal basis under existing international law for a *substantive legal obligation* to protect individuals from genocide, war crimes, and crimes against humanity. However, I would claim that R2P does provide the basis for a procedural obligation to justify non-intervention, especially an obligation of the permanent members of the Security Council to justify their veto in that body.[25]

8.3 Obligations to Protect in the Event of Natural Disasters

An international individual right to protection and humanitarian assistance has long been discussed within the context of disaster relief.[26] The memorandum by the secretariat of the International Law Commission on the protection of persons in the event of disasters in 2007 stated that the law as it stands in regard to any right to humanitarian assistance was unclear.[27]

[23] "I strongly believe that the first *obligation* of the international community is to do everything possible to ensure the immediate protection of civilians at demonstrable risk." UN Secretary-General Ban Ki-moon, Security Council, 6490th meeting, 25 February 2011 (UN Doc. S/PV.6490), p. 3 (italics mine).

[24] See Hobe, Responsibility to Protect 2011, 508 and other references.

[25] See Anne Peters, The Security Council's Responsibility to Protect, *International Organizations Law Review* 8 (2011), 1–40.

[26] See, especially, ILC, Protection of Persons in the Event of Disasters, Memorandum by the Secretariat, UN Doc. A/CN/590 of 11 December 2007 with Addendum of 26 February 2008 (UN Doc. A/CN/590/Add.1) and ILC, Report of the International Law Commission on its 60th session (5 May to 6 June and 7 July to 8 August 2008), UN Doc. A/63/10, Ch. IX ("Protection of Persons in the Event of Disasters"), esp. paragraphs 241–250 ("Right to Humanitarian Assistance"). See also Le droit à l'assistance humanitaire, Actes du colloque international organisé par l'UNESCO, Paris, 23–27 janvier 1996 (Paris: UNESCO).

[27] ILC, Protection of Persons in the Event of Disasters, Memorandum 2007 (n. 26), paragraph 257: "Existing positive law on the subject remains unclear." Paragraph 61: "Notwithstanding assertions of the existence of a generalized 'right to humanitarian assistance,' such position, to the extent that it imposes a 'duty' (as opposed to a 'right') on the international community to provide assistance is not yet definitively maintained as a matter of positive law at the global level." The "right" referred to here is the right of States to offer and grant assistance, not any right of individuals.

Bilateral or regional treaties in the context of disaster relief generally stipulate obligations that exist purely *between States* or define assistance mandates of special international organizations. In some cases, obligations are imposed on States parties to duly consider requests for assistance from other States parties.[28] Sometimes, specific obligations to assist are stipulated, but always depending on the State's capabilities.[29] Only in exceptional cases are State obligations to assist individuals mentioned, such as in Article 23 of the African Children's Charter and Article 146 of the Convention on the Law of the Sea.[30]

8.3.1 The ILC Draft Articles on the Protection of Persons in the Event of Disasters

In the absence of treaty rules, the ILC attempted to codify and further develop the law. Its Draft Articles on Disaster Protection[31] consist of the following elements: A general "duty to cooperate" among States and "other assisting actors" is stipulated (Article 7). The affected State has a primary role (Art. 10(2)); it has the duty to seek external assistance (Art. 11); its consent to external assistance is required, but its right to withhold such consent is limited (Art. 13). External actors are entitled to offer assistance and – controversially – they are obliged to give due

[28] Art. 12(2) ILC Draft Articles Disaster Protection 2016 (n. 4): "When external assistance is sought by an affected State by means of a request addressed to another State, the United Nations, or other potential assisting actor, the addressee shall expeditiously *give due consideration to the request* and inform the affected State of its reply." (italics mine).

[29] See numerous references in ILC, Protection of Persons in the Event of Disasters, Memorandum 2007 (n. 26).

[30] Article 23 of the African Charter on the Rights and Welfare of the Child of 11 July 1990: "Refugee Children: 1. States Parties to the present Charter *shall take all appropriate measures to ensure* that a child who is seeking refugee status or who is considered a refugee in accordance with applicable international or domestic law shall, whether unaccompanied or accompanied by parents, legal guardians or close relatives, *receive* appropriate protection and *humanitarian assistance* in the enjoyment of the rights set out in this Charter and other international human rights and humanitarian instruments to which the States are Parties" (italics mine). For instance, Article 98 of the Convention on the Law of the Sea (UNCLOS) stipulates a duty to render assistance in cases of distress at sea. Paragraph 1 of the provision, however, only sets out requirements for the States parties to provide for juridical rescue obligations of ship owners in their domestic law, and the article also requires States parties to establish a sea rescue service. Article 146 UNCLOS ("protection of human life") provides that the International Seabed Authority ensure effective protection of human life in the area (i.e., the seabed as referred to in Article 1(1)(1) UNCLOS).

[31] N. 4.

consideration to a request for assistance (Art. 12). I will in this Chapter focus mainly on the afflicted States' duty to seek assistance and on third States' duty to consider a request for assistance, because – if at all – these obligations might at some point be mirrored by individual rights to assistance.

First, the *territorial State*, by virtue of its sovereignty, has the primary duty to ensure the protection of persons concerned and provision of emergency assistance on its territory (Article 10 Draft Articles 2016).[32] This provision is constructed analogously to the concept of R2P by assuming that State sovereignty primarily consists in *responsibility for human beings.*

This "duty to ensure the protection" (in the words of Article 10 of the Draft Articles of 2016), which primarily accrues to the territorial State, is transformed into a "duty of the affected State to seek external assistance" (Art. 11). It is doubtful whether the postulated duty to seek external assistance already forms part of international customary law.[33] If accepted, it would constitute an independent primary obligation under international law, but only in the form of a due diligence-obligation of conduct, not as an obligation of result. It would potentially be a vertical obligation owed not to third States but *owed to the persons under the territorial State's jurisdiction.*[34] The legal consequences of the violation of this obligation of conduct are however unclear.

Scholarship occasionally asserted that the affected State which is unable to protect its population by itself *must* admit helpers and facilitate their access.[35] In contrast, the ILC Draft Articles uphold the consent-requirement (Article 13(1)). However, the territorial State may not "arbitrarily" withhold its consent to external assistance from third parties (Article 13(2)).[36] In other words, the territorial State may not arbitrarily

[32] Article 10, Role of the affected State: "1. The affected State has the duty to ensure the protection of persons and provision of disaster relief assistance in its territory, or in territory under its jurisdiction or control. 2. The affected State has the primary role in the direction, control, coordination and supervision of such relief assistance" (n. 4).

[33] See for its basis in international human rights law below pp. 245–46.

[34] Giulio Bartolini/Tommaso Natoli/Alice Riccardi, Report of the Expert Meeting on the ILC's Draft Articles on the Protection of Persons in the Event of Disasters, *International Law and Disasters Working Papers Series* 03 (2015), pp. 51–52.

[35] See Karel Wellens, Solidarity as a Constitutional Principle: Its Expanding Role and Inherent Limitations, in: Ronald St MacDonald/Douglas M. Johnston (eds), *Towards World Constitutionalism: Issues in the Legal Ordering of the World Community* (Leiden: Martinus Nijhoff 2005), 775–807 (785–786).

[36] Article 13(2): "Consent to external assistance shall not be withheld arbitrarily" (n. 4).

prevent assistance by third parties for the benefit of the persons concerned. So although it is still assumed that any provision of external assistance by third States requires the consent of the affected State,[37] the right of the afflicted territorial State to non-intervention has been modified on this point, namely in the sense that the State no longer has an unrestricted right to refuse assistance.[38] Although the prohibition of an "arbitrary" refusal is vague, it has the potential to effectively limit the affected State's options for refusal of assistance, and thus may really constitute an inroad into State sovereignty. Non-arbitrariness in substance requires a legitimate aim, and – in procedural terms – demands giving reasons for the refusal to grant access. Valid reasons may be the absence of unmet needs of the population, that the given offer of humanitarian assistance does not match the needs, that the offer emanates from questionable actors, or from actors with doubtful (hostile) motives. In armed conflict, imperative military necessities might also justify withholding consent.[39]

What are the consequences of the postulated obligation to cooperate for *third States*? In the literature, it has sometimes been demanded that third parties should be obligated to provide assistance.[40] Under the law as

[37] See in this sense also Institute of International Law, Sixteenth Commission, Humanitarian Assistance, rapporteur M. Budislav Vukas, Resolution of 2 September 2003, Article IV.2; Carlo Focarelli, Duty to Protect in Cases of Natural Disaster, in: Rüdiger Wolfrum (ed.), *The Max Planck Encyclopedia of Public International Law* (Oxford: Oxford University Press 2012), paragraphs 22–23.

[38] The two-step scheme: Need for consent to humanitarian assistance but tied back by the obligation of the affected States not to refuse consent in an arbitrary manner had already been envisaged by the Institut de Droit International in resolutions since 1989. See Article 5(2) of the 1989 IDI Resolution: "The Protection of Human Rights and the Principle of Non-Intervention in the Internal Affairs of States."

[39] Sivakumaran, Arbitrary Withholding 2015, 525. See for the parallel state of IHL Dapo Akande/Emanuela-Chiara Gillard, Arbitrary Withholding of Consent to Humanitarian Relief Operations in Armed Conflict, *International Law Studies*, 2016 (forthcoming).

[40] For example, according to Principle 33 of the Maastricht Principles of 2012 (n. 46), Obligation to provide international assistance: "As part of the broader obligation of international cooperation, States, acting separately and jointly, that are in a position to do so, *must provide international assistance* to contribute to the fulfilment of economic, social and cultural rights in other States, . . ." (italics mine). See also Principle 35, Response to a request for international assistance or cooperation: "States that receive a request to assist or cooperate and are in a position to do so must *consider the request in good faith*, and respond in a manner consistent with their obligations to fulfil economic, social and cultural rights extraterritorially . . ." (italics mine). *De lege ferenda* for a subsidiary guarantee obligation of third States "for reasons of the effectiveness of human rights protection", see Matz-Lück, Solidarität, Souveränität und Völkerrecht 2012, 158. For an obligation to assist *de lege ferenda*, see Anne-Laurence Brugères, Le

it stands, however, third States merely have the right to *offer* assistance (Article 12). The general obligation to cooperate does not include any obligation to provide assistance under customary law. This opinion was expressed by several States (including Switzerland, Austria, and Germany) in response to the question by the ILC on this point in the Sixth Committee of the General Assembly.[41] From this, the ILC Special Rapporteur concluded that "the duty to cooperate in relief matters does not currently include a legal duty for States to provide assistance when requested by an affected State".[42]

A more far-reaching question is whether the omission of a State with primary responsibility to seek assistance, or its refusal to accept an offer of assistance, not only constitutes a violation of human rights, but whether this would even constitute a crime against humanity.[43] Such a qualification would establish a connection with R2P, given that crimes against humanity, committed by state officials or para-State actors under the jurisdiction of the territorial State, be it actively or through omission, are a recognized trigger of the subsidiary responsibility to protect, to be exercised by the international community. Perpetration through omission by the territorial State's responsible office-holders' refusal to accept assistance would be an extension. This would require that not only the objective elements of the offence are fulfilled but also the subjective elements of the offence in the minds of the relevant actors. It is, however, unlikely that any court or decision-making body would qualify an official's refusal to accept assistance in the event of a humanitarian catastrophe as part of a widespread or systematic attack directed against any civilian population, with knowledge of the attack. The idea of an

droit international de l'assistance humanitaire en cas de catastrophes naturelles, in: Société française pour le droit international (ed.), *Colloque de Nanterre, La responsabilité de protéger* (Paris: Pedone 2008), 169–176 (175–176).

41 Fifth Report on the Protection of Persons in the Event of Disasters by Eduardo Valencia-Ospina, Special Rapporteur, 9 April 2012 (UN Doc. A/CN.4/652), paragraphs 51–52 and 68 and other references on statements by States.

42 Special rapporteur, Fifth Report (n. 41), paragraph 68.

43 See, e.g., Ashley McLachlan-Bent/John Langmore, A Crime Against Humanity? Implications and Prospects of the Responsibility to Protect in the Wake of the Cyclone Nargis, *Global Responsibility to Protect* 3 (2011), 37–60 (40–41). See also Nele Matz-Lück, Solidarität, Souveränität und Völkerrecht: Grundzüge einer internationalen Solidargemeinschaft, in: Holger P. Hestermeyer et al. (eds), *Coexistence, Cooperation and Solidarity: Liber Amicorum Rüdiger Wolfrum* (Leiden: Martinus Nijhoff 2012), 141–165 (162–163): Inaction in the face of a natural disaster should be assessed in the same legal ways as inaction in the face of a genocide on the State's own territory, since what matters are the consequences for the persons concerned, not the causes.

R2P-based "second pillar"-type quasi-obligation of third States to assist a State struck by a disaster is therefore rather far-fetched.

8.3.2 *Human Rights Based Reasoning*

Basically all the mentioned duties can also be based on human rights: Positive obligations to protect arise from human rights also in the event of a natural disaster, similar to the obligation to protect from acts of violence in an R2P situation.[44] In other words, human rights (e.g., the right to life, the right to food, water, and shelter, and numerous other human rights) may require positive measures, and may be violated through omission. These positive rights in any event are addressed to the territorial (or jurisdictional) State.

The positive dimension of human rights (obligations to fulfil and protect) furthermore demands (generally speaking, and specifically in the case of a natural disaster) that States work together internationally in order to "realize" the social human rights. The general obligation to cooperate as mentioned in Article 7 of the ILC Draft Articles on Disaster Protection is therefore equally based on human rights. If the State affected by a natural disaster is unable to adequately manage the consequences of the disaster, the State is legally obligated to cooperate – including on the basis of the human rights conventions.[45] Likewise, human rights conventions oblige a State which cannot effectively protect human rights of its population to seek assistance.[46]

For the right to food (Article 11 of the ICESCR), the UN Committee on Economic, Social and Cultural Rights has postulated a "duty to seek international support". A State party unable to supply its population with food itself must demonstrate that it has requested international

[44] See n. 15.

[45] See, e.g., Fourth Report on the Protection of Persons in the Event of Disasters by Eduardo Valencia-Ospina (n. 48), paragraph 60; ILC, Report of the International Law Commission on its Sixty-sixth session (5 May–6 June and 7 July–8 August 2014), Chapter V. "Protection of persons in the event of disasters", pp. 84–138 (120).

[46] See also the Maastricht Principles on Extraterritorial Obligations of States in the Area of Economic, Social and Cultural Rights of 29 February 2012 (a text drafted by a group of international legal and human rights experts), Principle 34, Obligation to seek international assistance and cooperation: "A State has *the obligation to seek* international assistance and cooperation on mutually agreed terms when that State is unable, despite its best efforts, to guarantee economic, social and cultural rights within its territory. That State has an obligation to ensure that assistance provided is used towards the realization of economic, social and cultural rights."

food assistance to no avail; otherwise, it is deemed to have violated its obligations arising from the ICESCR.[47]

The refusal of a State affected by a disaster (or mass crimes) to accept a third State's offer of assistance may constitute a violation of the right to life and food (through omission).[48] But even from the human rights perspective not every refusal but rather only the *arbitrary refusal* of external assistance violates human rights.[49]

8.4 Appraisal

8.4.1 Conceptual Problems of the Protection Regime

The debate on a possible right to humanitarian assistance is older than R2P, and cross-connections have been made especially since 2008 (in the wake of Cyclone Nargis).[50] The ICISS report on R2P in 2001 still mentioned natural disasters as possible triggers of the responsibility to protect, including protection through military intervention.[51] From a systematic perspective – i.e., from a humanitarian starting point – the application of R2P to situations of natural disasters would be entirely

[47] UN CESCR, General Comment No. 12, The Right to Adequate Food (Article 11) of 12 May 1999, paragraph 17: "… In determining which actions or *omissions* amount to a violation of the right to food, it is important to distinguish the inability from the unwillingness of a State party to comply. Should a State party argue that resource constraints make it impossible to provide access to food for those who are unable by themselves to secure such access, *the State has to demonstrate that every effort has been made* to use all the resources at its disposal in an effort to satisfy, as a matter of priority, those minimum obligations … A State claiming that it is unable to carry out its obligation for reasons beyond its control therefore has the *burden of proving that this is the case and that it has unsuccessfully sought to obtain international support* to ensure the availability and accessibility of the necessary food" (UN Doc. E/C.12/1999; italics mine).

[48] Fourth Report on the Protection of Persons in the Event of Disasters by Eduardo Valencia-Ospina, Special Rapporteur, 11 May 2011 (UN Doc. A/CN.4/643), paragraph 59.

[49] See for the non-arbitrariness-standard in human rights law, e.g., Articles 6, 9, and 17 ICCPR.

[50] For cross-corrections, see ILC, Report of the International Law Commission on its 60th session (2008) (n. 26), paragraphs 247–250.

[51] ICISS 2001 (n. 8), paragraph 4.19: "In the Commission's view, military intervention for human protection purposes is justified in two broad sets of circumstances, namely in order to halt or avert large scale loss of life, actual or apprehended, with genocidal intent or not, which is the product either of deliberate state action, or *state neglect or inability to act, or a failed state situation* …" (italics mine). Paragraph 4.20: "overwhelming *natural or environmental catastrophes*, where the state concerned is either unwilling or unable to cope, or call for assistance, and significant loss of life is occurring or threatened" (italics mine).

consistent.[52] Today, however, the two strands of the law have been strictly separated by the political actors including by the UN Secretary General.[53] R2P has expressly been excluded from the area of disaster law and from the ILC project in this field.[54]

The conceptual added value of both strands of ideas (humanitarian assistance in the event of disasters and R2P) – extending beyond the protective dimension of human rights that so far has been conceived primarily as unfolding with a State's territorial boundaries – consists in their *transnational or extraterritorial dimension*. At issue here is first of all to break through the sovereignty shield of the State, such as when the State prohibits the entry of emergency teams (as the regime of Burma/Myanmar did after the cyclone of 2008), then to obligate other actors to assist on a residual basis instead of the territorial State, and finally to recognize a corresponding individual right against *third parties*.

The first aspect, namely the limitation of the State right to non-intervention, may be explained as a temporary suspension of territorial integrity and the right to non-interference, i.e., the external sovereignty of the territorial State. This is recognized with regard to R2P (see pp. 236–40). In the context of natural disasters, a similar idea has been accepted by admitting that while interference in the form of assistance requires the consent of the affected State, that State is not allowed to withhold its consent arbitrarily (see pp. 242–43).

52 See in favour of an application of the legal idea of R2P to natural disasters, the chapter "Responsabilité de protéger et catastrophes naturelles: l'émergence d'un régime?" in: Société française pour le droit international (ed.), *Colloque de Nanterre, La responsabilité de protéger* (Paris: Pedone 2008), 149–185; Jarrod Wong, Reconstructing the Responsibility to Protect in the Wake of Cyclones and Separatism, *Tulane Law Review* 84 (2009), 219–263; Allan Craig/Thérèse O'Donnell, A Call to Alms? Natural Disasters, R2P, Duties of Cooperation and Unchartered Consequences, *Journal of Conflict and Security Law* 17 (2012), 337–371; McLachlan-Bent/Langmore, *Crime Against Humanity?* 2011, 37–60.

53 The UN-Secretary General found R2P not applicable in the area of disaster law: "The responsibility to protect applies, until Member States decide otherwise, only to the four specified crimes and violations: genocide, war crimes, ethnic cleansing and crimes against humanity. To try to extend it to cover other calamities, such as HIV/AIDS, climate change or the response to natural disasters, would undermine the 2005 consensus and stretch the concept beyond recognition or operational utility" (Secretary General, "Implementing the Responsibility to Protect" (UN Doc. A/63/677 of 12 January 2009), paragraph 10(b)).

54 See already the preliminary report by the Special Rapporteur (UN Doc. A/CN.4/598) of 5 May 2008, para. 55. During the discussions within the ILC, the idea to apply R2P doctrine to disaster law was firmly rejected (Yearbook ILC 2008, vol. II (Part Two) A/CN.4/598, paragraphs 247-250).

The next problem is the obligation of third States, international organizations, or even NGOs to provide assistance and protection. The *residual obligation of third States or international organizations to protect*, as postulated in both debates (on R2P and disaster relief), does not constitute a "hard" legal obligation according to existing law.

To render such an obligation to protect operational in law, its triggering and distribution criteria would have to be defined. The questions of "whether", "who", and "how" must be answered. The following passages speculate about the legal implications of any putative (currently non-extant) legal obligation to protect and show how difficult such legalization would be. First, it would have to be defined when this obligation is triggered, its addressee (which State?), and the way in which it would have to be fulfilled (what measures have to be taken?) must also be clarified. Speculatively, assuming that in principle such an obligation of third States (or other international legal persons) to protect persons were conceivable, it would surely arise only when key international legal goods have been endangered, when a certain threshold for intervention has been reached, when there is a sufficiently close relationship between the State and the victims, and when effective possibilities for intervention and protection are available.[55] The latter depends, for instance, on the geographical vicinity to the victims, the political relationships between the involved States, the state of knowledge of the third State, and other factors.

Any obligation to protect, if legalised, would in any case always be just an obligation to apply due diligence, not an obligation as to the result to be achieved. For this reason, a balance would always have to be struck: The State should not be disproportionately burdened by the protective measures.[56]

In my view, the permanent members of the Security Council have the status of guarantors in this context, both in the event of atrocity crimes and with regard to humanitarian crises which amount to a threat to the

[55] For these criteria for determining the obligations of third States to prevent in the case of genocide, see ICJ, *Application of the Convention on the Prevention and Punishment of the Crime of Genocide (Bosnia and Herzegovina v. Serbia and Montenegro)*, Judgment of 26 February 2007, paragraph 430. For a template with the three criteria (closeness of the protecting State to the injuring State, type of damage, and appropriateness of protective measures), see Monica Hakimi, State Bystander Responsibility, *European Journal of International Law* 21 (2010), 341–385 (354–376).

[56] For the obligations to protect human rights under the ECHR, see fundamentally *Osman v. UK*, No. 87/1997/871/1083, Judgment of 28 October 1998, Reports 1998-VII, 3124, paragraph 116.

peace.[57] The reason is that they have a special responsibility for preserving world peace and accordingly also for human security. A veto by one of them can prevent protective measures by the Security Council. Although, in the event of disasters, an "arbitral" refusal by the territorial State to accept humanitarian assistance would, according to the ILC Articles on Disaster Protection, be theoretically unlawful, no other (less politized) body than the Security Council seems to have the authority to make a determination on this,[58] and thus to authorize "imposed" assistance by outside actors. The status of the permanent members of the Security Council as guarantors is activated in regard to armed conflicts, mass crimes, and natural disasters because all three situations affect human security and world peace.[59] This means that the P 5 themselves should not be allowed to arbitrarily or abusively exercise their veto in such a context.

Furthermore, any legal speculation on a potential legal obligation to protect would have to fit this into the general law of State responsibility. If the obligation to protect were legalized, passivity might become unlawful and trigger State responsibility for omission (Article 2 of the ILC Articles on State Responsibility of 2001).[60] Moreover, if the humanitarian catastrophe results from an internationally wrongful act of the territorial State, aid or assistance by a third State could also be committed through omission (Article 16 of the ILC Articles on State Responsibility of 2001). A *lex specialis* in this regard is complicity in genocide under Article III(e) of the Genocide Convention. But of course the aiding-and-abetting norms do not in themselves create obligations of third States to protect persons; rather, a legal obligation to protect would be their prerequisite. The norms do show, however, that the mere passivity of third States and their merely indirect contributions to humanitarian disasters may in principle become legally relevant.

Finally, the relationship of obligation between the State directly violating international law through its actions or omissions and any other State merely indirectly violating international law due to a putatively legally relevant omission of protection (which might be categorized as

[57] See Peters, The Security Council's Responsibility to Protect 2011, 25–26.

[58] But see Sivakumaran, Arbitrary Withholding 2015, 528–530, arguing that the entity best placed to assess the absence of arbitrariness is the UN Emergency Relief Coordinator.

[59] Since 2007, the Security Council has recognized the relevance of climate change to peace and security. Most recently, see the statement of the Security Council (SC/10332) of 20 July 2011.

[60] ILC Articles on State Responsibility (UN Doc. A/CN.4/L.602, Rev.1 (2001)).

"complicity") would have to be clarified. A ranking of responsibility, in which the outsider State committing the omission would be responsible only on a subsidiary basis, would make sense. This would also correspond to the concept of aid and assistance.

In the ultimate analysis, numerous elements of any putative obligation to protect would have to be clarified, both within the framework of the R2P concept and in the context of disaster relief: What measures are legally permissible if the territorial State arbitrarily denies access? What situations (beyond the mass commission of core crimes) trigger the obligation to protect and assist? How should those subject to the obligation to protect be demarcated exactly? What is the relationship or ranking of several obligors? What would be the substantive scope of a conceivable obligation to protect? Currently, no tendency towards "hardening" of the responsibility to protect in the direction of a true legal obligation is visible, so that these questions remain theoretical.

8.4.2 No Extraterritorial Individual Right to Protection de lege lata

In the context of this study, the key question is whether any future legal obligation of third States to grant protection in R2P situations and humanitarian emergencies would correspond to *an individual right* to transnational protection from core crimes and to prevention, suppression, and prosecution of such crimes (and possibly to protection in other humanitarian emergencies). Not every objective legal obligation generates an individual right to fulfilment.[61]

Even if, as already discussed, an *obligation* to protect – not only of the territorial State but also of (some) *third* States and/or international organizations – might at some point emerge under objective law, this would not mean that a subjective international individual right to transnational humanitarian protection (i.e., to active protective intervention by third States and other subjects of international law) will be recognized.[62] Articles 98 and 146 of the UN Convention on the Law of the Sea are examples of this. These articles stipulate obligations of the State to rescue in situations of distress at sea and an obligation of the International Seabed Authority to protect human life in the case of

[61] See Chapter 15, pp. 474–79 (addressees of international individual rights).

[62] For example, the index of a new book on disaster relief does not once mention the word rights. David D. Caron/Michael J. Kelly/Anastasia Telesetsky (eds), *The International Law of Disaster Relief* (Cambridge: Cambridge University Press 2015).

activities on the seabed. It is unclear, however, whether these obligations to protect are owed directly to the affected individual and whether they give rise to individual rights – or whether they give rise only to rights and duties between States.[63]

In the absence of obligations to protect set out in treaties, extraterritorial obligations of third States to protect would have to be based on customary international law. Such obligations are controversial even in the domain of human rights.[64] Extraterritorial obligations, including the obligation to do something actively against human suffering, have been developed especially by a group of international legal and human rights experts in the Maastricht Principles on Extraterritorial Obligations of States in the Area of Economic, Social and Cultural Rights.[65] But even these principles are formulated not in the language of rights but rather in the language of ("objective") obligations.

Especially in the law of disaster relief, there are no binding treaty texts that set out an individual right of natural persons – the victims of natural disasters – to humanitarian assistance from third States. However, several soft law texts claim the existence of such an individual right, explicitly in the language of an individual entitlement. Relevant in this regard are, for instance, the Principles and Rules for Red Cross and Red Crescent Disaster Relief, which were established in 1969 by the International

[63] See Irini Papanicolopulu, The Law of the Sea Convention: No Place for Persons? *The International Journal of Marine and Coastal Law* 27 (2012), 867–874 (870): "These Articles clearly contain a positive obligation. But can they be interpreted to attribute a right to the person to be saved? . . . not clear to whom the obligations provided in Arts. 98 and 146 are owed . . ."

[64] For instance, Marko Milanovic entirely rejects extraterritorial positive human rights obligations ("to secure or ensure human rights"), in contrast to extraterritorial duties of omission (obligations to respect human rights in their defensive dimension), since the fulfilment of positive obligations to act would require a high degree of control, institutions, and procedures – i.e., means of fulfilment that are territorially bound. The positive obligations would be triggered only if a "jurisdictional threshold" is exceeded, while the duties of omission (e.g., the obligation to refrain from killing) are valid universally and without territorial limits (Marko Milanovic, *Extraterritorial Application of Human Rights Treaties: Law, Principles, and Policy* (Oxford: Oxford University Press 2011), 209–228).

[65] On extraterritorial obligations, especially the obligation to *actively do something*, see especially the Maastricht Principles (n. 46), Principle 9, Scope of jurisdiction: "A State has obligations to respect, protect and fulfil economic, social and cultural rights in any of the following: . . . b) situations over which State acts *or omissions* bring about *foreseeable effects* on the enjoyment of economic, social and cultural rights, whether *within* or *outside its territory*; . . ." (italics mine). Principle 28, General obligation: "All States must take action, separately, and jointly *through international cooperation*, to fulfil economic, social and cultural rights of persons within their territories *and extraterritorially* . . ." (italics mine).

Federation of Red Cross and Red Crescent Societies in consultation with the ICRC. According to Principle 2.1, "The Red Cross and Red Crescent in its endeavour to prevent and alleviate human suffering, considers it a *fundamental right* of all people to both offer and receive humanitarian assistance."[66] The Mohonk Criteria for Humanitarian Assistance in Complex Emergencies of 1994 state: "Everyone has the *right* to request and receive humanitarian assistance necessary to sustain life and dignity from competent authorities or local, national or international governmental or nongovernmental organizations."[67] A resolution of the International Law Institute of 2003 stipulates: "The victims of disaster are *entitled* to request and receive humanitarian assistance."[68] These documents generally derive the "right" to humanitarian assistance from fundamental human rights (to life, physical integrity, food, shelter, etc.).[69] Some scholars also assume that an individual right to humanitarian assistance is already part of existing law.[70] Hector Gros Espiell even wanted to categorize the right to

[66] Reprinted in IRRC No. 310, pp. 55–130 (of 29 February 1996, Annex IV); italics mine. See also the Guiding Principles on the Right to Humanitarian Assistance by the Council of the International Institute of Humanitarian Law of San Remo, April 1993: "Principle 1: Every human being *has the right to humanitarian assistance* in order to ensure respect for the human rights to life, health, protection against cruel and degrading treatment and other human rights which are essential to survival, well-being and protection in public emergencies" (www.iihl.org; italics mine). See further Principle 3(2) of the UN Human Rights Commission's "Guiding Principles on Internal Displacement", stipulating that "Internally displaced persons have *the right to request and to receive protection* and humanitarian assistance from [national] authorities" (UN Doc. E/CN.4/1998/53/Add.2 of 11 February 1998; italics mine).

[67] http://pao.chadwyck.co.uk/PDF/1288958599975.pdf; reprinted also in HRQ 17 (1995), 192 et seq. (196) with an introduction by John M. Ebersole (italics mine). The Mohonk Criteria were established in 1994 by the Task Force on Ethical and Legal Issues in Humanitarian Assistance of the Programme on Humanitarian Assistance of the World Conference for Religion and Peace. They refer to complex emergencies. This was a private initiative funded in part by UNICEF, US authorities, and various NGOs. The Mohonk Criteria were formulated as a guideline for States and emergency relief organizations, including the Red Cross, and were meant to serve as a reference point for political debates and practice.

[68] IDI, Resolution of 2 September 2003 (n. 37), Article II (2) (italics mine).

[69] See also ILC, Report of the International Law Commission on its 60th session (2008) (n. 26), paragraph 244: Some ILC members qualified the right to humanitarian assistance as an individual right that was implicitly contained in international humanitarian law and international human rights.

[70] See, affirmatively, Wellens, Solidarity as a Constitutional Principle 2005, 785: "The existence of a right to receive humanitarian assistance . . . appears now to be widely accepted." In a later publication, the author denied the existence of an individual right of victims to assistance in current law, but he did assume an objective obligation to provide assistance (Karel Wellens, Revisiting Solidarity as a (Re-) Emerging Constitutional

humanitarian assistance as part of peremptory international law.[71] Other authors qualify that right as a procedural human rights substitute in situations where human rights are violated by the emergency, similar to a right to compensation.[72] Furthermore, the right to assistance might be construed by analogy to the right to humanitarian assistance guaranteed in armed conflict (Article 38(1); Articles 59, 62, and 108 of the Geneva Convention (IV); Article 70 of AP I). This analogy makes even more sense in complex emergencies. Ultimately, all of these considerations are merely *de lege ferenda.*

8.5 Conclusion

The firm exclusion of R2P considerations from the law of disaster response in the relevant political and law-making circles has obfuscated that the underlying issues are – from the perspective of the victims – basically the same: The question is whether they are entitled to protection not only by the State under whose jurisdiction they find themselves but also by outside actors should their own State be unwilling or unable to protect them. Within the triangle formed by the affected natural persons, the territorial State, and third party actors, relationships of rights and duties might emerge under international law.

Any evaluation of possible direct international individual rights to protection against acts of violence and forces of nature must distinguish between rights vis-à-vis the territorial State (or the State exercising sovereignty) and rights vis-à-vis third-party subjects of international law. An individual right to assistance in emergencies vis-à-vis the *territorial State* (or State of jurisdiction) might form the counterpart of the novel duty of an afflicted State whose national response capacity is

Principle: Some Further Reflections, in: Rüdiger Wolfrum/Chie Kojima (eds), *Solidarity: A Structural Principle of International Law* (Heidelberg: Springer 2009), 3–38 (17–18). Antonio Cassese reached the opposite conclusion in the deliberations on the resolution of the Institute of International Law in the Annuaire de l'Institut de Droit International (AIDI) 70–2, 164: Rights of the individual to humanitarian assistance exist only vis-à-vis the territorial State. Third States are not required by international law to grant assistance. There is thus definitely no corresponding individual right vis-à-vis third States.

71 See Hector Gros Espiell, Intervention, in: *Le droit à l'assistance humanitaire: actes du colloque international organisé par l' UNESCO* (1996), 103–112 (103): "Le droit à l'aide humanitaire constituerait donc à l'heure actuelle un cas de *jus cogens*, entraînant la nullité de tout traité et de tout acte juridique international en conflit avec ce droit ou avec les mesures exigées par son application."

72 See Marie-José Domestici-Met, Intervention, in: UNESCO (ed.), *Le droit à l'assistance humanitaire: actes du colloque international organisé par l' UNESCO* (1996), 79–99 (88).

manifestly exceeded by a disaster to seek assistance from other States and other potential assisting actors, as postulated by Article 11 of ILC Draft Articles on Disaster Protection. This individual right to assistance may also be derived from that State's positive obligations to protect and fulfil the human rights to life and physical integrity, shelter, basic medical care, and so on. The question then arises whether there is any need for an additional right to be protected in a humanitarian catastrophe, superimposed on the already existing positive dimension of human rights. The ILC special rapporteur on the protection of persons in the event of disasters highlighted that the ILC's "work has not been geared to the development of yet another specialized human rights instrument".[73]

In any case, the established human rights to assistance are opposable only to the State on whose territory or under whose jurisdiction the affected person finds itself,[74] not to bystander States. And within the scope of application of R2P, and in the event of disasters, no individual rights to protection vis-à-vis third States exist.

In principle, a "rights-based approach" is likely to be useful in the context of natural disasters, mass crimes, and armed conflict in order to do justice to the status of the individual in the current international legal order. However, in the current debate, "rights-based" is only understood to mean that the human rights of the affected persons must be observed at all times (cf. Article 6 of the ILC Draft Articles on Disaster Protection). So far, the so-called rights-based approach has not implied any recognition of an extraterritorial individual right to protection beyond human rights.

Although the speculative right to protection from acute emergencies would not be a human right as such, it would nevertheless be motivated by the underlying human rights (right to life, food, water, shelter, and others). These form a strong basis of legitimacy for any rights to protection. However, the codification or recognition of a direct and transboundary international individual right to protection and assistance in acute emergencies vis-à-vis third-party subjects of international law is not only unlikely but would probably also be unwise in terms of legal policy, since such a right could easily be abused as an excuse for interventions and could in practice hardly or only selectively be enforced.[75]

[73] 8th Report on the protection of persons in the event of disasters, by Eduardo Valencia-Ospina, Special rapporteur (UN Doc. A/CN.4/697 of 16 March 2016), para. 121.

[74] See pp. 245 and 251.

[75] ILC, Report of the International Law Commission on its 60th session (2008) (n. 26), paragraph 242.

9

The International Legal Status of Victims of Crime

Guiding Principle 6 of the UN Secretary-General's Guidance Note on the United Nations Approach to Transnational Justice enshrines the "centrality of victims" in the design and implementation of the procedures and mechanisms for coming to terms with the past.[1] This raises the question to what extent this "centrality" is reflected as an international legal status, giving rise to direct international rights (and possibly obligations). Generally, rights to protection, participation, justice, and reparation are mentioned nowadays as rights of the victim.[2] This chapter takes a closer look at two rights, namely the (more substantive than procedural) right to justice and to demand punishment (Section 9.1) and the procedural right to participate in criminal proceedings before the International Criminal Court (Section 9.2). The rights to remedy and reparation for serious violations of human rights and international humanitarian law are dealt with in Chapter 6 in the context of international secondary rights; this chapter deals specifically with the rights of victims in criminal proceedings.

9.1 The Duty to Prosecute and Punish

Recent literature and international case law, especially of the Inter-American Court of Human Rights (IACtHR), show a tendency to link prosecution and punishment with the individual victim concerned. The existence of an extensive "international human rights duty to prosecute" is assumed, i.e., a *duty* of States to prosecute and punish that is based on human rights law. For instance, Principle 4 of the Basic Principles and Guidelines on the Right to a Remedy and Reparation for

[1] UN Secretary-General, Guidance Note on the United Nations Approach to Transitional Justice of 10 March 2010, Guiding Principle 6: "Ensure the centrality of victims in the design and implementation of transitional justice processes and mechanisms."

[2] See Jonathan Doak, *Victims' Rights, Human Rights and Criminal Justice* (Oxford: Hart 2008).

Victims of Gross Violations of International Human Rights Law and Serious Violations of International Humanitarian Law of 2006 states: "In cases of gross violations of international human rights law and serious violations of international humanitarian law constituting crimes under international law, States have the duty to investigate and, if there is sufficient evidence, the duty to submit to prosecution the person allegedly responsible for the violations, and, if found guilty, the *duty to punish* her or him."[3]

9.1.1 *Individual Right of Punishment?*

In the context of this study, it is of interest to examine an intensification and further development of the "duty to punish" referred to by the General Assembly, namely the assertion of a corresponding *individual right* of victims to have the State prosecute perpetrators.[4] Proponents of this further development of the objective duty to punish into an individual right tend to conflate the preventive and repressive elements of punishment.

The individual right of punishment is seen as a manifestation of an assumed individual right to justice.[5] From this perspective, punishment serves as a remedy for a human rights violation.[6] If a State fails to engage in effective criminal prosecution, it violates the individual right of the victim to an effective remedy.[7]

According to that view, the individual right of punishment should exist *alongside* the still existing duty of the State to punish in the public interest. The claimed parallelism of an international individual right and the objective duty to punish has two doctrinal consequences: Firstly, the

[3] Basic Principles and Guidelines on the Right to a Remedy and Reparation for Victims of Gross Violations of International Human Rights Law and Serious Violations of International Humanitarian Law, UN Doc. A/Res/60/147 (21 March 2006); italics mine.

[4] See, representatively, Raquel Aldana-Pindell, An Emerging Universality of Justiciable Victims' Rights in the Criminal Process to Curtail Impunity for State-Sponsored Crimes, *Human Rights Quarterly* 26 (2004), 605–685 (esp. 621); M. Cherif Bassiouni, International Recognition of Victims' Rights, *Human Rights Law Review* 6 (2006), 203–279. For the ECHR, on the basis of highly differentiated case law on the duty to investigate: "A *right* to criminal *prosecution* of third parties, not guaranteed by Article 6 . . ., can be derived from Article 2 in conjunction with Article 1" (Jens Meyer-Ladewig, *Europäische Menschenrechtskonvention: Handkommentar* (3rd ed. Baden-Baden: Nomos 2011), Art. 2, paragraph 26, translation and italics mine).

[5] See Bassiouni, Victims' Rights 2006, 263: "A victim's right to access to justice includes the State's duty to prosecute those responsible for human rights violations."

[6] On remedy, see Chapter 6. [7] See Bassiouni, Victims' Rights, 2006, 264.

still existing duty of the State to punish (as a duty under objective law) cannot be dismissed by any waiver of the victim to assert an individual right of punishment. Secondly, the victim (as the holder of the right of punishment) has legal standing that is not affected by the (also) public interest in criminal prosecution. The right of punishment is justiciable, according to that view.[8]

9.1.2 *General International Law and the Case Law of the Human Rights Bodies*

Despite the mentioned academic assertions that an individual right of punishment arises from international law, this is far from clear. There seems to be no right arising from *customary international law* to demand punishment, nor is there a general principle of law to this effect. A comparison of the national penal systems shows that numerous legal orders provide rights of victims to participate in criminal proceedings as well as provide mechanisms for private claims. But these do not include any right of the victim to co-determine *the outcome* of the proceedings and can therefore not be interpreted as national guarantees of an individual right of punishment.[9] For lack of general practice, no right of punishment belonging to the victims of serious violations of human rights has crystallized under customary international law. The thesis of a right of punishment is not unambiguously substantiated by international case law.[10]

9.1.2.1 IACtHR

The driver of the development in the case law can be found in the Inter-American human rights bodies. In the landmark case of *Velásquez*

[8] "Victims' claims to prosecution as a remedy has come to mean … that prosecutions become a justiciable right that victims should be able to claim against states. … [T]he fact that a right may take on a collective or general character intended to benefit the public as a whole does not mean that an individual may not have standing to assert that right" (Aldana-Pindell, Justiciable Victims' Rights 2004, 622). Along these lines, see also Bassiouni, Victims' Rights 2006, 263.

[9] Tatjana Hörnle points out, however, that the lack of procedural rights of disposition does not prove the non-existence of a right of punishment belonging to the victim; see Tatjana Hörnle, Die Rolle des Opfers in der Straftheorie und im materiellen Strafrecht, *JuristenZeitung* 61 (2006), 950–958.

[10] The excellent analysis by Anja Seibert-Fohr, *Prosecuting Serious Human Rights Violations* (Oxford: Oxford University Press 2009) has in part been superseded by newer, more progressive case law that points more clearly in the direction of a right of punishment.

Rodríguez, the IACtHR held: "The State has a *legal duty* to take reasonable steps to prevent human rights violations and to use the means at its disposal to carry out a serious investigation of violations committed within its jurisdiction, to identify those responsible, to impose the appropriate *punishment* and to ensure the victim adequate compensation."[11] In more recent judgments, the IACtHR considers the question of punishing the most serious violations of human rights, such as disappearances, under the heading of the "obligation to investigate the facts and to identify, prosecute and, where appropriate, punish those responsible"[12] or the "obligation to investigate, and, where appropriate, punish grave human rights violations".[13] In these cases, a legal duty (but not unambiguously an individual right) of punishment is assumed. Because the IACtHR initially mentioned the general "respect and ensure" clause in Article 1 of the ACHR as the primary legal basis,[14] it was possible to interpret this duty purely in terms of objective law. In a more recent fundamental judgment, however, the failure to prosecute and, where appropriate, punish was characterized by the IACtHR as a violation of the right to a fair trial (Article 8(1) ACHR) and of the right to judicial protection for violations of fundamental rights (Article 25(1) ACHR) in conjunction with the general obligation to guarantee the rights under the Convention and to properly conform domestic law (Article 1(2) and Article 2 ACHR).[15] This means that the IACtHR in fact assumes an individual right of punishment.

9.1.2.2 ECtHR

So far, the ECtHR has not derived an individual right of punishment from the ECHR. On the contrary, it has explicitly held that the ECHR does not grant *any independent right to prosecution or sentencing of a third party*.[16] However, Article 2 of the ECHR (right to life) requires the establishment of an effective system of justice. This may in turn

[11] IACtHR, *Velásquez Rodríguez* v. *Honduras*, 29 July 1988, Ser. C No. 4 (1988) esp. paragraph 174 (italics mine).

[12] IACtHR, *Gelman* v. *Uruguay*, 24 February 2011 (merits and reparations), paragraph 250.

[13] IACtHR, *Gomes Lund et al. ("guerrilha do Araguaia")* v. *Brazil*, 24 November 2010 (preliminary objections, merits, reparations and costs), paragraph 137.

[14] IACtHR, *Velásquez Rodríguez* (n. 11), paragraph 166.

[15] IACtHR, *Gomes Lund et al.* (n. 13), paragraph 180.

[16] ECtHR, *Vo* v. *France*, No. 53924/00, 8 July 2004, paragraph 90: "The right to have third parties prosecuted or sentenced for a criminal offence cannot be asserted independently." Such a right can in particular not be derived from the right to access to justice contained in Article 6 of the ECHR.

require that the State grant the possibility of criminal prosecution: "[A]n effective judicial system, as required by Article 2, may, and under certain circumstances *must, include recourse to the criminal law.*"[17] But in the event of unintentional violations of the right to life, the positive State duty to protect under Article 2 does not mean that the State must in all cases provide a remedy under criminal law. In the domain of medical malpractice, it suffices to grant an appropriate civil remedy.[18]

In the situation of acts of violence with a lethal outcome, the ECtHR has also derived a State duty to *carry out an official investigation* from Article 2 of the ECHR (right to life) in conjunction with the general duty of the State to secure rights and freedoms as set out in Article 1 of the ECHR.[19] The purpose of such a criminal investigation and prosecution is to ensure implementation of the domestic laws for the protection of life and also to hold State authorities and officials accountable when they are involved.[20]

This case law imposed a threefold obligation on the contracting parties to the ECHR. They must, firstly, classify certain acts (killings, etc.) as criminal offences at the level of substantive law.[21] Already in an earlier case, the Court classified the existence of judicial obstacles to the prosecution of the sexual abuse of a disabled woman as a violation of the right to a private life: "This is a case where fundamental values and essential aspects of private life are at stake. *Effective deterrence is indispensable in this area and it can be achieved only by criminal-law provisions.*"[22]

Secondly, the States must establish an effective judicial system, the procedures of which are capable of resolving cases involving violent

[17] *Ibid.* (italics mine). [18] See *ibid.*

[19] The investigation must be *ex officio,* it must be speedy and effective, and it must be subject to public control. The authorities must take reasonable steps. These include the taking of forensic evidence and, where appropriate, an autopsy. ECtHR, *Oğur* v. *Turkey*, No. 21594/93, 20 May 1999, paragraph 88; ECtHR, *Hugh Jordan* v. *UK*, No. 24746/94, 4 May 2001, paragraphs 102–109.

[20] See settled case law of the ECtHR, such as *Opuz* v. *Turkey,* No. 33401/02, 9 June 2009, paragraph 150.

[21] If, for instance, a State were not to prosecute "honour killings" as a homicide, this would already constitute a violation of Article 2 of the ECHR (see Ralf Alleweldt, Kapitel 10: Recht auf Leben, in: Oliver Dörr/Rainer Grote/Thilo Marauhn (eds), *EMRK/GG: Konkordanzkommentar* (Tübingen: Mohr Siebeck 2nd ed. 2013), 491–536, paragraph 86).

[22] ECtHR, *X and Y* v. *The Netherlands*, No. 8978/80, 26 March 1985, paragraph 27. In paragraph 30, the Court continued: "Thus, neither Article 248 ter nor Article 239 paragraph 2 of the Criminal Code provided Miss Y with practical and effective protection. It must therefore be concluded, taking account of the nature of the wrongdoing in question, that she was the victim of a violation of Article 8 (art. 8) of the Convention."

death. Of particular importance in this regard is the general requirement of the "effectiveness" of the remedy, which is functionally the converse of the German prohibition of insufficient action.[23] According to this requirement, the provisions of the legal order in general and the proceedings in the specific case involving an alleged *intentional* homicide *must be suitable* to result in an investigation and the *punishment* of the guilty party: "[T]he positive obligations laid down in the first sentence of Article 2 of the Convention also require by implication that an efficient and independent judicial system should be set in place by which the cause of a murder can be established and the guilty parties *punished*."[24]

Thirdly, the punishment imposed in the specific case must be sufficiently severe and proportionate to the affected human right in order to achieve the necessary deterrent effect. In the *Gäfgen* case, for instance, the Grand Chamber criticized that a German court had imposed a mere warning with a suspended sentence pursuant to § 59 of the German Criminal Code (with suspended monetary penalties in the amount of sixty or ninety daily rates), holding these were "almost token fines" and an insufficient response to a violation of Article 3: "Such punishment, which is manifestly disproportionate to a breach of one of the core rights of the Convention, does not have the necessary deterrent effect in order to prevent further violations of the prohibition of ill-treatment in future difficult situations."[25]

According to the case law, this obligation to investigate and prosecute is an obligation of conduct: "[I]t is clear that the obligation, like the obligation under Articles 2 and 3 of the Convention to conduct an effective investigation into loss of life or allegations of ill-treatment, *is one of means and not one of result*."[26] The intensity of this obligation of

[23] See BVerfG 88, 203, 254–258 (1993) – *Schwangerschaftsabbruch* (on abortion).

[24] ECtHR (Grand Chamber), 24 October 2002, *Mastromatteo* v. *Italy*, No. 37703/97, paragraph 90 (italics mine). See also ECtHR, *Oğur* v. *Turkey* (n. 19), paragraph 88; ECtHR, *Vo* v. *France* (n. 16), paragraph 90 *e contrario*.

[25] ECtHR (Great Chamber), 1 June 2010, *Gäfgen* v. *Germany*, No. 22978/05, paragraph 124, Description of the facts in paragraph 49. The legal consequence of a warning with a suspended sentence is ordered only very rarely in practice. At issue in this case was torture, which the ECtHR classified as inhuman treatment prohibited by Article 3 of the ECHR. The ECtHR's criticism of this sentence without punishment is understandable.

[26] ECtHR, *Blumberga* v. *Latvia*, No. 70930/01, 14 October 2008, paragraph 67. The Court continued: "[I]n other words, the obligation on the authorities to investigate and prosecute such acts *cannot be absolute*, as it is evident that many crimes remain unresolved or unpunished notwithstanding the reasonable efforts of the State authorities. Rather, the obligation incumbent on the State is to ensure that a proper and adequate criminal investigation is carried out and that the authorities involved act in a competent and

conduct depends on the gravity of the alleged crime and is more demanding if the human right to life and physical integrity are at issue. In the case of lesser offences, such as against property, the State breaches its obligation to investigate and prosecute only if the measures taken are evidently insufficient.[27]

9.1.2.3 UN Human Rights Committee and Other Bodies

Other special conventions expressly stipulate an obligation to punish, such as the Convention against Torture (CAT). Again, this could be read as an obligation only under objective law. The provision in Article 4 of the CAT requiring States parties to classify all acts of torture as criminal offences[28] does not explicitly grant a corresponding individual right of the victim to have the perpetrator punished. According to the African Commission on Human and Peoples' Rights, amnesties granting immunity from prosecution to violators of human rights infringe upon the victims' right to legal protection under Article 7(1) of the African Charter on Human and Peoples' Rights.[29]

In its views until 2007, the UN Human Rights Committee distinguished the objective obligation of the State from any individual right. According to that approach, the fundamental human rights of the ICCPR generated an *obligation of the State under objective law* to investigate and possibly punish the perpetrator, especially in cases involving disappearances and killings. But the Committee also emphasized that "[t]he Covenant *does not provide* that private individuals have the *right* to demand that the State criminally prosecute another person. ... The Committee nevertheless

efficient manner. Moreover, the Court is sensitive to the practical difficulties which the authorities may face in investigating crime and to the need to make operational choices and prioritise the investigation of the most serious crimes" (*ibid.*, italics mine).

27 ECtHR, *Blumberga* v. *Latvia* (n. 26), paragraph 67: "Consequently, the obligation to investigate is less exacting with regard to less serious crimes, such as those involving property, than with regard to more serious ones, such as violent crimes, and in particular those which would fall within the scope of Articles 2 and 3 of the Convention. The Court thus considers that in cases involving less serious crimes the State will only fail to fulfil its *positive obligation* in that respect where *flagrant and serious deficiencies in the criminal investigation or prosecution* can be identified" (italics mine).

28 Article 4 CAT: "1. Each State Party shall ensure that all acts of torture are offences under its criminal law. The same shall apply to an attempt to commit torture and to an act by any person which constitutes complicity or participation in torture. 2. Each State Party shall make these offences punishable by appropriate penalties which take into account their grave nature."

29 African Commission on Human and Peoples' Rights, *Mouvement Ivoirien des droits humains (MIDH)* v. *Côte d'Ivoire*, No. 246/2002, July 2008, paragraphs 97–98.

considers that the State party has *a duty to investigate* thoroughly alleged violations of human rights, particularly enforced disappearances and violations of the right to life, *and to criminally prosecute, try and punish* those deemed responsible for such violations. This duty applies *a fortiori* in cases in which the perpetrators of such violations have been identified".[30] In more recent views, the Committee has no longer made the distinction between the obligation of the State and the right of the victim or the victim's relatives. Instead, it now emphasizes that the failure to prosecute violates both the human right to life (Article 6) and the right to protection from torture and mistreatment (Article 7) as well as the right to an effective remedy under Article 2(3)(a) of the ICCPR.[31] "[C]riminal investigation and consequential prosecution are necessary remedies for violations of human rights such as those protected by articles 6 and 7 of the Covenant." Effective remedy as referred to in the Covenant requires the "initiation and pursuit of criminal proceedings".[32] "A violation of the Covenant may therefore arise as a result of a State party's failure to take appropriate measures *to punish*, investigate or redress such a violation. ... When a person dies in circumstances that might involve a violation of the right to life, the State party is bound to ... *ensure that there is no impunity*."[33] This means that in alleged cases involving the most serious attacks against physical integrity by organs of the State or enforced disappearance, the Human Rights Committee draws on the right to life and the right to an effective remedy in order to derive a human right to prosecution and, where appropriate, punishment.

9.1.2.4 Interim Conclusion

All human rights bodies – i.e., the ECtHR, the IACtHR, and the UN Human Rights Committee – have formulated a "positive obligation",[34]

[30] See the landmark decision of the UN Human Rights Committee in a case involving the kidnapping, torture, and killing of indigenous politicians by the Colombian military: *José Vicente et al.* v. *Colombia*, No. 612/1995, 19 August 1997, paragraph 8.8 (italics mine). See also *Messaouda Kimouché* v. *Algeria*, 10 July 2007, paragraph 9: "While the Covenant does not give individuals the right to demand the criminal prosecution of another person ... the Committee nevertheless considers the State party duty-bound ... to prosecute, try and punish the culprits."

[31] UN Human Rights Committee, *Sathasivam* v. *Sri Lanka*, No. 1436/2005, 8 July 2008, paragraphs 6.4 and 8; *Amirov* v. *Russian Federation*, No. 1447/2006, 2 April 2009, paragraphs 11.2 and 13; *Felipe and Evelyne Pestaño* v. *The Philippines*, No. 1619/2007, 23 March 2010, paragraphs 7.2 and 7.6.

[32] *Sathasivam* v. *Sri Lanka* (n. 31), paragraphs 6.4 and 8.

[33] *Felipe and Evelyne Pestaño* v. *The Philippines* (n. 31), paragraphs 7.2 and 7.6 (italics mine).

[34] *José Vicente et al.* v. *Colombia* (n. 30), paragraph 8.8.

a "legal duty",[35] or a "duty . . . to criminally prosecute, try and punish"[36] in the form of an obligation to investigate and, in the extreme case, to punish, but not necessarily in the form of an individual right (i.e., a right to demand punishment). At the current time, the case law of the ECtHR does not explicitly recognize individual treaty rights of victims of violent crimes to demand punishment of the perpetrators, but it does recognize corresponding obligations of the State to punish. In contrast, the decisions of the IACtHR and also, more recently, of the UN Human Rights Committee go farther and appear to postulate a *human right to prosecution and punishment*. The following section will discuss whether a distinction between a State obligation and a right of the affected person plays a role in the field of human rights or whether they are simply two sides of the same coin.

9.1.3 *Obligation to Investigate and Prosecute Exists Only under Objective Law*

One reason for the emergence of the idea of an international individual right to justice, which is claimed to include the right to demand punishment, is likely to be found in the enforcement mechanisms of the international human rights system.[37] Because country reports and the ensuing dialogue do not constitute an effective sanction and because State complaints are almost never lodged, the system depends significantly on *enforcement by affected individuals*. In those treaty regimes providing an individual complaint mechanism, such as the ACHR, the ECHR, and the ICCPR, it therefore has made sense to individualize the legal consequence of punishment and to construe a right to remedy. The ECtHR case law on the duty to investigate, for instance, was "born of necessity".[38] It was developed in relation to attacks by State security forces especially in Turkey, i.e., not with a view to violent crimes committed by private individuals. The context is the limited jurisdiction of the Court. The ECtHR has been able to take only a human rights approach, given that it is responsible only for sanctioning violations of human rights. It does not have any possibility of uprooting the deficient justice system

[35] IACtHR, *Velásquez Rodríguez* (n. 11), paragraph 174.
[36] *José Vicente et al.* v. *Colombia* (n. 30), paragraph 8.8.
[37] See Seibert-Fohr, *Human Rights Violations* 2009, 284.
[38] Meyer-Ladewig, *Europäische Menschenrechtskonvention* 2011, Art. 2, Rn. 29 (translation mine).

or forcing it to reform itself due to "objective" violations of the rule of law.

The progressive case law of the IACtHR, which – unlike that of the ECtHR – clearly assumes an individual right of punishment, must be seen in the specific historical context of the region. In Latin America, the main issue involves the widespread crimes committed by the military dictatorships of the 1960s to 1980s. Typically, the Court is responding to *legislation* such as amnesty laws and statutes of limitation that prevent the punishment of perpetrators. For instance, it has held the Brazilian amnesty law to be void and has expressly required the State to carry out a criminal investigation potentially leading to punishment of the individuals responsible for the enforced disappearance of the claimants' relatives during the military dictatorship (1964–1985).[39] In Latin America, individual complaints have been considered a promising way to combat the impunity of crimes committed by regimes. For this purpose, the literature has claimed an individual right of punishment, and the IACtHR has made a crucial contribution to this historical process of dealing with the past. The human right of punishment conceptualized here is thus a direct reaction to political transition and also compensates for the lack of a comprehensive international power to sanction and especially to punish that could be used to prosecute crimes (beyond individual complaints based on human rights claims).

The international individual right of punishment developed specifically in Latin America for these reasons thus plays an important legal–political role in that specific context. In cases concerning regime crimes (Algeria, Sri Lanka, the Russian Federation in regard to Chechnya, the Philippines), the UN Human Rights Committee has universalized these legal constructions.

The following practical and conceptual problems should, however, be seriously considered in this context: Firstly, the international human rights bodies are overextended by the comprehensive monitoring of domestic criminal law and procedural law. Tellingly, the Inter-American Court's sentences ordering States to investigate and prosecute are "almost never fully implemented".[40]

[39] See, especially, IACtHR, *Gomes Lund et al.* (n. 13), paragraphs 137–182 and 253–257, esp. 174 and 256.

[40] Michael J. Camilleri/Vivianna Krsticevic, Making International Law Stick: Reflections on Compliance with Judgments in the Inter-American Human Rights System, in: Joaquí Gonzalez Ibáñes (ed.), *Protección internacional de derechos humanos y estado de derecho* (Colombia: Grupo Editorial Ibàñes 2008), 235–247 (241). Statistically, these orders and

Even more significant is the conceptual objection: The criminal discourse in the field of human rights is strangely detached from the basic concepts of criminal law. Attention should be paid to these concepts. The starting point for these considerations should be the purpose of the punishment. The imposition and enforcement of a criminal penalty that sharply curtails the fundamental rights of the perpetrator is a sovereign instrument employed in the public interest. The main modern purposes of punishment are general and specific deterrence. Specific deterrence also includes the rehabilitation of the perpetrator and the protection of society. In today's law, punishment is in the public interest, not the private interest – regardless of which theory of punishment is followed in detail.[41] Even archaic theories of punishment such as theories of atonement and retribution focused on the interest of the community, not the victim. The key question of the *ownership of the right of punishment* will be considered once again in the chapter after the analysis of the status of victims in ICC proceedings (see Section 9.3, p. 276).

The purposes of punishment at the level of international law do not deviate considerably from the classic purposes in domestic criminal law. However, the Yugoslavia Tribunal specifically defined the purposes of punishment in international criminal justice as distinguished from domestic purposes of punishment.[42] In contrast to domestic criminal law, international criminal law is concerned only with very serious crimes. Public reprobation and stigmatization by the international community are the focus of the purposes of punishment at the international level, followed by deterrence and retribution. According to the Yugoslavia Tribunal, punishment also contributes to appeasement and gives "the chance to the people who were sorely afflicted to mourn those among them who had been unjustly killed".[43] Similarly, Principle 22(f) of the General Assembly's Basic Principles and Guidelines on the Right to a Remedy of 2006[44] mentions judicial sanctions as a form of satisfaction for the victim.

recommendations have so far been totally satisfied only in 10 per cent of the cases, while 13 per cent were partly satisfied, and 76 per cent were not satisfied (data from 2001 to 2006; in Fernando Basch et al., The Effectiveness of the Inter-American System of Human Rights Protection: A Quantitative Approach to Its Functioning and Compliance with Its Decisions, SUR –*International Journal of Human Rights* 7 (2010), 9–34 (18)).

41 But deviating from this view, see Tatjana Hörnle, *Straftheorien* (Tübingen: Mohr Siebeck 2011), 37–41.

42 ICTY, *The Prosecutor* v. *Drazen Erdemovic*, Sentencing Judgement, Case No. IT-96-22-T, Judgement of 29 November 1996, paragraphs 57–66.

43 *Ibid.*, paragraph 65. 44 n. 3.

Even from this perspective, satisfaction for the victim or the victim's family may be a side-effect of the punishment; but the rule of law requires that it cannot be the *reason* for the punishment. Imposing a punishment to appease a victim's need for satisfaction or revenge would be disproportionate.

From the perspective of human rights, the following insights are also important: Firstly, human rights are primarily directed at States. The commission of a criminal offence by private individuals (not sovereigns) is not in itself a violation of human rights. The human rights violation consists in the lack of protection by the State. The obligation to protect may manifest itself more strongly as an obligation to prosecute or even to punish if it cannot be fulfilled effectively by other, weaker sovereign means ("prohibition of insufficient action").[45] But only a small proportion of the acts that affect the human rights to life, physical integrity, individual freedom, non-discrimination, and human dignity are simultaneously also international criminal offences (such as war crimes) or obligate States to criminalize and prosecute them under their domestic law (such as torture, slavery, or apartheid). Other than the obligation to punish these serious crimes, current international law does not include any stronger obligation to protect in the sense of a comprehensive obligation to prosecute other serious violations of human rights.

Secondly, the individual rights to protection from private attacks against legal goods flanked by human rights are – as mentioned earlier – in principle only obligations of conduct, not obligations of result.[46] A strict right to a concrete State measure with a specific result (such as imposition of a penalty) is not even conceivable, because such a result cannot be guaranteed beforehand. In States governed by the rule of law, there can never be an abstract and result-oriented right of a victim to demand concrete punishment of a third party, because the third party's guilt must first be ascertained in judicial proceedings. The norm abbreviated as "right of punishment" can therefore always only be a guarantee of a sufficiently effective, but guilt-appropriate, criminal prosecution and punishment, which means it is always open in respect of the result.

Thirdly, the definition of conduct as a criminal offence and the imposition of the legal consequence of a penalty (i.e., the criminalization of an act) require a legal basis (*nullum crimen, nulla poena sine lege*). Mere

[45] As the German Constitutional Court put it in the abortion case (n. 23).
[46] See text with n. 26.

classification of an act as a violation of human rights is not sufficient for such an imposition.[47]

In our context, it is a crucial question whether an individual right corresponds to the State *obligation* of conduct postulated by case law. Is this merely a different way of expressing the same thing, or is there in fact a difference in terms of legal construction? In general, not every legal obligation corresponds to an individual right to have that obligation met. In all legal orders, including international law, there are numerous obligations solely under objective law that are not matched by any individual right. In *general international law*, obligations as a rule are more extensive than individual rights, i.e., there are *no corresponding individual rights to fulfilment*. In contrast, the doctrine of international human rights has so far not developed any divergence between "solely objective" obligations of States parties and obligations corresponding to individual rights. This is in part due to the fact that human rights have been conceived as individual rights from the outset. At the same time, the general treaty clauses that also establish the competence of the monitoring bodies are formulated in terms of objective law. For instance, Article 19 of the ECHR establishes the ECtHR's jurisdiction to ensure "the observance of the engagements" undertaken by the States parties. Specifically in the field of human rights, one should therefore assume a *symmetry of obligations and rights*: Normally, "rights" of the human being are inherent in the State obligations referred to here, so that the term "obligations" used in case law *indirectly* postulates a "right". The ECtHR uses the language of rights as well as the language of obligations: It has expressly held that Article 2 of the ECHR does *not* grant a right of the claimants for a third party to be prosecuted or punished. According to the Court, Article 2 also does *not* contain any obligation of result in the sense that every prosecution must end in a conviction or specific penalty. "L'article 2 ne peut pas être interprété comme impliquant, en tant que tel, un *droit* pour un requérant de faire poursuivre ou condamner au pénal des tiers, ou une *obligation de résultat supposant que toute poursuite doit se solder par une condamnation, voire par le prononcé d'une peine déterminée*."[48] The prohibition of insufficient action or the

[47] See BVerfG, *Schwangerschaftsabbruch* (n. 23), 292–293.

[48] ECtHR, *Zavoloka* v. *Latvia*, No. 58447/00, 7 July 2009, paragraph 34: "Article 2 cannot be interpreted as implying, in itself, *a right* of an applicant to have third persons prosecuted or criminally sentenced, and an *obligation of result* assuming that every criminal prosecution must be resolved by Judgement, that is to say by the pronouncement of a specific penalty" (translation and italics by the author).

requirement of effectiveness does, however, appear to entail a *de facto* obligation to punish in the case of attacks against life: "En revanche, les juridictions nationales ne doivent en aucun cas s'avérer disposées à *laisser impunies* des atteintes à la vie."[49]

In light of the reasons mentioned earlier – especially the purposes of punishment in a modern legal order – it is preferable to assume that in the context of criminal investigation and potential punishment, the *obligations of conduct are solely objective*, not mirrored by corresponding individual rights. The State obligation under objective law to investigate and punish does not generate an individual right to demand punishment. This legal interpretation is covered by the case law of the human rights bodies, even if the formulations chosen ("duty" or "obligation") might also be read as an indirect recognition of corresponding rights.

As the primary legal basis of the obligation of conduct to carry out criminal investigations and prosecutions, one might consider the general provisions of the human rights covenants and the general "ensure and respect" clauses of the Geneva Conventions on international humanitarian law.[50] In Article 2(2) of the ICCPR, for instance, the States parties undertake "to take the necessary steps . . . to adopt such laws or other measures as may be necessary to give effect to the rights recognized in the present Covenant". According to Article 1 of the ECHR, the High Contracting Parties shall "secure to everyone within their jurisdiction the rights" defined in the Convention. Article 1(1) of the ACHR states: "The States Parties to this Convention undertake to *respect* the rights and freedoms recognized herein and to *ensure* to all persons subject to their jurisdiction the free and full exercise of those rights and freedoms." According to common Article 1 of the Geneva Conventions, the High Contracting Parties undertake "to respect and to ensure respect for the present Convention in all circumstances". These clauses can be interpreted as "solely objective" and are thus better suited as legal bases for the obligation of conduct than the individual human rights guarantees set out in the treaties.

In the final analysis, victims of violence are protected under current international law by a *procedural* obligation of the States under whose jurisdiction the acts of violence took place to investigate and prosecute.

[49] "Correspondingly, the national jurisdictions must in no case show themselves disposed to leave unpunished attacks on life" (*Ibid.*, translation by the author).

[50] See Seibert-Fohr, *Human Rights Violations* 2009, 285.

This obligation under objective law does not, however, guarantee punishment.

9.2 The Legal Status of Victims in International Criminal Proceedings

9.2.1 Basic Concerns of the New Focus on Victims

The group of all potential victims is the traditional point of reference of criminal law. What is new about the victim orientation of recent criminal proceedings is the focus on the *current, specific* victim of the crime. In soft law texts, modern international law has developed principles for taking account of the concerns of victims of crime in domestic criminal law.[51] Moreover, it has established a strong legal status for victims in international criminal proceedings (pp. 270–75).

Inclusion of the specific victim in the criminal proceedings pursues legitimate purposes. Firstly, participation gives victims satisfaction. Victims are able to regain trust in the functioning of the legal order. Interaction with the victim can also make the perpetrator emotionally aware of the injurious character of her or his actions. The victim and the perpetrator are given the opportunity to process the conflict. Participation of the victim also makes prosecution more effective by making more information available. Finally, it can at least partially neutralize the harmful effects of the corruption of police, prosecutors, and judges that is widespread in many legal orders.

The statutes of the international *ad hoc* tribunals for the former Yugoslavia (1992) and Rwanda (1993) do not contain provisions on victim participation. This gap was widely criticized and was an incentive to include a detailed rule governing proceedings before the International Criminal Court (ICC).[52] Other international and hybrid

[51] See UN General Assembly Declaration of Basic Principles of Justice for Victims of Crime and Abuse of Power of 29 November 1985 (UN Doc. A/RES/40/34), paragraph 6. In this regard, see United Nations Office for Drug and Crime Prevention, Centre for International Crime Prevention, Handbook on Justice for Victims: On the Use and Application of the Declaration of Basic Principles of Justice for Victims of Crime and Abuse of Powers (New York 1999), 34–41. See also Council of Europe, Committee of Ministers, Recommendation No. R (85) 11 of 28 June 1985, On the Position of the Victim in the Framework of Criminal Law and Procedure.

[52] See Brianne McGonigle Leyh, *Procedural Justice?: Victim Participation in International Criminal Proceedings* (Cambridge: Intersentia 2011); Regula Echle, Die Stellung der Opfer

domestic–international criminal bodies (e.g., the Extraordinary Chambers in the Courts of Cambodia[53] and the Special Tribunal for Lebanon[54]) provide for intensive participation of victims in criminal proceedings, but these will not be discussed here. The participation of victims of crime in proceedings before the ICC – as specified in detail by the Rome Statute, the Rules of Procedure and Evidence of the ICC (hereinafter "Rules"[55]), and the case law of the ICC – grants victims a strong procedural status grounded in international law. A brief overview is provided below.

9.2.2 *The Legal Status of Victims under the ICC Statute*

The definition of victims: According to Rule 85, "victims" are primarily natural persons who have suffered harm as a result of the commission of any crime within the jurisdiction of the ICC.[56] The definition of victims thus includes four elements: person, harm, crime, and causality.[57]

Unlike in earlier soft law texts, family members of victims of crime are not explicitly defined as victims themselves.[58] In one of the first

in Verfahren vor dem Internationalen Strafgerichtshof, Master's Thesis at the Faculty of Law at the University of Basel, September 2010.

[53] The Extraordinary Chambers in the Courts of Cambodia were established to adjudicate the crimes of the Khmer Rouge. On victim participation, see Extraordinary Chambers in the Courts of Cambodia (ECCC), Rules and Procedures Committee, Practice Direction 02/2007/Rev. 1, Victim Participation, most recently amended on 27 October 2008; in the literature, see David Boyle, The Rights of Victims, *Journal of International Criminal Justice* 4 (2006), 307–313.

[54] See Article 17 (Rights of victims) of the Statute of the Special Tribunal for Lebanon (Annex to UNSC res. 1757 (2007) of 30 May 2007) and the Rules of Procedure and Evidence of 20 March 2009; in the literature, see Jérôme de Hemptine, Challenges Raised by Victims' Participation in the Proceedings of the Special Tribunal for Lebanon, *Journal of International Criminal Justice* 8 (2010), 165–179.

[55] Rules of Procedure and Evidence of the ICC (UN Doc. PCNICC/2000/1/Add.1 (2000)), esp. Chapter 4, Section III, Victims and witnesses (Rules 85–99).

[56] Rule 85, "Definition of victims: For the purposes of the Statute and the Rules of Procedure and Evidence: (a) 'Victims' means natural persons who have suffered harm as a result of the commission of any crime within the jurisdiction of the Court . . ."

[57] See ICC, PTC I, *Situation in the Democratic Republic of the Congo*, Decision on the Applications for Participation in the Proceedings . . . of 17 January 2006, ICC-01/04, paragraphs 77–94.

[58] In contrast, the definition of victims in the Declaration of Basic Principles of Justice for Victims of Crime and Abuse of Power of 1985 (n. 51) and Principle 8 of the General Assembly's Basic Principles and Guidelines on the Right to a Remedy of 2006 (n. 3) also includes family members.

cases before the ICC, however, the Pre-Trial Chamber recognized close family members as potential victims.[59] Under the Rules of Procedure of the ICC, organizations or institutions sustaining *direct* harm to their property dedicated to public purposes may also be victims.[60] By comparison, this means that natural persons may also be "indirect" victims.[61] In order to be recognized as a victim in a formal sense under the Statute, the affected person must make a written application to the ICC accompanied by sufficient evidence demonstrating the elements of a victim (Rules 89 and 85).[62] According to the wording of the relevant provisions, it cannot be ruled out that victims also serve as witnesses in criminal proceedings, and it is precisely this possible double role as victim and witness that might entail difficulties for the fairness of the proceedings.

The *basic provision on the participation of victims in proceedings* is Article 68 of the Rome Statute ("Protection of the victims and witnesses and their participation in the proceedings"). This provision is further specified by the Rules in Chapter 4, Section III, Subsection 3, "Participation of victims in the proceedings" (Rules 89–93). Article 68(3) of the Rome Statute states: "Where the *personal interests* of the *victims* are affected, the Court shall permit their views and concerns to be presented and considered at stages of the proceedings *determined to be appropriate* by the Court and in a manner which is not prejudicial to or inconsistent with the *rights of the accused* and a *fair and impartial trial* . . ." This means that when the Court decides on the participation of victims in proceedings, it must begin by considering two different elements: firstly, whether the person is a "victim", and secondly – and additionally – whether that person's "personal interests" are affected.

59 ICC, PTC I, Decision No. ICC-01/04-01/06 of 29 June 2006, p. 7: "where applicable, close family or dependents".

60 Rule 85 (b): "Victims may include organizations or institutions that have sustained *direct* harm to any of their property which is dedicated to religion, education, art or science or charitable purposes, and to their historic monuments, hospitals and other places and objects for humanitarian purposes" (italics mine).

61 The crime does not have to target the affected persons directly in order to make them victims. The definition of victims before the ICC is accordingly broader than under the rules of procedure of the Yugoslavia and Rwanda tribunals. See Rule 2(A) of the Rules of Procedure and Evidence of the ICTY and of the ICTR: "Victim: A person *against* whom a crime over which the Tribunal has jurisdiction has allegedly been committed" (italics mine).

62 The existence of the four elements of victims must be credibly shown (standard of "grounds to believe"), see ICC, PTC I, *Situation in the Democratic Republic of the Congo* (n. 57), paragraphs 95–101.

If the Court finds that these two preconditions are met (exercising a considerable margin of discretion), it – thirdly – has discretion regarding the manner of participation, also depending on the stage[63] of the investigation and prosecution. Fourthly, the ICC must weigh the desirability of victim participation against the opposing concerns of the rights of the accused and the fairness and impartiality of the proceedings.[64]

Triggering of criminal proceedings before the ICC: Victims themselves cannot trigger criminal proceedings before the ICC in the sense of a private action. However, the Prosecutor may receive all types of information, including information provided by victims or NGOs representing victims' interests (Article 15(2) of the Rome Statute). Moreover, when deciding whether to initiate investigations or not, the Prosecutor must take into account "the interests of victims" (Article 53(1)(c) of the Rome State). The Rome Statute specifies that the Prosecutor has the duty to respect the interests and personal circumstances of victims when exercising her or his powers (Article 54(1)(b) of the Rome Statute).[65] On the whole, the triggering of proceedings before the ICC is already significantly shaped by the interests of victims.

Consideration of the interests of victims: Beyond the decision on the initiation of investigations, the interests of the victims must be considered at all stages of the proceedings. Accordingly, the Pre-Trial Chamber may, pursuant to Article 57(3)(e) of the Rome Statute, seek the cooperation of States to take protective measures for the purpose of forfeiture, "in particular for the ultimate benefit of victims". According to Article 65(4) of the Rome Statute, the Trial Chamber may, even after an admission of guilt, order that the trial be continued or request the Prosecutor to present additional evidence, "in particular [in] the interests of the victims".

Participation of the victim includes *information on procedural steps*. Victims must be notified of the decisions of the organs of the Court.[66]

[63] From the investigation of a situation ("preliminary examination stage") and the hearings on jurisdiction and admissibility to the pre-trial proceedings (especially "confirmation of the charges hearing"), the trial, and appeals.

[64] On these four elements, see ICC, Appeals Chamber, Decision, *in limine*, on Victim Participation in the appeals of the Prosecutor and the Defence against Trial Chamber I's Decision entitled "Decision on Victims' Participation" of 16 May 2008 (ICC-01/04-01/06-1335), paragraph 36.

[65] Already in the hearings to authorize the Prosecutor's investigation, victims may make representations to the Pre-Trial Chamber (Article 15(3) of the Rome Statute).

[66] Rule 92; see also Rule 50(1) on the decision of the Prosecutor to seek authorization to initiate an investigation; Rule 50(5) on the Pre-Trial Chamber; Rule 59(1)(b) and 59(2): notification by the Registrar.

Victims also have the right to *legal representation* (Rule 90).[67] Participation furthermore includes the possibility for victims to make their own (oral or written) *observations.*[68] According to Article 15(3) of the Rome Statute, victims may make representations to the Pre-Trial Chamber during pre-trial proceedings. Article 19(3) of the Rome Statute states that victims may submit observations to the Court on questions of jurisdiction or admissibility. The participation of victims may in particular take the form of an opening or closing statement (Rule 89). According to Rule 93, a Chamber may also seek the views of victims not accorded formal participation status.

With reference to the general authority of the Court to request the submission of all evidence necessary for the determination of the truth (Article 69(3) of the Rome Statute) and the right of the victims' legal representatives to question witnesses, experts, and the accused (Rule 91(3)), Trial Chamber I decided that victims are also permitted to *introduce and examine evidence in proceedings* if, in the view of the Chamber, such evidence will assist the Court in the determination of the truth.[69] Based on the provisions requiring consideration of the views and concerns of the victims (Articles 68(3) and 69(4) of the Rome Statute), the Chamber concluded that the victims' legal representatives may challenge the admissibility or relevance of evidence.[70]

An important element of the proceedings is the *protection of victims* (and witnesses).[71] The Registrar has set up a Victims and Witnesses Unit (Article 43(6) of the Rome Statute). This unit must provide, in consultation with the Office of the Prosecutor, protective measures and security arrangements, counselling, and other appropriate assistance for witnesses and victims who appear before the Court.[72] Victims may

[67] According to Rule 91, legal representatives of victims have – beyond the rights accorded to victims themselves – the right to attend and participate in hearings.

[68] The Chamber concerned decides whether participation is effected through personal attendance and oral observations or whether only written submissions are permitted (Rule 91(2)).

[69] ICC, Trial Chamber I, Case No. ICC-01/04–01/06 (*Situation in the Democratic Republic of the Congo in the Case of the Prosecutor* v. *Thomas Lubanga Dyilo*), Decision of 18 January 2008, paragraphs 108–111.

[70] *Ibid.*, paragraph 110.

[71] Article 68 of the Rome Statute: "Protection of the victims and witnesses and their participation in the proceedings"; Rule 87 "Protective measures".

[72] See Article 57(3)(c) of the Rome Statute: victim protection measures of the Pre-Trial Chamber. According to Article 64(2) of the Rome Statute, the Trial Chamber must exercise its powers "with due regard for the protection of victims".

themselves request judicial orders to protect their safety, health, dignity, and privacy (Rule 87(1)).

9.2.3 *Balancing Opposing Concerns*

The Rome Statute made a basic decision that victims in principle have an opportunity to participate in proceedings (Article 68), but the scope of that participation must still be defined by case law. In doing so, the Court must take into account that the participation of victims in the trial is in tension with opposing concerns. These are mentioned in the basic provision of the Rome Statute on victim participation (Article 68(3)): At stake are "the rights of the accused and a fair and impartial trial". According to Article 67(1) of the Rome Statute, the accused has a general right to a fair and speedy trial. In detail, this includes the accused's rights to an effective defence (subparagraph (b)), a judgment "without undue delay" (subparagraph (c) and Rule 101), the right of the accused to confront witnesses (Article 67(1)(e) of the Rome Statute), and the presumption of innocence (Article 66 of the Rome Statute). Strengthening the legal status of the victim poses a danger to these rights.

If the participation of victims is too intensive, this might in the extreme case even call the objectivity and integrity of the investigation into question, or at least the appearance thereof.[73] Finally, victim participation extends the duration of the proceedings and ties up resources of the Court. It is thus inevitably in tension with the economy and practicability of the proceedings. The goal must therefore be a treatment of victims that is as efficient as possible, for instance by combining the legal representatives of victims during the proceedings.

Victim protection measures also make the defence more difficult. In principle, a witness must appear in person (Article 69(2) of the Rome Statute), except to the extent provided by the protective measures set forth in Article 68. Granting such protective measures is within the Court's discretion. By keeping victim-witnesses anonymous – which might be necessary for their protection – the accused is deprived of the possibility of effectively reviewing the suitability of evidence and the credibility of the testifying person. Weighing the concerns of witness/victim protection against the rights of the accused, the Yugoslavia Tribunal developed five

[73] See ICC, PTC I, *Situation in the Democratic Republic of the Congo* (n. 57), paragraphs 56–60.

criteria for the admissibility and scope of protective measures.[74] It remains to be seen whether the ICC will also apply these same criteria.

In light of these interests, the Statute leaves the scope of victim participation entirely to the discretion of the Court: According to Article 68(3) of the Rome Statute, victims may present their views and concerns only "at the stages of the proceedings *determined to be appropriate*" by the ICC,[75] only after the interests to the contrary are *weighed*, and only "where the Court *considers it appropriate*". In the *Lubanga* trial, for instance, the Appeals Chamber reconciled the participation of witnesses in the appeals proceedings with the rights of the accused by limiting the victims to presenting their views and concerns solely to the issues *that had already been raised* in the application to appeal.[76] According to the wording of the provision, this weighing of opposing concerns may, where the concerns are irreconcilable, also lead to a complete refusal for the victim to participate.

9.2.4 *Appraisal*

The design of the legal status of victims in proceedings before the ICC is considered one of the major innovations in international criminal law.[77] However, effective inclusion of victims requires legal and financial support for those affected.[78] Without such support, most victims would not be able to assert their rights of participation in the first place.

In the context of this study, it is significant that the Rome Statute, the Rules of Procedure and Evidence, and ICC case law have created *real international rights*; as the report of the ICC on its strategy in relation to

[74] ICTY, Trial Chamber, *Prosecutor* v. *Tadić*, Decision on the Prosecutor's Motion Requesting Protective Measures for Victims and Witnesses, 10 August 1995, paragraphs 62–66: (1) There must be real fear for the safety of the witness or her or his family, (2) the testimony of the witness must be important to the Prosecutor's case, (3) there must be no *prima facie* evidence that the witness is untrustworthy, (4) the normal witness protection programme must be ineffective, and (5) the protective measures that are least restrictive for the accused must be applied.

[75] This already includes the investigation of a situation. ICC, PTC I, *Situation in the Democratic Republic of the Congo* (n. 57), paragraphs 23–54.

[76] ICC, Appeals Chamber, Decision, *in limine*, on Victim Participation (n. 64), paragraph 50.

[77] See William Schabas, *An Introduction to the International Court* (3rd ed. Cambridge: Cambridge University Press 2008), 328: "one of the great innovations in the Rome Statute".

[78] For this reason, the ICC envisages support in certain cases, see ICC, Booklet: Victims before the International Criminal Court, 18.

victims emphasizes: “Victims’ participation is a statutory right, not a privilege.”[79] These rights may be addressed as part of the special legal remedies available in the criminal proceedings. In the proceedings before the ICC so far, the various adjudicating chambers have tended to treat victim participation generously. The admissibility decisions have sometimes been challenged by the Prosecutor.

A follow-up question is whether the design of victims’ rights must meet the minimum requirements set out in Article 6(1) of the ECHR.[80] First of all, this would require that the right to reparations set out in Article 75 of the Rome Statute be considered a “civil right” within the meaning of Article 6(1) of the ECHR. The legal nature of reparations under Article 75 of the Rome Statute is unclear, however. It might be a kind of compensation claim under civil law or part of the criminal penalty. Secondly, the ICC proceedings would have to be subject to the “jurisdiction” of an ECHR member State within the meaning of Article 1 of the ECHR. Given the attribution criteria developed by case law, this is unlikely but not entirely absurd. The ECHR contracting parties cannot escape responsibility by establishing an international organization.[81] In that light, the rights of victims would firstly be addressed to an international organization (the ICC) and secondly (on a parallel or subsidiary basis) to the Member States of the ICC.

9.3 No Privatization of the Right of Punishment

Beyond the necessity already discussed in the preceding section to weigh the rights of the victim against the rights of the accused, the new design of the legal status of the current and specific victim raises the basic question of who owns the right of punishment.[82] This was already addressed in the

[79] Assembly of States Parties, Report of the Court on the Strategy in Relation to Victims, ICC-ASP/8/45, 10 November 2009, paragraph 45. See also Gioia Greco, Victims’ Rights Overview under the ICC Legal Framework: A Jurisprudential Analysis, *International Criminal Law Review* 7 (2007), 531–547 (539): In ICC proceedings, victims are no longer only observers or third parties but rather have achieved a “specific relevant role”.

[80] For example, the ECtHR has applied Article 6(1) to the civil party in a criminal trial under French law and reviewed that party’s right of access to a court. See ECtHR, *Berger* v. *France*, No. 48221/99, Judgment of 3 December 2002.

[81] See ECtHR, *Matthews* v. *UK*, No. 24833/94, 18 February 1999, paragraph 32.

[82] See, fundamentally, Kurt Seelmann, Paradoxien der Opferorientierung im Strafrecht, *JuristenZeitung* 44 (1989), 670–676; Christoph Safferling, Die Rolle des Opfers im Strafverfahren – Paradigmenwechsel im nationalen und internationalen Recht? *Zeitschrift für die gesamte Strafrechtswissenschaft* 122 (2010), 87–116.

discussion of the "human right of punishment" postulated especially in Latin America (pp. 257–58) and will be discussed in more detail here.

9.3.1 *The Governmentalization of the Right of Punishment as a Characteristic of Modern Criminal Law*

In the case of modern domestic criminal proceedings, the exclusion of current victims of crime was intentional. Over the course of history, the State has taken the place of the specific victim when responding to violations of rights. By revoking the right to revenge, criminal law was made more rational, and the perpetrator–victim relationship was made less dramatic. This corresponded to the new orientation of the purposes of punishment, which placed the protection of society front and centre – especially through specific and general deterrence and by "putting away" the convict. It is therefore a principle of modern criminal proceedings conducted by the State that the individual conflict between the perpetrator and the specific victim has been mediated in universally valid proceedings under the rule of law. "The focus is on the breach of law, not on the bilateral violation. In the abstract proceedings, the prosecutor takes over the protection of the interests of the public, which include the interests of the victim, while private interests are precisely not to be taken into account."[83] In the protection of legal goods, the victims are "objectified".[84] The fact that – like the role of the perpetrator – the role of the victim is likewise a social attribution speaks against a prominent role of the specific victim in all types of criminal proceedings. The focus on the specific victim ignores the fact that the offences are (also) due to a social conflict that affects third parties. The increased emphasis on the specific perpetrator–victim relationship does not do justice to this social dimension.[85] In this light, bracketing the specific victim is a crucial characteristic of the modernity of criminal proceedings conducted by the State: "Criminal law *of the State* arises with the neutralization of the

[83] Safferling, Rolle des Opfers 2010, 88–89 (translation mine).

[84] Seelmann, Paradoxien der Opferorientierung 1989, 670.

[85] "The exclusive orientation toward the current victim suffers . . . especially from the fact that such an orientation is itself the result of an impermissible abstraction," it "abstracts away . . . from the impact of the conflict on others" (*ibid.*, 674–676, quote on 676, translation mine).

victim", writes Winfried Hassemer.[86] Consequently, the new focus on the victim is in tension with this achievement of modernity.

9.3.2 The International Community's Power to Punish

The question is now whether international law and criminal proceedings and the situation of victims are so fundamentally different from the domestic situation that the very strong legal status of victims being developed at the international level appears justified. In fact, additional aspects do play a central role in international criminal jurisdiction, which is intended to compensate for the deficits of criminal prosecution at the national level and which is meant to be complementary to national jurisdiction and limited to especially serious crimes. Special considerations are relevant here that shed a different light on the orientation towards victims than is the case in domestic criminal procedure.

The impact on society as a whole is especially clear in the case of international crimes and serious violations of human rights. These crimes and violations are typically committed in the context of armed conflicts, including civil wars, as well as in repressive and dysfunctional States. All these situations are highly relevant to third parties. Those victims who attain formal standing in criminal proceedings and/or assert reparation claims are individual privileged parties who in principle stand on behalf of a suffering society. In connection with this, many individuals involved in the massive interlinked crimes that are the object of proceedings before the ICC are both perpetrators and victims. It is difficult to determine who was a perpetrator and who was a victim and at what time. This speaks against an overly strong focus on the specific victim in international criminal proceedings.

On the other hand, the distance between perpetrators and victims that characterizes international crimes speaks in favour of including victims in international criminal proceedings. The victims are usually part of an anonymous mass. For that reason, their concern "to tell their story" is especially legitimate. With the special status going beyond their role as witnesses, victims can be given a voice. Even under this aspect, however, the assessment of the appropriateness of the legal status depends on the specific understanding of the function of international criminal jurisdiction. If punishment is seen as the main function of international criminal

[86] Winfried Hassemer, *Einführung in die Grundlagen des Strafrechts* (2nd ed. Munich: Beck 1990), 70 (translation and italics mine).

jurisdiction, then the inclusion of victims must be kept within limits. If its function is seen to consist also/or primarily in dealing with the past, then victims should be given more space to express their sufferings.[87] But it might be objected that an international criminal trial is anyway not the proper place to deal comprehensively with the social consequences of the kind of armed conflict that regularly lies at the bottom of such a trial.

Telling the story of the victim is more important in the macro-criminal international context than in a "bilateral" conflict between an individual perpetrator and an individual victim. The infiltration of all of society and the socio-psychological tension in the conflict areas must be reflected by a greater number of witnesses, including victim-witnesses, who must be given the opportunity to tell their story, even if the actual circumstances of the crime have already been reconstructed. The scale of the conflict, the gravity of the suffering, and the other factors mentioned earlier are relevant to the determination of guilt.[88]

Another special feature of international criminal proceedings is reparation (for more details, see Chapter 6, pp. 178–80). Because no international civil jurisdiction exists, the ICC itself has the power to order reparations by the perpetrator (Article 75 of the Rome Statute). The formalization of the status of victims prepares the way for the entitlement to reparations. This is a specific function of the participation of victims in proceedings before the ICC, described by the Pre-Trial Chamber as follows: "[T]he victims may participate ... in order to help contribute to the prosecution of the crimes from which they allegedly have suffered and to, where relevant, *subsequently be able to obtain reparations* for the harm suffered."[89]

Moreover, the *raison d'être* of the international criminal process is to combat impunity. At the international level, the participation of victims tends to be seen as a manifestation of the right to participation in the fight against impunity, as it is in the case law of the inter-American human rights bodies discussed earlier. Pre-Trial Chamber I of the ICC held that "article 68(3) of the Statute also gives victims *the right to participate in the*

[87] See Gauthier de Beco, Victim Participation in Proceedings Before the ICC: Resolving Contentious Issues, *Human Rights and International Legal Discourse* 3 (2009), 95–112 (112).

[88] See Safferling, Rolle des Opfers 2010, 114.

[89] ICC, Pre-Trial Chamber I, *The Prosecutor* v. *Thomas Lubanga Dyilo*, Decision on the Arrangements for Participation of Victims ... at the Confirmation Hearing of 22 September 2006, p. 5 (italics mine).

fight against impunity."[90] It should be considered in this context that international institutions are not given a monopoly on the use of force. The individual desire for retribution, satisfaction, or even revenge cannot be replaced entirely by a public right of punishment at the international level. It is true that, according to the Preamble of the Rome Statute, the international community – represented by the Prosecutor – is claimed to have a right of punishment.[91] But because of the fragility of international public power, individual satisfaction remains an important rationale for prosecution. This can be reflected in the criminal *proceedings*, but it should not lead to a replacement of the owner of the right of punishment.

It remains crucial who is seen as the *actual owner of the right of punishment*. In principle, a justified interest of the victim in a criminal conviction should be recognized. Along these lines, Tatjana Hörnle for instance advocates a right of the victim in German criminal law to have the perpetrator punished, as long as the crimes are *serious offences against the person*.[92] In international criminal law, these are almost always the offences at issue. The background of the victim's right postulated by Hörnle consists in legitimate desires for satisfaction that should be appeased by law and that conceptually can be distinguished from emotional forces, such as the desire for revenge. Because these kinds of escalating emotions (vendettas, etc.) must be tamed and controlled in the public interest, modern criminal law has denied the victim the possibility of personal punishment. "On the other side of the coin, this process should recognize the violation of the victim as an aspect of the criminal sentence," says Hörnle.[93] This gives the punishment an "expressive significance"; the sentence expresses sympathy and solidarity with the victim. Because, according to this thesis, the (domestic or international) judgment that the perpetrator has acted wrongly is also in the interest of the victim of the crime, the State or public power should be seen only as the trustee of the victim. Public power thus exercises the right of punishment (the substance of which belongs to the victim) only in a *fiduciary* capacity.[94] In the final analysis, this perspective postulates the existence of an individual right of the victim to have the State – or in the case of international crimes, the "international community" invoked

[90] ICC, PTC I, *Situation in the Democratic Republic of the Congo* (n. 57), paragraph 53 (italics mine).

[91] See the Preamble of the Rome Statute, according to which "the most serious crimes of concern to the international community as a whole must not go unpunished".

[92] Tatjana Hörnle, Rolle des Opfers 2006, esp. 952, 954. [93] *Ibid.*, 956 (translation mine).

[94] See Hörnle, *Straftheorien* 2011, 41.

by the Preamble of the Rome Statute – appropriately exercise *the victim's* right of punishment. In normative terms it is preferable, following Hörnle, to view the international community as a trustee of the victims. However, victims should not be deployed as replacement prosecutors. Any "privatization of criminal prosecution"[95] would call the modernity of international criminal proceedings into question and would not do justice to the rationale of criminal punishment. This basic consideration prohibits the casual and uncritical acceptance of an individual right of punishment beyond the Latin American context (pp. 257–58) and moreover marks the outer boundary for the expansion of the legal status of victims of crime under international law.

[95] Safferling, Rolle des Opfers 2010, 89 (translation mine).

10

Rights and Duties in Investment Protection Law

10.1 Definition of the Problem

Rights under international law beyond human rights arise in the field of international investment protection law. This chapter on investment protection differs from other chapters of the book because it concerns mostly moral persons (or economic associations) as opposed to natural persons (humans). The vast majority of investment arbitration cases are instituted by companies, and not by individual human beings.[1] This difference should matter for assessing the importance of acknowledging rights and obligations of investors.[2]

The focus of attention in this regard is on the special enforcement mechanisms under international law provided by investor–State arbitration. About two-thirds of all treaty-based proceedings known to the public are carried out under ICSID.[3] The remaining third of all treaty-based proceedings known to the public[4] follow the rules of the United Nations Commission on International Trade Law (UNCITRAL), the Arbitration Institute of the Stockholm Chamber of Commerce (SCC), and the International Chamber of Commerce in Paris (ICC).[5] The rise of ICSID is considered a "quiet revolution" in international law.[6] Under the

[1] According to a recent ICSID statistics on the South and East Asia and Pacific region, 93 per cent of cases in that region have been brought by legal associations (companies), and only 7 per cent by natural persons (ICSID Caseload – Statistics (Special Focus: South & East Asia & the Pacific Region, October 2015).

[2] On the difference between human rights and investor rights, see pp. 318–21.

[3] UNCTAD, International Investment Agreements (IIA), Issues Notes, Note No. 1, 25 March 2011: Latest Developments in Investor-State Dispute Settlement.

[4] For the relevant arbitration proceedings, see the website Investment Treaty Arbitration (www.italaw.com/), administered by Andrew Newcombe, University of Victoria.

[5] UNCTAD, Latest Developments in Investor-State Dispute Settlement, IIA MONITOR No. 1 (2009), UNCTAD/WEB/DIAE/IIA/2009/6, 2). I would like to thank Tillmann Rudolf Braun for this reference.

[6] John Collier/Vaughan Lowe, *The Settlement of Disputes in International Law: Institutions and Procedures* (Oxford: Oxford University Press 1999), 191.

ICSID Convention of 1965,[7] private investors who are nationals of a State party of ICSID may institute arbitration proceedings in regard to "any legal dispute arising directly out of an investment" against another Contracting State in which they have made an investment (host State) provided that the host State has consented in writing to ICSID arbitration (Article 36 in conjunction with Article 25 of ICSID). A directly investment-related legal dispute for the purposes of the Convention may arise not only from a breach of the "diagonal" investment-related contract between that State and the investor, but also from the breach of an international investment agreement (IIA), often a bilateral investment protection treaty (BIT) concluded between the home State of the investor and the host State. The investor may accordingly claim both a breach of the contract and a breach of a treaty before the ICSID tribunals.[8]

The ICSID Convention allows investors to institute arbitration proceedings on the basis of mutual consent (see p. 285). According to Article 25 of ICSID, "a national of [a] Contracting State" may "submit" a dispute to the International Centre for Settlement of Investment Disputes. Article 36, paragraph 1 of ICSID reads, "Any … national of a Contracting State wishing to institute arbitration proceedings shall address a request to that effect in writing to the Secretary-General …" This multilateral procedural framework for investor–State arbitration constitutes the starting point for reflections on the status of investors under international law. In investment protection law, the discussion of the legal status of investors – i.e., of legal or natural persons under private law – accordingly progresses in the opposite direction of the debate in international humanitarian law, which began with the *substantive legal* status of the individual (Chapter 7).[9] A second difference between the two discourses consists in their patterns of reliance on institutions under

7 Convention on the Settlement of Investment Disputes between States and Nationals of Other States of 18 March 1965, UNTS Vol. 575, 159.

8 The possibility of claiming a breach of the BIT is also derived from Article 42, paragraph 1, sentence 2 of ICSID, according to which the tribunal may apply such rules of international law as may be applicable if no choice of law is made. Such rules also include the BIT (see Christoph Schreuer, *The ICSID Convention: A Commentary* (2nd ed., Cambridge: Cambridge University Press 2009), Article 42, paragraphs 171–172).

9 According to the relevant treaty provisions of the Geneva Conventions, individuals are not only objects of duties of protection but also bearers of legal claims to protection. While the ownership of substantive rights by individuals is practically universally recognized under international humanitarian law, any derived status of individuals as bearers of secondary claims to reparation as well as the procedural power of individuals to file claims are controversial (for details, see pp. 202–10).

private versus public law. In international investment protection law, which is closely connected to private commercial arbitration, legal reasoning is sometimes more analogous to private law.[10] Accordingly, the request by the investor to institute arbitration proceedings under the ICSID Convention – whether the jurisdiction of the tribunal is based on an international treaty, a contract, or a national law – is construed as acceptance of the host State's *offer to arbitrate.*[11] In international humanitarian law, in contrast, legal reasoning tends to be borrowed from (national) public law. As in the field of international human rights adjudication, the power of private persons to file claims is, in IHL, seen as a result of an authorization (as understood under public law) unilaterally granted by the States which are parties to the respective treaties.

In this chapter, I discuss *three groups of rights* of investors: firstly, the power of investors to institute arbitration proceedings (Section 10.2); secondly, their substantive claims arising from contracts (Section 10.3) and treaties (Section 10.4); and thirdly, secondary claims that may accrue to investors from breaches of international law by the host State (Section 10.7). Especially in regard to the last two types of rights and claims, it is disputed whether they are attributable to the investors or only to their home States (in other words, whether they are "direct rights" or only "derivative rights", i.e., derived from the home State[12]). It is argued here that all three groups of claims are, or at least can be, real international-law-based rights.[13] Another question is their similarity to human rights (Section 10.5). I also discuss the practical legal consequences of acknowledging such investor rights (Section 10.6). Finally, a largely unexplored territory consists in the duties of investors, which I touch on briefly in Section 10.8 of this chapter and also in Chapter 4.

[10] See generally Anthea Roberts, Clash of Paradigms: Actors and Analogies Shaping the Investment Treaty System, *American Journal of International Law* 107 (2013), 45–94.

[11] See p. 286. [12] See on this misleading terminology below pp. 302–03.

[13] See also Tillmann Rudolf Braun, Globalization-Driven Innovation: The Investor as a Partial Subject in Public International Law: An Inquiry into the Nature and Limits of Investor Rights, *The Journal of World Investment and Trade* 15 (2014), 73–116. In his concurring opinion in the *Archer Daniels* case, Arbitrator Rovine referred to all three groups as autonomous rights of the investor: the "right to file a claim" as well as "an individual right, owed to him directly, and underlying the right to file and collect damages, not to have that obligation breached by defendant" (ICSID, *Archer Daniels Midland Company* v. *Mexico*, Case No. ARB(AF)/04/5 (NAFTA chapter 11), 21 November 2007, Concurring Opinion of Arthur W. Rovine, Issues of Independent Investor Rights, Diplomatic Protection and Countermeasures, paragraph 47).

10.2 The Procedural Right of Investors under International Law: Power to Institute Arbitration Proceedings

This section illustrates and argues that the power of the investor to institute arbitration proceedings, especially under ICSID, is a genuine, autonomous procedural right of the investor under international law. The arbitration system under the ICSID Convention is invoked by references in (substantive) legal texts. Such references to ICSID can be found either in the national laws of host States, in potentially transnationalized investment agreements between the investor and the host State (contracts), or in BITs[14] and multilateral treaties such as in the North American Free Trade Agreement (NAFTA)[15] and the Energy Charter Treaty.[16] Hereinafter, the agreements under international law are referred to as "treaties"; where IIAs are mentioned for the sake of simplicity, free trade agreements are also included.

10.2.1 Requirement of an Agreement to Arbitrate and the Question of Its Legal Nature

According to Article 25, the jurisdiction of an ICSID tribunal extends to legal disputes arising directly out of an investment "which the parties to the dispute *consent* in writing to submit to the [ICSID] Centre". This means that additionally to the general applicability of ICSID, a consensus resulting from corresponding offer and acceptance is required.[17] The striking feature of the ICSID system (and of *ad hoc* investment arbitration) is that the host State can make an offer for future disputes in advance, even to unknown parties. This offer may be contained in

[14] For instance, Article 10 of the German Model Treaty on the Encouragement and Reciprocal Protection of Investments of 2009 refers to ICSID. The model agreements of several countries can be found at http://italaw.com/investment-treaties.

[15] North American Free Trade Agreement of 17 December 1992, in force since 1 January 1994. Chapter 11 of NAFTA provides that investment disputes may be submitted to an ICSID tribunal under the Additional Facility Rules of ICSID or a tribunal under the UNCITRAL Arbitration Rules (Section B "Settlement of Disputes between a Party and an Investor of Another Party"; reference to ICSID in Article 1120 of NAFTA).

[16] Article 26 of the Energy Charter Treaty of 17 December 1994 (ECT) refers to ICSID for the settlement of investment disputes.

[17] "The fundamental condition is consent, the cornerstone of the jurisdiction of the Centre" (Aron Broches, The Convention on the Settlement of Investment Disputes between States and Nationals of other States, *Recueil des Cours* 136 (1972), 331–410 (352–353), citing the Report of the Executive Directors accompanying the text of the Convention).

a domestic law, in the arbitration clause of a contract with the investor, or in an international investment protection agreement such as an IIA, BIT, or the investment chapter of a trade agreement (e.g., Article 1122 of NAFTA). Acceptance by the investor (i.e., a natural or juridical person or a plurality of persons) may happen at a later time and is, in particular, implicit in the investor's decision to institute arbitration proceedings.[18] Once the investor has accepted, the host State may no longer withdraw the offer to arbitrate unilaterally (Article 25, paragraph 1, last sentence of ICSID). In the case of treaty-based investment arbitration, the host State's offer is not made directly to the particular investor; the consensus to arbitrate thus arises "indirectly", without prior direct contact between the parties to the dispute.[19]

The arbitration proceedings are accordingly based on this consensus, which is considered an agreement to arbitrate. The question is now to which legal sphere such an arbitration agreement between the State and the investor belongs. The special feature of investment treaty arbitration is that the investor accepts an offer that was made only indirectly to the investor as part of an international treaty concluded by the host State with the investor's home State. Does this acceptance somehow suggest a power of the investor *under international law* to "conclude" a treaty itself, in the sense that the diagonal arbitration agreement is also an international treaty? The predominant view is that this is not the case. The agreement to arbitrate, once perfected by the investor's acceptance of the treaty-based offer, is considered to be an ancillary *contract* arising under national or international law.[20] In the words of the Court of Appeals of England and Wales, "the agreement to arbitrate ... is not itself a treaty. It is an agreement between a private investor on the one side and the relevant state on the other."[21] This basic conclusion remains unaltered when the agreement to arbitrate has arisen from an international treaty, such as from Article 1122 of NAFTA: "In short, a treaty breeds a contract."[22] Through private choice of law,

[18] See ICSID, *Generation Ukraine* v. *Ukraine*, ARB/00/9, 16 September 2003, paragraphs 12.2–12.3.

[19] See Schreuer, ICSID Convention 2009, Article 25; paragraphs 374, 377, 382, 392–393, 417, 427–428.

[20] See James Crawford, Treaty and Contract in Investment Arbitration, *Arbitration International* 24 (2008), 351–374 (359–360).

[21] England and Wales Court of Appeal (Civil Division), *Occidental Exploration & Production Company* v. *Republic of Ecuador* [2005] EWCA Civ. 1116, Judgment of 9 September 2005, paragraph 33 (Lord Phillips et al.).

[22] Crawford, Treaty and Contract in Investment Arbitration, 2008, 360. *Crawford* justifies his view that the agreement to arbitrate is necessarily of a national, and especially private,

however, this agreement to arbitrate may again be made subject to international law: "[U]nder English [or other] private international law principles, the agreement to arbitrate may itself be subject to international law, as it may be subject to foreign law."[23] The functional internationalization of the agreement to arbitrate nevertheless becomes apparent when the State party's consent to arbitrate arises out of an IIA of some sort (BIT, NAFTA, Energy Charter Treaty). Such internationalization, arbitration proponents have long argued, is more likely to achieve the goal of protecting the investor by eliminating the host State's power to renege on the arbitration offer simply by amending its own domestic law.

10.2.2 Procedural Legal Relationship between the Host State and the Investor, and the Power under International Law *to Institute Proceedings*

The view that IIAs give rise to rights and duties only between States is not compatible with the insight that the mutual consent of the host State and the investor expressly required by Article 25 of ICSID has the legal result that an arbitration agreement between these actors is concluded once a particular IIA's investor–State dispute settlement clause is invoked. The procedural obligation of the host State to submit to the arbitration proceeding is simultaneously owed to the home State of the investor (i.e., the other contracting State to the relevant IIA), to the other contracting States to the ICSID Convention, *and to the private investor.* According to one of the intellectual authors of the ICSID Convention, Aron Broches, this obligation is firstly under international law and between States: "[A]n undertaking to have recourse to conciliation or arbitration was an international obligation and therefore bound a state vis-à-vis other states."[24] But, secondly, Broches says the obligation should

legal nature with reference to the fact that only then would the award be enforceable under the New York Convention (UN Convention on the Recognition and Enforcement of Foreign Arbitral Awards) of 10 July 1958 (UNTS vol. 300, p. 3). Recognition and enforcement under the New York Convention require an "agreement in writing" under which the parties undertake to submit to arbitration (Article II). According to Crawford, this agreement to arbitrate would have to be under private law. However, ensuring enforceability of ICSID awards does not require recourse to the New York Convention, since their enforceability is specially provided in Article 54 of the ICSID Convention.

23 England and Wales Court of Appeal (Civil Division), *Occidental Exploration & Production Company* v. *Republic of Ecuador* (n. 21), paragraph 33.

24 International Centre for the Settlement of Investment Disputes, Documents Concerning the Origin and Formulation of the Convention History, Vol. II Part 1 (Washington, DC:

also be addressed to the investor: "[T]he obligation was intended to be equally binding on the private party."[25]

Formally, the ICSID Convention neither contains the consent of the host State to arbitrate nor the consent of the investor to do so. A separate consent-granting instrument referring to ICSID arbitration is always required. What speaks against taking an overly formalistic view of the ICSID Convention's inter-State package of arbitration-related obligations, however, is the fact that the host State's obligation to submit to the arbitration proceeding as a respondent may arise not only from an international treaty, but also from the arbitration clauses of an investment contract that has nothing to do with the investor's home State. Even more importantly, the obligation of the host State always materializes only once the offer of arbitration is (implicitly or explicitly) accepted by the investor. The requirement of consensus (requirement of an arbitration agreement) expressed in Article 25 of ICSID supports the view that the procedural obligation on the part of the respondent to accept the arbitration proceeding is therefore *functionally* owed to the private investor as well as (*formally*) to the investor's home State.

Corresponding to this, the investor has a *procedural right* to arbitration under the consent-granting instrument, be it a treaty, contract, or statute As long as the host State has not withdrawn the offer (which is only possible to a limited extent, as discussed below), the investor may institute arbitration proceedings without further ado. Once the investor has accepted the offer, the host State may no longer withdraw it (Article 25, paragraph 1, last sentence of ICSID). Even before the investor has accepted the offer, it is difficult to withdraw in practice. An offer contained in an IIA can be revoked only by amending the treaty for future cases and hence only in accordance with the rules on amendment and denunciation under general international law or the IIA itself.[26] An offer contained in domestic legislation can be withdrawn by amending the law, but – as mentioned above – only before the investor has accepted it. Once it has been accepted, such as by instituting arbitration proceedings, any amendment of domestic legislation does not dissolve the consensus

ICSID 1968), 57. Aron Broches was General Counsel of the World Bank from 1959 to 1979 and ICSID Secretary-General from 1967 to 1980. As General Counsel, he chaired the expert meeting to prepare the new Convention.

25 *Ibid.*

26 Such terminations have occurred, though. Ecuador and Venezuela have terminated some BITs and announced that they will terminate more. Indonesia and South Africa are going through the process of systematically terminating all of their BITs.

already established.[27] Lastly, an offer contained in a contract with the investor can be withdrawn only by amending the contract, i.e., with the consent of the investor.

This procedural right of the investor to institute arbitration proceedings has its foundation in the arbitration agreement, but is also buttressed by the ICSID Convention (Articles 25 and 36 of ICSID) and other international treaties referring to it. The request by a national of an ICSID Contracting State to institute arbitration proceedings in accordance with Article 36 of ICSID need not be authorized by that person's home State.[28] A proposal to this effect was rejected during the ICSID Convention's negotiations.[29] This discussion point shows that an autonomous right of the investor was expressly intended here, not a right derived from the home State. Conversely, the home State also cannot compel the investor to submit a request for institution of arbitration proceedings.[30] This means the right of the investor to submit a request is entirely independent of the home State.

NAFTA refers to the ICSID Convention (Article 1120 of NAFTA), but it also contains its own provision on institution of arbitration proceedings. The heading of Article 1116 of NAFTA is "Claim by an Investor of a Party on Its Own Behalf". This wording also supports the claim that the investor's procedural right is autonomous.

In regard to arbitration proceedings arising from IIAs, tribunals have described the procedural right of the investor as follows: "The scheme of both the ICSID Convention and the bilateral investment treaties is that in this circumstance, the foreign investor *acquires rights* under the Convention and Treaty, including in particular the standing *to initiate international arbitration*."[31] Similarly, "[t]he procedural obligation under Section B of Chapter Eleven [NAFTA] to submit the investment dispute to arbitration ... is owed directly to the beneficiary of the obligation, in this case the investors .... The power to bring international arbitral proceedings under Section B, makes *the investor the holder of*

27 See Schreuer, ICSID Convention 2009, Article 25, paragraph 419.

28 *Ibid.*, Article 36, paragraph 9.

29 International Centre for the Settlement of Investment Disputes (n. 22), Vol. II Part 2, 982.

30 See ICSID, *AMT* v. *Zaire*, Case No. ARB/93/1, Award, 21 February 1997, n. 5.18: "[T]he two States cannot, by virtue of Article 25 of the Convention, compel any of their nationals to appear before the centre; this is a power that the Convention has not granted to States."

31 ICSID, *Gas Natural SDG* v. *The Argentine Republic*, Case No. ARB/03/10, Decision of the Tribunal on Preliminary Questions on Jurisdiction, 17 June 2005, paragraph 34 (italics mine). In the literature, see Zachary Douglas, The Hybrid Foundations of Investment Treaty Arbitration, *British Yearbook of International Law* 74 (2004), 151–290 (184).

a procedural right";[32] "the individual is vested with the right to bring claims of its own".[33] Referring to a clause of a BIT between Denmark and the Russian Federation stipulating, *inter alia*, that "the investor shall be entitled to submit the case" to arbitration, the tribunal stated that such treaty provisions "confer *independent third party rights* on investors".[34] In a 2010 award, another tribunal elaborated on "the Claimant's right to arbitration". It placed that right under international law by applying international State responsibility to its breach.[35]

The power of the investor to institute proceedings or file claims is therefore a specific procedural right created by the legal instrument containing the arbitration agreement and supported by the ICSID Convention and the legal texts referring to it. The arbitration agreement, which usually materializes through conduct (when the request for arbitration is submitted), makes this procedural right "perfect". But at a fundamental level, it arises already when the international investment protection treaty is concluded, and for this reason, the home State cannot prevent submission of the request for arbitration.[36]

Correspondingly, the host State has the procedural right (and also duty) to appear as a respondent in ICSID and other investment arbitration proceedings. The procedural legal relationship exists between these two actors.

The fact that one of the (several) preconditions for instituting proceedings, namely the arbitration agreement, is overwhelmingly interpreted to be a contract under national law (private or administrative law), as mentioned above, does not oppose qualification of the procedural power as being under international law, given that it is always an international treaty – either the ICSID Convention or other – that undergirds the unilateral possibility for the investor to trigger the proceedings.

[32] ICSID, *Archer Daniels Midland Co.* v. *Mexico* (n. 13), paragraph 177 (italics mine). See also paragraph 179: "[T]he only individual rights investors enjoy under Chapter Eleven is the procedural right under Section B to invoke the responsibility of the host State. In particular, Article 1116(1) gives investors the right to bring a claim on its own behalf."

[33] ICSID, *Corn Products International* v. *Mexico*, No. ARB(AF)/04/01, Decision on Responsibility (NAFTA Chapter 11), 15 January 2008, paragraph 173.

[34] SSC, *RosInvest Co. UK* v. *Russian Federation*, Case No. V079 (2005), Final Award of 12 September 2010, paragraph 153, on Art. 8(2) of the Danish–Russian BIT of 4 November 1993 (italics mine).

[35] ICSID, *ATA Construction, Industrial and Trading Company* v. *The Hashemite Kingdom of Jordan*, Case No. ARB/08/02, Award of 18 May 2010, paragraphs 129–132.

[36] Cf. Tillmann Rudolf Braun, *Ausprägungen der Globalisierung: Der Investor als partielles Subjekt im internationalen Investitionsrecht* (Baden-Baden: Nomos 2012), 102–103.

Ultimately, therefore, the power of the investor to institute proceedings before an ICSID or other investment tribunal is a procedural right of the investor under international law.[37]

10.2.3 *Rationale for the Investor's Procedural Right under International Law*

Recently, this procedural power of the investor has come under attack from a legal policy perspective. By giving private investors the possibility of filing an arbitration claim against the host State, enforcement of investment protection guarantees is left principally to such investors.[38] The ICSID system and its supporting IIA network have thus left realization of interests that are (arguably also) public in the hands of private parties.[39] This has been criticized as excessive privatization, with the danger that public interests are being marginalized. Apart from the one-sided power to file claims, the weaker institutional independence of arbitrators compared with real judges, the merely partial publicity of the proceedings, and finally the lack of a formal obligation to publish decisions are seen as deficits with regard to the rule of law.[40]

However, it can be argued in favour of the "privatization" of investor rights enforcement – e.g., as provided through the ICSID system – that despite these deficits, investment arbitration tribunals serve as neutral, independent, and impartial forums. The power of investors to file arbitration claims serves both to enforce investors' private business objectives and to realize the public interest, which includes proper application of international law. (This dual function is typical for the powers of individuals to file claims and complaints; see Chapter 15, pp. 472–74).

[37] See Patrick Dumberry, L'Entreprise, sujet de droit international? Retour sur la question à la lumière des développements récents du droit international des investissements, *Revue Générale de Droit International Public* 108 (2004), 103–122 (116) (without argumentation); Kate Parlett, *The Individual in the International Legal System* (Cambridge: Cambridge University Press 2011), 106; Braun, *Ausprägungen der Globalisierung*, 2012, 102–103.

[38] While most BITs also provide for State–State arbitration, they do not do so within the ICSID framework.

[39] On the possibility of States to file claims against investors under ICSID, see pp. 339–45.

[40] See Gus van Harten, *Investment Treaty Arbitration and Public Law* (Oxford: Oxford University Press 2007), especially 95–96, 153, 167–175; also Tai-Heng Cheng, Power, Authority, and International Investment Law, *American University International Law Review* 20 (2005), 465–520.

Compliance with the investment protection standards arising from the contract or treaty is of course in the interest of the investor. The fact that the investor (and not the home State, for instance) has historically borne the costs of instituting arbitration proceedings manifests the view that part of what is at stake are the investor's own, private interests. The power to institute arbitration proceedings constitutes a kind of *guarantee of access to arbitration*, comparable with the guarantee of access to justice arising from sources such as Article 6 of ECHR and national constitutions. From this perspective, the power to bring proceedings has not only a procedural significance but also the status of a substantive right. This substantive right is also reflected in the common IIA substantive guarantees of "fair and equitable treatment" and "full protection and security" (on substantive guarantees, see p. 301). Some arbitral tribunals have seen it this way: "[A]n arbitration clause, at least in the context of expropriation, is of the same protective value as any substantive protection."[41] Likewise, "[t]he Tribunal holds that provision for investor-state arbitration in bilateral investment treaties is a significant substantive incentive and protection for foreign investors".[42] However, it appears excessive to claim that the power to institute proceedings has a quality similar to that of human rights,[43] given that it typically serves to enforce economic interests and as a rule is asserted by legal persons or a plurality of persons, rather than by natural persons.

At the same time, the power to file arbitration claims serves to enforce international law, namely in a threefold way. Firstly, it opens up the possibility of *ex post* sanctioning of a violation of international law by actually instituting arbitration proceedings. Secondly, the legal framework which allows the investor to bring proceedings has an effect which is in the public interest of the host State itself: By submitting to arbitration in advance, host States have the opportunity to make a credible promise (in the form of a precommitment) to investors.[44] Only in that

[41] SCC (Arbitration Institute of the Stockholm Chamber of Commerce), *RosInvest Co UK* v. *Russia*, Case No. ARBV079/2005, Award on Jurisdiction (October 2007), paragraph 132.

[42] ICSID, *Gas Natural SDG* v. *The Argentine Republic* (n. 31), paragraphs 29, 31. See also the concurring opinion of arbitrator Rovine in the *Archer Daniels* case on the significance of the "right to remedy" and "right to legal redress" as a "substantive right" (Rovine, Concurring Opinion in ICSID, *Archer Daniels Midland Co.* v. *Mexico* (n. 13), paragraphs 45–47).

[43] Cf. Braun, *Ausprägungen der Globalisierung*, 2012, 101.

[44] See Anne Peters, Precommitment Theory Applied to International Law: Between Sovereignty and Triviality, *University of Illinois Law Review* (2008), 239–252.

way can host States create the necessary trust to trigger a capital flow into their country and to guarantee the objective of investment protection treaties, namely to promote foreign investments, which in turn serve the economic development of the host State at least in part.[45] And thirdly, the power to bring proceedings offers an incentive in the case of tension and conflict to find a negotiated solution "in the shadow" of the imminent arbitration proceedings.[46]

The procedural right of the investor under international law to institute ICSID proceedings is ultimately grounded in doctrine and appears sensible in terms of legal policy, both to secure the business interests of the investor and to achieve public development objectives.

10.3 Substantive Rights of Investors Arising from Contracts (Contract Claims)

Far more controversial than the procedural legal position of investors under international law, which is recognized in principle, is the legal quality of their substantive rights. On the traditional view, there is a split between the sphere of procedural rights and that of substantive rights: While investors may have the procedural power to bring proceedings, they are not assumed to be the owners of the substantive claims they assert. The question in this section is accordingly whether – deviating from the doctrine advocating this split – legal positions of the investors exist also at the level of substantive rights *under international law.* A distinction must be made in this regard between claims arising from contracts and claims arising from treaties. Today, investors in most ICSID arbitration proceedings invoke substantive provisions in the investment protection treaties under international law (treaty-based claims). The invoked treaty may be a BIT or a multilateral treaty. Contract claims under ICSID, which are less frequent, will be discussed here first.[47]

[45] See Stephan W. Schill, Private Enforcement of International Investment Law: Why We Need Investor Standing in BIT Dispute Settlement, in: Michael Waibel/Asha Kaushal/Kyo-Hwa Liz Chung (eds), *The Backlash Against Investment Arbitration: Perceptions and Reality* (Alphen aan den Rijn: Wolters Kluwer Law & Business 2010), 29–50 (31).

[46] Braun, *Ausprägungen der Globalisierung*, 2012, 203–204.

[47] Contract claims are overall numerically more frequent than treaty claims, but typically proceed outside of ICSID (e.g., under the ICC or the SCC) and hence are not publicly known.

On a regular basis, foreign investments are based on a contractual arrangement between the private investor and the host State, which is often referred to as a "State contract". Substantive claims from that contract belong to the investor, not the investor's home State. As an English court formulated it in regard to claims arising from the contract, it would be "both artificial and wrong in principle" to suggest that an investor is in reality pursuing a claim vested in the investor's home State and that the only difference to diplomatic protection is procedural.[48] The problem here is not that of the proper owner of the claim, but rather of the legal nature of these claims.

10.3.1 Claims under International Law Due to Internationalization of the Contract?

Since the first legal disputes arising from oil and commodity concession contracts starting in the 1930s, it has been discussed whether and under what conditions these State contracts are contracts under private law, administrative law, international law, or even *sui generis*.[49] The background of this debate is the effort by investors to make the contractual arrangement as independent as possible from the legal order of the host State. If, namely, the contract is subject only to the law of the host State, the investor is at the mercy of changes to the law, e.g., after a change of government. The investors therefore try to protect themselves from unilateral changes to the law by the host State, which may extend even to expropriations. For this reason, investors are often

[48] England and Wales Court of Appeal (Civil Division), *Occidental Exploration & Production Company* v. *Republic of Ecuador* (n. 21), paragraph 17.

[49] See Karl Heinz Böckstiegel, *Der Staat als Vertragspartner ausländischer Unternehmen* (Frankfurt a. M: Athenäum 1971); Esa Paasivirta, *Participation of States in International Contracts and Arbitral Settlement of Disputes* (Helsinki: Finnish Lawyers' Publishing Company 1990); Stephen J. Toope, *Mixed International Arbitration: Studies in Arbitration between States and Private Persons* (Cambridge: Grotius Publications 1990), 75–90 (very sceptical about the applicability of international law to State contracts); Uwe Kischel, *State Contracts* (Stuttgart: Boorberg 1992), especially Part 3 (p. 233, advocates an "internationalization in accordance with conflict of laws", i.e., applicability of international law by virtue of choice of law); Ivar Alvik, *Contracting with Sovereignty: State Contracts and International Arbitration* (Oxford: Hart 2011). The PCIJ only ever considered the attribution of a contract to either international law or the national law of a State, and it never saw the possibility of a third legal order to which a contract might belong. PCIJ, *Case Concerning the Payment of Various Serbian Loans Issued in France*, PCIJ Series A Nos. 220/21, p. 41: "Any contract which is not a contract between States in their capacity as subjects of international law is based on the municipal law of some country."

interested in a "delocalization" or internationalization of the contracts, i.e., *separation from the law of the host State* (and placement under a different legal order, e.g., international law).

This point is crucial for the definition of this study's problem, since one can only speak of primary claims of investors *under international law* if the investment contracts are international treaties as a whole or at least in part. In favour of qualification of State contracts as international treaties (and of a corresponding international legal personality and power of companies to conclude treaties), it is argued from an international legal perspective that powerful companies deal with States as equals and in many cases (especially in the context of foreign investments) are even superior to States and are thus functionally internationalized. Host States implicitly, so the argument goes, recognize the economic actors as subjects of international law by concluding the treaty with them.[50]

The discussion is different in the field of private international law, and it appears to capture the problem of internationalization of a State contract better. From that perspective, internationalization can occur in two different ways: through choice of law by the parties or, where no choice of law is made, on the basis of an objective link.[51] According to arbitral practice, choice of law can be deduced not only explicitly, but also implicitly from stabilization clauses (freezing of the legal position at the time the contract is concluded)[52] or arbitration clauses.[53] Placement under international law has also been derived from the

[50] See the references in Chapter 4, p. 100, n. 104. For a critical view, cf. Peter Malanczuk, Multinational Enterprises and Treaty-Making: A Contribution to the Discussion on Non-State Actors and the "Subjects" of International Law, in: Vera Gowlland-Debbas (ed.), *Multilateral Treaty-Making: The Current Status of Challenges to and Reforms Needed in the International Legislative Process* (Dordrecht: Martinus Nijhoff 2000), 45–74.

[51] The choice-of-law approach to the choice of international law by the contracting parties has been propagated especially by Frederic A. Mann in numerous publications beginning in the 1940s (first reference Frederic A. Mann, The Law Governing State Contracts, *British Yearbook of International Law* 12 (1944), 11–33).

[52] See *Texaco Overseas Petroleum Company/California Asiatic Oil Company* v. *Libya* (Award on the merits of 19 January 1977), decided by arbitrator René-Jean Dupuy (*International Legal Materials* 12 (1978), 1 et seq. = *International Law Reports* 53 (1979), 420 et seq., paragraph 45).

[53] The appointment of neutral, international arbitrators has been taken as a negative sign that the parties did not want to place the contract under the law of the host State. See, e.g., arbitrator Pierre Cavon in *Sapphire International Petroleums* v. *National Iranian Oil Company*, Award of 15 March 1963, International Law Reports 35 (1967), 136 et seq. (170–175, especially 172); see also *Texaco Overseas Petroleum Company/California Asiatic Oil Company* v. *Libya* (n. 52), paragraph 44.

nature of the investment contracts as "economic development agreements".[54]

An objective linkage (which is admissible only where the parties have not made a choice of law) is foreseen in Article 42, paragraph 1 of ICSID, according to which the tribunals must "apply the law of the Contracting State party to the dispute . . . and such rules of international law as may be applicable".[55] The arbitral tribunals accordingly draw on international law to fill lacunae. It is even more important for the investors that the tribunals may also apply international law as a benchmark for evaluating the law of the host State and thus can find measures contrary to international law (such as encroachments on property contrary to international law) to be unlawful and compensable.[56] In such cases, international law has not only a "complementary" but also a "corrective function".[57]

10.3.2 *Classic Arbitral Practice on Internationalization*

Examples from the arbitral practice on the internationalization of State contracts (outside ICSID) include the famous cases *Lena Goldfields, Sapphire*, and *Texaco*. The *Lena Goldfields* arbitration case (1930) arose out of a mining concession agreement of 1925 that did not include a choice-of-law clause. The Goldfields company carried out mining on a large scale in Siberia and other locations, but its "capitalist" activities were massively curtailed after the introduction of the planned economy in autumn of 1927. The arbitral tribunal applied the general legal principles as referred to in Article 38, paragraph 1(c) of the ICJ Statute. It relied on the fact that the concession agreement was "signed not only on behalf of the Executive Government of Russia generally but by the Acting Commissary for Foreign Affairs, and that many of the terms of the

54 *Texaco Overseas Petroleum Company/California Asiatic Oil Company* v. *Libya* (n. 52), paragraph 45.

55 See, e.g., ICSID, *CMS Gas Transmission Company* v. *Argentine Republic*, Case No. ARB/01/8, Award of 12 May 2005, paragraphs 116–117 on the application of domestic and international law to the investment dispute.

56 This function of international law was controversial when the ICSID was negotiated, and it was initially combated by capital-importing States, but it has meanwhile been recognized (see Schreuer, *ICSID Convention*, 2009, Article 42, paragraphs 198 and 204). In this sense, see already Broches, Convention on the Settlement of Investment Disputes, 1972, 392–393: International law is applied "where the law of the Contracting State party to the dispute, or action taken under that law, violates international law. In this instance international law operates as a corrective to national law".

57 ICSID, *Autopista* v. *Venezuela*, Case No. ARB/00/5, Award of 23 September 2003, paragraph 102.

contract contemplated the application of international rather than merely national principles of law".[58] The arbitral tribunal then referred to the principle of unjust enrichment, which it found in "Continental", Russian, French, German, Scottish, and English law,[59] and it awarded a considerable sum of money to Goldfields.

In *Sapphire* (1967), a Swiss arbitrator qualified an investment contract relating to oil production and oil export between the Canadian oil company Sapphire and an Iranian national company as follows: "This contract has therefore a quasi-international character which releases it from the sovereignty of a particular system, and it differs fundamentally from an ordinary commercial contract."[60]

In the *Texaco* case (1977), arbitrator René-Jean Dupuy found that three elements effect a "delocalization" (in the sense of a separation of the automatic link to a national legal order[61]) and "internationalization" of the oil concession agreement between Western concessionaires and Libya. These elements were the reference to "general principles of law", the arbitration clause, and the nature of the contract as an economic development agreement with a stabilization clause.[62] "Internationalizing" a contract would mean, according to Dupuy, "to situate it within a specific legal order – the order of the international law of contracts".[63] But this would mean neither that the private party is equated with a State, "*nor that the contract entered into with it is assimilated to a treaty*".[64] Internationalization or transnationalization therefore does not turn a State contract into an international treaty per se.

This arbitral practice is very controversial, and it is ultimately only partially persuasive. It cannot be dismissed out of hand that at least older arbitral practice might not have been free from colonial reminiscences and might have favoured investor interests. The "objective" situating of a contract within international law solely on the basis of its "nature" is not tenable doctrinally. And the "subjective" approach by way of autonomy of the parties and choice of law is likewise tricky: Firstly, the clauses of the State contracts excluding or undermining local law are not necessarily

58 The arbitration between the *Lena Goldfields, Ltd. and the Soviet Government*, Award of 2 September 1930, paragraph 22. Original language German, first published in www.trans-lex.org/26130 (English in *Cornell Law Quarterly* 36 (1951), 31–53).

59 *Ibid.*, paragraph 23.

60 *Sapphire International Petroleums* v. *National Iranian Oil Company* (n. 53), 173.

61 *Texaco Overseas Petroleum Company/California Asiatic Oil Company* v. *Libya* (n. 52), paragraph 29.

62 *Ibid.*, paragraphs 41–45.

63 *Ibid.*, paragraph 44.

64 *Ibid.*, paragraph 46 (italics mine).

manifestations of free choice, given the investors' outsized negotiating power. Most importantly, the contract clauses refer much more frequently to general principles of law than to international law. Such a choice of law does not transform the contracts as a whole into international treaties. Besides, international law offers solutions only for exceedingly few aspects of an investment contract – although the important aspect of expropriation is one of them.

10.3.3 Internationalization of Contracts through Umbrella Clauses?

A special feature of many BITs are "umbrella clauses". A typical umbrella clause is worded as follows: "Each party shall observe any obligation it may have entered into with regard to investments."[65] With such an umbrella clause, the host State is required to respect *all* obligations with regard to investment, including those set out in a contract with the investor. It can now be argued that in this way, the rights and duties arising from the contract are also made subject to the BIT. This might mean that contract claims would be transformed into treaty claims ("elevating effect" or "mirror effect").[66] An arbitral tribunal described this legal effect of an umbrella clause as follows: "an 'umbrella clause' . . . *transforms contractual undertakings into international law obligations* and accordingly makes it a breach of the BIT by the respondent if it breaches a contractual obligation that it has entered into with the Claimant." "An umbrella clause is usually seen as transforming municipal law obligations into obligations directly cognizable in international law."[67] It is claimed that by way of the umbrella clause of the BIT, the States parties to the treaty have made violations of the contract equivalent to violations of international law in order to more effectively achieve the objectives of the treaty, so that violations of the contract likewise trigger responsibility under international law: "This means that, when negotiating a bilateral investment treaty, two States may create within the scope of their mutual agreement an exception to the rules deriving from the

[65] This clause was used in the US model treaty between 1984 and 1987. It was also used in the BIT between the United States and Romania giving rise to the ICSID case *Noble Ventures Inc.* v. *Romania*, Case No. ARB/01/11, 12 October 2005, as well as in the treaty between the Netherlands and Poland giving rise to the *Eureko* case (ICSID, *Eureko BV* v. *Republic of Poland*, Ad Hoc Arbitration, Partial Award, 19 August 2005, paragraph 244–260).

[66] See for an excellent discussion of these effects Jan Ole Voss, *The Impact of Investment Treaties on Contracts between Host States and Foreign Investors* (Leiden: Brill Nijhoff 2011), 235–276 with further references.

[67] ICSID, *Noble Ventures Inc.* v. *Romania* (n. 65), paragraphs 46 and 53.

autonomy of municipal law, on the one hand and public international law, on the other hand. In other words, two States may include in a bilateral investment treaty a provision to the effect that, in the interest of achieving the objects and goals of the treaty, the host State may incur *international responsibility by reason of a breach of its contractual* obligations towards the private investor of the other Party, the breach of the contract being thus 'internationalized', i.e. assimilated to a breach of the treaty."[68] Another more recent arbitration award likewise held that it was possible in principle for the contracting parties to a BIT to agree that all breaches of the contract could also be treated as breaches of the BIT, but that this would have to be expressed clearly in the wording of the BIT.[69]

According to most case law, however, an umbrella clause normally does not transform the investment-related obligations of the host State to which it has committed itself in the contract with the investor into obligations under international law. The ICSID tribunal in *SGS v. Philippines* can be cited as an example: The umbrella clause "makes it a breach of the BIT for the host State to fail to observe binding commitments, including contractual commitments, which it has assumed with regard to specific investments. But it does not convert the issue of the extent of content of such obligation into an issue of international law".[70] Also in the literature, the legal effect of the umbrella clauses is disputed. One side assumes that on the basis of such a clause, "contracts might be considered as treaties from the point of view of their legal effects".[71] The opposing view, which is probably preferable, is that the contractual claims remain contractual and are governed by the contract.

[68] *Ibid.*, paragraph 54.

[69] ICSID, *SGS Société Générale de Surveillance SA* v. *Islamic Republic of Pakistan*, Case No. ARB/01/13, Decision of the Tribunal on Objections to Jurisdiction of 6 August 2003, paragraphs 163–174, especially 173.

[70] ICSID, *SGS Société Générale de Surveillance SA* v. *Philippines*, Case No. ARB/026, 29 January 2004, paragraph 128: Following this, see also ICSID, *Eureko BV* v. *Republic of Poland* (n. 59), paragraphs 255–257. Also ICSID, *CMS Gas Transmission Company* v. *Argentine Republic* (n. 49), Annulment Proceeding, Annulment Decision of 25 September 2007, paragraph 95 (c): "The effect of the umbrella clause is not to transform the obligation which is relied on into something else; the content of the obligation is unaffected, as is its proper law."

[71] Francisco Orrego Vicuña, Of Contracts and Treaties in the Global Market, *Max Planck Yearbook of United Nations Law* 8 (2004), 341–357 (353). See also José Alvarez, Are Corporations Subjects of International Law?, *Santa Clara Journal of International Law* 9 (2011), 1–36 (12): "[M]any BITs' and FTAs' umbrella clauses explicitly 'internationalize' investor–state contracts, thereby elevating such contractual assurances to the level of interstate pacts." See for a differentiated view Voss, *Impact of Investment Treaties*, 2011, 269–275.

The difference between the contract and the BIT persists despite the existence of an umbrella clause. The sole purpose of these clauses is to guarantee enforcement of claims, without transforming the legal nature and content of the underlying contract obligations.[72]

The transformation of the contract (or parts of it) by the umbrella clause occasionally assumed in the case law described above and in the probably prevailing literature can be seen as a special kind of internationalization of the contract.[73] If this mechanism does exist in principle, its operation in detail remains unclear. The following questions arise: Which treaty provisions should be understood as umbrella clauses? Which breaches of which contracts are "elevated" or "transformed"? The "indirect" internationalization brought about by the umbrella clause could refer to individual elements of the contract that would have to be specially determined.[74] Does the umbrella clause really change the proper law of the entire contract, or does it only bring the consequences of a breach of the contract into the realm of international responsibility of the host State?[75] But is that responsibility then, really, the normal responsibility under international law or something else?

Finally, it is an open question to whom the postulated international responsibility is owed. It can be assumed (but is not stated by the *Noble Venture* tribunal) that the investor would be the obligee (creditor) of the secondary legal relationship.

10.3.4 Conclusion

The possibility of a legal position of investors *under international law* arising from internationalized State contracts continues to be controversial. State contracts appear – if at all – to have international legal quality only in part, not as a whole. It would then have to be considered in detail for each contract claim asserted by an investor whether the basis of that claim should be qualified as being under international law. The view appears tenable that the legal positions arising from the contract interact

[72] See Crawford, Treaty and Contract in Investment Arbitration, 2008, 369.

[73] It is probably not a coincidence that the strong statements regarding transformation of the contract were made by an arbitral tribunal chaired by Karl-Heinz Böckstiegel, who in 1971 published a fundamental treatise on the internationalization of State contracts (Böckstiegel, *Staat als Vertragspartner ausländischer Unternehmen* 1971).

[74] Cf. ICSID, *Noble Ventures Inc.* v. *Romania* (n. 65), paragraph 61.

[75] See in this sense, e.g., Voss, *Impact of Investment Treaties*, 2011, 273–275.

with several standards under customary international law (and based on treaties) – especially the fair and equal treatment standard – in order to jointly realize the basic concern of international investment protection law, namely protection of the trust (legitimate expectations) of the investor. International law accordingly protects the legal positions arising from the contract. "To the extent that such standards protect interests created by contractual commitments, an investor acquires individual rights under international law by virtue of the contract."[76]

In any event, whether the claims from the contract can be qualified as being under international law plays a role only for the secondary legal consequences (for the State's responsibility). It depends on the qualification of the primary claims (and the primary legal relationship to the host State) whether a relationship of responsibility under international law arises between the investor and the host State in the event of a breach of the diagonal investment contract, and accordingly whether the international principles of State responsibility, including any grounds of justification, apply to such a relationship. This is discussed in Section 10.7 (see p. 331).

10.4 Rights Arising from Inter-State Investment Protection Treaties: The "Direct"/"Derivative" Rights Debate

In most investment protection treaties concluded bilaterally between States (BITs), the States parties typically undertake to comply with two standards, which in turn also apply under customary law. These are the fair and equitable treatment standard (FES), as well as full [and equal] protection and security.[77] Investment protection and free trade treaties often also stipulate the national treatment standard as well as most-favoured nation treatment.[78] Ultimately, what is protected either explicitly or implicitly, is property.

76 Alvik, *Contracting with Sovereignty*, 2011, 70; see also *ibid.*, 160.

77 See, e.g., Article 2, paragraph 2 of the German Model Treaty (n. 14): "Each Contracting State shall in its territory in every case accord investments by investors of the other Contracting State fair and equitable treatment as well as full protection under this Treaty." In the literature, see, e.g., M. Sornarajah, *The International Law on Foreign Investment* (2nd ed., Cambridge: Cambridge University Press 2007), 233–237.

78 See, e.g., Article 3, paragraph 1 of the German Model Treaty (n. 14): "Neither Contracting State shall in its territory subject investments owned or controlled by investors of the other Contracting State to treatment less favourable than it accords to investments of its own investors or to investments of investors of any third State."

In most of the current ICSID disputes, the claimed breach of a BIT plays the key role.[79] Before international arbitration bodies, foreign investors most frequently claim a violation of treaty standards.

However, many investment protection treaties do not state *to whom* the obligations to respect these standards are owed. They do not specify any obligees. So the question arises as to who are the owners of the primary claims (such as to fair treatment) and who are the bearers of the secondary claim in the event of their breach.[80] Even the protection of property by a treaty does not necessarily mean that property is protected as a personal right, because the idea of private property as opposed to State property is still not completely uncontested on the universal plane, and for example not codified in the ICCPR.

It does not necessarily follow from the aforementioned procedural standing of the investor that the private investor is also the owner of the substantive primary and secondary claims. The private power of the investor to bring claims before an arbitral tribunal could alternatively be conceptualised as a representative action by the investor acting on behalf of the State under international law. In such a legal conceptualisation, the investor is seen a kind of agent or trustee who asserts the rights of the State. The State is here seen as the principal who has delegated the right to bring an inter-State claim to the investor (agent).

The two possibilities are in the scholarly writings often referred to as the "derivative" and the "direct" model of the investor's power to bring proceedings against the foreign State. These terms have been coined in a seminal article by Zachary Douglas[81] but have unfortunately been

[79] See Schreuer, *ICSID Convention* 2009, Article 42, paragraph 172.

[80] See seminally Douglas, Hybrid Foundations, 2004, 160–184 under the heading: "To Whom are Investment Treaty Obligations Owed?"

[81] Douglas, Hybrid Foundations, 2004, 163–164. For a similar terminology, with the "derived right to bring an action" arising from the (substantive) law of the contracting State, see also Jeswald W. Salacuse, *The Law of International Investment Treaties* (Oxford: Oxford University Press 2008), 391. This terminology has been adopted by some arbitral tribunals, see, e.g., PCA, *HICEE BV* v. *The Slovak Republic*, Partial awards of 23 May 2011, PCA Case No. 2009–2011, paragraph 139, speaking of "an investor claiming derivatively through the rights procured for it by one of those States". Andrea Bjorklund speaks of the "delegated espousal" of a (State) claim (Andrea K. Bjorklund, Private Rights and Public International Law: Why Competition Among International Economic Law Tribunals Is Not Working, *Hastings Law Journal* 59 (2007), 241–307 (264)). Martins Paparinskis identifies three options: the investors as "right-holder", or as a "beneficiary", or as an "agent" of the State (Martins Paparinskis, Investment Treaty Arbitration and the (New) Law of State Responsibility, *European Journal of International Law* 24 (2013), 617–647, passim, esp. at 646).

distorted in the subsequent literature. The debate is nowadays often called the "'direct'/'derivative' rights debate".[82] In that parlance, the "direct rights" school asserts that the investor has own substantive rights flowing from an inter-State investment treaty; while the "derivative" rights school submits that the investor does not have own substantive rights. This terminology is somewhat misleading because it tends to mix up the procedural and the substantive rights of the investor, and the level of primary and secondary law. Still, I will sometimes use it because it is so widespread.

A yet different perspective is that private persons (investors) *enforce the public interest* and "objective law" (as opposed to "subjective" rights). This seems to be a typically public law approach, which has been prominent in the traditional French system of administrative legal protection. In contrast, the "private law" approach focuses more on "subjective" legal positions of specific entities. Because international law has traditionally been seen as analogous to private law, States have been considered to possess "rights" arising from international treaties. It is submitted here that the public law-approach to international law is more appropriate nowadays. That approach highlights that States are not ends in themselves, but rather instruments to secure the public interest. Therefore, it is – as a general matter – better to speak of the enforcement of objective law, and no longer of States' "rights". Specifically in the field of investment protection, this approach suggests that the obligations entered into by States in investment treaties have the broader "public interest" objective to promote foreign investment, and not in the first place to protect investors' rights.[83] However, even this public law-view does not prohibit treaty-makers and treaty-appliers to stipulate or acknowledge investors' substantive treaty-based rights. The public and "objective" legal regime to promote foreign investment may very well coincide with the establishment of "subjective" legal positions. This line of argument will be discussed again in the final chapter, Chapter 17, p. 526.

[82] See, e.g., Anastasios Gourgourinis, Investors' Rights "qua" Human Rights? Revisiting the "Direct"/"Derivative" Rights Debate in: Malgosia Fitzmaurice and Panos Merkouris (eds), *The Interpretation and Application of the European Convention on Human Rights* (Leiden: Brill Nijhoff 2013), 147–182; Eric de Brabandere, *Investment Treaty Arbitration as Public International Law: Procedural Aspects and Implications* (Cambridge: Cambridge University Press 2014), 60.

[83] This approach to investment arbitration has been particularly espoused by Eric de Brabandere, *Investment Treaty Arbitration as Public International Law*, 2014), see esp. at 70.

10.4.1 Are Primary Rights Flowing from the Treaty Owned by the State?

The traditional view is that while investment-related treaties – especially BITs and the North American Free Trade Agreement (NAFTA) – benefit the interests of investors, the actual treaty obligations are owed not to the private investor, but rather to the investor's home State or capital-exporting State party. According to this view, the home State is the rights-holder.[84]

Following this line of reasoning, some (arbitral) tribunal judgments and parts of the literature assume that investment protection treaties only give rise to substantive rights *of the State*. This view has been defended especially for chapter 11 of NAFTA.[85] Several tribunals in investment disputes have denied the existence of substantive rights arising from NAFTA for investors. In the first arbitration case discussing this question, *Loewen*, the arbitral tribunal rejected any analogy to arbitration cases under private law. It emphasized that NAFTA claims are claims under international law. According to the tribunal, the system was meant only to replace the possibility for States to pursue breaches of international law (through diplomatic protection) by a different, special kind of enforcement option. "There is no warrant for transferring rules derived from private law into a field of international law *where claimants are permitted for convenience to enforce what are in origin the rights of Party states.*"[86] In *Archer Daniels Midland Co.*, an arbitration award from 2007, the tribunal found "that the Chapter Eleven scheme establishes rights regarding the treatment of investors, but these rights are not owed by the host State to the investors, but to the investors' home State. Therefore, the rights provided by Section A only exist at the international plane between NAFTA Parties. Investors are the objects or mere beneficiaries of those rights".[87] In their statements in various investment protection cases (*Loewen, Metalclad*, and *Methanex*), the United States and Canada likewise repeatedly argued that the substantive rights contained in chapter 11 of NAFTA were owed solely to the States parties.[88] (But these awards are in contrast to others that expressly affirm substantive rights of investors

[84] Surya P. Subedi, *International Investment Law* (3rd. ed., Oxford: Hart 2016), 116, 131.

[85] NAFTA proceedings are never conducted according to the ICSID Convention, since neither Canada nor Mexico are States parties to ICSID. The ICSID Additional Facility may apply in some cases, however.

[86] ICSID, *Loewen* v. *United States*, Case No. ARB(AF)/98/3 (2003), Award of 26 June 2003, repr. in *International Legal Materials* 42 (2003), 811 et seq., paragraph 233 (italics mine).

[87] ICSID, *Archer Daniels Midland Co.* v. *Mexico* (n. 13), paragraph 178.

[88] Statements cited in ICSID, *Archer Daniels Midland Co.* v. *Mexico* (n. 13), paragraph 176.

arising from international treaties, especially chapter 11 of NAFTA (see below pp. 306–08).

In regard to BITs, some *domestic courts*, too, have denied that investors may have "direct" rights stemming from such treaties, and have insisted that these treaties create rights (and obligations) of States only. For example, the French Conseil Constitutionnel stated that the French–Algerian BIT created exclusively inter-State obligations ("ne crée d'obligations qu'entre les deux Etats signataires").[89] The Federal Constitutional Court of Germany explained the status of the investor as an agent of the State as follows: "[P]rivate parties may claim violations of an international agreement concluded between States. Substantively, this means that a claim is brought regarding the breach of an *obligation owed* not directly to the private claimant, but rather *to the claimant's home State*, even though the protective purpose of the agreement is guided by the interests of the private investors."[90] Put differently, from this perspective the States have – in the area of investment protection – only delegated the enforcement of the law (of the rights of the State) to private persons, "for convenience", as expressed by the *Loewen* tribunal, but States remain the rights-holders.

In scholarship, investor rights have been denied with the argument that investment treaty arbitration fulfils mainly *public* purposes of the involved States (as opposed to private purposes), and should therefore best be seen as "a legal mechanism to enforce international standards as a part of an inter-State bargain" (as opposed to a mechanism enforcing subjective rights). From that perspective, the appropriate "role of the claimant is more like that of a private attorney-general than the victim of a rights violation".[91]

The theory that rights flowing from the treaty are only those of the State – a theory which will be rejected in the next section – corresponds to the tradition of mediatization of the individual by the individual's home State, and it is tied to the assumption that the jurisdiction for investment arbitration *institutionalizes and strengthens the system of diplomatic protection*. Along these lines, an ICSID arbitral tribunal assumed that diplomatic protection is latently preserved as an option

89 French Conseil d'Etat, Décision No. 280264 of 21 December 2007, on Article 3 of the Accord entre le gouvernement de la République française et le gouvernement de la République algérienne démocratique et populaire sur l'encouragement et la protection réciproques des investissements of 13 February 1993.

90 BVerfG, 2 BvM 1/03, Ruling of the Second Senate of 8 May 2007, paragraph 51 (italics mine).

91 Gus van Harten, *Investment Treaty Arbitration and Public Law* (Oxford: Hart 2007), 143.

even in investment protection law: "To some extent, diplomatic protection is intervening as a *residual mechanism* to be resorted to in the absence of other arrangements recognizing the direct right of action by individuals."[92] If ICSID is the continuation of diplomatic protection by other means, then the underlying substantive claims would be *State* claims, not claims of the individual, in accordance with the *Mavrommatis* formula of the Permanent Court of International Justice (PCIJ).[93]

This view of investor–State investment arbitration as a *reinforcement* of the traditional system of diplomatic protection seems erroneous. It is strange because it switches the roles of the individual and the State in a kind of "protection diplomatique inversée":[94] Not the State sues on behalf of the individual but the individual on behalf of the State. The traditional legal fiction would be replaced by a new one, and would, if consistently pulled through, require that the investor would have to turn the reparation awarded to him to his home State.

10.4.2 Autonomous Substantive Treaty Claims ("Direct Rights") of the Investors

Contrary to the traditional view described above, the better arguments are in favour of acknowledging, as a matter of principle, the possibility of investors enjoying autonomous substantive rights, arising from investment protection treaties under international law ("direct rights"). Along these lines, an arbitral tribunal in *Corn Products* affirmed substantive rights of the investor-claimant arising under international law from

92 ICSID, *CMS Gas Transmission Company* v. *Argentine Republic* (n. 49), Decision on Objections to Jurisdiction of 17 July 2003, reprinted in *International Legal Materials* 42 (2003), 788–810, paragraph 45 (italics mine).

93 "[O]ne might argue that bilateral investment agreements in some sense institutionalize and reinforce (rather than replace) the system of diplomatic protection, and that in accordance with the Mavrommatis formula, the rights concerned are those of the state, not of the investor" (James Crawford, The ILC's Articles on Responsibility of States for Internationally Wrongful Acts: A Retrospect, *American Journal of International Law* 96 (2002), 874–890 (887–888)). On the Mavrommatis formula and diplomatic protection, see Chapter 12. If one holds the modern view that substantive rights of the individual (not of the State) can be asserted even *within* diplomatic protection, the argument in favour of a substantive ownership of rights by the investor is independent from the relationship of ICSID to diplomatic protection. See below pp. 308–11.

94 Mathias Forteau, La contribution au développement du droit international général de la jurisprudence arbitrale relative aux investissements étrangers, *Anuário Brasileiro de Direito Internacional* 4 (2009), 11–39, 38. Forteau therefore considers this legal construct to be "conservative" and "legally incorrect" (*ibid.*, 37).

chapter 11 of NAFTA: "In the Tribunal's view, the NAFTA confers upon investors substantive rights separate and distinct from those of the State of which they are nationals."[95] The arbitral tribunal justified its opinion with reference to the wording of the NAFTA treaty, the assumption of a convergence of procedural and substantive legal positions, the natural view, and the object and purpose of investor–State arbitration to offer an alternative to the insufficient system of diplomatic protection: "In the case of Chapter XI of the NAFTA, the Tribunal considers that the intention of the Parties was to confer substantive rights directly upon investors. That follows from the language used and is confirmed by the fact that Chapter XI confers procedural rights upon them. The notion that Chapter XI conferred upon investors a right, in their own name and for their own benefit, to institute proceedings to enforce rights which were not theirs but were solely the property of the State of their nationality is counterintuitive."[96] In a similar case constellation, an arbitral tribunal in *Cargill* referred to "specific obligations owed to *nationals* of the offending State".[97]

Other tribunals have gone in the same direction. In *El Paso*, a tribunal stated: "Contrary to the Respondent's allegation, El Paso is not claiming *for* the Argentinian companies; nor is it acting for their benefit or on their behalf. The claims filed by El Paso in these proceedings are those of an investor requesting compensation for the breach by the State of a certain number of guarantees provided by the BIT, an international treaty. El Paso is therefore claiming in its own right, not in somebody else's. ... [paragraph 551] The Argentinian companies' decisions and their agreements with the GOA therefore have no impact on El Paso's rights under the BIT, the breach of which is the cause of action in these proceedings."[98] Yet other tribunals qualified investors as "beneficiaries" and quite obviously meant investor rights flowing from the respective treaty: "Article 1 [of the investment treaty] in defining the concept of 'national' not only defines the scope of persons and entities that are to be regarded as the *beneficiaries of the substantive rights of the* BIT but also defines those persons and entities to whom the offer of arbitration is

[95] ICSID, *Corn Products International* v. *Mexico* (n. 33), paragraph 167; see also paragraph 174.

[96] *Ibid.*, paragraph 169.

[97] ICSID, *Cargill* v. *Mexico*, Case No. ARB (AF)/05/2(NAFTA) (Pryles/Caron/MCRae), 18 September 2009, published on 21 February 2011, paragraph 422 (italics in the original).

[98] ICSID, *El Paso Energy International Company* v. *Argentina*, Case No. ARB/03/15, Award of 27 October 2011, paragraphs 550 and 551.

directed and who thus are potential claimants."[99] "The beneficiaries of Article 1102(1) and (2) [NAFTA] are both investors and their investments."[100]

The granting of substantive rights of investors by an investment treaty was justified in detail by an English appellate court. According to that court, the investor can plausibly be said to be a bearer of claims arising from the BIT from the outset (or at least from the point in time when the investor asserts claims).[101] In her dissenting opinion on the German Constitutional Court ruling on German government bonds, Judge Lübbe-Wolff also assumed "investor rights" arising from the Argentine–German BIT.[102] Finally, the more recent literature argues that the investors themselves, not their home States, can be the holders of substantive rights arising from BITs and the Energy Charter Treaty.[103]

10.4.2.1 ICSID as an Alternative to Diplomatic Protection

The view of the investor as having – as a rule – rights arising from BITs is supported especially by the conception of the ICSID system as an alternative to diplomatic protection – not as one of its variants. This view is shared by the ICJ, which in the *Ahmadou Sadio Diallo* case saw ICSID practice as a special regime that is not relevant to the customary international law of diplomatic

[99] ICSID, *Aguas del Tunari SA* v. *Bolivia*, Case ARB no. 02/3, Decision on Respondent's Objection to Jurisdiction of 21 October 2005, paragraph 242.

[100] ICSID, *ADF Group Inc.* v. *United States*, Case No. ARB(AF)/00/1, Award of 9 Jan. 2003, paragraph 152.

[101] England and Wales Court of Appeal (Civil Division), *Occidental Exploration & Production Company* v. *Republic of Ecuador* (n. 21), paragraphs 17–22. It is difficult to explain the emergence of the claim only from the time of assertion, however. What legal position is the investor supposed to have before that – some kind of international claim-in-waiting?

[102] BVerfG, 2 BvM 1/03, Ruling of the Second Senate of 8 May 2007, dissenting opinion of Judge Lübbe-Wolff, paragraph 73.

[103] See Douglas, Hybrid Foundations, 2004, 168; Ole Spiermann, Individual Rights, State Interests and the Power to Waive ICSID Jurisdiction under Bilateral Investment Treaties, *Arbitration International* 20 (2004), 179–211 (185); Bjorklund, Private Rights, 2007; Alvik, *Contracting with Sovereignty*, 2011, 77; Voss, *Impact of Investment Treaties* 2011, 161; Braun, *Ausprägungen der Globalisierung* 2012, passim. For direct, autonomous claims of investors arising from the Energy Charter Treaty (ECT), Article 26 of which refers to dispute settlement by ICSID, see Richard Happ, The Legal Status of the Investor vis-à-vis the European Communities: Some Salient Thoughts, *International Arbitration Law Review* 10 (2007), 74–81 (76). See also ILC Commentary on Article 33 of the ILC Draft Articles (ILC Yearbook (2002), Vol. II, Part 2, 94–95 (95, paragraph 4)).

protection.[104] The opposing view of the ICSID system as institutionalized diplomatic protection with the consequence of State ownership of primary rights arising from the BITs is unconvincing as will be explained in this section.

The relevant treaty provision in Article 27 of the ICSID Convention does not give an unambiguous answer to the question of the structural relationship of ICSID arbitration and diplomatic protection. According to Article 27, submission to ICSID arbitration in regard to a concrete dispute is considered a "mandatory" exclusion of diplomatic protection.[105] However, there is merely a "suspension" of the power to grant diplomatic protection under general international law;[106] this power can – as clearly stated by the ICSID Convention – be revived if the host State fails to abide by and comply with the ICSID award rendered (Article 27, end of paragraph 1).

Despite this, the understanding of ICSID arbitration as "extended" diplomatic protection misses the point. The qualitative difference between ICSID arbitration and diplomatic protection is seen in the fact that the traditional preconditions for diplomatic protection are not applied in the ICSID context or if so, only in a modified form. The requirement of exhaustion of local remedies prevailing in the law of diplomatic protection does not apply under ICSID, unless the host State requires exhaustion of such remedies as a condition of its consent to arbitration (Article 26 of ICSID).[107] The rule–exception relationship is thus reversed in comparison with general international law: The rule is direct access to ICSID. The exception – i.e., prior exhaustion of local remedies – is seldom used in practice.[108] Also in this way, the involved

104 ICJ, Case Concerning Ahmadou Sadio Diallo (*Republic of Guinea* v. *Democratic Republic of the Congo*), Judgment on Preliminary Objections of 24 May 2007, ICJ Reports 2007, 582 (paragraphs 86–90). See also Parlett, *Individual*, 2011, 105–106.

105 Schreuer, *ICSID Convention* 2009, Article 27, paragraph 5.

106 *Ibid.*, Article 27, paragraph 30.

107 Article 26 of ICSID: "Consent of the parties to arbitration under this Convention shall, *unless otherwise stated*, be deemed consent to such arbitration to the exclusion of any other remedy. A Contracting State *may require the exhaustion* of local administrative or judicial remedies as a condition of its consent to arbitration under this Convention" (italics mine). The possibility for a State party to demand prior exhaustion of local remedies is therefore expressed twice, in sentences 1 and 2 of the provision. The States can express this demand in various legal acts, just like their consent to arbitration, i.e., in a BIT, a national law, or a State contract.

108 For instance, the 2009 German Model Treaty (n. 14) does not provide for exhaustion of local remedies.

States show that they do not have their own legal interests in the matter.[109]

Moreover, the rule of continuity of nationality relevant to the law of diplomatic protection does not apply. According to the continuity of nationality formula, the affected person must be in continuous possession of the nationality of the State exercising protection from the time the right is violated until at least the time the State takes up the matter. In contrast, ICSID does not rely on a time period, but instead on critical dates: The investor must, at the time of submission to arbitration and at the time of registration of the request to institute concrete proceedings, be in possession of the nationality of an ICSID Contracting State.[110] Finally, the nationality of claims rule is modified in respect of another important point. The requirement of a genuine link prevailing in diplomatic protection does not apply to the relationship between the investor and the home State in the ICSID system of arbitration.[111]

All these structural differences were introduced by the ICSID Convention and ICSID case law to establish ICSID as an alternative to diplomatic protection, not as an institutionalization thereof. ICSID arbitration was meant precisely to avoid the disadvantages of diplomatic protection. The deficit of diplomatic protection from the perspective of investors is that investors have no legal claim to diplomatic protection by their home State.[112] And for the home State, the exercise of diplomatic protection entails the danger of political tension; the State must decide between supporting its export economy and preserving untroubled political relations with the host State.

Politicization of the instrument of diplomatic protection, the associated legal uncertainty, and disruption of international relations were meant to be overcome in the field of investment protection. The goals of excluding diplomatic protection under Article 27 of ICSID included transferring the dispute from the domain of politics and diplomacy into the domain of law.[113]

[109] See Douglas, Hybrid Foundations, 2004, 178–179.

[110] See Schreuer, *ICSID Convention* 2009, Article 25, paragraphs 679 and 684; ICSID, *Siag* v. *Egypt*, Case No. ARB/05/15, Decision on Jurisdiction of 11 April 2007, paragraph 205.

[111] See ICSID, *Micula et al.* v. *Romania*, Case No. ARB/05/20, 24 September 2008, reprinted in *International Legal Materials* 51 (2009), paragraph 100.

[112] On this problem, see also Chapter 12, pp. 396–405.

[113] See International Centre for the Settlement of Investment Disputes (n. 24), Vol. II Part 1, 242, 273, 303, 372, 464; see also Schreuer, *ICSID Convention* 2009, Article 27, paragraph 14.

Overall, the ICSID framework was intended to abandon the flexibility of diplomatic protection in favour of achieving stability, predictability, and enforceability of the obligations of the host State.[114] The mandatory exclusion of diplomatic protection by ICSID is also a positive incentive for the host State to submit to ICSID arbitration.[115]

Ultimately, it should be concluded that the *raison d'être* of the ICSID system is not a continuation of diplomatic protection by other means. On the contrary, ICSID is precisely an answer to the deficits of diplomatic protection. In other words: ICSID dispute settlement was not developed as a way to strengthen diplomatic protection, but rather as an alternative to diplomatic protection. It was conceived as an alternative because diplomatic protection turned out to be an impracticable way to effectively protect business interests in contemporary economic life.[116] Accordingly, the fiction of State rights prevailing in diplomatic protection cannot be transferred to ICSID.

10.4.2.2 Further Justification of the Possibility of "Direct Rights" (Investor Rights Arising from the Treaty)

The possibility that primary rights of investors may arise under international law from BITs can be justified in different ways. According to the terminology of German private law, investment protection treaties are contracts for the benefit of third parties. Interpretation is used to determine whether they are "true" contracts for the benefit of third parties, i.e., whether they confer on a third party (in this case the investor) a legal right to performance of the contract.[117] In the common law tradition, investment protection treaties can be compared to contracts without privity:[118] "[A] standard bilateral or regional

[114] See Schill, Private Enforcement, 2010, 40.

[115] See Schreuer, *ICSID Convention* 2009, Article 27, paragraph 4.

[116] See Douglas, Hybrid Foundations, 2004, 181–182.

[117] See § 328 of the German Civil Code (BGB): "(1) Performance to a third party may be agreed by contract with the effect that *the third party acquires the right* to demand the performance directly. (2) In the absence of a specific provision it is to be *inferred from the circumstances*, in particular from the purpose of the contract, whether the third party is to acquire the right, whether the right of the third party is to come into existence immediately or only under certain conditions, and whether the power is to be reserved for the parties to the contract to terminate or alter the right of the third party without his approval" (italics mine). English translation available at www.gesetze-im-internet.de /englisch_bgb/englisch_bgb.html#p1154 (as of 12 November 2013).

[118] In common law, the doctrine of privity states that a contract cannot confer rights or duties upon third parties. The possibility of entitling third parties has, however, been demanded repeatedly in both English case law and the literature, and it has been codified

investment treaty is an interstate agreement, to which individual investors are not privy."[119] The conferral of treaty-based rights on third parties is thus compatible with the contract law traditions of various legal systems.

The concept of treaties providing for the rights of third entities also exists in international law. Article 36 of the Vienna Convention regulates "treaties providing for rights for third States". One arbitral tribunal has applied this provision in order to explain that an investor, analogously to a third State, derives substantive own rights from the investment treaty. On that analogy, said the tribunal, "the 'secondary right-holder' under a bilateral treaty (the investor) . . . is conferred certain rights, being in no different position from 'the third State' (mentioned in Article 36)".[120]

In contrast to that award, it is submitted here that the understanding of international law as being analogous to private law, according to which international treaties between States are comparable to private law contracts, is no longer appropriate. The citizens of States are not "third parties" standing outside the States, but rather they constitute the States and are their basis of legitimation.

Within the framework of a more recent understanding of international law as *public* international law, it is more coherent to compare a treaty to a law (an Act or a Statute) instead of to a private law contract. This analogy is reflected in the traditional term of a "law-making treaty". While investment protection treaties are – unlike classic *traités-lois* – not multilateral, but rather as a rule only bilateral or at best regional treaties, they have created a network of objective law, such as through most-favoured nation clauses and mutual citation of arbitral tribunals – i.e., they have been "multilateralized".[121] A quasi-multilateralized set of rules that is functionally similar to a Statute can without further ado confer rights (and obligations) on natural persons,

by an English law, the Contracts (Rights of Third Parties) Act 1999. This law has hence created a legal exception to the principle of privity of contract. Edwin Peel, *Treitel: The Law of Contract* (London: Sweet & Maxwell 2007), Chapter 14: Third Parties (613–713).

[119] Crawford, *The ILC's Articles*, 2002, 887.

[120] ICSID, *Wintershall* v. *Argentina*, Case No. ARB/04/14, Award of 8 December 2008, paragraph 114.

[121] Stephan W. Schill, *The Multilateralization of International Investment Law* (Cambridge: Cambridge University Press 2009). See also Jeswald W. Salacuse, The Emerging Global Regime for Investment, *Harvard International Law Journal* 51 (2010), 427–473.

even if those persons were not themselves directly involved in creating those rights.[122]

The assumption that BITs regularly confer autonomous substantive rights on investors and should be interpreted and applied in this way in the absence of indications to the contrary – i.e., as the normal case – is in conformity with the system of international investment protection law for several reasons. Firstly, it should be noted that enforcement of rights – even those arising from the BIT – is reserved to the investor (and the host State) through the ICSID arbitral tribunals. Under ICSID, the home State of the investor *cannot* institute arbitration proceedings against the host State. The home State must instead rely on other enforcement mechanisms under international law. Along the same lines, most BITs provide for arbitration between the participating States, but only outside ICSID. Diplomatic protection for the benefit of the investor is – as discussed above – ruled out in principle by Article 27 of ICSID (during the actual arbitration proceedings). This legal design places legal protection in the hands of the investor. Conversely, home States have no control over institution of arbitration proceedings by the investor. There have been situations in which the home State (unsuccessfully) attempted to prevent assertion of rights arising from the treaty.[123] If enforcement of objective international law were the only goal, or a goal of equal importance, then it would make more sense to give States the possibility of enforcing that law alongside private actors, as is the case in human rights law, or even to reserve completely the law enforcement for States, as in WTO law.

Further systemic components are the subrogation clauses (rules governing the transfer of claims) common in investment protection treaties. Where the investor has secured investments using an investment guarantee and realizes this guarantee in the event of damage, the claim against the host State arising from the BIT is transferred from the investor as the previous owner of the claim to the home State.[124] These treaties

[122] On this aspect and the consequent question of the democratic legitimation of international law, see Chapter 17, pp. 544–51.

[123] ICSID, *Gami* v. *Mexico*, Written Observation of the United States of America, cited in Final Award, 15 November 2004, paragraph 29. The arbitral tribunal in ICSID, *Corn Products International* v. *Mexico* (n. 33), paragraph 173, refers to this case in justifying its opinion that the investor asserts an autonomous substantive right. See also Braun, *Ausprägungen der Globalisierung*, 2012, 92.

[124] See, e.g., Article 6 of the 2009 German Model Treaty (n. 14) and similar clauses in the model investment protection treaties of other States. The Canadian model subrogation clause expressly refers to "rights of an investor" (see below n. 133).

assume that the investor – not the State – is the owner of the rights; otherwise, the subrogation provisions would be superfluous.[125]

Another consideration is the following: If the investor were representing the State's interests, the investor's conduct would have to be attributed to the State and deemed State practice. But this conclusion is not drawn in practice and would hardly be accepted by States.[126]

It also makes sense to see the rights arising from the international treaty and those arising from the State contract as being parallel. In ICSID arbitration, a violation of both the treaty and the contract is often claimed. The right flowing from the contract certainly belongs to the investor. Since it appears artificial to split up the ownership of the rights, it makes sense to speak of investor rights as arising from the BITs.[127]

Tax law measures of the host States affecting the property of an investor form a special constellation. As a rule, expropriation standards in BITs do not grant the investor an autonomous right under international law to protection *from taxation* if the arbitration complaint of the investor can be prevented by a "joint tax veto" of the States parties.[128] If an investor institutes arbitration proceedings in tax matters with a complaint of expropriation, some treaties foresee that the tax authorities of both States parties have the right to determine consensually within a specified time period that the measure in question does not constitute a breach of the BIT.[129] This treaty-based right of intervention

[125] See Braun, *Ausprägungen der Globalisierung*, 2012, 95–96. [126] *Ibid.*, 103.

[127] See England and Wales Court of Appeal (Civil Division), *Occidental Exploration & Production Company* v. *Republic of Ecuador* (n. 21), paragraphs 18 and 20.

[128] See Braun, *Ausprägungen der Globalisierung*, 2012, 105–110.

[129] Examples: Article 2103 No. 6 of NAFTA is worded as follows: "Article 1110 (Expropriation and Compensation) shall apply to taxation measures except that no investor may invoke that Article as the basis for a claim under Article 1116 (Claim by an Investor of a Party on its Own Behalf) or 1117 (Claim by an Investor of a Party on Behalf of an Enterprise), where it has been determined pursuant to this paragraph that the measure is not an expropriation. . . . If the competent authorities do not agree to consider the issue or, having agreed to consider it, fail to agree that the measure is not an expropriation within a period of six months of such referral, the investor may submit its claim to arbitration under Article 1120 (Submission of a Claim to Arbitration)." Article 21 of the US Model Treaty (2012) provides: "Article 6 [Expropriation] shall apply to all taxation measures, except that a claimant that asserts that a taxation measure involves an expropriation may submit a claim to arbitration under Section B only if: (a) the claimant has first referred to the competent tax authorities of both Parties in writing the issue of whether that taxation measure involves an expropriation; and (b) within 180 days after the date of such referral, the competent tax authorities of both Parties fail to agree that the taxation measure is not an expropriation . . .".

lends itself to the converse conclusion: If the right of intervention by the State were normal (which would indicate that the investor only asserts rights of the State anyway), the explicit specification of such a right of intervention by the States would not be necessary.[130]

In light of all these considerations, private investors *can* in principle ultimately be considered the holders of rights flowing from (bilateral) investment treaties or from chapter 11 of NAFTA – but this will not inevitably and automatically be so.

10.4.2.3 BIT-by-BIT Interpretation

Whether in a concrete case, the investors are actually owners of the substantive rights such as fair and equitable treatment, national treatment, most-favoured nation treatment, or respect for their property arising from an international investment protection treaty depends primarily on how the guarantees are set out in the respective treaty. "It is a matter of interpretation whether the primary obligations ... created by such a treaty are owed to qualified investors directly, or only to the other contracting state(s)."[131] The determination of investor rights requires evaluation on the basis of the *specific treaty in question*, i.e., a "BIT-by-BIT" evaluation.[132] The starting point is the wording of the BITs. For example, the BITs stipulate that the State "shall accord" fair treatment, or the investor "shall not be subject" to discrimination. Occasionally, treaties state that investors "shall have the right" to a certain treatment. Some model treaties on investment protection expressly accord autonomous rights to investors. The 2004 Canadian model BIT speaks of the "rights of an investor" in the subrogation clause (Article 15, paragraph 2).[133] Article 13, paragraph 2 of the Energy Charter Treaty accords an individual right to national remedies (analogous to Article 13 of ECHR).[134]

[130] See Braun, *Ausprägungen der Globalisierung*, 2012, 110.

[131] Crawford, *The ILC's Articles*, 2002, 887. [132] Parlett, *Individual*, 2011, 112.

[133] "Agreement between Canada and ... for the Promotion and Protection of Investments," available at http://italaw.com/investment-treaties, Article 15, paragraph 2: "A Party or any agency thereof which is subrogated to the *rights of an investor* in accordance with paragraph 1 of this Article, shall be entitled in all circumstances to the same rights as those of the investor in respect of the investment. Such rights may be exercised by the Party or any agency thereof, or by the investor if the Party or any agency thereof so authorizes" (italics mine).

[134] Article 13, paragraph 2: "The *Investor affected shall have a right* to prompt review, under the law of the Contracting Party making the Expropriation, by a judicial or other competent and independent authority of that Contracting Party, of its case, of the valuation of its Investment, and of the payment of compensation, in accordance with the principles set out in paragraph (1)" (italics mine).

The assumption of autonomous ("direct") rights of the investor is compatible with these and similar formulations in the treaties or is suggested by some of the provisions.[135] It is important that individual entitlements cannot be sweepingly assumed for all guarantees set out in the international treaty. Some treaty provisions may grant rights to investors, while others grant only rights to the State or protect objective legality.[136] The standard formula of a "denial of benefits" is ambiguous, however. On the one hand, a benefit is, in technical juridical language, normally distinct from a right. The clause could therefore be interpreted as not granting investor rights.[137] On the other hand, various tribunals have used the term "beneficiary" interchangeably with "rights-holder".[138]

Another question is whether the intent of the States parties should authoritatively determine the interpretation. Along these lines, an arbitral tribunal asked whether granting of individual rights had been intended by the States parties (here, of NAFTA).[139] In the advisory opinion of the Permanent Court of International Justice on *Danzig*, this intent of the parties is the decisive factor in affirming an individual right grounded in international treaty law.[140] In *LaGrand*, however, the ICJ did not consider the intent of the States parties, but rather looked only at the wording of the VCCR.[141] The interpretation of investment treaties should also follow this method of interpretation.

Taking this even further, a legal presumption could be envisaged that investors (not States parties) own the rights. If, as is usually the case, the wording of the treaty is open in regard to ownership of the right, this assumption would apply. Upon such an assumption, BITs would normally be understood as generating "direct" treaty rights of the investor, unless something else would expressly be derived from the norms set out in such treaties in individual cases.[142]

135 See Bjorklund, Private Rights, 2007, 266.
136 See Parlett, *Individual*, 2011, 112.
137 See in this sense Paparinskis, Investment Treaty Arbitration, 2013, 627.
138 ICSID, *Aguas del Tunari* (n. 99); ICSID, *ADF* (n. 100).
139 ICSID, *Corn Products International* v. *Mexico* (n. 33), paragraph 176.
140 PCIJ, Jurisdiction of the Courts of Danzig, PCIJ Ser. B, No. 15 (1928). For more details, see Chapter 2, pp. 29–31.
141 ICJ, LaGrand Case (*Germany* v. *United States of America*), ICJ Reports 2001, 466. For more details, see Chapter 11, p. 352.
142 See Braun, *Ausprägungen der Globalisierung*, 2012, 85.

However, the presumption of autonomous investor rights arising from a treaty seems to be an "oversimplification".[143] The proper course seems to be to analyse each investment treaty on its own terms without shying away from the finding of individual substantive, "direct" investor rights which will frequently impose itself. This is an adequate way to take account of the object and purpose of the international treaty as well as investment protection law in general. The goal of this legal regime in general is to protect foreign investments. This serves on the one hand to protect the private interests of the investor, but also of the host State, which seeks welfare effects by attracting capital.

Against this background, it is not necessary to take an either/or approach.[144] The normal legal situation will be the coexistence of State rights *and* investor rights flowing from a given investment treaty.[145] The follow-up questions of the relationship among these two sets of rights and the procedural consequences of such a coexistence will not be dealt with here.[146] In any case, in the ICSID-system, the investor claim enjoys a procedural priority: Art. 27(1) ICSID prohibits the investor's home State to institute any proceedings once the investor is involved in an ICSID arbitration.

143 Parlett, *Individual*, 2011, 113–114 and 118–119.

144 Anthea Roberts, State-to-State Investment Treaty Arbitration: A Hybrid Theory of Interdependent Rights and Shared Interpretive Authority, *Harvard International Law Journal* 55 (2014), 1–70, 37.

145 See for a presumption in this sense the extremely nuanced discussion of the question of investor rights Evelyne Lagrange, L'application des accords à l'investissement dans les ordres juridiques internes, in: Sabrina Cuendet (ed.), *Le droit des investissements étrangers: approche globale* (Paris: Larcier 2016 forthcoming). Lagrange shows that the acceptance of substantive investor rights flowing from investment treaties is from a legal perspective the proper conceptualization, but that political considerations by the tribunals motivates their denial. What really matters is the lacking invocablity of those rights in domestic courts. A more ready acceptance of the direct effect of investment treaties and the re-introduction of domestic remedies in the host State (against what is foreseen in Art. 26 ICSID-Convention as the regular course) would remedy the normative problem of a potentially undue "gouvernement des arbitres" which is tainted by legitimacy problems and therefore currently regarded with scepticism.

146 The two sets of rights could even be seen as "interdependent" in the sense of being shared and qualified (Roberts, State-to-State Investment Treaty Arbitration, 2014, 39–49). The infringement of State rights might be seen as possibly entailing violations of investor rights, and vice versa. This would also mean that arbitration claims launched by investors and home States could be coordinated under the headings of *lis pendens* or *res iudicata* so as to avoid duplicative claims, contradictory results, and duplicative damages. In such a framework, either the investor or the home State could bring a claim, but not both. Preclusion could operate on a temporal basis, or by prioritizing the one or the other claim.

10.5 Investor Rights Are Not Human Rights

The international substantive rights of investors ("direct rights") that bilateral or multilateral investment treaties may create, and which are normally enforceable by the investor himself through international tribunals, are best not understood as human rights in themselves – maybe with the exception of the right to property.[147] The main reason is not that most investors are moral as opposed to natural persons and thus not human beings with human interests and needs. Moral persons may also enjoy those human rights which do not presuppose human features: Business actors are normally accorded the right to property, right to business activity, right of association, right to privacy (business secrecy) and so on. However, this Section (as the book in general) does not deal with human rights but with other rights.

Without the additional and separate category of international rights outside the realm of human rights, we could neither explain the investors' position properly nor assess their normative significance adequately. In the absence of an additional category of rights, we would be compelled to qualify investors' rights as "quasi-human rights".[148] But this would be, it is submitted here, analytically misleading, and it would convey the wrong normative message.

The distinction between investor rights and human rights suggested here does not overlook the similarities and the overlaps which do exist. First, both international investment law and human rights law have grown out of the same historical roots, namely out of the law of State responsibility of injuries to aliens. Second, both bodies of law seek to address a structurally similar challenge. They both address asymmetric legal relations between sovereign States and individuals (including corporations), and the dangers arising from the superior position of the State vis-à-vis those actors.[149] Third, the investors' right to property forms the

[147] "Property" is today mostly, but not uniformly acknowledged to be a human right. It is however, due to its contestation, not codified in the ICCPR. Also, it is often mentioned as the prime case of a "not fundamental" human right (see the references in note 188).

[148] See in this sense Anastasios Gourgourinis, Investors' Rights "qua" Human Rights?, 2013, 147–182, 159. That author insists on "intimate affiliations and similarities" between both types of rights (158).

[149] Mosche Hirsch, Investment Tribunals and Human Rights: Divergent Paths, in: Pierre-Marie Dupuy/Francesco Francioni/Ernst-Ulrich Petersmann (eds), *Human Rights and International Investment Law and Arbitration* (Oxford: Oxford University Press 2009), 97–114 (107).

background of the rights to fair and equal treatment or full protection and security.

A putative dividing line has to do with the public/private split, but this distinction is not fully convincing. The distinguishing narrative is the following: The law of human rights offers protection to humans in their personal interest and also as an element of public order, reflecting fundamental values of the international community. States undertake international human rights obligations towards the international community as a whole (*erga omnes*) which is also the reason why other States are entitled to raise inter-State complaints for violations of human rights, independently of whether these infringements concern their nationals or not. Human rights treaties are part of the body of international constitutional law creating "objective obligations" "over and above" reciprocal engagements between States, to use the words of the European Court of Human Rights.[150] In contrast, investment obligations primarily bind the host State and the foreign investor and his home State *inter se*.[151] Concomitantly, investor rights are "inherently and inextricably linked" to the synallagmatic character of the inter-State investment treaties.[152] The identification of such features of investment law as contrasted to human rights law lead some observers to conclude that human rights law belongs to the field of public international law proper whereas investment law is in structural terms more of a "private law" type.[153] The follow-up debate then is whether investment law should be more "publicized" too.[154]

That follow-up debate shows that the mentioned difference between human rights and investor rights is less clear-cut than it appears at first sight. Investment protection as well has a "public" purpose, namely the protection of capital flows and the ensuing welfare benefits. In fact, the assumption that egoistic interests of human beings *may* coincide with an overarching public interest, and that exploiting the individuals' egoistic motivation to pursue and defend their own interests will, as a beneficial

[150] ECtHR, *Ireland* v. *United Kingdom*, Nr. 5310/71 (1978), 82: "Unlike international treaties of the classic kind, the Convention comprises more than mere reciprocal engagements between contracting states. It creates, over and above a network of mutual, bilateral undertakings, objective obligations which, in the words of the Preamble, benefit from a 'collective enforcement.'"

[151] Hirsch, Investment Tribunals and Human Rights, 2009, 109.

[152] Gourgourinis, Investors' Rights "qua" Human Rights?, 171.

[153] Hirsch, Investment Tribunals and Human Rights, 2009, 107–114.

[154] See, e.g., de Brabandere, *Investment Treaty Arbitration as Public International Law*, 2014.

side-effect, *also* promote the general interest, is a foundational tenet of liberalism and capitalism. From that perspective, it is Adam Smith's invisible hand, transferred into the legal realm, which guides not only the requests for arbitration of investors but also the individual complaints of victims of human rights violations. The expectation is that the common good will be promoted through the pursuit and legal defence of individual interests. This idea is one of various possible justifications for empowering and encouraging individuals to act as *gardiens*, as enforcers of "objective" international law (for detail, see Chapter 15, pp. 472–74).

Also, the new BITs negotiated or already concluded by the EU formulate a novel type of fair and equitable treatment standard. In order to enhance legal certainty, the relevant provisions list host State action which violates that standard. These lists in part resemble guarantees of procedural human rights (denial of justice and due process), and human rights to non-discrimination. For example, the CETA prohibits "targeted discrimination on manifestly wrongful grounds, such as gender, race or religious belief".[155]

Despite these commonalities, the better view is that both bodies of law, human rights law and investment law, "have evolved along radically divergent paths";[156] and that the differences between human rights and investor rights prevail over their similarities. Investor rights are not accorded to the investors for the sake of human flourishing. They are mainly instrumental, an incitement for the exportation of capital which is supposed to generate welfare effects in the host State. Second, enforceable investor rights are incumbent only to few and extremely wealthy entities (often moral and not natural persons) who are affluent enough to institute an extremely costly investment arbitration proceeding. The fact that "wealth is a legal as well as a practical precondition of access to justice",[157] and the "selectivity" going with it stands in contrast to the idea of human rights which are granted to human beings qua human beings and which

[155] Article X.9 ("Treatment of Investors and of Covered Investments") of the EU–Canadian Comprehensive Economic and Trade Agreement (CETA), consolidated text of 26 September 2014. See similar language in Art. 3 (2) lit. d) of the Transatlantic Trade and Investment Partnership (TTIP) – Trade in Services, Investment and E-Commerce, chapter II, EU text proposal of 12 November 2015.

[156] Hirsch, Investment Tribunals and Human Rights, 2009, 107.

[157] Gus van Harten, *Investment Treaty Arbitration and Public Law* (Oxford: Hart 2007), 142. Van Harten concludes – unlike this study – that investors have no rights at all: "More than anything, it is this selectivity of the legal entitlement to protection that undermines the investor rights view."

are thus universal and not selective. Third, international human rights are primarily protected by domestic courts (sometimes placed under the control of an international body) and thereby "domesticated", whereas the investor rights are safeguarded by international arbiters only, and thereby completely denationalized.[158] The two types of rights thus have a different telos, and arguably have a different weight, too.[159]

Nevertheless, the acknowledgment of substantive (not merely procedural) investor individual rights – even short of human rights – makes a difference to the mere objective protection of investors by international law. By relying on rights, investors are emancipated from their home States, are protected from too burdensome interpretive statements, enjoy protection during the survival period in the event of denunciation and termination of an investment protection agreement, and ultimately are immunized to a certain extent against countermeasures by the host States. These legal consequences are outlined briefly in the following section.

10.6 Practical Consequences of Individual Rights ("Direct Rights") Arising from Treaties

The question of the ownership of rights arising from BITs is not merely academic. It influences the solution of several problems that are relevant in practice.

10.6.1 Interpretation of BITs

First of all, the ownership of the rights could play a role for the interpretation of BITs. It has been argued that the subsequent practice of the States parties (as referred to in Article 31, paragraph 3(b) of VCLT) could not be an interpretive consideration under the assumption that the treaties grant substantive investor rights. But this argument seems flawed. Even if a BIT creates rights of third entities (investors), States remain the High contracting parties and accordingly remain entitled to interpret the treaty. Subsequent practice of the investor's home State (manifested, for example, in observations made during ICSID proceedings) may be taken into account. Despite

[158] Evelyne Lagrange, L'application des accords à l'investissement dans les ordres juridiques internes, in: Sabrina Cuendet (ed.), *Le droit des investissements étrangers: approche globale* (Paris: Larcier 2016), sec. B.1 b) ii.

[159] Paparinskis, Investment Treaty Arbitration, 2013, 623.

the strategical motivations and the political substance of such governmental subsequent practice, this is not an impermissible residue of the mechanism of diplomatic protection that would have to be completely kept outside any interpretation of the treaty by a tribunal.[160]

A question that has already arisen in practice is whether the States parties are able to modify their interpretation to the detriment of the investor, especially during arbitration proceedings that have already commenced.[161] Since, according to what has been argued above, a BIT normally gives rise to rights of the investor, the BIT must be interpreted in good faith (see Article 31, paragraph 1 of VCLT) in light of the *legitimate expectations of the investor*. In particular, this means that the autonomous legal position of the investor tends to shape the standards of treatment under the contract, such as the fair and equitable treatment clauses, in a manner friendly to the investor. While these treaty provisions – as discussed above – must first of all be interpreted "BIT-by-BIT" to determine whether they grant investors autonomous rights, any such legal position – once determined – leads to a further strengthening of the standards as part of a self-reinforcing process. An even more radical consequence would be to find impermissible any interpretive statements by the involved States that burden the investor as a third-party, non-State actor *during* the arbitration proceedings (or as part of proceedings between States).[162]

Furthermore, the legal position of the investor suggests an interpretation of investment standards guided by the human rights approach.[163] This means the human rights case law of the ECtHR relating to property should be considered in particular (Article 1 of Protocol No. 1). The individualistic construction is accordingly suited to defend against the accusation that an investment arbitration tribunal is exceeding its powers if it wishes to draw on that ECtHR case law. Such an approach seems adequate although investor rights (beyond the right to property)

[160] See Anthea Roberts, Power and Persuasion in Investment Treaty Interpretation: The Dual Role of States, *American Journal of International Law* 104 (2010), 179–225 (185, 217–219).

[161] See Braun, *Ausprägungen der Globalisierung*, 2012, 170–174.

[162] *Ibid.*, 174. UNCTAD finds a joint authoritative interpretation by the States parties to an investment protection agreement during ongoing arbitration proceedings to be problematic in light of due process considerations (UNCTAD, IIA Issue Note, No. 2, Reform of Investor-State Dispute Settlement: In Search of a Roadmap (May 2013), 6 n. 25). For a note of caution, see Alvarez, Are Corporations Subjects of International Law?, 2011, 24.

[163] See Braun, *Ausprägungen der Globalisierung*, 2012, 175.

are not as such human rights but form a distinct category (see above pp. 318–21 and Chapter 14).

Finally, the individualistic legal construction leaves no room for the interpretative maxim of *in dubio mitius* (according to which the interpretation granting stronger protection to the sovereignty of the State party in question should be chosen when in doubt).[164]

10.6.2 Denunciation and Revocation of a BIT and Survival Clauses

The individual entitlement of the investor is relevant to the possibility of destruction of the treaty guarantees through unilateral denunciation or consensual termination of the BIT. If the treaty guarantees were claims of the home State, the home State would in any event be able to dispose of them, renounce them, or limit them, such as by denouncing the BIT. In the classic law of diplomatic protection, this is indeed assumed. If the investment protection treaties did not grant autonomous rights to investors, their protection would be terminated immediately upon denunciation of the treaty.

If autonomous investor rights are acknowledged, on the other hand, the principle of protection of legitimate expectations must be observed. It could then be argued that the protection originally granted under the treaty should persist in relation to investments already made.[165] This is in any event already expressly provided in many BITs. Typically, BITs provide a survival period for the protection of the investor's legitimate expectations, i.e., a continuation of treaty protection even beyond the time of denunciation. Such survival clauses grant investors protection between ten and twenty years beyond the moment of termination.[166] In principle, survival clauses are intended for the event of unilateral denunciation (typically by the host State).

The question now arises whether such clauses also can be activated to protect the investor if the States parties consensually revoke the BIT. Wouldn't the States then also be able to revoke the survival clause consensually and thus immediately deprive the investor of protection? The assumption argued above that treaties generally give rise to autonomous investor rights suggests that the clauses should be interpreted as an expression of a general legal concept. Unless their wording is clearly to the contrary, the clauses should be interpreted so that they can be applied

[164] *Ibid.*, 184. [165] See, e.g., Bjorklund, Private Rights, 2007, 267–268.
[166] See Braun, *Ausprägungen der Globalisierung*, 2012, 168–169 with examples.

even on other termination grounds. For instance, Article 13 of the German Model Treaty permits unilateral "denunciation". The survival clause refers systematically to unilateral denunciation, but its wording is not limited to such situations. Rather, the survival period of twenty years for the benefit of the investor is stipulated for the situation of consensual "termination". According to Article 13, paragraph 3 of the Model Treaty, "in respect of investments made prior to the date of termination of this Treaty, the provisions of the above Articles shall continue to be effective for a further period of *twenty years from the date of termination* of this Treaty." Where BITs are interpreted individualistically, protection during the survival period must be granted even if the BIT is revoked consensually by the State parties. Accordingly, "States have themselves relinquished the option of intervening in regard to the survival period even when the treaty is terminated consensually."[167] This construction may be of considerable practical relevance to the investor and accordingly may have the effect of building trust and promoting capital exports even before an investment decision is made.

10.6.3 Waiver of Access to International Tribunals

The ownership of the claim plays a role in examining the controversial question of waiver – but does not give an unequivocal and definite answer to it. The (primarily private law, internationalized) contracts between the investor and the host State often contain jurisdiction clauses in favour of domestic courts or domestic arbitral tribunals.[168] The question arises whether such clauses imply that investors have waived their access to international arbitral tribunals.[169] (A similar question arises in the law of armed conflict: According to the non-renunciation clauses of the 1949 Geneva Conventions, protected persons may not renounce their substantive rights under the conventions because it is assumed that such renunciation would normally not be voluntary, but rather under pressure by the captor State. See Chapter 7, pp. 196–97).

167 *Ibid.*, 170.

168 The waiver of access to an international and especially ICSID arbitral tribunal may be contained explicitly in an exclusive jurisdiction clause or implicitly in a domestic forum election clause. It may also be specified in a law of the host State.

169 In favour of such an (implicit) waiver, see Spiermann, Individual Rights, 2004; against the effect of such jurisdiction clauses as waivers, see Salacuse, International Investment Treaties, 2008, 390–392.

If the waiver is effective, the host State can assert this fact as a defence should the investor – contrary to the agreement in the investor's contract – lodge an application for instituting international arbitration proceedings. The international tribunal must then decline jurisdiction. Arbitral tribunals have so far not taken a uniform approach.[170] Such a uniform approach could be found more easily if the ownership of the claims (arising from the contract and/or the treaty) could be clarified. It must first be considered whether the substantive claims are contractual claims or treaty claims. The investor can very well dispose of its own contractual claims (unless we assume that the investor, akin to a consumer, needs to be protected from disposing and renouncing carelessly or under pressure, and must be paternalized to that extent). *Prima facie*, a jurisdiction clause in the contract foreseeing, e.g., domestic jurisdiction, constitutes an effective waiver by the investor of the right to assert contract claims before an international investment tribunal and accordingly sets aside and precludes the jurisdiction of the tribunal for dealing with contract claims. Most dispute settlement bodies which have been seized on the basis of a jurisdictional clause have distinguished between contract claims and treaty claims in this way, applying jurisdiction agreements which include or imply waivers only to the contract claims, and allowing that treaty claims may in principle go forward to international arbitral tribunals.[171]

The fate of treaty claims under a contractual waiver is, however, unsettled. The case law has not yet decided the question whether the investor can expressly waive access to international arbitration in which the treaty would be examined. At this point, the ownership of the claims seems to play a role. However, opposite conclusions have been drawn in scholarship from that ownership.

[170] For arguments against the possibility of a waiver of ICSID jurisdiction by contract, see, e.g., ICSID, *Compañia de Aguas de Aconquija SA and Vivendi Universal* v. *Argentine Republic*, Decision on Annulment of 3 July 2002, paragraph 101: "[T]he existence of an exclusive jurisdiction clause in a contract between the claimant and the respondent state or one of its subdivisions cannot operate as a bar to the application of the treaty standard." For arguments in favour of the effectiveness of a waiver, see ICSID, *Aguas del Tunari* (n. 99) and ICSID, *SGS* (n. 178).

[171] See, e.g., ICSID, *Toto Costruzioni Generali SPA* v. *Lebanon*, Award of 30 May 2012, Case No. ARB/07/12, paragraph 85: "[T]he Tribunal is concerned by claims of Treaty breaches, and not by breaches of the Contract. Toto's waiver of its right to invoke the CEGP's liability under the Contract to claim contractual damages does not affect its right to invoke Lebanon's breach of the Treaty before this Tribunal."

One line of argument is the following: If the treaty claims were to belong to the home State, waiver clauses in the (private) investor–State contract could not effectively exclude the possibility of international (and especially ICSID) proceedings and of diplomatic protection. The formalist explanation is that the rights held by the State (not by the investor) cannot be contracted away by the investor. Along these lines, it has been argued that the rules contained in BITs are "objective legal positions"; BITs do not constitute "true contracts for the benefit of third parties". The investors benefited by the contract are accordingly not free to give up that legal position.[172] Put differently, only the owner of the original right, the State, may validly make such a waiver. The underlying reason would be that the rights of the home State (or the "objective" body of law) designed to protect the public interest, namely to strengthen economic relations between the high contracting States, and to promote foreign investment, should not be undermined by a private investor. Because not only the regime itself but also the investor's access to arbitration is, from that "public law" perspective, one element for achieving these objectives, a private person should not be allowed to thwart the effective enforcement of this body of law securing the public interest through a waiver of international arbitration.[173]

This appraisal turns out differently if the company itself is seen as the bearer also of the international treaty claims ("direct rights"). The contractual choice of law clauses common in practice could then be interpreted as an effective waiver of ICSID protection (or diplomatic protection), as an arbitral tribunal found: "[I]t would appear that an investor could also waive its right to invoke the jurisdiction of ICSID."[174] Because this statement did not influence the decision in the case in question, however, it should not be given too much weight. If the investor's "own" treaty rights are at stake, the investor can dispose of their actionability. Concomitantly, the State would not be able to determine whether these rights are actionable or not, and could surely not waive them.[175] The acceptance of investors' contractual waivers by some tribunals shows that the involved parties do not assume that State claims are at stake.[176]

172 Jörn Griebel, *Internationales Investitionsrecht* (Munich: Beck 2008), 105.
173 de Brabandere, *Investment Treaty Arbitration as Public International Law*, 2014, 69.
174 See, e.g., ICSID, *Aguas del Tunari* (n. 99), paragraph 118.
175 For the disposal of States of rights of their nationals to reparation in the field of IHL, see pp. 213–16.
176 See Douglas, Hybrid Foundations, 2004, 176–177.

However, the entire question could also be answered exactly in the opposite sense.[177] If the investor enjoys substantive treaty rights ("direct rights"), it might be adequate to protect him from disposing of those rights. This is the stance in human rights law, where the rights are deemed "inalienable". In contrast, if we consider the investor to act only as the agent of the State, enforcing State rights or "objective" law of investment protection (the "indirect rights" theory), one might be tempted to allow him to waive also his access to an international tribunal because what is at stake is the objective regime of investment protection which would in that case have to be enforced by someone else.

The solution also depends on our assessment of the function of the umbrella clause in a BIT, if such a clause exists. Anyone assuming that an umbrella clause upgrades the contractual claims into treaty claims will tend to conclude that the waiver agreed in the contract is ineffective, since it does not affect the claims (which have been "elevated" to treaty claims and have been indirectly internationalized, so to speak). This argumentation by an investor was rejected by the ICSID tribunal in *SGS* v. *Pakistan*, however. Here, the contractual waiver of ICSID legal protection (at least for contract claims) was seen as possible in principle.[178]

In conclusion, it must be noted that by recognizing the possibility of a real legal position of investors arising from a treaty (as a "direct" right), the question of the permissibility of the waiver has not yet been answered definitively. Permissibility should be appropriate to interests. But our judgment about what is appropriate depends on our view of the power relations upon conclusion of the investment contract and an assessment of the public policy dimension of international arbitration. Invocation of international, and especially ICSID arbitration, not only protects the investor but also serves to enforce objective law. A contractual waiver of such arbitration puts the investor in a worse position and prevents realization of rights. If one assumes that the negotiating position of an investor is in principle structurally weak compared with that of the host State, so that the host State can practically force the contractual waiver of ICSID on the investor, one will tend to view the waiver as ineffective, as is the case in consumer protection law. The consideration from the perspective of objective law, according to which the arbitration proceedings have a public policy function, leads to the same result. If the host State

[177] In that sense, see Paparinskis, Investment Treaty Arbitration, 2013, 644.

[178] ICSID, *SGS Société Générale de Surveillance SA* v. *Islamic Republic of Pakistan* (n. 69), paragraph 165, see also paragraphs 159 and 161.

were able to invoke an earlier (often implied) waiver by the investor as a defence in order to prevent arbitration proceedings, the ordering function of investment protection treaties under international law would be undermined – irrespective of whether those treaties additionally protect rights of the investor or not.[179]

From the perspective of individual rights, the interests of the investor are paramount: If one believes the investors are not in a structurally weak negotiating position, one will not see a need to protect them from themselves. Anyone holding this position will find the investors' contractually declared waiver of international arbitration to be effective, despite the negative consequences for their legal protection, because no grounds for paternalistically restricting the investors' party autonomy exist. In reality, the latter view is more likely to do justice to the typical power relations. The assumption therefore exists that private investors can effectively waive referral to an arbitral tribunal, even in relation to treaty claims. The presumption of a public interest in implementing the BIT does not pose an obstacle to this private power of disposal.[180]

10.6.4 Countermeasures of the Host State

The next practical problem whose solution depends on who owns the claims arising from the treaty involves the countermeasures taken by the host State against the home State of the investor. According to Articles 22 and 49(1) of the ILC Articles on State Responsibility, a measure contrary to international law per se (e.g., non-performance of a treaty) may be justified as a countermeasure.[181] But the effect of this justification is relative and limited to the relationship between the offending State and the responsible State. It covers only those countermeasures directed against another State, which in turn had previously committed a breach of international law – but not interference with the rights of third-party subjects of international law. When sufficiently important autonomous rights of the investor based on an international treaty are at stake,

[179] See Braun, *Ausprägungen der Globalisierung*, 2012, 110–116.

[180] See also Spiermann, Individual Rights, 2004, 207.

[181] Article 22 of the ILC Articles on State Responsibility: "The wrongfulness of an act of a State not in conformity with an international obligation towards another State is precluded if and to the extent that the act constitutes a countermeasure taken against the latter State in accordance with chapter II of Part Three." Article 49, paragraph 1: "An injured State may only take countermeasures against a State which is responsible for an internationally wrongful act in order to induce that State to comply with its obligations under Part Two" (UN Doc. A/CN.4/L.602, Rev.1 (2001)).

countermeasures by the host State are not permissible. The fact that the host State declares a measure to be a countermeasure is unable to undo its unlawfulness.

In the NAFTA *Corn Products* dispute, the respondent State Mexico argued that the levy of a certain tax prohibited by NAFTA was justified as a countermeasure against the United States. The ICSID tribunal competent under the Additional Facility found that the rights arising from NAFTA (to national treatment, etc.) were attributable to the investor. Since the tax therefore affected *rights* and not merely interests of third parties, the treaty breach could not be justified as a countermeasure.[182] The arbitral tribunal in the *Cargill* case found likewise: "The Tribunal determines that countermeasures operate only to preclude the wrongfulness of an act that is not in conformity with an obligation owed to the offending state, not in regard to obligations owed to a third state nor those, *as here, owed to the nationals of the offending state*."[183] If the investor had been seen only as a beneficiary of NAFTA, not as an owner of claims under the international treaty, the tax in violation of NAFTA would have been justified as a countermeasure against the United States.

This arbitration case law must be analysed critically. It depends on whether an independent obligation of the host State towards the investor exists. If so, then a violation of the investor's rights has occurred, which makes the countermeasure (which should be directed against the State, not the investor) impermissible. Similarly important is the question of which rights of the investor are likely to catapult a trade policy out of the protective zone of the countermeasure. This concerns the delineation between acceptable collateral damage to the investor and (prohibited) interference with the investor's rights. The starting point of these considerations is that the countermeasures may indeed have an adverse effect on third-party States or other parties and traditionally have done so. Especially in the domain of foreign investments, countermeasures – both of the home State and of the host State – have affected the nationals of the other State. According to the authoritative commentary, "indirect or consequential effects of countermeasures on third parties, *which do not involve an independent breach of any obligation to those third parties*, will not take a countermeasure outside the scope of Article 22".[184] "This does not mean that countermeasures may

[182] ICSID, *Corn Products International* v. *Mexico* (n. 33), paragraph 176.

[183] ICSID, *Cargill* v. *Mexico* (n. 97), paragraph 553 (italics mine).

[184] James Crawford, *The International Law Commission's Articles on State Responsibility: Introduction, Text and Commentaries* (Cambridge: Cambridge University Press 2002), 169.

not incidentally affect the position of third states or indeed other *third parties. ... If they have no individual rights in the matter they cannot complain*. Similarly, if as a consequence of the suspension of a trade agreement, trade with the responsible State is affected and one or more companies lose business or even go bankrupt. Such indirect or *collateral effects* cannot be entirely avoided."[185]

A dilution of total investor protection is reasonable:[186] Countermeasures must be allowed to affect investors. Otherwise, weak States would never have a chance to build up pressure. They have no other option than to use countermeasures to hit investor assets in particular. Complete protection of such assets would go too far. This is all the more obvious given that (depending on the design of the treaty), governmental investors may also fall within the scope of the treaty. Protecting these State actors from countermeasures would be entirely inappropriate. Additionally, investors are sometimes also at fault for breaches of international law committed by their home State. Also in such cases, investors do not appear worthy of protection.

On the basis of these considerations, not all individual rights of third parties should be protected against possible interference by countermeasures. According to this value-based judgment, "third parties" for purposes of the law of countermeasures should only include uninvolved third parties, such as uninvolved nationals of third-party States or international organizations.[187] Moreover, not all kinds of rights should enjoy equal protection. The evaluation made in Article 50, paragraph 1(b) of the ILC Articles on State Responsibility can be cited in this regard: "Countermeasures shall not affect ... (b) obligations for the protection of fundamental human rights." The usual investor rights are not "fundamental human rights" in this sense.[188] This means that, even under the assumption

[185] Crawford, *International Law Commission's Articles*, 2002, 285 (italics mine).

[186] See Braun, *Ausprägungen der Globalisierung*, 2012, 139. [187] See *ibid.*, 152.

[188] See on the distinction between investor rights and human rights above p. 318. See also Gaetano Arangio-Ruiz, Fourth Report on State Responsibility, Yearbook ILC 1992, Vol. II(1) A/CN 4 Ser. A/1992/Add.1 (Part 1), 32 (paragraph 83): "[T]he human rights which should be considered inviolable by countermeasures – the 'more essential' human rights – are not understood to include property rights." Generally speaking, some authors distinguish between "fundamental" human rights and "other" human rights, and relegate notably the right to property to the category of less fundamental rights. See Theo van Boven, Distinguishing Criteria of Human Rights, in: Karel Vasak/Philip Alston (eds), *The International Dimension of Human Rights* (Westport, CT: Greenwood Press and UNESCO: Paris 1982), 43–59, 43.

that a treaty grants the investor autonomous rights, these rights are not automatically fully immune to reprisals.

An intermediate solution should be sought:[189] On the one hand, it cannot be assumed that States have fully renounced the right to countermeasures, even by granting investors autonomous rights. On the other hand, investors should not be held fully to bear the brunt, since their interests are worthy of protection to a certain extent and under certain circumstances.

Protection of the investor can be realized by a compensation claim against the host State for damage suffered because of these countermeasures. This compensation is referred to in Article 27(b) of the ILC Articles on State Responsibility: "The invocation of a circumstance precluding wrongfulness in accordance with this chapter is without prejudice to: . . . (b) the question of compensation for any material loss caused by the act in question." The arbitral tribunal in *CMS Gas Transmission* assumed that this provision reflects valid customary international law and that the involved States should agree on compensation of the "sacrificed" investor rights: "[T]he plea of state of necessity may preclude the wrongfulness of an act, but does not exclude the duty to compensate *the owner of the right* which had to be sacrificed."[190]

However, the ability of the host State to exert pressure should again not be completely undermined by having to fully compensate the investor for damage caused by the countermeasure. In the final analysis, the assumption of autonomous investor rights based on international law entails that these rights may potentially (in the extreme case) make countermeasures impermissible, but are especially likely to trigger a compensation claim by the investor.[191]

10.7 Secondary Claims of the Investor under International Law

The question of ownership of the rights arising from a treaty has consequences for the State responsibility of the host State (beyond the question of countermeasures). If the guarantees in a BIT were to stipulate

[189] See Braun, *Ausprägungen der Globalisierung*, 2012, 154.

[190] ICSID, *CMS Gas Transmission Company* v. *Argentine Republic* (n. 55), Award of 12 May 2005, paragraphs 388–394, especially 388 (italics mine).

[191] Tillmann Rudolf Braun points out that even this claim for compensation arises only in the extreme case, e.g., when an expropriation is at issue and would be impermissible as a countermeasure. Moreover, an investor – analogously to Article 27(b) of the ILC Articles mentioned above – need be compensated only for immediate damage to the investment, but not for loss of profits (see Braun, *Ausprägungen der Globalisierung*, 2012, 159–161).

only substantive rights between States, the *relationship of responsibility (secondary level of international law)* after a treaty breach would consequently likewise arise only between the host State and the home State of the investor. But this is not the predominant view, as will be shown in this section.

In an investment dispute, the investor generally asserts claims for breach of the investor's contract with the host State and, nowadays, also for breach of the treaty between States. The investor can also claim a breach of customary international law, general principles of law, or all at once.[192] For determination of the relief, i.e., the content of the secondary claim, arbitral tribunals apply national law and in some cases international law (see Article 42, paragraph 1 of ICSID). The basic principle of investment arbitration appears to be that an arbitral tribunal may award any relief it deems appropriate, unless the law applicable to the dispute limits this power in a specific way.[193] The ICSID Convention implies that ICSID awards may impose a "pecuniary obligation" on the offending State simply by mentioning the State Parties' duty to enforce such obligations (Article 54 of ICSID). In practice, the most common relief is in fact monetary compensation.[194] This compensation is awarded to the investor, not the investor's home State, and is paid out to the investor.

It is much discussed to what extent secondary claims in investment protection law are governed by (general) international law and especially whether the ILC Articles on State Responsibility are applicable to investor–State arbitration. This question became relevant in the context of the Argentine state of emergency. During that crisis, Argentina and some of its provinces invoked necessity as referred to

[192] The complaints depend not least of all on the breadth of the consent clause. Some BITs, NAFTA, and the Energy Charter Treaty, for instance, provide only for arbitral jurisdiction in the event of claimed breaches of the treaty itself. Other BITs provide for jurisdiction in the event of "any dispute concerning an investment". But depending on the wording of the consent clause, an assertion of contract claims is, according to case law, also permissible in principle if the jurisdiction of the tribunal was based solely on an international treaty (plus arbitration agreement) and not on a clause contained in the contract. See ICSID, *Salini Costruttori et al.* v. *Kingdom of Morocco*, Case No. ARB/00/4, Decision on Jurisdiction of 23 July 2001, paragraph 59.

[193] See Sergey Ripinsky/Kevin Williams, *Damages in International Investment Law* (London: British Institute of International and Comparative Law 2008), 51.

[194] *Ibid.*, 59. See also Article 1135 (1) of NAFTA, which lets tribunals grant only monetary damages or restitution of property and no other form of redress.

in Article 25 of the ILC Articles as a ground for non-performance of loan agreements concluded by the public authorities with foreign private persons.

From the perspective of this study, the specific question is whether and when the investor has *secondary rights under international law*. According to current arbitral practice and the literature, the ILC Articles (or rather the rules on State responsibility under customary international law expressed therein) are in principle also relevant to diagonal investment disputes.[195] But it does not follow from this that the secondary rights under international law are held by the investors. The relationship of responsibility under international law arising from the breach of law may have been established solely between the States. According to Article 33(2) of the ILC Articles, however, secondary claims arising from the international responsibility of States towards non-State actors are possible.[196] The ILC Commentary expressly refers to the claims of investors arising from the breach of a bilateral or regional investment protection treaty by way of example.[197] Formally, Part 2 of the ILC Articles on State Responsibility as such is only applicable to inter-State obligations (and to *erga omnes* obligations). So formally, this Part 2, which regulates the *content* of the responsibility of the State, does not apply to secondary claims of natural or legal persons such as investors (Article 33(1) of the ILC Articles). Part 3 of the ILC Articles on *implementation* of the international responsibility of a State is likewise not applicable, since that Part refers solely to the invocation of State responsibility by one or more States (not by other actors). Accordingly, the special mechanism of ICSID for invoking breaches of the law is not subject to the ILC Articles.

An expert in investment protection law even concluded from the non-applicability of Parts 2 and 3 that this area of the law does not involve "true" State responsibility in the sense of general international law: "[A]n ICSID award does not create a truly 'international' liability at the inter-State level of responsibility such as would be the case, for example, with a judgment of the International Court of Justice . . . The liability created by this subsystem of international responsibility is perhaps more

[195] See Schreuer, *ICSID Convention* 2009, Article 42, paragraphs 192–193 and other references.

[196] For details on State responsibility toward individuals and the correlating individual claims, see Chapter 6.

[197] ILC Commentary on Article 33 of the ILC Articles (Yearbook of the ILC (2001), Vol. II, Part 2, 94–95 (95, paragraph 4)).

adequately described as having a transnational commercial nature in view of the commercial interests at the heart of the dispute."[198] Also in the older literature, it was argued that no relationship of responsibility under international law could arise between the private investor and the host State. This would mean that the investor would have to rely solely on the contractual remedies incurred by a breach of the contract.[199]

But I believe that this view unnecessarily fragments international law. Rather, it should be assumed in line with ICSID case law that the customary legal principles of State responsibility underlying the ILC Articles also apply in principle to arbitration cases between individuals or business partnerships and the host State.[200] The precondition is, however, that the primary right of the private complainant is of an international legal nature. The international responsibility of the State towards individuals in general is dealt with in Chapter 6. The following remarks discuss only secondary rights of private persons under international law specific to investment protection law. In this regard, the secondary rights arising from breach of the contract must be distinguished from those arising from breach of the treaty.

10.7.1 Secondary Claims for Breach of the Contract

The international law of State responsibility governs the claims of an investor arising from breach of the investor's contract with the host State only if these primary claims are of an international legal nature, not subject to domestic (private) law.[201] The Federal Constitutional Court of Germany assumed the latter in the *Argentina* case and denied any international legal nature of the investor claims. The court qualified Argentina's government bonds bought by private German creditors as purely private law contracts, denying the applicability of the international

[198] Zachary Douglas, Investment Treaty Arbitration and ICSID, in: James Crawford/ Alain Pellet/Simone Olleson (eds), *The Law of International Responsibility* (Oxford: Oxford University Press 2010), 815–842 (820–821).

[199] See Toope, *Mixed International Arbitration*, 1990, 243–244. The advocates of this view argue in part with reference to the provision in Article 42 (1), sentence 2 ICSID, according to which the tribunal may apply only such rules of international law as may be "applicable", claiming that the law of State responsibility is not "applicable".

[200] See, e.g., ICSID, *MTD* v. *Chile*, Decision on Annulment of 21 March 2007, paragraph 99; ICSID, *Franck Charles Arif* v. *Moldova*, Case ARB/11/23, Award of 8 April 2013, paragraphs 559–572.

[201] For the discussion on delocalization and internationalization of State contracts, see above pp. 294–301.

legal justification of necessity in regard to these contracts. The court distinguished strictly between the inter-State BIT, to which international legal principles are applicable, and the "private law contract between the investor and the State". According to the Federal Constitutional Court, Argentina's non-performance of the contracts with private persons therefore could not be justified under the principles of Article 25 of the ILC Articles.[202]

In contrast, Constitutional Judge Lübbe-Wolff's view was less formalistic and more holistic. She qualified the necessity defence as a general principle of law supported by the conviction that the enforceability of claims must in some cases be subordinated to general concerns of the common good.[203] According to Lübbe-Wolff, this constellation of interests exists irrespective of whether the claimant is a State or a private person. "In this context, the assumption that the scope of the necessity defence is limited to the legal relationship covered by the ILC Articles on State Responsibility does not suggest itself."[204] Lübbe-Wolff argued that "the object and purpose of the legal concept of necessity do not support the view that it protects the debtor State from a foreign private creditor any less than from another State".[205] It would therefore not make sense to "separate the spheres of validity".[206]

Deviating from the strict separation of contracts from international law put forward in the majority opinion of the Federal Constitutional Court, an internationalization of the State contracts is possible instead, as discussed above (see pp. 294–301). The arguments put forward by Constitutional Judge Lübbe-Wolff support this outcome.

As mentioned, an umbrella clause in a BIT concluded between the host State and the home State of the investor could be an especially suitable path to internationalization. It can thus not be ruled out entirely that

[202] BVerfG, 2 BvM 1/03, Ruling of the Second Senate of 8 May 2007, especially paragraph 51. Customary international law did not provide for a way to "reach through to a relationship under private law" (*ibid.*, paragraph 12).

[203] BVerfG, 2 BvM 1/03, Ruling of the Second Senate of 8 May 2007, dissenting opinion of Judge Lübbe-Wolff, paragraph 81.

[204] *Ibid.*, paragraph 85. [205] *Ibid.*, paragraph 86.

[206] *Ibid.*, paragraph 89. A final argument by the judge in favour of the overarching validity of the necessity defence is less convincing. Lübbe-Wolff argued that since the State courts deciding the private law dispute are organs of the State, the State is involved in that way. According to Lübbe-Wolff, the "way in which State courts deal with the necessity defence asserted by a State in private law disputes accordingly falls within the scope of international law just as much as a defence of necessity asserted by a State immediately before an international court" (*ibid.*, paragraph 90). Following this line of argument, any legal dispute involving a (foreign) State would become international law.

individual contractual claims of the investor might have an international legal nature. This can be determined by interpreting the contract and examining the context of the investment, including the treaty.

It cannot be assumed, however, that the mere breach of the contract as such is apt to trigger the international responsibility of the host State. Rather, the interplay of standards under customary international law and of the contact must be considered, with the ultimate goal of protecting the legitimate expectations of the investor. The standards of treatment under international law as such are not violated by a simple breach of contract. "The law of state responsibility is not directly linked to the contract as obligation, only *indirectly* as a legal fact taken into account by the relevant international obligation."[207] The rights arising from the contract thus play an indirect role in determining a violation of international law, namely as a legal fact.

10.7.2 Secondary Claims for Breach of the International Investment Protection Treaty

The second constellation is the breach of an international investment treaty, especially of a BIT (not only of the contract). Also in this regard, the question of application of the ILC Articles to the Argentina crisis became relevant in practice.[208] Our question is whether the investor can be the owner of secondary rights, this time arising from the breach of a treaty. This is denied by an expert in investment protection law: "[T]he breach of the treaty creates an international obligation *between state parties* to the treaty and no benefits or rights flow directly to the individual."[209] According to this view, the relationship of responsibility relevant to the secondary claims exists between States, and so the owner of the secondary claims is only the home State of the investor.

In contrast, the case law rather seems to consider the investor as the owner of the secondary rights. Practice of ICSID tribunals cited above

[207] Alvik, *Contracting with Sovereignty*, 2011, 76.

[208] In an annulment proceeding, an ICSID tribunal distinguished strictly between the typical "necessity" clauses in BITs and the general state of necessity justification. If the necessity clause in the contract applies, the BIT was never breached and Article 25 of the ILC Articles does not have to be considered. ICSID, *CMS Gas Transmission Company* v. *Argentine Republic* (n. 55), paragraphs 130–134.

[209] Muthucumaraswamy Sornarajah, State Responsibility and Bilateral Investment Treaties, *Journal of World Trade Law* 20 (1986), 79–98 (93; italics mine).

of granting relief in principle to the investor, not to the investor's home State, indicates that the investor, not the State, is seen as the owner of the secondary claims that (also) arise from a breach of an investment treaty.

Moreover, investors appear able to dispose of their compensation claims. For instance, the CMS Gas Company, one of the first investors awarded damages against Argentina by an ICSID tribunal, assigned its claim in the amount of USD 133.2 million to a branch of the Bank of America specialized in collecting debts.[210]

Finally, the idea that the secondary rights are held by the investor finds support in the practice of assessing damages. This practice refers to the investor, in contrast to assessment of State damages in inter-State relationships. In the latter case, the principle applies that the damages of the State are deemed to be *of a different kind*, even if the State is affected in the person of one of its citizens. In the words of the Permanent Court of International Justice: "The damage suffered by an individual is never therefore identical in kind with that which will be suffered by a State."[211]

It is also true that ICSID tribunals have raised the amount of compensation when several investors from the same State were injured by different incidents. The amount of compensation is accordingly assessed on the basis of the purely economic damages of investors. This would not make sense if the home State were the injured party, injured in the form of its citizens, or if the investors were deemed trustees of purely public interests.[212]

In line with the position defended in this Chapter, namely that primary treaty rights may be considered to be "direct rights", held by private persons, it is coherent to accept that the secondary relationship likewise arises between the host State and the investor. But this parallelism is not absolutely necessary from a purely doctrinal and formal perspective. It is, in legal terms, feasible to split the ownership of the claims between the primary and secondary levels.[213] For instance,

[210] See Christopher M. Ryan, Discerning the Compliance Calculus: Why States Comply with International Investment Law, *Georgia Journal of International Law* 38 (2009), 63–95 (84).

[211] PCIJ, *Case Concerning the Factory at Chorzów (Claim for Indemnity – Merits)*, PCIJ Series A, No. 17 (1928), 28 (paragraph 68).

[212] See Douglas, Hybrid Foundations, 2004, 180.

[213] Such a split, but in the opposite direction so to speak, has been assumed by some courts in decisions on international humanitarian law: They assume that the owner of a claim at the primary level is the individual, but at the secondary level only the individual's home State. But this appears artificial and is not plausible prima facie. See Chapter 7, p. 206.

James Crawford assumes that the ownership of the primary claims is a question of interpreting the BIT in question, but that even if the State is determined to be the owner of the primary claims, the secondary relationship of responsibility is always established between the host State and the investor, and not the investor's home State. From that standpoint, the investor would in all cases be the owner of the secondary right under international law.

Finally, in line with the view that investment treaties as a rule generate both investor rights and State rights (level of primary law), *both* the State and the investor could be considered as the holders of secondary rights based on the idea that both are "injured".[214]

As far as the procedure is concerned, in the ICSID system, only the investor, and not the investor's home State, may institute proceedings to claim the breach of the primary obligation (arising from a treaty), regardless of to whom that primary obligation was owed in theory.[215] But this does not yet determine the *content* of the State responsibility of the host State towards the investor. This content might be quite specific or *sui generis*. On top, the entire relationship of responsibility between private persons (here, the investor) and the State (here, the host State) need not even necessarily follow the rules of normal international State responsibility. The general rules of State responsibility (which are tailored to purely inter-State relationships) might have to be modified. This has already been discussed in a preceding chapter on secondary individual claims under general international law (Chapter 6).

In the final analysis, the assumption of the investors' ownership of secondary claims arising from BITs corresponds to practice and is well-founded in terms of doctrine. Viewed in this light, the "pecuniary obligations" referred to in Article 54 of ICSID can be qualified as compensation for the purposes of Article 36 of the ILC Articles (analogously or *mutatis mutandis*).[216]

214 Paparinskis, Investment Treaty Arbitration, 2013, 640.

215 See Crawford, *The ILC's Articles*, 2002, 887–888; Crawford, Treaty and Contract in Investment Arbitration, 2008, 354. As noted, most BITs additionally provide for ad hoc arbitration between States, but not within the ICSID framework.

216 Formally – as mentioned – Part 2 of the ILC Articles on State Responsibility cannot be applied to secondary rights of individuals (Article 33, paragraph 2 of ILC). For this reason, Zachary Douglas claims that "it cannot be assumed that ICSID tribunals are competent to order the different forms of reparation set out in Chapter II of Part Two" (Douglas, Investment Treaty Arbitration and ICSID, 2010, 820).

10.8 Obligations of Investors under International Law

A final question concerns the substantive and procedural obligations of investors under international law.[217] Rights are not logically tied to duties. A person (e.g., an infant) may have rights without being saddled with any duties. However, it is normally considered fair that those who enjoy rights should also be under some obligations (on the question of "fundamental duties" of individuals under international law, see Chapter 4, pp. 110–13). Therefore, it does not come as a surprise that the quest for a "balanced" system of investment protection (balancing both rights and duties of investors, and rights and duties of host States) is currently voiced.[218]

10.8.1 Material Standards

Generally speaking, international legal obligations of investors could arise from the inter-State investment treaties, they could be stipulated in (internationalized) investor–State contracts, they could also flow from general principle of international law (such as good faith, *neminem laedere*, the prohibition of abuse of rights, or the international *ordre public*), and finally they could arise from human rights.

The intensely discussed question whether and under which conditions business actors (which often invest in foreign States) are directly bound by international human rights has already been dealt with in Chapter 4, (pp. 99–110). I recapitulated that *de lege lata* business is not under a hard law duty to respect, fulfil, and protect human rights. But business actors are under a soft "responsibility" (using the

[217] Mehmet Toral/Thomas M. Schultz, The State: A Perpetual Respondent in Investment Arbitration? Some Unorthodox Considerations, in: Michael Waibel/Asha Kaushal/Kyo-Hwa Liz Chung/Claire Balchin (eds), *The Backlash Against Investment Arbitration: Perceptions and Reality* (Alphen aan den Rijn: Wolters Kluwer Law & Business 2010), 577–602; Laborde, Case for Host State Claims, 2010; Braun, *Ausprägungen der Globalisierung*, 2012, 187–202; Dai Tamada, Investor's Responsibility Toward Host-States? Regulation of Corruption in Investor-State Arbitration, in: Noemi Gal-Or/Cedric Ryngaert/Math Noortmann (eds), *Responsibilities of the Non-State Actor in Armed Conflict and the Market Place* (Leiden: Brill 2015), 203–216.

[218] See Julie Anne Maupin, *Reconciling Public and Private Rights and Interests in International Investment Law* (Thesis Geneva 2014), chapter V. Maupin demonstrates that the international regime on investments has vacillated back and forth from arrangements one-sidedly privileging particular foreign interests to a regime which favours host State interests, and in the past decades back to a very (maybe too) investor-friendly regime, a regime which is currently under attack.

terminology of the Ruggie Principles[219]) in that regard. I also argued that, in the future, the direct imposition of legal obligations on business to observe international human rights would require a proper legal basis, would need fine-tuning to balance against countervailing legal positions of business, and should not detract from the primary obligations of host States and home States (see above pp. 105–10).

The thousands of existing IIAs have hardly ever imposed obligations on investors so far, although this is being suggested by proponents of sustainable or responsible investment. For example, an NGO-authored model agreement of 2005 contains a part entitled "Obligations and Duties of Investors and Investments". Article 14 of that model agreement states that "(C) Investors and investments shall act in accordance with core labour standards as required by the ILO Declaration on Fundamental Principles and Rights of Work, 1998; (D) Investors and investments shall not manage or operate the investments in a manner that circumvents international environmental, labour and human rights obligations to which the host state and/or home state are Parties."[220]

In the practice of investor–State arbitration, international law has rarely been applied by arbitral tribunals as a barrier to investor activity, not to speak of direct obligations flowing from various branches of international law which would be placed on investors. For example, host States have occasionally relied on a purely auxiliary fashion on international law to bolster their policies directed against investors, for instance, for identifying public purposes which would allow, e.g., an expropriation. Examples are environmental law,[221] cultural heritage

219 Report of the Special Representative of the Secretary-General on the issue of human rights and transnational corporations and other business enterprises, with Guiding Principles in the Annex (UN Doc. A/HRC/17/31) of 21 March 2011.

220 International Institute for Sustainable Development (IISD), Model International Agreement on Investment for Sustainable Development, drafted by Howard Mann, Konrad von Moltke, Luke Eric Peterson, Aaron Cosbey (2005).

221 In the *Vattenfall* case, German authorities had denied or delayed water and emission permits for a Swedish power plant project in order to comply (at least so it was argued) with commitments under international environmental law such as the EU Water Framework Directive and the UNFCCC (cf. ICSID, *Vattenfall* v. *Germany*, Request for Arbitration (30 March 2009), paragraph 17). This stood in tension with the State's obligations under the Energy Charter Treaty not to expropriate foreign investors and to accord them fair and equitable treatment. See also ICSID, *Compania del Desarrollo de Santa Elena, S.A.* v. *Republic of Costa Rica*, Case No. ARB 96/1, Final Award of 17 February 2000: In this case, the right of the State to expropriate the investor for the public purpose of protecting the environment (in conformity with the general international law on protection of property) was not in dispute. The dignity of the public interest had no impact on the amount of the compensation.

law,[222] and human rights law. Human rights-based obligations have mostly become acute in the course of the privatization of infrastructure (*service public*), notably water services. Such privatizations have partly been required by the World Bank from developing States, and have often attracted foreign investors. Measures taken by host States such as repudiation of lease contracts, failure to improve facilities, negative propaganda, or lowering of water prices have been implicitly or explicitly justified by host States with the need to protect social human rights of their populations. They were then attacked by investors before arbitral tribunals. The *Biwater Gauff* tribunal suggested that "human rights and sustainable development issues are factors that condition the nature and extent of the investor's responsibilities, and the balance of rights and obligations as between the investor and the host State". This would mean that "foreign corporations engaged in projects intimately related to human rights and the capacity to achieve sustainable development . . ., have the highest level of responsibility to meet their duties and obligations as foreign investors, before seeking the protection of international law. This is precisely because such investments necessarily carry with them very serious risks to the population at large".[223] Two pending proceedings against Zimbabwe involve expropriations or evictions of foreign investors through the Zimbabwean land reforms. An association

[222] NAFTA chapter 11, Arbitration, *Glamis Gold* v. *United States of America*, Counter-memorial of the United States of 19 September 2006, 33–35: The defendant justified its regulations requiring backfilling and grading for mining operations in the vicinity of Native American sacred sites by relying, inter alia, on the principles of the UNESCO World Heritage Convention concerning the preservation of historic and cultural property which arguably limit investor's rights under NAFTA. The State relied on "principles of cultural preservation . . . that reflect the 'policy' of the international community" (p. 35). The Award of 8 June 2009 mentioned the UNESCO Convention only in the statement of the relevant legal instruments (pp. 46–47). See already ICSID, *Southern Pacific Properties (Middle East) Limited* v. *Arab Republic of Egypt*, Case ARB/84/3, Award of 20 May 1992, YB Commercial Arbitration 19 (1994), 51–104, paragraph 158: expropriation through cancellation of a tourist development project for the public purpose to protect antiquities.

[223] ICSID, *Biwater Gauff (Tanzania) Ltd.* v. *United Republic of Tanzania*, Case No. ARB/05/22, Award of 24 July 2008, paragraph 380 (*amici* submission, summarized by the Tribunal); see also paragraph 723 (host State's defence). See further ICSID, *Azurix Corp.* v. *The Argentine Republic*, Case No. ARB/01/12, Award of 14 July 2006: The province of Buenos Aires had privatized the water services. Subsequent regulations were alleged by the concessionaire to amount to expropriation. The province raised the issue of the compatibility of the BITs with human rights treaties, but the Tribunal "fail[ed] to understand the incompatibility in the specifics of the instant case", because water services to the consumer continued to be provided without interruption (paragraph 261).

of Zimbabwean traditional chiefs and a European human rights NGO filed an *amicus* brief in the dispute. They argued that the indigenous right of access to ancestral lands would be affected by the resolution of the case. The tribunal denied the *amicus* petition with the argument that "the putative rights of the indigenous communities as 'indigenous peoples' under international human rights law" was "a matter outside of the scope of the dispute, as it is presently constituted".[224] In no decision has international human rights law been thought to impose a direct international-law-based obligation on investors. It is, however, conceivable that either general international law principles or customary human rights should function as a guideline for the interpretation of both investment treaties and investor–State contracts. This guideline function of human rights would be perfectly in line with the idea of business "responsibility", as endorsed by the Ruggie Principles.[225]

Increasingly, host States have been alleging fraud, coercion, or corruption on the part of investors in investment arbitration.[226] Tribunals have relied on international legal principles for their interpretation of the investor–State contracts. For example, a contract brought about by fraud or corruption does not give rise to "legitimate expectations" worthy of protection.[227] Tribunals have also resorted to general international principles for determining whether an investor–State contract is tainted or even void so that claims based on such contract cannot be successful. For example, in *World Duty Free*, the tribunal stated that "bribery is contrary to the international public policy of most, if not all States, or, to use another formula, to transnational public policy" and concluded that "claims based on contracts of corruption or on contracts obtained by corruption cannot be upheld by this Arbitral Tribunal".[228]

[224] ICSID, *Border Timbers Limited, Border Timbers International (Private) Limited, and Hangani Development Co. (Private) Limited* v. *Republic of Zimbabwe*, Case No. ARB/10/25 and *Bernhard von Pezold and Others* v. *Republic of Zimbabwe*, Case No. ARB/10/15, Procedural Order No. 2 of 26 June 2012, paragraph 60.

[225] Note 219.

[226] On this case law, see Aloysius P. LLamzon, *Corruption in International Investment Arbitration* (Oxford: Oxford University Press 2014), esp. 198–199; Sébastien Manciaux, *Investissements étrangers et arbitrage entre Etats et ressortissants d'autres Etats* (Dijon: Litec-CREDIMI 2004), 325–382.

[227] ICSID, *Inceysa* v. *El Salvador*, Case No. ARB/03/26, Award of 2 August 2006, paragraphs 46 and 248; UNCITRAL, *International Thunderbird Gaming Corporation* v. *United Mexican States*, Award of 26 January 2006, separate opinion Thomas Wälde, dated December 2005, paragraph 112.

[228] ICSID, *World Duty Free Company Limited* v. *The Republic of Kenya*, Case No. ARB/00/7, Award of 4 October 2006, paragraph 157.

While this investment arbitration case law has not yet formulated direct international legal obligations binding the entrepreneur in the proper sense, some tribunals have reacted to investor misconduct. In *Plama Consortium*, for instance, Plama's request for arbitration on the basis of the Energy Charter Treaty was denied with the following reasoning: "[T]he tribunal found that the investor had violated the following general principles of law: (i) the principle of good faith ... and (ii) the principle of *nemo auditur propriam turpitudinem allegans* – that nobody can benefit from his own wrong – understood as the prohibition for an investor to 'benefit from an investment effectuated by means of one or several illegal acts'" and, thirdly, "'the respect for the law' which is a principle of international public policy".[229] In *Inceysa* v. *El Salvador*, a tribunal reviewed whether the investment was compatible with the general principles of law as referred to in Article 38, paragraph 1(c) of the ICJ Statute. The BIT between Spain (home State of Inceysa) and El Salvador referred to this source of law as applicable to investments. The tribunal found that the investor had violated several general principles of law, so that the BIT parties' consent to submit to investment arbitration was void and the tribunal accordingly had to refuse jurisdiction.[230]

However, such punishment has not always withstood scrutiny. In *Klöckner*, the tribunal (first instance) decided that Klöckner had violated the duty of disclosure postulated by the tribunal.[231] On the investor's application to have the award annulled, the *ad hoc* committee (second instance) found that the prior tribunal's argumentation constituted an obvious excess of powers and an obvious lack of impartiality, and it annulled the award.[232] This meant that Klöckner's conduct in the end went unsanctioned.

10.8.2 Procedural Options

The next question is who could invoke any potential international obligation or responsibility incumbent on investors, notably their human

229 ICSID, *Plama Consortium Limited* v. *Republic of Bulgaria*, Case No. ARB/03/24, Award of 27 August 2008, paragraph 141.

230 ICSID, *Inceysa* v. *El Salvador* (n. 227), paragraphs 224–257.

231 ICSID, *Klöckner Industrie-Anlagen GmbH* v. *Cameroon*, Case No. ARB/81/2, Award of 21 October 1983.

232 ICSID, *Klöckner*, Annulment Decision of 3 May 1985, paragraphs 64–79, 97–99.

rights responsibility, in which forum, and which additional procedural mechanisms or sanctions exist.

The mere denial of jurisdiction as reported above does not imply any imposition of a legal duty on the investor. But in the mentioned case of *Plama*, the tribunal penalized the claimant who was declared "guilty of fraudulent misrepresentation in obtaining the investment in Bulgaria", by imposing "all of the fees and expenses of the Tribunal and ICSID's administrative charges plus the reasonable legal fees and other costs incurred by respondent".[233]

In investor–State arbitration, "indirect" obligations or responsibilities of investors have mainly emerged as a result of successful defences raised by the host State in proceedings instituted by the investors. Only very few host States have themselves instituted arbitration proceedings.[234] While Article 36 of ICSID mentions the possibility for a host State to request the institution of proceedings, the host State only has the right to do so if the treaty providing for referral to ICSID in fact grants that right to the host State. NAFTA, for instance, permits only investors to institute arbitration proceedings (Articles 1116 and 1117 of NAFTA). The arbitration clauses in many BITs grant both contracting parties and hence also the host State the power to institute investment arbitration proceedings before *ad hoc* arbitral tribunals, but these are beyond the scope of ICSID. Such treaty clauses can be considered consent by the host State to arbitration proceedings *on the claimant side*.

Jurisdiction of the Centre for Settlement of Investment Disputes according to Article 25 of ICSID is available only if both parties to the dispute agree, i.e., if there is consensus. Accordingly, the consent of the investor is required. When proceedings are instituted by the host State, unlike in the normal constellation, the required consent of the investor (his "acceptance" of the host State's offer of arbitration) cannot be found in the request for institution of proceedings, since the investor as the respondent does not submit such a request. The investor's consent must theoretically be derived from the treaty or from the investor's contract with the host State, or the investor must declare consent in the individual case once the dispute arises. These two latter forms of consent are conceivable, but apparently very rare in practice.

233 ICSID, *Plama* (n. 229), paragraph 322.

234 Gustavo Laborde, The Case for Host State Claims in Investment Arbitration, *Journal of International Dispute Settlement* 1 (2010), 97–122 mentions three proceedings instituted since 1976.

The first-mentioned possibility for the investor's consent is difficult to explain in terms of doctrine. Since the investor is not a contracting party to the treaty, *the investor's* consent to arbitration cannot be derived from that treaty without further ado. This *prima facie* impossibility of a treaty-based path for the host State to bring proceedings against the investor has led to the famous qualification of ICSID arbitration as "arbitration without privity", understood here as an asymmetry or lack of reciprocity to the detriment of the host State.[235] Recently, it has been demanded that the arbitration clauses of BITs be interpreted so that they contain the consent of the host State to appear on the claimant side and govern the legal status of investors as potential respondents.[236] But this would be possible only if the establishment of private obligations by an international treaty of the home State were viewed as permissible and not as a prohibited contract at the expense of the investor as a third party. (This question is discussed in more detail in the chapter on individual obligations; see Chapter 4, pp. 72–74.)

All in all, the interpretation of the investor–State contracts (or of the BITs) in the light of general principles has so far not created any additional, international-law-based obligations for investors. But these techniques do increase the responsibility of investors, in its broader sense.[237] The enforceability of such responsibility appears limited at first sight, because host States can rarely institute investment proceedings themselves. However, the host State's active use of corruption as a defence functions as a severe penalty on investors because it may lead to inadmissibility and denial of jurisdiction and thus foreclose scrutiny of the substance of investors' claims. The ensuing protection of the host State is noteworthy because, e.g., bribery necessarily involves State organs' participation in the first place.

As a matter of legal policy, and in light of the recent criticism of one-sided preferential treatment given to investors notably under the ICSID system, more attention should be paid to carving out investor obligations, under due respect for the principle of legality.

[235] Jan Paulsson, Arbitration without Privity, *ICSID Review: Foreign Investment Law Journal* 10 (1995), 232–257.
[236] See Laborde, Case for Host State Claims, 2010.
[237] Tamada, Investor's Responsibility, 2015, 214.

10.9 Conclusion

This analysis has shown that the actual owners of the procedural and substantive primary and secondary rights in investment protection law may (also) be the investors, and not only the States parties. The procedural power to bring claims is an international legal position of the investor. The secondary claims belong almost indisputably to the investors, and the international legal responsibility of the host States is towards those investors. The primary rights accruing from the contract to the investor may, depending on the design of that contract, be internationalized and accordingly have an international legal nature. Moreover, investment treaties, notably BITs, may also generate rights of investors ("direct rights") which normally coexist with the rights of the State party.

This understanding of the legal positions involved corresponds to the description given by Jan Paulsson in his groundbreaking essay in 1995: "The possibility of direct action – international arbitration without privity – allows *the true complainant* to face the true defendant."[238]

The persistence of the question whether rights of the State and/or of the investor are in play on the three levels of procedure, substantive law, and responsibility – a question that appears purely doctrinal and academic only at first glance – reflects the dualism of investment protection. Investment protection is both a "private" and a "public" institution. The goals of BITs and investment arbitration, notably under the ICSID system, are not only to satisfy the private interests of investors in a facilitation of capital flow and secure conditions for investment but also to take account of the regulatory objectives of the host States and the interest of the capital-exporting States. Moreover, the interest in the free flow of capital must be weighed against other, potentially conflicting regulatory objectives such as environmental protection. The idea of diagonal investor–host State arbitration is intended to secure both the individual rights of investors and respect for reciprocal interstate treaty obligations.[239]

Relevant international legal texts emphasize the public interests. For instance, the preamble of the ICSID Convention places private foreign investments in the service of economic development and international

[238] Paulsson, Arbitration without Privity, 1995, 256 (italics mine).

[239] In the words of one of the creators, Aron Broches: "The purpose of the Convention is to promote foreign investment by improving the investment climate for investors and host States alike. The drafters have taken great care to make it a balanced instrument serving the interests of host States as well as investors" (Broches, Convention on the Settlement of Investment Disputes, 1972, 348).

cooperation.[240] The usual preambles of BITs also cite the strengthening of economic cooperation between the States parties or the increase of the prosperity of peoples as overarching goals of the treaty.[241]

From a rather "French" or public law perspective, the investor may be seen primarily as the trustee of these public interests. An ICSID tribunal formulated this idea as follows: "Although under modern international law, treaties may confer rights, substantive and procedural, on individuals, they will normally do so in order to achieve some public interest."[242] However, instrumentalization of the investor to realize the public interest does justice to the investor's private goals (which are legally secured by the freedom to conduct a business) only if private and public interests are congruent. But this is not necessarily the case for foreign investments. Alongside the economic interest in capital export that the home State shares with the investor, the home State as a rule has additional political, geostrategic, or other interests that may conflict with the private economic interests.

In fact, home States are hardly interested in the claims arising from BITs and the State contracts or in the enforcement thereof. Empirically, this can be seen in the fact that in arbitration proceedings instituted by businesses, the home States of those investors are far more likely to intervene as third parties in favour of the respondent State than in favour of their own business.

The acknowledgment or reinforcement of autonomous procedural and substantive rights of investors under international law underscores the market-economic and liberal sub-component of investment arbitration's hybrid quality. The danger of over-liberalization and one-sided preferential treatment of investors can be minimized by recognizing and expanding investor *obligations* under international law.

240 The preamble begins with the words: "The Contracting States, considering the need for international cooperation for economic development, and the role of private international investment therein . . ."

241 The preamble of the 2009 German Model Treaty (n. 14) states that "the encouragement and contractual protection of such investments are apt to stimulate private business initiative and to increase the prosperity of both nations" (italics mine).

242 ICSID, *SGS Société Générale de Surveillance SA* v. *Philippines* (n. 70), paragraph 154 (footnotes omitted).

11

Individual Rights in Consular Law

This chapter discusses the rights of the individual asserted against the so-called "receiving State", i.e., rights that allow individuals to contact the consulate of their home country ("sending State") or to have such a contact established by the receiving State. A separate question would involve a right asserted against the sending State to consular protection (which does not exist under current international law).[1] The right of individuals to contact their consulate and other related individual entitlements have great practical significance in times of globalization and increased mobility of individuals. In the negotiations on the Vienna Convention on Consular Relations (VCCR[2]) in 1963, the access of individuals to their home country consulate was so controversial that the adoption of the treaty was at risk because of this very question.[3] The special rights of foreign detainees to notify their consulate of their arrest and to have their communications forwarded to their consulate are not exotic rights relevant to just a handful of unlucky individuals. Criminality or suspected criminality abroad has increased significantly due to labour migration and foreign tourism, and therefore the risk of being taken into pre-trial or criminal custody has increased as well. Providing services to persons detained abroad in the wake of brawls, football hooliganism, or drug offences has already proven to be overwhelming for many consulates.[4]

Article 36 (1) of the VCCR[5] addresses the issue as follows:

"With a view to facilitating the exercise of consular functions relating to nationals of the sending State: (a) consular officers shall be free to communicate with nationals of the sending State and to have access to

1 On the parallel question of a right to diplomatic protection, see Chapter 12, pp. 396–409.
2 Vienna Convention on Consular Relations of 24 April 1963, 596 UNTS 261.
3 See Luke T. Lee/John Quigley, *Consular Law and Practice* (3rd ed., Oxford/New York: Oxford University Press 2008), 143.
4 See *ibid.*, 139–140.
5 Art. 36 VCCR: "Communication and contact with nationals of the sending State" (italics mine).

them. *Nationals of the sending State shall have the same freedom* with respect to *communication* with and *access* to consular officers of the sending State; (b) *if he so requests*, the competent authorities of the receiving State shall, without delay, *inform* the consular post of the sending State if, within its consular district, a national of that State is arrested or committed to prison or to custody pending trial or is detained in any other manner. Any *communication* addressed to the consular post by the person arrested, in prison, custody or detention shall be forwarded by the said authorities without delay. The said authorities shall inform the person concerned without delay of *his rights* under this subparagraph; (c) consular officers shall have the right to *visit* a national of the sending State who is in prison, custody or detention, to *converse* and *correspond* with him and to arrange for his legal *representation*. They shall also have the right to visit any national of the sending State who is in prison, custody or detention in their district in pursuance of a judgment. Nevertheless, consular officers shall refrain from taking action on behalf of a national who is in prison, custody or detention *if he expressly opposes such action*."

11.1 The Right to Consular Contact

Article 36(1)(a) sets out the general rule governing contact of all nationals of the sending State with their home consular officers. "Communicate with" and "have access to" are the forms of contact mentioned.

According to the wording, this is first of all (first sentence) a right of the sending State ("consular officers shall be free . . ."). This corresponds to the traditional right of the sending State to grant consular protection (see Article 5(a) of the VCCR[6]). In the classical bilateral consular agreements (prior to adoption of the VCCR), the contracting parties were regularly accorded reciprocal rights to grant protection.[7] This right of the State is also recognized under customary international law.

According to the newer, "individualized" view, however, this is also an international individual right of the citizen located abroad. This is mentioned in the second sentence: "*Nationals of the sending State shall have the same freedom* with respect to *communication* with and *access* to consular officers of the sending State." According to this view,

[6] Article 5 VCCR: "Consular functions consist in: (a) protecting in the receiving State the interests of the sending State and of its nationals, both individuals and bodies corporate, within the limits permitted by international law; . . ."

[7] See Lee/Quigley, *Consular Law and Practice*, 2008, 124.

the second sentence is not only the mirror image of the consular power referred to in the first sentence, but is also in fact a genuine right of the affected person. The Inter-American Court of Human Rights held that Article 36(1)(a) of the VCCR serves a dual protective purpose: firstly, that of "recognizing a State's right to assist its nationals through the consular officer's actions and, correspondingly, that of recognizing the correlative right of the national of the sending State to contact the consular officer to obtain that assistance".[8]

The follow-up question is how potential conflicts between the State's right to grant protection and the individual's right to contact for the purpose of obtaining protection can be resolved. In other words, does a State right exist to grant protection to unwilling nationals who refuse consular protection? In practice, receiving States do not like the exercise of protection for the benefit of reluctant individuals and oppose such protection.[9] This practice probably allows the conclusion that the State right to grant protection is recognized under customary law only subject to the consent of the affected individual. The individual aspect of the right appears to outweigh the interest and right of the State.

11.2 Rights of Detained Foreigners

The special situation of detained foreigners is governed by Article 36(1)(b) and (c) of the VCCR. These provisions are not limited to accused persons in criminal proceedings abroad, but rather they apply generally to all persons who have been deprived of their liberty abroad for various reasons, such as to avert danger or for their own protection (e.g., detention pending deportation in asylum proceedings,[10] quarantine, compulsory placement in a closed psychiatric facility), or for the execution of a sentence. The ICJ judgment in the *LaGrand* case concerned only the provisions in subparagraphs (b) and (c), not (a).[11]

[8] Inter-American Court of Human Rights (IACtHR), Advisory Opinion OC-16/99, *The Right to Information on Consular Assistance in the Framework of the Guarantees of the Due Process of Law* (1 October 1999), paragraph 80.

[9] See Lee/Quigley, *Consular Law and Practice*, 2008, 125.

[10] See Federal Court of Justice of Germany (BGH), 6 May 2010 – AZ V ZB 223/09; BGH, 28 October 2010 – V ZB 210/10; BGH, 18 November 2010 – V ZB 165/10; BGH, 12 May 2011 – V ZB 23/11; BGH, 14 July 2011 – V ZB 275/10.

[11] However, the ICJ formulated the key holding of the *LaGrand* judgment, namely that "Article 36, paragraph 1, creates individual rights", as a general statement about the entire paragraph 1 (ICJ, *LaGrand Case* (*Germany* v. *United States of America*), ICJ Reports 2001, 466, paragraph 77).

Four elements are at issue: (1) informing the consular post when a national is deprived of liberty, but only if the national so requests (subparagraph (b), first sentence); (2) forwarding of communications addressed to the consular post by the detained person (subparagraph (b), second sentence);[12] (3) informing the person concerned "without delay" of the person's rights referred to in the first two sentences (subparagraph (b), third sentence);[13] and (4) communication in the form of "visiting", "conversing" with the consul, and "corresponding" with the consul in writing (Article 36(1)(c), first sentence).

11.2.1 (Only) State Rights?

The question now is whether the four elements mentioned above (information about arrest, forwarding of communications, information provided to the person, written and oral communication) are rights of the individual concerned or only rights of the individual's sending State. The traditional view was that these were (only) rights of the sending State. Even the information provided to the detained person about that person's rights was and is construed as a right of the sending State vis-à-vis the receiving State to have the detained person informed of her or his rights.[14]

In the *LaGrand* case before the ICJ, the United States unsuccessfully defended the view that Article 36(1)(b) and (c) granted only rights between States. In his separate opinion, ICJ Judge Shi cited the arguments in favour of a statist interpretation:[15] The wording of the chapeau of

[12] The right of a detained person to have the consular post of the home State notified of the arrest and to have the communication forwarded is in lieu of the general right to contact the consular officers pursuant to subparagraph (a), because the detained person cannot appear at the consular post in person.

[13] Element 3 (informing of rights) is important because the receiving State has to contact the consulate of the home State only "if the person concerned so requests". Without being informed of the possibility to request contact, the detained person would not be able to make effective use of that right, and the right to establish contact would be empty. The information must be provided "without delay". See BGH, 28 October 2010 – V ZB 210/10 (deprivation of liberty), paragraph 7: Information provided to the asylum-seeker at the beginning of detention suffices; it does not have to be provided already at the hearing before detention is ordered (concerning an asylum application submitted while in criminal custody).

[14] See Niklas Wagner/Holger Raasch/Thomas Pröpstl, *Wiener Übereinkommen über konsularische Beziehungen vom 24. April 1963: Kommentar für die Praxis* (Berlin: Wissenschafts-Verlag 2007), 255.

[15] ICJ, *LaGrand Case*, Separate Opinion of Vice-President Shi. From the literature arguing against the individual rights content of Article 36 of the VCCR, see Christian Hillgruber,

Article 36(1) – "With a view to facilitating the exercise of consular functions relating to nationals of the sending State" – refers to the powers of the State. The systematic interpretation in the light of Article 5 of the VCCR,[16] which enumerates consular functions, also points in the direction of State interests. Finally, Shi referred to the drafting history of Article 36.

Along similar lines, the US Supreme Court, which has often had to consider Article 36 of the VCCR, has so far explicitly left open whether the provision grants individual rights.[17] Lower US federal courts are split on this question,[18] and state courts have so far rejected individual rights.[19] In particular the Supreme Court of the US state of New Mexico has rejected the individual rights content of Article 36 of the VCCR.[20]

11.2.2 *Individual Rights*

The better arguments recognize that all four elements mentioned in subparagraphs (b) and (c) *also* have the character of individual rights. The wording of Article 36 describes the notification of the home country consulate and the forwarding of communications addressed to the consular post as "his rights", i.e., the rights of the detained person. While the interpretation of Article 36 as an individual right cannot be justified solely with reference to the supposedly "clear" wording, the wording does constitute one of several interpretive considerations.

Secondly, the fact that the notification of the consular post about the detention of a national is linked to the request of the detained person shows that this notification is in principle at the disposal of the detained person. This legal construction likewise speaks in favour of an individual

Anmerkung zu LaGrand, *JuristenZeitung* 57 (2002), 94–99; Bernd Grzeszick, Rechte des Einzelnen im Völkerrecht, *Archiv des Völkerrechts* 43 (2005), 312–344.

16 Text in n. 6.

17 In *Breard* v. *Greene*, 523 US 371, 376 (1998), the US Supreme Court "arguably" assumed that the Vienna Convention grants the detained individual the right to consular assistance, but it did not decide the question. See, similarly, US Supreme Court, *Sanchez-Llamas* v. *Oregon, Bustillo* v. *Virginia*, 548 US 331 (2006).

18 In favour of an individual right: US Court of Appeals, *Jogi* v. *Voges*, 480 F.3d 822 (7th Circ. 2007), paragraph 51. Tending to reject an individual right: US Court of Appeals, *Cornejo* v. *County of San Diego*, 504 F.3d 853, 856–864 (9th Circ. 2007).

19 See John Quigley/William C. Aceves/S. Adele Shank, *The Law of Consular Access: A Documentary Guide* (London: Routledge 2010), 74 and other references.

20 Supreme Court of New Mexico, *State* v. *Martinez-Rodriguez*, 131 N.M. 47, 33 P.3d 267, 274 (2001), Judgment of 14 September 2001, without reference to the *LaGrand* decision of the ICJ of 27 June of the same year.

right *prima facie*. The rationale of this treaty clause is complex, however. Before the VCCR was adopted, the receiving State had an obligation under customary international law to notify the consular post of the sending State immediately if a national of the sending State was detained. By virtue of pre-conventional customary international law, this was true irrespective of the will of the person concerned. For the States parties to the VCCR, Article 36 is a derogation from the obligation under customary international law for the receiving State to automatically notify the sending State that one of its nationals has been detained, irrespective of any request of the detained person. Alongside this rule, some pre-conventional bilateral treaties exist which provide obligations to notify the foreign consular post even without or against the will of the national concerned. These treaties remain in force in accordance with Article 73 of the VCCR.[21]

At the 1963 Vienna Conference on Consular Relations, there were differences of opinion among States as to whether a receiving State should always be obliged by the Convention to notify the detention of a foreigner to that person's sending State.[22] During the time of the Cold War, many States were interested in automatic notification of the detention of their nationals due to mistrust. Other States, in contrast, were concerned that the receiving State would incur too heavy a burden if it automatically had to notify the home country consulate every time a foreigner was detained. On the other hand, the danger of abuse counselled against making notification dependent on the detained person's request: The authorities of the receiving State might claim at any time that the detained person had not wanted to notify his or her consulate of the detention.

The compromise at the Vienna Conference was to link the notification of the sending State regarding detention to the request of the person concerned, combined with the receiving State's obligation to inform the person concerned that he or she could demand notification (and forwarding of communications to the consulate). The intention of this rule was to prevent the above-mentioned abuse by local authorities and to balance the rights of the involved States and the individual.[23] This means that Judge Shi's reference to the origins of the VCCR is not a sound argument against the individual rights character of the elements in

[21] See Wagner et al., *Kommentar für die Praxis*, 2007, 255–256.
[22] On the VCCR negotiations, see Lee/Quigley, *Consular Law and Practice*, 2008, 143–146.
[23] See *ibid.*, 146.

subparagraph (b). Due to the objections by Venezuela at the Vienna Conference against the International Law Commission (ILC) draft, in which the right of the individual to consular contact was first mentioned, merely the ordering of the provisions in Article 36 of the VCCR was changed, and the duty to notify was made dependent on the request of the person concerned. The substance was not touched, however.[24]

Thirdly, the possibility of an explicit objection by the pre-trial detainee or the convict (paragraph 1(c), third sentence of the VCCR) within the scope of application of subparagraph (c) (consular access in the form of visitation, conversation, and correspondence) points in the direction of the individual rights content of consular access.[25] The individual's right to an explicit objection was not contained in the original draft of the ILC. It was introduced during the Vienna Conference to "take greater account of the detainee's personal decision".[26]

From all of these considerations, it follows that the provisions in Article 36(1)(b) and (c) of the VCCR should not be interpreted as guaranteeing merely obligations between States, as the United States unsuccessfully argued in the *LaGrand* case. The understanding of all four elements in subparagraphs (b) and (c) as individual rights of detained foreigners has won out in case law and State practice. In its 1999 advisory opinion, the Inter-American Court of Human Rights (IACtHR) found that Article 36(1)(b) "is unequivocal in stating that rights to consular information and notification are 'accorded' to the interested person. In this respect, Article 36 is a notable exception to what are essentially States' rights and obligations accorded elsewhere in the Vienna Convention on Consular Relations. As interpreted by this Court in the present Advisory Opinion, Article 36 is a notable advance over international law's traditional conceptions of this subject".[27] On Article 36 of the VCCR as a whole, the Court held that the provision "endows a detained foreign national with individual rights that are the counterpart to the receiving State's correlative duties".[28]

In the later *LaGrand* case, the ICJ relied on the clear wording of the provision and decided "that Article 36, paragraph 1, creates individual rights, which, by virtue of Article I of the Optional Protocol, may be invoked in this Court by the national State of the detained person".[29]

[24] See *ibid.*, 164–165 and other references.

[25] See IACtHR, 1999 Advisory Opinion (n. 8), paragraph 83.

[26] Wagner et al., *Kommentar für die Praxis*, 2007, 261 (translation mine).

[27] IACtHR, 1999 Advisory Opinion (n. 8), paragraph 82. [28] *Ibid.*, para 84.

[29] ICJ, *LaGrand Case* (n. 11), paragraph 77.

European countries and their domestic case law have followed this view. In a joint brief submitted in the *Medellín* case, for instance, the EU brief that was joined by the Council of Europe and the four EFTA states confirmed the existence of an international individual right to be informed about the right to contact with the sending State's consulate (alongside the right of the sending State itself); the brief furthermore urged that it should be possible under domestic law for the person concerned to contest a sentence in court by complaining of the violation of consular law.[30]

According to the preferable view, the guarantees arising from Article 36(1) of the VCCR are rights of the detained person *and* of the sending State.[31] The ICJ found that these two rights are in a relationship of interdependence with each other: A violation of the rights of the individual may entail a violation of the rights of the sending State, and conversely, a violation of the rights of the State may entail a violation of the rights of the individual.[32]

11.2.3 Individual Rights to Consular Contact in Other Treaties

Individual rights to consular contact are also granted by other treaties.[33] According to Article 6(3) of the UN Convention against Torture of 1984, any foreign person in custody on suspicion of torture must be given the opportunity to communicate immediately with the person's consulate.[34] According to the Protection of Diplomats Convention of 1973, the States parties must grant persons detained for an offence against diplomats the

[30] See Brief of *Amici Curiae* The European Union and Members of the International Community in Support of Petitioner, in *Medellín* v. *Dretke*, 544 US 660 (2005) (*Medellín I*).

[31] See ICJ, *LaGrand Case* (n. 11), paragraph 128 (3). See also Germany's submission to this effect in paragraph 75.

[32] See ICJ, *Case Concerning Avena and other Mexican Nationals* (*Mexico* v. *United States of America*), ICJ Reports 2004, 12, paragraph 40.

[33] For instance, the European Convention on Consular Functions of 1967 – which has not yet entered into force – states that a national of the sending State "shall at all times be entitled to communicate with the appropriate consular officer", European Convention on Consular Functions of 11 December 1967 (ETS no. 061), Article 5. See in general Articles 4–6. The Convention has been ratified by only four States and requires five ratifications for entry into force.

[34] The person "shall be assisted in communicating immediately with the nearest appropriate representative of the State of which he is a national", Article 6(3) of the Convention against Torture and Other Cruel, Inhuman or Degrading Treatment or Punishment of 10 December 1984 (GAOR, 39th sess., Resolutions, Supplement No. 51, UN Doc. A/39/51, p. 197).

right to communicate with the nearest appropriate representative of the person's sending State.[35] The most modern special human rights treaties, namely the Migrant Workers Convention[36] and the Convention against Enforced Disappearance,[37] likewise guarantee the right of consular contact. The leading manual on consular law characterizes these treaty norms as follows: "These are rights-giving provisions, designed to ensure fair treatment in the course of criminal proceedings."[38]

11.3 The Quality of Individual Rights Arising from Article 36 of VCCR

The follow-up question is whether the rights of the detained foreigner to consular contact (and to receive information about that right of contact) are human rights or "ordinary" international individual rights below the threshold of human rights. This is not a merely academic question, because the answer is relevant to legal protection and the legal consequences of the breach of the individual right.[39]

11.3.1 Protective Purpose of Article 36 VCCR

Any classification of the right to have consular contact arranged and to be provided with information about that right must take account of the object and purpose of those rights. Similarly, any classification of those rights as human rights depends in part on the protective purpose of the norm. In none of its judgments has the ICJ expressed an opinion on the rationale of the provision set out in Article 36(1)(b) of the VCCR.

[35] Article 6(2)(a) of the Convention on the Prevention and Punishment of Crimes against Internationally Protected Persons, including Diplomatic Agents of 14 December 1973, UNTS vol. 1035, 167.

[36] Article 16(7) of the International Convention on the Protection of the Rights of All Migrant Workers and Members of Their Families of 18 December 1990. See also the General Assembly resolution on protection of migrants (UNGA res. 58/190 of 22 December 2003), paragraph 10, which specifically reaffirms the duty of States parties arising from Article 36 of the VCCR towards foreign nationals, regardless of their immigration status.

[37] According to Article 17(2)(d) of the International Convention for the Protection of All Persons from Enforced Disappearance of 20 December 2006, the States parties must "[g]uarantee that any person deprived of liberty shall be authorized ... if he or she is a foreigner, to communicate with his or her consular authorities, in accordance with applicable international law".

[38] Lee/Quigley, *Consular Law and Practice*, 2008, 167.

[39] See Chapter 14, p. 365.

The rationale must be derived in light of the entire Convention and consular practice as expressed in the relevant service instructions.

The right to consular contact is not necessarily linked to the human right to a fair trial. The same right also applies in other situations of deprivation of liberty. The focus is on the classical consular responsibility to grant *protection to the State's own citizens abroad*. A key function of consulates is maintaining contact with citizens detained abroad. But in no event is the protective function of consulates directed solely – or even primarily – at improving criminal defence. Protection is also extended to persons serving a prison sentence or confined in psychiatric institutions. Consular officers are called upon to monitor whether convicts are physically abused. They are asked to ensure better medical care, nutrition, and other amenities. They must protect the property of convicts, explain foreign procedures to them, and help them deal with their stress.[40] Consulates may also work towards obtaining transfer to the home country.

One of the rationales of the right to notification and access is *protection from unnoticed disappearances* – but this is not the only rationale. Initially, however, the German Federal Court of Justice endorsed this narrower interpretation when it found that notification of the consulate was intended to prevent nationals of the sending State – who might have only minimal or no social contacts outside their home State – from being disappeared by the receiving State.[41] While the International Convention for the Protection of All Persons from Enforced Disappearance conceives of access to consular authorities as additional protection against disappearances,[42] this does not exhaust the function of consular access as set out in the VCCR and other treaties.

Typically, foreigners are more exposed to the power of the State than citizens, because they are less familiar with the legal order and often do not speak the national language. Support by their consulate can help compensate for these disadvantages. The special duties imposed on the receiving State (duty to notify the sending State, to provide information on the right of consular access, etc.) are intended to make consular protection by the sending State possible. The purpose of these duties is

[40] Lee/Quigley, *Consular Law and Practice*, 2008, 147–150.

[41] See BGHSt, Ruling of 7 November 2001 (5 StR 116/01). This ruling was overturned by the Federal Constitutional Court because it did not sufficiently consider the ICJ's *LaGrand* judgment and thus violated the constitutional duty of consideration.

[42] Article 17(2)(d) of the International Convention for the Protection of All Persons from Enforced Disappearance of 20 December 2006 (for the wording, see n. 37).

to compensate for the presumed *de facto* disadvantages for detained foreigners.[43] From the perspective of the person concerned, the rights set out in Article 36(1) of the VCCR are *rights to compensatory unequal treatment of foreigners to prevent their indirect discrimination.*

In reality, not all detained foreigners are in special need of protection, especially not those who have been living in the receiving State for a long time, are integrated there, and speak the national language. However, the inner logic of all provisions protecting from discrimination is to rely on (stereotypical) characteristics, the bearers of which are in general vulnerable to a specific danger of discrimination, even if individual bearers of those characteristics are not in fact in need of protection. Accordingly, the ICJ in the *LaGrand* case applied the provision set out in Article 36 of the VCCR to the German LaGrand brothers without restriction, even though they had lived in the United States for decades. A teleological reduction of the provision – in the sense of non-applicability to foreigners who are not in need of special protection – is not permissible.[44]

Only part of consular protection (albeit an important one) is related to *criminal defence*. The consulate may arrange for a defence counsel familiar with the home country who may be more committed, more likely to take a skilled approach, and – for instance in the United States – more able to achieve a favourable plea agreement. In particular, the consulate can help uncover exonerating life circumstances in the home country and in this way have a favourable effect on sentencing.[45] In the *Fierro* case decided by the Inter-American Commission on Human Rights, the parents of the accused were in police custody in their home country of Mexico. In part due to the accused's concern for their well-being, the accused made self-incriminating statements. His consulate would have been able to give him more detailed information on his parents' situation, thus permitting him to weigh his statements better.[46] The consulate can

[43] See BVerfGK 9, 174 (2 BvR 2115/01, 2 BvR 2132/01, 2 BvR 348/032010) of 19 September 2006, reprinted in *Neue Juristische Wochenschrift* 61 (2007), 499, paragraph 74: "The primary purpose of the provision is to protect foreign nationals in the light of their weaker legal and psychological position as compared with citizens" (translation mine).

[44] See *ibid.*, paragraph 66.

[45] See *LaGrand Case*, Memorial of the Federal Republic of Germany, Vol. 1, paragraph 4.61.

[46] Inter-American Commission on Human Rights (IAComHR), *Fierro* v. *United States*, Case No. 11.331, Report No. 99/03 of 29 December 2003, paragraph 67. See also Oklahoma Court of Criminal Appeals, *Osbaldo Torres* v. *the State of Oklahoma*, Ruling of 13 May 2004 (order granting stay of execution and remanding case for evidentiary hearing), Judge Chapel, specially concurring. In his concurring opinion, Judge Chapel

also act if the trial is delayed unreasonably or if a judge appears to be biased. Even just the presence of the consular officer at the trial may help counter any discrimination against the accused foreigner. On the other hand, the provision does not grant a right to consular assistance per se, but rather only to access and communication.

11.3.2 Human Rights?

Do these protective purposes justify the classification of rights derived from Article 36 of the VCCR as human rights? The IACtHR emphasized that a treaty such as the VCCR "can concern human rights regardless of what the principal purpose of that treaty might be".[47] The Rwanda Tribunal likewise referred to the right to notification of consular officers of the sending State as a "fundamental right" of the detained suspect.[48] In the *LaGrand* case, Germany had (unsuccessfully) argued that the individual's right under Article 36 of the VCCR to have the consulate of the sending State immediately notified of the arrest had "today assumed the character of a human right".[49] In *LaGrand*, the ICJ expressly did not find it necessary to consider this additional argument.[50] In its later *Avena* judgment, the ICJ apparently believed any classification as a human right was irrelevant, but nevertheless tended to negate the human rights quality.[51]

carried out an exemplary "review and reconsideration" procedure. He determined that the accused's home State of Mexico systematically assisted its citizens facing serious charges in the United States (observation of the trial; monitoring of the defence counsel; collection of evidence, especially exonerating circumstances). The judge concluded that the violation of the VCCR had created "a possibility of significant miscarriage of justice" and that the case would therefore have to be retried.

47 IACtHR, 1999 Advisory Opinion (n. 8), paragraph 76, also paragraph 85.

48 Appeals Chamber, *The Prosecutor* v. *Juvénal Kajelijeli*, Case No. ICTR-98-44A-A, Judgement of 23 May 2005, paragraph 221.

49 ICJ, *LaGrand Case* (n. 11), paragraph 78.

50 *Ibid.* In doing so, the ICJ signalled that it was not a supranational court of appeal that would adjudicate the legal position of the individual under domestic law. A possible motive of the ICJ might also have been that it wanted to cut off debate about the demand for recognition of a human rights claim to diplomatic (and consular) protection (Enrico Milano, Diplomatic Protection and Human Rights before the International Court of Justice, *Netherlands Yearbook of International Law* 35 (2004), 85–142 (131)).

51 See ICJ, *Case Concerning Avena and other Mexican Nationals* (n. 32), paragraph 124: "Whether or not the Vienna Convention rights are human rights is not a matter that this Court need decide. The Court would, however, observe that neither the text nor the object and purpose of the Convention, nor any indication in the travaux préparatoires, support the conclusion that Mexico draws from its contention in that regard." This paragraph is

The *travaux préparatoires* of the VCCR do provide a few weak indications of the human rights character of the right to consular contact. During the VCCR treaty negotiations, the Australian delegate referred to the right of nationals of the sending State to communication with their consular representation as a "fundamental right". Ecuador stated that this right came within the scope of the 1948 Declaration of Human Rights rather than of the VCCR.[52] The constitutions of Venezuela and Guatemala also deem the right of detainees to contact the consulates of their sending States to be so important that they have included them as special constitutional norms, in the case of Guatemala even under the heading of "human rights".[53] In conclusion, the view that the rights derived from Article 36 of the VCCR are human rights is prevalent especially in Latin America.

11.3.3 *Component of the Human Right to a Fair Trial*

For the important subgroup of people who face criminal charges abroad and have not yet been sentenced, the rights derived from Article 36 of the VCCR are ancillary to the human right to a fair trial. In its 1999 Advisory Opinion, the IACtHR made this determination without giving further reasons: Because consular assistance concerns the rights of the accused and can help the accused, such assistance is relevant to a fair trial and the procedural guarantees. According to the IACtHR, non-observance of Article 36 of the VCCR is prejudicial to the guarantees of the due process of law.[54]

The Inter-American Commission on Human Rights decided similarly. It held the right of a foreign detainee to information under Article 36(1)(b) of the VCCR to be a "fundamental component" of a fair trial and deemed the failure to respect that right to be a violation of the right to a fair trial and due process under Articles 18 and 26 of the American Declaration of

most likely a compromise between two opposing views on the qualification of the right among the judges.

[52] Statements of Australia and Ecuador, UN Conference on Consular Relations, UN Doc. A/Conf.25/C.2/SR.15, 15th meeting of the Second Committee, Meeting of 14 March 1963, Official Records Vol. 1, pp. 329–334 (p. 331, paragraph 34 and p. 333, paragraph 47).

[53] Article 44 of the Bolivarian Republic of Venezuela of 30 December 1999; Article 19(c) of the Political Constitution of the Republic of Guatemala as amended on 17 November 1993.

[54] IACtHR, 1999 Advisory Opinion (n. 8), paragraph 137, see also paragraphs 124 and 129.

the Rights and Duties of Man.[55] The academic literature has often followed this opinion.[56]

The Federal Constitutional Court of Germany likewise adopted this position in the wake of *LaGrand* and *Avena*. It deemed the violation of the VCCR to be a violation of the thematically relevant fundamental right of the Basic Law in conjunction with the principle of the rule of law, namely a violation of the fundamental right to a fair trial under Article 2(1) of the Basic Law.[57] In its ruling of 2010, the Court emphasized that "a fair trial . . . is structured not only by the provisions of the Code of Criminal Procedure, but also by the provisions of international law".[58] The Federal Constitutional Court furthermore held that "Article 36(1) of the VCCR, as an individual right to consular assistance . . . pursuant to the opinions of the International Court of Justice, constitutes the procedural status of the accused in this regard".[59] With this formulation, the Federal Constitutional Court hinted that exclusion of evidence might be considered: According to the settled case law of the Federal Court of Justice, exclusion of evidence must be considered especially when the breached procedural norm serves "to safeguard the basic principles of the procedural status of the suspect or accused in the criminal proceedings".[60] (On enforcement of the right through exclusion of evidence, see pp. 376–83.)

11.3.4 Component of Due Process in Administrative Proceedings

In situations involving detention outside criminal proceedings, the Federal Court of Justice of Germany states that information about the right to consular contact pursuant to Article 36(1)(b), the third

[55] IAComHR, *Martinez Villareal* v. *United States*, Case No. 11.753, Report No. 52/01 of 10 October 2002, paragraphs 84 and 69; similarly, IACtHR, *Fierro* v. *United States* (n. 46), paragraph 40; IAComHR, *Medellín, Ramirez Cardenas and Leal García* v. *United States*, Case No. 12.644, Report No. 90/09 of 7 August 2009, paragraphs 124–132.

[56] See, e.g., Martin Mennecke, Towards the Humanization of the Vienna Convention of Consular Rights, *German Yearbook of International Law* 44 (2001), 430–468 (453) for classification of the right to consular contact as a human right, namely as part of the fair trial guarantee ("functional link"); see also Andreas Paulus/Jörn Müller, Konsularische Information vor deutschen Gerichten - Never Ending Story oder Happy End?, *Strafverteidiger* 29 (2009), 495–502 (500).

[57] See BVerfGK 9, 174, 1st Chamber of the 2nd Senate, 2 BvR 2115/01 of 19 September 2006, paragraph 47.

[58] BVerfGK 17, 390, 2nd Chamber of the 2nd Senate, Ruling of 8 July 2010 - BvR 2485/07 (translation mine).

[59] *Ibid.* (translation mine).

[60] BGHSt 38, 214, 220 (1992; translation mine).

sentence of the VCCR, constitutes a fundamental procedural guarantee, i.e., an element of due process. Outside of criminal law, Article 36 of the VCCR is especially relevant to detention pending deportation. In such a case, the Federal Court of Justice held: "Providing this information is an *indispensible component of due process*. . . . If no information is provided at the time of detention, the order of deprivation of liberty suffers from a *basic procedural defect* entailing its unlawfulness."[61] In another case involving detention pending deportation, the Federal Court of Justice established a documentation requirement: "Because the *rights* arising from the Vienna Convention on Consular Relations are *procedural guarantees*, their observance must be traceable by the appellate bodies and thus be documented."[62] Consequently, the rights arising from Article 36 of the VCCR can plausibly be described as individual procedural guarantees even outside criminal proceedings.

11.3.5 Other Human Rights Involved: Privacy and Data Protection

In addition to the detainee's right to consular contact, other human rights are relevant to situations involving detention. Coupling the duty to notify the sending State of the deprivation of liberty to a request by the detainee fulfils a dual protective purpose. It serves not only to reduce the burden on the receiving State, but it especially also serves to safeguard the detainee's legitimate interest in keeping the detention confidential and thus ultimately to protect the detainee's privacy and his right to data protection as guaranteed under human rights law.

Does this mean that the receiving State must refrain from notifying the sending State about the detention if the detainee does not make a request in this regard, i.e., that the detainee has a corresponding right to confidentiality regarding the fact of his or her detention? This is not the case.[63] Article 36(1)(c), the third sentence of the VCCR, expressly prohibits the consular officer only from assisting the person concerned against his or her will. Notifications of detention are not covered by the individual's right to objection. In particular, the human rights in question

[61] BGH, Ruling of 6 May 2010, AZ V ZB 223/09 (concerning deprivation of liberty due to detention pending deportation), paragraph 25 (translation and italics mine). See also BGH, 28 October 2010 – V ZB 210/10 (case involving deprivation of liberty), paragraph 7.

[62] BGH, 18 November 2010 – V ZB 165/10 (case involving detention pending deportation; applicant for asylum), paragraph 5 (translation and italics mine).

[63] See Lee/Quigley, *Consular Law and Practice*, 2008, 163, n. 136; Wagner et al., *Kommentar*, 2007, 255.

are not absolute, but rather are subject to the usual limitations. The interests of the receiving State and the person concerned must be reconciled in a reasonable way. If the public interest is sufficient (e.g., in effective prosecution), the receiving State may notify the sending State about the detention even without or against the will of the detainee. This entails conversely that a detainee does not have a strict right to prevent the sending State from being notified of the detention. If the receiving State notifies the sending State against the will of the detainee (where the public interest is sufficient), the receiving State is not in breach of Article 36 of the VCCR or of the human right to informational self-determination. This means that under certain circumstances, notifications of detention are permissible even against the declared will of the foreigner.

11.3.6 *Interim Conclusion*

The functional link between consular access and the criminal proceedings entails that the fair trial guarantees under human rights law must be interpreted in conformity with the VCCR.[64] The applicable guarantees set out in the universal and regional human rights texts must be interpreted systematically in the light of Article 36 of the VCCR. Article 36 of the VCCR is a "relevant rule of international law" within the meaning of Article 31(3)(c) of the Vienna Convention on the Law of Treaties and thus must be taken into account when interpreting the human rights treaty in question.

The failure to observe the provisions of the VCCR that protect individuals also constitutes a violation of the human rights that are functionally linked to the right derived from Article 36 of the VCCR. In *criminal proceedings*, the violation of obligations under the VCCR (and the corresponding individual rights under Article 36(1)(b) and (c) of the VCCR, i.e., notifying the consular post about a detention, forwarding of communications, informing the detainee of these rights, right of the consular officer to visit) also entails a violation of the human right to a fair trial (e.g., pursuant to Article 14(1) of the ICCPR: a "fair hearing"). But this is true only if the procedural flaw is not corrected in the course of the domestic criminal proceedings or is not taken into account in review

[64] Due process guarantees in administrative proceedings are not expressly set out in the universal and regional human rights agreements, but they can be derived as a procedural limb from other human rights, such as the right to respect for private life.

proceedings that fulfil the requirements of international case law (see pp. 369–75). If the trial against a defendant whose rights under the VCCR have been deprived ends in a death sentence, the enforcement of that sentence also violates the right to life.[65]

The right to consular contact should best be understood not as an independent new human right, but rather as a sub-right within the framework of procedural guarantees, which in turn ultimately serve to protect human rights. The following considerations argue against classification as a new human right: The rights to access and information are linked to citizenship and the associated special relationship to a State. By definition, only individuals with a citizenship have this right; it is not accorded to stateless persons. The right also presupposes the existence of consular relations between the two involved States. The right to consular contact does not protect a central area of human life in the way a civil liberty does. Instead, it should be considered supplemental protection for the equal treatment of foreigners (see pp. 357–58). Accordingly, the Federal Court of Justice of Germany describes the right to information about the right to consular contact as a "non-central blanket special right" for foreigners.[66] Similarly, in his partial dissent from the 1999 Advisory Opinion of the IACtHR, Judge Jackman emphasized that this right concerned the relatively special context of the law governing aliens: "[I]t is difficult to see how a provision such as that of Article 36.1.(b) . . . can be elevated to the status of a fundamental guarantee, universally exigible as a *conditio sine qua non* for meeting the internationally accepted standards of due process."[67]

Finally, the persons concerned do not have a right against their sending State for the sending State's consulate to actually assist them. Arrangement of access by the receiving State is merely a procedural step that does not entail any substantive rights of the person concerned.

These aspects (dependence on citizenship and the existence of consular relations, safeguarding of equal treatment, no guarantee of result) do not prevent these rights from being accorded the quality of a human

[65] See IACtHR, 1999 Advisory Opinion (n. 8), paragraph 137; IAComHR, *Martinez Villareal* v. *United States* (n. 55), paragraph 85; IAComHR, *Fierro* v. *United States* (n. 46), paragraph 41.

[66] BGH (5 St 116/01) of 25 September 2007, Section II 1 (d) (translation mine). This classification was criticized in BVerfGK 17, 390 of 8 July 2010 (n. 58), however.

[67] IACtHR, 1999 Advisory Opinion (n. 8), Partially Dissenting Opinion of Judge Oliver Jackman, paragraph 9.

right per se, since even recognized human rights are affected by these or similar aspects. Classification as a human right should not be made on a formal and formalistic basis, but rather on a substantive and functional basis. To ensure the practical efficacy of human rights, they must be open to developments. A strict separation between human rights and other rights would tend to contravene this goal (on the distinction between human rights and "ordinary" international individual rights, see Chapter 14). "Ordinary" rights generally exist against the backdrop of human rights, just as the rights derived from the VCCR exist against the backdrop of the human rights to a fair trial and due process.

11.4 Enforcement of the Individual Right

The disputed question – left open by the ICJ – of whether the right to consular contact is a human right has practical consequences for enforcement of the right.

11.4.1 International Human Rights Bodies

Under the assumption that the rights to consular access and information are a functional component of the fair trial guarantee, claims regarding violations of Article 36 of the VCCR can be made indirectly in conjunction with claims regarding the relevant human rights (Article 14 of the ICCPR or Article 6 of the ECHR). These claims can be brought as individual complaints to the international or regional *human rights bodies*. This is not a tacit and impermissible extension of the human rights procedures to cover other international treaties, as some critics have argued.[68] The human rights bodies are authorized to interpret the human rights treaties under their jurisdiction in a systematic way and in the light of every other applicable and relevant rule of international law (Article 31(3)(c) of the VCLT). A foreign defendant in criminal proceedings may thus file a claim with the UN Human Rights Committee, the Inter-American Commission on Human Rights (IAComHR), thus indirectly with the IACtHR, or with the ECtHR. Because human rights apply *erga omnes*, the theoretical possibility also exists that a third country might claim a violation of human rights by filing an inter-State complaint with the competent international bodies.[69]

[68] See Grzeszick, Rechte des Einzelnen, 2005, 333.

[69] Art. 48 (1) lit. b) ILC Articles on State responsibility. See Milano, Diplomatic Protection, 2004, 85–142 (131).

11.4.2 Direct Application of Article 36 VCCR by National Courts

Under the principle of subsidiarity, violations of international individual rights should primarily be sanctioned by domestic bodies. This is possible if the international legal norm in question, in this case Article 36(1)(b) of the VCCR, has direct effect or is mirrored in domestic law. The direct application of Article 36 of the VCCR by domestic courts[70] does not depend on the human rights character of the asserted rights. This question has not been addressed by any of the international bodies, but it has been addressed by domestic courts.

In its *Sanchez-Llamas* judgment of 2006, the US Supreme Court found that the VCCR did not prescribe specific judicial remedies for a violation of Article 36 VCCR, but that it was a matter for domestic law to implement Article 36.[71] In its *Medellín II* judgment of 2008, the US Supreme Court rejected direct effect of the ICJ's *Avena* judgment for US state courts in the absence of federal implementing legislation.[72] In the wake of this judgment, Mexico invoked Article 60 of the ICJ Statute and requested the ICJ to interpret its *Avena* judgment of 2004. The ICJ found that the question of the direct effect of its *Avena* judgment had not been decided in the judgment itself. Instead, implementation of the ICJ judgment had been left to the United States. Therefore, this question could not be the object of an interpretative decision under Article 60 of the ICJ Statute.[73]

According to the Federal Constitutional Court of Germany, the provision in Article 36 of the VCCR is "sufficiently precise to be applied directly by German law enforcement authorities; it does not require implementing legislation, but rather is self-executing".[74] However, the question of the direct effect of the VCCR is not relevant in practice

[70] See on the muddled concepts of of direct effect, direct application, and self-executingness Chapter 16.

[71] US Supreme Court, *Sanchez-Llamas* v. *Oregon, Bustillo* v. *Virginia* (n. 17). This judgment dealt specifically with the question whether the exclusion of evidence in a criminal proceeding was the proper remedy. Although the Court seems to suggest that the VCCR is "a self-executing treaty" (see p. 11 of the slip opinion), the judgment is mostly considered as the key case for the US American rejection of a "direct effect" of the VCCR (in the sense of its applicability by domestic courts).

[72] See US Supreme Court, *Medellín* v. *Texas*, 552 US 491 (2008) (*Medellín II*). On direct effect and for more details on *Medellín*, see Chapter 16, pp. 510–11.

[73] See ICJ, *Request for Interpretation of the Judgment of 31 March 2004 in the Case Concerning Avena and Other Mexican Nationals (Mexico v. United States of America)*, Judgment of 19 January 2009, paragraph 44.

[74] BVerfGK 9, 174 (2006) (n. 43), paragraph 53 (translation mine).

if the provisions have been reflected precisely in domestic law. Since 1 January 2010, for instance, the German Code of Criminal Procedure has included the obligation to inform a detained suspect without delay of his or her right to notify the home country consulate and to have communications forwarded.[75] This means Article 36(1)(b) of the VCCR does not have to be applied directly by German law enforcement authorities. The legal consequences of a violation of this new obligation to provide information have not been set out explicitly in the Code of Criminal Procedure, but rather they continue to be governed by the general principles (see pp. 377–85).

11.4.3 *Enforcement by Way of Constitutional Complaint*

In Germany, violations of the international individual right derived from the VCCR can also be remedied through the constitutional obligation to consider international law. A violation of that obligation can be claimed by way of a constitutional complaint. This route has been taken by several foreigners who were sentenced by German courts on serious criminal charges. The Federal Court of Justice did not want to apply Article 36 of the VCCR to foreigners whose centres of life were in the receiving State (Germany).[76] This deviation from ICJ case law, without considering that case law, amounted to a violation of the constitutionally derived duty of consideration established by the Federal Constitutional Court in the *Görgülü* judgment of 2004.[77] The obligation of German courts "to take note of and consider the relevant case law of international courts with jurisdiction for Germany"[78] follows from "the principle of the openness of the Basic Law to international law in conjunction with the principle that the judiciary is bound by law and justice (Article 20(3) of the Basic Law in conjunction with Article 59(2) of the Basic Law), which includes the decisions of an international court established under international law in accordance with the content of the incorporated international treaty".[79] The duty of consideration is a "direct constitutional" duty,[80] so

[75] § 114b(2), last sentence of the German Code of Criminal Procedure, in force since 1 January 2010: "A foreign national shall be advised that he may demand notification of the consular representation of his native country and have messages communicated to the same." According to § 114b(1), first sentence, the information must be provided "without delay and in writing in a language [the detainee] understands".

[76] See BGHSt, Ruling of 7 November 2001 – 5 StR 116/ 01.

[77] BVerfGE 111, 307 (2004) – *Görgülü*.

[78] BVerfGK 9, 174 (2006) (n. 43), paragraph 54 (translation mine).

[79] *Ibid.*, paragraph 58 (translation mine). [80] *Ibid.*, paragraph 54 (translation mine).

that any breach thereof can be claimed by way of a constitutional complaint. ICJ judgments rendered in proceedings against other countries also have a "normative guiding function" and "orienting effect" for German courts.[81] If a German court fails to give adequate consideration to an international legal norm (as interpreted by the competent international court), this represents a violation of the thematically relevant fundamental right under the Basic Law in conjunction with the principle of the rule of law.[82] In the case involving a failure to consider Article 36 of the VCCR, this therefore represented a violation of the fundamental right to a fair trial under Article 2(1) of the Basic Law.[83]

11.5 Legal Consequences of the VCCR Violation, Especially in Criminal Proceedings

The legal consequences of the VCCR violation are of importance to practice. The breach of international law gives rise to a secondary right under international law. According to the view defended here, the individual concerned *and* the individual's sending State are the holders of the secondary rights (as they are of the primary right derived from Article 36(1) of the VCCR).[84] According to the general principles of State responsibility, the violator State must cease the wrongful act, guarantee non-repetition, and make reparation (primarily *restitutio in integrum*, secondarily in the form of monetary compensation).

Contradicting this view that the rights are owed to both the individual and the State, the traditional argument is that the secondary rights under international law are owed only to the injured *State*. Following this view, Guinea demanded monetary damages for itself in a case before the ICJ involving Article 36 of the VCCR, including compensation for loss of earnings of the Guinean national Ahmadou Sadio Diallo, on the basis of the State responsibility of the Democratic Republic of the Congo "to the Republic of Guinea".[85] The disputed question of the right of *individuals*

[81] *Ibid.*, paragraphs 55 and 61–62; the Federal Constitutional Court speaks of a "*de facto* precedent" (translation mine).

[82] See, fundamentally, BVerfG 111, 307 (2004) – *Görgülü*.

[83] See BVerfGK 9, 174 (2006) (n. 43), paragraph 47.

[84] See Lee/Quigley, *Consular Law and Practice*, 2008, 167: "a wrong is committed towards both the sending State and its national."

[85] ICJ, *Case Concerning Ahmadou Sadio Diallo* (*Republic of Guinea* v. *Democratic Republic of the Congo*), Judgment on Preliminary Objections of 24 May 2007, paragraph 11. The ICJ's view on the holder of the right to compensation is not clearly identifiable in ICJ, *Ahmadou Sadio Diallo (Republic of Guinea v. Democratic Republic of the Congo)*

(not of their home States) to (monetary) compensation under international law when international individual rights are violated is discussed in Chapter 6.

Additionally, the specific design and implementation of these secondary obligations under international law are a question for domestic law, and they must be fit into each State's legal order. For instance, the international obligation to restore the *status quo ante* may be achieved by releasing the person concerned.[86] However, especially in the frequent situation of deprivation of liberty in the context of criminal proceedings, this remedy is opposed by the concerns of effective prosecution. Numerous other remedies under domestic law are conceivable in such cases.[87] These will be discussed in the following section.

11.5.1 Requirement under International Law: Review and Reconsideration Must Examine Prejudice and Causal Link

In the *LaGrand* judgment, the ICJ held that in cases where the individuals concerned have been subjected to prolonged detention or convicted and sentenced to severe penalties, an apology would not suffice. In such cases, the State must "allow the review and reconsideration of the conviction and sentence by taking account of the violation of the rights set forth in the Convention. This obligation can be carried out in various ways. The choice of means must be left to the United States [i.e., the injuring State]".[88] As the ICJ emphasized in the subsequent *Avena* case, this freedom in the choice of means is "not without qualification".[89] Here, the ICJ required that after a violation of the VCCR, the domestic courts must examine the *causal link*. In the review and reconsideration process, the courts must determine whether the

(compensation owed by the Democratic Republic of the Congo to the Republic of Guinea), Judgment of 19 June 2012, paragraphs 57, 161, 165 (7). See also Section 12.2.2 in Chapter 12.

86 See German Federal Court of Justice, Ruling of 6 May 2010, AZ V ZB 223/ 09: Because the asylum applicant from Sierra Leone, who was taken into custody pending deportation, was not informed of his right to consular contact, the Court found that the deprivation of liberty was unlawful.

87 See Thomas Weigend, Der Fall LaGrand – Völkerrecht bricht Strafprozeßrecht, in: Cornelius Prittwitz/Michael Baurmann/Klaus Günther (eds), *Festschrift für Klaus Lüderssen* (Baden-Baden: Nomos 2002), 463–479 (473 et seq.) on legal consequences in German criminal procedure.

88 ICJ, *LaGrand Case* (n. 11), paragraph 125.

89 ICJ, *Case Concerning Avena and Other Mexican Nationals* (n. 32), paragraph 131.

violation of the Convention has *caused actual prejudice* to the defendant in the trial.[90]

The question of the legal consequences must be considered in each specific case by the domestic courts as part of the review and reconsideration process called for under international law.[91] The review and reconsideration required by the *LaGrand* judgment must be effective. It must take account of the violation of the right under the VCCR. The review must also guarantee that the breach of the Convention (i.e., the failure to inform the person concerned) and the *possible prejudice caused by that breach* are fully examined and taken into account in the review and reconsideration process. Finally, review and reconsideration must be both of the sentence and of the conviction.[92] This process must give full weight to the violation of international law, whatever may be the actual outcome of the review and reconsideration.[93]

In summary, in cases where the individuals concerned have been subjected to prolonged detention or convicted and sentenced to severe penalties, the legal consequences of any breach of the Convention in the domestic trial must be examined and taken into account in the course of the review and reconsideration required under international law. According to the ICJ, the judicial process in particular is suited to this task.[94] Furthermore, the review and reconsideration process must include an examination of the prejudice and of the causal link between the breach and that prejudice.

However, the question remains as to what constitutes "prejudice" as referred to by the ICJ. For instance, does a self-incriminating statement made after consultation with the defence counsel arranged by the

[90] *Ibid.*, paragraph 121: ". . . with a view to ascertaining whether in each case the violation of Article 36 committed by the competent authorities *caused actual prejudice*". *Ibid.*, paragraph 122: "The question of whether the violations of Article 36, paragraph 1, are to be regarded as having, *in the causal sequence* of events, ultimately led to convictions and severe penalties is an integral part of criminal proceedings before the courts of the United States and it is for them to determine in the process of review and reconsideration" (italics mine).

[91] See *ibid.*, paragraph 127. The Federal Constitutional Court of Germany summarized the comments of the ICJ in *Avena*, paragraph 127, as follows: "Accordingly, the review and reconsideration of the conviction is effective in accordance with Article 36(2) of the VCCR only if the question is answered as to whether the failure to provide information has actually prejudiced the procedural status of the person concerned, i.e. whether the person has suffered a disadvantage due to the violation of the VCCR" (translation mine). BVerfGK 17, 390 (n. 58).

[92] See ICJ, *Case Concerning Avena and Other Mexican Nationals* (n. 32), paragraph 138.

[93] See *ibid.*, paragraph 139. [94] See *ibid.*, paragraph 140.

consulate already constitute prejudice, or is prejudice reflected only in the greater severity of the punishment? The follow-up question arises as to who carries the burden of proof (or at least the burden of presenting his case) in determining whether the failure to inform the person concerned (and the consequent lack of consular assistance) has caused this prejudice. (In German criminal procedure, this question would arise in the judicial assessment of the grounds for the appeal, when the court considers whether the judgment "was based" upon a violation of the law as set out in § 337 of the Code of Criminal Procedure; see p. 374.) Because normally the principle of *ex officio* investigation applies in continental European criminal procedure, this causal link would probably have to be assumed in favour of the defendant if the facts cannot be determined.

The consular officer's function (or the function one believes the consular officer can perform) plays a role in this examination of the causal link. As already remarked, the consular officer is not only able to arrange a better defence counsel, but he may also be able to ascertain the life circumstances in the defendant's home country, for instance, which might lead to a less severe sentence. Viewed in this way, any unlawful failure to provide information to the defendant may indirectly result in prejudice with regard to *sentencing*. The causal link of the VCCR violation is less plausible in regard to the actual *determination of guilt*. If all these aspects are already considered "prejudice", the requirement of a causal link is ultimately an empty one, because some form of prejudice is always caused (or the causation cannot be ruled out). This would mean that a breach of the VCCR would automatically vitiate the criminal proceedings and judgment. It is a separate question as to what consequences should be drawn under the domestic criminal law in question (more on this below).

11.5.2 *Requirement of Effectiveness: Duty to Remove Procedural Obstacles, Especially Preclusionary Rules*

According to the general international law of State responsibility, breaches of international law must be remedied effectively. The provision in Article 36(2) of the VCCR likewise contains a requirement that the individual rights guaranteed by Article 36(1) be *effective*, although the provision as a whole is ambivalent. According to paragraph 2, "[t]he rights referred to in paragraph 1 of this article shall be exercised in conformity with the laws and regulations of the receiving

State, subject to the proviso, however, that the said laws and regulations must enable full effect to be given to the purposes for which the rights accorded under this article are intended." The first clause of this provision, namely the reference to domestic laws and regulations, was cited by the United States in the *LaGrand* case to justify the procedural default rule (a preclusionary rule) under US law. However, the second clause of Article 36(2) limits the applicability of domestic legal provisions again. Domestic law is not allowed to thwart realization of the individual's rights.

Because of this requirement of effectiveness,[95] the States parties must also eliminate any procedural obstacles to a review of the breach on appeal or on retrial by changing the applicable legislation or interpreting it in conformity with international law. In the specific criminal proceedings at issue in *Avena*, the procedural default rule did not result in a complete inability for judicial assessment of the case, so that the ICJ at first did not find a violation of Article 36(2) of the VCCR.[96]

The US Supreme Court refused to modify the procedural default rule in the light of the VCCR requirement or to declare it inapplicable.[97] In some cases, US state courts have now implemented the ICJ requirement of review and reconsideration of death sentences imposed on foreign criminals as part of their internal procedural rules. For instance, the Supreme Court of Nevada assumed that the Mexican national Gutierrez had "arguably suffered actual prejudice" due to the lack of consular assistance. The court ordered a "post-conviction evidentiary hearing" to determine whether the failure to inform Gutierrez of his rights under the VCCR had caused actual prejudice.[98]

The "objection rule" favoured by the 1st Criminal Senate of the German Federal Court of Justice also constitutes a preclusionary rule. According to this case law, the defendant or the defence counsel must object in a timely manner to impermissible use of evidence. According to the Senate, this also applies in the case of violations of Article 36 of the VCCR.[99] However, this objection requirement is difficult to reconcile

[95] On the requirement of effectiveness, see *ibid.*, paragraph 138. [96] Ibid., paragraph 113.

[97] See US Supreme Court, *Sanchez-Llamas* v. *Oregon, Bustillo* v. *Virginia* (n. 17), 350–360. In his dissent, Justice Breyer argued in favour of the inapplicability of the procedural default rule under certain conditions (*ibid.*, 392 and 397).

[98] Nevada Supreme Court, *Gutierrez* v. *State*, No. 53506, 2012 Nev. Unpub. LEXIS 1317 (19 September 2012), order of reversal; excerpts in *American Journal of International Law* 107 (2013), 216–218.

[99] See BGH, Ruling of 11 September 2007 – 1 StR 273/07.

with the principle of *ex officio* investigation, it is difficult to apply consistently in practice, and it entails hardship especially for defendants without counsel.[100] On these systematic, practical, and fairness considerations, the objection rule should therefore not be applied to violations of Article 36 of the VCCR.

11.5.3 *Annulment of the Conviction (VCCR Violation as a Ground for Appeal or Retrial)?*

The most far-reaching consequence would be an *annulment of the conviction* at the end of a trial in which a violation of Article 36 of the VCCR occurred. Along these lines, the IACtHR recommended that the defendant either be afforded a new trial or alternatively released, in the light of the violation of the guarantees of due process and a fair trial arising from the breach of Article 36 of the VCCR.[101] In German criminal procedure, this legal consequence could be achieved in technical terms by recognizing the violation of international law as a *relative* or even *absolute ground for appeal*, or, if the conviction has become legally effective, as a *ground for a retrial.*

The assertion that the individual rights arising from the VCCR have the character of human rights generally serves the purpose of justifying such a far-reaching remedy. In the *Avena* case, for instance, Mexico argued that the right to consular notification and consular communication was so fundamental that its infringement would *ipso facto* produce the effect of vitiating the entire process of the criminal proceedings.[102] Mexico had accordingly requested *restitutio in integrum* in the form of restoring the *status quo ante* by annulling the sentences of all fifty two Mexican nationals.[103] The ICJ expressly held, however, that partial or total annulment of the conviction or sentence did not provide the necessary and sole remedy, and that neither the text nor the object and purpose of the VCCR, nor any indication in the *travaux préparatoires*, supported Mexico's conclusions (in regard to the legal consequences of the breach of the Convention).[104]

[100] See the arguments of Sabine Gless, in: Volker Erb et al. (eds), *Löwe-Rosenberg, Die Strafprozessordnung und das Gerichtsverfassungsgesetz*, Vol. 4 (26th ed. Berlin: De Gruyter 2007), comment on § 136 StPO, paragraphs 82–85.

[101] See IAComHR, *Martinez Villareal* v. *United States* (n. 55), paragraph 87; see also IAComHR, *Fierro* v. *United States* (n. 46), paragraph 42.

[102] See ICJ, *Case Concerning Avena and Other Mexican Nationals* (n. 32), paragraph 124.

[103] See *ibid.*, paragraphs 116–117.

[104] See *ibid.*, paragraphs 123–124.

On the other hand, the concept of review and reconsideration introduced by the ICJ requires – as already explained – that the causal link between the procedural error and the conviction (including the sentence) must be examined.[105] In German criminal procedure, this can be done by recognizing the failure to provide information as a so-called "relative" (as opposed to "absolute") ground for appeal (§ 337 of the Code of Criminal Procedure).[106] On appeal, the impact of the failure to provide information on the conviction and sentencing must be examined (even if evidence is not excluded, see pp. 377–83). In a 2013 decision, the German Federal Constitutional Court explained how the ICJ standards may be fit into the German law of criminal procedure through this entry point: "According to the case-law of the International Court of Justice, Art. 36 (1) lit. b) sentence 3 VCCR constitutes the basis of a subjective right of the person concerned (ICJ, *Lagrand*, paragraph 77). Art. 36 (1) lit. b) sentence 3 must therefore be seen *as the basis of a right of the accused, which creates a procedural legal position* [in domestic criminal procedure law] for him, and which allows for a 'review and reconsideration' of the decision. This is realized by allowing him to invoke the omission of information as such as a relative ground of appeal [*relativer Revisionsgrund*] in the second instance proceeding [*Revisionsverfahren*]."[107]

The Judges' recognition of a new ground of appeal derived from international law is compatible with the wording of § 337 of the German Code of Criminal Procedure. The VCCR is considered a component of the German legal order pursuant to ratification of the Convention and thus constitutes a "legal norm" within the meaning of § 337 of the Code, the violation of which may constitute a relative ground for appeal if the judgment is based on that violation.

The possibility of a relative ground for appeal as set out in German criminal procedure also meets the ICJ's demand that domestic courts must examine whether the violation of the VCCR has caused actual prejudice to the defendant.[108] Thus, for German criminal procedure, the requirement of effectiveness set out in Article 36(2) of the VCCR is

105 See, explicitly, *ibid.*, paragraph 138.

106 § 337 of the Code of Criminal Procedure: "(1) An appeal on law may be filed only on the ground that the judgment was based upon a violation of the law. (2) Failure to apply a legal norm or erroneous application of a legal norm shall constitute a violation of the law."

107 BVerfG 2 BvR/1579/11, decision on inadmissibility of 5 November 2013, paragraph 18 (italics mine).

108 The ICJ demanded examination of "actual prejudice" or "possible prejudice" (ICJ, *Case Concerning Avena and Other Mexican Nationals* (n. 32), paragraphs 121 and 138).

met by interpreting § 337 of the Code of Criminal Procedure in conformity with international law.

The duty to inform set out in § 114b of the German Code of Criminal Procedure has now created legal clarity. Violation of this new legislative requirement is unlikely to result in annulment of a sentence, however, because the defendant generally will not be able to prove that the failure to provide information about the right to consular contact may have led to a less favourable sentence. While the criminal courts in Germany must examine *ex officio* whether a reversible procedural error has occurred, the burden of presenting his case in the petition to appeal, however, is high in practice.[109]

The same considerations apply *mutatis mutandis* to the reopening of the proceedings concluded by a final judgment under § 359 of the Code of Criminal Procedure. Either an unwritten ground for reopening proceedings must be recognized under customary international law or a new ground must be introduced by the legislature.

Neither the ICJ nor the German Federal Constitutional Court of Germany requires an *absolute ground for appeal* that would lead to the annulment of a conviction completely independent of whether the conviction is based on the procedural violation. The ICJ called for an examination of the causal link and thus in effect did not deem an absolute ground for appeal to be necessary.[110] Under German constitutional law, an absolute ground for appeal should be assumed only if an examination of the causal link (i.e., an examination of whether the conviction is based on the procedural error) is especially difficult or impossible, meaning that the procedural error would regularly go unpunished.[111] This is not the case for the failure to provide information under the VCCR. The courts can (and must) determine whether the conviction is based on the failure to inform. For these reasons, violation of individual rights arising from the VCCR will rarely lead to annulment of a conviction in German criminal procedure. This tends to contradict the ICJ's demand to consider any "possible prejudice" (see p. 370).

[109] BVerfG 2 BvR/1579/11 (n. 107), paragraph 19. See also BGH, Ruling of 26 August 2003 – 1 StR 284/03 on the strict requirements for the petition to appeal when a violation of Article 36(1)(b) of the VCCR is claimed.

[110] See ICJ, *Case Concerning Avena and Other Mexican Nationals* (n. 32), paragraphs 121, 122, and 138.

[111] BVerfG 2 BvR/1579/11 (n. 107), paragraph 28; BVerfGK 9, 174 (2006) (n. 43), paragraph 76.

11.5.4 Exclusion of Evidence?

Another possible legal consequence is the exclusion of evidence obtained due to a violation of the VCCR, i.e., statements made by the defendant. This legal consequence is currently the most disputed, and the case law of different domestic courts diverges in this regard.

11.5.4.1 International Legal Requirement and Its Implementation in Several Legal Orders

In the *Avena* case before the ICJ, Mexico claimed that statements and confessions obtained prior to informing the defendant of the right to consular contact should be excluded in any subsequent criminal proceedings.[112] Mexico also argued that this exclusionary rule applies in both common law and civil law jurisdictions and thus, as a general principle of law within the meaning of Article 38(1)(c) of the ICJ Statute, should be considered part of international law.[113] The ICJ refused to adjudicate the legal nature of any exclusion of evidence in general, but it did note that the question of the legal consequences of the failure to provide information must be examined under the concrete circumstances of each case by the competent domestic court.[114] In this way, the ICJ (implicitly) also demanded that exclusion of evidence should be considered.

In contrast, the US Supreme Court rejected the exclusion of evidence. Its reasoning was that Article 36 of the VCCR does not grant defendants any right to assistance, but rather only a right to have their home country consulate notified. In most circumstances, according to the Supreme Court, there is likely to be little connection between an Article 36 violation and evidence or statements obtained by police. According to US constitutional case law, the exclusionary rule serves to punish unlawful coercion and to exclude unreliable evidence. In the view of the US Supreme Court, both protective purposes are irrelevant in the context of Article 36 of the VCCR. The defendant is adequately protected by other legal and constitutional guarantees, especially the guarantee of due process. Article 36 adds little to these procedural protections. Instead of the exclusionary rule, other legal remedies protect the same interests of the defendant, according to the Supreme Court.[115] One Canadian trial court has likewise declined to

[112] See ICJ, *Case Concerning Avena and Other Mexican Nationals* (n. 32), paragraphs 117 and 126.

[113] See *ibid.*, paragraph 126. [114] See *ibid.*, paragraph 127.

[115] See US Supreme Court, *Sanchez-Llamas* v. *Oregon, Bustillo* v. *Virginia* (n. 17), 343–350. In his dissent, Justice Breyer argued in favour of a relative exclusionary rule (*ibid.*, 397).

exclude evidence when Article 36 of the VCCR is violated. In contrast, Australian and English courts have applied the exclusionary rule.[116]

11.5.4.2 Exclusion of Evidence in German Criminal Procedure

11.5.4.2.1 Rejection of the Exclusionary Rule in Case Law According to the balancing rule prevalent in German criminal procedure, there is no consistent or absolute exclusion of impermissibly obtained evidence. The courts decide whether the exclusionary rule applies by balancing different interests deemed to be relevant. On the side of the prosecution, the interest consists primarily in determining the facts; on the side of the defendant, the objective severity of the violation of the procedural requirement and its protective purpose factor in. This purpose is mainly framed by the question of whether the rule "safeguards the foundations of the procedural status of the suspect or accused".[117] This consideration is derived from the prevailing view in earlier case law, according to which a person could invoke the exclusionary rule only if his or her legal sphere ("*Rechtskreis*") was also affected by the unlawful gathering of evidence.[118] In general, the case law balances the interest of the State in the smooth functioning of its administration of justice – which also includes determination of the facts to the greatest possible extent, especially in serious criminal cases – with the objective severity of the violation of the procedural requirement. Generally, this balancing test is combined with a reference to the protective purpose of the norm, thus emphasizing that violations are especially severe if they affect the procedural status of the defendant. But unlike earlier case law, courts today no longer primarily resort to the idea of the rights of the defendant, but instead also take into account the abstract need for protection expressed by the procedural guarantee: Certain formal requirements must be observed, irrespective of the specific circumstances of a given case, in order to ensure that justice serves its protective purpose.[119]

As late as 2007, several Criminal Senates of the Federal Court of Justice held that neither German constitutional law nor international law required the exclusion of evidence in response to a violation of individual

[116] For a comparative overview, see Quigley et al., *Law of Consular Access*, 2010, 162–175.
[117] See settled case law since BGHSt 24, 125, 130 et seq. (1971); BGHSt 31, 304, 308 (1983); BGHSt 38, 214 (1992); BGHSt 44, 243, 249 (1998); BGHSt 51, 285, 289–290 (2007). See also BVerfGK 9, 174 (2006) (n. 43), paragraphs 71–72 (translation mine).
[118] See BGHSt (GrS) 11, 213, 214 et seq. (1958) and other references.
[119] See BVerfGE 103, 142, 155 (2001); BGHSt 51, 285, 297 (2007).

rights arising from the VCCR.[120] The Federal Court of Justice reasoned as follows: Taking account of the various concerns involved, especially the nature and severity of the legal flaw on the one hand, and the necessity to reach a criminal verdict on the other hand, the procedural error of having omitted the information on consular contact is a different matter than the omission of advice that has to be given to the accused under § 136(1), second sentence of the Code of Criminal Procedure. The latter obligation to advise is about the right to remain silent and the right to consult with defence counsel. And for this latter situation, the case law recognizes the exclusionary rule, at least if the defendant objects to use of the evidence. According to the Court, the possible prejudice to the defendant who has not been informed about his right to contact with his consul arising from the taking of evidence is not so great. The duty to inform a defendant about consular matters under the VCCR applies only upon detention, not as early as upon initial questioning. The Court held that the right of information about the consular contact offers "merely supplementary protection" to foreign detainees. The foreigners concerned could otherwise fully rely "on all due process standards for their defence". The right to information ultimately represented merely a "non-central blanket special right" for all foreigners.[121] But in regard to the questioning of suspects, the Federal Court of Justice believes that the role of the information provided pursuant to Article 36 of the VCCR overlaps with that of § 136 of the Code of Criminal Procedure concerning the right to consult with defence counsel. If the latter information is properly provided, the failure to inform pursuant to Article 36 of the VCCR is less severe, according to the Federal Court of Justice.[122] According to the case law, it also matters whether the defendants object to the use of specific statements or whether they demand the exclusion of evidence in general.[123]

Another argument against the exclusion of evidence is derived from the fact that, according to Article 36(1)(b) of the VCCR, the person

[120] See BGHSt 52, 48 et seq. (5 St 116/01) of 25 September 2007, Section B II 1 (d). See also BGHSt 52, 110 et seq. (Judgment of 20 December 2007, 3 StR 318/07); BGH (1 StR 251/10), Ruling of 13 July 2010.

[121] BGHSt 52, 48 et seq. (5 St 116/01) of 25 September 2007, Section B II 1 (d) (translation mine).

[122] BVerfGK 9, 174 (2006) (n. 43), paragraphs 71–72.

[123] See *ibid.*, paragraph 73. It is also said to matter whether they have raised an objection relating generally to the topic of the evidence or relating specifically to a piece of evidence (*ibid.*). But these distinctions turn out to be empty phrases. Statements of the defendant should not and in principle cannot be edited. Either they are used as evidence or they are not.

concerned must be informed (merely) "without delay". The ICJ has interpreted this clause to mean that information does not have to be provided immediately upon arrest. This means that commencing interrogation prior to the provision of information does not yet violate Article 36 of the VCCR, according to the ICJ's *Avena* judgment.[124] On the assumption that exclusion of evidence is the proper way to implement protection from self-incrimination, it has been concluded from this passage in the judgment that the ICJ itself does not expect application of the exclusionary rule.[125] But this assumption is dubious, as will be discussed below.

11.5.4.2.2 A Constitutional Duty to Consider Exclusion of Evidence

In 2010, the Federal Constitutional Court of Germany found that, by failing to consider the specific passage in the *Avena* judgment that discussed exclusion of evidence, the German Federal Court of Justice had breached the constitutional duty of consideration.[126] This breach of the Basic Law is irrespective of the result reached by the Federal Court of Justice; it consisted solely in the failure to consider the international case law. It therefore does not matter whether the argumentation of the Federal Court of Justice is plausible from the perspective of German law, and also not "whether the result may be upheld taking into account the International Court of Justice's requirements for review and reconsideration of the conviction".[127] This means the duty of consideration is purely procedural. The Federal Constitutional Court left open whether, in specific cases, proper fulfilment of the duty of consideration might necessarily entail a specific legal solution, so that a substantive deviation

[124] See ICJ, *Case Concerning Avena and Other Mexican Nationals* (n. 32), paragraph 87: Art. 36 "cannot be interpreted to signify that the provision of such information must necessarily precede any interrogation, so that the commencement of interrogation before the information is given would be a breach of Article 36". See generally on interpretation of the phrase "without delay" *ibid.*, paragraphs 83–88. If the law enforcement authorities did not have any indication that the arrested person was a foreign national, it would be unobjectionable under international law if the information was provided five days (of which three were working days) after arrest (*ibid.*, paragraph 97). But if there were indications from the outset that the person was a foreign national, the provision of information on consular rights forty hours after the arrest would be considered to be too late (*ibid.*, paragraph 89).

[125] This tends to be the argument in BVerfGK 9, 174 (2006) (n. 43), paragraphs 71–72.

[126] See BVerfGK 17, 390 (n. 58). On the constitutional duty of consideration, see Chapter 15, pp. 485–87.

[127] BVerfGK 17, 390, pp. 404–405 (translation mine).

from an international judgment might give rise to a breach of the Basic Law. According to the Federal Constitutional Court, the review and reconsideration process required by *Avena* leaves open the possibilities of remedy and also permits the domestic appellate proceedings to reject exclusion of evidence. However, international law requires that any prejudice arising to the complainant due to the failure to provide information must be examined and *considered*. For this reason, exclusion of evidence cannot be ruled out from the start. According to the Federal Constitutional Court, this is a question of ordinary law that the ordinary court must answer in accordance with the international legal requirement. The Federal Constitutional Court's scope of review on this point is limited: The Federal Constitutional Court merely reviews whether the lower court has made a *recognizable error in receiving* a decision of an international court.[128]

In the view of the Federal Constitutional Court, the review and reconsideration demanded by the ICJ, which must be neutral in regard to the result, requires that the possibility of exclusion of evidence must at least be kept open "on the basis of the specific circumstances of each case, i.e., due to prejudice in the further course of the proceedings arising from the failure to inform". Exclusion of evidence cannot be "generally ruled out".[129] Since then, the German Federal Court of Justice has examined the possibility of excluding evidence if information is not provided pursuant to Article 36(1)(b), the third sentence of the VCCR.[130]

11.5.4.2.3 Towards Exclusion of Evidence as a Rule In this section, I examine how the German Federal Constitutional Court's demand that the exclusion of evidence must be possible as a remedy for a violation of Article 36 of the VCCR can be satisfied. To this end, the case law of the German criminal courts discussed earlier needs to be modified. The proposal here is to recognize exclusion of evidence as a rule, either by abandoning or by modifying the traditional balancing approach.[131]

[128] See also p. 486. [129] BVerfGK 17, 390 (n. 58), pp. 401–402 (translation mine).
[130] See BGH, 7 June 2011 - 4 StR 643/10, paragraphs 16–25 (evidence admissible, because no prejudice).
[131] But see BVerfG 2 BvR/1579/11, decision on inadmissibility of 5 November 2013, paragraphs 22–26. See Sabine Gless/Anne Peters, Verwertungsverbot bei Verletzung der Pflicht zur Belehrung nach Art. 36 WÜK?, *Der Strafverteidiger* 31 (2011), 369–377. For an automatic exclusion of evidence for every statement made in violation of Article 36 of the VCCR, see already Paulus/Müller, Konsularische Information, 2009, 495–502; Tonio Walter, Der deutsche Strafprozess und das Völkerrecht, *Juristische Rundschau*

In fact, exclusion of evidence is not the obvious outcome of the balancing test when the information duty under Article 36 of the VCCR is breached, unlike when § 136(1), second sentence of the Code of Criminal Procedure is breached. The latter provision is generally regarded as so crucial to safeguarding the accused's freedom to make a statement or not that the violation thereof must result in the exclusion of evidence.[132] In contrast, Article 36 of the VCCR is primarily about protecting a detained foreigner. Detention is not necessarily related to criminal proceedings; rather, detention pending trial is only one subcategory of the deprivation of liberty.

In the balancing paradigm, a violation of the obligation to inform a detained foreigner about the right to consular contact tends not to weigh that heavily, especially when compared with other information obligations that apply immediately when the suspect is interrogated, such as about his right to remain silent or to contact a lawyer. The right of the detained foreigner to contact his or her home country consulate does not depend on a situation in which evidence is being gathered, but rather is formally a general right of protection enjoyed by all persons who have been deprived of liberty abroad for whatever reason.[133]

The balancing approach is worthy of criticism in general, however, and is inadequate specifically in cases involving a foreign country. A first point of criticism is that courts applying the balancing test have not always paid sufficient attention to the object and purpose of exclusionary rules. One function of exclusionary rules is to protect fundamental rights. The German criminal law doctrines of the "right to control information"[134] and of "the power to dispose of evidence"[135] convincingly draw attention to those aspects of rules of criminal procedure that protect individuals as well as the applicability of those rules

82 (2007), 99–104. For arguments against exclusion of evidence, cf. Claus Kreß, Die verfassungsrechtliche Pflicht der deutschen Strafverfolgungsbehörden zur Berücksichtigung des Wiener Konsularrechtsübereinkommens, *Goltdammer's Archiv für Strafrecht* 154 (2007), 296–308 (305–306).

[132] For the turnaround in the case law, see BGHSt 38, 214 (1992). [133] See p. 357.

[134] Knut Amelung, *Informationsbeherrschungsrechte im Strafprozess: Dogmatische Grundlagen individual-rechtlicher Beweisverbote* (Berlin: Duncker & Humblot 1990), 20 et seq.

[135] Matthias Jahn, *Verhandlungen des 67. Deutschen Juristentages Erfurt 2008*, Bd. I: Gutachten/Teil C: Beweiserhebung und Beweisverwertungsverbote im Spannungsfeld zwischen den Garantien des Rechtsstaates und der effektiven Bekämpfung von Kriminalität und Terrorismus (Munich: Beck 2008), C (C 66 et seq.).

to all State action. The pragmatic balancing test hardly does justice to those aspects.

Secondly, exclusionary rules serve as a general deterrent. They can prevent law enforcement authorities from obtaining evidence illegally. In that sense, the prohibition of using evidence obtained in violation of procedural requirements can be considered a disciplinary measure to punish all kinds of procedural errors. This was discussed in the literature in the 1960s, when it was argued that a negative incentive directly linked to the procedural breach would be the most efficient way to prevent the persons immediately involved from violating procedural norms.[136] This disciplinary function is not taken into account by German case law, but it is recognized in Anglo-American criminal proceedings, which are adversarial in principle, as well as in other European codes of criminal procedure.[137] In fact, exclusion of evidence would probably be the most effective way to implement the duty to inform set out in Article 36(1)(b), the third sentence of the VCCR, because then the incentive would be the strongest for law enforcement authorities to provide information immediately and properly.[138]

Thirdly, exclusion of evidence would follow the international legal principle of restitution most precisely, i.e., the principle that a violation of international law should be remedied as fully as possible by restoring the *status quo ante*.[139]

It should also be noted that the protective purpose of Article 36 of the VCCR mentioned earlier, which in part aims to prevent (indirect) discrimination against foreigners on trial, should be given substantial importance.[140] Informing the detainee of the right to consular contact does not primarily serve to protect the detainee from self-incriminating statements during questioning, but rather – as discussed earlier – to make the exercise of consular protection possible, which in turn has a significantly more extensive purpose than that of aiding with criminal defence.[141] However, by far the most frequent situation is that of arrest on suspicion of a crime. In this situation, Article 36 of the VCCR must also be able to

[136] Gerald Grünwald, Beweisverbote und Verwertungsverbote im Strafverfahren, *JuristenZeitung* 21 (1966), 489–501 (499). See also Gless/Peters, Verwertungsverbot 2011, 373–374 and other references.

[137] In regard to the Swiss Code of Criminal Procedure, see Sabine Gless, Art. 139-Art. 141 Beweismittel, in: Marcel Niggli/Marianne Heer/Hans Wiprächtiger (eds), *Basler Kommentar, Schweizerische Strafprozessordnung, Jugendstrafprozessordnung* (Basel: Helbing und Lichtenhahn 2010), Art. 139 paragraph 27 and Art. 141 paragraph 6.

[138] See Paulus/Müller, Konsularische Information, 2009, 499. [139] See *ibid.*, 499.

[140] See BVerfGK 9, 174 (2006) (n. 43), paragraph 74. [141] See pp. 357–58.

perform its protective function. If the situation of arrest leads to a situation of interrogation, then access of an arrested foreign suspect by the home country consulate also serves to protect the effective criminal defence of the arrested person: If he or she refutes the suspicion, the reason for arrest is also eliminated. If the consular officer is particularly experienced and skilful, the assistance may constitute specific added value compared with that of a defence counsel, so that the failure to inform the detainee of the possibility of consular access does actually interfere with criminal defence.

In summary, the constitutional duty of consideration – i.e., the duty to effectively protect (individual) interests rooted in international law within the framework of the Basic Law's requirements – suggests that the exclusionary rule should apply. Currently, however, application of the exclusionary rule to a violation of Article 36 of the VCCR is *de facto* prevented by the objection requirement and the traditional balancing approach under German criminal law.

To satisfy the constitutional and international legal requirements in criminal proceedings, the prevailing doctrine on the use of evidence should be modified so that exclusion of evidence should not *de facto* be ruled out in response to a violation of an international legal norm. Case law accordingly has two possibilities: either it treats internationally guaranteed individual interests the same way as the internationally guaranteed interests of third countries, and it should consider those interests as a priority or outside the usual balancing model,[142] or the public authorities fulfil their duty to consider international law by examining *ex officio* whether, in specific cases of violations of Article 36 of the VCCR, individual interests have been interfered with or whether prejudice can be ruled out, such as when a detained foreigner demonstrably did not desire assistance from the home country consulate in a case where Article 36 of the VCCR applied. Only in the latter case is the use of the detainee's statements not prohibited.

11.5.5 Compensation through the Length of Sentences Served and Consideration in Clemency Proceedings?

In principle, it is possible to carry out the review and reconsideration process demanded by the ICJ solely as part of clemency proceedings.[143]

[142] See BVerfG, Ruling of 8 June 2010 – 2 BvR 432/07, 2 BvR 507/08, 2 BvR 432–07, 507/08; BGH, Judgment of 9 April 1987 – 3 StR 11/87, NJW 40 (1987), 2168 (2171).

[143] See ICJ, *Case Concerning Avena and Other Mexican Nationals* (n. 32), paragraph 141.

The practice in US clemency proceedings at the time of the judgment did not meet the ICJ's review requirements, however.[144]

The Federal Court of Justice of Germany wanted to redress the breach of the duty to inform by granting *compensation through the length of the sentence served*. According to the Federal Court of Justice, the VCCR violation could be compensated by deeming a certain part of the imposed sentence of imprisonment to have been already served.[145] In its 2007 ruling, the 5th Criminal Senate left open whether in cases of lesser gravity (in which no sentence of imprisonment is imposed) compensation for the breach of international law might occur in other ways, e.g., through payment of damages. In the case of such minor sentences and where the procedural error had been "corrected" by providing the information required under the third sentence of Article 36(1)(b) of the VCCR "as soon as possible", "compensation might be dispensed with entirely", according to the 5th Criminal Senate.[146]

The convicted persons in those proceedings filed a successful constitutional complaint against the rejection of the appeal by the Federal Court of Justice. Because "in its examination of the consequences resulting from a violation of the third sentence of Article 36(1)(b) of the Vienna Convention on Consular Relations, the Federal Court of Justice [yet again] failed to adequately consider the case law of the International Court of Justice governing that Convention", the Federal Constitutional Court held that the fundamental right of the complainant to a fair trial had obviously been violated.[147] While the "length-of-sentence solution" of the Federal Court of Justice was not deemed unconstitutional as such, the Federal Constitutional Court did find that the Federal Court of Justice had "not guaranteed the examination of the specific case required under international law in regard to the question of the prejudice incurred by the affected person in the further course of the proceedings, where that prejudice resulted from the failure to provide information in accordance with the third sentence of Article 36(1)(b) of

[144] See *ibid.*, paragraph 143.

[145] See BGHSt 52, 48 et seq. (5 St 116/01) of 25 September 2007, Section B II 1 (e) and (f). In this specific case, the length of the sentences deemed already served was six months.

[146] *Ibid.*, Section B II 1 (f) (translation mine). In contrast, the 3rd Criminal Senate – like the Federal Constitutional Court later – considered the length-of-sentence solution to be unlawful and inappropriate to the subject matter, because the State could not simply make up for procedural violations by granting a reduced sentence, which would lead to an unacceptable relativization of the law of criminal procedure (BGH 52, 110 et seq. (2007)).

[147] BVerfGK 17, 390 (n. 58) (translation mine).

the VCCR".[148] According to the Federal Constitutional Court, the Federal Court of Justice had "ruled out precisely the result-neutral examination of the question very clearly demanded by the International Court of Justice as to whether, in the course of the criminal proceedings in this specific case, the affected person had incurred a prejudice arising from the failure to provide information".[149]

It has been argued persuasively in the literature that the "length-of-sentence solution" does not satisfy the international legal requirements.[150] This "solution" does not follow comprehensible standards. Unlike cases where proceedings are excessively long, there is no time component involved in the violation of the VCCR. This means the question of how to assess and "quantify" the violation of the VCCR is left entirely to the judge's discretion. Symptomatically, the 5th Criminal Senate did not even give reasons for the amount of its reduction of the sentence (six months). According to Andreas Paulus, that approach "borders on arbitrariness".[151] Moreover, the length-of-sentence solution violates the requirement of effectiveness set out in Article 36(2) of the VCCR: Compensation is easy to circumvent if the court, deliberately or not, imposes a higher sentence from the outset in anticipation of the reduction of the sentence.

Finally, the length-of-sentence solution ignores the ICJ's demand that where criminal proceedings are undermined by errors of international law, the determination of guilt and the sentence pronounced at the end of such proceedings must be reviewed and reconsidered. Under the length-of-sentence solution, the pronouncement of the sentence itself remains unchanged, and only part of the sentence is deemed to have been already served.

11.6 Conclusion

With *LaGrand*, the ICJ has "crossed the rubicon of individual rights".[152] Certainly, the *LaGrand* judgment and the subsequent case law have made a contribution to the "humanization" of international law overall.[153] But it appears sensible in this context not to undertake a "maximum expansion of the domain of human rights",[154] but rather to conceive of the new

148 *Ibid.* (translation mine). 149 *Ibid.*, Section B I 2 (b) (bb) (translation mine).
150 See Paulus/Müller, Konsularische Information, 2009, 500–502.
151 *Ibid.*, 501 (translation mine). 152 Milano, Diplomatic Protection, 2004, 129.
153 Mennecke, Humanization of the Vienna Convention, 2001, 468.
154 Kreß, Die verfassungsrechtliche Pflicht 2007, 308 (translation mine).

international individual right to consular access and the associated right to information as "ordinary" international individual rights. While these rights are an element of the fair trial guarantee for foreigners, they are not human rights per se. However, the ICJ itself cannot harmonize the new individual right with other human rights, such as the right to a fair trial and equal treatment (e.g., of candidates for the death penalty as compared with other accused persons), because it does not have jurisdiction to do so. Human rights bodies would probably be best positioned to draw the specific international legal conclusions from the "individualized" interpretation of the VCCR.[155] At the level of international law, this entire set of questions is characterized by an oscillation between an individual rights approach and a more classical intergovernmental approach. The tension between these two radically different conceptions of international law has not been resolved.[156]

In a legally sound manner, the domestic authorities and courts must fit the international legal requirements into the domestic legal order alongside the building blocks of domestic law, and this is where the greatest difficulties lie. The individual rights for foreign defendants in criminal proceedings arising from Article 36 of the VCCR, which were placed in the spotlight by the *LaGrand* affair, have triggered intensive jurisprudential work by international and domestic courts and other bodies. Effective implementation of the treaty guarantees by providing domestic remedies for breaches has not yet been sorted out conclusively in various domestic legal orders. The conceivable solutions range from annulment of the conviction to consideration in clemency proceedings, exclusion of evidence, monetary compensation, subsequent correction of the error, mitigation of the sentence, and compensation through the length of sentences served.

In German criminal procedure as shaped by the case law, the consequences of a VCCR violation are often blunted: The defendant must object in a timely manner to the use of any statements made without the benefit of information on consular access. Moreover, the exclusionary rule is applied only if the VCCR violation weighs heavily in comparison to the countervailing interests of prosecution. Even if exclusion of evidence is accepted, the violation constitutes only a relative ground of appeal under German law, not an absolute ground of appeal. The conviction therefore has to be

[155] See Simonetta Stirling-Zanda, Obtaining Judicial Enforcement of Individual Conventional Rights, *Archiv des Völkerrechts* 42 (2004), 184–216 (200 and 203).

[156] See Milano, Diplomatic Protection, 2004, 132.

annulled only if it is based upon the violation of the exclusionary rule (§ 337 of the Code of Criminal Procedure). And finally, the defendant must sufficiently demonstrate the procedural violation and the causal link in the petition to appeal.

As already mentioned, this relativization of the effectiveness of the requirement set out in Article 36 of the VCCR and especially the routine rejection of the exclusionary rule hardly satisfy the requirements of international law. Implementation of the international individual right arising from the Vienna Convention on Consular Relations remains a challenge.

12

Individual Rights in Diplomatic Protection

This chapter deals with two controversies in the law of diplomatic protection: firstly, whether the State exercising protection asserts international rights of the individual *against the injuring State*; and secondly, whether there is a potentially justiciable right to have protection exercised, which the individual can assert *against the home State*. Both disputes concern the international status of the individual and any rights asserted by the individual. Before these questions can be analysed, the mesh of involved legal positions must be examined.

12.1 Foundations and Definition of the Question

Diplomatic protection is a mechanism or process to demand respect for international legal norms that protect individuals. States in which foreigners are present must comply with their contractual obligations laid down in traditional treaties of establishment, commerce, and navigation, and in investment protection agreements. States must respect the human rights of aliens, and they must observe international law relating to aliens where such law goes beyond human rights, such as in regard to the protection of property.

Under current international law, the alien concerned may have his or her *own* international primary rights against the State of residence, especially in regard to human rights. When these primary rights are violated, the injured individual in principle has his or her own international secondary rights arising from the law of State responsibility (see Chapter 6, pp. 168–69). A separate question is whether the injured individual can assert those secondary rights autonomously at the level of international law. Because this is often not the case, the individual depends on assistance from the home State in the form of diplomatic protection.

In the traditional view, the legal mechanism for this is as follows: The person injured by the breach of international law committed by a third State (typically the State where the individual finds itself) turns to his or her home State in accordance with the provisions of domestic law; the home State then intervenes on his or her behalf at the international level (or not). According to the *Mavrommatis* formula of the Permanent Court of International Justice (PCIJ), the dispute becomes an international dispute – between the two States – only once the home State becomes active. The PCIJ held: "In the case of the Mavrommatis concessions it is true that the dispute was at first between a private person and a State – i.e. between M. Mavrommatis and Great Britain. Subsequently, the Greek Government took up the case. The dispute *then entered upon a new phase; it entered the domain of international law and became a dispute between two States.*"[1] The dispute is thus "translated" into a dispute under international law, so to speak.

There are two questions of interest here: First, is there a right of the individual against the home State to have diplomatic protection granted? This right would be a right to performance, directed at proper efforts performed by the home State. The second question concerns the legal norms triggering protective action and the violation thereof. An international individual right to protection against the home State would make more sense if the primary and secondary rights which are violated by the foreign State and which give rise to the request for protection are also attributed to the individual. This latter question will therefore be discussed first.

12.2 Rights against the Injuring State: The End of the Vattelian Fiction

12.2.1 *The Open* lex lata

By way of diplomatic protection, the home State complains of a breach of international law and asserts another State's responsibility. Often, the State's right to bring a claim is termed a *procedural* "right" of the State. This means that the home State of the injured person is entitled by international law to exercise diplomatic protection against the injuring State. The exercise of protection consists primarily in procedural acts in political or, in extreme cases, judicial forums. The home State does not need to have an actual right to exercise protection against the injuring State, because the home State is in any event free to take diplomatic steps and, if

[1] PCIJ, *Mavrommatis Palestine Concessions Case*, Ser. B, No. 3 (1924), 12 (italics mine).

an international court has jurisdiction, to initiate proceedings against the injuring State. These activities do not constitute impermissible interventions in the affairs of the injuring State. The right of the home State to exercise diplomatic protection does not create an additional basis for jurisdiction. The talk of the "right" of a State to exercise diplomatic protection refers less to its relationship to the injuring State than to its relation with its national. The term "right" (and not obligation) is used for denying any duty of the State towards the individual concerned. Another confusing linguistic usage is to refer to the right to bring a claim as a "secondary rule" (like the rules of State responsibility).

Another question concerns who is the holder of the violated *substantive* primary and secondary rights? The classic view was that the State asserted its own primary and especially secondary rights (to reparation) here, not those of its national. The rights were simply assigned to the State by way of a legal fiction (the "Vattelian fiction"). In case law and the literature, it is not always clear whether these are "really" State rights or whether they are merely fictions. For the sake of simplicity, the following discussion will refer to them as a legal fiction. The background to this fiction is that the spheres of domestic and international law are traditionally viewed as strictly separate. Certainly, diplomatic protection relies on the possibility of an individual to assert his or her own claim under *domestic* law (of the injuring State and directed against it), because the individual concerned would otherwise not be able to exhaust legal remedies in the injuring State.[2] But according to the traditional view, this has nothing to do with any rights of the individual *under international law*.

Emer de Vattel had postulated that any ill treatment of a citizen by a third State indirectly injured that citizen's home State: "Whoever ill-treats a citizen *indirectly injures the State*, which must protect that citizen. The sovereign of the injured citizen *must* avenge the deed and, if possible, force the aggressor to give full satisfaction or punish him, since otherwise the citizen will not obtain the chief end of civil society, which is protection."[3] According to Vattel, the home State is considered injured in the person of its citizen. In *Mavrommatis*, the PCIJ construed the right of the State somewhat differently: "By taking up the case of one

[2] See BVerfGE 94, 315, 330 (1996) – *jüdische Zwangsarbeiter*.

[3] Emer de Vattel, *Le droit des gens ou Principes de la loi naturelle* (London 1758), Book II Chapter 6, p. 309 (engl. transl. of the edition of 1758 by Charles G. Fenwick, *The Law of Nations or the Principles of Natural Law Applied to the Conduct and to the Affairs of Nations and of Sovereigns, Classics of International Law*, Carnegie Institution 1916, Vol. III, p. 136; italics mine).

of its subjects and resorting to diplomatic action or international judicial proceedings on his behalf, *a State is in reality asserting its own right* – its right to ensure, in the person of its subjects, respect for the rules of international law."[4] In *Barcelona Traction*, the ICJ summarized this as follows: "[W]hether claims are made on behalf of a State's national or on behalf of the State itself, *they are always a claim of the State.*"[5] This attribution (or fiction) of State rights has practical consequences, as will be shown at pp. 393–94.

In the literature on diplomatic protection, it is sometimes argued that certain legal positions (those of the minimum standard under international law) are always the individual's own rights under international law (not merely granted under domestic law), and that the State asserts these rights on the individual's behalf.[6] The ICJ's *LaGrand* judgment did not decide this doctrinal dispute conclusively. In that case, Germany submitted that by breaching the VCCR, the United States had violated *two* duties owed to Germany, because Germany held two legal positions: firstly, the genuine State right to compliance with the treaty; and secondly, the (State) right to the exercise of diplomatic protection for the benefit of the individual whose international individual right arising from the VCCR had been violated.[7] The ICJ appeared to understand this as a doubling of the substantive rights, namely as individual rights alongside State rights.[8] The ICJ's formulations can be read as postulating a representative action by the State on behalf of the individual's rights.[9] Unlike the applicant and the respondent, however,[10] the ICJ did not mention that Germany was asserting an individual right by way of

[4] PCIJ, *Mavrommatis Palestine Concessions Case* (n. 1), 12 (italics mine).

[5] ICJ, *Barcelona Traction, Light and Power Company (New Application 1962) (Second Phase)*, ICJ Reports 1970, 4 et seq., paragraph 85. See also *ibid.*, paragraph 35.

[6] See, fundamentally, Karl Doehring, *Die allgemeinen Regeln des völkerrechtlichen Fremdenrechts und das deutsche Verfassungsrecht* (Cologne: Carl Heymanns 1963), 109–113. It was earlier pointed out that ICJ case law "leaves sufficient latitude for dissociating rights to ensure respect for international law from the substantial rights to be ensured as a part of international law" (Arnold Jan Pieter Tammes, The Obligation to Provide Local Remedies, in: *Volkenrechtelijke Opstellen – Aangeboden aan Professor Dr. Gesina H. J. van der Molen* (Kampen: J. H. Kok NV 1962), 152–168 (167)). More recently, see Roland Portmann, *Legal Personality in International Law* (Cambridge: Cambridge University Press 2010), 278. For a cautious view and *de lege ferenda*, see Felix Chittaranjan Amerasinghe, *Diplomatic Protection* (Oxford: Oxford University Press 2008), 71 and 345.

[7] See ICJ, *LaGrand Case* (*Germany* v. *United States of America*), ICJ Reports 2001, 466, paragraph 65.

[8] See *ibid.*, paragraphs 73 and 75.

[9] See *ibid.*, paragraph 77.

[10] See *ibid.*, paragraphs 75 and 76.

diplomatic protection (other than when citing Germany's submission). The ILC Draft Articles on Diplomatic Protection of 2006 also deliberately left open the question of whether the State asserts its own right, the right of its citizen, or both.[11] The *lex lata* is therefore open in regard to who holds the substantive international legal positions underlying a request for protection.

12.2.2 *Towards Substantive Individual Rights*

A new reading of the right to diplomatic protection could and should recognize underlying substantive international rights of the individual against the injuring State. This would not require any explicit change to written law, because the Vattelian fiction is a judicial and academic construction that can be rebuilt by way of a new reading.

The genuinely political nature of the legal instrument of diplomatic protection is cited as the main argument against its "individualization" or "humanization".[12] According to this criticism, individualization of the involved legal positions is superfluous; the legal fiction must be maintained that diplomatic protection merely calls for respecting the rights of (and between) States at the international level.[13] Ultimately, according to this view, enforcement effectively happens only between States. In fact, individuals are largely powerless against third States without the assistance of their home State. With the exception of the human rights bodies and the ICSID tribunals, which function more or less well, there is a lack of forums at the international level to which the individual might have access. Legal proceedings in the domestic courts of the injuring State are burdensome and not very promising. Claims against the injuring State before the courts of the home State fail on grounds of State immunity. States thus still appear to be "the natural guardians of the rights of their nationals"[14] at the level of international law. From this standpoint, autonomous rights belonging to the individual do not contribute anything to the individual's protection.

[11] ILC Commentary on Article 1 of the Draft Articles on Diplomatic Protection of 2006, YB ILC 2006 II, Part Two, 26 (commentary on Article 1, paragraph 5).

[12] For a critical view, see Vasileios Pergantis, Towards a "Humanization" of Diplomatic Protection?, *Zeitschrift für ausländisches öffentliches recht und Völkerrecht* 66 (2006), 351–397. Pergantis argued that "humanization" is neither taking place nor should it. On the political nature of diplomatic protection, see *ibid.*, 393.

[13] See Annemarieke Vermeer-Künzli, As If: The Legal Fiction in Diplomatic Protection, *European Journal of International Law* 18 (2007), 37–68.

[14] Christian Tomuschat, Die Europäische Union und ihre völkerrechtliche Bindung, *Europäische Grundrechte-Zeitschrift* 34 (2007), 1–12 (11).

However, the anachronistic nature and doctrinal inconsistency of the construction argue against focusing solely on the rights of the State as the object of the request for diplomatic protection. The idea that the State is injured in the person of its citizens originated in an international legal era in which the individual did not have any rights whatsoever at the level of international law, i.e., did not exist as a legal subject. To elevate a dispute to the level of international law in the first place, the citizen had to be seen as part or "chattel" of the State, or a State right had to be made up as a fiction. This is no longer necessary in the era of human rights and the crystallization of other individual legal positions under international law.

Moreover, the assumption that the rights asserted through diplomatic protection are State rights gives rise to the following doctrinal inconsistencies: Firstly, the local remedies rule is self-contradictory, because the State would thus lose "its" right if the individual does not resort to local remedies. If this really were a State right, then its expiry would not depend on the act or omission of someone else. The requirement of continuous nationality is also incompatible with the existence of a right belonging merely to the State: If an individual changes nationalities, no State is entitled to diplomatic protection any longer. These inconsistencies are eliminated merely in a formal sense by deeming the State right a mere fiction. But this does not resolve the substantive inconsistencies.

Because individuals largely lack possibilities to assert their international legal positions against foreign States in practice, diplomatic protection is anything but obsolete. But effective protection does not depend on a fiction of State rights. The home State can always *assert the international rights of the individual on the individual's behalf.*

This construal of the rights as individual rights has practical consequences. Firstly, if primary and secondary rights are assumed to belong solely to the State, then the State would not have to include individuals in the proceedings to assert those rights, since – from this perspective – the individuals are affected only *de facto*, not *de jure*. As soon as individual rights are at stake, however, the State must involve the individuals concerned.

The other very relevant practical consequence of individual rights against foreign States is the following: If the fiction is valid, Calvo clauses in agreements between foreign investors and host States (i.e., contractual waivers of legal protection) must be considered invalid, because the investor cannot effectively waive the right of his or her home State to exercise diplomatic protection.[15] Under the assumption of individual rights, however, the investor can normally effectively waive these rights as well as legal remedies. A variant of this question is currently being disputed in ICSID case law.[16]

The substantive rights whose violation is asserted by the home State must be distinguished from the *secondary rights* to reparation (such as in the form of monetary compensation) arising from international legal responsibility.[17] In diplomatic protection proceedings, these rights are demanded by the home State in all cases, but it is unclear who the actual owner of the right to compensation is. The current practice of States on this point is, as the ILC Special Rapporteur on this topic emphasized, "contradictory": While some judicial decisions, both international and domestic, emphasize that the individual concerned has no right to claim any reparation or compensation, more recent decisions suggest that the compensation received must be disbursed to the individual.[18]

With regard to human rights violations under the ECHR, the ECtHR recently clarified that, "according to the very nature of the Convention, it is the individual, and not the State, who is directly or indirectly harmed and primarily 'injured' by a violation of one or several Convention rights. Therefore, if just satisfaction is afforded in an inter-State case, it should always be done for the benefit of individual victims".[19] This indeed sounds as if the individual is also the *titulaire* of the secondary claim to just satisfaction which is regulated in Art. 41 ECHR as a *lex specialis*. (In the terminology of the general international law – which also governs the responsibility of the States parties to the Convention for violations of any of its provisions[20] – the ECtHR's award granting money falls under

[15] See Mohamed Bennouna, Special Rapporteur, Preliminary Report on Diplomatic Protection (ILC, 50th sess. (1998)), UN Doc. A/CN.4/484 of 4 February 1998, paragraph 51.

[16] At issue there is the admissibility of contractual waivers by investors, not of diplomatic protection, but of access to ICSID tribunals. See Chapter 10, pp. 324–28.

[17] Secondary rights of the individual arising from international legal responsibility, especially rights to remedy and reparation in the event of serious violations of human rights and international humanitarian law, are discussed in Chapter 6.

[18] John R. Dugard, Seventh Report on Diplomatic Protection, International Law Commission, Fifty-eighth session (1 May–9 June and 3 July–11 August 2006) (UN Doc. A/CN.4/567), paragraphs 93–103: "The right of the injured national to receive compensation" and other references; quote in paragraph 96.

[19] ECtHR (Grand Chamber), *Cyprus* v. *Turkey*, No. 25781/94, Judgment (just satisfaction) of 12 May 2014, paragraph 46.

[20] The commentary on the preliminary draft Convention underscored the conformity of the projected power of the Court to grant just satisfaction with the general rules of

the heading of "compensation" in the sense of Art. 36 of the ILC Articles on the Responsibility of States for Internationally Wrongful Acts.[21])

Disbursement to the individual was also required by the ICJ in the *Ahmadou Sadio Diallo* case. Diallo's home State of Guinea had exercised diplomatic protection for the benefit of the investor, bringing a claim against the Democratic Republic of the Congo before the ICJ. The ICJ recognized a violation of Diallo's human rights (liberty of person and right of abode, Articles 9 and 13 of the ICCPR and parallel provisions in the African Charter on Human and Peoples' Rights) and awarded USD 95,000 to be paid by the Democratic Republic of the Congo (only a fraction of the amount sought). According to the ICJ, this compensation was "due to Guinea for the injury suffered by Mr. Diallo".[22] This formulation could be understood as meaning that the ICJ regarded the home State, not the individual concerned, as the owner of the secondary right, although the holder of the primary rights (human rights) clearly was Diallo. On the other hand, the amount was calculated on the basis of the personal material and immaterial damages to the individual concerned. The ICJ also emphasized that "the sum awarded to Guinea in the exercise of diplomatic protection of Mr. Diallo is *intended to provide reparation for the latter's injury*".[23] So this judgment likewise does not give an entirely clear answer to the question of who is the holder of the secondary right, but should be read in that sense. Judge Cançado Trindade stated in his separate opinion that the *titulaire* of the right to reparation was clearly the individual, Mr. Diallo, not the State.[24] While it

international law: "This provision is in accordance with the actual international law relating to a violation of an obligation by a State. In this respect, jurisprudence of a European Court will never, therefore, introduce any new element or one contrary to existing international law." Doc. CDH(70)17, 30 April 1970, 21.

21 This means that "just satisfaction" in Art. 41 ECHR seems to have a different meaning than the term "satisfaction" as nowadays used in the general international law of state responsibility. When the ECHR was drafted in 1950, the legal framework and legal terminology of the law of state responsibility was not yet fully elaborated and was not codified.

22 ICJ, *Ahmadou Sadio Diallo (Republic of Guinea* v. *Democratic Republic of the Congo)*, ICJ Reports 2010 (II), 692 (Judgment of 30 November 2010 on the merits), paragraph 161, see also paragraph 165 (7).

23 ICJ, *Ahmadou Sadio Diallo (Republic of Guinea* v. *Democratic Republic of the Congo)* (compensation owed by the Democratic Republic of the Congo to the Republic of Guinea), *Judgment of* 19 June 2012, paragraph 57.

24 See ICJ, *Ahmadou Sadio Diallo (Republic of Guinea* v. *Democratic Republic of the Congo)* (compensation owed by the Democratic Republic of the Congo to the Republic of Guinea), Judgment of 19 June 2012, Separate Opinion of Judge Cançado Trindade, paragraphs 5, 13, 100.

is conceivable to split the ownership of primary and secondary rights, a parallel construction would be the clearest in terms of the law.[25] The conclusive consequence of recognizing the individual's ownership of the right at the primary level would thus be a *corresponding secondary right of the individual* arising from the international responsibility of the injuring State and thus an individual right to compensation, e.g., in the form of monetary compensation. In practical terms, the home State would have to transfer to the victim any monetary compensation obtained,[26] as indeed explicitly held by the ECtHR in *Cyprus* v. *Turkey*.[27]

12.3 International Right to Diplomatic Protection vis-à-vis the Home State?

According to existing international law, individuals do not have a specific and autonomous international right to diplomatic protection vis-à-vis their home State. Any rights are traditionally seen as a purely domestic question, as the ICJ put it in *Barcelona Traction*: "The municipal legislator may lay upon the State an obligation to protect its citizens abroad, and may also confer upon the national a right to demand the performance of that obligation, and clothe the right with corresponding sanctions. However, all these questions remain within the province of municipal law and do not affect that position internationally."[28]

My thesis is that a potential right to protection – in contrast to the view expressed in the quote – has an international dimension. Such a conceivable international right of the individual against the home State to exercise diplomatic protection would, in any event, only be a right to proper and fair consideration when making an official decision about whether and how to proceed against a third State. Such a "soft" right in this sense could flow from four sources, alternatively or cumulatively: a special treaty rule, customary international law, general principles of law, and international human rights.

[25] On the possible split between primary and secondary rights (right to compensation for a violation of international humanitarian law), see Chapter 7, pp. 205–06.

[26] See Riccardo Pisillo Mazzeschi, Impact on the Law of Diplomatic Protection, in: Menno T. Kamminga/Martin Scheinin (eds), *The Impact of Human Rights Law on General International Law* (Oxford: Oxford University Press 2009), 211–233 (221).

[27] ECtHR (Grand Chamber), *Cyprus* v. *Turkey* 2014 (n. 19), holding 4 c) and 5 c).

[28] ICJ, *Barcelona Traction* (n. 5), paragraph 78.

12.3.1 Lack of Special Treaty Right to Protection vis-à-vis the Home State

For the codification of the international law of diplomatic protection, ILC special rapporteur John Dugard had recommended requiring States to exercise protection in the case of *jus cogens* breaches.[29] However, this proposal in the first ILC report on diplomatic protection predominantly met with rejection. Article 19 of the 2006 ILC draft now only says that a State entitled to exercise diplomatic protection "*should* ... [g]ive due consideration to the possibility of exercising diplomatic protection, especially when a significant injury has occurred".[30] The special rapporteur noted that, despite the continued insistence by States on the discretionary nature of diplomatic protection, "international law already recognizes the existence of some obligation on the part of a State to *consider* the possibility of exercising diplomatic protection on behalf of a national who has suffered a significant injury abroad".[31] So, while there is currently no right to diplomatic protection codified in special treaties, Dugard states that there is an international obligation to consider such protection.

12.3.2 Right Arising from Customary International Law or a General Principle of Law: Domestic Trends towards Limiting State Leeway

Many constitutions, especially modern Eastern European constitutions, require the State to protect its nationals abroad, and some even contain explicit individual rights or guarantees of protection.[32] In constitutional

[29] See John R. Dugard, First Report on Diplomatic Protection, UN Doc. A/CN4/506 (of 7 March 2000), Article 4(1), 27 and paragraphs 75 et seq. Agreeing with this view, see Amerasinghe, *Diplomatic Protection*, 2008, 90.

[30] Report of the International Law Commission, Fifty-eighth session (1 May–9 June and 3 July–11 August 2006), General Assembly Official Records, Sixty-first session, Supplement No. 10 (A/61/10), 94 (italics mine).

[31] John R. Dugard, Commentary on Article 19, *ibid.*, 96–97 (italics mine).

[32] For example Albania: Article 8(2) of the Constitution of 5 July 1995; Bosnia and Herzegovina: Article 7(e) of the Constitution of 1 December 1995; Bulgaria: Article 25(5) of the Constitution of 12 July 1991; Croatia: Article 10 of the Constitution of 21 December 1990; Estonia: Article 13(1) of the Constitution of 28 June 1992; Georgia: Article 13(1) of the Constitution of 24 August 1995; Hungary: Article 69(3) of the Constitution of 20 August 1949; Poland: Article 36 of the Constitution of 2 April 1997; Portugal: Articles 14 and 59(2)(e) of the Constitution of 2 April 1976; Romania: Article 17 of the Constitution of 8 December 1991; Russia: Article 61 of the Constitution of 12 December 1993; Spain: Article 42 of the Constitution of 29 December 1978; Ukraine: Article 25 of the Constitution of 28 June 1996. On these provisions, see Enikö Horvath, Mandating Identity: Citizenship, Kinship Laws and Plural Nationality in the

States without special provisions of this sort, a State duty of protection can in principle be derived from the constitutional *fundamental rights.* A defensible argument would be that the home State must protect fundamental rights if there is a danger that third parties, including third States, are about to or have already violated such rights. The constitutional literature often postulates a "conditional" right to diplomatic protection of fundamental rights.[33] Moreover, duties of protection may be derived from the general prohibition of arbitrary action and the principle of the protection of legitimate expectations.[34] In none of these constructions, however, do strict rights of protection exist. If individual rights are recognized, these rights always refer only to the *proper exercise of discretion.*[35] However, and this is remarkable, there is

European Union (Leiden: Kluwer International 2008), Chapter III (esp. 141–142). A historical protection norm that became notorious due to Hitler's abuse of it was Article 112(2) of the Weimar Constitution of the German Reich of 11 August 1919: "All German citizens within and without the boundaries of the Reich have the right of protection by the Reich against foreign countries."

33 For a right to protection under German law, see, e.g., Alfred Scheidler, Der Schutz deutscher Staatsangehöriger gegenüber der Hoheitsgewalt ausländischer Staaten, *Die öffentliche Verwaltung* 59 (2006), 417–423. For a right of citizens arising from fundamental rights to have a State consider exercising diplomatic protection without abuse of discretion, see Eckhart Klein, Diplomatischer Schutz und grundrechtliche Schutzpflicht, *Die öffentliche Verwaltung* 30 (1977), 704–710 (707 and 710). For the possibility of a development of a conditional right of the citizen to diplomatic protection in conformity with the Swiss legal system, see Norbert Brunner, *Die Frage nach dem Anspruch des Bürgers auf diplomatischen Schutz* (Frankfurt a. M.: Peter Lang 1983), esp. 153–154.

34 For Germany, see the landmark *Rudolf Hess* case concerning diplomatic protection exercised against the Allies for the benefit of the Nazi criminal Hess. Broad discretion exists, since this falls within the scope of foreign policy. Discretion is only (but nevertheless) limited by fundamental rights and the prohibition of arbitrary action set out in Article 3(1) of the Basic Law (BVerfGE 55, 349 (1980), paragraphs 37–42). In the Swiss legal order, there is no legal norm granting Swiss citizens a strict legal right to the exercise of diplomatic protection. In this area, the Confederation has discretion limited only by the prohibition of arbitrary action (Decision of the Federal Council of 14 January 2004 (VPB 68.78), Consideration 4). See, e.g., Federal Supreme Court of Switzerland, BGE, *Groupement X* v. *Conseil fédéral*, 4A.1/2004, Judgment of 2 July 2004 (not in the official compilation), on diplomatic protection vis-à-vis CERN, especially Consideration E. 1.1.

35 In a comparative study Karl Doehring carried out in 1959, he concluded that diplomatic protection was seen as a matter of discretion in all legal orders he examined. Judicial review concerning abuse of discretion was in principle possible in these legal orders, but – despite the progressing trend toward justiciability in regard to action in the field of foreign affairs – such review was being denied with reference to principles such as the political question doctrine or *acte de gouvernement.* Claims due to the abuse of official discretion in regard to diplomatic protection were hardly ever likely to succeed (Karl Doehring, *Die Pflicht des Staates zur Gewährung diplomatischen Schutzes* (Cologne: Carl Heymanns Verlag 1959), 89–90).

currently a global trend towards *tightening restrictions* on discretion in numerous legal orders.[36] Current national judicial practice is moving in the direction of reviewing "reasonableness" (meaning, roughly, proportionality) or arbitrariness in government decisions on whether and how diplomatic protection should be exercised. The traditionally broad leeway of public authorities and governments in the field of foreign affairs is increasingly being restricted, especially in regard to fundamental rights. The contrary political question and *acte de gouvernement* doctrines are being pushed back.

Some more recent decisions by domestic and international courts on diplomatic protection have found that nationals abroad who request diplomatic protection have a right to substantively and procedurally proper consideration of their request, that governments must give reasons for their decision, that protection may not be denied arbitrarily, and that legitimate expectations may arise.[37] In connection with the detention of a British national at Guantanamo Bay, the Court of Appeal in England deviated from the traditional position that diplomatic protection is a matter beyond judicial review. In that case, the court held the complaint of a British detainee to be admissible. The British national was dissatisfied with the protection measures the UK government had taken, so he sued the government so that it would assert the illegality of his detention against the United States. Although the court rejected the claim that there was a general right to the exercise of specific acts of protection, it did accept that expectations worthy of protection may exist in this context.[38]

[36] See Annemarieke Vermeer-Künzli, Restricting Discretion: Judicial Review of Diplomatic Protection, *Nordic Journal of International Law* 75 (2006), 279–307; John R. Dugard, Diplomatic Protection, in: Rüdiger Wolfrum (ed.), *The Max Planck Encyclopedia of Public International Law* (Oxford: Oxford University Press 2012), paragraphs 13–15; Pisillo Mazzeschi, Diplomatic Protection, 2009, 221.

[37] See, especially, the Constitutional Court of South Africa, *Samuel Kaunda and Others* v. *President of the Republic of South Africa and Others*, Judgment of August 4, 2004, reprinted in *International Legal Materials* 44 (2005), 173, esp. Ngcobo, C.J., paragraph 192: "In my view, the duty of the government entails a duty to properly consider the request for diplomatic protection. The government must carefully apply its mind to the request and respond rationally to it. This would require, amongst other things, the government to follow a fair procedure in processing the request and it may be required to furnish reasons for its decisions. The request for diplomatic protection cannot be arbitrarily refused."

[38] See UK Supreme Court of Judicature – Court of Appeal, Civil Division, *Abbasi* v. *Secretary of State for Foreign and Commonwealth Affairs*, Case No. C/2002/0617A; 0617B, Judgment of 6 November 2002, reprinted in *International Legal Materials* 42 (2003), 355. See also High Court of Justice, *R. (Al-Rawi and Others)* v. *Secretary of State for Foreign and Commonwealth Affairs* [2006] EWHC 972 (Admin), paragraphs 89–93, and

In the area of targeted sanctions, there has been a particularly clear trend towards accepting a duty of protection rooted in fundamental rights. If the domestic investigation and prosecution of a person whose name is on a black list for counterterrorism sanctions leads to a negative result, the home State of the victim of the sanction (who, from a domestic perspective, has turned out not to be suspicious) sometimes, though not always, is motivated to support its national in proceedings against the United Nations. The question arises whether, in the special situation of listing (see Chapter 4, p. 95), there is a duty of the home State under international or constitutional law to assist a person against the sanctions committee. This would represent a special form of diplomatic protection against an international organization.

The case law of several jurisdictions accepts such a duty. For instance, the Federal Supreme Court of Switzerland held that Switzerland must assist a complainant in the delisting procedure, since Switzerland itself is not allowed to strike the person out from the list.[39] The legal basis for this duty of assistance is not clearly stated, though the basis appears to be the ECHR and Swiss constitutional law. In several sanctions cases, the European Court of First Instance (CFI) decided that the Member States (in the view of the CFI, pursuant to European fundamental rights) are required to act promptly to ensure that the person's case is presented without delay and fairly and impartially to the sanctions committee, with a view to its re-examination.[40] In the *Yusuf* case, the CFI stated that it is open to the persons affected by targeted sanctions to bring an action for judicial review based on *domestic law* against any *wrongful refusal* by the competent national authority to submit their cases to the sanctions committee for re-examination.[41] This aspect was not addressed by the ECJ on appeal. The CFI thus appeared to assume the existence of

Court of Appeal, *R. (Al-Rawi and Others)* v. *Secretary of State for Foreign and Commonwealth Affairs* [2006] EWCA 1279, QB 2008–2012, paragraph 148.

[39] See Federal Supreme Court of Switzerland, BGE 133 II 450 (2007) – *Youssef Nada*, paragraph 9 (reprinted in *Europäische Grundrechte-Zeitschrift* 35 (2008), p. 66 et seq.).

[40] See CFI, Case T-49/04, *Hassan* v. *Council of the European Union*, Judgment of 12 July 2006, paragraph 119, also paragraph 116; and CFI, Case T-253/02, *Ayadi* v. *Council of the European Union*, Judgment of 12 July 2006, paragraph 149. These statements of the law were not attacked by the applicants in the appeals proceedings and were not addressed by the ECJ judgments on appeal.

[41] See CFI, Case T-306/01, *Yusuf* v. *Council of the European Union*, Judgment of 21 September 2005 [2005] ECR II-3649, paragraph 317.

a common European, justiciable prohibition of abuse or arbitrary action in the field of diplomatic protection.[42]

The significance of this domestic and EU judicial practice is not limited solely to domestic law. It might be considered an expression of an emerging general principle of law. Most importantly, it can in principle bring about the creation of a norm of customary international law that gives rise to a universal (or at least European regional) standard of proper exercise of discretion in regard to diplomatic protection.

12.3.3 Right to Diplomatic Protection Arising from Human Rights?

A potential right to diplomatic protection as such cannot be considered an autonomous, isolated human right.[43] However, it can be understood as an element of the positive protective dimension of the human rights involved. Normally, the situations in which an individual requests diplomatic protection from his or her home State are due to violations of human rights (property, personal freedom, fair trial, economic freedom).

Duties of protection and the corresponding individual rights have been recognized in the field of international human rights and international criminal law (protection from genocide).[44] These rights are not limited to protection from injurious private activities, but they also may extend to protection from *foreign sovereigns*.[45] In principle, this means that parallel rights with identical objectives but differing substantive content exist: against the injuring State to refrain from the human rights violation, and against the home State to prevent and protect.

In the doctrine of human rights and criminal rights, "protection" encompasses both preventive and reactive measures. Diplomatic

[42] See Christian Storost, Der Fall Abbasi: Wegbereiter eines gemeineuropäischen Anspruchs auf diplomatischen Schutz?, *Archiv des Völkerrechts* 42 (2004), 411–424.

[43] But cf. Pieter H. Kooijmans, Is the Right to Diplomatic Protection a Human Right?, *Studi di diritto internazionale in onore di Gaetano Arangio-Ruiz* (Naples: editoriale Scientifica 2004), Vol. 3 (1984), 1975–1984. Kooijmans assumes the emergence of an implicit human right to diplomatic protection.

[44] See UN Human Rights Committee, General Comment No. 31 [80], Nature of the General Legal Obligations Imposed on State Parties to the Covenant (CCPR/C/21/Rev.1/Add. 13 (26 May 2004), paragraph 8). For the ACHR, see Inter-American Court of Human Rights, *Velásquez Rodriguez* v. *Honduras*, Ser. C No. 4 (1988), paragraphs 172–177. For the ECHR, see Cordula Dröge, *Positive Verpflichtungen der Staaten in der Europäischen Menschenrechtskonvention* (Berlin: Springer 2003).

[45] For the first comprehensive analysis in the literature beyond human rights, see Monica Hakimi, State Bystander Responsibility, *European Journal of International Law* 21 (2010), 341–385.

protection is primarily reactive; its objective is to bring ongoing violations to an end, but especially also to achieve restitution. Such reactive measures are also considered "protection" in human rights case law.

Within the scope of the ECHR, the protective dimension of human rights has already been activated specifically in regard to the exercise of diplomatic protection. According to the settled case law of the European Commission of Human Rights, no "right to diplomatic protection ... as such" is guaranteed by the ECHR.[46] But in certain circumstances, this does not prevent us to derive a duty of protection from the general obligation to secure human rights set out in Article 1 of the ECHR in conjunction with the rights specifically affected. In the 1970s, the European Commission of Human Rights decided that Article 1 of the ECHR did *not* give rise to any obligation on the High contracting parties to secure that non-contracting States, acting within their own jurisdiction, respect the rights and freedoms guaranteed by the Convention, even though their failure to do so might have adverse effects on persons within the jurisdiction of a contracting party;[47] but since then, the extraterritorial application of the ECHR has steadily been expanded.[48] The ECtHR decided that, even in the absence of effective control by Moldova over the Transdniestrian region, "Moldova still has a positive obligation under Article 1 of the Convention to take the *diplomatic*, economic, judicial or other measures that it is in its power to take and are in accordance with international law to secure to the applicants the rights guaranteed by the Convention."[49]

12.3.4 Systematic and Legal Policy Foundation of an Individual Right to Diplomatic Protection

It has been argued against juridification of the institution of diplomatic protection (by granting international legal rights to the individual against

[46] EComHR, *Bertrand Russell Peace Foundation Ltd* v. *UK*, no. 7597/76 of 2 May 1978, DR 14, p. 117 et seq.; EComHR, *G. Kapas* v. *UK*, no. 12822/87 of 9 December 1987; EComHR, *Dobberstein* v. *Germany*, no. 25045/94 of 12 April 1996; EComHR, *A. Leschi et al.* v. *France*, no. 37505/97 of 22 April 1998. The benchmark *Bertrand Russell Peace Foundation* case was about the alleged violation of the secrecy of correspondence and privacy by the Soviet Union, which was not a contracting party. In other cases, the deprivation of real property in non-contracting States was at issue.

[47] See EComHR, *Bertrand Russell Peace Foundation Ltd* v. *UK* (n. 46), p. 124.

[48] See Anne Peters, Die Anwendbarkeit der EMRK in Zeiten komplexer Hoheitsgewalt und das Prinzip der Grundrechtstoleranz, *Archiv des Völkerrechts* 48 (2010), 1–57.

[49] ECtHR, *Ilascu* v. *Moldova*, no. 48787/99, Judgment of 8 July 2004, paragraph 331 (italics mine).

the home State) that this would undermine the separation of powers between the executive branch, which has primary responsibility for foreign affairs, and the judicial branch. According to the traditionalists, not only are the courts functionally unsuited to consider delicate foreign policy considerations in their decisions, but they also do not have the democratic legitimacy to do so.[50]

The most important response to this objection is that under the rule of law, the political bodies are in principle subject to law, which implies a certain degree of judicial oversight. Constitutional, economic, and fiscal considerations of the home State often prevent it from acting overly assertive in relation to foreign governments. Without judicial protection, individuals would be exposed to arbitrary action by their governments and would be largely without any protection at all, since they are hardly able to defend themselves against a foreign State on their own.

Certainly, actionability in a domestic court does not depend on an international legal right to diplomatic protection. In many countries, claims may also be brought on the basis of the domestic fundamental rights set out in the respective national constitution.[51] But as is the case in regard to human rights, an international guarantee is not superfluous in order to stipulate an international minimum standard for legal orders that do not provide sufficient protection under domestic law.

To the extent that peremptory international law has been breached, a specific argument can be added. Every breach of a peremptory norm of international law triggers the obligation of all States to not recognize the situation as lawful and to cooperate to bring an end to the breach.[52] But if States are required by international law to refuse any recognition of breaches of peremptory international law and to cooperate for the purpose of eliminating the breach, they should *a fortiori* also be required to exercise diplomatic protection for the benefit of their citizens.[53]

In terms of legal construction, an international obligation of the home State to exercise due diligence (more on this later) in regard to the

[50] See Pergantis, "Humanization" of Diplomatic Protection, 2006, 386.

[51] See n. 32 with accompanying text.

[52] Article 41 of the ILC Articles on Responsibility of States for Internationally Wrongful Acts (2001), A/CN.4/L.602, Rev. 1., also as an annex to the UN General Assembly resolution taking note of them (A/Res/56/83 [2002]). See ICJ, *Legal Consequences of the Construction of a Wall in the Occupied Palestinian Territory*, Advisory Opinion of 9 July 2004, ICJ Reports 2004, paragraph 159.

[53] See Anna Maria Helena Vermeer-Künzli, *The Protection of Individuals by Means of Diplomatic Protection – Diplomatic Protection as a Human Rights Instrument* (Leiden: PrintPaertners Ipskamp 2007), 215.

protection of its citizens against foreign States should be seen as a necessary correlate of the Vattelian fiction. In Vattel, the assumption that the injury of foreigners interfered with a State right was coupled to the duty to protect. According to Vattel, the home State was required to protect its citizens against abuse: The sovereign of the injured citizen "*must* avenge the deed." Vattel used contract theory to derive this duty to protect from the purpose of the social contract, that is to safeguard the security of citizens speaking of "the chief end of civil society, which is protection".[54] Vattel considered the home State to be injured because the mistreatment of its citizen *forces* it to engage in protective activities. This limits the State's freedom of action, which – from a Vattelian perspective – constitutes the actual breach. But if the State is not required to respond to the breach, the State is also not limited in respect of its freedom, so that the basis for the assumption of a breach no longer applies. The two can therefore not be combined without contradiction: State ownership of the right, and the lack of an obligation for the State to act.

Furthermore, the law of State immunity offers a key argument in favour of recognizing an international right of the individual against the home State that is in principle justiciable, namely to have the home State properly consider its decision on the exercise of diplomatic protection. State immunity prevents the person concerned from bringing claims against foreign States before the courts of other States. If State immunity is preserved even in the case of serious breaches of human rights, this could and should be compensated by reducing the discretion of the victim's home State when deciding on the exercise of diplomatic protection.[55] The detailed criteria for triggering and circumscribing the duty of diplomatic protection are still unclear.

As discussed in Chapter 8, duties of protection are emerging for bystander States in the international legal subareas of human rights protection, R2P, disaster relief, international criminal law, and international humanitarian law. The addressees of these duties are not only the home States of the victims, but also third States. These duties are about protecting natural persons from serious breaches of international law (committed by the host State or private individuals). The right of diplomatic protection must be fitted into these recent legal developments.

[54] See n. 3. The French original for "protection" is "sûreté".

[55] See François Flauss, Vers un aggiornamento des conditions d'exercice de la protection diplomatique?, in: Flauss (ed.), *La protection diplomatique: Mutations contemporaines et pratiques nationales* (Brussels: Bruylant 2003), 29–61 (53).

It would be a contradiction to the trend in other areas of international law if of all States the home State of the victims were exempt from the duties of protection, even though it is the home State which per se has a close legal relationship with the victims.

An international individual right to proper exercise of due diligence when deciding on whether to grant diplomatic protection can therefore be derived from international human rights (and international criminal law). While the threshold for activating the duty of protection is frequently not reached, the duty can nevertheless be triggered in extreme cases.

12.4 Conclusion

The "humanization" of the law of diplomatic protection, which extends in two dimensions, can be justified in legal terms and, with reservations, should be welcomed in terms of legal policy. In the first dimension, namely the relationship between the person concerned and the injuring State, autonomous individual rights should be recognized. The rejection of the attribution (or fiction) of rights belonging solely to the State (i.e., rights of the individual's home State against the injuring State) fits better into contemporary international law and has practical consequences, as mentioned earlier (inclusion of the individual in the proceedings, permissibility of waiver).

"Humanization" in the second dimension, namely the relationship between the injured individual and the home State, should be deemed positive in principle as well. The fact that the nature of the institution of diplomatic protection is also political does not mean that it exists in a legal vacuum. Both domestic principles of the rule of law and the international rule of law prohibit arbitrary action and require discretion instead. By definition, discretion is subject to legal limits.

As already discussed, an increasing number of legal orders recognize State obligations to do something for the protection of their citizens who have been injured by a foreign State. Already the domestic request of the injured person for protection has an international legal dimension, especially because this request usually arises from a human rights violation. A right to diplomatic protection (or to proper exercise of discretion), although it is formally granted under domestic law, can therefore be considered as a *functional* international individual right.

Moreover, an international obligation to properly consider the possibility of exercising diplomatic protection should be recognized.

The limitation of State discretion (in virtue of international law) by the *rights of the individual* would be a progressive development. The proposal to further develop international law by requiring States under international law to grant their citizens diplomatic protection in principle should be welcomed.[56]

Such an obligation rooted in international law could never be an obligation of result, but rather only an obligation to take all reasonable steps, i.e., an obligation of conduct. Countervailing public interests would also have to be weighed in this regard. But these public interests would always have to be legitimate and could not be exhausted simply by referring to mere *raison d'Etat*. The interests of the individual concerned should not be overemphasized. Protection should not always be granted at any price. The individual's interest must be weighed not only against the concerns of the home State, but also against those of the injuring State.[57] Such a weighing of interests and the resulting limitation of the duty of protection are systemically compatible with human rights. Even as a duty rooted in international law, the duty to exercise diplomatic protection proposed here would only be a duty to properly exercise State discretion.

Another question is whether this duty is mirrored (and reinforced) by an international individual right. In any event, such a right would likewise be "soft", i.e., not a strict right. With this restriction, however, it would still be justiciable in domestic courts, which in turn are required to apply international law, including the customary international law of diplomatic protection.

A further question concerns the legal contents of the proposed international individual right to proper exercise of discretion in deciding whether and which diplomatic protection measures should be taken. A procedural component is the procedural right of the person concerned to be *informed of the reasons of the home State* if it decides not to grant protection.[58]

If this is an international individual right to proper exercise of discretion, *non-fulfilment* would have to trigger the *international responsibility* of the home State towards the individual. In the field of human rights, this is accepted without further difficulties. However, even in the field of human rights there are only limited options for the individual to enforce

[56] See also Amerasinghe, *Diplomatic Protection*, 2008, 90. [57] See *ibid.*, 344.

[58] See Constitutional Court of South Africa, *Samuel Kaunda and Others* v. *President of the Republic of South Africa and Others* (n. 37), paragraph 192.

these rights against the home State under international law. Claims against home States for violations of duties of protection, in cases where no or only insufficient protection measures were taken against third States, have sometimes been brought before the European human rights bodies, but usually without success.[59] The (still) incomplete actionability of international individual rights changes nothing about their possible existence, however.[60]

Overall, the emerging "humanization" of diplomatic protection described in both of these legal relationships can be considered a further development of international law that fits to the extant law. It simultaneously manifests the international legal status of the individual and can contribute to consolidating that status.

[59] See n. 46.

[60] On the distinction between substantive individual rights and the procedural right to bring claims, see Chapter 3, pp. 44–50.

13

The Legal Basis for the International Legal Personality of the Individual and the Question of its Independence from the State

The overview of the branches of international law has shown that in recent years individuals have acquired an increasingly wide range of international rights. At the same time, international legal duties are being imposed on individuals, such as in the law of armed conflict. These rights and duties can be found at both the primary and the secondary levels. Individuals may therefore also be participants in the international relationship of responsibility that arises from a breach of international law. The newness of the current legal situation does not consist in the fact that individuals (are able to) have international rights and duties at all, but rather that the quantity of these rights and duties has increased dramatically.

It would be a significant paradigm shift if the legal status of the individual was emancipated from States (at least to a certain extent). The answer to the question of whether or not the international legal personality of the individual is autonomous of the State depends crucially on the legal basis from which that international legal personality is derived. The individual positions under international law that have been identified in the preceding chapters presuppose, in terms of legal logic, the existence of an international legal personality of the individual. The implicit recognition of the legal subjectivity of the individual can therefore be deduced from the legal positions afforded by treaties. A stable international legal personality of the individual requires an additional legal basis, however. This will be discussed in the following section.

13.1 States as Overlords?

It would be a serious deficit of the international legal personality of the individual if the individual's legal status necessarily had to be granted by the State. At first glance, individuals in fact do not appear to be "the masters of their international rights" and of their legal personality.[1] The progress made in the legal personality of individuals "remains dictated by the States".[2] This statement expresses that individuals are unable to confer international legal rights and duties upon themselves. The States still appear to be the "overlords".[3] At any time, States are able to set aside a treaty that grants an individual right or establishes a monitoring mechanism and thus to destroy the legal status of the individual.[4] Individual rights conferred under customary international law can likewise fall into *desuetudo* pursuant to State practice.[5]

Fully in line with this analysis, the classic literature assumed that the international legal status of individuals was based on a treaty concluded between States for the benefit of a third party (*pactum in favorem tertii*).[6] Until recently, a distinction was made among three types of international treaties: Firstly, treaties granting private third parties (individuals) actionable "direct" rights against contracting States in international legal proceedings (e.g., the ECHR); secondly, treaties which only benefit private third parties (in the sense that the treaty obliges contracting States to grant rights to third parties (individuals) as part of their domestic law, such as TRIPS); and thirdly, treaties that benefit private individuals as

[1] Michel Cosnard, Rapport introductif, in: Société française pour le droit international (ed.), *Colloque de Mans: Le sujet en droit international* (Paris: Pedone 2005), 13–53 (51; translation mine).

[2] "This progress in the extension of the legal personality of the individual remains *dictated by the States*. These consent only to respond to the dominant expectations of each category of private persons which differ from one group to the other; and this prohibits to unequivocally take stock of their international legal personality." Patrick Daillier/ Alain Pellet, *Droit International Public* (7th ed., Paris: LGDJ 2002), 652 (translation and italics by the author).

[3] Antonio Cassese, *International Law* (2nd ed., Oxford: Oxford University Press 2005), 149.

[4] For the field of investment protection law, see ICSID, *Archer Daniels Midland Company*, Case No. ARB(AF)/04/5 (NAFTA chapter 11), of 21 November 2007, Concurring Opinion of Arthur W. Rovine, Issues of Independent Investor Rights, Diplomatic Protection and Countermeasures, paragraph 51: "[T]he legal capacity of governments to amend or repeal rights of non-state actors does not signify that the rights were never there, and do not remain as long as the rights are not amended or terminated."

[5] See Christian Dominicé, L'émergence de l'individu en droit international public, in: Dominicé, *L'ordre juridique international entre tradition et innovation* (Paris: PUF 1997) (orig. 1987), 109–123 (123).

[6] See Marek Korowicz's summary of the justification of the international legal personality of the individual dominant until the 1950s (within the group of proponents, which was opposed by a group of opponents that was at least as large): Marek St Korowicz, The Problem of the International Personality of Individuals, *American Journal of International Law* 50 (1956), 534–562 (542).

third parties only "by rebound".[7] The mark of all these entitlements or benefits is that they can be nullified by the contracting parties.

To the extent that the rights and duties in question imply international legal capacity, it might be argued within this paradigm that the withdrawal of rights and duties simultaneously means a withdrawal of the status as a legal subject upon which the rights and duties depend. From this perspective, the international legal personality of the individual would be unstable and revocable: "In this way, the individual as addressee of international norms, be they substantive norms or procedural ones, is always in a precarious situation." [8] This is often expressed by claiming that the individual at best is a "passive" or derivative international legal subject, or not a full or real subject at all.[9]

Kate Parlett distinguishes between "autonomous" and "passive" international legal subjects.[10] In contrast to the latter, the former are characterized by two "capacities": Firstly, autonomous subjects have control over the recognition of their own rights, obligations, and capacities. These are imposed only when the autonomous subject consents.

[7] See Rolf Schwartmann, *Private im Wirtschaftsvölkerrecht* (Tübingen: Mohr Siebeck 2005), 19–22. See also Chapter 17 on the distinction between having rights and being only the beneficiary of another actor's obligations. In Chapter 10, pp. 301–17 it was discussed whether investors derive "direct" rights from BITs, or whether they only benefit from inter-State rights and obligations.

[8] Dominicé, L'émergence de l'individu, 1997, 123 (translation by the author). In the older literature, see Korowicz, Problem of International Personality, 1956, 536: "Today the existence of such international personality of individuals is still entirely dependent on the states which created it, and it is always revocable according to the decisions of these states."

[9] See Antoine Favre, *Principes du droit des gens* (Fribourg: Editions Universitaires 1974), 310: "One can thus consider as passive subjects of the law of nations those entities *which do not have the capacity to make international law* but which are constituted by international law as addressees of the rules of the law of nations, *rules which determine their rights and obligations* of an international character: and this is true . . . in certain cases for individuals." (translation and italics by the author). See also Dominicé, L'émergence de l'individu, 1997, 111; Robert Kolb, Nouvelle observation sur la détermination de la personalité juridique internationale, *Zeitschrift für öffentliches Recht* 57 (2002), 229–241 (esp. 236 and 239); Joe Verhoeven, *Droit International Public* (Brussels: Larcier 2000), 296: The international legal personality of the individual remains "overall purely passive . . . which hardly offers them [the individuals] the means of any autonomous conduct" (translation by the author). See in this sense also Gerhard Hafner: "Individuals . . . derive their legal status only from the will of States (and international organizations) and cannot influence it. . . Accordingly, one cannot contend that individuals are subjects of international law" (Gerhard Hafner, The Emancipation of the Individual from the State under International Law, *Recueil des Cours* 358 (2011), 263–453 (437–441)).

[10] Kate Parlett, *The Individual in the International Legal System* (Cambridge: Cambridge University Press 2011), 357–358.

In contrast, rights and obligations can be imposed upon passive subjects without their consent. Secondly, only autonomous subjects have control over the delegation of functions and capacities to other entities and are therefore "gatekeepers". As Parlett summarizes, "Entities which possess these two capacities enjoy qualitatively meaningful participation in the international legal system." It is evident that at the present time only States have these two capacities as autonomous subjects. So Parlett's distinction is also tantamount to a distinction between States and all other actors, but this distinction is justified and not simply quasi-definitional. In this scheme, individuals are not autonomous international legal subjects, but rather they are "passive recipients of rights and obligations in the international legal system".[11] Since, according to Parlett, individuals do not have the power to create rights, but rather they are only recipients of rights, their legal status is largely dependent on the State.[12] Individuals play a hybrid role: They are objects when it comes to acquiring rights and subjects for the purposes of exercising them.[13] "Thus, individuals remain subordinated in the international system, suspended between object and independent or autonomous subject."[14] Parlett emphasizes that States can impose both obligations and rights upon individuals (whether the latter want them or not): "Individuals cannot agree to the conferral of rights or the imposition of obligations, for example, through participating in international treaties. In general, there has been little concern as to whether individuals consent to bearing rights, obligations and capacities."[15] Parlett even sees a strengthening of the dominance of States in the international system in the current, quasi-paternalistic legal constellation: "[T]he conferral of rights and obligations on individuals – which is exclusively controlled by states – actually reinforces the dominant position of states in the international legal system."[16]

[11] Parlett, *Individual*, 2011, 353.

[12] *Ibid.*, 362: "[T]he role of individuals in the international legal system has remained heavily, if not exclusively, dependent on state consent." *Ibid.*, 353: "[T]he exercise of rights is dependent on a pre-existing grant (which like any treaty is revocable in certain circumstances) . . . [S]tates have remained central and in control of the extent to which individuals may engage in the international legal system: the extent to which individuals are given rights, obligations and capacities is dependent on a specific grant from the primary actors in the international legal system, dominated by states."

[13] *Ibid.*, 361. [14] *Ibid.*, 359–360. [15] *Ibid.*, 352. [16] *Ibid.*, 370.

13.2 International Legal Personality Independent of the State?

In contrast to the views described above, only few contemporary authors explicitly affirm an "original" international legal personality of the individual, independent of the State, at least in regard to certain key rights. According to Robert McCorquodale, "each State no longer has complete control over the continuance, development, and interpretation of individuals' rights ... [A] number of the rights of individuals in the international system are now, to some extent, separate from the specific control and direction of States, at least as they are protected by customary international law (or by *jus cogens*), and are independent rights within the international legal system."[17] In his concurring opinion to an advisory opinion of the Inter-American Court of Human Rights, Judge Antônio Cançado Trindade believed that the "juridical personality of the individual" was "no longer conditioned by the law emanated from the public power of the State."[18]

Christopher Barbara notes that globalization has created a new social context that suggests a primary international legal personality of the individual: "This new social context is trying to inform the law that secondary legal personality is no longer an acceptable solution to the position of the individual at international law."[19] Janne Nijmann sees international legal personality as part of a "cosmopolitan" identity, permitting a fundamental change in perspective: According to this view, the individual is "an originary and primary international legal person".[20] Roland Portmann assumes an *a priori* international legal personality of individuals in relation to international crimes and fundamental human rights. Portmann is primarily concerned with obligations:

> "[T]here is a rebuttable presumption that individuals possess personality in international law when international crimes and basic human rights are concerned. By implication, *as a matter of fundamental legal principle,*

[17] Robert McCorquodale, The Individual in the International Legal System, in: Malcolm Evans (ed.), *International Law* (3rd ed., Oxford: Oxford University Press 2010), 284–310 (291).

[18] IACtHR, *Juridical Status and Human Rights of the Child*, Advisory Opinion OC-17/02 of 28 August 2001, Concurring Opinion of Judge Cançado Trindade, paragraph 50.

[19] Christopher Barbara, International Legal Personality: Panacea or Pandemonium? Theorizing About the Individual and the State in the Era of Globalization, *Austrian Review of International and European Law* 12 (2007), 17–58 (38).

[20] Janne E. Nijman, Paul Riceur and International Law: Beyond "The End of the Subject." Towards a Reconceptualization of International Legal Personality, *Leiden Journal of International Law* 20 (2007), 25–64 (64).

individuals are a priori international persons in this limited context. It follows that there is no need to separately establish whether international crimes *bind* individual human beings: they automatically do so *on the basis of legal principle* without a statutory provision or customary practice necessarily indicating so."

The legal basis of this (substantively limited) international legal personality is thus, according to Portmann, not positive international law but rather natural law: "just a matter of them being individual human beings and as such under an obligation to respect fundamental international norms."[21]

The positions cited here that affirm the quality of independence from the State or of "originality", as opposed to the quality of being dependent and derived from the State, i.e., the "derivative" quality of the international legal personality of the individual, do not connect this dispute with existing theory on the legal sources of international law. But in fact, the legal basis of international legal personality is what significantly determines its independence from the State. For this reason, the following subsections will seek out this legal basis. The premise is that the legal principle recognizing the international legal personality of an actor must be attributable to one of the recognized sources of international law. In other words, any norm stipulating that individuals have international legal personality would have to be found in customary international law, an international treaty provision, or in a general principle of law (Article 38(1) of the ICJ Statute).

13.3 Treaty Basis

Explicit treaty provisions granting international legal subjectivity to an actor are only apparent in regard to international organizations. According to the first sentence of Article 4(1) of the Rome Statute of the International Criminal Court, for instance, "[t]he Court shall have international legal personality." Parallel norms that might explicitly grant international legal personality to individuals, analogous to national legal provisions such as § 1 of the German Civil Code or Article 11 of the Swiss Civil Code, do not exist.

[21] Roland Portmann, *Legal Personality in International Law* (Cambridge: Cambridge University Press 2010), 273 (italics mine). For Portmann, international legal personality is otherwise in principle an empty *a posteriori* concept, namely a bundle of rights and obligations (*ibid.*, 272). But in regard to international crimes and human rights, he makes the exception mentioned above.

13.3.1 *Implicit Conferral of International Legal Personality as the Normal Case*

International treaties may contain an implicit statement on the international legal personality of an entity. For instance, the constituent treaties of some international organizations implicitly grant international legal personality to the organization they constitute. In the *Reparation for Injuries* case, the International Court of Justice (ICJ) derived the international legal subjectivity of the UN from the fact that the UN Charter entrusted the organization with certain functions. In order to discharge those functions, the UN requires international legal subjectivity. Therefore, the UN Charter implicitly assigned international legal subjectivity to the organization.[22] But transferring such a functionalist argumentation to human beings would hardly be compatible with the image of human beings as ends in themselves – an image that underlies the Universal Declaration of Human Rights.

A different, probably more common way to justify the international legal personality of individuals in terms of treaty provisions is the inference drawn from the conferral of an individual right to the unwritten norm contained therein, namely that the individual has the capacity to hold this right. *Just like the explicit right itself, the implicit legal personality (as a precondition of the specific right) would in this case also be treaty-based and hence selective.* Along these lines, it was already determined as a "well-established principle of international law" in the 1950s that States may, by common agreement, recognize the international legal personality of individuals.[23]

Even less than twenty years ago, it was still claimed that all international individual rights were ultimately based on treaties, i.e., individuals had not a single international right in virtue of customary international law.[24] It then matters crucially which treaty provisions actually grant individual rights. Until recently, treaty interpretation contained an

[22] See ICJ, *Reparation for Injuries Suffered in the Service of the United Nations*, Advisory Opinion, ICJ Reports 1949, 174–220 (179–180).

[23] See Korowicz, Problem of International Personality, 1956, 561: "[S]tates may, *by common agreement*, recognize the international personality of individuals not only in their duties and responsibilities, but also in their capacity for international procedural action" (italics mine).

[24] See Albrecht Randelzhofer, The Legal Position of the Individual under Present International Law, in: Randelzhofer/Christian Tomuschat (eds), *State Responsibility and the Individual: Reparation in Instances of Grave Violations of Human Rights* (The Hague: Martinus Nijhoff 1999), 231–242 (234).

unspoken presumption *against* individual rights. Even where treaties explicitly granted rights to individuals, such as the Geneva Conventions on international humanitarian law[25] or the slavery convention mentioned in Chapter 2,[26] international treaty rights and duties of individuals were generally rejected.

Such an unspoken presumption against individual rights (and thus the underlying legal personality) can no longer be justified. International individual rights and duties are no longer the exception that has to be specially proven. Instead, when examining the individual rights content of treaties, the usual interpretation methods should be used to determine whether the treaties actually grant individual rights or duties. Furthermore, a doctrine of international protective norms should be developed, as Oliver Dörr proposes. Here, the substantive preconditions for direct international individual rights would have to be defined. According to Dörr, a treaty norm generates a right only if, firstly, the norm's purpose is aimed at the protection of individuals and, secondly, "the norms solidify in such a way that the individual is granted a right to have the norm observed as part of the individual's own legal sphere, and that right corresponds to the State duty of conduct".[27] This approach is promising. The other conditions mentioned by Dörr, however, lead to an excessive narrowing of the international legal position of the individual. Dörr's requirement that the text of the treaty must clearly show the intention of the contracting parties to "establish … a true entitlement"[28] comes close to the old presumption against individual rights, is static due to its recourse to the original intent of the lawmakers, and is in opposition to the dynamic approach taken by the ICJ in *LaGrand* (see below). This narrow view also led to the implausible conclusion that "the inventory of genuine individual rights is significantly smaller than the group of norms commonly referred to as 'human rights'".[29]

25 See Chapter 7, pp. 194–96.

26 See General Act of the Brussels Conference Relating to the African Slave Trade of 2 July 1890, *American Journal of International Law* 3 (1909), Supplement p. 29 at 41. See also pp. 13–14.

27 Oliver Dörr, Völkerrechtliche Deliktsansprüche Privater – auf der Grundlage und in den Grenzen einer völkerrechtlichen Schutznormlehre, in: Martin Breuer/Astrid Epiney/ Andreas Haratsch/Stefanie Schmahl/Norman Weiß (eds), *Der Staat im Recht: Festschrift Eckart Klein zum 70. Geburtstag* (Berlin: Duncker & Humblot 2013), 765–782 (776) (translation mine).

28 *Ibid.*, 777 (translation mine).

29 *Ibid.*, 780 (translation mine).

In contrast to Dörr's unspoken presumption against the grant of individual rights by treaties, the normative centrality of the human being that is recognized today in international law might even provide the basis for the converse presumption: The accumulation of selective individual rights and duties in conjunction with the ripple effect of international human rights and the increasingly strong orientation of current international law towards the individual now permit the presumption that international treaty norms directly affecting the interests of individuals also regularly protect individuals. This means they contain international individual rights and thus implicitly presume the legal personality of the individual.[30] Such a presumption can refer to the principle that international treaty interpretation should be in conformity with human rights. As long as the wording of a treaty provision is not contradicted, an interpretation recognizing the existence of an individual right is in conformity with the system and is teleologically justified. This was precisely the approach taken by the International Court of Justice in *LaGrand*. Based on the clear wording of Article 36 of the Vienna Convention on Consular Relations (VCCR), and contrary to the *travaux préparatoires*, the ICJ derived individual rights to contact the home State consulate.[31] This interpretation of the VCCR by the ICJ is thus an example of a dynamic and "individualized" interpretation of an international treaty. Because of the underlying statement about the international personality of individuals, the rapid increase of international (treaty) provisions addressed to individuals represents a solidification and strengthening of their status as subjects of international law.[32]

Nevertheless, the inductive derivation of a (so to speak point by point) legal personality from the conferral of certain rights remains unsatisfactory – even with the help of the presumption of individual entitlement. Functionally, the concept of legal personality is a *general* precondition for

[30] For the possibility of an implicit recognition of individual rights in international treaties, see Irini Papanicolopulu, The Law of the Sea Convention: No Place for Persons? *The International Journal of Marine and Coastal Law* 27 (2012), 867–874 (871): "While rights of persons may implicitly follow from the rights and duties of States, they are often uncertain."

[31] See ICJ, *LaGrand Case* (*Germany* v. *United States of America*), ICJ Reports 2001, 466, paragraph 77.

[32] Daillier/Pellet, *Droit International Public*, 2002, 651 note that "a rapid growth of norms whose direct and indirect addressees are private persons, a phenomenon of the current epoch which is in itself worth discussing, in order to deduce a decisive progress of their legal personality..." (translation by the author).

the ownership of specific rights and duties. The concept is unable to fulfil this task if legal capacity is determined only *ad hoc* from case to case.

13.3.2 Quasi-Irreversibility of the Treaty Basis through Precommitment and Prevention of Rollback

Another serious problem associated with international legal personality conferred upon individuals by treaties appears to be that such personality (and the specifically granted rights or duties) can be nullified by cancelling the treaty, i.e., solely by a State decision. The objection that privileges conferred (and revocable) by the State could never be genuine "rights" is well known from German late constitutionalism, and it was countered at the time in German public law by Georg Jellinek and his idea of individual "subjective" public rights. Is treaty-based international legal personality merely the "fruit of a haphazard and changing will"[33] of States, and can there accordingly be no individual rights independent of the State, i.e., no genuine international individual rights?

My response is that even "merely" treaty-based international legal personality is more stable than it appears at first glance. Revocation of treaty-based international legal personality (and individual treaty rights) can be ruled out if a rollback prohibition is posited. One can argue that States governed by the rule of law may not (and, due to political lock-in, cannot) simply reverse positive stipulations of individual rights.

In political science, the (irreversible) self-binding of the State is referred to as *precommitment*, using rational choice terminology.[34] Simply put, precommitment means that by engaging in certain acts, a State sends a political signal that it is committing itself *irreversibly* to certain conduct, thus enhancing its credibility.

In parallel, a prohibition of rollback is assumed in the area of social human rights. According to a General Comment of the Committee on Economic, Social and Cultural Rights, "any deliberately retrogressive measures in that regard would require the most careful consideration and would need to be fully justified by reference to the totality of the rights provided for in the Covenant and in the context of the full use of

[33] *Ibid.*, 649.

[34] However, this view regards States as black boxes and ignores that the binding arrangements they enter into are based on the decisions of several political actors (acting in succession), so that the idea of "self"-binding appears simplistic. See Anne Peters, Precommitment Theory Applied to International Law: Between Sovereignty and Triviality, *University of Illinois Law Review* (2008), 239–252.

the maximum available resources".[35] Similarly, the IACtHR postulated a rollback prohibition in regard to the optional recognition of the jurisdiction of the Inter-American Court of Human Rights by a Latin American party to the ACHR. Here, Peru tried to withdraw the declaration it had made under Article 62(1) of the ACHR in order to release itself from the court's jurisdiction. The court found that this withdrawal was impermissible without denunciation of the ACHR as a whole.[36] Finally, the UN Human Rights Committee has espoused the view that "international law does not permit a State which has ratified or acceded or succeeded to the Covenant [the ICCPR] to denounce it or withdraw from it".[37]

Considered as a legal rule, the prevention of rollback postulated here could be transferred to other legal positions beyond human rights and acceptance of the jurisdiction of international monitoring bodies. This means that the objection "what the State has given, the State can take away" does not thwart the possibility of stable international legal personality of individuals, even if such personality is conferred only by a treaty.

13.3.3 Limits to the Private Law Analogy

A final problem with the idea of treaty-based international legal personality of individuals is the underlying analogy with private law. The classic justification of the derivative legal status of third parties (here, individuals) in analogy with private law by positing an agreement "for the benefit of a third party" is fundamentally Statist. Individuals are placed here as "third parties" outside the States. That construction ignores the fact that citizens – from a democratic perspective – are the legitimizing point of departure for the State, that States represent these citizens (and should not displace them), and that States are ultimately instruments to make the coexistence of individuals possible. This perspective is not only political but also a component of current international law. International

[35] CESCR General Comment No. 3 (1990), UN Doc. E/1991/23, paragraph 9.

[36] IACtHR, *Ivcher Bronstein Case, Competence*, Judgment of 24 September 1999, paragraphs 32 et seq., esp. paragraphs 50–51.

[37] UN Human Rights Committee, General Comment No. 26, *Continuity of Obligations*, of 8 December 1997, paragraph 5; see also paragraph 3: "Furthermore, it is clear that the Covenant is not the type of treaty which, by its nature, implies a right of denunciation . . . As such, the Covenant does not have a temporary character typical of treaties where a right of denunciation is deemed to be admitted, notwithstanding the absence of a specific provision to that effect."

law includes a rule in favour of democratic development,[38] i.e., the requirement that newly created States must adopt a democratic form of government and that existing States should work in that direction. In that sense, the private law analogy does not do justice to existing international law and its democratic aspiration.

For this reason, this study prefers a public law perspective: Rights and duties may legitimately be imposed on individuals even without their *direct* consent, if this is foreseeable and legally clear for the person subject to the right, or in other words if the (international legal) principle of legality is observed (see Chapter 4, pp. 79–85) – and even if the direct democratic legitimacy of the international legal basis for the rights and duties is relatively weak (for details, see Chapter 17, pp. 544–51). This also means that the legal capacity (legal personality) underlying the potential rights and duties cannot meaningfully be derived from a treaty "for the benefit of third parties".

13.4 Customary International Law

A general and permanent legal basis for international legal personality might also be found outside treaty law. In my view, the norm that individuals are subjects of international law already exists under customary international law.[39] This customary norm is implicitly contained in those guarantees of international humanitarian law and key human rights that belong to *jus cogens* and thus cannot be abolished by treaty. Additionally, there has been the new phenomenon of a massive expansion of international individual rights and duties beyond human rights, as described in the preceding chapters.

This significant and relatively new pattern of imposing rights and duties on individuals can be seen as a general, sufficiently continuous

[38] See Niels Petersen, *Demokratie als teleologisches Prinzip: Zur Legitimität von Staatsgewalt im Völkerrecht* (Heidelberg: Springer 2009); Anne Peters, Dual Democracy, in: Jan Klabbers/Anne Peters/Geir Ulfstein, *The Constitutionalization of International Law* (2nd ed., Oxford: Oxford University Press 2011), 263–241 (273–286); Frithjof Ehm, *Das völkerrechtliche Demokratiegebot* (Tübingen: Mohr Siebeck 2013).

[39] See in this sense also Rosalyn Higgins, *Problems and Process: International Law and How We Use It* (Oxford: Clarendon Press 1995), 53–54. See further Julie Cassidy, Emergence of the Individual as an International Juristic Entity: Enforcement of International Human Rights, *Deakin Law Review* 9 (2004), 533–572 (571): "Such modern day state practice provides strong support for the existence of a new customary international law recognizing indiviuals as an international juristic entity, with international rights and procedural capacity."

practice that generates customary law. The holdings of international and domestic courts and the statements of foreign policy actors also show that objections in principle to the legal personality of individuals have largely become irrelevant. The *opinio juris* of numerous States thus appears to be moving in the direction of self-evident acceptance of international legal personality of the individual that is no longer merely selective *per se*. This means that the two elements (practice and *opinio juris*) of a customary rule of international law are satisfied.

Moreover, international individual rights, especially many human rights, are also rooted in customary law. For instance, Antonio Cassese argues that it "would be not only consistent from the viewpoint of legal logic but also in keeping with new trends emerging in the world community" to recognize rights that directly accrue to individuals under customary international law. "[T]hey are entitled to respect for their life and limbs, and for their dignity; hence they have a right not to become a victim of war crimes, crimes against humanity, aggression, torture, terrorism."[40]

While some authors still do not even recognize human rights as individual rights in principle,[41] the thesis that human rights are only objective law (as opposed to rights) contradicts both the wording of the human rights treaties as well as their object and purpose. "If the requirement to respect human rights were solely objective law, the concept of inalienable human rights would lose its meaning."[42]

So if we assume that international human rights in principle are individual rights, and if we furthermore accept that many of them – such as the right to life and physical integrity – are considered to be customary international law, then the international legal personality (specifically the human rights personality) presupposed by them is rooted in customary law.

[40] Antonio Cassese, *International Law* (2nd ed., Oxford: Oxford University Press 2005), 145. See also Christian Tomuschat for a "personal right [of the individual] not to be subjected to genocide" (Christian Tomuschat, Individual Reparation Claims in Instances of Grave Human Rights Violations: The Position under General International Law, in: Albert Randelzhofer/Christian Tomuschat (eds), *State Responsibility and the Individual: Reparation in Instances of Grave Violations of Human Rights* (The Hague: Martinus Nijhoff 1999), 1–25 (13)).

[41] See Randelzhofer, Legal Position, 1999, 235: Only a precise interpretation could show whether a specific norm of a human rights treaty confers individual rights.

[42] Karl Doehring, *Völkerrecht* (2nd ed., Heidelberg: C. F. Müller 2004), paragraph 249 (p. 113) (translation mine). A human rights violation is not only a violation of the rights of other States or of all States (in the style of an *erga omnes* or *erga omnes partes* obligation). If that were the case, the person concerned would not even be able to exercise self-defence (*ibid.*, paragraph 248 (p. 112)).

13.5 General Principle of Law

A further legal basis to be considered for the status of the individual as a subject of international law is a general principle of law as referred to in Article 38(1)(c) of the ICJ Statute. Hersch Lauterpacht's conception went in this direction. He postulated a general principle according to which individuals are the ultimate addressees of all law: "[H]aving regard to the inherent purposes of international law, of which the individual is the ultimate unit, he is in that capacity a subject of international law."[43] According to Lauterpacht, the international legal personality of the individual has "a source independent of the will of States", without requiring an explicit or even just implied consent of the States. On this point, State practice is "essentially declaratory".[44] (Lauterpacht understood every general principle to be simultaneously a principle of natural law, see below.)

Is there in fact such a general principle of law establishing the international legal personality of the individual? General principles of law within the meaning of the ICJ Statute can only be principles which, firstly, are widespread in domestic law and, secondly, are transposable at the international level.[45] Both elements must be considered in turn.

13.5.1 The Legal Personality of the Individual in Domestic Law

In domestic law, the legal capacity of the individual was recognized first in the area of private law and later in the area of public law. Since the Enlightenment and Idealism, legal personality – as the capacity to have individual rights – has been considered a "necessary attribute of the human being as a moral person".[46] Notably Kant placed the distinction made in Roman law between things and persons on a new basis: "rational beings, by contrast, are called *persons*, because their nature already marks

[43] Hersch Lauterpacht, The Subjects of the Law of Nations, *Law Quarterly Review* 63 (1947), 428–460, repr. in Elihu Lauterpacht (ed.), *International Law: Being the Collected Papers of Hersch Lauterpacht* (Cambridge: Cambridge University Press 1975), 526. On Lauterpacht, see Portmann, *Legal Personality*, 2010, 127–133.

[44] Lauterpacht, Subjects of the Law of Nations, 1947/1975, 532–533.

[45] See Alain Pellet, Article 38, in: Andreas Zimmermann/Christian Tomuschat/Karin Oellers-Frahm/Christian Tams (eds), *The Statute of the International Court of Justice: A Commentary* (2nd ed., Oxford: Oxford University Press 2012), 832–840, paragraphs 250–269 (esp. paragraph 254 (p. 834)).

[46] Helmut Coing, Der Rechtsbegriff der menschlichen Person und die Theorien der Menschenrechte, in: Ernst Wolff (ed.), *Beiträge zur Rechtsforschung* (Berlin/Tübingen: de Gruyter/Mohr 1950), 191–205, 201 (translation mine).

them out as ends in themselves, i.e., as something that may not be used merely as means, hence to that extent limits all arbitrary choice".[47] Consequently, "[e]very human being . . . has a legitimate claim to respect from his fellow human beings and is *in turn* bound to respect every other".[48] Not until Immanuel Kant (and John Locke) were individual rights upgraded in normative terms and in that way modernized.[49]

The Austrian Civil Code (ABGB) of 1811, which is still in force, was the first code of private law to incorporate the concept of the general legal personality of the individual, under the influence of Kant. The first sentence of § 16 ABGB is: "Every human being has rights by the fact of his birth and in the light of reason and is therefore considered as a person."[50] According to this understanding, general civil legal personality is in principle attributed to every person in the same way. The individual is a bearer of natural rights and thus a person and a subject of the law. This characteristic is essential to being human. It does not depend on the positive legal order, but it is rather its default rule.[51] As the understanding of legal personality in domestic law shows, the fact that the State sets out the rules governing legal personality (and thus also the possibility of removing them from positive law) does not interfere with the understanding of legal personality as an original, legally

[47] Immanuel Kant, *Groundwork for the Metaphysics of Morals*, edited and translated by Allen W. Wood (New Haven: Yale University Press 2002), 1–79, at 46 (orig. Immanuel Kant, *Grundlegung zur Metaphysik der Sitten* (1785), in: Wilhelm Weischedel, Werkausgabe Vol. 7 (Frankfurt a. M.: Suhrkamp), 60 [Ak 4:428]).

[48] Immanuel Kant, *The Metaphysics of Morals*, Section II, § 38, edited and translated by Mary Gregor (Cambridge: Cambridge University Press 1996), 209 [Ak 6:462] (orig. Immanuel Kant, *Metaphysik der Sitten* (1797), in: Wilhelm Weischedel, Werkausgabe Vol. 8 (Frankfurt a. M.: Suhrkamp), 600). According to Hegel, "Personality implies, in general, a capacity to possess rights, and constitutes the conception and abstract basis of abstract right. This right, being abstract, must be formal also. Its mandate is: Be a person and respect others as persons" (Georg Wilhelm Friedrich Hegel, *Philosophy of Right*, translated by Samuel Walter Dyde (Kitchener ON: Batoche Books 2001), 53, § 36 (1) (orig. Georg Wilhelm Friedrich Hegel, *Grundlinien der Philosophie des Rechts* (Hamburg: Felix Meiner Verlag 1995), § 36 (52)).

[49] See also Chapter 17, p. 529.

[50] Allgemeines Bürgerliches Gesetzbuch of 1 June 1811, in force since 1 January 1812 (translation mine).

[51] On Kant's influence on the implementation of his doctrines in the practice of Austrian private law by the Viennese natural law teacher Franz A. Edler von Zeiller (1753–1828), see Hermann Conrad, *Individuum und Gemeinschaft in der Privatrechtsordnung des 18. und beginnenden 19. Jahrhunderts* (Karlsruhe: C. F. Müller 1956), 21–28.

relevant characteristic belonging to human beings and thus to some extent independent of the State.

The later development in domestic *public* law is especially interesting due to its parallels with the international legal discussion. In German late constitutionalism, critics found that there could be no legal personality of the individual in public law and no individual public rights because there could be no rights against the State, or in other words, all rights necessarily had to be granted by the State itself. Georg Jellinek countered this objection by deriving individual public rights separately from the "voluntary" self-commitment of the State.[52] Also at the domestic level, the self-binding of public authority in the form of law was (and is) seen as the essence of the rule of law, and only then can one speak of "rights". Accordingly, the fact of the (mere) self-commitment of the State is no longer used in contemporary domestic law as an objection to the existence of individual (public) rights.

At this point in the discussion, we have to assure ourselves that the concept of individual rights asserted against the bearers of public authority does not arise merely from a single domestic legal tradition. In order to be considered a general principle of law, individual legal personality would have to be "recognized by civilized nations" (according to the wording of Article 38(1)(c) of the ICJ Statute). In contrast to the probably universal recognition of the legal personality of individuals in private law (i.e., in relation to legal transactions among private individuals),[53] the

[52] See Georg Jellinek, *System der subjektiven öffentlichen Rechte* (2nd ed., Tübingen: Mohr 1905), 85–86. See also Johannes Masing, *Die Mobilisierung des Bürgers für die Durchsetzung des Rechts: Europäische Impulse für eine Revision der Lehre vom subjektiv-öffentlichen Recht* (Berlin: Duncker & Humblot 1997), 63.

[53] For instance in Europe: Article 1 of the German BGB; Article 1 of the Italian Codice Civile; § 16 of the Austrian ABGB; Articles 29–34 of the Spanish Código Civil; Article 17 of the Civil Code of the Russian Federation, as of 23 December 2003. In Asia: General Principles of the Civil Law of the People's Republic of China (adopted at the Fourth Session of the Sixth National People's Congress, promulgated by Order No. 37 of the President of the People's Republic of China on 12 April 1986, and effective as of 1 January 1987), Chapter II Citizen (Natural Person), Section I: Capacity for Civil Rights and Capacity for Civil Conduct; Article 3 of the Japanese Civil Code Act No. 89 of 1896. In Latin America: Article 1 of the Brazilian Civil Code, Law No. 10.406 of 10 January 2002; Article 74 of the Chilean Civil Code. In North America: Civil Code of Québec, Book One: Persons; Title One: Enjoyment and Exercise of Civil Rights. In Africa: Zatu an VII 13 du 16 novembre 1989 portant institution et application d'un code des personnes et de la famille au Burkina Faso, Première partie: Des personnes, Titre I: Des personnes physiques, Chapitre I: De la jouissance des droits civils, Articles 1–7. Common law systems do not have legislative provisions governing legal capacity, but legal capacity is established by case law.

idea of rights of the individual against the State is less widespread. According to the traditional French view of the law, for instance, individuals are expected to enforce objective public law (not the individuals' own rights) before administrative courts, acting as guardians of legality. Not coincidentally, a French writer, Michel Villey, refers to individual rights as a "barbaric and confused notion".[54] It is doubtful whether individual *public* rights are recognized in other non-European legal cultures. While virtually all constitutions in the world at least pay lip service to human rights, "ordinary" rights going beyond this that might be asserted against the State and its institutions are likely mostly unknown. On the other hand, it should be considered that especially those legal orders with Anglo-Saxon roots do not distinguish strictly between private law and public law. With these considerations in mind, a universally shared legal view on the foundation of those aspects of the legal personality of individuals which are by continental European legal orders categorized as "private" legal personality might suffice as a generalizable recognition of the legal personality of individuals. In any event, this legal personality has been considered a necessary consequence of the autonomy of the human being since the Enlightenment. The specification of that legal personality in laws of the State is merely declaratory. The acceptance of this basic idea is possibly more important than the specific recognition or specification of individual *public* rights in the legal orders of the world.

13.5.2 Transposability to International Law

The second element of a general principle of law within the meaning of Article 38(1)(c) of the ICJ Statute, namely transposability of the justification of the legal personality of the individual under domestic private and public law to international law, causes more difficulties. Does the ultimately meta-legal conception outlined above fit into international law, or would it be alien to the system? Would not the recognition of a "natural" international legal personality of the individual transform the international legal order into a quasi-domestic system and thus obliterate it? Along these lines, Hans Kelsen remarked in relation to individual complaints:

> "If the individual State no longer stands exclusively between the individual and the international community, i.e., if the international

[54] Michel Villey, *La formation de la pensée juridique moderne: Cours d'histoire de la philosophie du droit* (Paris: Ed. Montchrestien 1975), 236.

community with its specific bodies is available directly to the individual and even against the individual's 'own' State, or if the individual State in some cases can act against its own subjects only with authorization from an international court, then the international legal order – i.e., the international legal order constituting this special international community – no longer differs significantly from the legal order of individual States in a technical legal sense."[55]

Joe Verhoeven claims that the recognition of an "active" international legal personality for individuals would mean that international relations would have to be reconstrued as a quasi-federal scheme, "which is the exact opposite of what contemporary international law is like".[56]

These views have a kernel of truth. Recognition of the original international legal personality of the individual is indeed accompanied by a transformation of the international legal order, and this entails a structural convergence of international law with domestic law. However, it is a different question as to how such an evolution should be evaluated and what consequences it has for the effectiveness of the international legal system as a whole. The convergence of international and domestic law in terms of content and structure is in no way a novel phenomenon. In times of globalization, it is referred to with the catchphrase "world internal law"[57] – which is already a platitude. The convergence and interplay of the levels of the law can strengthen rather than hinder the functioning of international law. Instead of a sweeping demonization of an international legal order that is becoming "too similar to a State", the focus must be on an actual appraisal of the structural characteristics of international law that might stand in the way of transposing the concept of individual legal personality.

Two factors are at the forefront. Firstly, international law deals with seven billion people and thus with a quantity that is difficult for the law to manage. It is conceivable that international law is no longer able to fulfil its coordinating role, given the sheer number of rights holders. Secondly, the addressees ("obligors") of international rights differ from the addressees of rights rooted in domestic law. Possible addressees of international rights include the home States, other States, international organizations,

[55] Hans Kelsen, Die Technik des Völkerrechts und die Organisation des Friedens, *Zeitschrift für öffentliches Recht* 14 (1934), 240–255 (253) (translation mine).

[56] Verhoeven, *Droit International Public*, 2000, 296 (translation by the author).

[57] Jost Delbrück, Prospects for a "World (Internal) Law"? Legal Developments in a Changing International System, *Indiana Journal of Global Legal Studies* 9 (2002), 401–431.

and non-State transnational actors. If the addressees are not sufficiently clear, this would hinder the transposability of the principle of individual legal personality, because rights make little sense without (at least potentially identifiable) bearers of the corresponding obligations.

These two structural differences between international law and internal law do not necessarily mean, however, that the concept of the inherent legal personality of the individual is inapplicable at the level of international law. The first factor, namely the sheer number of potential rights holders, is manageable, because the structural principle of subsidiarity assigns the responsibility for application and implementation of international individual rights to the "lower level", namely the nation-States. The second structural characteristic, namely the diversity of obligors, likewise does not pose insurmountable difficulties. The addressees of international individual rights are identifiable (for details, see Chapter 15).

With regard to transposability, the effects of the legal institution of individual legal personality are maybe less important than the comparability of the problem to which a solution has been found in domestic law. The institution of legal personality is a legal instrument used to ascribe rights and duties to an actor, in this case an individual. The ascription in turn has the purpose of protecting individuals and holding them responsible. Satisfying this purpose is relevant also to international law, due to the many ways in which international law affects individuals.

The rationale of the idea of the inherent legal personality of the individual is a strong argument in favour of transposing it to international law. Both in domestic law and in international law, a prime rationale is to emancipate the human being.[58] At an early development stage at the domestic level, opponents or sceptics regarding the rights of individuals against the State and its institutions claimed that paternalistic protection of the individual through objective law (without the conferral of rights) was sufficient. At the beginning of the twentieth century, Otto Mayer wrote that one should not assume "that individual rights play the same dominant role in administration as they do in private legal transactions. . . . Administrative law can also be exclusively in the service of objective law, maintenance of the legal order, and thus indirectly serve the interests protected by that legal order, which do not necessarily have the specific form of individual rights".[59] Similarly, writers such as Rainer

[58] For international law, see IACtHR, *Juridical Status and Human Rights of the Child* (n. 18), paragraph 15. See for further rationales of rights below pp. 536–41.

[59] Otto Mayer, *Deutsches Verwaltungsrecht*, Vol. 1, 3rd ed., 1924 (repr. Berlin: Duncker & Humblot 2004), 132 (translation mine).

Wahl continue to deny the existence of international individual rights entirely. According to Wahl, the individual "is *not himself or herself a rights holder* at the third level [i.e., the level of international law] and not a potential claimant; instead, the individual's interests and rights are represented at the international level by the State as the trustee of those rights and at the same time as the obligor of the individual in the basic relations governed by constitutional law".[60] According to that view (refuted in this study), "[t]he asymmetry of objective international legal rules, which benefit individuals but fail to grant them legal subjectivity and standing as claimants, . . . is not a structural deficit or a faulty design". The status of the individual is said to be "a composite legal position corresponding to the complementary relationship of international law and constitutional law".[61] International lawyers who argue today in the same vein as the individual rights sceptics in pre-constitutional domestic public law did are ignoring a surge in constitutionalism that encompasses the entire multi-level system of law in a globalized world. Mayer's model of the individual as an object of the State's administration appears paternalistic to us from today's perspective. A new edition of this model in international law should likewise be considered obsolete.

Doubts remain in current international law regarding the initial question of whether a general principle of law gives rise to individual legal personality that is independent of the State. These doubts are mitigated by the insight that at least with respect to private legal transactions numerous domestic legal orders recognize an inherent legal personality of the individual. Individual public rights (i.e., rights against the State) exist in the form of human rights guarantees with constitutional rank in a majority of States. The transposability of this basic idea to international law, which is also concerned with rights against States (and other subjects of international law), is not defeated by the structural differences between domestic law and international law. The rationale of emancipating the human being from the guardianship of the State is an argument in favour of transposing the concept of the inherent legal personality of the individual; it thus also is an argument in favour of the existence of a general principle of law according to which individuals are *original* or *a priori* subjects of international law.

[60] Rainer Wahl, Der Einzelne in der Welt jenseits des Staates, in: Wahl/Joachim Wieland (eds), *Das Recht des Menschen in der Welt: Kolloquium aus Anlass des 70. Geburtstags von Ernst-Wolfgang Böckenförde* (Berlin: Duncker & Humblot 2002), 59–109 (64; translation and italics mine).

[61] *Ibid.*, 72 (translation mine).

13.6 Natural Law

Ultimately, the independence of the individual's international legal personality from the State requires recourse to a basic principle that precedes the State. Hersch Lauterpacht was not alone in associating the general principles of law discussed above with natural law. According to ICJ Judge Tanaka, "in Article 38, paragraph 1 (c), some natural law elements are inherent".[62] This view is supported by the *travaux préparatoires* of the Statute of the Permanent Court of International Justice (which was later taken over by the ICJ). During the negotiations on the PCIJ Statute, the first formulation proposed by Baron Descamps was: "the rules of international law as recognized by the *legal conscience* of civilized nations".[63] This formulation was criticized by the other members of the advisory committee, however, because it relied too heavily on "subjective conceptions of the principle of justice" and thus expanded the jurisdiction of the planned PCIJ too broadly.[64] Descamps then specified that the source of law was "the *fundamental law of justice and injustice* deeply engraved on the *heart of every human being* and which is given its highest and most authoritative expression in the legal conscience of civilized nations".[65] The later, slight modification of the formulation, which omitted the explicit reference to "legal conscience" in favour of the "general principles of law recognized by civilized nations" changes nothing about the fact that human intuition formed the basis for the understanding of the general principles of law at the time, i.e., an understanding rooted in natural law.

Daillier and Pellet assume a basis in natural law for the international legal personality of the individual. The authors distinguish between treaty-based rights of the individual and rights and duties arising from customary international law (*directement en vertu du droit international*). These latter rights and duties can be found in human rights and international humanitarian law and are considered *jus cogens*. In this area,

[62] ICJ, *South West Africa Cases* (Ethiopia/South Africa; Liberia/South Africa), Second Phase, Judgment, ICJ Reports (1966), 6–505, Dissenting Opinion of Judge Tanaka, 250–324 (298).

[63] PCIJ, *Advisory Committee of Jurists*, Procès-Verbaux of the Proceedings of the Committee (16 June—24 July 2010) with annexes (The Hague: van Langenhuisen Brothers 1920), 306 (italics mine).

[64] See, especially, the US representative Root (*ibid.*, 307–310, quote on p. 309). See also Pellet, Article 38, Statute of the International Court of Justice 2012, 731 et seq., paragraph 251 (pp. 832–833).

[65] PCIJ, *Advisory Committee of Jurists* (n. 63), 310–311 (italics mine).

Daillier and Pellet claim the following: Even if these rights and duties were originally conferred upon individuals by States, their existence subsequently no longer depends on how States expressed their will at the time when the norm was created. These norms can continue to be asserted against the State without the State confirming its consent. Any refusal to grant explicit consent could then be deemed "ineffective" (*inefficace*).[66] According to Daillier and Pellet, these (few) mandatory provisions in the field of human rights and international humanitarian law form the basis for the natural law of the international legal personality of the individual:

> "Essentially designed to protect the dignity of the human person, who benefits from the principle of universal equality of this dignity, they [these guarantees] are surely not very numerous, but they constitute a sufficient basis for the recognition of *a 'natural' right* of individuals, of natural persons, *to an international legal personality*."[67]

Such a justification of the international legal personality of the individual solely in terms of natural law does not necessarily appear to satisfy the standards of a scientific theory. However, the justification of human rights does not stand on much more solid ground. This justification is also difficult philosophically and often ends up being tantamount to a trivial form of natural law. For human rights, perhaps we have to satisfy ourselves by referring to empirical evidence of a universal consensus of values in this regard. There may be an anthropologically "justifiable" minimum standard that can be derived empirically and *ex post* from an analysis of universal value judgments. This minimum standard would not be defined *a priori* but would rely on observations and could therefore be mutable. Referring back to value judgments instead of factual needs avoids a naturalistic fallacy.[68] Such a justification would be intersubjectively understandable and thus methodologically sound.[69] An empirical value consensus of this kind is also evolving in regard to the international legal personality of the individual.

[66] Daillier/Pellet, *Droit International Public*, 2002, 650: "invocables et opposables aux États sans qu'il soit nécessaire de s'assurer de leur consentement préalable, éventuellement même en rendant inefficace leur refus de donner un consentement explicite."

[67] *Ibid.*, 650 (translation and italics by the author).

[68] For a "dynamization of natural law", i.e., for a trial-and-error examination whether norms are deemed fundamental and universal, see Arnold Angenendt, *Toleranz und Gewalt* (Münster: Aschendorff 2008), 127.

[69] See Wolfgang M. Schröder, Natur- und Vernunftrecht, in: Arndt Pollmann/Georg Lohmann (eds), *Menschenrechte: Ein interdisziplinäres Handbuch* (Stuttgart: Metzler 2012), 179–185 (184) on the adequacy of respecting the basic conditions of existence and development of human beings. Respecting those basic conditions as

The general principles of law within the meaning of Article 38(1)(c) of the ICJ Statute may have the content of natural law, but the elements must necessarily have been juridified (formalized) in order to be considered international law.[70] As discussed above, this formalization occurred by recognizing the legal personality of the individual in domestic law. The original legal personality of the individual thus appears to be a kind of positivized natural law.

13.7 Human Right

Another legal basis of the international legal subjectivity of the individual can be found in the human right to legal personality. This justification in terms of human rights cuts across the traditional legal sources.[71] According to Article 6 of the Universal Declaration of Human Rights and Article 16 of the ICCPR, everyone has "the right to recognition *everywhere* as a person before the law".[72] These codifications are the historical response to the practice of totalitarian regimes to deny all rights to their political opponents ("civil death"). According to the original intent of the drafters, these provisions thus referred to the level of the nation-State, as a guarantee of legal personality in national law, especially civil law. The worldwide incorporation of the legal personality of natural persons in national legal orders and the non-derogability of these human rights even in times of public emergency under Article 4(2) of the ICCPR indicate that the right to legal personality is considered both customary international law and a general principle of law, at least within the traditional scope of application (i.e., within domestic law).

The wording "everywhere" permits a more expansive and dynamic interpretation of these texts. A teleological argument can be made that the guarantee would be devalued in times of globalization and of amalgamation of the domestic and international legal spheres if legal personality continued to be limited to domestic law. In light of the fact that international law has a substantial impact on human life, the lack of international legal status would affect individuals in a similar way as the

individual human rights is "adequate", "if one takes oneself and others seriously as human beings" (translation mine).

[70] See Pellet, Article 38, *Statute of the International Court of Justice*, 2012, n. 257 (p. 835).

[71] A human right may be positivized in the form of treaty law, customary international law, or a general principle of law.

[72] Article 6 of the Universal Declaration of Human Rights and Article 16 of the ICCPR (italics mine).

lack of domestic legal status formerly affected slaves and outlaws. The more that international law regulates the conduct of individuals, the more important become individual rights and duties relevant to international law.

For this reason, the human rights provisions mentioned above should be interpreted dynamically in such a way that they are not limited to the level of domestic law but also guarantee international legal personality. The historical focus on legal capacity under civil law does not speak against an internationalized interpretation, given that international law is neither civil law nor public law. According to this interpretation, Article 6 of the Universal Declaration of Human Rights and Article 16 of the ICCPR guarantee a human right to recognition as a person before international law.

This would mean that the international legal personality of individuals would no longer be deducible only from the rights recognized in various treaties as their implicit precondition, but rather it would be considered a human right itself. As a human right, the right to legal personality is ascribed to individuals in virtue of their humanity. The philosophical justification of this can remain open. If the legal personality of the individual is an expression of a human right, it is not limited in terms of content. However, no specific rights or duties arise from legal capacity anyway, since it is a potential only.[73] Because international legal personality does not imply any fixed inventory of rights, the label "comprehensive" does not fit in regard to either individuals or States.

13.8 Conclusion

There are good reasons to assume that the individual is now the natural person of international law. Only independence of the individual's international legal personality from the State offers a stable basis for this legal status of the individual. We have seen that all three sources of law referred to in Article 38(1) of the ICJ Statute may serve as a legal foundation for international legal personality. In light of this, the fabric of individual entitlements woven together out of treaty law and customary international law is becoming increasingly dense. This means the recognition of individual legal personality contained therein is increasingly becoming the normal case. In sum, the accumulation of international individual rights and duties as well as the teleologically interpreted

[73] See Chapter 3, pp. 35–36 and 41.

human right to be recognized as a person before the law is placing the international legal personality of individuals on a new legal basis.

While the first two sources of the triad set out in Article 38 of the ICJ Statute (treaty and customary law) appear largely independent of the State at first glance, it has been shown (at pp. 417–18) that international legal personality rooted in treaty law cannot be reversed without difficulties, given legal impediments to rollback and the political mechanism of precommitment. Overall, however, the treaty basis of international legal personality should be viewed critically, especially because it strangely implies that the individuals stand "outside" the intergovernmental treaty, which does not do justice to the fundamental democratic idea that citizens legitimize and constitute the State. Customary law as a basis of the international legal personality of the individual is likewise not independent of the State, because this legal basis is also primarily created by States and can in theory be abandoned by contrary State practice and changes to the *opinio juris* of States. Such a reversal is unlikely, however, especially given that according to the more modern view, the practice and *opinio juris* of non-State actors also shape the creation of customary law.[74] In the end, however, only recourse to general principles of law and to natural law – which is closely related to that source of law – allows the international legal personality of the individual to be established independently of the State. At the same time, this basis avoids the problematic private law analogy of the "agreement for the benefit of a third party".

Generally speaking, referring only to the "derivative" international legal status of the individual is not very helpful anyway. The dichotomy between "original" international legal subjects (the State) and "derivative" international legal subjects (all others) is based on a legal fiction. The supposed originality and non-derivative nature of States is not based on historical facts, but rather on an idealization of the institution and definitional fiat. This is paralleled by the view that being "non-derivative" is a key element of sovereignty and thus is reserved to States.[75] This

[74] See Chapter 17, p. 547.

[75] See Georg Jellinek, *Allgemeine Staatslehre* (3rd ed., Berlin: Verlag von O. Häring 1914), 489: "But the power of the State is sovereignty that is *not further derivable*, sovereignty exercised of one's own power and therefore in one's own right" (translation mine). *Ibid.*, 180: "[The State] is the only association that governs in virtue of its inherent, original power *not derived from any other power*" (translation and italics mine). See also Roman Herzog, *Allgemeine Staatslehre* (Frankfurt a. M.: Athenaeum 1971), 88: "[W]ith the attempt to demarcate the power of the State from the power of all other legal persons

terminology ignores that most actually existing States were "created" historically by peace treaties, secession, or the process of decolonization, i.e., by acts of international law, and were never entities "given" by nature. On the other hand, international organizations created by treaties and therefore considered derivative can in turn generate international law. Historically speaking, States – which had risen to the status of international legal subjects – monopolized the creation of international law during its "classical" period. And even today, they are the most important "creator-subjects".[76] But international organizations, other civil society actors, and even businesses now participate in the transnational creation of law (see Chapter 3, p. 54 and Chapter 17, pp. 544–51). States and intergovernmental organizations, as well as to some extent non-State actors, are therefore both products and producers of international law. According to this empirical view, several different categories of actors, not only States, are likewise "primary" subjects of international law.[77]

The difference between legal personality of the individual that is solely rooted in treaty law and the view advocated in this study – namely of legal subjectivity rooted in human rights, customary law, and general principles of law – has practical consequences. The legal basis determines the scope of legal personality. Legal personality deduced from rights and duties set out in treaties is per se only partial, because it relates only to the selective rights (and duties) recognized by the treaties. In contrast, international legal personality rooted in customary law, general principles of law, and human rights is not merely selective, but rather is a potential that is unlimited *a priori*. It is a separate question as to which rights will fulfil that potential.[78]

But does the international legal personality of the individual propagated here – independent of the State – simply pull itself up by its own bootstraps, obtaining new international individual rights surreptitiously?

under public law, the idea that sovereignty should be equated with the non-derivative nature of all State power gained substantial importance" (translation mine).

76 Anthony D'Amato, *International Law: Process and Prospect* (Irvington NY: Transnational Publishers 1995), 148.

77 See Simone Gorski, Individuals in International Law, in: Rüdiger Wolfrum (ed.), *The Max Planck Encyclopedia of Public International Law* (Oxford: Oxford University Press 2012), paragraph 53: "[I]ndividuals have fewer rights and duties compared to States as the traditional subjects of international law . . . The difference, however, is one of degree and is subject to further change."

78 See ICJ, *Reparation for Injuries Suffered in the Service of the United Nations* (n. 22), 178: "The subjects of law in any legal system are not necessarily identical . . . in the extent of their rights."

This is not the case, precisely because the analytic separation of legal personality and the inventory of rights breaks the cycle often found in the literature (deriving rights from the status as a subject, which in turn is derived from rights).

Finally, the assessment of the dependence of the individual's international legal status on the consensus of States is linked to the observer's view of the structure of the international legal order. The answer to the question of the legal basis of the international legal personality of the individual thus depends on the basic convictions of the observer regarding the manifestations ("sources") of international law. Under the premise that there is no super-positive international law and that all positive norms of international law – including metanorms such as international legal personality – can be created only by States, dependence on the State is inescapable. As long as positive international law is not generated by "direct" democratic procedures without mediation by the States, and as long as natural law is not an option, then international law is subject to ultimate control by the States.

A basis for the international legal personality of the individual that is independent of States is only conceivable if international law not created by States is deemed possible in the first place. Roland Portmann argues along these lines as follows:

> "[A]t least *some fundamental legal principles precede the existence of states* as international persons. With the acceptance of legal principles as sources of international law existing independently of expressions of state will, the circularity in international law between norms and legal persons is interjected. The starting-point is then not anymore an original international person enjoying absolute powers, but rather a set of legal principles endowing states and other entities with specific capacities in international law, including that of creating the law."[79]

Portmann thus assumes legal principles that precede States, but he does not indicate from where these principles might come. I have defended the view that moral philosophical considerations have led to a "juridified" natural law of the legal personality of the individual. The possibility and reality of international law not generated by States (which is also affirmed in this study) will be discussed at the end.[80]

The international legal personality of the individual continues to rely in many ways on acceptance by States. States are indispensable as enforcers of the international rights and duties of individuals. They are

[79] Portmann, *Legal Personality*, 2010, 275. [80] See Chapter 17, pp. 544–51.

essential not only as providers of domestic jurisdiction, which individuals may invoke to assert their international rights, but also as masters of the international enforcement mechanisms. When a State withdraws its subjection to the jurisdiction of an international monitoring body, individuals lose their protection again in that regard. But because of its emancipatory potential, a "right to rights" independent of the State – alongside the classical "right to rights" in Hannah Arendt's sense, namely citizenship itself[81] – is fundamental to an up-to-date international legal order.

[81] Hannah Arendt, *The Origins of Totalitarianism* (New York: Harcourt, Brace and Company 1951), 287–298, esp. 294.

14

Human Rights and Other Rights

14.1 Two Groups of International Individual Rights

The rights and obligations identified in the preceding chapters that are not human rights will be referred to as "ordinary" or "simple" international rights and obligations. The umbrella term of international individual rights thus includes *two groups of rights*: human rights and ordinary (simple) international individual rights. Human rights, in this sense, are a specific subgroup of international individual rights: "[L]es droits de l'homme constituent une catégorie spécifique *ratione materiae* de droits individuels."[1] The "simple" international individual rights are the other subgroup.[2] In addition to rights, international individual obligations also exist, but these cannot be usefully distinguished as "basic obligations" and other "ordinary" obligations (Chapter 4, pp. 110–13).

In my view, it is possible and advisable to compare the international legal order on this point (the legal status of the individual), which is meanwhile highly refined, with the legal orders of constitutional States. The latter typically set out fundamental rights (human rights), often in constitutions. But in addition to these fundamental rights, domestic legal orders also recognize other, simple individual rights vis-à-vis the organs of the State. These rights are often set out in administrative law: rights to issuance of economic authorizations and licences; rights to protection from neighbours, data protection, or access to documents; rights to issuance of a residence permit; rights to social services; and so on. These individual public rights under domestic administrative law are sometimes designed as strict rights, and sometimes as rights to proper exercise of discretion. Simple rights are more or less always directly set

[1] Christian Dominicé, Droits individuels et droits de l'homme, in: Marcelo Kohen (ed.), *Mélanges en l'honneur de Vera Gowlland* (Leiden and Boston: Martinus Nijhoff 2010), 287–292 (290).

[2] See for this terminology also Emmanuel Roucounas, Facteurs privés et droit international public, *Recueil des Cours: Collected Courses of The Hague Academy of International Law* 299 (2002), 9–419 (46, paragraph 42): "droits individuels ('subjectifs') ou simples."

against the backdrop of the constitutionally guaranteed fundamental rights of the individual: fundamental rights to economic freedom and exercise of one's profession, the right to a private life and information, to a life with dignity or to subsistence, to protection from discrimination, and so on. In that sense, administrative law spells out, specifies, and makes concrete constitutional law. Individual public rights in domestic legal orders thus are rooted in fundamental rights, but they are not themselves fundamental rights; all the while many serve to give expression and further detail to fundamental rights.

This study is based on the assumption that within the domain of international law, a constitution-like layer of norms has begun to crystallize and is being further developed. We refer to this as a process of constitutionalization of international law. International constitutional law includes the structural norms that define membership in the constitutional community, provisions on institutions and their powers, provisions governing the creation of law and conflict resolution, as well as substantive guidelines and principles embodying values. Human rights belong to the layer of international constitutional law. The simple individual rights do not belong to this layer, but rather (figuratively) to the layer of ordinary international law "below" that layer. This distinction between two layers of norms in international law, namely international constitutional law on the one hand (including international human rights) and ordinary international law on the other hand (including ordinary or simple individual rights), is still only rudimentary. So far, there are hardly any special law-making processes guaranteeing that international constitutional law would be more difficult to amend, thus implementing a hierarchy of norms within international law.

Another phenomenon not discussed here is the modification of numerous principles, institutions, and procedures of international law by human rights.[3] International law is increasingly interpreted by international and domestic bodies in conformity with human rights, or has been harmonized with human rights through formal revisions (changes to treaties, new customary law). This so-called humanization concerns

[3] See Bruno Simma, Der Einfluss der Menschenrechte auf das Völkerrecht: Ein Entwurf, in: Isabelle Buffard et al. (eds), *International Law between Universalism and Fragmentation: Festschrift in Honour of Gerhard Hafner* (Leiden and Boston: Martinus Nijhoff 2008), 729–745; Menno T. Kamminga/Martin Scheinin (eds), *The Impact of Human Rights Law on General International Law* (Oxford: Oxford University Press 2009); Erika de Wet/Jure Vidmar (eds), *Hierarchy in International Law: The Place of Human Rights* (Oxford: Oxford University Press 2012).

both the substantive commands and prohibitions of international law as well as the norms governing the creation, application, and enforcement of other international legal norms (secondary norms as referred to by Herbert Hart). In the final report of the International Law Association on the impact of human rights on general international law, Menno Kamminga mentions the following areas: the structure of international obligations (*erga omnes* obligations, *jus cogens*), the formation of customary international law, treaty law (interpretation, reservations, and State succession in treaties), the relationship between international law and domestic law, immunity, diplomatic protection and the right to consular notification, and finally State responsibility (attribution, positive obligations, and State crimes).[4] Modifications by human rights also are evidenced in numerous specialized areas of international law: the law of armed conflict and international criminal law, refugee law, labour law, deportation law, world trade law, and investment protection law. This structural evolution, which often leads to substantive convergence and reciprocal enrichment between these specialized areas and the protection of international human rights, is not affected by the idea of international individual rights. It is possible and useful to differentiate between human rights and other international individual rights, as the following discussion will show.

14.2 Possibility of a Distinction

According to which criteria can simple international individual rights be differentiated from human rights? Only little inspiration can be drawn from the historical debates on the human rights quality of social and economic rights and third-generation rights (rights to a clean environment, peace, and development). At the time, sceptics were concerned about making a distinction between these norms and civil and political rights.[5] Unlike the old discussion about second- and third-generation rights, the conceptualization of simple individual rights is not primarily

[4] See Menno T. Kamminga, Final Report on the Impact of International Human Rights Law on General International Law, in: Kamminga/Martin Scheinin (eds), *The Impact of Human Rights Law on General International Law* (Oxford: Oxford University Press 2009), 1–23.

[5] See, e.g., Jerome J. Shestak, The Jurisprudence of Human Rights, in: Theodor Meron (ed.), *Human Rights in International Law: Legal and Policy Issues* (Oxford: Clarendon 1984), 89–113 (74–75): "Which rights are human rights?"; Maurice Cranston, Human Rights, Real and Supposed, in: D. D. Raphael (ed.), *Political Theory and the Rights of Man* (London: Macmillan 1967), 43–54.

about whether certain legal content must be sufficiently determined or determinable in order to be justiciable.

A *formal approach* would be to define human rights only as those rights which officially are called human rights and are included in human rights conventions.[6] Another, likewise formal approach would be to rely on a universal consensus about a new human right in the form of a General Assembly resolution.[7] Such a purely formal qualification is not convincing, however. For instance, Article 24 of the Universal Declaration of Human Rights states: "Everyone has the right to rest and leisure, including reasonable limitation of working hours and periodic holidays with pay." Despite codification in the Declaration, the right proclaimed here is not, according to the prevailing view, a human right. The same goes for the "right to science", as stated in Article 15 ICESCR.[8]

Human rights must therefore be defined primarily using a *substantive* criterion, and at most secondarily using the formal criterion of general recognition, and thus be distinguished from simple rights. Only rights that are universally recognized and also exhibit certain characteristics can be human rights.[9] According to Christian Dominicé, human rights are distinguished from other international individual rights in view of their object ("objet") and purpose ("finalité").[10] Purpose is closely related to rationale. If purpose were decisive, the differentiation between human rights and other international individual rights would depend on the (normative) justification given to human rights. Rights that are justifiable in the terms preferred by the examiner would then be human rights. If, for instance, one derives human rights from the concept of "normative agency", as James Griffin does, one can only consider rights to be (moral) human rights if they arise from human agency and make such agency

6 See, e.g., Philip Alston, Core Labour Standards and the Transformation of the International Labour Rights Regime, *European Journal of International Law* 15 (2004), 457–521 (476): "In international law terms a right is a human right if it has been recognized by the United Nations in instruments such as the Universal Declaration of Human Rights."

7 See Philip Alston, Conjuring Up New Human Rights: A Proposal for Quality Control, *American Journal of International Law* 78 (1984), 607–621.

8 Article 15 ICESCR mentions "the right of everyone . . . to enjoy the benefits of scientific progress and its applications", as does Article 27 UDHR. But see for the qualification as a human right Mikel Mancisidor, Is There Such Thing as a Human Right to Science in International Law?, *ESIL Reflections* 4, issue 1 (4 April 2015).

9 See Sinai Deutch, Are Consumer Rights Human Rights?, *Osgoode Hall Law Journal* 32 (1994), 537–578 (549) with other references.

10 Dominicé, Droits individuels, 2010, 291.

possible in turn.[11] Because the justification of human rights depends on philosophical and ideological preconditions, there is no consensus in this regard beyond platitudes. It is therefore frequently recommended to do without a philosophical justification and to rely solely on "evidence".[12] This means the purpose of the rights is only of limited use for the classification of individual rights, but it still is a relevant factor.

Human rights (in contrast to simple rights) are intended to mark especially important, fundamental interests as worthy of protection and gain recognition for them. John Rawls put this as following: "Human rights . . . express a special class of urgent rights", in his model Law of the Peoples.[13] Contemporary analysis of the law as it stands echo this: "Human rights recognize *extraordinarily* special, basic interests, and this sets them apart from rights, even moral rights, generally." "[T]alk of human rights serves the recognitional function of singling out extraordinarily important interests."[14] In the domestic constitutional law of various States, it is common to identify human rights and fundamental rights in terms of their substantive importance when the goal is to uncover unwritten fundamental rights (which often correspond to human rights at the international level). In the United States, for instance, the question arises whether certain rights must be read into the 14th Amendment (due process) as unwritten guarantees and accordingly bind the States of the Union. Here, the Supreme Court asked whether a right is "implicit in the concept of ordered liberty" or whether it belongs to the "fundamental principles of liberty and justice which lie at the base of all our civil and political institutions".[15] The Federal Supreme Court of Switzerland has likewise developed "unwritten constitutional rights" in its case law. The Court accepted as constitutional fundamental rights only those rights "which form a prerequisite for the exercise of other freedoms (mentioned in the Constitution) or otherwise serve as indispensable components of the democratic and constitutional order of the Confederation". Moreover, the "guarantee in question must [correspond] to widespread constitutional

[11] See James Griffin, *On Human Rights* (Oxford: Oxford University Press 2008), esp. at 44–45: Griffin breaks down agency into autonomy, real choices, and liberty (at 33).

[12] The US Declaration of Independence relied only on evidence in justifying human rights: "We hold these truths to be self-evident . . ."

[13] John Rawls, *The Law of Peoples* (Cambridge MA: Harvard University Press 1999), 79.

[14] William A. Edmundson, *An Introduction to Rights* (2nd ed., Cambridge: Cambridge University Press 2012), 158 (italics mine).

[15] US Supreme Court, *Palko* v. *Connecticut*, 302 US 319, 325 (1937). See also US Supreme Court, *Moore* v. *City of East Cleveland*, 431 US 494, 503 (1977): "deeply rooted in this Nation's history and tradition".

reality in the Cantons" and be "supported by a general consensus".[16] Conversely, rights that are not indispensable for freedom, democracy, and the rule of law can be said not to merit the label of a fundamental or human right with a higher normative rank.

In a call to UN bodies responsible for setting human rights standards, the UN General Assembly similarly established a substantive criterion for the development (or identification) of new human rights: Human rights are only those rights that are "of *fundamental character* and *derive from the inherent dignity and worth of the human person*".[17] Despite its softness, this criterion is in principle a plausible way to distinguish human rights from other (international) rights. The following discussion will rely on this criterion.

Such a demarcation between human rights and other rights does not constitute a barrier to the dynamic development of human rights. Because the potential threats to human dignity change, new human rights may evolve in response to a new or newly perceived need for protection from new threats or due to changing social sensibilities. Theoretically, certain human rights might also disappear if the need for protection becomes obsolete.

The following objection might be made against the recognition of simple international individual rights. If these rights (in contrast to human rights) only protect non-fundamental human interests, then it might be inappropriate to lay them down at the international level. According to this concern, less important interests should be legally protected only at the domestic level in the wide variety of different national societies, not least of all in order to respect the diversity of values. In that view, it would be neither necessary nor desirable to harmonize mundane rights and duties through international regulation. However, this objection ignores, firstly, that such regulation already exists in fact, as the overview of the various areas of the law showed earlier; and secondly, that such regulation is also legitimate in light of the principle of subsidiarity. The justifying reason for global regulation is not the importance of the subject matter, but rather the transnational nature of many problems. The right to consular access, for instance, has to be regulated at the international level, because it becomes relevant only in

[16] BGE 121 I 367, Judgment of 27 October 1995, Consideration 2 (a) on the basic right to a livelihood.

[17] General Assembly resolution 41/120, 4 December 1986, Setting international standards in the field of human rights, paragraph 4(b).

transnational circumstances per se. A purely domestic regulation of this problem would be nearly pointless.

The demarcation proposed here does not mean that human rights and ordinary or simple international rights of the individual are two strictly separate compartments in the category of international individual rights. Evidently, human rights form the basis or at least the background for most of the individual rights discussed in the preceding chapters: The potential right to compensation for violations of international humanitarian law is ultimately motivated by the human right to life and physical integrity. The right to consular access is a component of the fair trial guarantee for detained suspects and a question of due process for detainees awaiting deportation. The right of victims of crimes to participate in proceedings before the ICC, which is not a human right per se, can be seen in the context of the human right to information and the right to seek redress.[18] Rights of investors arising from investment protection agreements should be seen against the backdrop of the right to property and protection of legitimate expectations.

Some of these background guarantees, such as the right to life and a fair trial, are not only principles of objective international law, but indisputably are also internationally guaranteed human rights. In the case of other background guarantees, such as the rights to property and due process, the human rights content is controversial.

Irrespective of any relevance to human rights of the individual rights discussed in this study, it appears mistaken to qualify these rights themselves as specific human rights. Returning to the criterion established by the UN General Assembly, most rights dealt with so far do not have a fundamental character as such, but rather only an ancillary character, and are linked only indirectly – if at all – to the dignity and worth of the human person.

It thus appears possible to distinguish human rights from ordinary international individual rights, without denying possible internal relationships between the two subgroups of international individual rights, and without disputing the openness of human rights to development.

[18] See Brianne McGonigle Leyh, *Victim Participation in International Criminal Proceedings* (Cambridge: Intersentia 2011), 340: "While not an explicitly recognized human right as such, the right to participate in criminal proceedings (to receive information, to provide information, and to seek redress) is undoubtedly linked with important human rights standards."

14.3 Desirability of the Distinction: Against the Trivialization of Human Rights

The distinction between human rights and simple international individual rights is not only possible, but it also makes sense. The new category of simple international rights (and duties) counteracts the risk of trivializing and overstraining international human rights. This risk of trivialization is expressed in the 1990 novel *Immortality* by the Czech writer Milan Kundera, which conveys the experiences of a Central Eastern European immediately after the collapse of the Socialist bloc:

> "But because people in the West are not threatened by concentration camps and are free to say and write what they want, . . . the fight for human rights . . . [becomes] a kind of universal stance of everyone toward everything, a kind of energy that turns all human desires into rights. The world has become man's right and everything in it has become a right: the desire for love the right to love, the desire for rest the right to rest, the desire for friendship the right to friendship, the desire to exceed the speed limit the right to exceed the speed limit, the desire for happiness the right to happiness, the desire to publish a book the right to publish a book, the desire to shout in the street in the middle of the night the right to shout in the street."[19]

The expansion of human rights as denounced in the novel has been ongoing in real life. In some cases, the identification of a new, unwritten human right seems entirely warranted – given the importance of the interests covered. An example is the human right to water and sanitation, which has been inferred from Article 11 of the ICESCR (right to food) in conjunction with Article 12 of the ICESCR (right to health).[20]

But other rights proclamations seem exaggerated. Examples comprise the promulgation by the UNESCO's International Charter of

[19] Milan Kundera, *Immortality*, translated from the Czech by Peter Kussi (New York: Harper Perennial 1992), 140.

[20] See Committee on Economic, Social and Cultural Rights, Twenty-ninth session (2003), General Comment No. 15: The Right to Water (Arts. 11 and 12 of the Covenant); Realization of the right to drinking water and sanitation, Report of the Special Rapporteur, El Hadji Guissé, UN Doc. E/CN.4/Sub.2/2005/25 of 11 July 2005; UNESCO & Green Cross International, Fundamental Principles for a Framework Convention on the Right to Water (2005), www.watertreaty.org/convention.php: Article 2: The Human Right to Water; Article 3: The Right to a Sufficient Quantity of Water; UN Human Rights Council, resolution on Human Rights and Equitable Access to Safe Drinking Water and Sanitation, UN Doc. A/HRC/15/9 of 30 September 2010.

Physical Education and Sport, of a basic right to sport,[21] and the United Nations Population Fund's postulation of a human right to family planning.[22] It has recently been explored whether there is a right to be breastfed and therefore to human milk redistribution.[23] The World Congress of Sexology has propagated rights to comprehensive sex education and sexual pleasure, and it notes that "sexual rights are fundamental and universal human rights".[24] In the preceding chapters, I have discussed the thesis of a human right to diplomatic protection,[25] consular protection,[26] and a specific human right to humanitarian assistance in the event of a disaster.[27] These claims are either nitty-gritty or specifications of broader basic rights. They seem too specific and/or not foundational enough to warrant the human rights label in themselves. These types of claims might – upon closer examination – lend themselves to be qualified as rights below the level of human rights.

New demands concern the structure of society and features of the legal system as a whole: A human right to globalization[28] and a human right to

[21] See UNESCO, International Charter of Physical Education and Sport, of 21 November 1978, Article 1(1): "Every human being has a fundamental right of access to physical education and sport, which are essential for the development of his personality. The freedom to develop physical, intellectual and moral powers through physical education and sport must be guaranteed both within the educational system and in other aspects of social life."

[22] See UNFPA State of World Population 2012, 14 November 2012: UNFPA EN-SWP 2012_Report.pdf.

[23] Mathilde Cohen, Regulating Milk: Women and Cows in France and the United States, *American Journal of Comparative Law* 65 (2017) forthcoming.

[24] 14th World Congress of Sexology, Declaration of Sexual Rights, Hong Kong, 26 August 1999.

[25] See Pieter H. Kooijmans, Is the Right to Diplomatic Protection a Human Right?, in: *Studi di diritto internazionale in onore di Gaetano Arangio-Ruiz*, Vol. 3 (Naples: Editoriale Scientifica 2004), 1975–1984 (1984). See also Chapter 12.

[26] See Chapter 11.

[27] See Boris Jakoljevic, International Disaster Relief Law, *Israel Yearbook on Human Rights* 34 (2004), 251–286 (258): "emerging customary rule of the right to humanitarian assistance for all the victims of disasters, a right whose enjoyment depends upon certain conditions to be fulfilled". J. Benton Heath, Disasters, Relief and Neglect: The Duty to Accept Humanitarian Assistance and the Work of the International Law Commission, *New York University Journal of International Law and Policy* 43 (2011), 419–477 (440): "[R]ecent trends in human rights law indicate that the international community is coming to recognize a distinct right to request and receive humanitarian assistance." See Chapter 8.

[28] See Michael D. Pendleton, A New Human Right – The Right to Globalization, *Fordham International Law Journal* 22 (1999), 2052–2095.

a corruption-free society[29] have been claimed in the academic literature. These types of demands are probably best not couched in the rights language at all. They should be analyzed as claims for legal reform on the international and domestic level which should give rise to new policies, measures, and higher legal standards including treaties and laws, but not as specific new rights.

Other constellations are even more ambiguous. For example, it needs to be discussed whether the special relation between some indigenous peoples and their land is best described as a right. On the one hand, the label "rights" does not fully fit because the link is much more ancient and less legalized than other aspects of life, and because it exists between the land and the entire collective. On the other hand, the relationship seems connected to modern rights such as the freedom of religion, right to food, and even property.

It is not being suggested here that none of the claims mentioned earlier might have the quality of rights or even human rights. The point is rather that the inflation of supposed human rights tends to lead to their devaluation.[30] Conferring the label of a human right too generously unintentionally promotes the trivialization of the overall idea of human rights.

In contrast, awarding the quality seal of a human right only sparingly contributes to preserving the high quality of human rights. My proposal for conferring and recognizing simple individual rights addresses the problem of cementing individual legal positions. It tries to defuse the problem by "rezoning" certain individual rights positions downward. Such a downward rezoning might work against the proliferation of assertions of human rights in international discourse as reported earlier.

The capacity of simple international individual rights to reduce the burden on human rights, as already described, can be illustrated by the example of *international environmental law*. In this context, a human right to a clean environment is often asserted or demanded.[31] In positive

[29] Ndiva Kofele-Kale, The Right to a Corruption-Free Society as an Individual and Collective Human Right: Elevating Official Corruption to a Crime under International Law, *International Lawyer* 34 (2000), 149–178; Andrew Brady Spalding, Corruption, Corporations and the New Human Right, *Washington University Law Review* 91 (2014), 1365–1428.

[30] See Alain Pellet, "Human Rightism" and International Law, *Italian Yearbook of International Law* 10 (2003), 3–16. Pellet uses the term "human rightism" to define and criticize an (academic) attitude that asserts the autonomy of a discipline of human rights protection distinct from general international law.

[31] In the literature, see Malgosia Fitzmaurice/Jill Marshall, The Human Right to a Clean Environment – Phantom or Reality?, The European Court of Human Rights and English Courts Perspective on Balancing Rights in Environmental Cases, *Nordic Journal of*

law, the Protocol of San Salvador to the American Convention on Human Rights of 1989 actually stipulates that everyone shall have the right to live in a healthy environment.[32] Such a "right" would not be operational in juridical terms, however, because it is completely indeterminate, and the content and obligors are open. The better legal strategy appears to be to confer international individual *procedural rights*, such as access to environmental information, public participation in environmental decision-making, and access to justice (such as in the triad of rights under the Aarhus Convention of 1998[33]). The exercise of these procedural rights contributes to preventing environmental damage and at the same time to safeguarding individual substantive interests. Such *procedural environment rights are not themselves human rights*. They may be based on human rights to life, physical integrity, and private life, the social right to health, and perhaps the specific rights of indigenous peoples. The exercise of international procedural environmental rights equally serves to protect the public interest in the conservation of a healthy environment and to realize the participatory-democratic ideal enshrined in contemporary international law.

This example shows that the recognition of ordinary international individual rights in addition to human rights makes it possible to transcend the framework of purely State rights and duties in international law without having to designate the new legal phenomena as human rights in an inflationary way. While conversely one might discern a risk of deflation of human rights or an overly minimalist view of human rights, the recognition of ordinary international individual rights does not enhance this risk.

The conceptualization of simple rights besides or below human rights seems less complicated than establishing different categories within the body of human rights, such as "fundamental" and less fundamental human rights.[34] Ultimately, the recognition that there might be individual rights "below" the normative level of human rights just like the notion

International Law 76 (2007), 103–151; Alice Palmer, An International Right to Environment: A New Generation?, *Interights Bulletin* 15 (2006), 141–143.

32 Article 11 of the Additional Protocol to the American Convention on Human Rights in the Area of Economic, Social and Cultural Rights of 17 November 1988, entry into force on 16 November 1999 (Protocol of San Salvador), *International Legal Materials* 1989, 161.

33 Convention on Access to Information, Public Participation in Decision-Making and Access to Justice in Environmental Matters of 25 June 1998, a convention of the UNECE (UN Economic Commission for Europe), UNTS 2161, No. 447.

34 But see for a distinction between normal human rights and the most "basic" human rights which constitute the "moral minimum" Steven Ratner, *The Thin Justice of International Law* (Oxford: Oxford University Press 2015), 75–77. Ratner's "basic" human rights are

of a "subjective" international individual right can keep the door open for an additional modernization of international law and at the same time prevent the normative power of human rights from being undermined.

14.4 Consequences of the Distinction

The distinction between simple international individual rights and human rights has practical legal consequences for the weight of the rights in question, legal protection, and their design and revocability.

Special bodies (human rights committees and regional human rights courts) are available to *enforce* international human rights at the international and especially the regional level. These bodies cannot be called upon when a simple international individual right is violated. However, as mentioned earlier (p. 442), since it can often plausibly be claimed that individual rights violations occur against the backdrop of human rights infringements, the special human rights bodies will typically not decline jurisdiction from the outset.

Classification of an international individual right as a right beyond or "below" human rights reduces its weight when being balanced against countervailing concerns. For example, when the host State of an investment seeks to regulate the investor's activities for reasons of public policy (environmental law, protection of an indigenous population, labour law, or the like), the curtailment of the investor's rights will appear more admissible when they are qualified as non-human rights which weigh less than the fundamental right to property.[35]

However, this distinction is a question of degree. With regard to investments, the right to property often forms the backbone of investors' rights, and may be affected by regulation as well. Its weight will thus also enter into the balance. Inversely, and generally speaking, even human rights are not necessarily given absolute precedence over conflicting principles of international law. In the *Nada* judgment, for instance, the ECtHR strived

roughly those which are normally qualified as *jus cogens*: protection against torture, slavery, genocide, and crimes against humanity. Beyond this very small group, Ratner considers as "basic" human rights also non-discrimination, the freedom to form or not to form a family, freedom of religion, "some" freedom of political expression, self-determination, "some" type of representative government, primary education, and a safe workplace. See also, e.g., Theo van Boven, Distinguishing Criteria of Human Rights, in: Karel Vasak/Philip Alston (eds), *The International Dimension of Human Rights* (Westport CT: Greenwood Press and UNESCO: Paris 1982), 43–59.

[35] See on the qualification of investor rights as different from human rights Chapter 10, pp. 318–21.

to harmonize the right to private life under Article 8 of the ECHR with Switzerland's obligation – arising from its UN membership – to implement the Security Council resolutions on targeted sanctions, and it thereby mitigated the conflict considerably.[36]

Furthermore, the qualification of an international right as not being a human right matters with a view to countermeasures. For example, we have seen that it is not adequate to qualify investor rights as "fundamental" rights in the sense of the prohibition of countermeasures by a host State under Article 50, paragraph 1(b) of the ILC Articles on State responsibility. Investor rights are therefore not completely immune from reprisals (for detail, see Chapter 10, pp. 328–31).

Finally, ordinary international individual rights may be *modified or even revoked* by States by way of treaty provisions or customary law, as long as such a change of law does not violate any human right that might underlie the ordinary right. This can be illustrated with the example of the international *right of option*. The right of option is the right of a person affected by a change of territory to choose between the citizenship of the successor State or the predecessor State by filing a declaration, without having to emigrate for nationality purposes.[37] The backdrop to the evolution of this right consists in border shifts, such as after 1918 when territory was ceded by peace treaties concluding the First World War, after 1945 in the course of decolonization, and after 1990 due to the dissolution of the Soviet Union and Yugoslavia. The question regularly arises in this context as to what citizenship the inhabitants of a territory subject to new statehood have. The classic solution is for the new sovereign to impose its (new) citizenship on the inhabitants. By way of international treaty or domestic legislation, however, inhabitants are often given the right of option, i.e., the choice between their old citizenship and the new one.

I propose understanding the option granted by treaty law as an ordinary international individual right of the persons concerned. This terminology changes the orientation of the discussion about this topic. The traditional question, especially since the First World War, which led to a comprehensive new territorial order in Europe,

[36] ECtHR (Grand Chamber), *Nada* v. *Switzerland*, No. 10593/08, Judgment of 12 September 2012.

[37] Venice Commission, Explanatory Report on the Declaration on the Consequences of State Succession adopted at its 28th Plenary Meeting, Venice, 13–14 September 1996, paragraph 13. The choice may also be made by refusing the new citizenship which the State had granted *ex lege* (*ibid.*).

was whether there was a right of option under customary international law, i.e., whether the States involved in the territorial changes were required – even without a treaty basis – to offer their citizenship to inhabitants (within a certain time period) and conversely to release individuals from such citizenship. The predominant opinion is that, for lack of sufficient State practice, no such right of option exists under customary international law.[38] In the course of the break-up of the Soviet Union, in fact, most former Soviet republics apparently did not offer an option, but rather imposed their (new) citizenship on the inhabitants of their territory without other actors condemning that practice as a breach of international law.[39]

The insight that the right of option is not itself a human right, although it has recently been backed by the generally recognized human right of the freedom of choice of nationality,[40] opens up a new perspective: Where there is no right of option granted by treaty or legislation, the denial of the option represents a restriction of the human right to choice of nationality in the special constellation of a territorial reorganization. This restriction serves the legitimate purpose of preserving stable international relations in a reasonable way and is thus not "arbitrary" within the meaning of Article 15 of the Universal Declaration of Human Rights. This means that the existing State practice has *de facto* prevented the emergence of a right of option under customary international law, and furthermore, this normal legal situation can also be accepted as legitimate from a normative human rights perspective.

[38] See Yael Ronen, Option of Nationality, in: Rüdiger Wolfrum (ed.), *The Max Planck Encyclopedia of Public International Law* (Oxford: Oxford University Press 2012), paragraphs 11–12.

[39] In any event, the citizenship laws of Azerbaijan, Kyrgyzstan, Kazakhstan, and Tajikistan did not grant a right to option. An option was granted by the Law on Citizenship of Moldova of 2 June 2000 (Chapter I, Article 3(2)); Federal Law No. 62-FZ of 31 May 2002 on Russian Federation Citizenship (Article 13(1)); the Law of the Republic of Turkmenistan on Citizenship of 30 September 1992 (Article 49); the Law on the Citizenship of the Republic of Uzbekistan of 28 July 1992 (Article 4(1) and (2)); and the Law on the Citizenship of Ukraine of 18 January 2001 (Article 2(1)). See www.legislationline.org/topics/topic/2.

[40] This right is not set out in either the ICCPR or the ECHR, but it can be found in Article 15 of the Universal Declaration of Human Rights and more recent human rights conventions. According to Article 15 of the Universal Declaration, "(1) Everyone has the right to a nationality. (2) No one shall be arbitrarily deprived of his nationality nor denied the right to change his nationality."

14.5 Superposition of Human Rights and New Orientation of a Regime: The Example of Refugee Law

14.5.1 Definition of the Question

The phenomenon of the superposition of human rights and – it is submitted – also of simple individual rights on a regime of intergovernmental obligations can be seen in refugee law. The main treaty basis was erected in the years after the Second World War: the Geneva Convention Relating to the Status of Refugees (in the following: Refugee Convention) was concluded in 1951, and the Protocol removing the temporal limits was concluded in 1967.[41] Historically speaking, the contracting States were not primarily interested in the well-being of the individuals concerned, but rather in channelling migration flows in their own State interest. "[T]he pursuit by states of their own well-being has been the greatest factor for shaping the international legal response to refugees since World War II. Current refugee law['s] ... purpose is not specifically to meet the demands of the refugees themselves ... but rather is to govern disruptions of regulated international migration in accordance with the interests of states."[42]

A dual question now arises: Firstly, what influence does the gradual increase in importance of international human rights have on the refugee law regime? Secondly, would the recognition of separate and specific refugee rights be useful or important *alongside* human rights? James Hathaway has dedicated an entire book to the "rights which follow from the refugee status", the "essential premise" of which "is that refugees are entitled to claim the benefit of a deliberate and coherent system of rights".[43] It is less clear whether other authors assume direct international legal rights of the refugee or not. When Guy S. Goodwin-Gill and Jane McAdam state in their standard work that "[i]n our view, the Convention's first point of reference is the individual, particularly as a rights-holder, rather than the system of government and its efficacy or intent in relation to protection",[44] they apparently are referring primarily to rights under domestic law. In this section, it is

[41] Convention Relating to the Status of Refugees of 28 June 1951 and Protocol Relating to the Status of Refugees of 31 January 1967.

[42] James C. Hathaway, A Reconsideration of the Underlying Premise of Refugee Law, *Harvard International Law Journal* 31 (1990), 129–183 (133).

[43] James C. Hathaway, *The Rights of Refugees under International Law* (Cambridge: Cambridge University Press 2005), 3 and 4.

[44] Guy S. Goodwin-Gill/Jane McAdam, *The Refugee in International Law* (3rd ed., Oxford: Oxford University Press 2007), 10.

argued that refugees hold rights directly under international law. This reinforces Hathaway's argumentative intent "to affirm the importance of refugee-specific rights".[45]

14.5.2 *From State Obligations to Individual Rights*

Similar to the 1949 Geneva Conventions on the law of armed conflict (Chapter 7), the Refugee Convention is primarily formulated in the language of *State obligations*. This corresponds to the State-centred telos of the refugee regime at the time it evolved. Today, the view of authoritative commentators is that the refugee regime has taken on a different primary purpose, namely protection of the interests of refugees: "fundamental *interests* which must be protected as a matter of law, if the inherent worth and dignity of the individual in flight are to be upheld".[46] However, this objective does not necessarily imply that the Convention grants individual rights directly under international law. The most important legal consequences of refugee status continue to be State obligations under international law: "The international legal status of the refugee necessarily imports certain legal consequences, the most important one of which is the *obligation of States to respect* the principle of non-refoulement through time."[47] Accordingly, the traditional view is that the Refugee Convention and its 1967 Protocol lay down obligations between States; the refugee appears (merely) as a beneficiary.[48] According to Vincent Chétail, the Refugee Convention "is a duty-based rather than a human-rights based instrument".[49]

But the Refugee Convention puts this State-fixated interpretation in perspective: The standards laid down in the Convention are either absolute, such as access to courts (Article 16),[50] or they are defined by reference to one

[45] Hathaway, *Rights of Refugees*, 2005, 13.

[46] Goodwin-Gill/McAdam, *Refugee in International Law*, 2007, 12. [47] *Ibid.*, 1.

[48] See Guy S. Goodwin-Gill, Refugees and Their Human Rights, *Refugee Studies Centre (RCS) Working Paper* No. 17 (Oxford 2004), 6–7.

[49] Vincent Chétail, Are Refugee Rights Human Rights?, in: Ruth Rubio-Marín (ed.), *Human Rights and Immigration, Collected Courses of the Academy of European Law* (Oxford: Oxford University Press 2014), 19–72 (40).

[50] Article 16(1) states: "A refugee shall have free access to the courts of law on the territory of all Contracting States."

of three contingencies: national treatment, most favoured nation treatment,[51] or treatment as aliens generally,[52]

Whether these obligations also correspond to rights of the refugees themselves is basically left open by the wording. Several provisions in the Geneva Convention on Refugees do at least mention the "rights" of refugees.[53] However, it is not usually clear whether the rights mentioned arise directly from the Convention itself or must first be created in the domestic law of the contracting parties. For instance, Article 26 on freedom of movement states: "Each Contracting State *shall accord* to refugees lawfully in its territory *the right* to choose their place of residence to move freely within its territory, subject to any regulations applicable to aliens generally in the same circumstances." This formulation sounds like a State obligation to create a right of residence under the domestic law of the contracting party.

The provision in Article 7(3) is ambiguous: "Each Contracting State shall continue to accord to refugees the *rights* and benefits to which they were already entitled, in the absence of reciprocity, at the date of entry into force of this Convention for that State." Here, it is again in doubt whether the rights arise directly from the Convention or must first be granted by domestic legislation. Commentaries assume that the passage

[51] See, for example, Article 15, Right of Association: "As regards non-political and non-profit-making associations and trade unions the Contracting States *shall accord* to refugees lawfully staying in their territory the *most favourable treatment* accorded to *nationals* of a foreign country, in the same circumstances" (italics mine). Article 17, Wage-Earning Employment: "1. The Contracting States *shall accord* to refugees lawfully staying in their territory the *most favourable treatment* accorded to nationals of a foreign country in the same circumstances, as regards the right to engage in wage-earning employment" (italics mine).

[52] See for example Article 13, Movable and Immovable Property: "*The Contracting States* shall accord to a refugee treatment as favourable as possible and, in any event, not less favourable than that accorded to *aliens generally* in the same circumstances, as regards the acquisition of movable and immovable property and other rights pertaining thereto, and to leases and other contracts relating to movable and immovable property" (italics mine). Article 18, Self-Employment: "The Contracting States *shall accord* to a refugee lawfully in their territory treatment as favourable as possible and, in any event, not less favourable than that accorded to *aliens generally* in the same circumstances, as regards the right to engage on his own account in agriculture, industry, handicrafts and commerce and to establish commercial and industrial companies" (italics mine). Article 19, Liberal Professions: "1. Each Contracting State *shall accord* to refugees lawfully staying in their territory who hold diplomas recognized by the competent authorities of that State, and who are desirous of practicing a liberal profession, treatment as favourable as possible and, in any event, not less favourable than that accorded to *aliens generally* in the same circumstances" (italics mine).

[53] For example Article 6: "... for the enjoyment of the *right* in question ..." (italics mine).

"accord ... rights" refers to individual rights under international law, where these rights are warranted.[54]

The provision in Article 7(5) gives an important indication of the rights content of the Refugee Convention: "The provisions of paragraphs 2 and 3 apply both to the *rights and benefits referred to* in articles 13, 18, 19, 21 and 22 of this Convention and to rights and benefits for which this Convention does not provide." Interestingly, the provisions enumerated in Article 7(5) (Articles 13, 18, 19, 21, and 22) do not "refer to" any rights at all, but rather are formulated in the language of State obligations: Articles 13, 18, 19, and 21 contain most favourable treatment clauses that relate to several areas of life, such as housing. Article 22 stipulates national treatment for public education. The reference in Article 7(5) leaves open whether the State obligations of most favourable treatment and national treatment correspond to *"rights"* or only *"benefits"* of the refugees. The wording of Article 7(5) also leaves open whether the Refugee Convention itself should accord rights or whether it only refers to individual rights in domestic law.

According to the presumption rule proposed in Chapter 13, the treaty guarantees of the Refugee Convention should as a rule be interpreted as genuine international individual rights, since the wording of the Convention permits that interpretation. In fact, commentaries affirm the direct international conferral of individual rights by the Refugee Convention in regard to Article 13 (protection of property),[55] Article 15 (right of association),[56] Article 17 (wage-earning employment),[57] and Article 22 (education).[58] In regard to the other guarantees, however,

[54] See Achilles Skordas, Article 7, in: Andreas Zimmermann (ed.), *The 1951 Convention Relating to the Status of Refugees and Its 1967 Protocols* (Oxford: Oxford University Press 2011), 715–754, paragraph 68 on Article 7(3), see also paragraph 127.

[55] See Scott Leckie/Ezekiel Simperingham, Article 13, in: Andreas Zimmermann (ed.), *The 1951 Convention Relating to the Status of Refugees and Its 1967 Protocols* (Oxford: Oxford University Press 2011), 883–893, paragraph 24 ("specific rights guaranteed under the 1951 Convention").

[56] See Michael Teichmann, Article 15, in: Andreas Zimmermann (ed.), *The 1951 Convention Relating to the Status of Refugees and Its 1967 Protocols* (Oxford: Oxford University Press 2011), 909–930, paragraph 43: "The right enshrined in Art. 15 has a subjective character and can be invoked by every refugee." Goodwin-Gill/McAdam, *Refugee in International Law*, 2007, 509 mention a "right of association".

[57] See Goodwin-Gill/McAdam, *Refugee in International Law*, 2007, 509: "right to engage in wage-earning employment".

[58] Despite the change of the formulation originally proposed in the draft, "refugees shall enjoy the rights" to "the Contracting States shall accord", the commentaries indicate that these are in fact rights. See Andreas Zimmermann/Jonas Dörschner, Article 22, in: Andreas Zimmermann (ed.), *The 1951 Convention Relating to the Status of Refugees*

Goodwin-Gill and McAdams mention "rights" only in quotation marks, namely for administrative assistance (Article 25), identity papers (Article 27), transfer of assets (Article 30), and naturalization (Article 34).[59]

14.5.3 Refugee Rights and Human Rights

In view of the above, numerous guarantees of the Refugee Convention create international individual rights. These are distinct from human rights. An important difference is that refugee rights are not linked to the quality of being human. They are linked to the quality of being a refugee. This quality is of a different nature than, for example, being a person of colour, a woman, a child, or a person with disabilities, each of whom enjoys particular human rights under specific international human rights conventions. The quality as a refugee is different because it is contingent and often temporary and does not flow from a personal or human quality (as one's sex or age) but from a mixture of political factors and personal choice.[60] The status as a refugee is characterized substantially by the traditional distinction between citizens and foreigners. A necessary but not sufficient precondition for refugee status is the lack of domestic citizenship – only foreigners can be refugees. The treatment standards to which the contracting parties commit adhere to five different levels of attachment: the mere refugee status[61] or various intensities of a link to the State territory, ranging from mere presence over "habitual residence"[62] to "lawfully staying in their territory".[63]

What additional role do human rights play – on top of the refugee status? While the management of uncontrolled flow of human beings was historically the primary motivation of the contracting States after the Second World War, the authors of the Refugee Convention

and Its 1967 Protocols (Oxford: Oxford University Press 2011), 1019–1042, paragraphs 31–32: "[T]here are good reasons to take the position that Art. 22 of the 1951 Convention, too, was meant to provide for an individual right."

59 See Goodwin-Gill/McAdam, *Refugee in International Law*, 2007, 512.

60 Although "gender" is to some extent a socially constructed feature, and the resulting discrimination, against which CEDAW protects women, is also an external and political factor imposed on women, I submit that the structure of refugee rights is different from women's rights because they attach to a legally circumbscribed status (Article I A of the Refugee Convention) which a person may acquire and loose, and which is subject to a legal determination by public authorities.

61 For example Article 13, Article 16(1) of the 1951 Refugee Convention.

62 For example Article 14, Article 16(2) of the 1951 Refugee Convention.

63 For example Article 15, Article 17, Article 18 of the 1951 Refugee Convention.

nevertheless did mention human rights. Already the introductory sentence of the preamble refers to the Universal Declaration of Human Rights.[64] Today, human rights are accorded far greater significance than in 1951. Commentators argue that human rights constitute the modern *raison d'être* of the entire Convention.[65] Refugee law expert Guy Goodwin-Gill points out the historical process of superposition: "[T]he idea of rights ... began also to attach to the status of a refugee, and to and in the process of claiming to be a refugee."[66] Goodwin-Gill leaves it open, however, whether these rights attaching to the status of a refugee today are human rights or special refugee rights alongside human rights.

It is increasingly claimed that the refugee regime is an "integral part" of the international regime for the protection of human rights.[67] In that sense, a standard treatise on refugee law begins with the sentence: "Refugee law may be the world's most powerful international human rights mechanism."[68] Some even go further and say that that "refugee law has been absorbed by human rights law", and the Refugee Convention has become "a human-rights treaty in its own right".[69] But does the Geneva Convention on Refugees now retain only symbolic relevance as a consequence of this transformation? It must be conceded that refugee status has become less important in practical terms because asylum seekers can now achieve the same benefits through the general application of human rights to foreigners.

In the final analysis, the superposition of international human rights onto the historically older refugee law has led not so much to absorption than to a far-reaching ideational and political reorientation of the regime, as examined in detail by Vincent Chétail.[70] While the refugee regime

64 "Considering that the Charter of the United Nations and the Universal Declaration of Human Rights approved on 10 December 1948 by the General Assembly have affirmed the principle that human beings shall enjoy fundamental rights and freedoms without discrimination ...".

65 See Chétail, Refugee Rights, 2014, 70–71: "[H]uman rights law considerably informs the very function of refugee law ... its *raison d'être* is to ensure effective respect for human rights." See also Goodwin-Gill, Refugees and Their Human Rights, 2004, 6–7.

66 Goodwin-Gill, Refugees and Their Human Rights, 2004, 7.

67 Chétail, Refugee Rights, 2014, 72.

68 James C. Hathaway/Michelle Foster, *The Law of Refugee Status* (2nd ed., Cambridge: Cambridge University Press 2014), 1. See also *ibid.*, 3, stating that the Refugee Convention is just one of the human rights treaties.

69 Chétail, Refugee Rights, 2014, 70.

70 *Ibid.*, 70: "[T]he conception of the Geneva Convention as a whole has been revisited and reframed through the lens of human rights law."

defines only the obligations of host States, the international human rights regime also addresses the obligations of the countries from which the refugees have fled. While refugee law is dedicated to the ideals of neutrality and humanity, international human rights embody a political programme. From the perspective of human rights, the issue is not charity but rather responsibility, and not only the responsibility of individual States but rather the collective responsibility of the international community.[71]

This fundamental reorientation does not make the specific refugee rights obsolete, for various reasons. Firstly, under international and domestic human rights law, States may grant civil rights (e.g., the right to exercise a profession, or the right to residence) unevenly (within the rather loose confines of the non-discrimination rule) to nationals and non-nationals. Most of all, the usual civil rights under the ICCPR are often insufficiently tailored to refugee needs, and they allow for an easier limitation on grounds of public order and public security, even short of an officially declared state of emergency.

In the field of economic, social, and cultural rights, special Refugee Convention-based rights are even more needed. The main reason is the allowance given by Art. 2(3) ICESCR to "developing countries" to "determine to what extent they would guarantee the economic rights recognized in the present Covenant to non-nationals". If refugees were to depend only on the Covenant's ESC rights, this exception would be fatal to the majority of them who find themselves in developing states. Second, the weak concept of "progressive implementation" in the ICESCR — even if bolstered by the notion of core content — does not begin to match the obligations of result imposed on States Parties to the Refugee Convention.[72]

Finally, the Refugee Convention contains several very concrete and specific guarantees that go beyond general human rights. These are guarantees regarding identity papers (Article 27), travel documents (Article 28), fiscal charges (Article 29), and transfer of assets (Article 30). According to the reading advocated here, these provisions generate genuine international individual rights that arise directly from the Convention, irrespective of whether the treaty norms are formulated in the language of rights or corresponding State obligations.[73] Here again,

[71] See *ibid.*, 72. [72] I thank James Hathaway for this observation.

[73] See, e.g., Article 27 of the Geneva Convention on Refugees, Identity Papers: "The Contracting States shall issue identity papers to any refugee in their territory who does not possess a valid travel document."

human rights are in the background, namely the right to legal personality (Article 16 of the ICCPR) and the right to property (Article 17 of the Universal Declaration of Human Rights).

The specific rights of refugees already mentioned might be interpreted as a further specification or extension of those human rights. James Hathaway emphasizes that "refugee rights will in the overwhelming majority of cases consist of an amalgam of principles drawn from both refugee law and the Covenants".[74] But the rights arising from the Refugee Convention are better tailored than human rights to the situation of refugees. In this way, refugee rights perform "surrogate or substitute protection of basic human rights".[75] Because refugee rights are not themselves human rights, these international individual rights may be curtailed or revoked by treaty amendments, as long as the human rights core is not affected. The more context-tailored nature of refugee rights makes them operational. Alongside human rights, they fulfil a lasting function in the design of the international legal status of the individual.

14.6 Divergences and Tensions between Simple Rights and Human Rights: The Example of International Labour Law

14.6.1 Problématique

Hundreds of conventions that have been elaborated since 1919 within the framework of the International Labour Organization are intended to address the concerns of workers. The interests of workers might potentially be satisfied by the granting and enforcement of international individual rights. Therefore, this area of the law can also be analyzed from the perspective of international individual rights; the idea of international individual rights might have explanatory power in this domain and might also make a normative contribution to improved protection. The question is therefore to what extent the already existing labour law regime grants such rights, to what extent these rights are distinct from international human rights, and to what extent labour rights – understood as their own category – are more operational than the more general category of human rights.

To answer these questions, workers' rights must first be identified in the ILO conventions. We have already seen that international agreements relevant to individuals, which include the ILO conventions, normally

[74] Hathaway, *Rights of Refugees*, 2005, 9. [75] *Ibid.*, 4, see also 14.

raise two questions. Firstly, who are the international obligees (creditors) of the duties stipulated here: only the States parties, or individuals? This question is discussed especially in regard to investment protection treaties (Chapter 10), but also in relation to the Geneva Conventions on international humanitarian law (Chapter 7). Secondly, what exactly do the State obligations aim at: merely the enactment of domestic laws with the desired content, or "directly" at the performance or omission of specific acts? For instance, the classic international suppression conventions obligate the contracting parties only to enact domestic criminal laws, in which the States are required to criminalize certain acts (see Chapter 5).

In the case of the ILO conventions, both questions arise alongside – crucially – a third aspect characteristic of and specific to this area of the law. Unlike the conventions on international humanitarian law, the Refugee Convention, and the investment protection agreements, the *respondents* of the claims are not the contracting States themselves, but rather *employers* (which are often private actors). Even if, technically speaking, these agreements normally set out rights and duties between States (rarely between States and individuals), the true interested parties are employers and employees. This constellation of interests is taken into account by the special system of ILO tripartism, in that the social partners participate in the negotiation of ILO conventions and recommendations directly through their own delegates and independent of the representatives of the States.

14.6.2 Openness of the Convention Texts

A review of the ILO conventions shows that they very seldom speak of the "rights" of workers. Instead, they explicitly set out State obligations. The wording typically leaves open whether the obligations correspond to workers' rights, i.e., whether international individual rights of workers are stipulated or whether workers are merely beneficiaries. Beyond this, it remains unclear whether the State obligations are directed at the enactment of domestic legal provisions or whether they contain direct international requirements and prohibitions.

We can divide the obligations enshrined in the conventions according to *four types*, depending on how obligations and rights are formulated: First, those whose wording is directed (only) at the enactment of domestic labour protection laws; second, those that define obligations of conduct under international law; third, those that are unclear (which includes most of these conventions); and fourth, very modern conventions that quite unambiguously accord international individual rights to workers. (Some conventions establish various legal relations which fall under several of those headings.)

The first group (obligation to enact domestic measures) includes the Discrimination Convention No. 111 (1958): "*Each Member* for which this Convention is in force *undertakes to declare and pursue a national policy* designed to promote, by methods appropriate to national conditions and practice, equality of opportunity and treatment in respect of employment and occupation, with a view to eliminating any discrimination in respect thereof."[76] The Minimum Age Convention No. 138 (1973) has similar wording: "*Each Member* for which this Convention is in force *undertakes to pursue a national policy* designed to ensure the effective abolition of child labour and to raise progressively the minimum age for admission to employment or work to a level consistent with the fullest physical and mental development of young persons."[77] The Collective Bargaining Convention No. 154 (1981) is also clear: "The provisions of this Convention shall, in so far as they are not otherwise made effective by means of collective agreements, arbitration awards or in such other manner as may be consistent with national practice, *be given effect by national laws or regulations.*"[78] In these conventions, the States are evidently undertaking to enact domestic law and to implement a specific policy.

The second group of conventions stipulates direct prescriptions or prohibitions: For instance, Article 3 of the Hours of Work (Commerce and Offices) Convention No. 30 (1930) stipulates: "The hours of work of persons to whom this Convention applies shall not exceed forty-eight hours in the week and eight hours in the day, except as hereinafter otherwise provided."[79] But the question remains open as to whom

[76] Article 2 of the Discrimination (Employment and Occupation) Convention (C111) of 25 June 1958 (italics mine).

[77] Article 1 of the Minimum Age Convention (C138) of 26 June 1973 (italics mine).

[78] Article 4 of the Collective Bargaining Convention (C154) of 3 June 1981 (italics mine). See also Articles 3 and 4 of the Maternity Protection Convention (C183) of 15 June 2000 ("adopt appropriate measures"; "as determined by national law") and Article 2 of the Tripartite Consultation (International Labour Standards) Convention (C144) of 21 June 1976 ("undertakes to operate procedures"; "in accordance with national practice").

[79] Article 3 of the Hours of Work (Commerce and Offices) Convention (C030) of 28 June 1930. See also Article 2 of the Medical Examination of Young Persons (Sea) Convention (C016) of 11 November 1921: "The employment of any child or young

compliance with these working time limits under international law is owed: only to the other States parties, or to the workers themselves? The wording does not indicate whether this provision sets out a direct international right of workers to working time limits.

The third and largest group encompasses conventions that are ambiguous and unclear both in regard to the precise content of the State obligations and in regard to possible ownership of the rights. Some examples illustrate this finding of ambiguity. For instance, Article 2 of the Freedom of Association Convention No. 87 (1948) states: "Workers and employers, without distinction whatsoever, shall have *the right* to establish and, subject only to the rules of the organisation concerned, to join organisations of their own choosing without previous authorisation."[80] This provision can be interpreted such that it guarantees a genuine right of workers directly under international law, namely the freedom of association. This interpretation is underlined by the fact that the freedom of association is the first of the so-called "fundamental rights at work" as endorsed by the ILO Declaration of 1998. Paragraph 2 of that declaration mentions "the fundamental *rights which are the subject of those Conventions*".[81] However, Article 1 of Convention No. 87 gives rise to doubts whether the convention really is intended to confer any international individual rights. This provision states: "Each Member of the International Labour Organisation for which this Convention is in force *undertakes to give effect* to the following provisions." The phrase "undertakes to give effect" is not unambiguous. This might mean the enactment of domestic legal provisions in which the contracting States parties must in turn grant the right of association. But it might also simply mean ratification of the Convention which – according to this interpretation – directly grants the right of association.

Another example of the typical ambiguity of the ILO conventions in regard to individual entitlements is the Collective Bargaining Convention No. 98 (1949). Article 1(1) reads: "Workers shall enjoy *adequate protection against* acts of anti-union *discrimination* in respect of their

person under eighteen years of age on any vessel, other than vessels upon which only members of the same family are employed, shall be conditional on the production of a medical certificate attesting fitness for such work, signed by a doctor who shall be approved by the competent authority."

[80] Freedom of Association and Protection of the Right to Organise Convention (C087) of 9 July 1948 (italics mine).

[81] Declaration on Fundamental Principles and Rights at Work and Its Follow-up, adopted by the International Labour Conference at its Eighty-sixth Session, Geneva, 18 June 1998 (italics mine). See on fundamental rights at work below pp. 462–68.

employment."[82] This provision might be interpreted as the conferral of an individual right to non-discrimination directly by the Convention. However, it could also be understood in a different way, namely that the "adequate protection" has to be realized only by the legal provisions of domestic law.

Also in other conventions, the content of the State obligation is already unclear from the wording, as well as the question of entitlement. For instance, Article 1 of the Forced Labour Convention No. 29 (1930) states: "*Each Member* of the International Labour Organisation which ratifies this Convention *undertakes to suppress* the use of forced or compulsory labour in all its forms within the shortest possible period."[83] Similarly, Article 2(1) of the Equal Remuneration Convention No. 100 (1951) reads: "*Each Member shall, by means appropriate* to the methods in operation for determining rates of remuneration, *promote* and, in so far as is consistent with such methods, *ensure the application* to all workers of the principle of equal remuneration for men and women workers for work of equal value."[84] Again, the question arises as to what "undertake" means here. Is this merely an obligation to enact domestic legislation, or do these provisions directly require the States to refrain from tolerating forced labour or to respect the principle of equal remuneration?

Fourthly, more recent conventions expressly stipulate individual rights. An important example is the Maritime Labour Convention of 7 February 2006 (in force since 2013), which has been ratified by more than 30 States that jointly make up 60 percent of global maritime shipping. Article IV of the Convention governs the employment and social rights of seafarers as follows: "1. *Every seafarer has the right* to a safe and secure workplace that complies with safety standards. 2. Every seafarer has a *right* to fair terms of employment. 3. Every seafarer has a *right* to decent working and living conditions on board ship. 4. Every seafarer has a *right* to health protection, medical care, welfare measures and other forms of social protection. 5. Each Member shall ensure, within the limits of its jurisdiction, that the

[82] Right to Organise and Collective Bargaining Convention (C098) of 1 July 1949 (italics mine).

[83] Article 1(1) of the Forced Labour Convention (C029) of 28 June 1930 (italics mine). See also Article 1 of the Abolition of Forced Labour Convention (C105) of 25 June 1957: "Each Member of the International Labour Organisation which ratifies this Convention *undertakes to suppress* and not to make use of any form of forced or compulsory labour" (italics mine).

[84] Article 2(1) of the Equal Remuneration Convention (C100) of 29 June 1951 (italics mine).

seafarers' employment and social rights set out in the preceding paragraphs of this Article are fully implemented in accordance with the requirements of this Convention. Unless specified otherwise in the Convention, such implementation may be achieved through national laws or regulations, through applicable collective bargaining agreements or through other measures or in practice." These rights to a safe and secure workplace, fair terms of employment, and medical care are, according to the wording of the convention, clearly rights of the individual that arise directly from the convention itself. The basis of these rights is international law, but the rights must be implemented by domestic law or collective bargaining agreements. The interplay between international law and domestic law necessary for the realization of the individual rights is expressly envisaged by the convention itself. These treaty rights rely in part on the human right to personal enjoyment of the highest attainable standard of health and on measures taken by the State to realize this human right in regard to the workplace (Article 12(2)(b) of the ICESCR on "industrial hygiene"). It would be inflationary, however, to refer to the individual rights set out in Article IV of the Maritime Labour Convention overall as human rights. As shall be explained at pp. 464–68 on the human rights content of labour rights, not all international individual rights in the field of labour are human rights. It seems that the Maritime Labour Convention mostly stipulates such rights below the threshold of human rights. In the final analysis, the wording of this and other ILO conventions (not analysed in detail here) does not rule out the existence of international individual rights held by workers.

14.6.3 (Fundamental) Rights at Work

On the basis of the presumption justified in Chapter 13 in favour of individual rights directly under international law, the "individualistic" reading of an international treaty should be preferred, as long as that reading is permitted by the open wording and there is no consideration on principle against it. The question is therefore whether there is a reason of principle against the acceptance of an individual right to freedom of association based directly on Convention No. 87, against a direct international individual right to equal treatment/non-discrimination based on Convention No. 98, against a right to equal remuneration based on Convention No. 100, against a right to protection from forced labour based on Convention No. 29, and so on.

Such a reason of principle might be found in the specific nature of international labour law. This is characterized by the fact that the direct threats to labour rights are not the States, but rather the employers, who in most countries in the world today are predominantly private individuals and not State actors. This state of affairs is an argument in favour of understanding the State obligations imposed by the treaty primarily as *implementation obligations*: The contracting States are being addressed first and foremost in their role as protectors and guarantors. They must enact legislation and take other measures to regulate the employer side in accordance with the ILO guarantees set out in the treaty. Because States are not the primary threats, and because employers are not formally parties to the ILO conventions, the domestic laws obligating companies appear to be the most adequate instruments.

In practical terms, the treaty obligations must be substantiated with the help of domestic law. But in terms of legal construction, this does not rule out that employees (in the event of State inaction) might derive rights directly from the convention (namely against the States). Such rights against the contracting States derived directly from the convention would be *entitlements to protection* by the States from threats arising from the employers (in contrast to claims to forbearance (omissions) by the States themselves). But these rights to protection are not different from the rights to protection arising from constitutional fundamental rights. The latter rights may also generate an obligation to enact new and effective legal provisions. From the viewpoint of the person concerned, it is irrelevant whether the source of this duty of protection is the domestic constitution or an international convention. The ILO conventions therefore have a quasi-constitutional function in this regard, i.e., they require the contracting States to take protective measures using the instruments of ordinary law, just as domestic constitutions do. The effectiveness of this function is strengthened by the recognition of corresponding individual rights, because labour representatives can invoke them within the framework of the ILO complaint procedures.

A *different* question concerns any additional rights directly vis-à-vis the *employer* to have the labour rights in question fulfilled. Such rights addressed directly to private parties may under certain circumstances also be derived from several ILO conventions as part of a dynamic interpretation. The *pacta tertiis* principle does not defeat this reading, but the principle of legality must be observed (foreseeability of the obligation imposed on the companies/employers). The special problem of private actors as potential addressees of international individual rights is discussed in Chapter 4.

The interpretation of the ILO agreements proposed here is in conformity with the terminology of the ILO itself. The organization refers to the guarantees promoted by it and enshrined in the ILO's Fundamental Conventions as "fundamental rights at work" and as an expression of the "constitutional principles" of the ILO.[85]

14.6.4 *Labour Rights Distinct from Human Rights*

But is the extrapolation of specific workers' rights from the ILO conventions superfluous because the need for protection is satisfied by human rights? Numerous guarantees relevant to employees and enumerated in the ILO conventions are simultaneously enshrined in international human rights instruments: the freedom of association and the right to organize (Article 23(4) of the Universal Declaration of Human Rights; Article 22 of the ICCPR; Article 8 of the ICESCR), rights to equal treatment/non-discrimination (Article 7 of the Universal Declaration of Human Rights; Article 26 of the ICCPR; Article 2(2) and Article 3 of the ICESCR), the prohibition of slavery also in modern forms of forced labour (Article 4 of the Universal Declaration of Human Rights; Article 8 of the ICCPR), the right to social security (Article 22 of the Universal Declaration of Human Rights), a right to work (Article 23 of the Universal Declaration of Human Rights; Article 6 of the ICESCR), just and favourable conditions of work (Article 7 of the ICESCR), and limitation of working hours (Article 24 of the Universal Declaration of Human Rights).

For several reasons, these general guarantees do not render specific labour rights superfluous. Firstly, the human rights quality of the provisions already mentioned is in some cases controversial, even though they are referred to in the human rights texts. There is general agreement that the mere mention of a guarantee, such as to "periodic holidays with pay" in Article 24 of the Universal Declaration of Human Rights, does not yet make it a human right.

A second consideration is the current controversy surrounding the stronger principle-based approach taken by the ILO, as expressed in the ILO Declaration on Fundamental Principles and Rights at Work of

[85] Preamble of the ILO Declaration on Fundamental Principles and Rights at Work (n. 81).

1998[86] and the ILO Declaration on Globalization of 2008.[87] The critics of this strategy portray "principles" as being in opposition to rights, and the declaration of principles is denounced as "use of a regressive terminology".[88] Taking into account the economic and legal background of the new ILO strategy, however, this opposition appears to be misleading and the criticism exaggerated. Firstly, the ILO wants to counter the growing challenge that globalization – with the concomitant increase in the power of transnational and globally mobile enterprises – poses specifically to the protection of workers. Secondly, it aims to counter the low number of ratifications of ILO conventions and the poor record of compliance. In its 1998 Declaration, the International Labour Conference thus committed all ILO members to the fundamental principles of the ILO Constitution, irrespective of ratification of the ILO conventions. The "core labour standards" (freedom of association and right to collective bargaining, prohibition of forced labour, abolition of child labour, and prohibition of discrimination) make up the constitutional core of the entire ILO regime and thus also the foundation of the "specific rights and obligations" as set out in the special ILO conventions.[89] The intention of the ILO conference was not to weaken or replace those "specific" international individual rights – rooted in treaty law – but rather to underpin them with fundamental principles that are already included in the ILO Constitution itself.

There is a danger that international labour law will be diluted if the ILO is satisfied in substantive terms with mere guidelines instead of strict requirements and prohibitions, and in formal terms with codes of conduct and voluntary commitments of businesses rather than hard treaties.

Not least of all for that reason, probably the majority of labour specialists today call for the recognition of labour rights *as* human rights. For example, Nicolas Valticos writes that "international labour standards, as a body, constitute a special category of human rights".[90]

[86] ILO Declaration on Fundamental Principles and Rights at Work (n. 81) (Annex revised 15 June 2010).

[87] ILO Declaration on Social Justice for a Fair Globalization adopted by the International Labour Conference at its Ninety-seventh Session, Geneva, 10 June 2008.

[88] Alston, Core Labour Standards, 2004, 483.

[89] ILO Declaration on Fundamental Principles and Rights at Work (n. 81), paragraphs 2 and 1 (b).

[90] Nicolas Valticos, International Labour Standards and Human Rights: Approaching the Year 2000, *International Labour Review* 137 (1998), 135–147 (136–137). See also, seminally, Virginia A. Leary, The Paradox of Workers' Rights as Human Rights, in: Lance A. Compa/Stephen F. Diamond (eds), *Human Rights, Labour Rights, and International*

Claire La Hovary opines: "[L]les droits du travail devraient être conçus comme faisant partie intégrante des droits de la personne et non comme formant une catégorie á part."[91] This recognition is mainly intended to guarantee the *high quality* of the rights in question: "[T]here is a significant risk that ... labour rights will become just one more consideration to be taken into account in shaping the clauses underpinning a liberalized global economy ... [T]here is little reason to expect that labour rights will be accorded anything near the sort of *priority which is inherent in the very notion of a human right.*"[92] From that perspective, the recognition of labour rights *as* human rights has the merit of highlighting which values are really at stake – which seems particularly acute in times of globalization and deregulation. It is hoped that reading the norms of labour law through a human rights lens gives them the necessary "ethical seal". The objective is to acknowledge an "intrinsic value" of labour rights, and to "neutralise" them by removing them from the sociopolitical antagonism between employers and employees.[93] The basic consideration here is that labour rights are given sufficient weight when being balanced against conflicting goods (such as free trade) only if they are envisaged "as human rights". This argument is important, but it should not be sustained at the cost of internal contradictions.

The better view, contrary to the voices just heard, is to conceptualize labour rights as a distinct category of international rights, besides human rights, while acknowledging a considerable area of overlap. (For example, the right to non-discrimination in employment is both a labour right and a human right.) Such a distinction does justice to the relevant differences between labour rights and human rights.[94]

Trade (Philadelphia: University of Philadelphia Press 1996), 777–798. See for a philosophical justification for counting labour rights as human rights, Mathias Risse, A Right to Work? A Right to Leisure? Labor Rights as Human Rights, *Law & Ethics of Human Rights* 3 (2009), 1–39.

91 Claire La Hovary, *Les droits fondamentaux au travail: Origines, statut et impact en droit international* (Paris: Presses Universitaires de France 2009), 37.

92 Philip Alston, Labour Rights as Human Rights: The Not So Happy State of the Art, in: Philip Alston (ed.), *Labour Rights as Human Rights* (Oxford: Oxford University Press 2005), 1–24 (23; italics mine).

93 La Hovary, *Les droits fondamentaux*, 2009, 40 (translation by the author).

94 See on these differences Kevin Kolben, Labor Rights as Human Rights?, *Virginia Journal of International Law* 50 (2010), 449–484; Hugh Collins, Theories of Rights as Justifications for Labour Law, in: Guy Davidov/Brian Langille (eds), *The Idea of Labour Law* (Oxford: Oxford University Press 2011), 137–155 (142–143); Patrick Macklem, *The Sovereignty of Human Rights* (Oxford: Oxford University Press 2015), 89–94.

Importantly, the non-human rights quality of many specific labour rights, such as rights on working hours and working conditions, is not owed to the fact that we are here in the area of economy and social security. Social, economic, and cultural rights (ESC rights) are, as a matter of principle, "real" and full-fledged human rights. Rather, the key conceptual difference between labour rights and human rights, already mentioned, is that international labour rights direct material claims *against employers*, which are predominantly private actors in market economies. In contrast, the classical human rights are directed against States which are potential threats. Again, there is an overlap: On the one hand, human rights also trigger the States' duty to protect individuals (including workers) against harmful private actors (including employers). On the other hand, labour rights' claims against employers need to be regulated and enforced by States. However, the actual principal addressee differs. Also, labour rights do not benefit everyone universally, but only those in an employment relationship.

Other differences between labour rights and human rights are of a more incremental nature. The interests protected by labour rights do not appear as compelling as, for instance, liberty, security, and subsistence. Notably, rights such as fair pay and a reasonable holiday depend strongly on the affluence of the relevant society. There is arguably no minimum standard (as with human dignity and liberty) below which the degree of protection awarded to labourers may never lawfully fall. Next, human rights are often conceived as securing timeless universal (human) needs, whereas labour rights may evolve according to the systems of production. Moreover, labour rights have a slightly stronger collective focus than human rights, which are accorded to the individual (even if the ties of the individual to the community are recognized). Another conceptual difference is that labour rights have a stronger emphasis on process than human rights, which are primarily outcome-oriented. These differences should not be exaggerated, because human rights as well are to some extent contextual and flexible as opposed to abstract, absolute, and rigid.

But in addition, the nuances of the realization strategy differ as well. The labour movement tends to take a less legalistic approach than the human rights movement, and it tends to think of law less as a value in itself than as an instrument of social reform. Especially the mainstream human rights discourse is not as interested as the labour discourse in analyzing the basic economic constellation of society and, where necessary, calling it into question.[95]

[95] See Kolben, Labor Rights, 2010, 484.

A labour lawyer therefore warns against an excessive transposition of the human rights paradigm into (international) labour law. There are "differences between human and labour rights, both as concepts and as movements. While associating with the international human rights movement and adopting its discourse clearly has some potential benefits for labour advocates, both within and without the trade union movement, there are also some serious pitfalls".[96] Along the same line, another author entertains "a significant doubt whether labour rights are properly classified as universal human rights".[97]

The slogan "labour rights as human rights" illustrates the problem of inflationary claims of human rights. This inflation needs to be dampened with due regard for the intersections between international labour law and international human rights law: Some human rights are a necessary precondition for the exercise of labour rights, such as freedom of expression. At the same time, the key labour rights are in fact human rights, and as such they are protected by the international human rights conventions. Finally, the regional human rights courts are increasingly taking into account international labour law instruments when interpreting and applying convention rights and have thus been aligning the substance of human rights case law with ILO law.[98] Overall, international labour law and human rights law intersect in various dimensions, and "the relationship between the labour rights and the human rights discourse is close, with often overlapping regulatory objectives".[99] However, numerous specifications in regard to working hours, health standards, paid leave, and wages should not be understood as human rights, but rather as simple international individual rights. This classification does justice to the moral weight of the claims, the universality, the strictness of the standard, and the variability over time. Labour rights, classified not as human rights but as a distinct category of international rights, fulfil necessary functions in the area of international labour law. They provide a stable protection against utilitarian balancing of conflicting interests and policy objectives, while safeguarding the specific moral weight of human rights proper.

[96] *Ibid.* [97] Collins, Theories of Rights, 2011, 143.

[98] Franz Ebert/Martin Oelz, Bridging the Gap between Labour Rights and Human Rights: The Role of ILO Law in Regional Human Rights Courts, Discussion Paper DP212/2012 (International Institute for Labour Studies 2012).

[99] *Ibid.*, 2.

14.7 A Practical Conception of Human Rights

My proposal of a distinction on principle between international human rights and other international individual rights, which in turn can be – but do not have to be – manifestations or further specifications of human rights, is easily compatible with the interesting current versions of the "practical" or "political" conception of human rights in contemporary political philosophy (John Rawls,[100] Charles Beitz,[101] Cristina Lafont[102]). Cristina Lafont describes this orientation as follows: The traditional approach attempts to determine what human rights are "on the basis of some independently grounded account of human nature or human freedom". In contrast, the "so-called political or practical approach . . . takes contemporary human rights practice as a guide in order to figure out what human rights actually are".[103]

Hardly sustainable, on the other hand, is the conception of Joseph Raz, which in turn illustrates the problem of *human rights inflation.*[104] According to Raz, *human rights are everything that justifies international interference*: "Individual rights are human rights if they disable a certain argument against interference by outsiders in the affairs of a state. They disable, or deny the legitimacy of the response: I, the state, may have acted wrongly, but you, the outsider are not entitled to interfere. I am protected by my sovereignty. Disabling the defence 'none of your business,' is definitive of the political conception of human rights."[105] Human rights are then international per se (because they are only relevant to cross-border situations), but they are not universal in the sense that they would be valid for all times and for all people. They have and need no further internal justification (what Joseph Raz calls "human rights without foundation"[106]).

The contrast to the proposal advanced here of recognizing international individual rights beyond human rights is obvious: Raz derives the

[100] See John Rawls, *The Law of Peoples* (Cambridge MA: Harvard University Press 1999), 79: "Human rights are a class of rights that play a special role in a reasonable Law of Peoples: they restrict justifying reasons for war and its conduct, and they specify limits to a regime's internal autonomy."

[101] See Charles R. Beitz, *The Idea of Human Rights* (Oxford: Oxford University Press 2011).

[102] See Cristina Lafont, *Global Governance and Human Rights* (Spinoza Lecture Amsterdam: Van Gorcum 2012).

[103] *Ibid.*, 14.

[104] See Joseph Raz, Human Rights Without Foundations, in: Samantha Besson/ John Tasioulas (eds), *The Philosophy of International Law* (Oxford: Oxford University Press 2011), 321–337.

[105] *Ibid.*, 332. [106] *Ibid.*

quality of human rights from the internationalization of the protective concern. Internationalized simple rights (defined by international law and subject to practical protection through international action) cannot exist within this framework, because internationalization by definition entails the quality of a human right: All international relations (to the extent they recognize individual rights at all) become human rights policy.[107] The human rights label is not reserved for especially "basic" or "very important" norms: "[T]he rights will lose much of the aura of exceptional standing which is currently associated with 'human rights'."[108]

The Razian conception of human rights is not compatible with current international law, and it does not appear to offer much explanatory power for legal discourse or inspiration for legal practice. It ignores that human rights are primarily protected by domestic law and by means of domestic institutions, and that this primacy of the domestic legal level makes sense, because it contributes to both the effectiveness and the legitimacy of protection. Raz's conception does not answer the question of how human rights can be demarcated from other rights or claims of rights. It can identify human rights only *ex post facto* and does not contain a normative criterion for determining a human right: A human right exists – according to Raz – when the protection thereof is deemed a concern of the international community. It remains open whether this "internationalization" (openness to intervention in form of human rights policies) is in normative terms appropriate or not. Raz's proposition seems empty: He says that whether a concern is in fact a human right or not depends on the political interference by other States and organizations it triggers. I would inversely say that the appropriateness of such interference should be judged in dependency on the fact whether a human right is at stake or not. But exactly that normative follow-up question of when an outside interference ("piercing" the shield of sovereignty) *should* be allowed is not answered by Raz's human rights narrative. The Razian re-conceptualization will therefore be left aside here.

Simple individual rights are also possible and make sense from the perspective of practical human rights philosophy. While the goal of the advocates of the so-called practical human rights approach is not to

[107] See *ibid.*, 334: "[T]he politics of international human rights is drifting towards becoming just the politics of international relations, in so far as they acknowledge individual rights."

[108] *Ibid.*, 337.

compile an exhaustive list of international human rights, the proclaimed objective of that practical conception is to instead provide an alternative to any abstract approaches that aim to reduce international human rights to a principle (such as reason, autonomy, or the like). The practical approach has the advantage that it does not rely on a single principle of justification and it is thus accessible to an overlapping consensus. In this way, the practical approach attempts to avoid the accusation of provincialism and Eurocentrism, so that human rights remain dynamic and open to development.

But even the practical approach establishes necessary (albeit not exhaustive) characteristics of human rights. Cristina Lafont mentions three "core elements" of all human rights norms: Firstly, they are about "fundamental interests". Secondly, these are subject typically to political, economic, or social threats. Thirdly, these interests are amenable to institutionalized protection (i.e., they are not merely a private matter).[109]

From the perspective of the practical approach, juridical rights that do not satisfy these minimum conditions are not human rights. However, a strict demarcation between human rights and other rights would not be in keeping with the practical approach. Instead, the practical approach emphasizes that human rights can be instrumental, and it wants to leave room for future, as of yet unknown functions of human rights that might make sense in a changed world.

The practical conception of Charles Beitz is the most developed. Beitz wants to place human rights on a "middle ground" between principles of domestic social justice on the one hand and a "moral minimum" in the sense of permanently valid rights for all people at all times on the other hand. Human rights stand between these two extremes and are "critical public standards distinguished by their special role as elements of the global normative order we inhabit today".[110] This understanding of human rights is perfectly compatible with the recognition of further international individual rights beyond human rights. The model presented here thus finds support in current political philosophy.

[109] Lafont, *Global Governance*, 2012, 31. [110] Beitz, *Idea of Human Rights*, 2011, 198.

15

The Individualized Enforcement of International Law

15.1 Individuals as Guardians of the International Legal Order

The recognition of primary international legal personality strengthens the role of the individual as a functionary, trustee, or *gardien vigilant* of (objective) international legality.[1] This seems to be paradoxical at first sight, but it is not. From the perspective of the overall system, the empowerment of the individual counts less than the individual's efforts to enforce the international legal order. In a system with decentralized enforcement such as the international legal system, this role of the individual is especially important for ensuring the system's effectiveness. Assigning the role of guardian does not entail an inhuman instrumentalization of the individual, nor does it generate any contradiction with the status of the individual as a legal subject.

There have been and continue to be international treaties and regimes that take individuals into their service. For instance, the individual right of access to environmental information guaranteed under the Aarhus Convention is granted "not only to protect the legal interests of the individual, but also – in contrast to 'pure human rights' – to realize the role of the individual in pursuing certain interests of the common good".[2] One well-known case involves the early versions of the European integration treaties, in which individuals appeared as "market citizens" whose assertion of their freedoms was intended to advance European integration.[3] Especially, the concept of direct application of European

[1] The expression *gardien vigilant* is part of French administrative legal tradition, which does not demand the assertion of individual rights in order to bring claims (*intérêt à agir*) in *ultra vires* actions (*recours pour excès de pouvoir*), but rather only requires *de facto* concern.

[2] Astrid Epiney/Martin Scheyli, *Die Aarhus-Konvention: Rechtliche Tragweite und Implikationen für das schweizerische Recht* (Fribourg: Universitätsverlag 2000), 94 (translation mine).

[3] See ECJ, Case 26/62 [1963] ECR 1, 26 – *Van Gend & Loos*: "The vigilance of individuals concerned to protect their rights amounts to an effective supervision in addition to the supervision entrusted . . . to the diligence of the Commission and the Member States."

directives by domestic courts was criticized from the perspective of the (potentially objectionable) instrumentalization of the citizen.[4] In fact, the EU freedoms – unlike human rights – are linked to cross-border activities, and they serve to create a Common Market. Nevertheless, these freedoms are increasingly being accorded a purpose that is more akin to fundamental rights, i.e., they serve human flourishment and dignity.[5] The direct effect of EU directives also has a dual motivation: It serves both the protection of individual interests, and safeguards the uniform effectiveness of Union law. Both rationales seem to be equally important.[6]

The dual function of individual rights (individual empowerment and strengthening "objective" legality) is not a legal anomaly. The Preamble of the International Covenant on Civil and Political Rights combines the instrumental and the intrinsic justifications of the treaty-based protection of international human rights:

> "The States Parties to the present Covenant, Considering that, in accordance with the principles proclaimed in the Charter of the United Nations, recognition of the inherent dignity and of the equal and inalienable rights of all members of the human family *is the foundation of freedom, justice and peace in the world*, Recognizing that these rights derive from the inherent dignity of the human person."[7]

Invocation of the civil and political human rights set out here as an instrument for safeguarding world peace did not, in the view of the drafters of the treaty, undermine the simultaneous grounding of those rights in the dignity of the human being.

Also in national constitutional traditions, "functional" conceptions of fundamental rights – i.e., those that emphasize the promotion of general welfare through fundamental rights – stand alongside "autonomous" conceptions – i.e., those that view fundamental rights as a manifestation of

[4] See, critically, Johannes Masing, *Die Mobilisierung des Bürgers für die Durchsetzung des Rechts: Europäische Impulse für eine Revision der Lehre vom subjektiv-öffentlichen Recht* (Berlin: Duncker & Humblot 1997), esp. 176–181. For a response, see Martin Nettesheim, Subjektive Rechte im Unionsrecht, *Archiv des öffentlichen Rechts* 132 (2007), 333–392 (esp. 355).

[5] See Thorsten Kingreen, *Die Struktur der Grundfreiheiten des Europäischen Gemeinschaftsrechts* (Berlin: Duncker & Humblot 1999); Alexander Schultz, *Das Verhältnis von Gemeinschaftsgrundrechten und Grundfreiheiten des EGV* (Berlin: Duncker & Humblot 2005).

[6] See Stefan Kadelbach, *Allgemeines Verwaltungsrecht unter europäischem Einfluss* (Tübingen: Mohr Siebeck 1996), 77.

[7] ICCPR of 19 December 1966, UNTS Vol. 999, p. 171 (italics mine).

human autonomy and dignity.[8] The reference to purposes lying outside the fundamental right in question (such as safeguarding a functioning democracy and ascertaining the truth with the help of freedom of opinion and speech) does not devalue fundamental rights per se. The case law of various domestic courts and the ECtHR often draws on both types of justification, depending on the fundamental right at issue. Both conceptions can generate arguments for a higher or lower level of protection, and both are legally sustainable. Irrespective of the functions of fundamental rights, the enforcement of law in some legal orders tends to be left to individuals rather than to *ex officio* enforcement. Competition law, for instance, tends to be enforced by governmental agencies in Europe, while it tends to be enforced by individuals in the United States.

The individual's task of safeguarding international legality is therefore a consequence of the status of the individual as a subject of international law; that job does not devalue the individual's status, but rather the two mutually reinforce each other: The conception of human beings in the contemporary international order is that humans are ends in themselves and, in light of their quality as humans, must be respected, protected, and empowered by international law. Mobilizing their self-interest for the purpose of enforcing international law does not contradict that view, but rather it pursues the same goal. Because individuals are not forced to bring claims, they are not instrumentalized and not made into objects. As long as enforcement of the law in the hands of individuals does not become a burden on them and does not endanger the common good, there should be no objection to this mechanism. If individuals decide to institute legal proceedings against violators of international law in order to safeguard their individual interests, then those individual interests and the public interest converge.

15.2 Addressees of International Individual Rights

A key question is that of the addressees bound by international individual rights (i.e., the obligors). Against whom are these rights directed?

[8] See Antje von Ungern, Autonome und funktionale Grundrechtskonzeptionen unter besonderer Berücksichtigung der Rechtsprechung des EGMR, in: Mathias Hong/ Nele Matz-Lück (eds), *Grundrechte und Grundfreiheiten im Mehrebenensystem – Konkurrenzen und Interferenzen* (Berlin: Springer 2011), 69–108.

15.2.1 States and Other Obligors

In the paradigm of international law as existing between States and analogous to private law, State obligations always correspond to rights of other States,[9] because from that perspective, the entire international legal order is constituted by the network of reciprocal right – obligation relationships. But as soon as international law is thought of as international public law, enacted in the global public interest, obligations no longer necessarily have to be tied to rights. From the public law perspective, international legal subjects may be bound by obligations to which no right corresponds, i.e., obligations that exist "only" in the public interest. This is especially true vis-à-vis individuals. Numerous commands and prohibitions of international law, most of which are addressed to States, do not correspond to international individual rights. Individuals do not have a general right to compliance with international law that would be actionable or otherwise enforceable.

But where rights are recognized, those rights often enjoy normative priority over obligations, and their content can often not be determined exhaustively simply by enumerating the obligations that arise from them. Rights have a dynamic character; when the circumstances change, rights may lead to the emergence of new obligations. There is no exhaustive list of obligations that correspond to a particular right.[10] "Rights are a reason for the emergence of obligations, but they are not equivalent to them."[11] This open-ended range of (possible) obligations also applies *ratione personae*, i.e., in relation to their addressees. One can sensibly speak of rights – even international rights – of the individual even where there is no actualized, individualized counterpart. A "latent obligation" is enough.[12]

9 See Roberto Ago, Special Rapporteur on State Responsibility, Second Report on State Responsibility, ILC Yearbook 1970 II, 177 et seq. (192–193), paragraph 46: "[I]t seems perfectly legitimate, in international law, to regard the idea of the breach of an obligation as the exact equivalent of the idea of the impairment of the subjective rights of others ... The correlation between a legal obligation on the one hand and a subjective right on the other admits of no exception; as distinct from what is said to be the situation in municipal law, there are certainly no obligations incumbent on a subject which are not matched by an international subjective right of another subject or subjects, or even, for those who take a view referred to in the previous section, of the totality of the other subjects of the law of nations."

10 See Marietta Auer, Subjektive Rechte bei Pufendorf und Kant, *Archiv für die civilistische Praxis* 208 (2008), 584–634 (598).

11 *Ibid.*, 599.

12 See Johannes Saurer, *Der Einzelne im europäischen Verwaltungsrecht: Die institutionelle Ausdifferenzierung der Verwaltungsorganisation der Europäischen Union in individueller Perspektive* (Tübingen: Mohr Siebeck 2013), 80.

The obligor of international individual rights is therefore not a single authority. In line with the decentralized structure of international law, international individual rights are directed against a *multitude of actors*. States are the primary obligors. To the extent that international treaties concluded between States grant individual rights, which must be determined through interpretation, the individuals as beneficiaries hold a genuine international right to have those individual rights respected by the contracting States.

However, in light of the transformation of statehood through globalization, the deterritorialization of markets, the associated increase in the power of transnational companies, and the growing law-making and law-enforcing power of international organizations and institutions, the question arises whether it still makes sense to focus on individual rights that are recognized by the State and (only) directed against it.[13] Whether *natural persons or legal persons under (domestic) private law* are in turn obligated to satisfy international individual rights was discussed in Chapter 4. Here, only the most important obligors in addition to States, namely international organizations, will be considered.

15.2.2 *Obligations of International Organizations*

The international obligations of international organizations towards individuals have so far been discussed only in relation to human rights. The arguments in that debate will be recapitulated here first and then, in a second step, their validity for other international individual rights will be examined.

An expansion of human rights obligations to cover international organizations is in line with the general objectives of human rights. Human rights are intended to protect individuals against the abuse of public power at any level at which authority is wielded. It is a truism that human rights must be not merely theoretical but rather practical and effective.[14] This objective would be met if human rights could be asserted not only against States but also against international actors such as international organizations, agencies, and conferences. Using this teleological reasoning, several authors call for international organizations to become addressees of (some) international human rights guarantees.[15]

[13] See Catherine Colliot-Thélène, Après la souveraineté: que reste-t-il des droits subjectifs?, *Jus Politicum: Revue de droit politique* (2008) (www.juspoliticum.com/).

[14] ECtHR, *Airey* v. *Ireland*, No. 6289/73, 9 October 1979, paragraph 24.

[15] See Cristina Lafont, Accountability and Global Governance: Challenging the State-Centric Conception of Human Rights, *Ethics & Global Politics* 3 (2010), 193–215.

Going further, some authors argue that these obligations of international organizations are already part of existing international law.[16] Questions remain, however, regarding which organizations are covered, which human rights are extended in this way, and what types of obligations (to respect, protect, or fulfil) the organizations would be bound by.

In the context of this study, we are interested in international individual rights beyond human rights. Such rights are also affected especially by the activities of international organizations; one need only think of rights to participate and be heard in project approval procedures, social standards, access to aid, and so on. International non-human rights have so far only rarely been asserted against international organizations, however. Until now, they have mainly become relevant in proceedings before the International Criminal Court, which is an international organization with its own international legal personality (Article 4 of the Rome Statute of the ICC). The participation rights of victims and a right to reparations are elaborated in detail in the Rome Statute (see Chapter 9, pp. 270–76; Chapter 6, pp. 178–79).

How can the binding nature of international human rights in regard to international organizations be constructed in legal terms? Firstly, the constituent documents must be interpreted in conformity with the international obligations of their Member States. This follows from the rule of interpretation set out in Article 31(3)(c) of the VCLT, according to which "[a]ny relevant rules of international law applicable in the relations between the parties" "shall be taken into account". Obligations arising from international treaties vis-à-vis individuals that have been accepted by all Member States of an organization, such as those arising from the international humanitarian law conventions, are "relevant" and "applicable" in the sense of this rule of interpretation. They must therefore "be taken into account" in the interpretation of constituent documents, such as of the UN, the World Bank, and the WTO.

[16] For the international financial institutions, see Sigrun I. Skogly, *The Human Rights Obligations of the World Bank and the International Monetary Fund* (London: Cavendish 2001); Mac Darrow, *Between Light and Shadow: The World Bank, the International Monetary Fund and International Human Rights Law* (Oxford: Hart 2003); for the WTO, see Holger Hestermeyer, *The WTO and Human Rights: The Case of Patents and Access to Medicine* (Oxford: Oxford University Press 2007); for the United Nations, see Anne Peters, Article 25, in: Bruno Simma//Daniel-Erasmus Khan/Georg Nolte/Andreas Paulus (eds), *A Commentary to the Charter of the United Nations*, Vol. 1 (3d ed., Oxford: Oxford University Press 2012), 787–854 (paragraphs 109–123); for all international organizations, see Anne Peters, The Constitutionalisation of International Organisations, in: Neil Walker/ Jo Shaw/Stephen Tierney (eds), *Europe's Constitutional Mosaic* (Oxford: Hart 2011), 253–285 (266–269).

Secondly, every interpretation of the constituent documents must observe the principle enshrined in existing law that States are not authorized to avoid their international obligations by transferring powers to an international organization ("no flight into international organizations"[17]). To prevent the adverse consequences of an "upward rezoning" of public tasks to the international level, Member States must retain residual responsibility. But this cannot prevent gaps in legal protection if the organizations are not themselves obligated in parallel. This means that the systematic interpretation of the constituent documents of international organizations must include the unwritten obligation of organizations to take into account the international legal obligations of their Member States in the context of their own activities. This duty of consideration is a relatively soft obligation of the organizations, comparable to the general obligation of States to protect human rights.

Thirdly, international organizations – independently of treaty provisions – could be bound directly and fully by general international law (customary law and general principles of law).[18] One standard textbook assumes that international organizations are bound by customary international law "in principle", unless the norm in question is not "suitable to be applied" to international organizations.[19] In my view, it must in addition always be examined whether these norms actually bind the (new) addressees alongside States. For instance, the normal obligors of human rights – including those under customary law – are States. It is not clear that these rights have received a different direction of obligation. To include organizations as obligors, the structure of the international legal norm in question (but not its content) must have changed in order for it to address organizations (in addition to States). It is doubtful whether such a legal development can simply be presumed where there are no indications to the contrary.[20] One should therefore tend to

[17] See ECtHR, *Matthews* v. *UK*, No. 24833/94, 18 February 1999, paragraph 32, in regard to the attempts of EU Member States to avoid human rights obligations under the ECHR.

[18] On the human rights obligations of the United Nations, see Ian Cameron, The European Convention on Human Rights, Due Process, and the United Nations Security Council Counter-Terrorism Sanctions, Report Commissioned by the Council of Europe (2006), 21.

[19] See Henry G. Schermers/Niels M. Blokker, *International Institutional Law* (5th ed., Dordrecht: Martinus Nijhoff 2011), § 1579.

[20] Along these lines, see Holger Hestermeyer, who argues that the WTO is bound by human rights, because WTO law does not contradict that presumption and the WTO has not implicitly contracted itself out (Hestermeyer, *The WTO and Human Rights*, 2007, 99–102).

assume that this change in direction must rely on practice and accompanying *opinio juris*. Such practice and *opinio juris* can be observed only rudimentarily so far.

15.3 The Enforcement of International Individual Rights

15.3.1 Individual Enforcement of International Law as a Recognized Practice

The primary international individual rights to fulfilment and the corresponding secondary rights in the case of infringement[21] must, in order to be effective, be enforceable by individuals through institutional means. The legal guarantee of this enforceability is referred to as the guarantee of legal protection or as access to justice.[22]

The individualized enforcement of international law – before international and domestic bodies – is a phenomenon historically well established in international law. It began with the right of prize and reprisal in the thirteenth century[23] and ranges from claims for compensation under the US Alien Tort Claims Act[24] to the ICSID arbitration system.[25] Other examples include communications to the Compliance Committee of the Aarhus Convention on environmental information by "members of the public",[26] where "the public" is legally defined as NGOs and individuals.[27] Not least of all, there are the individual claims and complaints procedures under human rights law.

[21] To be consistent, the recognition of an individual right would have to be accompanied by the recognition of corresponding individual rights at the level of secondary law if the primary right is violated. When an international individual right is violated, the owner of that right is therefore also the bearer of rights arising from international responsibility. For details, see Chapter 6.

[22] See Antônio Augusto Cançado Trindade, *The Access of Individuals to International Justice* (Oxford: Oxford University Press 2011).

[23] See Grover Clark, *The English Practice with Regard to Reprisals by Private Persons*, *American Journal of International Law* 27 (1933), 694–723.

[24] See Beth Stephens, Translating Filartiga: A Comparative and International Law Analysis of Domestic Remedies for International Human Rights Violations, *Yale Journal of International Law* 27 (2002), 1–57.

[25] See Chapter 10.

[26] ECE, Decision I/7 Review of Compliance, adopted at the first meeting of the Parties, Annex: "Structure and Functions of the Compliance Committee and Procedures for the Review of Compliance", MOP 1 (2002), Doc. ECE/MP.PP/2/Add.8 (2004), Sec. VI "Communications from the Public."

[27] See the definition in Article 2(4) of the Aarhus Convention (UNECE Convention on Access to Information, Public Participation in Decision-Making and Access to Justice in Environmental Matters) of 25 June 1998, *International Legal Materials* 38 (1999), 517–533.

Generally speaking, individual enforcement contributes substantially to improving the effectiveness of the international legal norms in question and also reduces the burden on relations between States (so-called plaintiffs' diplomacy).[28] Enforcement of international law by individuals is thus well known.

15.3.2 Legal Protection against States Primarily through Domestic Bodies

International individual rights are and should be primarily enforced through domestic institutions. For instance, the enforcement of rights arising from the Vienna Convention on Consular Relations (VCCR) is mainly accomplished through the domestic law of criminal procedure.[29] A breach of the VCCR may constitute a reason for review or reconsideration or may lead to the exclusion of evidence (Chapter 11). A second example can be found in the individual enforcement possibilities for asserting secondary rights arising from international responsibility for the violation of provisions of the law of armed conflict. These possibilities are currently insufficient. Here again, the primary bodies for enforcement are the domestic courts. For this purpose, domestic courts must, firstly, recognize individuals as the owners not only of the primary rights but also of the secondary rights and, secondly, qualify the relevant provisions of international humanitarian law as directly applicable (see, in detail, Chapter 7). Current practice is moving in that direction, albeit hesitantly.

15.3.2.1 The Right to a Local Remedy as a Correlate of the Local Remedies Rule

This section will show that international individual rights include a right to a local remedy. Classification of an international norm as one that

[28] "By including the individual in the legal structure, the set of procedural instruments for the enforcement of the deliberately promoted body of law becomes substantially more effective . . . While States must always ask themselves the question before deciding on the initiation of formal proceedings whether this also makes sense politically, individuals generally are not concerned with such considerations. In the vast majority of cases, they work to safeguard the law very simply for their own personal advantage." Christian Tomuschat, Article 25 GG, in: *Bonner Kommentar* (140th update, June 2009), paragraph 97 (translation mine). Tomuschat refers to this phenomenon as "democratization".

[29] See ICJ, *Case Concerning Avena and Other Mexican Nationals* (*Mexico* v. *United States of America*), ICJ Reports 2004, 12, paragraph 40. Here, the ICJ affirmed an international individual right arising from the VCCR, but it nevertheless demanded that this right be enforced in the first place within the domestic legal system of the United States.

protects individual rights gives rise to an international individual right to the provision of a *domestic* enforcement mechanism. This is in any event true of rights against the State, but less so for rights directed against international organizations (on the latter, see pp. 488–92).

The international right to a local remedy when international legal norms are violated by a State is already established in existing international law as a correlate of the local remedies rule. The local remedies rule is an old principle of the law of aliens in the sense that private individuals injured by a foreign State must first avail themselves of the legal remedies in the injuring State before claiming diplomatic protection from their home State. Secondly, in the domain of international human rights protection, the principle of local remedies is considered a precondition for the admissibility of individual complaints or communications before the international monitoring bodies. In both contexts,[30] the rationale of the rule is traditionally seen primarily as protecting the sovereignty of the host State, because this gives the host State the opportunity to remedy the problem on its own and without interference by an international body. However, exceptions to the principle of exhaustion of local remedies are now recognized for the individual's benefit, and in a given case a balancing between State sovereignty and the individual's interest in legal protection is required.[31] Additionally, new protective purposes have accrued to the requirement of exhaustion of local remedies in the global multi-level system, as will be examined in the following discussion.

Consideration of the injured individual's interests as demanded by international law as it stands does not require us to set aside the requirement that local remedies must be exhausted. The mechanism could also work the other way around – as might even be proper according to the principle of subsidiarity (see below). Individual interests can be realized by recognizing an obligation of the injuring State to make local remedies

[30] The scope of application of diplomatic protection overlaps with that of human rights protection. Diplomatic protection by the home State applies only when the international rules relating to foreigners are interfered with by the host State. It is thus limited *ratione personae*, but it may be triggered by all kinds of breaches of international law. The human rights protection mechanisms are limited *ratione materiae*, but they are available to all persons and are directed against the State under whose jurisdiction the affected person is placed; this may be a foreign State or the person's home State.

[31] See Felix Chittarajan Amerasinghe, *Diplomatic Protection* (Oxford: Oxford University Press 2008), 142–190 (esp. 189–190).

available.[32] The obligation postulated here to make local remedies available can be derived from several existing principles of international law. Firstly, it can be derived from the principle identified in the literature as the basis of the local remedies rule, namely the principle of engaging domestic courts – in the interest of the international community – for the effective and fair adjudication of a dispute.[33] Secondly, this obligation to make remedies available also arises from the functional linkage: If the exhaustion of domestic remedies is a precondition of admissibility for exercising diplomatic protection (and also a precondition for seizing international human rights bodies), then there must be a corresponding *international obligation to make such remedies available*. Otherwise, that precondition would be meaningless: Diplomatic protection and the work of the international human rights institutions would be empty concepts. In other words, the local remedies rule obligates States to make a remedy available, because the additional first instance (the domestic court) serves to improve the legal protection of individuals and also to reduce the burden on the international dispute settlement body.

Thirdly, within the domain of human rights, the obligation to make a local remedy available arises not only from the requirement of the exhaustion of domestic remedies but also from the special prescriptions under human rights conventions to provide a remedy in the domestic legal system for the examination of arguable claims relating to the human rights guaranteed by the convention (Article 2(3) of the ICCPR; Article 25 of the ACHR; Articles 12–14 of the CAT; Article 47 of the EU Charter of Fundamental Rights; for details, see Chapter 6, pp. 180–83).

The complementary relationship between the requirement of the exhaustion of domestic remedies and the obligation to make such remedies available has been formulated by Arnold Jan Pieter Tammes as follows: "Since international law does recognize the preference of States for having, in private claims, their international obligations and those of their nationals decided by their own courts,

[32] See, e.g., Riccardo Pisillo Mazzeschi, International Obligations for Reparation Claims?, in: Albrecht Randelzhofer/Christian Tomuschat (eds), *State Responsibility and the Individual: Reparation in Instances of Grave Violations of Human Rights* (The Hague: Martinus Nijhoff 1999), 149–172 (156).

[33] See Felix Chittarajan Amerasinghe, *Local Remedies in International Law* (2nd ed., Cambridge: Cambridge University Press 2004), 62–63 and 427. On this functional duality of domestic courts, see n. 52 below.

there is room for the complementary principle that local remedies should be optimally organized."[34]

15.3.2.2 The Right to a Local Remedy as a Requirement of the Principle of Subsidiarity

Both the subsidiarity principle (e.g., for the EU pursuant to Article 5(3) of the TEU) as well as practical considerations suggest recognizing domestic institutions not merely as equal forums, but rather as primary forums.[35] Decentralized enforcement by domestic authorities and courts offers the advantage of proximity to the subject matter, facilitates the consideration of local particularities, and reduces the burden on centralized bodies.

In the EU, this division of labour is required as part of the multi-level juridical system. According to Article 19(1) subsec. (2) of the TEU, "Member States shall provide remedies sufficient to ensure effective legal protection in the fields covered by Union law." The Treaty on European Union therefore presupposes that Union law makes substantive rights available that must be enforced by the domestic courts. In other words, within the EU, the level at which rights are established and the level at which legal protection is granted institutionally are often not the same. European rights of the individual are established at the European level, while their judicial protection is generally the responsibility of the Member States.[36] The decentralized enforcement of EU law by the courts of the Member States ultimately *also* serves to protect the rights of individuals.[37] Naturally, the EU regime differs from general international law in that the courts of the Member States are forced directly or indirectly by the ECJ to exercise their role as guardians (via preliminary rulings or infringement procedures brought against the Member States). The basic principles of subsidiarity and division of labour also apply in general international law, however.

[34] Arnold Jan Pieter Tammes, The Obligation to Provide Local Remedies, in: *Volkenrechtelijke Opstellen – Aangeboden aan Professor Dr. Gesina H. J. van der Molen* (Kampen: J H Kok NV 1962), 152–168 (153).

[35] On the important role of domestic courts in the further development of international law, see Anthea Roberts, Comparative International Law? The Role of National Courts in International Law, *International and Comparative Law Quarterly* 60 (2011), 57–92.

[36] See Saurer, *Der Einzelne im europäischen Verwaltungsrecht*, 2013, 382 and further references.

[37] On the right of individuals to invoke EU directives before domestic courts, see ECJ, Joined Cases C-6/90 and C-9/90, *Francovich* [1991] ECR I-5357, paragraph 32: The national courts must "ensure that those rules [of Union law] take full effect *and must protect the rights which they confer on individuals*" (italics mine).

The primacy of domestic courts is established especially in human rights practice. Here, the international institutions (human rights bodies and regional courts) can be invoked only after domestic remedies have been exhausted (see, e.g., Article 41(1)(c) of the ICCPR; Article 34 of the ECHR). For the ECHR, the ECtHR's settled case law holds: "[T]he machinery of protection established by the Convention is subsidiary to the national systems safeguarding human rights."[38] Similarly, the implementation and further development of regional human rights law is being significantly influenced by the case law of domestic courts, especially in Latin America.[39]

However, decentralized enforcement of international law is no panacea. In the ideal case – when the domestic courts respect the rule of law – decentralized enforcement is generally more legitimate and more effective than centralized enforcement by international bodies, given that the legitimacy and effectiveness of the latter are precarious. But there are disadvantages of decentralized enforcement as well, such as the potential lack of uniformity of legal interpretation, the danger of improper application or non-application of international law, and non-compliance with universally recognized procedural standards. In practice, legal protection is deficient in many States, measured against the minimum requirements of international law. Self-appointed guardians of dubious legitimacy may interpret the applicable international legal norms divergently (and thus threaten the unity of international law), and in addition there is the danger of unfair domestic proceedings.[40]

This tension can be resolved dialectically in accordance with the general principle of complementarity (based on and generalizing Article 17 of the Rome Statute of the ICC) by giving national or even local bodies primacy in the application of international law only *as long*

[38] ECtHR, *Handyside* v. *UK*, No. 5493/72, 7 December 1976, paragraph 48. For a more recent strong emphasis on the subsidiarity principle, see the Brighton Declaration of the High Level Conference on the Future of the European Court of Human Rights of 20 April 2012, Principles 3, 11, 12, and 28. See, generally, Paolo G. Carozza, Subsidiarity as a Structural Principle of Human Rights Law, *American Journal of International Law* 97 (2003), 38–79.

[39] See Kathryn Sikkink; *The Justice Cascade: Human Rights Prosecutions and World Politics* (New York: W.W. Norton & Co. 2011).

[40] For a critical view, see ICJ, *Arrest Warrant* (*Democratic Republic of the Congo* v. *Belgium*), ICJ Reports 2002, 3 et seq., Separate Opinion of President Guillaume, paragraph 15: The unlimited conferral of universal jurisdiction upon domestic courts would "encourage the arbitrary for the benefit of the powerful, purportedly acting as agent for an ill-defined 'international community'".

as they are effective and legitimate, which in turn must be assessed using a universal benchmark. In other words, the principle of complementarity stipulates that international bodies may and shall act if domestic enforcement of international law is ineffective or illegitimate. Under this principle, international courts do not necessarily have jurisdiction if there is merely a danger of divergent interpretations at the domestic level. Such divergences are not illegitimate per se, but rather they may correspond to regional cultural needs. Consideration of these needs contributes to ensuring acceptance of an international norm by legal subjects and by those applying the law at the domestic level. In the interplay between domestic and international enforcement institutions, the balance between regional/local interpretation and the necessary uniformity of interpretation and application of international legal provisions must always be struck anew and operationalized using legal techniques such as the margin of appreciation, etc.

15.3.2.3 International Rights May Also Be Rights under Domestic Law

The qualification of an international norm as an international individual right does not necessarily correspond to specific domestic law qualifications. For example, a given international right is not automatically also an individual public right (*subjektives öffentliches Recht*) in the sense of the German Basic Law with the consequence that Article 19(4) of the Basic Law would apply. This provision would grant a *constitutional* right to a remedy in the event of an infringement of that right by State institutions, which in turn could be asserted by way of a constitutional complaint. This consequence is not automatically entailed, because the quality of being an individual *public* right is governed by the criteria of domestic administrative and constitutional law.[41] However, a parallelism may arise from the constitutionally protected obligation of domestic bodies to take into account/to consider international norms according to the interpretation given by an international court.[42] In Germany, e.g., courts are obliged "to take note of and consider the relevant case law of the international courts with jurisdiction for Germany".[43] This follows

41 See Eberhard Schmidt-Aßmann, Commentary on Article 19 of the Basic Law, in: Theodor Maunz/Günter Dürig (eds), *Grundgesetzkommentar* (57th ed., Munich: Beck 2010), Article 19 Abs. 4 GG, paragraph 152.

42 See for Germany BVerfGE 111, 307 (2004), paragraph 30 – *Görgülü*.

43 BVerfGK 9, 174 (2006) (First Chamber of the Second Senate), 2 BvR 2115/01, 2 BvR 2132/01, 2 BvR 348/032010, of 19 September 2006, paragraph 53 (= *Neue Juristische*

from "the principle of openness of the Basic Law to international law in conjunction with the principle that the judiciary must be bound by law and justice (Article 20(3) of the Basic Law in conjunction with Article 59(2) of the Basic Law), which includes the decisions of an international court established under international law in accordance with the content of the incorporated international treaty".[44] The duty of consideration is a "direct constitutional" duty,[45] so that any breach thereof can be claimed by way of a constitutional complaint. If a German court fails to give adequate consideration to an international legal norm (as interpreted by the competent international court), this represents a violation of the thematically relevant fundamental right under the Basic Law in conjunction with the principle of the rule of law.[46]

In a 2010 ruling, the Federal Constitutional Court of Germany further defined how tightly it would review compliance with the duty of consideration.[47] This review must take into account how difficult it is for regular courts to consider the decisions of international courts. For this reason, the Federal Constitutional Court refused to evaluate all the details of an international decision and then to measure the regular court's consideration against such a detailed evaluation. Instead, the ordinary court must disclose "that it has taken note of and considered the relevant case law". "With regard to the question of whether a regular court has attributed the correct content to a decision of the International Court of Justice, a violation of the constitutional duty of consideration may be assumed *only if a recognizable error has been made in the legal reception of the decision.*"[48] According to the Federal Constitutional Court, only in that way can "constitutional review take into account the difficulties that result from the increasing international embeddedness of the German legal order, especially also for the regular courts".

After the ICJ qualified the right of a foreign detainee to receive information about his right to consular access as an international individual right in the *LaGrand* case,[49] the duty of consideration

Wochenschrift 61 (2007), 499 = Europäische Grundrechte-Zeitschrift 33 (2006), 684 et seq.; translation mine).

44 *Ibid.*, paragraph 58 (translation mine).

45 *Ibid.*, paragraph 54 (translation mine).

46 See, fundamentally, BVerfG, *Görgülü* (n. 42), paragraph 63.

47 See BVerfG, Second Chamber of the Second Senate, Ruling of 8 July 2010 – BvR 2485/07.

48 *Ibid.* (translation and italics mine).

49 ICJ, *LaGrand Case* (*Germany* v. *United States of America*), ICJ Reports 2001, 466, paragraph 77. See Chapter 11.

required the German courts likewise to accept the existence of an individual right, the violation of which could constitute a grounds of appeal in a criminal trial.[50]

15.3.2.4 Interim Conclusion

According to what has been said above, one way for domestic courts to protect international individual rights effectively is to sanction violations of those rights by organs of the State, in accordance with the procedures and forms made available under domestic law. But the practical objections against individual enforcement of international rights before domestic courts must be taken seriously. Especially in the law of armed conflict, there is a danger of a flood of complaints if individual victims of war crimes and of other breaches of international humanitarian law – which typically are mass phenomena – are granted the power to institute proceedings. Particularly, States that are fragile in a post-conflict situation may be overwhelmed by mass complaints, which would endanger the goal of re-establishing peace. Compromises must be found in this regard in order to reconcile the goals of individual justice and of stabilization, such as by permitting objections claiming a national emergency (see also Chapter 7, p. 212).

The fact that in many instances, only domestic law and procedures exist for enforcing international norms which protect individuals does not mean that these norms could in no case be qualified as conferring genuine international individual rights.[51] In a multi-level system, the domestic courts are the functional equivalent of international courts and arbitration bodies ("*dédoublement fonctionnel*").[52] This function is assigned to domestic courts not only by international law, but it can also be required in parallel by domestic law. For instance, the Federal

[50] See BVerfGK 9, 174 (2006) (n. 43).

[51] See Evelyne Lagrange, L'efficacité des normes internationales concernant la situation des personnes privées dans les ordres juridiques internes, *Recueil des Cours* 356 (2012/III), 243–552 (275): "The realisation of an international subjective right and the sanctioning of an international obligation which saddles a private person may be sought in more than in the legal order of one State" (translation by the author).

[52] See Georges Scelle, Le phénomène juridique du dédoublement fonctionnel, in: Walter Schätzel/Hans-Jürgen Schlochauer (eds), *Rechtsfragen der internationalen Organisation: Festschrift für Hans Wehberg zu seinem 70. Geburtstag* (Frankfurt a. M.: Vittorio Klostermann 1956), 324–342. Hans Kelsen referred to domestic criminal courts as organs of the international community that apply domestic law and international law simultaneously (Hans Kelsen, *Principles of International Law* (2nd ed., Robert W. Tucker (ed.), New York: Holt Rinehart and Winston 1966), 205–206 and 210).

Constitutional Court of Germany assumes that "the Basic Law directly places the organs of the State in the service of enforcement of international law".[53] A necessary precondition for legal protection before domestic courts is the *direct effect* of the breached international norm, as discussed in Chapter 16. In the final analysis, the practical legal consequence of interpreting an international rule as an individual right is that the associated right of access to domestic procedures for protecting individual rights improves the procedural protection of the individual in the obligated State.[54]

15.3.3 Legal Protection against International Organizations

15.3.3.1 European Union

If international individual rights can be directed against international organizations, it would be consistent to allow for instituting proceedings against these organizations. Such complaints before domestic courts regularly fail due to the immunity of the organizations. Before international courts, complaints are so far possible only to a very limited extent against the EU, namely in the form of an individual or direct complaint to the ECJ to annul an act of an EU body in accordance with Article 263(4) of the TFEU.[55] Symptomatically, however, direct complaints by individuals against the EU bodies are admissible only subject to stricter conditions than against the Member States when they are executing EU law. While so far, no violation of rights has had to be asserted for individual complaints and it has sufficed for individual interests to be affected in fact ("direct and individual concern"), the ECJ has been interpreting this precondition increasingly narrowly. According to the *Plaumann* formula, individuals can challenge a measure of general application only if that measure affects them "by reason of certain attributes peculiar to them, or by reason of a factual situation which differentiates them from all other persons and distinguishes them individually in the same way as the addressee of

[53] BVerfGK 9, 174 (2006) (n. 43), paragraph 58 (translation mine).

[54] For a sceptical view, see Bernd Grzeszick, Rechte des Einzelnen im Völkerrecht, *Archiv des Völkerrechts* 43 (2005), 312–344 (337).

[55] Article 263(4) TFEU states: "Any natural or legal person may, under the conditions laid down in the first and second paragraphs, institute proceedings against an act addressed to that person or which is of direct and individual concern to them, and against a regulatory act which is of direct concern to them and does not entail implementing measures."

a decision".[56] It is important in this regard that in the case law, the power of the individual to institute proceedings was precisely *not* linked to the existence of a "right", but rather it was linked to direct (and individual) concern. While the ECJ does consider interference with individual rights when determining the power to institute proceedings, it apparently does not consider such interference to be a relevant precondition for direct concern.[57]

There is thus a tendency to restrict individual rights protection asserted directly against the EU's own administration. By comparison, it is often easier to bring claims under the law of Member States against decentralized acts of enforcement by the authorities of the Member States, which in turn apply EU law. A discrepancy therefore exists between judicial review of acts by the EU's own administration and the decentralized administrations of Member States. This discrepancy is intended to protect the functioning of the EU's own administration. But it is problematic from the perspective of the rule of law.

For this reason, it should be welcomed that the Treaty of Lisbon has expanded the wording of the provision slightly. According to Article 263(4) of the TFEU, legal protection is now granted against all acts (no longer only decisions), as long as the "act" is "of direct and individual concern to a person", "and against a regulatory act which is of direct concern to them and does not entail implementing measures". In the view of some commentators, this amendment does not represent a change to the substance, but rather it has simply adjusted the wording of the treaty to the case law. Contrary to this view, however, one could argue that the reformulation gives new, autonomous significance to the characteristic of individual concern. Individual concern could then

[56] ECJ, Case 25/62, *Plaumann & Co.* v. *Commission* [1963] ECR 95, p. 238. Contrary to the Opinion by the Advocate General to expand the individual's power to institute proceedings, confirmed in ECJ, Case C-50/00 P, *Unión de Pequeños Agricultores* [2002] ECR I-6677, paragraph 36.

[57] In *Jégo-Quéré*, the Court of First Instance had interpreted the requirement of direct and individual concern in the sense of legal concern when it wrote that "a natural or legal person is to be regarded as individually concerned by a Community measure of general application that concerns him directly if the measure in question affects his legal position, in a matter which is both definite and immediate, by *restricting his rights or by imposing obligations on him*" (cited in paragraph 37 of the ECJ's judgment on appeal; italics mine). The ECJ found in this regard: "Such an interpretation has the effect of removing all meaning from the requirement of individual concern set out in the fourth paragraph of Article 230 EC" (ECJ, Case C-263/02 P, *Commission* v. *Jégo-Quéré* of 1 April 2004 [2004] ECR I-3425, paragraph 38).

be elevated to a key element of the provision (which would accordingly be subject to a new interpretation).[58]

But it is an open question whether this legal development contains a new orientation towards individual *rights*. Two considerations speak in favour of this view: Firstly, a goal of the Lisbon reform was to "put citizens at the centre of the European project".[59] Secondly and most importantly, the Lisbon reform made the Charter of Fundamental Rights of the European Union legally binding. The "right to an effective remedy" and to an "impartial tribunal" laid down in Article 47 of the Charter of Fundamental Rights makes legal protection dependent on violated "*rights* and freedoms".[60] This fundamental right introduces the logic of individual rights into the EU's legal protection system. The new legally binding nature of the Charter of Fundamental Rights requires any interpretation of the TFEU's preconditions for instituting proceedings to be compatible with fundamental rights. This may signal a movement towards individualizing actions for annulment (and thus turning away from the "French" objective-law approach to instituting proceedings). Among international organizations, the EU enjoys a special position. The fact that individual rights protection directed against EU bodies is rudimentary, despite the strong EU judicial system, gives an indication of how far removed such protection is in relation to other organizations.

15.3.3.2 Other International Organizations

The following mechanisms for protecting individual rights against international organizations are in the process of being strengthened: Against the World Bank, groups of two or more complainants who believe their rights are violated by projects funded by the World Bank may request an inspection. The Inspection Panel of the World Bank then examines whether the Bank has failed to follow its operational policies and relevant agreements with respect to the design, appraisal, and/or implementation of a project financed by the Bank and thus has had a material adverse

[58] See Matthias Kottmann, Plaumanns Ende: Ein Vorschlag zu Art. 263 Abs. 4 AEUV, *Zeitschrift für ausländisches öffentliches Recht und Völkerrecht* 70 (2010), 547–566.

[59] José Manuel Barroso, President of the European Commission, in: Press release of the Commission dated 13 December 2007, IP/07/1922.

[60] Article 47(1) of the Charter of Fundamental Rights states: "Everyone whose *rights* and freedoms guaranteed by the law of the Union are violated has the right to an effective remedy before a tribunal in compliance with the conditions laid down in this Article" (italics mine).

effect on the rights or interests of the complainants.[61] The intellectual father of the World Bank Inspection Panel and Senior Vice President of the World Bank at the time, Ibrahim F. I. Shihata, referred to his project as part of the "phenomenal expansion of the rights of individuals and private groups derived directly from international law".[62]

Furthermore, two different institutions exist to monitor compliance with human rights standards by the two principal international actors in Kosovo. First, the United Nations Mission in Kosovo (UNMIK) is monitored by the UNMIK Human Rights Advisory Panel (HRAP)[63] which was established in 2006 and began its work in 2007.[64] Second, the European Union Rule of Law Mission in Kosovo (EULEX) is reviewed by the Human Rights Review Panel (HRRP) in Pristina (operational since 2010).[65] The benchmark for review to be applied by HRRP (its "accountability concept") is not fully clear. It forms part of EULEX's Operational Plan.[66] But the relevant EU Council Joint Action states that EULEX Kosovo shall "ensure that all its activities respect international standards concerning human rights and gender mainstreaming".[67]

[61] The legal basis is International Bank for Reconstruction and Development and International Development Association, Resolution No. IBRD 93-10 and Resolution No. IDA 93-96, "The World Bank Inspection Panel" of 22 September 1993, *International Legal Materials* 34 (1995) 520–523. The Operating Procedures (OP) of the Inspection Panel are reprinted in: The World Bank Inspection Panel, Accountability at the World Bank – The Inspection Panel 10 Years On (Washington 2003), Annex VIID.

[62] Ibrahim F. I. Shihata, *The World Bank Inspection Panel: In Practice* (2nd ed., New York: Oxford University Press 2000), 262.

[63] www.unmikonline.org/human_rights/index.htm.

[64] The legal basis for the Human Rights Advisory Panel is UNMIK Regulation No. 2006/12 on the Establishment of the Human Rights Advisory Panel of 23 March 2006, amended by UNMIK Regulation No. 2007/3 Amending UNMIK Regulation No. 2006/12 on the Establishment of the Human Rights Review Panel of 12 January 2007. Also relevant are the Administrative Direction No. 2009/1 Implementing UNMIK Regulation No. 2006/12 on the Establishment of the Human Rights Advisory Panel of 17 October 2009 (based on Article 19 of Regulation No. 2006/12) and the Rules of Procedure of the Human Rights Advisory Panel; the Rules of Procedure were adopted by the Panel on 5 February 2008. The Rules of Procedure have been revised several times. See European Commission for Democracy through Law (Venice Commission) of the Council of Europe, Opinion on the Existing Mechanisms to Review the Compatibility with Human Rights Standards of Acts by UNMIK and EULEX in Kosovo, No. 545/2009, adopted at its 85th Plenary Session on 17–18 December 2010, CDL-AD(2010)051.

[65] The Rules of Procedure (hereinafter: Rules) were adopted on 9 June 2010. The first regular session was held from 9 to 11 June 2010.

[66] See Annual Report Human Rights Review Panel 2014, p. 8, note 1.

[67] Article 3(i) of the Council Joint Action 2008/124/CFSP on the European Union Rule of Law Mission in Kosovo of 4 February 2008.

Against the Security Council, individuals affected by targeted sanctions can turn to the Office of the Ombudsperson, which took up work in 2010.[68] The Ombudsperson procedure for delisting is precisely defined in Annex II of the Working Guidelines of the sanctions committee (latest version of 2013), including time periods.[69] The persons on whom sanctions are imposed have "*subjective rights vis-à-vis the United Nations* that derive from the UN Charter", according to the Fassbender study.[70] Overall, the possibilities for the affected persons themselves to enforce international individual rights against international organizations are only rudimentary.

15.4 International Individual Rights as the Foundation of the Emerging International Guarantee of Access to Justice

Currently, "a trend can be observed worldwide toward recognizing the individual right to effective review by an independent body as an important characteristic of the international legal order".[71] This goes beyond the right to a local remedy against human rights violations as guaranteed, e.g., by Article 13 ECHR (see Chapter 6, pp. 180–82 and in this

[68] UNSC res. 1904 (2009), paragraphs 20–27. In 2010, the Secretary-General appointed Kimberley Prost as the first Ombudsperson (UNSC 282 of 4 June 2010). UNSC res. 1989 (of 17 June 2011) extended and expanded the mandate of the Ombudsperson. In particular, the Ombudsperson may now make a recommendation on a delisting decision, from which the members of the Sanctions Committee may deviate only by consensus; otherwise, the recommendation becomes binding after sixty days or a shorter period (the latest resolution is SC res. 261 of June 2014 which extended the ombudsperson's mandate until December 2017 (paragraph 41). It is controversial whether this procedure, which is tantamount to "*de facto* judicial review", meets the demands of due process. See Katalin Tünde Huber/Alejandro Rodiles, An Ombudsperson in the United Nations Security Council: A Paradigm Shift?, *Anuario Mexicano de Derecho Internacional* 10 (2012), 107–142; Watson Institute for International Studies/The Graduate Institute Geneva (ed.), Due Process and Targeted Sanctions: An Update of the "Watson Report" by Sue Eckert and Thomas J. Biersteker (2012) with a positive assessment (quote on p. 24).

[69] Security Council Committee pursuant to Resolutions 1267 (1999) and 1989 (2011) concerning al-Qaida and associated individuals and entities, Guidelines of the Committee for the Conduct of Its Work (adopted on 7 November 2002, as amended on 10 April 2003, 21 December 2005, 29 November 2006, 12 February 2007, 9 December 2008, 22 July 2010, 26 January 2011, 30 November 2011, and 15 April 2013). Important points had been revised in 2011.

[70] Bardo Fassbender, Targeted Sanctions Imposed by the UN Security Council and Due Process Rights: A Study Commissioned by the UN Office of Legal Affairs and Follow-Up Action by the United Nations, *International Organisations Law Review* 3 (2006), 437–485 (438; italics mine).

[71] Eberhard Schmidt-Aßmann/Timo Rademacher, Rechtsschutzgarantien des internationalen Rechts, *Jahrbuch des öffentlichen Rechts der Gegenwart* 61 (2013), 61–88 (62; translation mine).

Chapter p. 482). We see the beginnings of an "overarching guarantee of protection of individual rights against acts of public power under international law". This guarantee extends across sectors and levels. This overarching or "integrative" principle rounds off the existing selective guarantees of judicial protection and strengthens them. In this way, individuals are protected better in the "intermediate areas", i.e., where various regimes intersect. This principle of international law also serves as a guideline for the interpretation of domestic guarantees of access to justice.[72] There is a "trend towards judicial protection" under international law. This novel international-law-based right to a remedy relates not only to alleged violations of domestic legal positions of the individual but arguably also to violations of international rights (human rights and others). According to Eberhard Schmidt-Aßmann and Timo Rademacher, "[w]ithin this flexible framework, one can now speak of a right in principle to judicial legal protection recognized by international law. Any deviations from this basic model require justifying reasons and sufficient compensatory rules."[73]

In our context, it is especially significant that international individual rights provide additional legitimacy to the demand for individual rights protection (through domestic and international bodies). Here, one might raise the critical objection that international law does not provide compulsory jurisdiction, and hence even States do not have automatic access to legal protection. Why should such access be granted to individuals? The answer must start with the insight that only individuals have rights for their own sake. In contrast, States have powers and competences that allow them to carry out tasks in the interest of human beings. The State is an institution that serves human beings, not an end in itself.[74]

[72] *Ibid.*, 86-87. [73] *Ibid.*, 88 (translation mine).

[74] This consideration was a main argument for international legal scholars of the interwar period who fought for the international legal personality of the individual. "Since the dogma of absolute sovereignty has been shaken, since the State has been dismantled of any mystical personification, and since finally the conviction has established itself that the State is not an end in itself, but only a means for satisfying individual needs, one begins to remember that all law – and consequently the law of nations itself – ultimately exists only for the protection of individuals" (Jean Spiropoulos, L'individu et le droit international, *Recueil des Cours* 30 (1929/V), 191–270 (197; my translation)); See also Nicolas Politis, *Les nouvelles tendances du droit international* (Paris: Hachette 1927), 55–93 (76). The advocates of the international legal personality of the individual thus opposed the Hegelian hypostasis of the State: "The state does not exist for the sake of the citizens; it might rather be said that the state is the end and the citizens are its instruments" (Georg Wilhelm Friedrich Hegel, *Vorlesungen über die Philosophie der Geschichte, Bd. I:*

International legal protection for States and against other States is thus motivated differently than international legal protection for individuals. Legal protection between States can be justified only functionally, not existentially. At the same time, such protection is also limited due to State-specific grounds: In relations between States, it is State sovereignty that stands in the way of compulsory international jurisdiction and also grants immunity from the courts of foreign countries. But the principle of State sovereignty and equality cannot easily justify the reduction of legal protection for the purpose of safeguarding rights of persons against State power.

The legitimizing role played by international individual rights in regard to the just-mentioned overarching right to a remedy can be compared with that of Jellinek's individual public right in German late constitutionalism.[75] While qualifying an international legal norm as an individual right does not entail automatic enforceability, the conceptualization of international individual rights does provide a theoretical basis for the existing practice of international individual enforcement, and it can thus also provide the intellectual foundation for the expansion thereof.

Einleitung – Die Vernunft in der Geschichte (Georg Lasson (ed.), Leipzig: Felix Meiner Verlag 1920), 91; translation mine).

75 See Masing, *Mobilisierung des Bürgers*, 1997 (n. 4), 65–66 with n. 47.

16

Direct Effect of Norms Establishing Individual Rights and Duties

16.1 Definition of the Problem

In the global multi-level system, the practical effectiveness of the international rights and duties of the individual depends on the ability to enforce them through domestic courts and authorities. The international status of the individual is determined significantly by the direct effect of international legal norms.

While older judicial practice on direct effect was primarily concerned with treaty provisions that benefited individuals, more recently the issue has also been the direct application of international criminal law by domestic courts. This is of practical relevance at least during the interim period – which may last long – before international criminal norms are incorporated verbatim or in spirit into domestic criminal law (see Chapter 5, p. 126). Another important area is the direct effect of norms of the law of armed conflict that create entitlements and obligations (see Chapter 7).

The direct effect of international legal norms is a complex matter: Superficially, it concerns the technical suitability of the norms, but underneath lie questions concerning the separation of powers and the principles of legality and democracy. These constitutional principles are in turn intertwined with politics.[1] The issue is not primarily whether authorities and courts can apply international legal norms, but rather whether they legitimately may or should. The principles involved here are those of the domestic constitutional law of democratic States organized according to the rule of law, the ultimate purpose of which is to protect individuals from arbitrary action by power-holders and to secure their liberty. Starting from the premise that the law has at least some

[1] Hélène Ruiz Fabri, Is There a Case – Legally and Politically – For a Direct Effect of WTO Obligations? *European Journal of International Law* 25 (2014), 151–173 (151): "[T]he issue of direct effect always becomes a political question", the core of the matter is "who decides for what purposes".

independent life from the political processes in which it is embedded, the highly political character of the issue of direct effect does not render a legal and constitutional analysis obsolete.

16.2 Terms and Distinctions

16.2.1 Foundations

In this chapter, the terms "direct effect" and "self-executingness"[2] are used synonymously. According to my usage, an international legal provision has direct effect, is directly applicable, or is self-executing if a domestic body can apply the norm and is authorized or required to do so, and if the application of the norm might entail – in combination with the primacy of international law over domestic law – that a contrary domestic legal provision is no longer controlling within the domestic jurisdiction. A complementary concept is the indirect effect of international law, i.e., interpretation of domestic law in conformity with international law.

The domestic body applying international law may be a public authority or an administrative, civil, or domestic court, since the question of direct effect may arise both in the context of domestic (non-contentious or contentious) administrative proceedings and in the context of civil or criminal proceedings. Depending on the constellation, application of the relevant international legal norm can be to the benefit or the detriment of the individual concerned. In the beneficial constellation, the individual will typically *invoke* the international legal norm. In some cases, authorities and courts may or must apply international legal norms *ex officio*, e.g., in criminal proceedings.[3]

Direct effect understood in that way must be distinguished from two other aspects, namely the inclusion of the international legal norms in the domestic legal order (systemic aspect) and the imposition of substantive individual rights or duties (substantive aspect).

[2] The term "self-executing" originated in US law and is common in the United Kingdom; it is also familiar in continental European case law and literature. For the first mention, see Justice Field in *Bartram* v. *Robertson*, 122 US 116, 120 (1887).

[3] See ECJ, Joined Cases C-300/98 and C-329/98, *Dior et al.* v. *Tuk Consultancy* [2000] ECR I-11307, paragraph 48, where two possibilities are mentioned, namely "that the legal order of a Member State should accord to individuals the right to rely directly on the rule laid down by Article 50(6) of TRIPs or that it should oblige the courts to apply that rule of their own motion".

Both international treaty law and customary international law may be self-executing. The case law and literature focus almost exclusively on the former. The following discussion refers initially to treaty norms and only briefly broaches the application of customary international law.

Finally, self-executing international or European norms are not automatically also individual public-law-based rights for the purposes of domestic law, e.g., in the sense of Article 19(4) of the German Basic Law or of any domestic law-administrative procedure. In Germany, for instance, it has been discussed whether and under what preconditions German administrative courts should hear complaints which are based only on the plaintiff's assertion that a policy violated an EU provision. Does such a violation grant standing? This discussion is still in flux: While direct effect of international or EU law does not replace the requirements of administrative procedure under domestic law, it might – e.g., in Germany – modify the traditional requirement of plausible reliance an individual public-law-based right (*subjektives öffentliches Recht*) as a prerequisite of standing before administrative tribunals.

16.2.2 *Direct Effect Is (Also) a Question of International Law*

Direct effect is governed both by international law and by the domestic law in question; the principle is of a "mixed international/domestic nature".[4] According to a traditional view, direct effect was solely a question of domestic law, the answer to which was entirely left to the domestic courts. The reasoning for that view was that the issue was primarily one of *implementing* international law or of fulfilling international legal obligations. International law itself demanded only that it be implemented, but it left the way in which it was implemented to the States. The way in which it was implemented fell within the *domaine réservé* and thus – from this perspective – also the decision on direct or merely indirect effect.[5]

[4] André Nollkaemper, *National Courts and the International Rule of Law* (Oxford: Oxford University Press 2011), 127.

[5] On the direct effect of WTO law within the internal legal sphere of the EU, see ECJ, Case C-149/96, *Portugal* v. *Council*, Judgment of 23 November 1999 [1999] ECR I-8395, paragraph 35: "[A]ccording to the general rules of international law there must be bona fide *performance* of every agreement. Although each contracting party is responsible for executing fully the commitments which it has undertaken *it is nevertheless free to determine the legal means appropriate for attaining that end in its legal system* . . ." (italics mine). According to ECJ, Joined Cases C-300/98 and C-329/98, *Parfums Christian Dior SA* v. *Tuk*

In contrast, it is argued here that direct effect should primarily be understood as a question of *interpretation* of the treaty provision concerned.[6] The ascription of direct effect depends crucially on the content of the norm, and thus inevitably requires interpreting the treaty provision.[7] The interpretation of an international treaty's provisions must meet international requirements, even if the interpretation is made by a domestic court. The rules for interpreting international treaties are codified in the Vienna Convention on the Law of Treaties and have been further specified by international (and domestic) case law. As the English House of Lords recalled, "multilateral treaties . . . must be given an independent meaning derivable from the sources mentioned in articles 31 and 32 [Vienna Convention on the Law of Treaties] and . . . without taking colour from distinctive features of the legal system of any individual contracting state. *In principle therefore there can be only one true interpretation.*"[8]

However, determining whether an international norm is self-executing is the responsibility of the domestic authorities and courts called upon in the specific dispute. This situation corresponds to the normal case of international (decentralized) application of the law. The existence of centralized international requirements cannot guarantee that they are actually applied identically in concrete individual cases. Along these lines, the Swiss Federal Council stated in its first dispatch (*Botschaft*) on the GATT that the issue involved "the question of the direct effect of individual provisions of the various WTO agreements, which arises for all international treaties in accordance with the general rules of interpretation of the law of treaties (Article 31 of the Vienna Convention on the Law of Treaties . . .) *and* Swiss administrative and judicial practice".[9]

Consultancy [2000] ECR I-11307, paragraphs 45–48, esp. 48, different answers in different member States are possible (in regard to Article 60(6) of TRIPS).

6 As it is in BGE 136 I, 290–295, *X.* v. *Z.* (4 May 2010), Considerations 2.3.1.–2.3.2.: Direct effect is a question of interpretation that must be undertaken in accordance with the guiding principles of the VCLT.

7 See Nollkaemper, *Rule of Law*, 2011, 129: "Still, when the question of direct effect is made contingent on the substantive qualities of the norm, the distinction between the international and national level collapses and the possibility of an international institution giving effect to that norm becomes highly relevant to the question of whether a national court should do so."

8 House of Lords, *R* v. *Secretary of State for the Home Department*; ex parte Adan and Aitseguer, 2000 UKHL 67 of 19 December 2000 (referring to the Refugee Convention, italics mine).

9 Dispatch on approval of the GATT/WTO agreements (Uruguay Round) of 19 September 1994, BBl. 1994 IV 1 et seq., 418 (italics mine).

Direct effect is thus a question whose answer must be found not only in domestic law but *also* in international law itself.[10] Accordingly, the question may be decided by international courts, as was the case in the PCIJ's *Danzig* opinion.[11] Application of an international legal norm by domestic *and* international bodies should follow rules that are in turn compatible with each other, because both levels are linked as reciprocal catch-all mechanisms due to the local remedies requirement and the principle of subsidiarity.

16.2.3 Direct Effect, "Validity" of International Law, and Monism/ Dualism

The multidimensional problem of legitimacy is the deeper reason for the frequent conflation of the question of direct effect with the question of the inclusion of a treaty into the domestic legal order, especially in Anglo-American practice and literature.[12] In the United Kingdom, direct effect

[10] For a detailed and convincing justification, see Arnold Koller, *Die unmittelbare Anwendbarkeit völkerrechtlicher Verträge und des EWG-Vertrages im innerstaatlichen Bereich* (Bern: Stämpfli 1971), 114–124. Along these lines, see also Joe Verhoeven, La notion d' "applicabilité directe" du droit international, *Revue belge de droit international* 15 (1980), 243–264 (258–259); Nollkaemper, *Rule of Law*, 2011, 126–129. For a weaker form of the argument, see Karen Kaiser, Treaties, Direct Applicability, in: Rüdiger Wolfrum (ed.), *The Max Planck Encyclopedia of International Law* (Oxford: Oxford University Press 2012), paragraphs 6 and 8: The question is ultimately answered by domestic law, but international law must be observed in this regard, especially the interpretation of a provision by international bodies. But see André Nollkaemper, The Duality of Direct Effect of International Law, *European Journal of International Law* 25 (2014), 105–125 (108): International law allows the domestic authorities and courts to shape and apply doctrines of direct effect to fulfil two functions: either to shield domestic law from international law or to protect individuals with help of international law.

[11] PCIJ, *Jurisdiction of the Courts of Danzig*, PCIJ Ser. B, No. 15 (1928).

[12] In *Medellín*, for example, the US Supreme Court formulated self-execution primarily as a question of the validity of a treaty *"as" international law* or *"as" domestic law*: "This Court has long recognized the distinction between treaties that automatically have effect *as domestic law*, and those that – *while they constitute international law commitments* – do not by themselves function as binding federal law" (US Supreme Court, *Medellín* v. *Texas*, 552 US 491 (504) (Judgment of 25 March 2008 – *Medellin II*). In its explanatory footnote, the Supreme Court conflated the aspect of including an ICJ judgment in the domestic legal order with the aspect of implementing that decision through a (domestic) law: "The label 'self-executing' has on occasion been used to convey different meanings. What we mean by 'self-executing' is that the treaty has automatic *domestic effect as federal law* upon ratification. Conversely, a 'non-self-executing' treaty does not by itself give rise to domestically enforceable federal law. Whether such a treaty has domestic effect depends upon implementing legislation passed by Congress" (*ibid.*, n. 2, italics mine).

is seen as a *prerequisite* for including the treaty in the law of the United Kingdom. If a provision is not self-executing, it is not considered part of the English legal order. According to the House of Lords, "as a matter of the constitutional law of the United Kingdom, the Royal Prerogative, whilst it embraces the making of treaties, does not extend to altering the law or *conferring rights upon individuals* or *depriving individuals of rights* which they enjoy in domestic law without the intervention of Parliament. Treaties, as it is sometimes expressed, are *not self-executing*. Quite simply, a treaty is *not part of English law* unless and until it has been incorporated into the law by legislation. So far as individuals are concerned, it is res inter alios acta from which they cannot derive rights and by which they cannot be deprived of rights or subjected to obligations; and it is outside the purview of the court not only because it is made in the conduct of foreign relations, which are a prerogative of the Crown, but also because, as a source of rights and obligations, it is irrelevant."[13] While this judgment refers to the rights and duties of individuals (at the substantive level), not to procedural invocability, this changes nothing about the underlying question of legitimacy. Because in the United Kingdom international treaties are traditionally concluded without the involvement of Parliament, they enjoy only minor democratic legitimacy.[14] For this reason, an implementing act of Parliament is required for the treaty to be valid in domestic law (i.e., for it to be included in the domestic legal order), so that – in regard to international treaties – the UK system is strictly dualist.

Preferable, however, is a distinction that contrasts with the Anglo-American tradition described above. The question of including the international legal norm in domestic law (the question of "domestic validity") should be distinguished from that of its direct effect.[15] This

[13] House of Lords, *Australia & New Zealand Banking Group* v. *Australia*, Judgment of 26 October 1990, [1990] 2 AC 418 (italics mine).

[14] On the reform efforts for a Constitutional Renewal Bill, stagnating since 2009, see HL Bill 34, Government response (Cm 7688, 20 July 2009) on the Draft Constitutional Renewal Bill (Cm 7342).

[15] See also Gaby Buchs, *Die unmittelbare Anwendbarkeit völkerrechtlicher Vertragsbestimmungen* (Baden-Baden: Nomos 1993), 28–30; Kaiser, Treaties, 2010, paragraph 2; Rudolf Geiger, *Grundgesetz und Völkerrecht* (4th ed., Munich: Beck 2009), 143. Unfortunately, in a recent decision on Article 36 of the VCCR, the Federal Constitutional Court of Germany associated the inclusion of a treaty by way of an approving formal legal act of Parliament with its direct effect by referring to the "understanding underlying Article 59(2) of the Basic Law, according to which international treaty law as interpreted by the competent international court is *not directly applicable* domestically" (BVerfGK 9,

would also mean that direct effect is independent of the "monist" or "dualist" tradition of a State.[16] The inclusion of a treaty (or of customary law) can be accomplished "monistically" or "dualistically", and it is a subsequent question of whether an international legal norm is then self-executing or not. A norm that is included in the domestic legal order but not directly applicable by authorities and courts is not totally useless, because the legislature and the government must ensure compliance with the norm through further domestic action.[17]

16.3 Direct Effect and the Substantive International Legal Status of the Individual

Direct effect of international legal norms should be distinguished from the existence of substantive individual rights and duties.[18] This is often not the case in practice (and the literature).[19] In the *Jurisdiction of the Courts of Danzig* opinion, the PCIJ treated the conferral of rights and their invocability or actionability before domestic courts as a single set of issues.[20] Linking these aspects does make sense especially in constellations that are qualified under domestic law as belonging to civil law, administrative law, or constitutional law. In civil law, actionability is normally linked to a substantive right, and the public law of many

174 (2 BvR 2115/01, 2 BvR 2132/01, 2 BvR 348/032010) of 19 September 2006, paragraph 62; italics mine).

[16] The interpretations of the *Danzig* opinion of the PCIJ corresponded, however, to the respective views of monism and dualism. The strict dualist Anzilotti interpreted the opinion such that conferring individual rights was (only) possible under domestic law (see Chapter 2, p. 30). On the independence of the question of the legal status of the individual from monism/dualism, see Chapter 3, pp. 54–58.

[17] See Geiger, *Grundgesetz und Völkerrecht*, 2009, 143.

[18] Because of the distinction between the direct effect of an international legal norm and its character as an individual right, the limited actionability of social, economic, and cultural rights, for instance, does not automatically entail that they lack the quality of individual rights. The UN Committee on Economic, Social and Cultural Rights assumes that certain provisions must be applied directly by domestic courts, and it furthermore assumes that domestic implementing legislation can create justiciable claims for other rights under the ICESCR. See Committee on Economic, Social and Cultural Rights, General Comment No. 3 (UN Doc. E/1991/23, Annex II, 86 (1991), esp. paragraphs 4–6).

[19] See, e.g., the Federal Supreme Court of Switzerland, BGE, *X.* v. *Z.* (n. 6). The judgment rejects the direct effect of Article 7(d) of the ICESCR on holidays with pay and equates the question of whether the norm is directly applicable ("directement applicable") with the question of whether it grants individual rights ("droits subjectifs") (Considerations 2.3.1. and 2.3.2).

[20] See PCIJ, Jurisdiction of the Courts of Danzig (n. 11).

States also links the possibilities for individuals to protect their rights under administrative law to the existence of substantive (individual) rights of the individual (in contrast to norms that exist merely under objective law). The linkage or lack thereof is then, however, a question solely for domestic law – a question that arises equally when provisions of domestic law (especially domestic public law) are invoked. It is therefore not astonishing that domestic courts often consider the conferral of rights upon individuals to be a precondition for the direct effect of a provision[21] – or conversely view the conferral of rights as a consequence of direct effect.[22] Practice on this point is therefore "confused (or fused)".[23]

In terms of the legal system, however, direct effect cannot be equated with the conferral of individual rights for the following reasons.[24] Firstly, international legal norms can set out not only individual rights but also duties, or neither of the two. Secondly, direct effect is generally reviewed

[21] For the United States, e.g., see US Supreme Court, *Head Money Cases*, 112 US 580, 598–599 (1884): "A treaty, then, is a law of the land, as an act of Congress, whenever its provisions prescribe a rule by which the *rights* of the private citizen or subject may be determined." If the treaty contains detailed specific individual rights, it is more probable that it is addressed to the courts (US Supreme Court, *Medellín* v. *Texas* (n. 12), Justice Breyer, dissenting (p. 538 et seq. (550)). For Switzerland, see BGE 126 I 240, p. 242, Consideration 2.b. (2000) – *Studiengebühren ZH II* on Article 13(2)(b) and (c) of the ICESCR (quote below, n. 27). For Germany, see RGZ 117, 280, 284 (1927) on Chapter 18 of the implementing provisions of the German-Polish agreement on Upper Silesia of 1922: "Since this provision, as its content shows, is not a general international legal provision, but rather a legislative measure governing the legal relationships of the parties concerned, the individual can also derive rights from it" (translation mine). For France, see, e.g., Conseil d'Etat: Because Article 9 of the Convention on the Rights of the Child "does not grant rights to individuals", the provision is not self-executing: "Considérant que les stipulations de l'article 9 de la convention relative aux droits de l'enfant signée à New-York le 26 janvier 1990 *créent seulement des obligations entre Etats sans ouvrir de droits aux intéressés*; que les époux X. . . . ne peuvent donc utilement se prévaloir de cet engagement international pour demander l'annulation des arrêtés ordonnant leur reconduite à la frontière" (Décision No. 143866 of 29 July 1994; italics mine).

[22] See BGE, *Maison G.Sprl contre Direction générale de douanes* of 2 September 1986, BGE 112 Ib, 183 et seq., Consideration 2a): "pour autant qu'elles apparaissent directement applicables, les règles conventionnelles sont susceptibles d'imposer des obligations et de conférer des droits non seulement aux autorités, mais également aux particuliers".

[23] John Jackson, Status of Treaties in Domestic Legal Systems: A Policy Analysis, *American Journal of Internatinal Law* 86 (1992), 310–340 (317).

[24] From case law, see the opinions of Advocate General Walter van Gerven in ECJ, Case 70/87, *Fediol* v. *Commission*, Judgment of 22 June 1989 [1989] ECR 1797, p. 1806. From the literature, see Buchs, *Anwendbarkeit völkerrechtlicher Vertragsbestimmungen*, 1993, 40 and 89; Geiger, *Grundgesetz und Völkerrecht*, 2009, 143; Nollkaemper, *Rule of Law*, 2011, 121–122.

by domestic courts as a precondition for admissibility, and the lack of direct effect entails inadmissibility of the complaint. In contrast, individual rights are a concept of substantive law, the procedural consequence of which may be actionability, but it does not necessarily have to be. Thirdly, the rationale of an individual right consists in the owner's individuality and status as a person. In contrast, the direct effect test, as an upstream filter for the actual application of international law, is motivated primarily by institutional considerations. A positive outcome of the test leads to the decentralized enforcement of international law. Overall, the preliminary examination of the direct effect of an international legal norm ensures the division of functions and powers of the executive, legislative, and judicial branches (which in turn serves to safeguard freedom, however). This institutional background explains why, especially in the jurisprudence of the ECJ on WTO law, the overall structure of an international treaty is examined as a preliminary question to assess the suitability of a specific norm for direct effect.[25] When, in contrast, the issue is the qualification of a norm as an individual right, the overall structure of the treaty is not able to serve as a filter in this sense. In sum, the direct effect of an international legal norm and the existence of an (international) individual right are different legal concepts.[26]

[25] For the WTO agreements, see ECJ, *Portugal* v. *Council* (n. 5); for other international treaties, see Conseil d'Etat, 9 November 2007, *Ligue pour la préservation de la faune sauvage et la défense des non-chasseurs*: criterion of "économie générale" of an agreement.

[26] For a clear distinction, see, e.g., BVerfGE 46, 342 et seq. (Ruling of 13 December 1977 – *philippinische Botschaftskonten*): Even general rules of international law, the regulatory content of which is directed solely at States, must "be observed by all law-making and law-applying bodies of the Federal Republic of Germany as *norms of objective law* and *applied*, depending on their definition and the content of the regulation. Private individuals – like foreign States – may equally 'invoke' these general rules of international law within the jurisdiction of the Federal Republic of Germany and within the framework of the applicable procedural law, as they may invoke other objective law, even though they must be observed *ex officio* within this framework even without being invoked. Depending on their content and, as a rule, as a preliminary question, they may have an effect as objective law on the legal request by the individual and thus be relevant to the decision. Along these lines, they may also generate legal effects for and against the individual." (p. 363). The general international legal rules on post-judgment measures of constraint "do not give rise to an individual right of the private person to carry out measures of constraint against foreign States within the jurisdiction of the Federal Republic of Germany to the extent permitted by general international law, nor do they provide the basis for an individual duty not to engage in measures of constraint against a foreign State to the extent prohibited by general international law" (p. 503, translation and italics mine). This ruling concerned the immunity of States from post-judgment measures of constraint. The Federal Constitutional Court of Germany found

The relationship between these concepts is reciprocal. In practice, courts often reject the direct effect of an international legal norm in order to curtail substantive claims. Common to an international individual right and a self-executing international legal norm is that their quality is determined by interpretation, and that similar criteria are employed for their qualification. In particular, the interpretation of both legal concepts relies on the fact that their protective purpose is directed at the individual. In summary, the question of direct effect could be described as an additional filter that has the potential to weaken the practical effectiveness of the international legal status of the individual; when employing this filter, the courts must therefore also consider the substantive rights of the individual in advance (in addition to other considerations).

16.4 Traditional Criteria of Direct Effect

The practice of the courts of different States regarding the direct effect of international treaty law is guided by parallel principles and does not diverge significantly, either from the "classical" international requirements or from each other.

The first criterion is the intention of the contracting parties and of the bodies of the State involved in domestic conclusion of the treaty, e.g., the US Senate. The domestic courts normally take the intentions of these actors into consideration. Traditionally, this has even been the primary consideration. The courts review whether the parties as a whole or individual State bodies wanted the provision in question to be self-executing.[27] This intention must often be derived from objective factors such as the wording, the circumstances under which the treaty was concluded, implications that private parties are permitted to bring claims, etc. Recently, the focus on the will of the historical law-making bodies, which previously had been dominant, appears to be easing somewhat.

a prohibition of compulsory execution in regard to objects serving sovereign purposes, as a general rule of international law as referred to in Article 25 of the Basic Law.

[27] § 111(4) of the Restatement (Third) of Foreign Relations Law (1987): "An international agreement of the United States is 'non-self-executing' (a) if the agreement manifests an intention that it shall not become effective as domestic law without the enactment of implementing legislation, (b) if the Senate in giving consent to a treaty, or Congress by resolution, requires implementing legislation, or (c) if implementing legislation is constitutionally required."

In the formulation of the Federal Administrative Court of Germany, the other criteria are the "wording, purpose, and content" of an international treaty provision.[28] Courts review especially whether the specific provision is suitable for judicial application. This encompasses primarily its *specificity*.[29] In addition, its *unconditionality* (completeness) is required, in the sense that no implementing steps by authorities or lawmakers are necessary.[30] Often, the courts consider the object, the

[28] BVerwGE 80, 233 et seq., 235 (27 September 1988) on the requirement of approval set out in the final protocol of the German-Iranian settlement agreement: "Pursuant to the approving parliamentary act . . ., the treaty provision has become directly applicable under domestic law, because it is suitable in terms of its *wording, purpose, and content* to have legal effect in the same way as a domestic legal provision" (translation and italics mine). According to BVerwGE 87, 11, 13 (16 October 1990) on the 1954 Convention relating to the Status of Stateless Persons, "the transformation of an international treaty through an approving Parliamentary act leads to the direct effect of a treaty norm, if it is suitable in terms of *wording, purpose, and content* and sufficiently specific to have legal effect in the same way as a domestic legal provision, i.e., it does not require any further normative elaboration" (translation and italics mine). See also BVerwG, Judgment of 4 June 1991, AVR 29 (1991), 409 (412) on the Geneva Convention on Refugees. The older case law (Imperial Court of Justice and Federal Court of Justice) used the synonymous formula "content, purpose, and formulation", see, e.g., RGZ 117, 284, 285 (1927); RGZ 121, 7, 9 (1928); RGZ 124, 204, 206 (1931) on an agreement between Germany, Poland, and the Free City of Danzig (an implementing agreement for Article 98 of the Treaty of Versailles); BGHZ 11, 135 et seq., 138 (6 November 1953) of the Berne Convention for the Protection of Literary and Artistic Works; BGHZ 17, 309, 313 (24 May 1955) on an interzonal agreement of the German and Soviet railroad administrations.

[29] For Switzerland, see BGE, *Studiengebühren ZH II* (n. 21) on Article 13(2)(b) and (c) of the ICESCR: "The complainant may . . ., however, only invoke such norms that are self-executing; the treaty complaint serves only to enforce those treaty provisions that govern the legal status of the individual directly . . . This requires that the invoked treaty norm is sufficiently specific in terms of content and sufficiently clear to form the basis of a decision in a given case. The required specificity is not given especially in the case of mere programmatic articles. Specificity is also lacking in the case of norms which only sketch the regulation of a subject matter, which give the contracting State considerable discretion or scope for decision-making, or which merely contain guiding principles, i.e., which are not addressed to the administrative and judicial authorities but rather to the legislative bodies . . ." (translation mine). See, similarly, BGE 120 Ia 1, p. 11 Consideration 5.b (1994) – *Studiengebühren ZH I*. For France, see Jean Matringe, Note, *Revue Générale de Droit International Public* 112 (2008), 210–212 (211), who calls for individual consideration of the provisions and mentions the criteria of specificity and unconditionality of the norms. Similarly, see Commissaire du Gouvernement Ronny Abraham, Conclusions of 23 April 1997, in the *Groupe d'information et de soutien des travailleurs immigrés (GISTI)* case, reprinted in *Revue française de droit administrative* (RFDA) 13 (1997), 585–595 (589–590) (on the Convention on the Rights of the Child).

[30] See RGZ 117, 284, 285 (1927) on Article 365 of the Treaty of Versailles: "without the need for further international or domestic legal acts . . ." (translation mine). See also BVerwG, Judgment of 4 June 1991, *Archiv des Völkerrechts* 29 (1991), 409 (412): "does not require any further normative elaboration" (translation mine). On the criterion of "perfection" in

purpose,[31] and the overall structure of the treaty.[32] In his dissenting opinion in *Medellín*, Justice Breyer distilled from previous US Supreme Court cases the criteria of textual language, drafting history, and *subject matter* of the treaty.[33] Also relevant are the *purpose of individual protection* (but note that pursuing the general interest and individual protection are not mutually exclusive)[34] and the *addressee* of a norm: An international legal norm is not self-executing if it is addressed only to States (overall, as a black box).[35]

French practice, see Denis Alland, L'applicabilité directe du droit international considérée du point de vue de l'office du juge: des habits neufs pour une vieille dame?, *Revue Générale de Droit International Public* 102 (1998), 203–244 (221).

31 See, e.g., BVerfGE 40, 141, 164–165 (1975) on the German treaties with the countries of Eastern Europe: The limited purpose of the treaties was to create a favourable political climate. This meant that, in cases of doubt, the contracting parties did not intend to establish specific obligations of action for individuals. For the United States, see, e.g., US Court of Appeals for the Fifth Circuit, *United States* v. *Postal*, 589 F.2d 862 (5th Circ. 1979), paragraph 64: "the purposes of the treaty and the objectives of its creators, the existence of domestic procedures and institutions appropriate for direct implementation, the availability and feasibility of alternative enforcement methods, and the immediate and long-range consequences of self- or non-self-execution".

32 See, e.g., for the criterion of the "économie générale" of a treaty, Conseil d'Etat, *Ligue pour la préservation de la faune sauvage et la défense des non-chasseurs* (n. 25), on Article 3 of the (regional) Paris Convention for the Protection of Birds Useful to Agriculture of 19 March 1902: "[L]'ensemble des stipulations créent seulement des obligations entre les Etats parties et ne produisent pas d'effet direct dans l'ordre juridique interne." It followed that Article 3 of the Convention (prohibition of the employment of traps, nets, lime-twigs, etc.) "ne peut, en tout état de cause être utilement invoqué".

33 See the list of decisions compiled by Breyer in which the Supreme Court qualified a treaty provision as *self-executing* and also applied the provision to invalidate a state law or measure contrary to the treaty (US Supreme Court, *Medellín* v. *Texas* (n. 12), Justice Breyer, dissenting, Appendix A (p. 568 et seq.)). A peace treaty, for instance, is addressed to the political bodies. A treaty on the settlement of property disputes, commercial dealings, or civil claims for damages might also be addressed to the judiciary (see *ibid.*). Using these criteria, Justice Breyer found the provisions of Article I of the Optional Protocol to the VCCR and Article 94 of the UN Charter to be self-executing (p. 15).

34 See Advocate General Alber in ECJ, Cases C-93/02 and C-94/02, *Biret International* v. *Council* and *Etablissements Biret et Cie SA* v. *Council*, Opinion of 15 May 2003, paragraphs 115 and 118–119: The SPS Agreement is *also* intended to protect individual traders.

35 See Conseil d'Etat, *Commune de Breil sur Roya*, Décision No. 204756 of 8 December 2000: no direct effect of Articles 6 and 9 of the Bern Convention (Convention of 19 September 1979 on the Conservation of European Wildlife and Natural Habitats): "Considérant toutefois que ces stipulations *ne créent d'obligations qu'entre les Etats parties* à la convention et ne produisent pas d'effet direct dans l'ordre juridique interne" (italics mine). Conseil d'Etat, *Commune de Groslay*, Décision No. 292942 of 6 June 2007 rejected the application of Article 6(4), (6), (8), and (9) and of Articles 7 and 8 of the Aarhus Convention, but it did affirm application of Article 6(2) on public information.

In sum, the criteria of direct effect recognizable in (largely convergent) State practice concern both *the (substantive) legal status of individuals* as well as the division of powers of the State authorities dealing with international law.

16.5 The Direct Effect of Secondary Law

16.5.1 Security Council Resolutions

Security Council resolutions may impose obligations on individuals directly under international law (Chapter 4, pp. 93–99). For this reason, the question arises whether the legal commands contained in the resolutions are directly applicable by State bodies. This is regularly rejected in the very sparse case law[36] and literature.[37] One justification of this view is that UN member States have not transferred any sovereign rights to the United Nations, but rather they only have limited their own exercise of sovereign powers.[38] The assumption underlying this explanation that where "domestic" sovereign power is lacking, there can be no legal effect in the domestic legal space, is not very plausible.

The acknowledgement or negation of direct effect of Security Council resolutions should be guided by the same criteria as the provisions of international treaty law for two reasons. Firstly, the binding effect of a Security Council resolution is similar to that of a treaty from the perspective of those applying the law domestically. Secondly, the binding effect of the resolutions arises from a treaty, namely the UN Charter. For this reason, Security Council resolutions that address individuals directly

The provisions mentioned above "*créent seulement des obligations entre les Etats parties* à la convention et ne produisent pas d'effets directs dans l'ordre juridique interne; qu'elles ne peuvent par suite être utilement invoquées".

[36] Without more detailed reasoning and merely with reference to the "limited nature of the United Nations Resolutions", see US District Court for the District of Columbia, Civil Action No. 74-1292, Memorandum of 13 May 1975, *Diggs* v. *Dent*, reprinted in ILM 14 (1975), 797–805 (803). See also BGHSt 41, 127, 129 (Judgment of 21 April 1995).

[37] See, e.g., André Nollkaemper, Introduction, *European Journal of International Law* 20 (2009), 853–887 (864). For an overview of State practice, see Vera Gowlland-Debbas, The Domestic Implementation of UN Sanctions, in: Erika de Wet/P. André Nollkaemper (eds), *Review of the Security Council by Member States* (Mortsel: intersentia 2003), 63–76 (70).

[38] See Jochen A. Frowein, Implementation of Security Council Resolutions Taken under Chapter VII in Germany, in: Vera Gowlland-Debbas (ed.), *United Nations Sanctions and International Law* (Dordrecht: Kluwer 2001), 253–265 (258); Norbert Weiss, *Kompetenzlehre internationaler Organisationen* (Heidelberg: Springer 2009), 185 and other references.

should, like treaty norms, be examined in regard to whether they are sufficiently specific and unconditional or whether they require implementing legislation.[39] These traditional criteria are often met by particular provisions of Security Council resolutions. This means that these provisions can – technically speaking – deploy direct effect.

And this means that here again, the question of legitimacy is ultimately key: *Should* a Security Council resolution be applied by domestic institutions?[40] Once more, the answer should be guided by principles of legitimacy such as liberty/democracy, legality, and legal certainty. Especially the principle of legality (see Chapter 4, pp. 79–85) must be preserved when individual legal obligations are imposed by Security Council resolutions. This is all the more true if they have implications under criminal law.[41] Democratic considerations might also motivate the rejection of direct effect of Security Council resolutions, because the resolutions are concluded in a non-inclusive and hardly deliberative procedure.

In sum, there is no evident reason why the direct effect of Security Council resolutions imposing burdens on individuals should be ruled out from the start. Domestic authorities that do not want to apply a resolution specifically addressing individuals must justify their refusal; the best way to do this is on the basis of the principles mentioned above, which ultimately protect the freedom of the individual.

The concrete consequences of this legal assessment become apparent with regard to the already mentioned resolution on foreign terrorist fighters (resolution 2178). Here, the Security Council "demands that all foreign terrorist fighters disarm and cease all terrorist acts and participation in the conflict".[42] Under due respect for the principle of legality, notably in its strict version of *nulla poena*, resolution 2178 surely cannot deploy any criminalizing effects. But the obligations to cease and desist from all terrorist acts *directly* flow from the Security Council resolution

[39] See Emilio J. Cárdenas/Mariano Garcia-Rubio, Argentina, in: Vera Gowlland-Debbas (ed.), *National Implementation of United Nations Sanctions: A Comparative Study* (Leiden: Martinus Nijhoff 2004) 81–101 (85, 89–92): The need for supplemental legislation and the addressees of the resolutions should be the determinative points of the examination.

[40] This also applies to binding decisions of subsidiary bodies of the Security Council, especially the sanctions committees, which manage targeted sanctions. Here, there are additional problems of delegation, which make the question even more complex.

[41] After the entry into force of the Kampala amendments to the Rome Statute of the ICC, every determination by the Security Council of an act of aggression within the meaning of Article 39 of the UN Charter will imply a (non-judicial) determination of a crime, which will trigger the criminal responsibility of the perpetrator.

[42] Resolution 2178 (2014), paragraph 1.

2178. It could even be argued (although with some difficulty) that the individuals' obligation *not to travel* into a region to participate in the financing, planning, preparation, or perpetration of terrorist acts also flows from the resolution itself.[43] That would mean that a domestic authority, in the absence of a domestic boundary control law, could – from the perspective of international law – rely on resolution 2178 to refuse the issuance of a passport, for example. It would have to respect international humans rights law, namely the human right to leave one's country (12(2) ICCPR), for this. It seems as if the limits spelt out in Article 12(3) of ICCPR are *prima facie* satisfied, because the travel ban and control is "provided by law", and seems to be "necessary" to protect national security, public order, and the rights and freedoms of others.[44]

16.5.2 Decisions of International Dispute Settlement Bodies

In an era of more intensive activity of international courts and arbitral tribunals, the question of the direct effect of international judicial decisions becomes even more urgent. The issue is not primarily the interpretation of treaty norms applied by the international body in disputes, but rather the norms that define the position and power of the international dispute settlement body.[45] With a view to the legal status of the individual, three different approaches to the problem will be described here by way of example, namely the approach taken by the Federal Constitutional Court of Germany in regard to ICJ and ECtHR judgments, that of the US Supreme Court in regard to ICJ judgments, and that of the EU courts in regard to decisions of the WTO Dispute Settlement Body.

[43] *Ibid.*, paragraphs 1, 6 and 8.

[44] Anne Peters, Security Council Resolution 2178 (2014): The "Foreign Terrorist Fighter" as an International Legal Person, *EJIL Talk! Blog of the European Journal of International Law*, 21 November 2014.

[45] The Federal Constitutional Court of Germany, Ruling of 14 October 2004 (2 BvR 1481/04 – *Görgülü*), BVerfGE 111, 307, paragraph 37 is unclear in this regard: "The legal effect of the decisions of an international court constituted by a treaty is measured on that basis *in accordance with the content of the incorporated international treaty* and the applicable validity requirements under the Basic Law. If the treaty law of the European Convention on Human Rights and, concomitantly, the federal legislative power have ordered the direct effect of the legal decisions on the basis of Article 59(2) of the Basic Law, then such legal effect is ranked lower than that of constitutional law. Determining this legal effect at the domestic level is first of all the responsibility of the competent specialized courts" (translation mine).

16.5.2.1 Approach Taken by the Federal Constitutional Court of Germany

The Federal Constitutional Court of Germany finds "that judgments of the International Court of Justice in any event have an effect within the domestic legal order if ... norms protecting individuals are at issue".[46] Otherwise, the Court treats the question of the legal effects of decisions by international courts purely as a question under German law (not international law) and rejects their direct effect. Instead, it derives from the principle of the rule of law in conjunction with the approval act for the treaty regime in question a "direct constitutional obligation on the German courts to take note of and consider relevant rulings of the international courts whose jurisdiction extends over Germany".[47] This *duty of consideration* applies only to decisions rendered against Germany. Judgments against other States instead have an "orienting effect" and a "normative guiding function", i.e., the German institutions must follow them "*de facto*", according to the Federal Constitutional Court.[48]

16.5.2.2 Approach Taken by the US Supreme Court

In *Medellín*, the majority of the US Supreme Court rightly did not consider the provision contained in Article 36 of the VCCR, about which the case appeared to be on the surface. In a memorandum to the US Attorney General, the US President had declared that (and how) the ICJ's *Avena* judgment[49] had to be followed by the state courts. According to that memorandum, the state courts would have had to carry out a "review and reconsideration" of several trials. The Mexican citizen Medellín was one of 51 death row inmates who, only after being convicted by Texas courts, claimed that Article 36 of the VCCR had been violated at the time of his arrest years before, invoking the *Avena* judgment and the President's memorandum. According to a criminal procedural provision of the state of Texas, his appeal was actually not admissible. The case made it to the US Supreme Court, which interpreted

[46] BVerfGK 9, 174 (2 BvR 2115/01, 2 BvR 2132/01, 2 BvR 348/032010) of 19 September 2006, paragraph 59.

[47] *Ibid.*, paragraph 54 (translation mine). See, fundamentally, BVerfGE, *Görgülü* (n. 45), paragraphs 45–48.

[48] BVerfGK 9, 174 (n. 46), paragraphs 55 and 61–62; the Federal Constitutional Court also speaks of a "*de facto* precedent".

[49] ICJ, Case Concerning Avena and Other Mexican Nationals (*Mexico* v. *United States of America*), ICJ Reports 2004.

Article 94 of the UN Charter and considered Article I of the Optional Protocol to the VCCR as well as the ICJ Statute.[50] The interpretation of those provisions led the Supreme Court to opine that the relevant international agreements did not provide for implementation of ICJ judgments through direct enforcement by state courts.[51]

The Supreme Court in *Medellín* therefore held that Art. 94 of the UN Charter is "non-self-executing". In the opinion of the Court, the expression "undertake to comply . . ." in Article 94 of the UN Charter means that UN members have committed merely to take measures in the future through their political bodies (especially their legislatures) to implement a judgment. In the view of the Supreme Court, this reading is also supported by Article 94(2) of the UN Charter: If an ICJ judgment is not complied with, the Security Council may be called upon to act, which in turn is a political procedure (in which the US also has veto power). In the Supreme Court's opinion, these two considerations entail that the judgments are addressed only to the State as a whole as a subject of international law, but not to its individual authorities. This means that an ICJ judgment must first be implemented by US legislation. Of its own power, the judgment does not bind domestic courts. Because, on grounds of federalism and the separation of powers, the Supreme Court believed the President was not authorized to prescribe that the individual states implement the ICJ judgment, the Texas rule was upheld, according to which the belated claim of a violation of the VCCR was found inadmissible.

16.5.2.3 Approach Taken by the EU Courts

In *Biret*, the European Court of First Instance took the easy way out and simply found that decisions of the WTO Dispute Settlement Body were "inescapably and directly linked to the plea alleging infringement of the SPS Agreement" and hence shared its fate of lack of direct effect.[52] In contrast, the Advocate General of the EU, Siegbert Alber, had argued in this case *for* the direct effect of the decisions of the WTO Dispute

[50] See US Supreme Court, *Medellín* v. *Texas* (n. 12), 506–514. [51] See *ibid.*, 511.

[52] CFI, Case T-174/00, *Biret International SA* v. *Council* [2002] ECR II-17, paragraph 67. On appeal, the ECJ found this argument to be insufficient, but it did not itself consider the issue further, because the CFI's legal error had not been relevant to the decision (ECJ, Case C-93/02, *Biret International SA* v. *Council*, Judgment of 30 September 2003 [2003] ECR I-10497, paragraphs 55–60).

Settlement Body.[53] He emphasized that while non-compliance with a report of the Dispute Settlement Body was a political option, it was not lawful. Irrespective of the terminology, which was soft on political grounds, WTO members are legally required to follow the decisions of the Dispute Settlement Body (Article 21(1) of the Dispute Settlement Understanding (DSU)). The trade policy option of (temporary) non-compliance is available only because the reports are not subject to compulsory enforcement. According to Alber's commendable view, the principle of legality prohibits non-observance of the Dispute Settlement Body decisions on those grounds alone.[54]

Moreover, the non-fulfilment of WTO law and the non-compliance with associated decisions of the WTO dispute settlement bodies – a behaviour which according to the traditional view is within the "lee-way" of the foreign policy institutions – can lead to retaliatory measures by the other WTO parties. These sanctions in turn can cause massive damage to private economic operators in the EU. In this situation, such "victims of retaliation" have claimed damages against the EU. In the case of disproportionate and massive damage, these economic operators can – according to the more recent view – derive rights to compensation from the general principles of law, e.g., from the (European) fundamental freedom to pursue a trade or business, the principle of protection of legitimate expectations, and the principle of equal treatment, irrespective of the direct effect or non-applicability of WTO law or decisions of its dispute settlement bodies.[55] The deeper justification of this preferable view is that the status of the individual as a subject – recognized by EU law – cannot simply be negated in relation to the foreign policy and foreign economic policy of the EU. The EU must pay for its unlawful non-compliance with WTO law through compensation to affected EU citizens. Although these citizens cannot enforce compliance by the EU with the primary obligations of WTO law by invoking WTO law before

[53] Opinion of Advocate General Alber, *Biret International* v. *Council* and *Etablissements Biret et Cie SA* v. *Council* (n. 34), paragraphs 86–88.

[54] Opinion of Advocate General Alber, *ibid.*, paragraph 88.

[55] See Anne Thies, The Impact of General Principles of EC Law on Its Liability Regime towards Retaliation Victims after *Fabbrica Italiana Accumulatori Motocarri Montechio Spa (FIAMM) v. Council, European Law Review* 34 (2009), 889–913; Anne Thies, EU Membership of the WTO: International Trade Disputes and Judicial Protection of Individuals by EU Courts, *Global Constitutionalism* 2 (2013), 237–261. For a contrary opinion, however, see ECJ, Joined Cases C-120/06 P and C-121/06 P, *Fabbrica Italiana Accumulatori Motocarri Montechio Spa (FIAMM)* v. *Council of the EU*, Judgment of 9 September 2008 [2008] ECR I-6513.

EU courts, they must be compensated and are thus owners of a European secondary right to damages. The prospect of such claims for damages might motivate the EU in the direction of compliance. In this way, *a third track* (instead of claims before the Dispute Settlement Body, which are not available to private individuals, or claims for compliance with WTO law before EU courts) would help enforce norms of WTO law that benefit individuals.

16.5.2.4 Interim Conclusion

In conclusion, the criteria of specificity and unconditionality do not pose a problem in regard to international rulings. Judicial or quasi-judicial decisions meet these criteria without difficulties.[56] What is crucial for the application of these decisions – even more clearly than in the case of the direct effect of treaty norms – is the question of legitimacy: *Should* the decisions of international judicial or quasi-judicial bodies also bind domestic authorities and courts (as true precedents or at least as normative guidelines)? If a domestic court were to respond too easily to this question in the affirmative, this would constitute interference by the court in the matters of the domestic political bodies, in that the international decisions would be recognized as having an effect that the treaty-concluding "political" bodies did not intend.

A different question is that of the possible effects of judgments by international courts which do not ask for legal measures to be taken by domestic authorities but rather for *actual* measures. Some judgments have, for instance, ordered the return of property, the immediate release of a convict, and the opening of a school and a medical dispensary. These are not novel legal consequences that contradict existing domestic laws, but rather the measures may already be provided for by domestic law. What is special here is (only) that an international court, not a domestic authority, is ordering those measures. Were one to follow the *Medellín* logic of the US Supreme Court, such international judgments could never provide for such measures of their own accord, because they lack political legitimacy. According to a view advocated in the literature, such judgments are in contrast "applicable in the domestic legal sphere directly".[57]

[56] In the case of the WTO Dispute Settlement Reports, however, only after expiry of the (at most) fifteen-month implementation period set out in Article 21(3) of the DSU.

[57] Menno T. Kamminga, Final Report on the Impact of International Human Rights Law on General International Law, in: Menno T. Kamminga/Martin Scheinin (eds), *The Impact of Human Rights Law on General International Law* (Oxford: Oxford University Press 2009), 1–22 (14).

"Although these decisions may still require implementation by domestic authorities, their room for manoeuvre in such cases is very limited indeed."[58]

According to the view argued here, application of international rulings should be the normal case. No legitimacy handicap should be imposed on either international legal norms or on the decisions of international dispute settlement bodies. This approach would also strengthen the procedural standing of the individual whose rights and duties are at stake in these constellations.

16.6 Rejection of Direct Effect as a Mechanism of Legitimacy

The criteria mentioned above that can be identified in practice to determine the direct effect of international legal norms are borne by institutional considerations, which will be outlined briefly in this section.

16.6.1 Justiciability (Separation of Powers between Judicial and Legislative Branches)

One function of the concept of direct effect is to regulate the relationship between the domestic legislative power and the judicial power. Under that rationale, direct effect must be granted to international provisions which do not require implementation by the legislative power, but which are rather equivalent to legislation themselves.[59] The law-like character of the provision depends necessarily and primarily on its content. If the treaty provision is abstract-general and at the same time specific enough to be operational, it can act as a *legislative* norm. It is suitable to be applied by a judge. In a US leading case on this issue, *Foster & Elam* v. *Neilson* in 1829, Chief Justice Marshall clearly addressed the relationship between the legislative and judicial branches: "Our Constitution declares a treaty to be the law of the land. It is consequently to be regarded in courts of justice as equivalent to an act of the legislature whenever it

[58] *Ibid.*

[59] See US Supreme Court, *Whitney* v. *Robertson*, 124 US 190, 193 (1888): "If the treaty contains stipulations which are self-executing – that is, require no legislation to make them operative – to that extent they have the force and effect of a legislative enactment." See also already US Supreme Court, *Head Money Cases* (n. 21): "self-executing, that is, require no legislation to make them operative". More recently, see, e.g., BGE, *X.* v. *Z* (n. 6), Consideration 2.3.3: "En l'occurrence, on ne voit pas qu[e] . . . son article 7 let d. [of the ICESCR] doive être considérée comme directement applicable. Il apparaît au contraire que cette norme s'adressait au législateur."

operates of itself, without the aid of any legislative provision. But when the terms of the stipulation import a contract, when either of the parties engage to perform a particular act, the treaty addresses itself to the Political, not the Judicial Department, and the Legislature must execute the contract before it can become a rule for the Court."[60] At this level of the problem, the issue thus concerns the justiciability of a provision.[61] This aspect is *not specific to international law*, but rather it concerns all legal norms. It should not be assessed differently in regard to international legal norms than in regard to other norms.

16.6.2 *Political Scope for Manoeuvre (Separation of Powers between Judicial and Executive Branches)*

The suitability of the content of a treaty provision for application by a court also concerns the separation of powers between the branch responsible (in the ideal-typical constellation) for shaping foreign policy (i.e., the executive, in democratic States usually in cooperation with the legislature) and the branch that applies the law (the judiciary), acting (in the ideal-typical constellation) technically and "apolitically". Accordingly, the dividing line between self-executing and non-self-executing treaty provisions should be drawn so that the courts do not inappropriately interfere with the foreign policy leeway of the executive (and legislative) branch. Because the typical constellation is that individual plaintiffs argue before the courts of a given State that a previous executive or legislative measure of that very State has violated an international treaty, the room for manoeuvre at issue mainly refers to *whether and how the State organs should respond to (alleged) violations of international treaties through prior measures of that same State, or – put differently – whether the State should comply with international law or not.* This consideration frequently forms the basis for court decisions on direct effect, but is seldom stated as explicitly as in the US Supreme Court judgment in the *Medellín* case (which was about the direct effect of an ICJ judgment, not of a treaty): "In sum, Medellín's view that ICJ decisions are automatically enforceable as domestic law is fatally undermined by the

60 US Supreme Court, *Foster & Elam* v. *Neilson*, 27 US 253, 314 (1829), Chief Justice Marshall.

61 On the direct effect of Article 13 of the ECHR, see Federal Supreme Court of Switzerland, 29 May 1985, BGE 1b, 111, 68, p. 72., *X.* v. *Federal Department of Justice and Police*, Consideration 1: "which depends on whether the provision is justiciable, i.e., can be implemented by the judge in the real world . . ." (translation mine).

enforcement structure established by Article 94. His construction would eliminate the option of noncompliance contemplated by Article 94(2), *undermining the ability of the political branches to determine* whether and how to comply with an ICJ judgment. Those *sensitive foreign policy decisions would instead be transferred to state and federal courts* charged with applying an ICJ judgment directly as domestic law. And those courts would not be empowered to decide whether to comply with the judgment – again, always regarded as *an option by the political branches* – any more than courts may consider whether to comply with any other species of domestic law."[62] The Federal Supreme Court of Switzerland argued similarly in a judgment on a bilateral transport agreement. Because of the clear wording, which provides for the establishment of a system on the basis of reciprocity, the treaty provision was held to be non-self-executing. It could not be invoked by the Belgian company before Swiss courts to achieve elimination of the heavy vehicle fee on trucks registered in Belgium on grounds of a treaty violation. Enforcing compliance with a treaty, or sanctioning its violation was held to be possible *only at the international level (by means of an inter-State claim brought by Belgium).*[63]

The practice regarding the WTO agreements clearly illustrates that the question of direct effect is primarily about separation of powers and respect for political leeway.[64] Domestic courts[65] and the EU courts[66] have rejected the direct effect of the GATT, as have the WTO dispute settlement institutions themselves.[67] In the United States, the possibility of direct effect of the GATT was expressly ruled out by law in 1994.[68] This

[62] US Supreme Court, *Medellín* v. *Texas* (n. 12), 511 (italics mine). On the direct effect of *judgments* and on the facts of the case, see pp. 510–11.

[63] See BGE, *Maison G.Sprl contre Direction générale de douanes* (n. 22), Consideration 2b on Article 7 of the ancillary agreement between the Swiss Federal Council and the Government of the Kingdom of Belgium on road transport of 25 February 1975 (RS 0.741.619.172).

[64] See Anne Peters, The Position of International Law Within the European Community Legal Order, *German Yearbook of International Law* 40 (1997), 9–77 (61–66).

[65] For Switzerland, leaving the question open, see Federal Supreme Court, *X. SA* v. *Federal Office of Agriculture*, 14 July 1997.

[66] See ECJ, Case C-149/96, *Portugal* v. *Council* [1999] ECR I-8395, paragraphs 34–52; ECJ, Case C-377/02, *Léon Van Parys NV* v. *Belgisch Interventie-en Restitutiebureau* [2005] ECR I-1465, paragraphs 38–54.

[67] WTO Panel, *US – Section 301–310 of the Trade Act of 1974*, WT/DS152/R (22 December 1999), no appeal, paragraph 7.72. Instead, the GATT should be said to have "indirect effect" (paragraph 7.78). See also below n. 71.

[68] Sec. 102 (a) and (b) (2) of the Uruguay Round Agreement Act, 19 USCA 3512.

rejection cannot be based on the wording of the relevant treaty provisions, since the GATT guarantees – such as most favoured treatment and non-discrimination – are formulated almost identically to the parallel guarantees under the TFEU.[69] The latter are directly applied by the courts of the member States, in accordance with the ECJ requirements, for the benefit of individual claimants. The ECJ mandates that the institutions of the member States apply the EU provisions directly, even though it rejects the direct effect of practically identical GATT provisions itself (in its capacity as an internal court of the EU). To justify the different assessment, the ECJ can merely cite the overall structure of the treaties in question but not the wording of individual provisions. The flexible nature of the GATT, the numerous exemption clauses, and especially the negotiability of the responses of WTO members to treaty breaches – in short, the supposedly diplomatic-political nature of the GATT – are claimed to oppose the direct effect of the GATT.

In regard to the WTO agreements, the ECJ clearly formulates the argument in favour of leaving political leeway for responses to claimed treaty breaches. The Court rejects the direct effect of these agreements especially because judicial application (or non-application of internal EU law contrary to the WTO) would deprive the EU institutions responsible for foreign policy "of the possibility ... of entering into negotiated arrangements", i.e., of their "scope for manoeuvre".[70]

The "scope for manoeuvre" respected by the courts here refers to the sanctioning of treaty breaches. This reasoning presupposes that not all treaty breaches caused by internal acts entail normal and full legal consequences. The normal consequence would be that the internal act which caused the breach of the treaty is illegal *tout court*. By denying this normal consequence and allowing for a scope of manoeuvre in this regard, international law is ultimately denied the nature of "hard" law.

In the context of this study, what matters is that the devaluation of international legal provisions with the objective of protecting individuals into soft norms that are subject to intergovernmental negotiations

[69] The first sentence of Article III(2) of the GATT states: "The products of the territory of any contracting party imported into the territory of any other contracting party shall not be subject, directly or indirectly, to internal taxes or other internal charges of any kind in excess of those applied, directly or indirectly, to like domestic products." Article 30 of the TFEU states: "Customs duties on imports and exports and charges having equivalent effect shall be prohibited between Member States."

[70] ECJ, *Portugal* v. *Council* (n. 5), paragraphs 40 and 46.

ultimately undermines the legal status and the legal protection of individuals; this devaluation is what underlies the rejection of their direct effect. The filter of direct effect is employed by the ECJ as a mechanism for fending off the genuinely legal consequences of GATT breaches. Since one of the primary goals of the GATT is to protect market participants from the protectionist policy of States, which is excessively influenced by the particular interests of lobbyists, the observance of GATT rules primarily benefits these individuals. Conversely, the rejection of direct effect primarily injures those market participants in the end.[71] A change of perspective so that GATT law is considered normal and hard law, breaches of which must be remedied in the normal case, would in principle have to entail its direct application by domestic and European institutions. This change of perspective would at the same time imply the concession that non-compliance with this law cannot be punished by way of negotiations between the injuring State and the injured State. This perspective would do justice to the rationale of the GATT, which is to protect individuals as well as the legal status of the economic operators in question.

16.6.3 Democracy

Another important aspect is the (democratic) legitimacy of international treaty law. Even if a treaty provision is sufficiently specific and thus technically suitable for application by a court, it might still be deficient in terms of legitimacy and should therefore not be applied. In existing international law, the democratic legitimacy of treaties is secured merely

[71] The panel in the *US – Section 301–310* case emphasized this goal of the GATT to protect individuals, but it nevertheless rejected the direct effect thereof: "7.72. Under the doctrine of direct effect, which has been found to exist most notably in the legal order of the EC but also in certain free trade area agreements, obligations addressed to States are construed as creating legally enforceable rights and obligations for individuals. Neither the GATT nor the WTO has so far been interpreted by GATT/WTO institutions as a legal order producing direct effect. Following this approach, the GATT/WTO did not create a new legal order the subjects of which comprise both contracting parties or Members and their nationals. 7.73. However, *it would be entirely wrong to consider the position of individuals is of no relevance* to the GATT/WTO legal matrix. Many of the benefits to Members which are meant to flow as a result of the acceptance of various disciplines under the GATT/WTO depend on the activity of individual economic operators in the national and global market places. The purpose of many of these disciplines, indeed *one of the primary objects of the GATT/WTO as a whole, is to produce certain market conditions which would allow this activity to flourish*" (WTO Panel, *US – Section 301–310 of the Trade Act of 1974*, WT/DS152/R (22 December 1999), no appeal; italics mine).

transitively, i.e., through the involvement of the legislatures of the States concluding the treaty, but not through democratic procedures at the international level.[72] For this reason (because of the role of the national legislatures), the legality and legitimacy aspects of the domestic separation of powers overlap with the legitimacy of the treaty as such.

If domestic courts are seen as gatekeepers of the legitimacy of the law applicable within the domestic legal sphere, and especially as the guardians of domestic constitutional principles, they play the important role of preventing international legal norms from violating domestic constitutional principles by rejecting their direct effect.[73] However, firstly, the situation of a threat to domestic constitutional law by international law is relatively rare. Secondly, some legal orders (such as in Switzerland) tend to assign the role of gatekeeper to legislatures rather than to courts. In this tradition, once the legislature has approved an international treaty, the compatibility of that treaty with the constitution has explicitly or implicitly been affirmed. Finally, the courts are able to play their role as gatekeepers even if their review treats direct effect as the normal case, which is the approach advocated in the following section.

16.7 Direct Effect as the Normal Case

The international legal status of the individual will only be fully regularized once the direct effect of international law is considered the normal case. The current structure of international law, its interaction with domestic law, and legitimacy considerations make this possible.

In its *Danzig* opinion, the PCIJ still held that international treaties normally did not generate individual rights that were actionable in domestic courts. Implicitly, it therefore established a presumption against direct effect.[74] It is plausible that this happened mainly on tactical grounds, to make the opinion palatable to statists, even within the Court.[75] Such a presumption against the direct effect of a treaty was

[72] See Anne Peters, Dual Democracy, in: Jan Klabbers/Anne Peters/Geir Ulfstein, *The Constitutionalization of International Law* (2nd ed., Oxford: Oxford University Press 2011), 263–341.

[73] See Armin von Bogdandy, Pluralism, Direct Effect, and the Ultimate Say, *International Journal of Constitutional Law* 6 (2008), 397–413 (401–412).

[74] See PCIJ, *Jurisdiction of the Courts of Danzig* (n. 11), 17: "[B]eing an international agreement, [it] *cannot, as such*, create direct rights and obligations for private individuals" (italics mine).

[75] See Hersch Lauterpacht, *The Development of International Law by the International Court* (2nd ed., London: Stevens 1958), 174.

also the basis for older case law in the courts of various States.[76] The German Imperial Court of Justice, and following it even still in the 1960s the German Federal Court of Justice, found that an individual could derive rights from a treaty norm only "*to the extent this follows with complete clarity* from the treaty itself . . .".[77]

The progressive development of international law has eliminated the basis for that presumption. There is no categorical difference between international law and other law. It is the normal case for law of any kind that it can be applied by public authorities and by courts.[78]

Because the question of direct effect – as discussed above – must be distinguished from the questions of inclusion of international law in the domestic legal order and the conferral of individual rights, there is in principle no obstacle to the direct and regular application of international legal norms by domestic institutions. Quite to the contrary, the normal maxims of the interpretation of international treaties point towards their "direct" application. The ICJ highlights that "[t]he principle of good faith obliges the Parties to apply [a treaty, in that case a bilateral one] in a reasonable way and *in such a manner that its purpose can be realized*".[79] From this, one might infer that "in some circumstances perhaps the only reasonable way to apply a treaty that protects or benefits individuals is for national courts to be available for individuals to litigate claims arising from the treaty".[80] In the more recent literature, this is referred to as an international legal presumption *in favour* of the direct

[76] For the presumption against the conferral of "enforceable" individual rights by international treaties, when such rights were not entirely unambiguously granted, see US courts in cases involving Article 36 of the VCCR (Supreme Court of New Mexico, *State* v. *Martinez-Rodriguez*, 131 N.M. 47, 33 P.3d 267, 274 (2001); US Court of Appeals, *Cornejo* v. *County of San Diego*, 504 F.3d 853, 858-9-864 (9th Circ. 2007)). These judgments do not clearly state whether this presumption relates to the substantive right or to invocability in domestic courts.

[77] RGZ 121, 7, 9 (29 March 1928) on Articles 74 and 297i of the Treaty of Versailles (rejecting the right). Along these lines, see also BGHZ 52, 371, 383 (1969). This case law conflates direct effect with the question of the substantive right.

[78] See, fundamentally (with reference to EU law), Pierre Pescatore, The Doctrine of "Direct Effect": An Infant Disease of Community Law, *European Law Review* 8 (1983), 155–177 (177).

[79] ICJ, *Case Concerning the Gabčíkovo-Nagymaros Project (Hungary* v. *Slovakia)*, Judgment of 25 September 1997, ICJ Reports 1997, 7, paragraph 142 (italics mine).

[80] Sean D. Murphy, Does International Law Obligate States to Open Their National Courts to Persons for the Invocation of Treaty Norms That Protect or Benefit Persons?, in: David Sloss (ed.), *The Role of Domestic Courts in Treaty Enforcement: A Comparative Study* (New York: Cambridge University Press 2009), 61–119 (67).

effect of international legal norms.[81] According to this view, domestic authorities or courts not wanting to apply international law must expressly show that a norm is not specific enough to be justiciable and/or that it only governs relations between States and does not have the purpose of protecting individuals, and especially that fundamental considerations of legitimacy oppose the application of the norm.

In actual practice, courts in relevant legal orders might simply apply international law without making an issue of its direct effect. But this speculation is difficult to substantiate with precise statistics.[82] An example is the 2010 ruling of the Federal Constitutional Court of Germany on the principle of speciality in mutual legal assistance law: "'The domestic validity of international treaties . . . requires a domestic order to apply them in the form of federal legislation as referred to in Article 59(2) of the Basic Law. Where such an order exists, *German courts must observe and apply international treaties in the same way as federal laws within the framework of methodologically acceptable interpretation.*"[83] In this passage, the Federal Constitutional Court made a clear – and I think proper – distinction between inclusion of an international legal norm in the domestic legal order and the application thereof (as a consequence of inclusion). The Court also considered application to be the normal case.

The fact that the application of international law should be the normal case is even more evident in the case of customary international law than in the case of treaty law. However, there is far less judicial practice in this regard. In Germany, for instance, the inclusion of customary

[81] Especially in French practice and literature; see Commissaire du Gouvernement Ronny Abraham, Conclusions of 23 April 1997 (n. 29), 589; Evelyne Lagrange, L'efficacité des normes internationales concernant la situation des personnes privées dans les ordres juridiques internes, *Recueil des cours* 356 (2012/III), 243–552 (448). But see with the claim of a presumption *against* the direct effect of international treaty norms, Ruiz Fabri, Is There a Case, 2014, 152. See in favour of the presumption of direct effect for EU law Christian Wohlfahrt, Veränderungen des Lissabon-Vertrages im Hinblick auf die Doktrin der unmittelbaren Wirkung, *Zeitschrift für ausländisches öffentliches Recht und Völkerrecht* 70 (2010), 523–545 (537–544).

[82] Nollkaemper, Duality of Direct Effect, 2014, 108, claims that on the basis of the reports in "International Law in Domestic Courts" (ILDC, Oxford University Press), the number of States which do not grant international law direct effect "far exceeds" the number of States where such practice exist. However, I doubt that the unproblematic situations where administrative authorities and courts simply apply the relevant provisions of international treaties without further ado are actually reported in that series.

[83] BVerfG, Ruling of 8 June 2010 – 2 BvR 432/07, 2 BvR 507/08, paragraph 27 – *Komplex Schreiber*, internal citations omitted; italics mine.

international law in the domestic legal sphere is governed by Article 25 of the Basic Law. This provision governs neither the question of direct effect in the sense of invocability nor the substantive legal question of the individual right. It says only that the general rules of international law have the same legal effects to the benefit and to the detriment of individuals as other domestic law and – to the extent their content allows – may also generate individual rights and duties.[84] According to the Federal Constitutional Court, "If an international norm has been elevated to the rank of customary law, German courts are in principle prevented by Article 25 of the Basic Law from interpreting and applying domestic law in a way that violates the norm."[85] Formulated in positive terms, the courts are required to apply the norm of customary international law.

The normal case of the applicability of international treaty law is also clearly reflected in French case law. Usually, a treaty provision relevant to the dispute is simply applied,[86] sometimes with the remark that these provisions "produisent des effets directs à l'égard des particuliers".[87] An explicit justification is provided – if at all – in cases of non-applicability ("que les ... ne produisent pas d'effet direct").[88] The thesis

[84] See Geiger, *Grundgesetz und Völkerrecht*, 2009, 151.

[85] BVerfG, *Komplex Schreiber* (n. 83; translation mine).

[86] See, e.g., Conseil d'État, *Botéro*, Décision No. 159999 of 21 May 1997 (application of Article 1(A)(2) of the Geneva Convention on Refugees).

[87] Conseil d'Etat, Décision No. 163043 of 23 April 1997 on Article 4.1 of ILO Convention No. 118. The same decision rejected the direct effect of Articles 24(1), 26(1), and 27(1) of the UN Convention on the Rights of the Child.

[88] However, in accordance with the dearth of justifications given in French court judgments, reasons are often not provided in such cases either. See, e.g., Conseil d'Etat, *Ministère du budget*, Décisions Nos. 37772 and 37774 of 20 April 1984, on Article 4.4 of the European Social Charter: "Cons., en troisième lieu, que Mlle X. ... invoque les termes de l'article 4-4 de la Charte sociale Européenne, selon lesquels 'En vue d'assurer l'exercice effectif du droit à une rémunération équitable, les parties contractantes s'engagent ... à reconnaître le droit de tous les travailleurs à un délai de préavis raisonnable, dans le cas de cessation de l'emploi'; que cette clause ne produit pas d'effet direct à l'égard des nationaux des états contractants; qu'ainsi, en tout état de cause, la requérante ne peut se prévaloir utilement de la violation de la clause de l'article 4-4." Conseil d'Etat, *Raut*, Décision No. 152417 of 15 May 1995, on Article 12 of the European Social Charter: "ces clauses ne produisent pas d'effet direct à l'égard des nationaux des Etats contractants; qu'ainsi, en tout état de cause, le requérant ne peut se prévaloir utilement de leur violation". Conseil d'Etat, *Collectif contre l'handiphobie*, Décision No. 24857 of 26 September 2005, on Article 12 of the ICESCR (right to health): "Considérant ... que les stipulations de l'article 12 du pacte international relatif aux droits économiques, sociaux et culturels du 19 décembre 1966 aux termes duquel les Etats parties ...reconnaissent le droit qu'a toute personne de jouir du meilleur état de santé physique et mentale qu'elle soit capable d'atteindre sont dépourvues d'effet direct dans l'ordre juridique interne." Conseil d'Etat, 11 January 2008, No. 292493: Article 1, Article 2(4), and Article 5(2) of the Aarhus

that the (direct) application of international law – without a legitimacy handicap – should be normal thus corresponds to the empirical finding that it *is* in fact normal.

16.8 Conclusion

The decision of a domestic institution (especially of a court) to apply a provision of international law directly or not may, from the perspective of international law, be guided by domestic law, but international legal requirements must be met. Because this decision substantially shapes the real effectiveness of the international legal status of the individual, the interests of the individual should – according to the view advocated here – be incorporated into the decision-making process. It is important in this regard that the normative considerations of separation of powers and democratic legitimacy, which (also) motivate this decision, are not institutional ends in themselves, but rather they ultimately also serve the freedom of the individual. Moreover, regular application of international law in turn strengthens its output legitimacy (in the sense that international law actually contributes to the realization of the rights and duties of individuals). The routine rejection of direct effect would thus lead to a vicious circle of delegitimation of international law.

To argue that it is imperative to grant political leeway to the genuinely political bodies of the State, which may then decide whether they in fact want to comply with a treaty (e.g., the GATT) or with the judgment of an international court – *or not*, implies a downgrading of the legal-ness of international law. A rule which is not meant to be complied with resembles more a political guideline than a legal norm. The marginalization of individual concerns by making general references to the overall structure of a treaty also tends to contain such a denial of the legal quality of the norms involved. Under the premise that international treaties constitute genuine law, their violation must – from the perspective of the rule of law – be actionable in principle (as a rule), i. e., in domestic courts. The domestic courts are, for reasons of subsidiarity and in light of the gaps in international jurisdiction, primarily responsible for the implementation of international law. Such a standpoint is not inevitably naïve in the sense that it disregards the political implications of the legal analysis but simply insists that law cannot be completely

Convention of 25 June 1998 "ne produisent pas d'effets directs dans l'ordre juridique interne et ne peuvent, par suite, être utilement invoqués" (without reasons).

dissolved into or reduced to politics. From that perspective, we may admit that "[b]eyond these arguments lies the reality of power".[89] However, we cannot admit that "*[a]ll* depends on the ability to resist and bargain over implementation".[90] To the contrary, under the rule of law, not "all" depends on power only. From that perspective, exceptions from applicability must be specially justified. A general reference to the lower level of legitimacy of international law in principle is not a convincing argument against the normal case of application of the law postulated here.

The primary criteria for determining the direct effect of an international legal provision should therefore be those concerning their justiciability (suitability for application by a court), i.e., their specificity and unconditionality. These criteria apply to all norms, including those of domestic law.

Certainly, the application of international legal norms by domestic courts carries the risk of diverging and mutually contradictory case law. Deviating interpretations of the same norms are given not only by domestic courts, however, but also by international courts and arbitral tribunals. Decentralized application of international law is thus already intrinsic to the existing system of international law. The risk of legal fragmentation through the increased application of international law by domestic bodies is not different in nature from the current situation that already exists due to the "proliferation" of international dispute settlement bodies. In practice, domestic institutions have not regularly proven to be less professional than international bodies. The dialogue of the courts, the recourse to common and overarching principles, and mutual citation can help counter the fragmentation of international law, even where a generally accepted hierarchy of norms is lacking and where there is no overarching appeals procedure all the way to a single supreme court. Substantive contradictions may nevertheless arise and persist, yet that is the price that has to be paid in an institutionally decentralized legal system that includes a plurality of bodies applying the law.

From the perspective of the individual and with a view to the freedom that should be protected by the international rule of law, international legal norms imposing obligations on the individual (and in some cases also those norms that entitle the individual) should be applied directly only to the extent that doing so respects the *principle of legality* (Chapter 4, pp. 79–85). In particular, the *legal* obligations of the

[89] Ruiz Fabri, Is There a Case, 2014, 173. [90] *Ibid.*, italics mine.

individual must be traceable back to a specific, accessible, and foreseeable legal foundation. The problem is compounded in regard to the norms of international criminal law, the application of which must respect the strict *nullum crimen* principle (Chapter 5, pp. 127–37).

The conclusion of this chapter is that provisions of international treaties should normally be qualified as *self-executing* in the sense described above (although it is unclear, as an empirical matter, whether law-applying authorities and courts worldwide accept this), as long as the norms *prima facie* meet minimum requirements of specificity and unconditionality (i.e., the usual preconditions for justiciability, no different from domestic legal provisions). Recognizing this normal case strengthens the legal status of the individual invoking international law in his or her favour, but it also shapes the individual's international legal status as the bearer of duties (obligations) under international law.

17

The International Individual Right

The term of the international individual right encapsulates the legal status of the individual in international law, where that legal status is not based purely on the consensus of States. The term of the international individual right is meant to encode the *primary* international legal personality of the individual. "Primary" is here meant in an ethical and doctrinal sense. I will in the following use the word subjective international right as a synonym, because in some legal traditions the term of the subjective right is well known. The concept of an international individual right is not unknown to international law.[1] It is found in international case law and decisions of regional human rights courts as "individual right"[2] or "personal right",[3] without detailed explanation or questioning of these terms. On various occasions, EU courts[4] (i.e., the

[1] See for a discussion of "droits 'subjectifs'" of the individual in international law Emmanuel Roucounas, Facteurs privés et droit international public, *Recueil des Cours* 299 (2002), 9–419 (42–48), with further references.

[2] ICJ, *LaGrand Case* (*Germany* v. *United States of America*), ICJ Reports 2001, 466, paragraph 77 ("individual rights"); ICJ, *Case Concerning Avena and Other Mexican Nationals* (*Mexico* v. *United States of America*), ICJ Reports 2004, 12, paragraph 40 ("individual rights"); Inter-American Court of Human Rights, *The Right to Information on Consular Assistance in the Framework of the Guarantees of the Due Process of Law*, Advisory Opinion OC-16/99 of 1 October 1999, paragraph 84 ("individual rights").

[3] ECtHR, *Emine Araç* v. *Turkey*, No. 9907/02, 23 December 2008, paragraph 24 (education as a "personal right" and accordingly a "civil right" as referred to in Article 6 ECHR); ECtHR, *Enea* v. *Italy*, No. 74912/01, 23 September 2008, paragraph 103 (social contact of a prisoner as a "personal right" and accordingly a "civil right" as referred to in Article 6 ECHR). The civil right required for application of Article 6 ECHR normally arises from national law. Because the ECtHR interprets the term autonomously, there need not be a right as defined by the legal order of the Member State, i.e., the right in question is functionally an international right as a prerequisite for the European guarantee of access to justice.

[4] On this case law, see Johannes Saurer, *Der Einzelne im europäischen Verwaltungsrecht: Die institutionelle Ausdifferenzierung der Verwaltungsorganisation der Europäischen Union in individueller Perspektive* (Tübingen: Mohr Siebeck 2013), 74–75.

ECJ,[5] the EGC,[6] and the CST[7]) and the Advocates General of the ECJ[8] speak of "individual rights" or, more rarely in English, "subjective rights" (in German more commonly *subjektive Rechte* and in French *droits subjectifs*). Beyond the operationalization of individualized enforcement discussed above (Chapter 15), recognition of the subjective international right has tangible juridical consequences and numerous doctrinal, systemic, and legal policy advantages.

17.1 Rights as a Paradigm of Modernity

The international individual right can benefit from the emancipatory potential of the concept of rights. Normally, rights are divided into, firstly, claim rights in the sense of the ability to legally demand the act from the addressee of the obligation; secondly, liberty rights (permissive rules); and thirdly, powers, i.e., the right to change a legal relationship, which may in turn be bilateral or *erga omnes*.[9]

5 ECJ, Case 118/75, *Lynne Watson* [1976] ECR 1185, Summary 1; ECJ, Case 130/87, *François Retter* v. *Caisse de pension des employés privés* [1989] ECR 865, paragraph 13; ECJ, Case C-578/08, *Rhimou Chakroun* v. *Minister van Buitenlandse Zaken* [2010] ECR I-0183, paragraph 41. In ECJ, Case C-445/06, *Danske Slagterier* v. *Federal Republic of Germany* [2009] ECR I-02119, Opinion of Advocat General Verica Trstenjak of 4 September 2008, paragraphs 59–73, the Advocat General discussed whether a directive confers an "individual" or "subjective" right and answered this question in the negative (at most a "legal effect by rebound", paragraph 72). The ECJ affirmed a "legal position", a "right" arising from Article 28 EC (free movement of goods) that was given concrete expression by the directives in question (Judgment of 24 March 2009, paragraphs 18–26).

6 EGC, Case T-227/95, *AssiDomän Kraft Products AB, AB Iggesunds Bruk, Korsnäs AB, MoDo Paper AB, Södra Cell AB, Stora Kopparbergs Bergslags AB and Svenska Cellulosa AB* v. *Commission of the European Communities* [1997] ECR II-1185, paragraph 90; EGC, Case T-251/00, *Lagardère SCA and Canal+ SA* v. *Commission of the European Communities* [2002] ECR II-4825, paragraphs 139, 142, 150; EGC, Case T-25/04, *González y Díez, SA* v. *Commission of the European Communities* [2007] ECR II-3121, paragraphs 97, 119.

7 CST, Case F-51/07, *Philippe Bui Van* v. *Commission of the European Communities*, Judgment of 11 September 2008, paragraphs 55, 67: "subjective rights".

8 ECJ, Case C-408/08 P, *Lancôme parfums et beauté & Cie SNC* v. *Office for Harmonisation in the Internal Market (Trade Marks and Designs) (OHIM)* [2010] ECR I-01347, Opinion of Advocate General Ruiz-Jarabo Colomer of 15 October 2009, paragraphs 64, 75: "individual rights" and "personal legal rights"; "subjektive Rechte" in German, and "droits subjectifs" in French.

9 See fundamentally Wesley Newcomb Hohfeld, Fundamental Legal Conceptions as Applied in Judicial Reasoning, *Yale Law Journal* 23 (1913), 16–59 and *Yale Law Journal* 26 (1917), 710–770. See generally Eva Schulev-Steindl, *Subjektive Rechte: Eine rechtstheoretische und dogmatische Analyse* (Vienna: Springer 2008).

Human rights provisions often contain several different types of subjective rights.[10]

The subjective right has a Roman prehistory. However, the term *ius* (in contrast to *lex*) was used in different meanings by classical Roman jurists: It often, but not always, referred to an individual (so-called subjective) right or a claim in the contemporary sense. There was also no scientific systematization.[11]

According to Michel Villey, the term *ius* was used in a meaning close to the contemporary understanding by William of Ockham in the fourteenth century and was further developed by Thomas Hobbes.[12] Throughout his entire legal career, Hugo Grotius considered *ius* in the sense of subjective right and analysed the problem in several works.[13] According to Richard Tuck, *De iure belli ac pacis* is "in fact the first reconstruction of an actual legal system in terms of rights rather than laws. Consequently it is the true ancestor of all the modern codes which have rights of various kinds at their centre."[14]

[10] In the contemporary view, all "generations" of human rights contain the "obligations to respect, protect, and fulfil"; see fundamentally (not yet in that terminology) Henry Shue, *Basic Rights* (Princeton: Princeton University Press 1980), 35–64.

[11] *Ius* influenced by natural law tended to be used in the sense of fair allocation. See fundamentally Michel Villey, *La formation de la pensée juridique moderne: Cours d'histoire de la philosophie du droit* (Paris: Ed. Montchrestien 1975); Annabel S. Brett, *Liberty, Rights and Nature: Individual Rights in Later Scholastic Thought* (Cambridge: Cambridge University Press 1997). According to Michel Villey, the contemporary concept of the subjective right is a *contresens commis sur le langage romain* (*ibid.*, 236). For a review of Villey's reading, see Charles Donahue, Ius in the Subjective Sense in Roman Law: Reflections on Villey and Tierney, in: Domenico Maffei et al. (eds), *A Ennio Cortese*, Vol. 1 (Rome: Il Cigno Edizioni 2001), 506–535 (especially 508 et seq.). See also Helmut Coing, Zur Geschichte des Begriffs "subjektives Recht", in: Helmut Coing/Frederick H. Lawson/Kurt Grönfors (eds), *Das subjektive Recht und der Rechtsschutz der Persönlichkeit* (Frankfurt a. M.: Metzner 1959), 7–23.

[12] See fundamentally Villey, *La formation de la pensée juridique moderne*, 1975 (n. 11), 225–272, who explains the shift in meaning with reference to Ockham's nominalism; on Hobbes *ibid.*, 649–676.

[13] According to Grotius's definition, "ius est qualitas moralis personae competens ad aliquid iuste habendum vel agendum" ("Ius is the moral quality of a person enabling that person to have something or do something rightfully"); Hugo Grotius, *De iure belli ac pacis libri tres* (1625), liber primus, caput 1, n IV, ed. B. J. A. de Kanter-van Hettinga Tromp (Leiden: E. J. Brill 1939; online 2009 dbnl). See Peter Haggenmacher, Droits subjectifs et système juridique chez Grotius, in: Luc Foisneau (ed.), *Politique, droit et théologie chez Bodin, Grotius et Hobbes* (Paris: Editions Kimé 1997), 73–130. See also Peter Pavel Remec, *The Position of the Individual in International Law According to Grotius and Vattel* (The Hague: Martinus Nijhoff 1960).

[14] Richard Tuck, *Natural Rights Theories: Their Origin and Development* (Cambridge: Cambridge University Press 1979), 66.

The individual right (in the modern sense) can be seen as accompanying the rise of the sovereign State. The ideology of individualism in the sense of an awareness of moral and juridical rights of the individual evolved, in any event, parallel with the consolidation of the modern sovereign State. This development was favoured by the mathematical-quantitative thinking of natural law theory in the seventeenth century because "the reduction of law to the individual was an abstraction, analogous to mathematics, of the legal substrata to the 'smallest necessary particle'".[15] It can remain an open question here whether the rise of the State was a cause of individualism and of the conception of subjective rights.[16] In any event, as other institutions (guilds, local rules, the Church) were pushed into the background, the individual entered into a direct legal relationship with the State.

Not until John Locke, and especially Immanuel Kant, was the "central position of the subjective right in modern legal thinking" established.[17] Kant grounded individual rights in the innate liberty of the human being, allowing him "to base his legal justification on the justificatory structure of normative individualism. . . . As such, the form of the subjective right according to Kant becomes the normative essence of the legal concept of liberty".[18] Subjective rights in the post-Kantian sense are, as Marietta Auer has convincingly argued, the "legal paradigm of modernity". They are an "indicator of a change in legal thinking". Since Kant, the subjective right has been "the normative basis for a social order that identifies the general and the socially expected with the specific in the exercise of individual discretion and thereby claims to resolve the contradiction

[15] Dieter von Stephanitz, *Exakte Wissenschaft und Recht: Der Einfluß von Naturwissenschaften und Mathematik auf das Rechtsdenken und Rechtswissenschaft in zweieinhalb Jahrtausenden: Ein historischer Grundriß* (Berlin: de Gruyter 1970), 70–71.

[16] For a critical view, cf. Antony Black, Individuals, Groups and States: A Comparative Overview, in: Janet Coleman (ed.), *The Individual in Political Theory and Practice* (Oxford: Clarendon 1996), 329–340 (330). Cf. also Kurt Seelmann, Die Denkfigur des "subjektiven Rechts" in der spanischen Spätscholastik, in: Reyes Mate/ Friedrich Niewöhner (eds), *Spaniens Beitrag zum politischen Denken in Europa um 1600* (Wiesbaden: Harrassowitz Verlag 1994), 141–151, with a critical view of the "legend" of the development of "subjectivity" in the context of the Reformation. The development of the concept of subjective rights was "extremely complicated" with "numerous breaks and countercurrents" (*ibid.*, 151; translations mine).

[17] Marietta Auer, *Der privatrechtliche Diskurs der Moderne* (Tübingen: Mohr Siebeck 2013), 24–29, 27 (translation mine).

[18] *Ibid.*, 35–36. On Kant's "invention" of autonomy, see Jerome B. Schneewind, *The Invention of Autonomy: A History of Moral Philosophy* (Cambridge: Cambridge University Press 1998).

between the general and the specific by making the latter into an absolute".[19] The subjective right understood in this way is the "paradigmatically modern answer" to the basic problem of every society, namely the separation between individual reason and a social order no longer experienced as necessary but rather as malleable.[20] And exactly these "modern" issues have also become relevant for the international legal order, as highlighted by Emmanuel Roucounas: "Jusqu'à présent il y a peu d' intérêt de la part des auteurs pour une théorisation des droits 'subjectifs' en droit international. ... Néanmoins, il faut rappeler que depuis le milieu du XXème siècle la question des droits subjectifs repose sur des postulats de grande importance pour tous les systèmes juridiques, à savoir ceux de la responsabilité morale de l' homme, sa liberté, sa sociabilité, et la finalité de ses actions."[21]

17.2 The Postmodern Critique of Rights

But if rights are the paradigm of modernity, the critique of and farewell to rights is the hallmark of postmodernity.[22] Notably, human rights have recently been declared superfluous or even counterproductive, and their "twilight"[23] or even "end"[24] has been announced. So does it make sense to "individualize" the international legal order even more by conceptualizing (more) international rights even beyond human rights? Would this not be moving exactly in the wrong direction, in contradiction to current trends? The merit of the concept of an international subjective right depends on the value of rights as such. We therefore need to address the critique of rights.

I will not deal here with the cultural relativist critique raised, e.g., by Islamic and East Asia voices and with the problem of universality for two reasons. First, that critique is most relevant for human rights which are not the subject of this book. Second, the difficulty of reaching universal acceptance arises not specifically with regard to rights but also with regard to setting and implementing standards of objective law, as evidenced in international treaty making.

[19] Marietta Auer, Subjektive Rechte bei Pufendorf und Kant, *Archiv der civilistischen Praxis* 208 (2008), 584–634, 633 (translation mine).

[20] *Ibid.*

[21] Roucounas, Facteurs privés, 2002, 47 (paragraph 43; emphasis omitted, translation by the author).

[22] See already Chapter 2, pp. 21–23.

[23] Eric Posner, *The Twilight of Human Rights Law* (Oxford: Oxford University Press 2014).

[24] Costas Douzinas, *The End of Human Rights: Critical Legal Thought at the Turn of the Century* (Oxford: Hart 2000).

17.2.1 "Critical", Communitarian, Democrat, and Welfarist Critiques

Contemporary critiques of rights feed on the following, partly overlapping ideational sources: first, critical legal studies (which often suggest political action as an alternative to legalism and rights), sometimes inspired by neo-Marxism (which considers rights to be a pure superstructure in the service of those which hold economic and hence also political power); secondly, communitarianism (which highlights the importance of community, responsibility, and virtue alongside or instead of rights); thirdly, democratism (which considers entrenched legal rights as an undue obstacle to political process); and fourthly, welfarism (which opposes the overemphasis of so-called liberal rights which serve the wealthy). Finally, the law and economics view on human rights is that, as an empirical matter, international human rights treaties have not or only marginally improved the well-being of people and therefore recommends "that humanitarians should abandon the utopian aspirations of human rights law for the hard-won truths of development economics".[25] I will not address this recommendation, because human rights in particular are not the topic of this book.

In a *seminal critique of rights*, Mark Tushnet has highlighted that rights are instable, indeterminate, empty abstractions, and in practical terms useless. Rights may even counterproductively impede advances by social forces.[26] His "Essay on Rights" (being the paradigmatic postmodernist critique) takes, in Tushnet's own words, "a strong relativist position; it insists that rights-talk is meaningful only when it is placed within a full social and legal context".[27] The critique culminates in the charge of the "pragmatic disutility" of rights. But, as Tushnet recognizes, "pragmatic assessments are impossible in a completely relativized system, in which there are no criteria by which to evaluate whether something is pragmatically useful or not". This is the "paradox of relativism".[28] Tushnet's attempts to dissolve or overcome this paradox fail to convince me. Also, Tushnet ironizes the belief that rights have an emancipatory potential by insisting that "there is no such thing as a transcendent humanity lying around waiting to be emancipated or even to emancipate itself".[29] I interpret Tushnet's observation that "[o]ne sides with the party of humanity because it is defined as the party in opposition to what exists"[30] as saying that not the law but (only) politics may help to combat

[25] Posner, *Twilight*, 2014, 7–8.
[26] Mark Tushnet, An Essay on Rights, *Texas Law Review* 62 (1984), 1363–1403.
[27] *Ibid.*, 1394. [28] *Ibid.* [29] *Ibid.*, 1398. [30] *Ibid.*

and redress injustice. This type of legal nihilism cannot be addressed by any legal argument.

In line with this rights-scepticism, critical authors have spoken out in favour of reviving doctrines of objective law (as opposed to subjective rights). According to John Milbank, for example, objective law will "better protect, and also help to discriminate and mediate between those various more-or-less good causes of human dignity and freedom of action which we now try to protect through incoherent notions of 'human rights'".[31] Building on Michel Villey's work on the origin of the notion of *ius*, Milbank recalls that the "buried foundation" of human rights lies in a "questionable theological voluntarism and a questionably atomizing metaphysic".[32] Milbank also opines that the Dominican Middle Ages ideas of "just partition" and "virtuous usage" are better suited to achieve freedom and dignity than just relying on the ostensibly "emancipatory" promise of human rights. Without that retrieval, finds Milbank, the "cause of the West" clothed in the human rights language, might be lost.[33]

In the second intellectual camp, a *communitarian* worldview that emphasizes the belonging of an individual to the community forms the background of another strand of critique. In her work "Rights Talk", Mary Ann Glendon asks "whether an undifferentiated language of rights is really the best way to address the astonishing variety of injustices and forms of suffering that exists in the world".[34] The Polish legal scholar Wiktor Osiatyński sees a conflict between inflationary claims of rights and human happiness. According to Osiatyński, rights are overused and misused. Rights-holders do not have to belong somewhere and do not have to make compromises. He claims that juridification therefore weakens human bonds, limits trust, and prevents intimacy.[35] In this view, rights are only a "fall-back" or a "background guarantee" in case social and moral responsibility fails ("when justice replaces affection").[36]

[31] John Milbank, Against Human Rights: Liberty in the Western Tradition, in: Costas Douzinas/Conor Gearty (eds), *The Meanings of Rights: The Philosophy and Social Theory of Human Rights* (Cambridge: Cambridge University Press 2014), 39–70 (70).

[32] *Ibid.*, 68. See on Villey *supra* n. 11.

[33] Milbank, Against Human Rights, 2014, 70.

[34] Mary Ann Glendon, *Rights Talk: The Impoverishment of the Political Discourse* (New York: The Free Press 1991), 16.

[35] See Wiktor Osiatyński, Beyond Rights, in: András Sajo (ed.), *Abuse: The Dark Side of Fundamental Rights* (Utrecht: Eleven 2006), 309–327. See also Wiktor Osiatyński, *Human Rights and Their Limits* (Cambridge: Cambridge University Press 2009), esp. 187–188.

[36] Jeremy Waldron, When Justice Replaces Affection: The Need for Rights, *Harvard Journal of Law and Public Policy* 11 (1988), 625–647.

From such a communitarian perspective, Martti Koskenniemi has argued that "the turn to rights is adverse to a political culture of negotiation and critique" because it colonizes "political culture by a technocratic language that leaves no room for the articulation or realisation of conceptions of the good".[37] Koskenniemi claims that "despite its claim for value-neutrality, rights-rhetoric is constantly reduced to conflicting and contested arguments about the political good .... To this extent, the 'priority of the right over the good' proves an impossible demand, and insisting upon it will leave political discretion unchecked".[38] Koskenniemi rightly points out that "[s]ocial morality cannot ... be translated exhaustively into rights language".[39] Injustice may arise from economic and social causes, and "posing the normative issue in terms of individual rights fails to grasp its social meaning".[40] Koskenniemi also highlights the importance of the community for human flourishing: "Rights protect personal autonomy but autonomy is possible only if various collective goods are available. In a society that offers no choices, autonomy is meaningless. The extent of the availability of such collective goods again is a pure issue of political value; of struggle and compromise between alternative views about what a good society would be like. ... [R]ights refer back to contested notions of the political good."[41] The "indeterminacy" of rights "exists far beyond ... simple semantic openness ... The main point is that rights not only determine and limit policies, but that policies are needed to give meaning, applicability and limits to rights".[42] Overall, concludes Koskenniemi, reliance on rights is a veiled "enforcement of invested political preferences":[43] The "choice of the relevant language ('frame of reference') – whether the normative field is seen in terms of 'human rights' or, for example, 'economic development' or 'national security' – reflects upon a prior political decision independent of the language finally chosen, often having to do with which authority should have the competence to deal with a matter".[44] Thereby, politics is being transformed into technocracy: "As politics lose

[37] Martti Koskenniemi, The Effects of Rights on Political Culture, in: Martti Koskenniemi, *The Politics of International Law* (Oxford: Hart 2011), 133–167 (133).

[38] *Ibid.* See for a classic liberal proposition implying a priority of the right over the good, e.g., Michael Ignatieff, Human Rights as Politics, in: Amy Gutman (ed.), *Human Rights as Politics and Idolatry* (Princeton: Princeton University Press 2001), 3–52 (20–21): "When two sides recognize one another's claim of right, the dispute ceases to be – in their eyes – a conflict between right and wrong and becomes a conflict of rights."

[39] Koskenniemi, The Effects of Rights, 2011, 136. [40] *Ibid.*, 139.

[41] *Ibid.*, 139, internal references omitted. [42] *Ibid.*, 147–148. [43] *Ibid.*, 140.

[44] *Ibid.*, 141.

their creative, 'imaginative' character, they are transformed from their core sense as human vita activa into an exercise of technical competence by experts."[45]

That critique of depoliticization overlaps with the classic *democratic concern* that is directed primarily against the overlegalization of certain rights. Democrats (especially in the British tradition) see the specification of human rights primarily as an impermissible circumvention of the normal democratic process. They point out that the more rights are entrenched in a constitution (or international treaty), the less room there is for democracy (including for the right of each citizen to participate in votes), public debate, and – as also highlighted by the communitarians – social compromise.[46]

Coming from a yet different perspective which might be called *welfarist* or social(ist), other sceptics oppose an overemphasis on "liberal" and economic, i.e., "Western", rights. The German-American political scientist Friedrich Kratochwil calls the "proliferation of rights" a "rhetorical gambit" to support the desiderata of a certain lifestyle around the turn of the millennium.[47] The critique is here that problems of social life are translated into a catalogue of individual rights. Thus, the understandable preference for a democratic form of government suddenly becomes a "right to democracy". According to Kratochwil, this is a "category mistake of the first order".[48] Overall, the harshest critique finds that "the common discourse about rights ... is an intellectual stopgap and a political dead end".[49]

17.2.2 Responses to the Critique

The four strands of critique of the rights discourse referred to usefully point to drawbacks and dangers of rights, but they are in part exaggerated, confused, or flawed. For example, the reproach that the "rights talk" risks losing sight of the importance of shouldering responsibilities is one-sided. As Cass Sunstein has shown, a general critique of rights does not

[45] *Ibid.*, 150.

[46] See, e.g., Jeremy Waldron, A Rights-Based Critique of Constitutional Rights, *Oxford Journal of Legal Studies* 13 (1993), 18–52.

[47] Friedrich Kratochwil, How (Il)liberal is the Liberal Theory of Law?, Some Critical Remarks on Slaughter's Approach, *Comparative Sociology* 9 (2010), 120–145 (136–137). Kratochwil in particular opposes the idea of a "human right to free trade".

[48] *Ibid.*

[49] Martti Koskenniemi, Rights, History, Critique, in: Adam Etinson (ed.), *Human Rights: Moral or Political?* (Oxford: Oxford University Press 2016).

make much sense. Empirically, in our contemporary societies, no general shift from responsibilities to rights is occurring. Conceptually, rights also engender responsibilities, and are no opposite to those. The question is not whether to have rights but what rights in which settings.[50] And, we might add, who will be granted rights.

Importantly, rights critics do not distinguish between the supposed problem of inflationary recourse to rights in general and specifically the proliferation of *human* rights (a subgroup of especially important rights of high quality that enjoy stronger legal and moral protection).

Second, critics do not properly distinguish between individual public rights directed against the State (and possibly against other wielders of political power) and *rights directed against private persons*, either in the form of rights flowing from private law (contracts, torts, and so on), or in situations of conflicting fundamental rights (such as privacy versus free press). When Koskenniemi rightly points out that "the solidarity of friendship" and "the sexual relations between man and woman, can only with a loss of meaning be described in rights language",[51] he misses the direction of the international rights that are discussed in this book. Within personal relationships, the invocation of rights may weaken human bonds, undermine trust, and prevent personal closeness. But these concerns are irrelevant for rights directed against political, public institutions notably States.

Finally, the criticism of rights has been mainly formulated with a view to national societies and within the framework of a mature, highly differentiated domestic legal system, and has its merit there. But the exaggeration of individual rights seems much less an issue on the level of international law, where rights (of humans) are anyway still the exception and sparse. Notably, the democratic objection that an excessive focus on actionable (constitutionally guaranteed) rights weakens the democratic political process is almost totally beside the point for the international legal system, because law-making here is not democratic anyway.

The same observation is true for the critique of depolitization and technocracy. Legal rights, especially human rights, can be and should best be conceived as being not above or beyond politics, but as being both the result of political struggles, and as being usable for political ends

[50] Cass Sunstein, Rights and Their Critics, *Notre Dame Law Review* 70 (1999), 727–768, esp. 756.

[51] Koskenniemi, The Effects of Rights, 2011, 138.

themselves. "Human rights is nothing other than a politics, one that must reconcile moral ends to concrete situations and must be prepared to make painful compromises not only between means and ends, but between ends themselves."[52] While the language of rights adds an additional register to the political process, rights are not hermetically sealed off from the latter. Moreover, on the international level, genuinely political processes (in the sense of deliberation about the common good of a society, using the mode of arguing and persuasion) – as opposed to diplomacy (in the sense of pursuing national interests in the mode of bargaining and package deals) – are anyway rare. The relative lack of politization is not mainly owed to any exaggerated focus on rights but to other factors.

17.2.3 The Added Value of Rights

The four types of critique of rights just discussed fail to convince ordinary political and social actors. In the practice of states, governments, activists, and individual victims themselves, the attraction and the pull of rights, notably human rights, is incessant. The quest for recognizing, committing to, and implementing rights both in domestic law and in international law is as strong as it was in the 1990s. For example, the heads of State and governments in the United Nations' 2012 General Assembly Declaration on the Rule of Law at the National and International Levels emphasized "the importance of awareness-raising concerning legal rights" notably among the members of vulnerable groups in society.[53] Apparently, rights resonate both in the political and in the layperson's sphere. This section examines whether the prestige of rights is justified.

One question is the rationale of rights. In private law in German-speaking Europe, the (subjective) right has been and continues to be justified in terms of "will" (paradigmatically by Friedrich Carl von Savigny[54]) or "interests"

[52] Ignatieff, Human Rights as Politics, 2001, 22–23. See for the political character of rights also David Kinley, Human Rights Fundamentalisms, *Sydney Law Review* 29 (2007), 545–575 (567–568).

[53] Declaration of the High-level Meeting of the General Assembly on the Rule of Law at the National and International Levels, of 30 November 2012 (UN Doc. 67/1), paragraph 14.

[54] Friedrich Carl von Savigny defines "right in a subjective sense" as "the power justly appertaining to the individual person: a territory in which his will rules and rules with our consent. This power we call a right of this person synonymous with privilege; some call it right in a subjective sense" (Friedrich Carl von Savigny, *System of the Modern Roman*

(paradigmatically by Rudolf von Ihering[55]). In Anglo-Saxon law, these two directions correspond to "choice"- and "interest"-based views.[56] Nowadays, the foundation in interests seems to prevail. For example, Jospeh Raz defines: "'X has a right' if and only if X can have rights, and, other things being equal, an aspect of X's well-being (his interest) is a sufficient reason for holding some other person(s) to be under a duty."[57] It is also possible to combine both views, as Georg Jellinek had done, when defining the subjective right as "the human power of will recognized and protected by the legal order and directed at a good or interest".[58]

I will not dwell further on the essentially contested foundation of rights but only look at what rights actually do for human beings.[59] What are the benefits and the added value of so-called subjective rights as opposed to mere objective legal standards of protection? These benefits may unfold in different dimensions of social life. Rights may be practically useful in a hands-on sense, they may be theoretically and doctrinally more appealing to lawyers, and their utility may lie in the realm of emotions, expressivity, and symbolism.

A first and very practical advantage of rights is to facilitate proceedings in court. Indeed, some legal systems have traditionally defined rights by their judicial enforceability: "no rights without remedy" (see on this pp. 45–47). However, justiciability is no universal feature of all kinds of rights in all legal systems. For example, when an international human right is violated, there is virtually no international judicial remedy available. Moreover, many domestic legal orders acknowledge rights which cannot, or not directly, be vindicated in courts.[60] This state of the law

Law, Vol. I, transl. by William Holloway (Madras: J. Higginbotham 1867), 7. German original: *System des heutigen römischen Rechts*, Vol. 1 (Berlin: Veit 1840), 7).

55 Rudolph von Ihering, *Geist des römischen Rechts auf den verschiedenen Stufen seiner Entwicklung*, Part Three, Section One (3rd ed., Leipzig: Breitkopf und Härtel 1877), 339: "Rights are legally protected interests" (translation mine).

56 Matthew H. Kramer, Rights Without Trimmings, in: Matthew H. Kramer/Neil E. Simmonds/Hillel Steiner (eds), *A Debate over Rights: Philosophical Enquiries* (Oxford: Oxford University Press 2000), 7–111 (60–101).

57 Joseph Raz, *The Morality of Freedom* (Oxford: Clarendon 1988), 166.

58 Georg Jellinek, *System der subjektiven öffentlichen Rechte* (Tübingen: Mohr 1905), 44 (translation mine).

59 *Cf.* in that sense Michael Ignatieff, Human Rights as Idolatry, in: Amy Gutman (ed.), *Human Rights as Politics and Idolatry* (Princeton: Princeton University Press 2001), 53–100 (54).

60 In France, citizens can only since 2008 complain directly about fundamental rights violations before the *Conseil constitutionnel* (Question prioritaire de constitutionnalité, QPC). In the United Kingdom, citizens can only since 1998 invoke fundamental rights as endorsed in the British Human Rights Act. However, British courts are not allowed to

shows that, as a matter of legal theory and practice, the question of possessing a right (as a part of substantive law) and the question of how and in which forums to enforce it (procedural law) are two separate issues. The usefulness of a right can lie elsewhere than in its judicial enforceability.

The second main function of rights lies in their emancipatory potential. Rights empower people, if not judicially then at least politically.[61] As Cass Stunstein put it: "It is surely plausible that the recognition of rights often converts people from victims into citizens. Certainly a major point of rights guarantee is to do precisely this."[62]

Thirdly, and importantly, the advantage of having rights as opposed to being merely beneficiaries of standards of conduct is an increased and stronger protection. The recognition of rights carries with it a powerful message of prima facie inviolability (which the metaphors of "trump",[63] "stop-sign", "shield" or "armour",[64] and the like express). The protection is not absolute, but it is stronger than without rights. Rights are not absolutes, because they can be interfered with, curtailed, or restricted up to a certain point. The heightened protection offered by a right lies in the fact that curtailments and restrictions of rights must *be specifically justified*. Acknowledging a right places a burden of explanation and justification on the actor who wants to restrict the right (in the case of public rights this is notably the State). Only if the justification fails, the right is deemed to be violated.[65]

Exactly this burden of justification implies that cloaking the question of our social and political interactions and of the ensuing conflicts between antagonist interests in the language of rights *channels the discourse*. "Introducing the notion of something having a 'right' (simply speaking that way), brings into the legal system a flexibility and open-

disregard, amend, or annul a law violating those rights. They can only issue a statement of incompatibility. In Switzerland, social rights (called "social objectives") under Article 41 of the Federal Constitution are excplicitly not justiciable in court (Article 41(4)).

61 See, e.g., Ignatieff, Human Rights as Idolatry, 2001, 57: Rights language is a language of empowerment.

62 Sunstein, Rights and Their Critics, 1999, 754.

63 Ronald Dworkin, Rights as Trumps, in: Jeremy Waldron (ed.), *Theories of Rights* (Oxford: Oxford University Press 1984), 153–167.

64 Frederick Schauer, A Comment on the Structure of Rights, *Georgia Law Review* 27 (1993), 415–434 (429).

65 I here follow the terminology of the European Court of Human Rights with regard to human rights: interference/restriction – justification – violation.

endedness that no series of specifically stated legal rules like R1, R2, R3, ... R. can capture. Part of the reason is that 'right' (and other so-called 'legal terms' ...) have meaning – vague but forceful – in the ordinary language, and the force of these meanings, inevitably infused with our thought, becomes part of the context against which the 'legal language' of our contemporary 'legal rules' is interpreted."[66] This modification of the discourse is in turn apt to impact on behaviour, as social constructivists have argued. The rights discourse and the burden of justification going with it "socializes" the relevant actors. This has been empirically shown with regard to human rights, as an effect of endorsing and ratifying international human rights conventions.[67]

Fourth, the rights-related balancing *differs from the utilitarian calculus* directed at identifying the "greatest happiness of the greatest number", to use Jeremy Bentham's words.[68] Although the identification of the point where an interference with a right amounts to an inadmissible violation of that right involves balancing, too, the right confers a legal position which changes the equation. As Jeremy Waldron points out: "There are differences between the trade-offs involved in utilitarian theory and the sorts of trade-offs that might be adopted as a solution to conflicts of rights."[69] For example, balancing the protection of civilians (as in the humanitarian law standard of "military necessity") is structurally biased against civilians. In contrast, individual rights flowing from international humanitarian law would allow a fair balancing in which the proper value of fundamental human interests (such as the interest to live) could be integrated.

[66] Christopher D. Stone, Should Trees have Standing?, Toward Legal Rights for Natural Objects, *Southern California Law Review* 45 (1972), 450–501 (488).

[67] Beth A. Simmons, *Mobilizing for Human Rights: International Law in Domestic Politics* (Cambridge: Cambridge University Press 2009); Ryan Goodman/Derek Jinks, *Socializing States: Promoting Human Rights Through International Law* (Oxford: Oxford University Press, 2013); Thomas Risse/Stephen C. Ropp, Introduction and Overview, in: Thomas Risse/Stephen C. Ropp/Kathryn Sikkink (eds), *The Persistent Power of Human Rights: From Commitment to Compliance* (Cambridge: Cambridge University Press 2013), 3–25 on the "spiral model of human rights change" which social constructivist authors had developed since 1998.

[68] Jeremy Bentham posited as a "fundamental axiom, it is the greatest happiness of the greatest number that is the measure of right and wrong" (Jeremy Bentham, *A Fragment on Government, or, A Comment on the Commentaries, Edited with an Introduction by Francis Charles Montague* (Oxford: Clarendon Press 1891; original 1776), 93).

[69] Jeremy Waldron, Rights in Conflict, in: Jeremy Waldron, *Liberal Rights: Collected Papers 1981–1991* (Cambridge: Cambridge University Press 1993), 203–224 (210–211).

Fifthly, the usefulness of rights lies in their dynamic and overshooting content. Neither the substance nor the addressees of rights are entirely determined, but may change. As Joseph Raz writes, "one may know of the existence of a right . . . without knowing who is bound by duties based on it or what precisely are those duties".[70] This means that the protection created through rights may become stronger (or weaker) with the circumstances. In the field of human rights (which are otherwise not treated in this book), the evolution of prisoners' rights may serve as an example. In 1993 still, the ECtHR denied that a prisoner's right to be treated humanely (Article 3 ECHR) was violated by his detention in a cell of 6 m^2.[71] This was in spite of the determination, in 1992, by the European Committee for the Prevention of Torture and Inhuman or Degrading Treatment of Punishment of 7 m^2 per prisoner as a "rough guideline" for a detention cell.[72] In a 2002 judgment, the ECtHR found that a prison cell in Russia, measuring between 17 m^2 (according to the applicant) and 20.8 m^2 (according to the Government), designed for eight inmates but normally occupied by eighteen to twenty-four inmates, was "severely overcrowded", and that detention in such conditions amounted to degrading treatment in the sense of Article 3 ECHR.[73] The outreach and substance of that specific right not to be treated in an inhuman or degrading way has changed and will probably continue to change, due to improved building and housing and sanitary conditions, and due to increased sensibilities.

In a 1999 judgment on beatings by the police, the ECtHR explicitly raised the human rights standards. It considered "that certain acts which were classified in the past [only] as 'inhuman and degrading treatment' as opposed to 'torture' could be classified differently in future". The Court took "the view that the increasingly high standard being required in the area of the protection of human rights and fundamental liberties correspondingly and inevitably requires greater firmness in assessing breaches of the fundamental values of democratic societies".[74]

[70] Raz, *The Morality of Freedom*, 1988, 184.

[71] European Commission of Human Rights, *Delazarus* v. *United Kingdom*, No. 17525/90, Decision of 16 February 1993: The detention for fourteen weeks in a single cell measuring three by two metres (i.e., 6 m^2) "with a high ceiling" for twenty-three hours a day with two thirty minute exercise breaks in an individual pen, the size of a tennis court, did not constitute a violation of Article 3 ECHR. See also ECtHR, *Case of Guzzardi* v. *Italy*, No. 7367/76, Judgment of 6 November 1980 (compulsory residence for three years at Cala Reale on the island of Asinara): no violation of Article 3.

[72] CTP, 2nd General Report – CPT/Inf (92) 3, of 13 April 1992, paragraph 43.

[73] ECtHR, *Kalashnikov* v. *Russia*, No. 47095/99, Judgment of 15 July 2002.

[74] ECtHR, *Selmouni* v. *France*, No. 25803/94, Judgment of 28 July 1999, paragraph 101.

Related to the added value of the rights' dynamism over time as illustrated by the case law of prisoners' rights is a sixth one, the jurisgenerative quality of rights. "[H]aving rights is a generalized legal competence, whereas being the beneficiary of the obligations of others breaks down into a series of specialized, specific rules." Also, "the idea of having 'rights' includes a notion of moral rights that can inform existing law or even *push it in a certain direction*".[75]

Overall, the difference between having a right and being the object of protective standards looks not so much like a difference in kind but seems rather a matter of degree. Because rights trigger an obligation to justify their curtailment, because of the weight afforded to rights in a balancing exercise, because of their overshooting tendency and the indeterminacy of the obligations flowing from rights, legal rights offer a stronger protection than the concrete and selective obligations to accord humans a specific treatment under international law.

17.2.4 Specific Problems of Individual Rights in International Law

So far I have discussed the merits and flaws of rights in general. Additional problems arise in the international legal system. The rights-based model might be superfluous from an output-oriented perspective. Facially, the added value of the recognition of an international individual right over a system of objective standards (through legal effects by rebound) is not clear. Along this line, Kate Parlett opines that "it should not be assumed that direct rights necessarily connote better protection in a particular context, than would be possible under a state-centred model of international law".[76] In the preceding section, I have argued that the position created through legal rights is – as a matter of principle – stronger than protecting by rebound, *inter alia* because it creates a burden of justification for curtailments. And even if objective international standards were able to bring about equal legal protection, this would still correspond to a *paternalistic* model of international law, in which the State is understood as a trustee of the welfare of the individual. The purely objective model of international law lacks the practical, theoretical, and symbolic advantages of rights as just explained (pp. 536–41).

[75] Anthony D'Amato/Sudhir K. Chopra, Whales: Their Emerging Right to Life, *American Journal of International Law* 85 (1991), 21–62 (51) (italics mine).

[76] Kate Parlett, *The Individual in the International Legal System* (Cambridge: Cambridge University Press 2011), 363 and 372.

Second, it has been asserted that international individual rights, especially when associated with the possibility to file individual complaints under international law, may be counterproductive in terms of legal policy. Their exercise might give rise to resistance by the States, which would in turn undermine the practical functioning of the international legal order. An example of backlash is the withdrawal from the Optional Protocol to the Vienna Convention on Consular Relations (VCCR) by the United States as a consequence of the *LaGrand* judgment, in which the ICJ had found the United States to be in violation of the VCCR.[77] The withdrawal allowed the United States to remove itself from the jurisdiction of the ICJ in the future.[78] Another example is the denunciation of the Optional Protocol to the ICCPR by Trinidad and Tobago in response to criticism by the UN Human Rights Committee of its death penalty policy (especially the very long time served by prisoners on death row) in 1998. The small State re-joined the Optional Protocol, which grants the possibility of individual complaints, on the same day, but with a reservation excluding all complaints on behalf of prisoners in respect of matters relating to the death penalty.[79] In both cases, the States withdrew from monitoring mechanisms and in that way limited the practical effectiveness of the international legal protection of the individual.

Admittedly, the threat of individual complaints influences the cost–benefit calculus of a State in regard to its participation in an international regime, including the monitoring bodies established therein.[80] However, withdrawal from submission to an international court by a State is not necessarily linked to or triggered by the recognition of individual rights. Already in 1986, after being found in breach of the prohibition of force, i.e., an inter-State norm *par excellence*, the United States had withdrawn its general declaration recognizing the jurisdiction of the ICJ.

It is a sociological truism that law which is too strict and too intensly contrary to interests of those subjected to the law will provoke backlashes that undermine the normative force of the law in general. Because of the

[77] Chapter 11.

[78] Letter of withdrawal by the US Secretary of State to the UN Secretary-General dated 7 March 2005.

[79] UN Human Rights Committee, *Kennedy* v. *Trinidad and Tobago*, Communication No. 845/1998 (UN Doc. CCPR/C/67/D/845/1999), Decision on admissibility of 31 December 1999.

[80] This is probably one reason why the United States, although it accepts the American Declaration of the Rights and Duties of Man, has not joined the American Convention on Human Rights and accordingly does not recognize the treaty-based jurisdictions of the Inter-American human rights bodies.

ever-present threat of a backlash, the normative demands on the States should not be overstretched by overlegalizing the international rights of individuals.[81]

On the other hand, law – if it is to deserve its name – is counterfactual. It is not and should not simply reflect the actually existing power relationships and interests. Rather, the purpose of every legal norm is to influence the interests and conduct of those subject to that norm and to guide them in the direction desired by the law-makers. Then, law, including international law, itself has a reality-shaping significance. Put differently, social reality, including international relations, is constituted in part by law and especially by rights.[82] This interaction has been theorized and empirically demonstrated by the constructivist strands of political science. As already discussed, States can be "socialized" by international legal norms under certain conditions.[83] More specifically even, changes to the international system (through the emergence of many new States) have been often or even mainly brought about through the struggles of individuals for human rights and their predecessor, religious tolerance. Historical examples are the emergence of the Westphalian system of States, the independence of Latin American States, the reorganization of Europe after the First World War, and the collapse of the Soviet Union.[84]

Although this constructive power of law – and of legal rights of the individual in particular – is precarious, an anticipatory resignation of legal scholars in light of political resistance would mean to give up exploiting the factual power of normativity and would betray the counterfactual nature of law and of rights.

[81] See Laurence R. Helfer, Overlegalizing Human Rights: International Relations Theory and the Commonwealth Caribbean Backlash Against Human Rights Regimes, *Columbia Law Review* 102 (2002), 1832–1911.

[82] See Emanuel Adler, Constructivism, in: Walter Carlsnaes/Beth Simmons/Thomas Risse (eds), *Handbook of International Relations* (2nd ed., Los Angeles: Sage 2013), 112–144 (113).

[83] See pp. 538–39 on the socialization through international human rights norms, esp. note 67. See further Martha Finnemore, *National Interests in International Society* (Ithaca: Cornell University Press 1996), 128.

[84] Christian Reus-Smit, Struggles for Individual Rights and the Expansion of the International System, *International Organisation* 65 (2011), 207–242; Christian Reus-Smit, *Individual Rights and the Making of the International System* (Cambridge: Cambridge University Press 2013).

17.3 The Lack of Global Citizenship

The status of the human being in international law is similar to the status of the citizen in the German constitutionalism of the nineteenth century, to whom certain basic rights (property and liberty) were granted, but not a general democratic right to vote. As was the case one hundred years ago in most national legal orders, natural persons' say in law-making is hardly developed in today's international law – there is no democratic law-making.[85] Hence, the international legal status of man currently largely lacks a political dimension.[86]

In this regard, the processes at two legal levels must be distinguished, the interplay of which gives rise to international law. Normally, individuals are involved only at the level of the State. In democratic States, the governments concluding treaties are representatives elected by their citizens. In so far, the creation of international law (i.e., the conclusion of international treaties) can be understood as indirect law-making *by the* individuals. However, the chains of legitimacy are long and often interrupted, so that the real influence of individuals on the concrete legal product is minimal. Moreover, representation of the individuals is extremely distorted, since the principle of "one State, one vote" applies in conferences and for the conclusion of treaties. Finally, governments that are not democratically legitimized and do not reflect the views of their States' inhabitants also participate in the negotiation of treaties. For all these reasons, the idea of an indirect international law-making process by individuals via governments is largely a legal fiction.

17.3.1 The Participation of Individuals in the Creation of Norms at the International Level

What about the inclusion of individuals in the creation of law directly at the level of international law? On a large scale and with a great degree of diversity, transnationally operating businesses, arbitral tribunals, NGOs, and all of them together in transnational multi-stakeholder initiatives

[85] Anne Peters, Dual Democracy, in: Jan Klabbers/Anne Peters/Geir Ulfstein (eds), *The Constitutionalization of International Law* (2nd ed. Oxford: Oxford University Press 2011), 263–341 (286–296).

[86] By political dimension, I mean the participation of natural persons in public, controversial, and deliberative procedures in which political answers are given and laid down in the form of *legal* – and thus in form of relatively stable but nevertheless reversible – norms in order to tackle problems of global society.

and public–private partnerships act as global standard setters.[87] This means that nowadays, natural and legal persons under national law participate *alongside* States in generating norms also at the international level. A first channel of influence is offered by the participation arrangements for NGOs at treaty conferences and in the context of international organizations and bodies that enact secondary law. NGOs are permitted to observe and comment on the negotiation of international treaties and the enactment of secondary norms in international treaty regimes. Firstly, however, these NGOs are not elected representatives of citizens, and secondly, they do not have co-decision powers at the same level as government representatives in any existing body.[88]

Another channel for influencing the creation of international law consists in parliamentary assemblies in international organizations, representing the citizens of Member States either as direct representatives (as in the European Parliament) or as members of the parliaments of the Member States. However, these assemblies – with the exception of the European Parliament – have only consultative powers.[89] And the most powerful international organizations, namely the UN and the WTO, have no parliamentary assembly at all.

Another example is the creation of law within the framework of the ILO: Delegates of the social partners, together with the representatives of the ILO Member States, negotiate and adopt the ILO conventions and recommendations by a majority decision. These delegates are appointed by the Member States (with the agreement of the professional organizations), but they exercise their voting rights freely (i.e., without instructions) (Article 3(1) and (5); Article 4(1) of the ILO Constitution). As a result, the social partners participate at the same level as government representatives in the development of hard and soft ILO law. In the case of ILO conventions requiring ratification by the States at a second stage in order to enter into force, however, the States remain the gatekeepers due to the ratification requirement.

Furthermore, the new transparency requirements for the creation of international law might be seen as an indirect strengthening of the

[87] Anne Peters/Lucy Koechlin/Till Förster/Gretta Fenner Zinkernagel (eds), *Non-State Actors as Standard Setters* (Cambridge: Cambridge University Press 2009).

[88] See Anne Peters, Membership in the Global Constitutional Community, in: Jan Klabbers/Anne Peters/Geir Ulfstein (eds), *The Constitutionalization of International Law* (2nd ed., Oxford: Oxford University Press 2011), 153–262 (225–227).

[89] See Isabelle Ley, *Opposition im Völkerrecht* (Heidelberg: Springer 2014), chapter 12 (215–254).

participation of private persons and members of global civil society.[90] Transparency makes it possible for the public to gain knowledge of law-making projects (e.g., treaty projects), which is a precondition for public criticism and protest. These are negative and informal forms of participation in the development of law.

According to a recent view, transnational companies, i.e., legal persons under (national) private law, also have the competence to conclude quasi-international legal or transnationalized treaties with States.[91] These are bilateral treaties, not global regulatory agreements.

Finally, minorities and indigenous peoples participate in the creation of soft law, for instance according to the rules of the World Bank and private financial institutions.[92] One type of participation is provided in the safeguard policies adopted by the World Bank since 1997. Although these policies do not refer to international human rights treaties, some of them provide for the participation and empowerment of people affected by projects funded by the World Bank. For instance, the operational policy on indigenous peoples requires free, prior, and informed consultation of the affected communities during the entire project cycle.[93] The operational policy on involuntary resettlement emphasizes that "[t]he involvement of involuntary resettlers and hosts in planning prior to the move is critical".[94]

The Equator Principles, the third version of which was adopted by financial institutions in 2013, are another example. These are standards of the international financial sector for determining, assessing, and managing social and environmental risks of project financing. One principle concerns consultation and dialogue. The banks committed to the Equator Principles pledge that they will not provide loans for projects where the borrower or the State has failed to consult the affected communities in a structured and culturally appropriate manner.[95] For projects with significant impact on the affected communities, a special "Informed Consultation and Participation process" must be conducted. This process requires an in-depth exchange of views intended to ensure

[90] See Andrea Bianchi/Anne Peters (eds), *Transparency in International Law* (Cambridge: Cambridge University Press 2013).

[91] See Chapter 10, pp. 294–301. [92] See Peters, Membership, 2011 (n. 88), 159–161.

[93] Operational Policy 4.10: Indigenous Peoples of January 2005, Article 1.

[94] Operational Policy 4.12: Involuntary Resettlement of January 2001 (the operational policy statement was updated in March 2007), Article 8.

[95] Equator Principles III (June 2013), Principle 5: Stakeholder Engagement. The financing institutions require the client "to demonstrate effective Stakeholder Engagement as an ongoing process in a structured and culturally appropriate manner with Affected Communities and, where relevant, Other Stakeholders" (www.equator-principles.com).

that the opinions of the affected communities are taken into account in the decision-making process.[96]

Similar in nature are participation rights contained in the transnationalized negotiation processes for indigenous rights, such as fishing rights, between indigenous peoples and States. The Human Rights Committee has interpreted the minority protection clause in Article 27 ICCPR to mean that the States parties must include representatives of minorities in law-making processes if rules are enacted that affect the rights of a minority.[97] All these (soft) legal requirements for consultation are only a very limited way to empower affected individuals and communities. Those affected are not, for instance, empowered to initiate a project themselves.

Another question is whether individuals can contribute to the creation of *customary* international law.[98] To do so, the conduct of natural persons (or of NGOs as their proxies) would have to be considered relevant practice and be taken into account as an objective element of the emergence of law. The Appeals Chamber of the Yugoslavia tribunal affirmed this in passing in the *Tadic* decision on jurisdiction: It held that the behaviour of insurgents contributes to the formation of new rules in the law of armed conflict.[99] Public opinion and the legal opinions of individuals, as may be manifested in the filing of individual claims and complaints or as may be determined in opinion surveys, would then be considered relevant *opinio iuris*. The customary law formed in this way could be called "customary transnational law".[100] Overall, the forms of participation of individuals and groups in the creation of law are diverse and of very different intensities (from mere transparency and

[96] "Informed Consultation and Participation is an in-depth exchange of views and information and an organized and iterative consultation that leads the client to incorporate the views of Affected Communities, on issues that affect them directly (such as proposed mitigation measures, the sharing of development benefits and opportunities, and implementation issues), into their decision-making process" (Equator Principles III of June 2013, Exhibit I: Glossary of Terms, 17).

[97] UN Human Rights Committee, *Apirana Mahuika et al.* v. *New Zealand*, Communication No. 547/1992, CCPR/C/70/D/547/1993 (2000), paragraphs 9.6.–9.8.

[98] Christiana Ochoa, The Individual in Customary International Law Formation, *Virginia Journal of International Law* 48 (2007), 119–186.

[99] ICTY, Case No. IT-94-1-AR72, *Prosecutor* v. *Duško Tadić*, Decision on the Defence Motion for Interlocutory Appeal on Jurisdiction, Appeals Chamber of 2 October 1995, paragraph 108: "In addition to the *behaviour* of belligerent States, Governments and *insurgents*, other factors have been instrumental in bringing about the *formation of the customary rules* at issue" (italics mine).

[100] Till Müller, Customary Transnational Law: Attacking the Last Resort of State Sovereignty, *Indiana Journal of Global Legal Studies* 19 (2008), 19–47.

contestation to participation in the conclusion of treaties). Not every involvement of every actor (from indigenous peoples to transnational companies) should be welcomed equally in normative terms. In our context, we are interested in pointing out that the phenomenon of privatized and hybrid standard setting exists, but the normative appraisal thereof shall remain an open question here.

17.3.2 Is International Law Being Produced Here?

The practice sketched above, including the conceptualization proposal, cannot hide the fact that quantitatively and qualitatively significant production of norms by non-State actors does not fit into the traditional categories of international law. It is questionable whether these activities really generate actual, hard international law or whether they give rise only to *non-legal* or at best soft legal norms. Global legal pluralism conceptualizes the new phenomenon as the creation of real law.[101] The various strands of global legal pluralism negate the monopoly of the State to create law (so-called legal centralism) and hold the norms produced by non-State groups or institutions to be similarly effective as State law (or even more effective and legitimate).[102] It is a question of legal theory whether the social actors should be deemed to have original power to create law or whether the norms emerging from (transnational) civil society can achieve the quality of law only if the State orders it to be valid. From a normative perspective, the view that there can be no justice outside State law[103] is not

[101] See fundamentally Gunther Teubner, Globale Bukowina: Zur Emergenz eines transnationalen Rechtspluralismus, *Rechtshistorisches Journal* 15 (1996), 255–290. See also Brian Z. Tamanaha, Understanding Legal Pluralism: Past to Present, Local to Global, *Sidney Law Review* 30 (2008), 375–411 with the proposal to do without a definition of "law", and instead to recognize that State law has a special status. For a good overview of the literature, see Ralf Michaels, Global Legal Pluralism, *Annual Review of Law and Social Science* 5 (2009), 243–262. For a new attempt to conceptualize transnationally, privately created law, see Gralf-Peter Calliess/Peer Zumbansen, *Rough Consensus and Running Code* (Oxford: Hart 2010). The authors assume that the "rough" consensus suffices to make these norms legitimate and effective.

[102] See fundamentally James Griffiths, What is Legal Pluralism?, *Journal of Legal Pluralism and Unofficial Law* 24 (1986), 1–50; Franz von Benda-Beckmann, Rechtspluralismus: Analytische Begriffsbildung oder politisch-ideologisches Programm, *Zeitschrift für Ethnologie* 119 (1994), 1–16.

[103] Cf. still Léon Duguit/Hans Kelsen, Préface, *Revue internationale de la théorie du droit* 1 (1926–1927), 1–4 (3). For the normative arguments against a State monopoly on lawmaking, see Ferdinand Kirchhof, *Private Rechtsetzung* (Berlin: Duncker und Humblot 1987), § 3. For more details, see Gregor Bachmann, *Private Ordnung* (Tübingen: Mohr Siebeck 2006): What is decisive for the validity claim of a rule is not its origin (public or

accurate with respect to the current transnationalized lifeworld. In any event, it is empirically clear on the one hand that a State monopoly for the production of global norms does not exist (anymore), but on the other hand that natural persons as individuals (unlike various organizational units) play only a marginal and subordinate role here as well.

17.3.3 Creation of Law through the Power to Bring Claims?

The actionability of breaches of international law arising from the international individual right, especially before national courts (see above Chapter 15), is not a real alternative to the underdeveloped democratic participation of natural persons in the creation of international law. This is true even though the power of individuals to bring claims or complaints through which individuals can institute international judicial or arbitration proceedings, such as before the European Court of Human Rights or ICSID arbitral tribunals, does generate a corpus of case law. This case law develops international law in general, and it has strengthened and expanded the rights and duties of natural persons as well. Also in (international) criminal proceedings, the accused individuals serve as catalysts for the development of international criminal law. The work of the international criminal courts, human rights bodies, and committees is therefore seen as an indicator of the consolidation of the individual international legal personality: "This indicates a growth of the international legal personality ... of individuals."[104] Because international judges and arbitrators enjoy judicial independence, this further development of the law occurs without direct government control.

This can again be compared with German late constitutionalism, in which representatives of the people had no general power of democratic law-making. The "subjective, public law-based right" (*das subjektive öffentliche Recht*) at the time precisely did not permit the actionability of universal concerns, but rather only of "private" interests, just as parliament did not claim co-responsibility for "political" questions.[105]

private), but rather its legitimacy. Bachmann makes an ideal-typical distinction between two forms of legitimacy: the "private law" mechanism of consent and the "public law" mechanism of orientation towards the common good. These two may complement each other or also compensate legitimacy deficits in the other "camp" (*ibid.*, 415).

104 Kenneth S. Gallant, *The Principle of Legality in International and Comparative Criminal Law* (Cambridge: Cambridge University Press 2009), 10.

105 Johannes Masing, *Die Mobilisierung des Bürgers für die Durchsetzung des Rechts: Europäische Impulse für eine Revision der Lehre vom subjektiv-öffentlichen Recht* (Berlin: Duncker & Humblot 1997), 66–67.

Is the individual power to bring claims a functional equivalent of the regular power to create international law that is primarily vested in States? Hardly. The accountability of public authority triggered by judicial proceedings is only *ex post* accountability and is not anticipatory. When the courts fence in public authority, they do so on the basis of law and cannot take account of interests that have no legal basis. Constraints on public authority concern individual cases and not the public in general. Possibilities for bringing claims and complaints at the national and international level are therefore no substitute for democratic international law-making processes. The individual is not yet able to play the part of an international citizen who could have a key role in the process of transforming the international legal order from a Vattelian, inter-State system into a universal constitutional democracy.[106]

A universal constitutional democracy, in which the individual is not only vested with international rights and duties but also is (directly) represented, and within the framework of which individuals can participate in the individual law-creating and law-applying institutions, is still far away. The so-far only rudimentary political dimension of the international legal status of the individual could be beefed up by establishing structures of a "dual democracy" which would consist of a transitive statist track of democratic procedures coupled with a direct track of democratic procedures on the international level.[107] The international individual right constitutes one building block for the construction of such mechanisms, but the construction site is still enormous.

17.3.4 Preliminary Conclusion

The inclusion of natural persons in the production of norms which, given what was just said above, might deserve the label of international law should be further developed, and the currently weak trend towards upgrading individuals not only as bearers of individual rights but also as creators of law should be continued. The legal starting point for this purpose is the human right to take part in political decision-making (Article 25 ICCPR). Similarly to the human right to legal personality, it can be argued that in a world of increasingly intensive global governance, Article 25 should be interpreted also as conferring a right to take part in

[106] Janne E. Nijman, *The Concept of International Legal Personality: An Inquiry into the History and Theory of International Law* (The Hague: TMC Asser Press 2004), 424.
[107] Peters, Dual Democracy, 2011.

the creation of international law. All told, the internationally guaranteed formal *rights of participation* of non-State actors blur the lines between creators of law and mere bearers of rights. It can be said that the rights to participation are halfway between mere ownership of rights and the capacity to make law.

17.4 The Global Bourgeois

The goal of this book has been to systematically analyse the practice and legal opinion on the status of the individual in various sub-areas of international law. The core findings in terms of doctrine and legal policy can be summarized as follows.

The individual possesses numerous rights under international law as it stands. But his/her political participation rights in the production of international law are scarce.[108] Alongside international individual rights, the individual's legal responsibility has been examined. Criminal legal responsibility of the individual is established. But non-criminal international legal responsibility of the individual can be seen only in a rudimentary form.[109] And so far, there has hardly been any indication of a global political responsibility of the individual.[110]

The massive increase of simple legal rights of the individual and the operationalization of the individual's duties not only have quantitative significance but are also an indicator of a *qualitative leap*. This qualitative leap lies in the fact that the practice and *opinio iuris* of acknowledging rights and duties on a large scale has at the same time crystallized – it is submitted here – an original (primary) international legal personality of the human being. I have argued that a customary international legal norm or a general principle of law concerning the original international legal personality of the individual has come into being. This norm is supported by the reinterpretation of the human right to legal capacity. As shown,[111] Article 6 of the Universal Declaration of Human Rights and Article 16 (2) ICCPR can and should be interpreted expansively such that the human right to personality also confers international legal personality. Such a purposive (teleological) interpretation is warranted with a view to the provisions' rationale. If their purpose is to offer to humans

[108] See above pp. 544–48. [109] See Chapter 5.
[110] But cf. Janne E. Nijman, Paul Riceur and International Law: Beyond "The End of the Subject." Towards a Reconceptualization of International Legal Personality, *Leiden Journal of International Law* 20 (2007), 25–64 (61).
[111] See Chapter 13, pp. 430–31.

protection from the arbitrary exercise of political power on whichever level of governance, a legal personality of human beings restricted to the national sphere is no longer sufficient. To conclude, the individual is a full, i.e., a primary, original, *erga omnes* subject in the international community, a potential bearer of new international rights and duties. The catchphrase for describing this new legal status, including the totality of rights under international law, might be the international individual right.

What are the benefits of this novel, emancipated, and legally independent status of the individual? The old paradigm of protection, representation, and mediation of individuals was deficient. The representation of individuals at the international level by their States could and can, on practical and systemic grounds, function only to a limited extent. The position of the State as trustee is *de facto* often a custodianship, either because the State is not a democracy, or because foreign policy, economic, or fiscal considerations – i.e., the reason of State – interfere with its engagement on behalf of the interests of an individual. Without the conferral of the international individual right, the human being would (despite the banishment of an explicit positivistic "object theory" from the current textbooks) remain a "derivative", "partial", and "particular" subject of international law. All these qualifications merely veil the human being's situation ultimately as an object of the legal relations between States.

The novel legal status of the individual is significant for international law as a whole, as, e.g., Evelyne Lagrange notes: The increasingly consolidated status of the individual as a subject in international law, the fact that "the private person . . . is simply, more and more often, a subject who effectively holds subjective rights whith an international origin" denotes "the true change" of current international law.[112] The normality of individual rights and duties is an expression of a fundamentally changed understanding of the law: Individuals, not States, have become the natural persons under international law.[113]

[112] Evelyne Lagrange, L'efficacité des normes internationales concernant la situation des personnes privées dans les ordres juridiques internes, *Recueil des Cours* 356 (2012/III), 243–552 (258). Already the recognition of the individual in principle as a unit capable of having an effect in international law (irrespective of the theoretical justification) represents a "breakthrough" that allows the growing role of non-State actors (including NGOs) to be accompanied and ordered by international law (Georg Dahm/Jost Delbrück/ Rüdiger Wolfrum, *Völkerrecht*, Vol. I/2 (2nd ed., Berlin: De Gruyter 2002), 267).

[113] See Roland Portmann, *Legal Personality in International Law* (Cambridge: Cambridge University Press 2010), 2–3: In certain situations, individuals are "a priori international persons". In this sense also Andreas Müller, Zum Primat der juristischen Person im

At this point, a dim and rough historical analogy is in order. In current international law, the human being can be likened to a global *bourgeois* in the dual sense of an economic actor and bearer of so-called unpolitical international rights that secure his or her personal freedom and development.[114] This evolution can be compared to the historic effect of the crystallization of subjective rights in (German) national law. There as well, the subjective, public-law-based right was a decisive vehicle for the development from subject (*Untertan*) to citizen.[115] Already with the contours given to the subjective (private) right by the Pandectists in the nineteenth century, the idea of individual liberty was recognized as the rationale of private law.[116] The subsequent construction of subjective, public law-based rights was a key factor in pushing back the (German) authoritarian State and for the crystallization of a modern, liberal State.[117] Drawing lessons from this historic episode does not mean to predict or tout a world State. It simply suggests bidding farewell to the persisting anachronism of paternalism in the international legal system (with States as overlords).

We may evaluate the "true change" of the international legal order both from the vantage point of moral theory and from the vantage point of international legal principles. From the philosophical perspective, the new international legal status of the human being is an expression of a normative individualism. The idea here is that politics and law ultimately should be guided and justified by the concerns of the persons affected by them.[118] That paradigm does not dispute that people live

internationalen Recht: Zugleich ein Beitrag zur „Rehabilitierung" der natürlichen Person als Völkerrechtssubjekt, *Contributions of the Austrian Ludwig Wittgenstein Society*, Vol. X, 25th International Wittgenstein Symposium, 2002, 176–178 (178): Individuals as the "primary" subjects of international law.

114 See Manfred Riedel, Bürger, Staatsbürger, Bürgertum, in: Otto Brunner/Werner Conze/Reinhart Kosellek (eds), *Geschichtliche Grundbegriffe, Historisches Lexikon zur politisch-sozialen Sprache in Deutschland*, Vol. I: A–D (5th ed., Stuttgart: Klett-Cotta 1997), 672–725 (692, 707, 714).

115 See Hartmut Maurer, *Allgemeines Verwaltungsrecht* (18th ed., Munich: Beck 2011), § 8, paragraph 4 (173–174): "Without autonomous rights, the individual would in contrast be merely a subject, or an object of State action. Guaranteeing subjective rights is one of the basic conditions of a State characterized by freedom, democracy, social justice, and the rule of law. For this reason, subjective rights have been upgraded considerably even after enactment of the [German] Basic Law" (translation mine).

116 "The conception of the subjective right keeps the conviction alive that individual liberty is one of the most basic ideas for the sake of which private law exists" (Coing, Concept of "subjective right" 1959, 23 (translation mine).

117 Masing, *Mobilisierung des Bürgers*, 1997, 56 and 62.

118 Dietmar von der Pfordten, Normativer Individualismus und das Recht, *JuristenZeitung* 60 (2005), 1069–1080 (1069). Fernando Tesón defines normative individualism as the

socially (i.e., in communities), that their identity is constituted in part by those communities, that people act jointly, and that they have and should have collective goals. These collective projects must, however, ultimately be measured by the needs and interests of the persons affected and are not an end in themselves. From that perspective, precisely this orientation towards the individual in (different, overlapping, changing) communities justifies international law as a whole. At the same time, the recognition of genuinely *international* individual rights runs counter to the Hegelian view according to which the individual can be free and a legal subject only within and through the State.[119] The international individual right rather is an element of the *ius cosmopoliticum* in the Kantian sense.[120]

From the perspective of international legal basic principles, the recognition of the overarching concept of the international individual right fits. Acknowledging this concept presupposes that the welfare of the human being is a universal concern and a task of the entire international community. That starting-point is well anchored in international law. The Charter of the United Nations affirms that one of the purposes of the Organization and one of the "common ends" "of nations" is "promoting and encouraging respect for human rights and fundamental freedoms" (Articles 1(3) and (4) UN Charter). To realize this "common end of nations", international law normally relies on the most powerful political

insistence "that our moral concepts should be referred in the last analysis to individual rights and interests" (Fernando Tesón, *A Philosophy of International Law* (Boulder, CO: Westlake 1998), 27.

119 See Georg Wilhelm Friedrich Hegel, *Vorlesungen über die Philosophie der Geschichte, Vol. I: Einleitung – Die Vernunft in der Geschichte* (Georg Lasson (ed.), Leipzig: Felix Meiner Verlag 1920), 89–90: "This essential being is the union of the subjective with the rational Will: it is the moral Whole, the State, which is that form of reality in which the individual has and enjoys his freedom . . . In the State alone has man rational existence. The sole purpose of education is for the individual not to remain subjective, but to become objective in the State . . . Everything man is, all spiritual reality, he has solely through the State." *Ibid.*, 97: "Society and the State are the very conditions in which Freedom is realized." For an English translation, see J. Sibree, *The Philosophy of History, George Wilhelm Friedrich Hegel* (Kitchener: Batoche Books 2001), 53 (56) (translation modified by the author). See also Christoph Enders, *Die Menschenwürde in der Verfassungsordnung: Zur Dogmatik des Art. 1 GG* (Tübingen: Mohr Siebeck 1997), 243: "Anyone wishing to be recognized as free must enter into the condition of the State: Only within the State is he a person, a legal subject" (on Hegel) (translation mine).

120 Immanuel Kant, *Zum Ewigen Frieden* (Stuttgart: Reclam 1984 (orig. 1795)), Abschnitt II, Dritter Definitivartikel. See also Immanuel Kant, Die Metaphysik der Sitten, erster Theil, metaphysische Anfänge der Rechtslehre (orig. Königsberg 1798), in: Kant, Metaphysik der Sitten, Werkausgabe (eds), von Weischedel, Vol. 8 (Frankfurt a. M.: Suhrkamp 1978), § 62 (476) on "ius cosmopoliticum" (which Kant did not consider to be a right to political participation).

units, the States. But where interests of the State and individual human interests and needs diverge, international law should have a set of instruments at its disposal to at least leave the possibility for finding a legal solution which benefits the individual. This set of instruments must be placed in the individual's own hands or must allow for his or her participation. If this were not the case, the normative centrality of the human being as proclaimed by Article 1 of the UN Charter and all human rights instruments would be empty rhetorics.

Making explicit – through scholarly analysis – the existence of the so-far hidden and implicit overarching concept of an international individual right in positive international law creates a tension with current assertions of a re-sovereignization of international law. But this only shows the usefulness of that conceptualization for putting the latter claims into perspective: Pure Statism would be an exaggeration, just like the human-rightism of the 1990s – this time in the opposite direction. The time has come for the international individual right.

BIBLIOGRAPHY

Adler, Emanuel, Constructivism, in: Walter Carlsnaes/Beth Simmons/ Thomas Risse (eds), *Handbook of International Relations* (2nd ed. Los Angeles: Sage 2013), 112–144.

Akande, Dapo, Sources of International Criminal Law, in: Antonio Cassese (general ed.), *The Oxford Companion to International Criminal Justice* (Oxford: Oxford University Press 2009), 41–53.

Akande, Dapo/Gillard, Emanuela-Chiara, Arbitrary Withholding of Consent to Humanitarian Relief Operations in Armed Conflicts, *International Law Studies*, 2016 (forthcoming).

Aldana-Pindell, Raquel, An Emerging Universality of Justiciable Victims' Rights in the Criminal Process to Curtail Impunity for State-Sponsored Crimes, *Human Rights Quarterly* 26 (2004), 605–685.

Aldrich, George H., Individuals as Subjects of International Humanitarian Law, in: Jerzy Makarczyk (ed.), *Theory of International Law at the Threshold of the 21st Century: Essays in Honour of Krysztof Skubiszewski* (The Hague.: Kluwer Law International 1996), 851–858.

Alland, Denis, L'applicabilité directe du droit international considerée du point de vue de l'office du juge: des habits neufs pour une vieille dame?, *Revue générale de droit international public* 102 (1998), 203–244.

Alleweldt, Ralf, Kapitel 10: Recht auf Leben, in: Oliver Dörr/Rainer Grote/ Thilo Marauhn (eds), *EMRK/GG: Konkordanzkommentar* (2nd ed. Tübingen: Mohr Siebeck 2013), 491–536.

Alston, Philip, Conjuring up New Human Rights: A Proposal for Quality Control, *American Journal of International Law* 78 (1984), 607–621.

Alston, Philip, Core Labour Standards and the Transformation of the International Labour Rights Regime, *European Journal of International Law* 15 (2004), 457–521.

Alston, Philip, Labour Rights as Human Rights: The Not So Happy State of the Art, in: Alston (ed.), *Labour Rights as Human Rights* (Oxford: Oxford University Press 2005), 1–24.

Alston, Philip (ed.), *Non-State Actors and Human Rights* (Oxford: Oxford University Press 2005).

Alvarez, José, Are Corporations Subjects of International Law?, *Santa Clara Journal of International Law* 9 (2011), 1–36.

Alvik, Ivar, *Contracting with Sovereignty: State Contracts and International Arbitration* (Oxford: Hart 2011).

Ambos, Kai, *Treatise on International Criminal Law*, Vol. 1 (Oxford: Oxford University Press 2013).

Amelung, Knut, *Informationsbeherrschungsrechte im Strafprozess: Dogmatische Grundlagen individual-rechtlicher Beweisverbote* (Berlin: Duncker & Humblot 1990).

Amerasinghe, Felix Chittarajan, *Diplomatic Protection* (Oxford: Oxford University Press 2008).

Amerasinghe, Felix Chittarajan, *Local Remedies in International Law* (2nd ed. Cambridge: Cambridge University Press 2004).

Anderson, Gavin W., *Constitutional Rights after Globalization* (Oxford and Portland: Hart 2005).

Angenendt, Arnold, *Toleranz und Gewalt* (Münster: Aschendorff 2008).

Anzilotti, Dionisio, *Corso di Diritto Internazionale* (3rd ed. Rome: Athenaeum 1928).

Arangio-Ruiz, Gaetano, Dualism Revisited: International and Interindividual Law, *Rivista di diritto internazionale* 96 (2003), 909–999.

Arbour, Louise, The Responsibility to Protect as a Duty of Care in International Law and Practice, *Review of International Studies* 34 (2008), 445–458.

Arendt, Hannah, *The Origins of Totalitarianism* (New York: Harcourt, Brace and Company 1951).

Auer, Marietta, *Der privatrechtliche Diskurs der Moderne* (Tübingen: Mohr Siebeck 2013).

Auer, Marietta, Subjektive Rechte bei Pufendorf und Kant, *Archiv für die civilistische Praxis* 208 (2008), 584–634.

Avineri, Shlomo/De-Shalt, Avner (eds), *Communitarianism and Individualism* (Oxford: Oxford University Press 1992).

Aznar Gomez, Mariano J., *La administración internacionalizada del territorio* (Barcelona: Atelier 2008).

Bachmann, Gregor, *Private Ordnung* (Tübingen: Mohr Siebeck 2006).

Balkin, Jack M., Understanding Legal Understanding: The Legal Subject and the Problem of Legal Coherence, *Yale Law Journal* 103 (1993), 105–175.

Bank, Roland/Schwager, Elke, Is there a Substantive Right to Compensation for Individual Victims of Armed Conflicts against a State under International Law?, *German Yearbook of International Law* 49 (2006), 367–412.

Barbara, Christopher, International Legal Personality: Panacea or Pandemonium? Theorizing about the Individual and the State in the Era of Globalization, *Austrian Review of International and European Law* 12 (2007), 17–58.

Bartolini, Giulio, *Riparazione per violazione dei diritti umani e ordinamento internazionale* (Napoli: Jovene Editore 2009).

Bartolini, Giulio/Natoli, Tommaso/Riccardi, Alice, Report of the Expert Meeting on the ILC's Draft Articles on the Protection of Persons in the

Event of Disasters, *International Law and Disasters Working Papers Series* 03 (2015).

Basch, Fernando/Basch, Fernando/Filippini, Leonardo/Laya, Ana/Nino, Mariano/Rossi, Felicitas/Schreiber, Bárbara, The Effectiveness of the Inter-American System of Human Rights Protection: A Quantitative Approach to Its Functioning and Compliance with Its Decisions, *SUR – International Journal of Human Rights* 7 (2010), 9–34.

Bassiouni, M. Cherif, An Appraisal of the Growth and Developing Trends of International Criminal Law, *Revue internationale de droit pénal* 45 (1974), 405–433.

Bassiouni, M. Cherif, International Recognition of Victims' Rights, *Human Rights Law Review* 6 (2006), 203–279.

Baxter, Richard R., The Municipal and International Law Basis of Jurisdiction over War Crimes, in: M. Cherif Bassiouni/Ved P. Nanda (eds), *A Treatise on International Criminal Law*, Vol. II (Springfield IL: Charles Thomas Publisher 1973), 65–86.

Beco, Gauthier de, Victim Participation in Proceedings before the ICC: Resolving Contentious Issues, *Human Rights and International Legal Discourse* 3 (2009), 95–112.

Beitz, Charles R., *The Idea of Human Rights* (Oxford: Oxford University Press 2011).

Benda-Beckmann, Franz von, Rechtspluralismus. Analytische Begriffsbildung oder politisch-ideologisches Programm, *Zeitschrift für Ethnologie* 119 (1994), 1–16.

Benedek, Wolfgang, Das Individuum als Völkerrechtsubjekt, in: August Reinisch (ed.), *Österreichisches Handbuch des Völkerrechts, Band I: Textteil* (5th ed. Wien: Manzsche Verlags- und Universitätsbuchhandlung 2013), 290–297.

Bentham, Jeremy, *A Fragment on Government, or, A Comment on the Commentaries*, edited with an introduction by Francis Charles Montague (Oxford: Clarendon Press 1891; original 1776), 93.

Berber, Friedrich Josef, *Lehrbuch des Völkerrechts: Zweiter Bd.: Kriegsrecht* (2nd ed. Munich: Beck 1969).

Berman, Sir Franklin, Jurisdiction: The State, in: Patrick Capps/Malcolm Evans/Stratos Konstantinidis (eds), *Asserting Jurisdiction: International and European Legal Perspectives* (Oxford: Hart 2003), 3–15.

Bernstorff, Jochen von, The Public International Law Theory of Hans Kelsen: *Believing in Universal Law* (Cambridge: CUP 2014) (German original: Der Glaube an das universale Recht: Zur Völkerrechtstheorie Hans Kelsens und seiner Schüler (Baden-Baden: Nomos 2001)).

Besselink, Leonard F. M./Pennings, Frans/Prechal, Sacha (eds), *The Eclipse of the Legality Principle in the European Union* (Alphen aan den Rijn: Kluwer 2011).

Bjorklund, Andrea K., Private Rights and Public International Law: Why Competition among International Economic Law Tribunals Is Not Working, *Hastings Law Journal* 59 (2007), 241–307.

Black, Antony, Individuals, Groups and States: A Comparative Overview, in: Janet Coleman (ed.), *The Individual in Political Theory and Practice* (Oxford: Clarendon 1996), 329–340.

Blackstone, William, *The Commentaries on the Laws of England*, Vol. 4 (London: John Murray 1876) (orig. 1753).

Bleckmann, Albert, *Völkerrecht* (Baden-Baden: Nomos 2001).

Bluntschli, Johann Caspar, *Das moderne Völkerrecht der civilisirten Staten: als Rechtsbuch dargestellt* (3rd ed. Nördlingen: Verlag der C. H. Beck'schen Buchhandlung 1878).

Böckstiegel, Karl Heinz, *Der Staat als Vertragspartner ausländischer Unternehmen* (Frankfurt a. M.: Athenäum 1971).

Bogdandy, Armin von, Pluralism, Direct Effect, and the Ultimate Say, *International Journal of Constitutional Law* 6 (2008), 397–413.

Bogdandy, Armin von/Wolfrum, Rüdiger/Bernstoff, Jochen von/Dann, Philipp/Goldmann, Matthias (eds), *The Exercise of Public Authority by International Institutions* (Heidelberg: Springer 2010).

Bothe, Michael, Conflits armés et droit international humanitaire, *Revue générale de droit international public* 82 (1978), 82–102.

Bothe, Michael, The Role of National Law in the Implementation of International Humanitarian Law, in: Christophe Swinarski (ed.), *Studies and Essays on International Humanitarian Law and Red Cross Principles in Honour of Jean Pictet* (Dordrecht: Martinus Nijhoff 1984), 301–312.

Bottigliero, Ilaria, *Redress for Victims of Crimes under International Law* (Leiden: Martinus Nijhoff 2004).

Bourquin, Maurice, Règles Générales du Droit de la Paix, *Recueil des Cours: Collected Courses of The Hague Academy of International Law* 35 (1931/I), 5–229.

Boven, Theo van, Distinguishing Criteria of Human Rights, in: Karel Vasak/Philip Alston (eds), *The International Dimension of Human Rights* (Westport CT: Greenwood Press and Paris: UNESCO 1982), 43–59.

Boyle, David, The Rights of Victims, *Journal of International Criminal Justice* 4 (2006), 307–313.

Brabandere, Eric de, *Investment Treaty Arbitration as Public International Law: Procedural Aspects and Implications* (Cambridge: Cambridge University Press 2014).

Braun, Tillmann Rudolf, *Ausprägungen der Globalisierung: Der Investor als partielles Subjekt im internationalen Investitionsrecht* (Baden-Baden: Nomos 2012).

Braun, Tillmann Rudolf, Globalization-Driven Innovation: The Investor as a Partial Subject in Public International Law: An Inquiry into the Nature and

Limits of Investor Rights, *The Journal of World Investment and Trade* 15 (2014), 73–116.

Brady, Andrew Spalding, Corruption, Corporations and the New Human Right, *Washington University Law Review* 91 (2014), 1365–1428.

Brems, Eva, *Human Rights: Universality and Diversity* (The Hague: Martinus Nijhoff 2001), 424–441.

Brett, Annabel S., *Liberty, Rights and Nature: Individual Rights in Later Scholastic Thought* (Cambridge: Cambridge University Press 1997).

Brierly, James Leslie, Règles Générales du Droit de la Paix, *Recueil des Cours: Collected Courses of The Hague Academy of International Law* 58 (1936/IV), 5–237.

Broches, Aron, The Convention on the Settlement of Investment Disputes between States and Nationals of other States, *Recueil des Cours: Collected Courses of The Hague Academy of International Law* 136 (1972), 331–410.

Brugères, Anne-Laurence, Le droit international de l'assistance humanitaire en cas de catastrophes naturelles, in: Colloque de Nanterre (ed.), *Société française pour le droit international*, La responsabilité de protéger (Paris: Pedone 2008), 169–176.

Brunnée, Jutta, Of Sense and Sensibility: Reflections on International Liability Regimes as Tools for Environmental Protection, *International and Comparative Law Quarterly* 53 (2004), 351–368.

Brunner, Norbert, *Die Frage nach dem Anspruch des Bürgers auf diplomatischen Schutz* (Frankfurt a. M.: Peter Lang 1983).

Buchs, Gaby, *Die unmittelbare Anwendbarkeit völkerrechtlicher Vertragsbestimmungen* (Baden-Baden: Nomos 1993).

Bühler, Ottmar, *Die subjektiven öffentlichen Rechte und ihr Schutz in der deutschen Verwaltungsrechtsprechung* (Berlin: Kohlhammer 1914).

Bürger, Peter, *Das Verschwinden des Subjekts: eine Geschichte der Subjektivität von Montaigne bis Barthes* (Frankfurt a. M.: Suhrkamp 1998).

Burke-White, William W., Power Shifts in International Law: Structural Realignment and Substantive Pluralism, *Harvard International Law Journal* 56 (2015), 1–80.

Buszewski, Sinthiou Estelle, Das Individuum als Völkerrechtssubjekt, *Ad Legendum* 3 (2014) 178–183.

Calliess, Gralf-Peter/Zumbansen, Peer, *Rough Consensus and Running Code* (Oxford: Hart 2010).

Cameron, Ian, The European Convention on Human Rights, Due Process, and the United Nations Security Council Counter-Terrorism Sanctions, Report Commissioned by the Council of Europe (2006).

Camilleri, Michael J./Krsticevic, Vivianna, Making International Law Stick: Reflections on Compliance with Judgments in the Inter-American Human Rights System, in: Joaquí Gonzalez Ibáñes (ed.), *Protección internacional de derechos humanos y estado de derecho* (Colombia: Grupo Editorial Ibàñes 2008), 235–247.

Cançado Trindade, Antônio Augusto, International Law for Humankind: Towards a New Jus Gentium, *Recueil des Cours: Collected Courses of The Hague Academy of International Law* 316 (2005), 9–444.

Cançado Trindade, Antônio Augusto, *The Access of Individuals to International Justice* (Oxford: Oxford University Press 2011).

Cárdenas, Emilio J./Garcia-Rubio, Mariano, Argentina, in: Vera Gowlland-Debbas (ed.), *National Implementation of United Nations Sanctions: A Comparative Study* (Leiden: Martinus Nijhoff 2004), 81–101.

Caron, David D./Kelly, Michael J./Telesetsky Anastasia (eds), *The International Law of Disaster Relief* (Cambridge: Cambridge University Press 2015).

Carozza, Paolo G., Subsidiarity as a Structural Principle of Human Rights Law, *American Journal of International Law* 97 (2003), 38–79.

Cassese, Antonio, *International Criminal Law* (2nd ed. Oxford: Oxford University Press 2008).

Cassese, Antonio, *International Law* (2nd ed. Oxford: Oxford University Press 2005).

Cassese, Antonio, *The Human Dimension of International Law: Selected Papers*, edited by Paola Gaeta/Salvator Zappalà (Oxford: Oxford University Press 2008).

Cassese, Antonio, The Status of Rebels under the 1977 Geneva Protocol in Non-International Armed Conflict, *International and Comparative Law Quarterly* 30 (1981), 416–439.

Cassidy, Julie, Emergence of the Individual as an International Juristic Entity: Enforcement of International Human Rights, *Deakin Law Review* 9 (2004), 533–572.

Chang, Robert S., The End of Innocence or Politics after the Fall of the Essential Subject, *American University Law Review* 45 (1996), 687–694.

Cheng, Tai-Heng, Power, Authority, and International Investment Law, *American University International Law Review* 20 (2005), 465–520.

Chétail, Vincent, Are Refugee Rights Human Rights?, in: Ruth Rubio-Marín (ed.), *Human Rights and Immigration, Collected Courses of the Academy of European Law* (Oxford: Oxford University Press 2014), 19–72.

Chinkin, Christine, *Third Parties in International Law* (Oxford: Clarendon 1993).

Clapham, Andrew, *Human Rights in the Private Sphere* (Oxford: Clarendon 1993).

Clapham, Richard, *Human Rights Obligations of Non-State Actors* (Oxford: Oxford University Press 2006).

Clapham, Andrew, The Role of the Individual in International Law, *European Journal of International Law* 21 (2010), 25–30.

Clark, Grover, The English Practice with Regard to Reprisals by Private Persons, *American Journal of International Law* 27 (1933), 694–723.

Cohen, Mathilde, *Regulating Milk: Women and Cows in France and the United States, American Journal of Comparative Law* 65 (2017 forthcoming).

Coing, Helmut, Der Rechtsbegriff der menschlichen Person und die Theorien der Menschenrechte, in: Ernst Wolff (ed.), *Beiträge zur Rechtsforschung* (Berlin and Tübingen: de Gruyter und Mohr 1950), 191–205.

Coing, Helmut, Zur Geschichte des Begriffs "subjektives Recht," in: Helmut Coing/ Frederick H. Lawson/Kurt Grönfors (eds), *Das subjektive Recht und der Rechtsschutz der Persönlichkeit* (Frankfurt a. M.: Metzner 1959), 7–23.

Collier, John/Lowe, Vaughan, *The Settlement of Disputes in International Law: Institutions and Procedures* (Oxford: Oxford University Press 1999).

Collins, Hugh, Theories of Rights as Justifications for Labour Law, in: Guy Davidov/Brian Langille (eds), *The Idea of Labour Law* (Oxford: Oxford University Press 2011), 137–155.

Colliot-Thélène, Catherine, *Après la souveraineté: que reste-t-il des droits subjectifs?* (Jus Politicum: Revue de droit politique 2008).

Conrad, Hermann, *Individuum und Gemeinschaft in der Privatrechtsordnung des 18. und beginnenden 19. Jahrhunderts* (Karlsruhe: C. F. Müller 1956).

Cosnard, Michel, Rapport introductif, in: *Société française pour le droit international* (ed.), Colloque de Mans: Le sujet en droit international (Paris: Pedone 2005), 13–53.

Craig, Allan/O'Donnell, Thérèse, A Call to Alms? Natural Disasters, R2P, Duties of Cooperation and Unchartered Consequences, *Journal of Conflict and Security Law* 17 (2012), 337–371.

Cranston, Maurice, Human Rights, Real and Supposed, in: D. D. Raphael (ed.), *Political Theory and the Rights of Man* (London: Macmillan 1967), 43–54.

Crawford, James, *Brownlie's Principles of Public International Law* (8th ed. Oxford: Oxford University Press 2012).

Crawford, James, Continuity and Discontinuity in International Dispute Settlement: An Inaugural Lecture, *Journal of International Dispute Settlement* 1 (2010), 3–24.

Crawford, James, The ILC's Articles on Responsibility of States for Internationally Wrongful Acts: A Retrospect, *American Journal of International Law* 96 (2002), 874–890.

Crawford, James, *The International Law Commission's Articles on State Responsibility: Introduction, Text, and Commentaries* (Cambridge: Cambridge University Press 2002).

Crawford, James, The System of International Responsibility, in: Crawford/ Alain Pellet/Simone Olleson (eds), *The Law of International Responsibility* (Oxford: Oxford University Press 2010), 17–25.

Crawford, James, Treaty and Contract in Investment Arbitration, *Arbitration International* 24 (2008), 351–374.

D'Amato, Anthony, *International Law: Process and Prospect* (2nd ed. Irvington NY: Transnational Publishers 1995).

D'Argent, Pierre, *Les réparations de guerre en droit international public: La responsabilité internationale des États à l'épreuve de la guerre* (Brussels: Bruyant 2002).

Daes, Erica-Irene, *Freedom of the Individual under Law: A Study on the Individual's Duties to the Community and the Limitations on Human Rights and Freedoms under Article 29 of the Universal Declaration of Human Rights* (New York: United Nations 1990), 41–63.

Dahm, Georg/Delbrück, Jost/Wolfrum, Rüdiger, *Völkerrecht*, Vol. I/2 and I/3 (2nd ed. Berlin: De Gruyter 2002).

Daillier, Patrick/Pellet, Alain, *Droit international public* (7th ed. Paris: LGDJ 2002).

Darrow, Mac, *Between Light and Shadow: The World Bank, the International Monetary Fund and International Human Rights Law* (Oxford: Hart 2003).

David, Eric, *Principes de droit des conflits armés* (3rd ed. Brussels: Bruylant 2002).

de Wet, Erika/Vidmar, Jure (eds), *Hierarchy in International Law: The Place of Human Rights* (Oxford: Oxford University Press 2012).

Debuf, Els, *Captured in War: Lawful Internment in Armed Conflict* (Oxford: Hart 2013).

Delbrück, Jost, Prospects for a "World (Internal) Law"? Legal Developments in a Changing International System, *Indiana Journal of Global Legal Studies* 9 (2002), 401–431.

Deng, Francis Mading/Rothchild, Donald/Zartman, I. William, *Sovereignty as Responsibility: Conflict Management in Africa* (Washington DC: Brookings Institution Press 1996).

Deutch, Sinai, Are Consumer Rights Human Rights?, *Osgoode Hall Law Journal* 32 (1994), 537–578.

Diva, Surya, *Regulating Corporate Human Rights Violations: Humanizing Business* (New York: Routledge 2012).

Doak, Jonathan, *Victims' Rights, Human Rights and Criminal Justice* (Oxford: Hart 2008).

Doehring, Karl, *Die allgemeinen Regeln des völkerrechtlichen Fremdenrechts und das deutsche Verfassungsrecht* (Cologne: Carl Heymann 1963).

Doehring, Karl, *Die Pflicht des Staates zur Gewährung diplomatischen Schutzes* (Cologne: Carl Heymanns Verlag 1959).

Doehring, Karl, *Völkerrecht* (2nd ed. Heidelberg: C. F. Müller 2004).

Domestici-Met, Marie-José, Intervention, in: UNESCO (ed.), *Le droit à l'assistance humanitaire: actes du colloque international organisé par l'UNESCO* (Paris: UNESCO 1996), 79–99.

Domingo, Rafael, *The New Global Law* (Cambridge: Cambridge University Press 2010).

Dominicé, Christian, Droits individuels et droits de l'homme, in: Marcelo Kohen (ed.), *Mélanges en l'honneur de Vera Gowlland* (Leiden and Boston: Martinus Nijhoff 2010), 287–292.

Dominicé, Christian, *L'émergence de l'individu en droit international public, in: Dominicé, L'ordre juridique international entre tradition et innovation* (Paris: PUF 1997) (orig. 1987), 109–123.

Dominicé, Christian, *La prétention de la personne privée dans le système de la responsabilité internationale des Etats, in: Studi di diritto internazionale in onore di Gaetano Arangio-Ruiz* (Naples: Editoriale Scientifica 2004).

Donahue, Charles, Ius in the Subjective Sense in Roman Law: Reflections on Villey and Tierney, in: Maffei Domenico/Italo Birocchi/Mario Caravale (eds), *A Ennio Cortese* Vol. 1 (Rome: Il Cigno Edizioni 2001), 506–535.

Dörr, Oliver, Privatisierung des Völkerrechts, *JuristenZeitung* 60 (2005), 905–916.

Dörr, Oliver, Völkerrechtliche Deliktsansprüche Privater – auf der Grundlage und in den Grenzen einer völkerrechtlichen Schutznormlehre, in: Martin Breuer/ Astrid Epiney/Andreas Haratsch/Stefanie Schmahl/Norman Weiß (eds), *Der Staat im Recht: Festschrift Eckart Klein zum 70. Geburtstag* (Berlin: Duncker & Humblot 2013), 765–782.

Douglas, Zachary, The Hybrid Foundations of Investment Treaty Arbitration, *British Yearbook of International Law* 74 (2004), 151–290.

Douglas, Zachary, Investment Treaty Arbitration and ICSID, in: James Crawford/ Alain Pellet/Simone Olleson (eds), *The Law of Responsibility* (Oxford: Oxford University Press 2010), 815–842.

Douzinas, Costas, *The End of Human Rights: Critical Legal Thought at the Turn of the Century* (Oxford: Hart 2000).

Draper, Gerald Irving Anthony Dare, The Geneva Conventions of 1949, *Recueil des Cours: Collected Courses of The Hague Academy of International Law* 114 (1965/ I), 59–165.

Dröge, Cordula, *Positive Verpflichtungen der Staaten in der Europäischen Menschenrechtskonvention* (Berlin: Springer 2003).

Dugard, John R., Diplomatic Protection, in: Rüdiger Wolfrum (ed.), *The Max Planck Encyclopedia of Public International Law* (Oxford: Oxford University Press 2012).

Duguit, Léon, *Traité de droit constitutionnel* (2nd ed. Paris: E. de Boccard 1921).

Duguit, Léon/Kelsen, Hans, Préface, *Revue internationale de la théorie du droit* 1 (1926–1927), 1–4.

Dumberry, Patrick, L'Entreprise, sujet de droit international? Retour sur la question à la lumière des développements récents du droit international des investissements, *Revue Générale de Droit International Public* 108 (2004), 103–122.

Dunoff, Jeffrey L./Trachtman, Joel P., The Law and Economics of Humanitarian Law Violations in Internal Conflict, *American Journal of International Law* 93 (1999), 394–409.

Dupuy, Pierre-Marie, *Droit International Public* (7th ed. Paris: Dalloz 2004).

Dworkin, Ronald, Rights as Trumps, in: Jeremy Waldron (ed.), *Theories of Rights* (Oxford: Oxford University Press 1984), 153–167.

Ebert, Franz/Martin Oelz, Bridging the Gap between Labour Rights and Human Rights: The Role of ILO Law in Regional Human Rights Courts, Discussion Paper DP212/2012 (International Institute for Labour Studies 2012).

Echle, Regula, Die Stellung der Opfer in Verfahren vor dem Internationalen Strafgerichtshof, Master's Thesis in the Faculty of Law of the University of Basel, September 2010.

Edmundson, William A., *An Introduction to Rights* (Cambridge: Cambridge University Press 2nd ed. 2012).

Ehm, Frithjof, *Das völkerrechtliche Demokratiegebot* (Tübingen: Mohr Siebeck 2013).

Emmerich-Fritsche, Angelika, *Vom Völkerrecht zum Weltrecht* (Berlin: Duncker & Humblot 2007).

Enders, Christoph, *Die Menschenwürde in der Verfassungsordnung: Zur Dogmatik des Art. 1 GG* (Tübingen: Mohr Siebeck 1997).

Epiney, Astrid/Scheyli, Martin, *Die Aarhus-Konvention: Rechtliche Tragweite und Implikationen für das schweizerische Recht* (Fribourg: Universitätsverlag 2000).

Evans, Christine, *The Right to Reparation in International Law for Victims of Armed Conflict* (Cambridge: Cambridge University Press 2012).

Fassbender, Bardo, Can Victims Sue State Officials for Torture?, *Journal of International Criminal Justice* 6 (2008), 347–369.

Fassbender, Bardo, Targeted Sanctions Imposed by the UN Security Council and Due Process Rights: A Study Commissioned by the UN Office of Legal Affairs and Follow-Up Action by the United Nations, *International Organisations Law Review* 3 (2006), 437–485.

Favre, Antoin, *Principes du droit des gens* (Fribourg: Editions Universitaires 1974).

Feldman, David, International Personality, *Recueil des Cours: Collected Courses of The Hague Academy of International Law* 191 (1985/II), 343–413.

Ferdinandusse, Ward N., *Direct Application of International Criminal Law in National Courts* (The Hague: TMC Asser Press 2006).

Ferstman, Carla/Goetz, Mariana/Stephens, Alan (eds), *Reparations for Victims of Genocide, War Crimes and Crimes against Humanity: Systems in Place and Systems in the Making* (Dordrecht: Martinus Nijhoff 2009).

Feyter, Koen de/Parmentier, Stephan/Bossuyt, Marc/Lemmens, Paul (eds), *Out of the Ashes: Reparations for the Victims of Gross and Systematic Human Rights Violations* (Antwerp: intersentia 2005).

Finnemore, Martha, *National Interests in International Society* (Ithaca: Cornell University Press 1996).

Fiore, Pasquale, *Le droit international codifié et sa sanction juridique* (3rd ed. Paris: Pedone 1911).

Fischer-Lescano, Andreas, Subjektivierung völkerrechtlicher Sekundärregeln, *Archiv des Völkerrechts* 45 (2007), 299–381.

Fitzmaurice, Malgosia/Marshall, Jill, The Human Right to a Clean Environment – Phantom or Reality? The European Court of Human Rights and English Courts Perspective on Balancing Rights in Environmental Cases, *Nordic Journal of International Law* 76 (2007), 103–151.

Flauss, François, Vers un aggiornamento des conditions d'exercice de la protection diplomatique?, in: François Flauss (ed.), *La protection diplomatique: Mutations contemporaines et pratiques nationales* (Brussels: Bruylant 2003), 29–61.

Fleck, Dieter, The Role of Individuals in International Humanitarian Law and Challenges for States in Its Development, in: Michael Schmitt/Leslie Green (eds), *The Law of Armed Conflict: Into the Next Millennium, Naval War College*, Vol. 71 (Newport: Naval War College 1998), 119–139.

Focarelli, Carlo, Duty to Protect in Cases of Natural Disaster, in: Rüdiger Wolfrum (ed.), *The Max Planck Encyclopedia of Public International Law* (Oxford: Oxford University Press 2012).

Forteau, Mathias, La contribution au développement du droit international général de la jurisprudence arbitrale relative aux investissements étrangers, *Anuário Brasileiro de Direito Internacional* 4 (2009), 11–39.

Friedman, Milton, *Capitalism and Freedom* (Chicago: University of Chicago Press 1962).

Frowein, Jochen A., Implementation of Security Council Resolutions Taken under Chapter VII in Germany, in: Vera Gowlland-Debbas (ed.), *United Nations Sanctions and International Law* (Dordrecht: Kluwer 2001), 253–265.

Frühwald, Wolfgang, *Der Zerfall des Individuums: Über szientifisches Erschrecken in der Literatur* (Heidelberg: C. F. Müller 1993).

Gallant, Kenneth S., *The Principle of Legality in International and Comparative Criminal Law* (Cambridge: Cambridge University Press 2009).

Gärditz, Klaus Ferdinand, Bridge of Varvarin, *American Journal of International Law* 108 (2014), 86–93.

Geiger, Rudolf, *Grundgesetz und Völkerrecht* (4th ed. Munich: Beck 2009).

Geldermann, Heiner, *Völkerrechtliche Pflichten multinationaler Unternehmen* (Baden-Baden: Nomos 2009).

Glendon, Mary Ann, *Rights Talk: The Impoverishment of the Political Discourse* (New York: The Free Press 1991).

Gless, Sabine, in: Volker Erb/Robert Esser/Ulrich Franke/Kirsten Graalmann-Scheerer/Hans Hilger/Alexandr Ignor (eds), *Löwe-Rosenberg, Die Strafprozessordnung und das Gerichtsverfassungsgesetz*, Vol. 4 (26th ed. Berlin: De Gruyter 2007), commentary on § 136 StPO.

Gless, Sabine, Article 139–Article 141 Beweismittel, in: Marcel Niggli/Marianne Heer/Hans Wiprächtiger (eds), *Basler Kommentar, Schweizerische Strafprozessordnung, Jugendstrafprozessordnung* (Basel: Helbing und Lichtenhahn 2010).

Gless, Sabine/Peters, Anne, Verwertungsverbot bei Verletzung der Pflicht zur Belehrung nach Art. 36 WÜK?, *Der Strafverteidiger* 31 (2011), 369–377.

Goldsmith, Jack L./Posner, Eric A., *The Limits of International Law* (Oxford: Oxford University Press 2005).

Goodwin-Gill, Guy S., *Refugees and Their Human Rights*, Refugee Studies Centre (RCS) Working Paper No. 17 (Oxford 2004).

Goodwin-Gill, Guy S./McAdam, Jane, *The Refugee in International Law* (3rd ed. Oxford: Oxford University Press 2007).

Gorski, Simone, Individuals in International Law, in: Rüdiger Wolfrum (ed.), *The Max Planck Encyclopedia of Public International Law* (Oxford: Oxford University Press 2012).

Gourgourinis, Anastasios, Investors' Rights "qua" Human Rights? Revisiting the "Direct"/'Derivative" Rights Debate, in: Malgosia Fitzmaurice and Panos Merkouris (eds), *The Interpretation and Application of the European Convention on Human Rights* (Leiden: Brill Nijhoff 2013), 147–182.

Gowlland-Debbas, Vera, The Domestic Implementation of UN Sanctions, in: Erika de Wet/P. André Nollkaemper (eds), *Review of the Security Council by Member States* (Mortsel: intersentia 2003), 63–76.

Greco, Gioia, Victims' Rights Overview under the ICC Legal Framework: A Jurisprudential Analysis, *International Criminal Law Review* 7 (2007), 531–547.

Greiff, Pablo de (ed.), *The Handbook of Reparations* (Oxford: Oxford University Press 2006).

Griebel, Jörn, *Internationales Investitionsrecht* (Munich: Beck 2008).

Griffin, James, *On Human Rights* (Oxford: Oxford University Press 2008).

Griffiths, James, What Is Legal Pluralism?, *Journal of Legal Pluralism and Unofficial Law* 24 (1986), 1–50.

Grotius, Hugo, *De iure belli ac pacis libri tres (1625)*, liber primus, caput 1, n IV, edited by B.J.A. de Kanter-van Hettinga Tromp (Leiden: E.J. Brill 1939; online 2009 dbnl).

Grover, Leena, *Interpreting Crimes in the Rome Statute of the International Criminal Court* (Cambridge: Cambridge University Press 2014).

Grünwald, Gerald, Beweisverbote und Verwertungsverbote im Strafverfahren, *JuristenZeitung* 21 (1966), 489–501.

Grzeszick, Bernd, Rechte des Einzelnen im Völkerrecht, *Archiv des Völkerrechts* 43 (2005), 312–344.

Guzman, Andrew, *How International Law Works* (Oxford: Oxford University Press 2008).

Hafner, Gerhard, The Emancipation of the Individual from the State under International Law, *Recueil des Cours: Collected Courses of The Hague Academy of International Law* 358 (2011), 263–453.

Hafner, Felix/Loretan, Adrian/Spenlé, Christoph, Naturrecht und Menschenrecht: Der Beitrag der Spanischen Spätscholastik zur Entwicklung der

Menschenrechte, in: Frank Grunert/Kurt Seelmann (eds), *Die Ordnung der Praxis: Neue Studien zur Spanischen Spätscholastik* (Tübingen: Niemeyer 2001), 123–153.

Haggenmacher, Peter, Droits subjectifs et système juridique chez Grotius, in: Luc Foisneau (ed.), *Politique, droit et théologie chez Bodin, Grotius et Hobbes* (Paris: editions Kimé 1997), 73–130.

Hakimi, Monica, State Bystander Responsibility, *European Journal of International Law* 21 (2010) 341–385.

Happ, Richard, The Legal Status of the Investor vis-à-vis the European Communities: Some Salient Thoughts, *International Arbitration Law Review* 10 (2007), 74–81.

Harten, Gus van, *Investment Treaty Arbitration and Public Law* (Oxford: Oxford University Press 2007).

Hassemer, Winfried, *Einführung in die Grundlagen des Strafrechts* (2nd ed. Munich: Beck 1990).

Hathaway, James C., A Reconsideration of the Underlying Premise of Refugee Law, *Harvard International Law Journal* 31 (1990), 129–183.

Hathaway, James C., *The Rights of Refugees under International Law* (Cambridge: Cambridge University Press 2005).

Hathaway, James C./ Foster, Michelle, *The Law of Refugee Status* (2nd ed. Cambridge: Cambridge University Press 2014).

Heath, J. Benton, Disasters, Relief and Neglect: The Duty to Accept Humanitarian Assistance and the Work of the International Law Commission, *New York University Journal of International Law and Policy* 43 (2011), 419–477.

Heffter, August Wilhelm, *Das europäische Völkerrecht der Gegenwart auf den bisherigen Grundlagen* (8th ed. Berlin: Verlag von H. E. Müller 1888).

Hegel, Georg Wilhelm Friedrich, *Philosophy of Right*, translated by Samuel Walter Dyde (Kitchener ON: Batoche Books 2001) (orig. Hegel, Georg Wilhelm Friedrich, *Grundlinien der Philosophie des Rechts* (Hamburg: Felix Meiner Verlag 1995).

Hegel, Georg Wilhelm Friedrich, Vorlesungen über die Philosophie der Geschichte, Vol. I: *Einleitung – Die Vernunft in der Geschichte* (edited by Georg Lasson) (Leipzig: Felix Meiner Verlag 1920).

Heilborn, Paul, *Das System des Völkerrechts aus den völkerrechtlichen Begriffen* (Berlin: Springer 1896).

Heinegg, Wolff Heintschel von, Entschädigung für Verletzungen des humanitären Völkerrechts, *Berichte der Deutschen Gesellschaft für Völkerrecht* 40 (2003), 1–61.

Helfer, Laurence R., Overlegalizing Human Rights: International Relations Theory and the Commonwealth Caribbean Backlash against Human Rights Regimes, *Columbia Law Review* 102 (2002), 1832–1911.

Hemptine, Jérôme de, Challenges Raised by Victims' Participation in the Proceedings of the Special Tribunal for Lebanon, *Journal of International Criminal Justice* 8 (2010), 165–179.

Henckaerts, Jean-Marie/Doswald-Beck, Louise, *Customary International Humanitarian Law*, Vol. I, Rules (Cambridge: Cambridge University Press 2005).

Herdegen, Matthias, *Die Befugnisse des UN-Sicherheitsrates: Aufgeklärter Absolutismus im Völkerrecht?* (Heidelberg: C. F. Müller 1998).

Herdegen, Matthias, *Internationales Wirtschaftsrecht* (3rd ed. Munich: Beck 2002).

Herzog, Roman, *Allgemeine Staatslehre* (Frankfurt a. M.: Athenaeum 1971).

Hestermeyer, Holger, *The WTO and Human Rights: The Case of Patents and Access to Medicine* (Oxford: Oxford University Press 2007).

Higgins, Rosalyn, *Problems and Process: International Law and How We Use It* (Oxford: Clarendon 1995).

Hillgruber, Christian, Anmerkung zu LaGrand, *JuristenZeitung* 57 (2002), 94–99.

Hirsch, Mosche, Investment Tribunals and Human Rights: Divergent Paths, in: Pierre-Marie Dupuy/Francesco Francioni/Ernst-Ulrich Petersmann (eds), *Human Rights and International Investment Law and Arbitration* (Oxford: Oxford University Press 2009), 97–114.

Hobe, Stephan, The Responsibility to Protect and Security Council Action in Libya, *Indian Journal of International Law* 51 (2011), 502–512.

Hofmann, Rainer, Victims of Violations of International Humanitarian Law: Do They Have an Individual Right to Reparation Against States under International Law?, in: Pierre-Marie Dupuy/Bardo Fassbender/Malcolm N. Shaw/Karl-Peter Sommermann (eds), *Völkerrecht als Wertordnung/Common Values in International Law* (Kehl: Norbert Paul Engel Verlag 2006), 341–359.

Hold-Ferneck, Alexander, *Lehrbuch des Völkerrechts, erster Teil* (Leipzig: Felix Meiner 1930).

Holdsworth, William Searle, *A History of English Law*, Vol. 3 (3rd ed. London: Methuen 1923).

Holland, Thomas, *Studies in International Law* (Oxford: Clarendon 1898).

Hörnle, Tatjana, Die Rolle des Opfers in der Straftheorie und im materiellen Strafrecht, *JuristenZeitung* 61 (2006), 950–958.

Hörnle, Tatjana, *Straftheorien* (Tübingen: Mohr Siebeck 2011).

Horvath, Enikö, *Mandating Identity: Citizenship, Kinship Laws and Plural Nationality in the European Union* (Leiden: Kluwer International 2008).

Hummer, Waldemar, Internationale und transnationale Akteure an oder unter der Schwelle der Völkerrechtssubjektivität, in: Hans-Peter Neuhold/Waldemar Hummer/Christoph Schreuer (eds), *Österreichisches Handbuch des Völkerrechts*, Vol. 1 (4th ed. Vienna: Manz 2004), 233–243.

Ignatieff, Michael, Human Rights as Idolatry, in: Amy Gutman (ed.), *Human Rights as Politics and Idolatry* (Princeton: Princeton University Press 2001), 53–100.

Ignatieff, Michael, Human Rights as Politics, in: Amy Gutman (ed.), *Human Rights as Politics and Idolatry* (Princeton: Princeton University Press 2001), 3–52.

Ignatieff, Michael, The Attack on Human Rights, *Foreign Affairs* 80 (2001), 102–116.

Ihering, Rudolph von, *Geist des römischen Rechts auf den verschiedenen Stufen seiner Entwicklung, Dritter Teil, Erste Abtheilung* (3rd ed. Leipzig: Breitkopf und Härtel 1877).

International Centre for the Settlement of Investment Disputes, *Documents Concerning the Origin and Formulation of the Convention History*, Vol. II Part 1 and 2 (Washington DC: ICSID 1968).

Jackson, John, Status of Treaties in Domestic Legal Systems: A Policy Analysis, *American Journal of International Law* 86 (1992), 310–340.

Jahn, Matthias, Verhandlungen des 67. Deutschen Juristentages Erfurt 2008, Bd. I: Gutachten/Teil C: Beweiserhebung *und Beweisverwertungsverbote im Spannungsfeld zwischen den Garantien des Rechtsstaates und der effektiven Bekämpfung von Kriminalität und Terrorismus* (Munich: Beck 2008).

Jakovljević, Bosko, International Disaster Relief Law, *Israel Yearbook on Human Rights* 34 (2004), 251–286.

Jellinek, Georg, *Allgemeine Staatslehre* (3rd ed. Berlin: Verlag von O. Häring 1914).

Jellinek, Georg, *System der subjektiven öffentlichen Rechte* (Tübingen: Mohr 1905).

Jescheck, Hans Heinrich, Verbrechen gegen das Völkerrecht, in: *Deutsche Landesreferate zum IV. Internationalen Kongress für Rechtsvergleichung in Paris 1954* (Düsseldorf: Michael Triltsch Verlag 1955), 351–400.

Jessup, Philip C., *A Modern Law of Nations* (New York: Macmillan 1950).

Kadelbach, Stefan, *Allgemeines Verwaltungsrecht unter europäischem Einfluss* (Tübingen: Mohr Siebeck 1996).

Kaeckenbeeck, Georges, *The International Experiment of Upper Silesia* (Oxford: Oxford University Press 1942).

Kaiser, Karen, Treaties, Direct Applicability, in: Rüdiger Wolfrum (ed.), *The Max Planck Encyclopedia of International Law* (Oxford: Oxford University Press 2012).

Kalshoven, Frits, State Responsibility for Warlike Acts of the Armed Forces, *International and Comparative Law Quarterly* 40 (1991), 827–858.

Kamminga, Menno T., Final Report on the Impact of International Human Rights Law on General International Law, in: Menno T. Kamminga/Martin Scheinin (eds), *The Impact of Human Rights Law on General International Law* (Oxford: Oxford University Press 2009), 1–22.

Kamminga, Menno T./Scheinin, Martin (eds), *The Impact of Human Rights Law on General International Law* (Oxford: Oxford University Press 2009).

Kant, Immanuel, *Groundwork for the Metaphysics of Morals*, edited and translated by Allen W. Wood (New Haven: Yale University Press 2002), 1–79 (orig.: Kant, Immanuel, Grundlegung zur Metaphysik der Sitten (1785), in: Wilhelm Weischedel, Werkausgabe Bd. 7, 11 et seq. (Frankfurt a. M.: Suhrkamp 1977)).

Kant, Immanuel, *The Metaphysics of Morals*, edited and translated by Mary Gregor (Cambridge: Cambridge University Press 1996) (orig.: Kant, Immanuel, Die Metaphysik der Sitten (1798), in: Wilhelm Weischedel, Werkausgabe Bd. 8 (Frankfurt a. M.: Suhrkamp 1977)).

Kant, Immanuel, *Zum Ewigen Frieden* (1795) (Stuttgart: Reclam 1984).

Katz Cogan, Jacob, The Regulatory Turn in International Law, *Harvard International Law Journal* 52 (2011), 321–372.

Kaufmann, Wilhelm, *Die Rechtskraft des internationalen Rechtes und das Verhältnis der Staatengesetzgebung und der Staatsorgane zu derselben* (Stuttgart: F. Enke 1899).

Kelsen, Hans, Die Technik des Völkerrechts und die Organisation des Friedens, *Zeitschrift für öffentliches Recht* 14 (1934), 240–255.

Kelsen, Hans, Les rapports de système entre le droit interne et le droit international public, *Recueil des Cours: Collected Courses of The Hague Academy of International Law* 14 (1926/IV), 231–329.

Kelsen, Hans, *Principles of International Law* (2nd ed. edited by Robert W. Tucker, New York: Holt Rinehart and Winston 1966).

Kelsen, Hans, *Reine Rechtslehre* (Leipzig: Franz Deuticke 1934).

Kempen, Bernhard/Hillgruber, Christian, *Völkerrecht* (Munich: Beck 2007).

Kingreen, Thorsten, *Die Struktur der Grundfreiheiten des Europäischen Gemeinschaftsrechts* (Berlin: Duncker & Humblot 1999).

Kingsbury, Benedict/Donaldson, Megan, From Bilateralism to Publicness in International Law, in: Ulrich Fastenrath/Rudolf Geiger/Daniel-Erasmus Khan (eds), *From Bilateralism to Community Interest: Essays in Honour of Judge Bruno Simma* (Oxford: Oxford University Press 2011), 79–89.

Kinley, David, Human Rights Fundamentalisms, *Sydney Law Review* 29 (2007), 545–575.

Kirchhof, Ferdinand, *Private Rechtsetzung* (Berlin: Duncker und Humblot 1987).

Kischel, Uwe, *State Contracts* (Stuttgart: Boorberg 1992).

Klein, Eckhart, Diplomatischer Schutz und grundrechtliche Schutzpflicht, *Die öffentliche Verwaltung* 30 (1977), 704–710.

Kleinlein, Thomas, Der EGMR und das Völkerrecht im Rahmen von Art. 7 EMRK, *Europäische Grundrechte-Zeitschrift* 37 (2010), 544–560.

Knox, John H., Horizontal Human Rights Law, *American Journal of International Law* 102 (2008), 1–47.

Knox, John H., The Human Rights Council Endorses "Guiding Principles" for Corporations, *ASIL Insights* 15 (2011), 1 August 2011.

Knubben, Rolf, *Die Subjekte des Völkerrechts* (Stuttgart: Kohlhammer 1928).

Kofele-Kale, Ndiva, The Right to a Corruption-Free Society as an Individual and Collective Human Right: Elevating Official Corruption to a Crime under International Law, *International Lawyer* 34 (2000) 149–178.

Kolb, Robert, Nouvelle observation sur la détermination de la personalité juridique internationale, *Zeitschrift für öffentliches Recht* 57 (2002), 229–241.

Kolben, Kevin, Labor Rights as Human Rights?, *Virginia Journal of International Law* 50 (2010), 449–484.

Koller, Arnold, *Die unmittelbare Anwendbarkeit völkerrechtlicher Verträge und des EWG-Vertrages im innerstaatlichen Bereich* (Bern: Stämpfli 1971).

Kooijmans, Pieter H., Is the Right to Diplomatic Protection a Human Right?, *Studi di diritto internazionale in onore di Gaetano Arangio-Ruiz* (Naples: editoriale Scientifica 2004).

Korowicz, Marek St, The Problem of the International Personality of Individuals, *American Journal of International Law* 50 (1956), 534–562.

Koskenniemi, Martti, Rights, History, Critique, in: Adam Etinson (ed.), *Human Rights: Moral or Political?* (Oxford: Oxford University Press 2016).

Koskenniemi, Martti, The Effects of Rights on Political Culture, in: Martti Koskenniemi, *The Politics of International Law* (Oxford: Hart 2011), 133–167.

Kottmann, Matthias, Plaumanns Ende: Ein Vorschlag zu Art. 263 Abs. 4 AEUV, *Zeitschrift für ausländisches öffentliches Recht und Völkerrecht* 70 (2010), 547–566.

Krajewski, Markus/Singer, Christopher, Should Judges Be Front-Runners? The ICJ, State Immunity and the Protection of Fundamental Human Rights, *Max Planck Yearbook of United Nations Law* 16 (2012), 1–34.

Kramer, Matthew H., Rights without Trimmings, in: Matthew H. Kramer/Neil E. Simmonds/Hillel Steiner (eds), *A Debate Over Rights: Philosophical Enquiries* (Oxford: Oxford University Press 2000), 7–111.

Kratochwil, Friedrich, How (Il)liberal Is the Liberal Theory of Law? Some Critical Remarks on Slaughter's Approach, *Comparative Sociology* 9 (2010), 120–145.

Kreß, Claus, Die verfassungsrechtliche Pflicht der deutschen Strafverfolgungsbehörden zur Berücksichtigung des Wiener Konsularrechtsübereinkommens, *Goltdammer's Archiv für Strafrecht* 154 (2007), 296–308.

Kreß, Claus, International Criminal Law, in: Rüdiger Wolfrum (ed.), *The Max Planck Encyclopedia of International Law* (Oxford: Oxford University Press 2012).

Kundera, Milan, *Immortality, Translated from the Czech by Peter Kussi* (New York: Harper Collins 1999).

Laborde, Gustavo, The Case for Host State Claims in Investment Arbitration, *Journal of International Dispute Settlement* 1 (2010), 97–122.

Lafont, Cristina, Accountability and Global Governance: Challenging the State-centric Conception of Human Rights, *Ethics & Global Politics* 3 (2010), 193–215.

Lafont, Cristina, *Global Governance and Human Rights* (Spinoza Lecture Amsterdam: Van Gorcum 2012).

Lagrange, Evelyne, L'application des accords à l' investissements dans les orders juridiques internes, in: Sabrina Cuendet (ed.), *Le droit des investissements étrangers: approche globale* (Paris: Larcier 2016).

Lagrange, Evelyne, L'efficacité des normes internationales concernant la situation des personnes privées dans les ordres juridiques internes, *Recueil des Cours: Collected Courses of The Hague Academy of International Law* 356 (2012/III), 243–552.

La Hovary, Claire, *Les droits fondamentaux au travail: Origines, statut et impact en droit international* (Paris: Presses Universitaires de France 2009).

Lambert Abdelgawad, Elisabeth/Martin-Chenut, Kathia (eds), *Réparer les violations graves et massives des droits de l'homme: la Cour interaméricaine, pionnière et modèle?* (Paris: Société de législation comparé 2010).

Lapradelle, Albert Geouffre de, La Question Chinoise, *Revue Générale de Droit International Public* 8 (1901), 272–340.

Lauterpacht, Hersch, *International Law and Human Rights* (London: Stevens 1950).

Lauterpacht, Hersch, *The Development of International Law by the International Court* (2nd ed. London: Stevens 1958).

Lauterpacht, Hersch, The Grotian Tradition of International Law, *British Yearbook of International Law* 23 (1946), 1–53.

Lauterpacht, Hersch, The Subjects of International Law, in: Elihu Lauterpacht (ed.), *International Law: Being the Collected Papers of Hersch Lauterpacht* (1970–1978), Vol. I: The General Works (Cambridge: Cambridge University Press 1970), 279–307.

Lauterpacht, Hersch, The Subjects of the Law of Nations (Part I), *Law Quarterly Review* 63 (1947), 428–460, repr. in Elihu Lauterpacht (ed.), International Law: Being the Collected Papers of Hersch Lauterpacht Vol. 2: The Law of Peace Part I: International Law in General, Chapt. 18 (Cambridge: Cambridge University Press 1975).

Leary, Virginia A., The Paradox of Workers' Rights as Human Rights, in: Lance A. Compa/Stephen F. Diamond (eds), *Human Rights, Labour Rights, and International Trade* (Philadelphia: University of Philadelphia Press 1996), 777–798.

Le Fur, Louis, La Théorie du Droit Naturel Depuis le XVIIe Siècle et la Doctrine Moderne, *Recueil des Cours: Collected Courses of The Hague Academy of International Law* 19 (1927/III), 259–442.

Leckie, Scott/Simperingham, Ezekiel, Article 13, in: Andreas Zimmermann (ed.), *The 1951 Convention Relating to the Status of Refugees and Its 1967 Protocols* (Oxford: Oxford University Press 2011), 883–893.

Lee, Luke T./Quigley, John, *Consular Law and Practice* (3rd ed. Oxford and New York: Oxford University Press 2008).

Ley, Isabelle, *Opposition im Völkerrecht* (Heidelberg: Springer 2014).

Liszt, Franz von, *Das Völkerrecht systematisch dargestellt* (4th ed. Berlin: Verlag von O. Häring 1906).

Liszt, Franz von, Die deterministischen Gegner der Zweckstrafe, *Zeitschrift für die gesamte Strafrechtswissenschaft* 13 (1893), 325–370.

Llamzon, Aloysius P., *Corruption in International Investment Arbitration* (Oxford: Oxford University Press 2014).

Macklem, Patrick, *The Sovereignty of Human Rights* (Oxford: Oxford University Press 2015).

Maitland, Frederic William, *Equity, also the Forms of Action at Common Law: Two Courses of Lectures*, edited by Alfred Henry Chaytor/William Joseph Whittaker (Cambridge: Cambridge University Press 1910).

Malanczuk, Peter, *Akehurst's Modern Introduction to International Law* (London: Routledge 1997).

Malanczuk, Peter, Multinational Enterprises and Treaty-Making – A Contribution to the Discussion on Non-State Actors and the "Subjects" of International Law, in: Vera Gowlland-Debbas (ed.), *Multilateral Treaty-making: The Current Status of Challenges to and Reforms Needed in the International Legislative Process* (Dordrecht: Martinus Nijhoff 2000), 45–74.

Mälksoo, Lauri, *Russian Approaches to International Law* (Oxford: Oxford University Press 2015).

Manciaux, Sébastien, *Investissements étrangers et arbitrage entre Etats et ressortissants d'autres Etats* (Dijon: Litec-CREDIMI 2004).

Mancisidor, Mikel, Is There Such Thing as a Human Right to Science in International Law? *ESIL Reflections* 4, issue 1, April 4, 2015.

Mann, Frederic A., The Law Governing State Contracts, *British Yearbook of International Law* 12 (1944), 11–33.

Manner, George, The Object Theory of the Individual in International Law, *American Journal of International Law* 46 (1952), 428–449.

Marauhn, Thilo, Vorwort, in: Thilo Marauhn (ed.), *Die Rechtsstellung des Menschen im Völkerrecht* (Tübingen: Mohr Siebeck 2003).

Mares, Radu (ed.), *The UN Guiding Principles on Business and Human Rights: Foundations and Implementation* (Leiden: Martinus Nijhoff 2012).

Masing, Johannes, *Die Mobilisierung des Bürgers für die Durchsetzung des Rechts: Europäische Impulse für eine Revision der Lehre vom subjektiv-öffentlichen Recht* (Berlin: Duncker & Humblot 1997).

Matringe, Jean, Anmerkung, Revue générale de droit international public, *Revue* 112 (2008), 210–212.

Matz-Lück, Nele, Solidarität, Souveränität und Völkerrecht: Grundzüge einer internationalen Solidargemeinschaft, in: Holger P. Hestermeyer/Doris König/

Nele Matz-Lück/Volker Röben/Anja Seibert-Fohr/Peter-Tobias Stoll/ Silja Vöneky (eds), *Coexistence, Cooperation and Solidarity: Liber Amicorum Rüdiger Wolfrum* (Leiden: Martinus Nijhoff 2012), 141–165.

Maupin, Julie Anne, Reconciling Public and Private Rights and Interests in International Investment Law (Unpublished Thesis Geneva 2014).

Maurer, Hartmut, *Allgemeines Verwaltungsrecht* (18th ed. Munich: Beck 2011).

Mayer, Otto, *Deutsches Verwaltungsrecht*, Vol. 1, 1924 (reprinted without changes, 3rd ed. Berlin: Duncker & Humblot 2004).

McCorquodale, Robert, The Individual in the International Legal System, in: Malcolm Evans (ed.), *International Law* (3rd ed. Oxford: Oxford University Press 2010), 284–310.

McDougal, Myres, International Law, Power, and Policy: A Contemporary Conception, *Recueil des Cours: Collected Courses of The Hague Academy of International Law* 82 (1953/I), 133–260.

McGonigle Leyh, Brianne, *Procedural Justice?: Victim Participation in International Criminal Proceedings* (Cambridge: intersentia 2011).

McGonigle Leyh, Brianne, *Victim Participation in International Criminal Proceedings* (Cambridge: intersentia 2011).

McLachlan-Bent, Ashley/Langmore, John, A Crime against Humanity? Implications and Prospects of the Responsibility to Protect in the Wake of the Cyclone Nargis, *Global Responsibility to Protect* 3 (2011), 37–60.

Mejknecht, Anna, *Towards International Personality: The Position of Minorities and Indigenous People in International Law* (Antwerp: intersentia 2011).

Mennecke, Martin, Towards the Humanization of the Vienna Convention of Consular Rights, *German Yearbook of International Law* 44 (2001), 430–468.

Menon, P. K., The Legal Personality of Individuals, *Sri Lanka Journal of International Law* 6 (1994), 127–156 (148).

Meron, Theodor, *The Humanization of International Law* (Leiden: Martinus Nijhoff 2006).

Mettraux, Guénaël, *International Crimes and the Ad hoc Tribunals* (Oxford: Oxford University Press 2005).

Meyer-Ladewig, Jens, *Europäische Menschenrechtskonvention: Handkommentar* (3rd ed. Baden-Baden: Nomos 2011).

Michaels, Ralf, Global Legal Pluralism, *Annual Review of Law and Social Science* 5 (2009), 243–262.

Milano, Enrico, Diplomatic Protection and Human Rights before the International Court of Justice, *Netherlands Yearbook of International Law* 35 (2004), 85–142.

Milanovic, Marko, Is the Rome Statute Binding on Individuals? (And Why We Should Care), *Journal of International Criminal Law* 9 (2011), 25–52.

Milbank, John, Against Human Rights: Liberty in the Western Tradition, in: Costas Douzinas/Conor Gearty (eds), *The Meanings of Rights: The Philosophy and Social Theory of Human Rights* (Cambridge: Cambridge University Press 2014), 39–70.

Mohl, Robert von, *Staatsrecht, Völkerrecht und Politik*, Vol. 1 (Tübingen: Laupp & Siebeck 1860).

Mosler, Hermann, Die Erweiterung des Kreises der Völkerrechtssubjekte, *Zeitschrift für ausländisches öffentliches Recht und Völkerrecht* 22 (1962), 1–48.

Müller, Andreas, Zum Primat der juristischen Person im internationalen Recht: Zugleich ein Beitrag zur "Rehabilitierung" der natürlichen Person als Völkerrechtssubjekt, *Contributions of the Austrian Ludwig Wittgenstein Society*, X, 25th International Wittgenstein Symposium (2002), 176–178.

Müller, Till, Customary Transnational Law: Attacking the Last Resort of State Sovereignty, *Indiana Journal of Global Legal Studies* 19 (2008), 19–47.

Mullerson, Rein A., Human Rights and the Individual as Subject of International Law: A Soviet View, *European Journal of International Law* 1 (1990), 33–43.

Murphy, Sean D., Does International Law Obligate States to Open their National Courts to Persons for the Invocation of Treaty Norms that Protect or Benefit Persons?, in: David Sloss (ed.), *The Role of Domestic Courts in Treaty Enforcement: A Comparative Study* (New York: Cambridge University Press 2009), 61–119.

Nettesheim, Martin, Subjektive Rechte im Unionsrecht, *Archiv des öffentlichen Rechts* 132 (2007), 333–392.

Neuhäuser, Christian, *Unternehmen als moralische Akteure* (Berlin: Suhrkamp 2011).

Newcomb Hohfeld, Wesley, Fundamental Legal Conceptions as Applied in Judicial Reasoning, *Yale Law Journal* 23 (1913), 16–59 and Yale Law Journal 26 (1917), 710–770.

Nijman, Janne E., Paul Riceur and International Law: Beyond "The End of the Subject." Towards a Reconceptualization of International Legal Personality, *Leiden Journal of International Law* 20 (2007), 25–64.

Nijman, Janne E., *The Concept of International Legal Personality: An Inquiry into the History and Theory of International Law* (Den Haag: TMC Asser Press 2004).

Nipperdey, Hans Carl, *Grundrechte und Privatrecht* (Krefeld: Scherpe Verlag 1961).

Nkambo Mugerwa/Peter James, Subjects of International Law, in: Max Sørensen (ed.), *Manual of Public International Law* (London: Macmillan 1968), 247–310.

Nollkaemper, André, Responsibility of Transnational Corporations in International Environmental Law: Three Perspectives, in: Gerd Winter (ed.), *Multilevel Governance of Global Environmental Change* (Cambridge: Cambridge University Press 2006), 179–199.

Nollkaemper, André, Introduction, *European Journal of International Law* 20 (2009), 853–887.

Nollkaemper, André, *National Courts and the International Rule of Law* (Oxford: Oxford University Press 2011).

Nolte, Georg/Aust, Helmut Philipp, European Exceptionalism?, *Global Constitutionalism* 2 (2013), 407–436.

Nowak, Manfred, The Right to Reparation of Victims of Gross Human Rights Violations, in: George Ulrich/Louise Krabbe Boserup (eds), *Reparations: Redressing Past Wrongs, Human Rights in Development Yearbook 2001* (Dordrecht: Kluwer 2003), 277–308.

Nowrot, Karsten, *Normative Ordnungsstruktur und private Wirkungsmacht: Konsequenzen der Beteiligung transnationaler Unternehmen an den Rechtssetzungsprozessen im internationalen Wirtschaftssystem* (Berlin: Berliner Wissenschaftsverlag 2006).

Ochoa, Christiana, The Individual in Customary International Law Formation, *Virginia Journal of International Law* 48 (2007), 119–186.

Oppenheim, Lassa Francis Lawrence, *International Law: A Treatise*, Vol. I (London: Longmans Green 1905).

Orakhelashvili, Alexander, The Position of the Individual in International Law, *California Western International Law Journal* 31 (2001), 241–276.

Orrego Vicuña, Francisco, Of Contracts and Treaties in the Global Market, *Max Planck Yearbook of United Nations Law* 8 (2004), 341–357.

Osakwe, Chris, Contemporary Soviet Doctrine and the Juridical Nature of Universal International Organizations, *American Journal of International Law* 65 (1971), 502–521.

Osiatyński, Wiktor, Beyond Rights, in: András Sajo (ed.), *Abuse: The Dark Side of Fundamental Rights* (Utrecht: eleven 2006), 309–327.

Osiatyński, Wiktor, *Human Rights and Their Limits* (Cambridge: Cambridge University Press 2009).

Paasivirta, Esa, *Participation of States in International Contracts and Arbitral Settlement of Disputes* (Helsinki: Finnish Lawyers' Publishing Company 1990).

Palmer, A., An International Right to Environment: A New Generation?, *Interights Bulletin* 15 (2006), 141–143.

Palombo, Dalia, Chandler v. Cape: An Alternative to Piercing the Corporate Veil beyond Kiobel v. Royal Dutch Shell, British, *Journal of American Legal Studies* 4 (2015), 453–471.

Papanicolopulu, Irini, The Law of the Sea Convention: No Place for Persons? *The International Journal of Marine and Coastal Law* 27 (2012), 867–874.

Parlett, Kate, *The Individual in the International Legal System* (Cambridge: Cambridge University Press 2011).

Parlett, Kate, The PCIJ's Opinion in Jurisdiction of the Courts of Danzig. Individual Rights under Treaties, *Journal of the History of International Law* 10 (2008), 119–145.

Paulsson, Jan, Arbitration without Privity, *ICSID Review: Foreign Investment Law Journal* 10 (1995), 232–257.

Paulus, Andreas/Müller, Jörn, Konsularische Information vor deutschen Gerichten - Never Ending Story Oder Happy End? *Strafverteidiger* 29 (2009), 495–502.

Paparinskis, Martins, Investment Treaty Arbitration and the (New) Law of State Responsibility, *European Journal of International Law* 24 (2013), 617–647.

Peel, Edwin, *Treitel: The Law of Contract* (London: Sweet & Maxwell 2007).

Pellet, Alain, Article 38, in: Andreas Zimmermann et al. (eds), *The Statute of the International Court of Justice: A Commentary* (2nd ed. Oxford: Oxford University Press 2012), 832–840.

Pellet, Alain, Can a State Commit a Crime? Definitely, Yes!, *European Journal of International Law* 10 (1999), 425–434.

Pellet, Alain, "Human Rightism" and International Law, *Italian Yearbook of International Law* 10 (2003), 3–16.

Pendleton, Michael D., A New Human Right - The Right to Globalization, *Fordham International Law Journal* 22 (1999), 2052–2095.

Pergantis, Vasileios, Towards a "Humanization" of Diplomatic Protection?, *Zeitschrift für ausländisches öffentliches Recht und Völkerrecht* 66 (2006), 351–397.

Pescatore, Pierre, The Doctrine of "Direct Effect": An Infant Disease of Community Law, *European Law Review* 8 (1983), 155–177.

Peters, Anne, Article 25, in: Bruno Simma/Daniel-Erasmus Khan/Georg Nolte/Andreas Paulus (eds), *A Commentary to the Charter of the United Nations*, Vol. 1 (3d ed. Oxford: Oxford University Press 2012), 787–854.

Peters, Anne, Die Anwendbarkeit der EMRK in Zeiten komplexer Hoheitsgewalt und das Prinzip der Grundrechtstoleranz, *Archiv des Völkerrechts* 48 (2010), 1–57.

Peters, Anne, Dual Democracy, in: Jan Klabbers/Anne Peters/Geir Ulfstein (eds), *The Constitutionalisation of International Law* (2nd ed. Oxford: Oxford University Press, 2011), 263–341.

Peters, Anne, Humanity as the A and Ω of Sovereignty, *European Journal of International Law* 20 (2009), 513–544.

Peters, Anne, Membership in the Global Constitutional Community, in: Jan Klabbers/Anne Peters/Geir Ulfstein (eds,) *The Constitutionalization of International Law* (2nd ed. Oxford: Oxford University Press 2011), 153–262.

Peters, Anne, Nebenpflichten im Verwaltungsrechtsverhältnis?, *Die Verwaltung* 35 (2002), 177–221.

Peters, Anne, *Precommitment Theory Applied to International Law: Between Sovereignty and Triviality*, University of Illinois Law Review (2008), 239–252.

Peters, Anne, Rechtsordnungen und Konstitutionalisierung: Zur Neubestimmung der Verhältnisse, *Zeitschrift für öffentliches Recht* 65 (2010), 3–63.

Peters, Anne, Security Council Resolution 2178 (2014): The "Foreign Terrorist Fighter" as an International Legal Person, EJIL Talk! Blog of the European Journal of International Law, 21 November 2014.

Peters, Anne, Sind transnationale Unternehmen verpflichtet, (internationale) Menschenrechte zu respektieren und zu fördern?, in: Peter Kirchschläger/Thomas Kirchschläger/Andréa Belliger/David Krieger (eds), *Menschenrechte und Wirtschaft im Spannungsfeld zwischen State und Nonstate Actors* (Bern: Stämpfli 2005), 127–135.

Peters, Anne, The Constitutionalisation of International Organisations, in: Neil Walker/Jo Shaw/Stephen Tierney (eds), *Europe's Constitutional Mosaic* (Oxford: Hart 2011), 253–285.

Peters, Anne, The Position of International Law within the European Community Legal Order, *German Yearbook of International Law* 40 (1997), 9–77.

Peters, Anne, The Security Council's Responsibility to Protect, *International Organisations Law Review* 8 (2011), 1–40.

Peters, Anne, Transnational Law Comprises Constitutional, Administrative, Criminal, and Quasi-private Law, in: Pieter Bekker/Rudolf Dolzer/Michael Waibel (eds), *Making Transnational Law Work: Liber Amicorum Detlev Vagts* (Cambridge: Cambridge University Press 2010), 154–173.

Peters, Anne, Treaty Making Power, in: Rüdiger Wolfrum (ed.), *The Max Planck Encyclopedia of Public International Law* (Oxford: Oxford University Press 2012).

Peters, Anne/Koechlin, Lucy/Förster, Till/Fenner Zinkernagel, Gretta (eds), *Non-state Actors as Standard Setters* (Cambridge: Cambridge University Press 2009).

Petersen, Niels, *Demokratie als teleologisches Prinzip: Zur Legitimität von Staatsgewalt im Völkerrecht* (Heidelberg: Springer 2009).

Pfordten, Dietmar von der, Normativer Individualismus und das Recht, *Juristen-Zeitung* 60 (2005), 1069–1080.

Pictet, Jean (ed.), Commentary of the Geneva Conventions of 12 August 1949, Vol. I *Geneva Convention I for the Amelioration of the Condition of the Wounded and Sick in Armed Forces in the Field* (Geneva: ICRC 1952).

Pictet, Jean (ed.), Commentary of the Geneva Conventions of 12 August 1949, Vol. IV, *Geneva Convention IV Relative to the Protection of Civilian Persons* (Geneva: ICRC 1958).

Pictet, Jean (ed.), Commentary of the Geneva Conventions of 12 August 1949, Vol. III, *Geneva Convention III Relative to the Treatment of Prisoners of War* (Geneva: ICRC 1960).

Pinker, Steven, *The Better Angels of Our Nature: Why Violence Has Declined* (New York: Viking 2011).

Mazzeschi, Riccardo, International Obligations for Reparation Claims?, in: Albrecht Randelzhofer/Christian Tomuschat (eds), *State Responsibility and the Individual: Reparation in Instances of Grave Violations of Human Rights* (The Hague: Martinus Nijhoff 1999), 149–172.

Pisillo Mazzeschi, Riccardo, Impact on the Law of Diplomatic Protection, in: Menno T. Kamminga/Martin Scheinin (eds), *The Impact of Human Rights Law on General International Law* (Oxford: Oxford University Press 2009), 211–233.

Politis, Nicolas, *Les nouvelles tendances du droit international* (Paris: Hachette 1927).

Portmann, Roland, *Legal Personality in International Law* (Cambridge: Cambridge University Press 2010).

Posner, Eric, *The Twilight of Human Rights Law* (Oxford: Oxford University Press 2014).

Provost, René, *International Human Rights and Humanitarian Law* (Cambridge: Cambridge University Press 2002).

Quigley, John/Aceves, William C./Shank, S. Adele, *The Law of Consular Access: A Documentary Guide* (London: Routledge 2010).

Rama-Montaldo, Manuel, International Legal Personality and Implied Powers of International Organizations, *British Yearbook of International Law* 44 (1970), 111–155.

Randelzhofer, Albrecht, The Legal Position of the Individual under Present International Law, in: Albrecht Randelzhofer/Christian Tomuschat (eds), *State Responsibility and the Individual: Reparation in Instances of Grave Violations of Human Rights* (The Hague: Martinus Nijhoff 1999), 231–242.

Ratner, Steven, Business, in: Daniel Bodansky/Jutta Brunnée/Ellen Hey (eds), *The Oxford Handbook of International Environmental Law* (Oxford: Oxford University Press 2007), 807–828.

Ratner, Steven, Corporations and Human Rights: A Theory of Legal Responsibility, *Yale Law Journal* 111 (2001), 443–545.

Ratner, Steven, *The Thin Justice of International Law* (Oxford: Oxford University Press 2015).

Rawls, John, *The Law of Peoples* (Cambridge MA: Harvard University Press 1999).

Raz, Joseph, *The Morality of Freedom* (Oxford: Clarendon 1988).

Raz, Joseph, Human Rights without Foundations, in: Samantha Besson/ John Tasioulas (eds), *The Philosophy of International Law* (Oxford: Oxford University Press 2011), 321–337.

REDRESS, *Implementing Victims' Rights: A Handbook on Basic Principles and Guidelines on the Right to a Remedy and Reparation* (London: The Redress Trust 2006).

Rehm, Hermann, Untertanen als Subjekte völkerrechtlicher Pflichten, *Zeitschrift für Völkerrecht und Bundesstaatsrecht* 1 (1906), 53–55.

Remec, Peter Pavel, *The Position of the Individual in International Law According to Grotius and Vattel* (The Hague: Martinus Nijhoff 1960).

Reus-Smit, Christian, *Individual Rights and the Making of the International System* (Cambridge: Cambridge University Press 2013).

Reus-Smit, Christian, Struggles for Individual Rights and the Expansion of the International System, *International Organisation* 65 (2011), 207–242.

Richards, Julie-Anne/Boom Keely, *Big Oil, Coal and Gas Producers Paying for Their Climate Damage*, Vol. 39 (Berlin: Heinrich Böll Foundation, Series Ecology 2014).

Riedel, Manfred, Bürger, Staatsbürger, Bürgertum, in: Otto Brunner/ Werner Conze/Reinhart Kosellek (eds), *Geschichtliche Grundbegriffe, Historisches Lexikon zur politisch-sozialen Sprache in Deutschland* (5th ed. Stuttgart: Klett-Cotta 1997).

Ripinsky, Sergey/Williams, Kevin, *Damages in International Investment Law* (London: British Institute of International and Comparative Law 2008).

Riquelme Cortado, Rosa, Central American Court of Justice (1907–18), in: Rüdiger Wolfrum (ed.), *The Max Planck Encyclopedia of Public International Law* (Oxford: Oxford University Press 2012).

Risse, Mathias, A Right to Work? A Right to Leisure? Labor Rights as Human Rights, *Law & Ethics of Human Rights* 3 (2009), 1–39.

Risse, Thomas/Ropp, Stephen C., Introduction and Overview, in: Thomas Risse/ Stephen C. Ropp/Kathryn Sikkink (eds), *The Persistent Power of Human Rights: From Commitment to Compliance* (Cambridge: Cambridge University Press 2013), 3–25.

Risse, Thomas/Sikkink, Kathryn, Conclusions, in: Thomas Risse/Stephen C. Ropp/ Kathryn Sikkink (eds), *The Persistent Power of Human Rights: From Commitment to Compliance* (Cambridge: Cambridge University Press 2013), 275–295.

Rivero, Jean, La protection des droits de l'homme dans les rapports entre personnes privées, in: Institut International des Droits de l'Homme (ed.), *René Cassin Amicorum Disciplorumque Liber* Vol. 3 (Paris: Pedone 1971), 311–322.

Roberts, Anthea, Clash of Paradigms: Actors and Analogies Shaping the Investment Treaty System, *American Journal of International Law* 107 (2013), 45–94.

Roberts, Anthea, Comparative International Law? The Role of National Courts in International Law, *International and Comparative Law Quarterly* 60 (2011), 57–92.

Roberts, Anthea, Power and Persuasion in Investment Treaty Interpretation: The Dual Role of States, *American Journal of International Law* 104 (2010), 179–225.

Roberts, Anthea, State-to-State Investment Treaty Arbitration: A Hybrid Theory of Interdependent Rights and Shared Interpretive Authority, *Harvard International Law Journal* 55 (2014), 1–70.

Ronen, Yael, Option of Nationality, in: Rüdiger Wolfrum (ed.), *The Max Planck Encyclopedia of Public International Law* (Oxford: Oxford University Press 2012).

Roucounas, Emmanuel, Facteurs privés et droit international public, *Recueil des Cours: Collected Courses of The Hague Academy of International Law* 299 (2002), 9–419.

Ruiz Fabri, Hélène, Is there a Case – Legally and Politically – For a Direct Effect of WTO Obligations?, *European Journal of International Law* 25 (2014), 151–173.

Ruiz Fabri, Hélène, Les catégories de sujet du droit international, in: Société française pour le droit international (ed.), *Colloque de Mans: Le sujet en droit international* (Paris: Pedone 2005), 55–71.

Ryan, Christopher M., Discerning the Compliance Calculus: Why States Comply with International Investment Law, *Georgia Journal of International Law* 38 (2009), 63–95.

Safferling, Christoph, Die Rolle des Opfers im Strafverfahren – Paradigmenwechsel im nationalen und internationalen Recht? *Zeitschrift für die gesamte Strafrechtswissenschaft* 122 (2010), 87–116.

Salacuse, Jeswald W., The Emerging Global Regime for Investment, *Harvard International Law Journal* 51 (2010), 427–473.

Salacuse, Jeswald W., *The Law of International Investment Treaties* (Oxford: Oxford University Press 2008).

Sarooshi, Dan, *The United Nations and the Development of Collective Security: The Delegation by the UN Security Council of Its Chapter VII Powers* (Oxford: Oxford University Press 1999).

Sassòli, Marco, Reparation, in: Vincent Chétail (ed.), *Post-Conflict Peacebuilding: A Lexicon* (Oxford: Oxford University Press 2009), 279–290.

Sassòli, Marco, State Responsibility for Violations of International Humanitarian Law, *International Review of the Red Cross* 84 (2002), 401–434.

Sassòli, Marco/Bouvier, Antoine A., *How Does Law Protect in War?* (3rd ed. Geneva: ICRC 2011).

Saurer, Johannes, *Der Einzelne im europäischen Verwaltungsrecht: Die institutionelle Ausdifferenzierung der Verwaltungsorganisation der Europäischen Union in individueller Perspektive* (Tübingen: Mohr Siebeck 2013).

Savigny, Friedrich Carl von, *System des heutigen römischen Rechts*, Vol. 1 (Berlin: Veit und Comp. 1840).

Scelle, Georges, *Droit International Public* (Paris: Les Ed. Domat-Montchrestien 1944).

Scelle, Georges, Le phénomène juridique du dédoublement fonctionnel, in: Walter Schätzel/Hans-Jürgen Schlochauer (eds), *Rechtsfragen der internationalen Organisation: Festschrift für Hans Wehberg zu seinem* 70. Geburtstag (Frankfurt a. M.: Vittorio Klostermann 1956), 324–342.

Scelle, Georges, Précis de droit des gens: Principes et systématique, Vol. I, *Introduction, le milieu intersocial* (Paris: Sirey 1932).

Scelle, Georges, Règles générales du droit de la paix, *Recueil des Cours: Collected Courses of The Hague Academy of International Law* 46 (1933/IV), 327–703.

Scelle, Georges, Some Reflections on Juridical Personality in International Law, in: George A. Lipsky (ed.), *Law and Politics in the World Community* (Berkeley: University of California Press 1953), 49–58.

Schabas, William, *An Introduction to the International Court* (3rd ed. Cambridge: Cambridge University Press 2008).

Schauer, Frederick, A Comment on the Structure of Rights, *Georgia Law Review* 27 (1993), 415–434.

Scheidler, Alfred, Der Schutz deutscher Staatsangehöriger gegenüber der Hoheitsgewalt ausländischer Staaten, *Die öffentliche Verwaltung* 59 (2006), 417–423.

Schermers, Henry G./Blokker, Niels M., *International Institutional Law* (5th ed. Dordrecht: Martinus Nijhoff 2011).

Scheuner, Ulrich, *Die großen Friedensschlüsse als Grundlage der europäischen Staatenordnung zwischen 1648 und 1815*, reprinted in: Scheuner, Schriften zum Völkerrecht (edited by Christian Tomuschat (Berlin: Duncker & Humblot 1984)), 352–354.

Schill, Stephan W., Private Enforcement of International Investment Law: Why We Need Investor Standing in BIT Dispute Settlement, in: Michael Waibel/Asha Kaushal/Kyo-Hwa Liz Chung (eds), *The Backlash Against Investment Arbitration: Perceptions and Reality* (Alphen aan den Rijn: Wolters Kluwer Law & Business 2010), 29–50.

Schill, Stephan W., *The Multilateralization of International Investment Law* (Cambridge: Cambridge University Press 2009).

Schlag, Pierre, The Problem of the Subject, *Texas Law Review* 69 (1991), 1627–1743.

Schmidt-Aßmann, Eberhard, Commentary on Article 19 of the Basic Law, in: Theodor Maunz/Günter Dürig (eds), *Grundgesetzkommentar* (57th ed. Munich: Beck 2010).

Schmidt-Aßmann, Eberhard/Rademacher, Timo, Rechtsschutzgarantien des internationalen Rechts, *Jahrbuch des öffentlichen Rechts der Gegenwart* 61 (2013), 61–88.

Schneewind, Jerome B., *The Invention of Autonomy: A History of Moral Philosophy* (Cambridge: Cambridge University Press 1998).

Schreuer, Christoph, *The ICSID Convention: A Commentary* (2nd ed. Cambridge: Cambridge University Press 2009).

Schröder, Wolfgang M., Natur- und Vernunftrecht, in: Arndt Pollmann/Georg Lohmann (eds), *Menschenrechte: Ein interdisziplinäres Handbuch* (Stuttgart: Metzler 2012), 179–185.

Schücking, Walther, *Der Staatenverband der Haager Konferenzen* (Munich and Leipzig: Duncker & Humblot 1912), 141–148.

Schulev-Steindl, Eva, *Subjektive Rechte: Eine rechtstheoretische und dogmatische Analyse* (Vienna: Springer 2008).

Schultz, Alexander, *Das Verhältnis von Gemeinschaftsgrundrechten und Grundfreiheiten des EGV* (Berlin: Duncker & Humblot 2005).

Schwartmann, Rolf, *Private im Wirtschaftsvölkerrecht* (Tübingen: Mohr Siebeck 2005).

Schwarzenberger, Georg, *A Manual of International Law* (London: Stevens 1947).

Schweisfurth, Theodor, *Völkerrecht* (Tübingen: Mohr Siebeck 2006).

Seelmann, Kurt, Die Denkfigur des "subjektiven Rechts" in der spanischen Spätscholastik, in: Reyes Mate/Friedrich Niewöhner (eds), *Spaniens Beitrag zum politischen Denken in Europa um 1600* (Wiesbaden: Harrassowitz Verlag 1994), 141–151.

Seelmann, Kurt, Paradoxien der Opferorientierung im Strafrecht, *JuristenZeitung* 44 (1989), 670–676.

Seibert-Fohr, Anja, *Prosecuting Serious Human Rights Violations* (Oxford: Oxford University Press 2009).

Seyersted, Finn, *Objective International Personality of Intergovernmental Organizations: Do Their Capacities Really Depend Upon the Conventions Establishing Them?* (Copenhagen: Krohns Boy Trykkeri 1963).

Shestak, Jerome J., The Jurisprudence of Human Rights, in: Theodor Meron (ed.) *Human Rights in International Law: Legal and Policy Issues* (Oxford: Clarendon 1984), 89–113.

Shihata, Ibrahim F. I., *The World Bank Inspection Panel: In Practice* (2nd ed. New York: Oxford University Press 2000).

Shue, Henry, *Basic Rights* (Princeton: Princeton University Press 1980).

Sikkink, Kathryn, *The Justice Cascade: Human Rights Prosecutions and World Politics* (New York: W.W. Norton & Co. 2011).

Simma, Bruno, Der Einfluss der Menschenrechte auf das Völkerrecht: Ein Entwurf, in: Isabelle Buffard/James Crawford/Alain Pellet/Stephan Wittich (eds), *International Law between Universalism and Fragmentation: Festschrift in Honour of Gerhard Hafner* (Leiden and Boston: Martinus Nijhoff 2008), 729–745.

Sivakumaran, Sandesh, Binding Armed Opposition Groups, *International and Comparative Law Quarterly* 55 (2006), 369–394.

Sivakumaran, Sandesh, Arbitrary Withholding of Consent to Humanitarian Assistance in Situations of Disaster, *International and Comparative Law Quarterly* 64 (2015), 501–531.

Skogly, Sigrun I., *The Human Rights Obligations of the World Bank and the International Monetary Fund* (London: Cavendish 2001).

Skordas, Achilles, Article 7, in: Andreas Zimmermann (ed.), *The 1951 Convention Relating to the Status of Refugees and Its 1967 Protocols* (Oxford: Oxford University Press 2011), 715–754.

Sliedregt, Elies van, *Individual Criminal Responsibility in International Law* (Oxford: Oxford University Press 2012).

Sornarajah, Muthucumaraswamy, *The International Law on Foreign Investment* (2nd ed. Cambridge: Cambridge University Press 2007).

Spiermann, Ole, Individual Rights, State Interests and the Power to Waive ICSID Jurisdiction under Bilateral Investment Treaties, *Arbitration International* 20 (2004), 179–211.

Spiropoulos, Jean, L'individu et le droit international, *Recueil des Cours: Collected Courses of The Hague Academy of International Law* 30 (1929/V), 191–270.

Stammler, Philipp, *Der Anspruch von Kriegsopfern auf Schadensersatz* (Berlin: Duncker & Humblot 2009).

Stephanitz, Dieter von, *Exakte Wissenschaft und Recht: Der Einfluß von Naturwissenschaften und Mathematik auf das Rechtsdenken und Rechtswissenschaft in zweieinhalb Jahrtausenden. Ein historischer Grundriß* (Berlin: de Gruyter 1970).

Stephens, Beth, Translating Filartiga: A Comparative and International Law Analysis of Domestic Remedies for International Human Rights Violations, *Yale Journal of International Law* 27 (2002), 1–57.

Stirling-Zanda, Simonetta, Obtaining Judicial Enforcement of Individual Conventional Rights, *Archiv des Völkerrechts* 42 (2004), 184–216.

Stoerk, Felix, Staatsunterthanen und Fremde, in: Franz von Holtzendorff (ed.), *Handbuch des Völkerrechts auf Grundlage Europäischer Staatspraxis, Bd. 2: Die völkerrechtliche Verfassung und Grundordnung der auswärtigen Staatsbeziehungen* (Hamburg: Verlag von J. F. Richter 1887), 583–655.

Storost, Christian, Der Fall Abbasi: Wegbereiter eines gemeineuropäischen Anspruchs auf diplomatischen Schutz?, *Archiv des Völkerrechts* 42 (2004), 411–424.

Strupp, Karl, *Grundzüge des positiven Völkerrechts* (5th ed. Bonn: Röhrscheid 1932).

Subedi, Surya P., *International Investment Law* (3rd ed., Oxford: Hart University Press 2016)

Sunstein, Cass, Rights and Their Critics, *Notre Dame Law Review* 70 (1999), 727–768.

Tamada, Dai, Investor's Responsibility Toward Host-States? Regulation of Corruption in Investor-State Arbitration, in: Noemi Gal-Or/Cedric Ryngaert/ Math Noortmann (eds), *Responsibilities of the Non-State Actor in Armed Conflict and the Market Place* (Leiden: Brill 2015), 203–216.

Tamanaha, Brian Z., Understanding Legal Pluralism: Past to Present, Local to Global, *Sydney Law Review* 30 (2008), 375–411.

Tammes, Arnold Jan Pieter, The Obligation to Provide Local Remedies, in: Maria Nolte/ Gezina van der Molen/ Hermina Johanna, *Volkenrechtelijke Opstellen – Aangeboden aan Professor Dr. Gesina H. J. van der Molen* (Kampen: JH Kok NV 1962), 152–168.

Teichmann, Michael, Article 15, in: Andreas Zimmermann (ed.), *The 1951 Convention Relating to the Status of Refugees and Its 1967 Protocols* (Oxford: Oxford University Press 2011), 909–930.

Teitel, Ruti, *Humanity's Law* (Oxford: Oxford University Press 2011).

Tesón, Fernando, *A Philosophy of International Law* (Boulder CO: Westlake 1998).

Teubner, Gunther, Globale Bukowina: Zur Emergenz eines transnationalen Rechtspluralismus, *Rechtshistorisches Journal* 15 (1996), 255–290.

Thies, Anne, EU Membership of the WTO: International Trade Disputes and Judicial Protection of Individuals by EU Courts, *Global Constitutionalism* 2 (2013), 237–261.

Thies, Anne, The Impact of General Principles of EC Law on Its Liability Regime Towards Retaliation Victims after Fabbrica Italiana Accumulatori Motocarri Montechio Spa (FIAMM) v. Council, *European Law Review* 34 (2009), 889–913.

Tomuschat, Christian, Article 25 GG, in: Wolfgang Kahl/Christian Waldhoff/ Christian Walter (eds), Bonner Kommentar (140th update, June 2009).

Tomuschat, Christian, Die Europäische Union und ihre völkerrechtliche Bindung, *Europäische Grundrechte-Zeitschrift* 34 (2007), 1–12.

Tomuschat, Christian, Grundpflichten des Individuums nach Völkerrecht, *Archiv des Völkerrechts* 21 (1983), 289–315.

Tomuschat, Christian, *Human Rights between Idealism and Realism* (2nd ed. Oxford: Oxford University Press 2008).

Tomuschat, Christian, Individual Reparation Claims in Instances of Grave Human Rights Violations: The Position under General International Law, in: Albrecht Randelzhofer/Christian Tomuschat (eds), *State Responsibility and the Individual: Reparation in Instances of Grave Violations of Human Rights* (The Hague: Martinus Nijhoff 1999), 1–25.

Tomuschat, Christian, International Law: Ensuring the Survival of Mankind on the Eve of a New Century: General Course on Public International Law, Recueil des Cours: Collected Courses of The Hague Academy of International Law 11–438 (1999).

Tomuschat, Christian, The Responsibility of Other Individuals: Private Individuals, in: James Crawford/Alain Pellet/Simone Olleson (eds), *The Law of International Responsibility* (Oxford: Oxford University Press 2010), 317–329.

Tomuschat, Christian, Grundpflichten des Individuums nach Völkerrecht, *Archiv des Völkerrechts* 21 (1983), 289–315.

Toope, Stephen J., *Mixed International Arbitration: Studies in Arbitration between States and Private Persons* (Cambridge: Grotius Publications 1990), 75–90.

Toral, Mehmet/Schultz, Thomas M., The State, a Perpetual Respondent in Investment Arbitration? Some Unorthodox Considerations, in: Michael Waibel/Asha Kaushal/Kyo-Hwa Liz Chung/Claire Balchin (eds),

The Backlash against Investment Arbitration: Perceptions and Reality (Alphen aan den Rijn: Wolters Kluwer Law & Business 2010), 577–602.
Tourme-Jouannet, Emmanuelle, *Le droit international* (Paris: PUF Que sais-je 2013).
Trachtman, Joel P., *The Economic Structure of International Law* (Cambridge MA: Harvard University Press 2008).
Triepel, Heinrich, *Völkerrecht und Landesrecht* (Leipzig: Verlag von C. L. Hirschfeld 1899).
Triffterer, Otto, *Dogmatische Untersuchungen zur Entwicklung des Völkerstrafrechts seit Nürnberg* (Freiburg: Albert 1966).
Tuck, Richard, *Natural Rights Theories: Their Origin and Development* (Cambridge: Cambridge University Press 1979).
Tünde Huber, Katalin/Rodiles, Alejandro, *An Ombudsperson in the United Nations Security Council: A Paradigm Shift? Anuario Mexicano de Derecho Internacional* 10 (2012), 107–142.
Tushnet, Mark, An Essay on Rights, *Texas Law Review* 62 (1984), 1363–1403.
Ullmann, Emanuel, *Völkerrecht* (2nd ed. Tübingen: J. C. B. Mohr (P. Siebeck) 1908).
Ulrich, George, Introduction: Human Rights with a View to History, in: George Ulrich/Louise Krabbe Boserup (eds), *Human Rights in Development Yearbook 2001: Reparations: Redressing Past Wrongs* (Dordrecht: Kluwer 2003), 1–10.
Ulrich, George/Krabbe Boserup, Louise (eds), *Reparations: Redressing Past Wrongs, Human Rights in Development Yearbook 2001* (Dordrecht: Kluwer 2003).
Unger, Moritz von, *Menschenrechte als transnationales Privatrecht* (Berlin: Duncker & Humblot 2008).
Ungern, Antje von, Autonome und funktionale Grundrechtskonzeptionen unter besonderer Berücksichtigung der Rechtsprechung des EGMR, in: Mathias Hong/Nele Matz-Lück (eds), *Grundrechte und Grundfreiheiten im Mehrebenensystem – Konkurrenzen und Interferenzen* (Berlin: Springer 2011), 69–108.
Valticos, Nicolas, International Labour Standards and Human Rights: Approaching the Year 2000, *International Labour Review* 137 (1998), 135–147.
Vattel, Emer de, *Le droit des gens ou Principes de la loi naturelle* (London 1758, Classics of International Law, Carnegie Institution 1916, Vol. I ; engl. transl. of the edition of 1758 by Charles G. Fenwick, The Law of Nations or the Principles of Natural Law Applied to the Conduct and to the Affairs of Nations and of Sovereigns, Classics of International Law, Carnegie Institution 1916, Vol. III).
Vaurs-Chaumette, Anne Laure, *Les sujets du droit international pénal: Vers une nouvelle définition de la personalité juridique internationale?* (Paris: Pedone 2009).
Verdross, Alfred/Simma, Bruno, *Universelles Völkerrecht* (Berlin: Duncker & Humblot 1984).

Verhoeven, Joe, *Droit International Public* (Brussels: Larcier 2000).
Verhoeven, Joe, La notion d'"applicabilité directe" du droit international, *Revue belge de droit international* 15 (1980), 243–264.
Vermeer-Künzli, Anna Maria Helena, *The Protection of Individuals by Means of Diplomatic Protection – Diplomatic Protection as a Human Rights Instrument* (Leiden: PrintPaertners Ipskamp 2007).
Vermeer-Künzli, Annemarieke, As If: The Legal Fiction in Diplomatic Protection, *European Journal of International Law* 18 (2007), 37–68.
Vermeer-Künzli, Annemarieke, Restricting Discretion: Judicial Review of Diplomatic Protection, *Nordic Journal of International Law* 75 (2006), 279–307.
Villey, Michel, *La formation de la pensée juridique moderne: Cours d'histoire de la philosophie du droit* (Paris: Ed. Montchrestien 1975).
Virally, Michel, The Sources of International Law, in: Max Sørensen (ed.), *Manual of Public International Law* (London: Macmillan 1968), 116–174.
Vitoria, Francisco de, *Relectiones Theologicae*, De Indis (Original 1532) (The Classics of International Law, edited by Ernest Nys (Washington: Carnegie Institution 1917)).
Voss, Jan Ole, *The Impact of Investment Treaties on Contracts between Host States and Foreign Investors* (Leiden: Brill Nijhoff 2011).
Wagner, Niklas/Raasch, Holger/Pröpstl, Thomas, *Wiener Übereinkommen über konsularische Beziehungen vom 24. April 1963: Kommentar für die Praxis* (Berlin: Wissenschafts-Verlag 2007).
Wahl, Rainer, Der Einzelne in der Welt jenseits des Staates, in: Rainer Wahl/ Joachim Wieland (eds), *Das Recht des Menschen in der Welt: Kolloquium aus Anlass des 70.* Geburtstags von Ernst-Wolfgang Böckenförde (Berlin: Duncker & Humblot 2002), 59–109.
Waldron, Jeremy, A Rights-Based Critique of Constiutional Rights, *Oxford Journal of Legal Studies* 13 (1993), 18–52.
Waldron, Jeremy, Rights in Conflict, in: Jeremy Waldron (ed.), *Liberal Rights: Collected Papers 1981–1991* (Cambridge: Cambridge University Press 1993), 203–224.
Waldron, Jeremy, The Rule of International Law, *Harvard Journal of Law and Public Policy* 30 (2006), 15–30.
Waldron, Jeremy, When Justice Replaces Affection: The Need for Rights, *Harvard Journal of Law and Public Policy* 11 (1988), 625–647 (629).
Walter, Christian, Subjects of International Law, in: Rüdiger Wolfrum (ed.), *The Max Planck Encyclopedia of Public International Law* (Oxford: Oxford University Press 2012).
Walter, Tonio, Der deutsche Strafprozess und das Völkerrecht, *Juristische Rundschau* 82 (2007), 99–104.
Watson Institute for International Studies/The Graduate Institute Geneva (eds), Due Process and Targeted Sanctions: An Update of the "Watson Report" by Sue Eckert and Thomas J. Biersteker (2012).

Weigend, Thomas, Der Fall LaGrand – Völkerrecht bricht Strafprozeßrecht, in: Cornelius Prittwitz/Michael Baurmann/Klaus Günther (eds), *Festschrift für Klaus Lüderssen* (Baden-Baden: Nomos 2002), 463–479.

Weil, Prosper, Le droit international en quête de son identité: Cours général de droit international public, *Recueil des Cours: Collected Courses of The Hague Academy of International Law* 237 (1992/VI), 9–370.

Weiler, Joseph H. H., The Geology of International Law – Governance, Democracy and Legitimacy, *Zeitschrift für ausländisches öffentliches Recht und Völkerrecht* 64 (2004), 547–562.

Weill, Sharon, *The Role of National Courts in Applying International Humanitarian Law* (Oxford: Oxford University Press 2014).

Weiss, Norbert, *Kompetenzlehre internationaler Organisationen* (Heidelberg: Springer 2009).

Wellens, Karel, Solidarity as a Constitutional Principle: Its Expanding Role and Inherent Limitations, in: Ronald St. MacDonald/Douglas M. Johnston (eds), *Towards World Constitutionalism: Issues in the Legal Ordering of the World Community* (Leiden: Martinus Nijhoff 2005), 775–807.

Wellens, Karel, Revisiting Solidarity as a (Re-)Emerging Constitutional Principle: Some Further Reflections, in: Rüdiger Wolfrum/Chie Kojima (eds), *Solidarity: A Structural Principle of International Law* (Heidelberg: Springer 2009), 3–38.

Werle, Gerhard/Jessberger, Florian, *Principles of International Criminal Law* (3rd ed. Oxford: Oxford University Press 2014).

Westlake, John, Chapter VI: The Principles of International Law, in: Lassa Oppenheim (ed.), *The Collected Papers of John Westlake on Public International Law* (Cambridge: Cambridge University Press 1914), 78–85.

Wiessner, Siegfried/Willard, Andrew, Policy-Oriented Jurisprudence, *German Yearbook of International Law* 44 (2001), 96–112.

Wilde, Ralph, *International Territorial Administration: How Trusteeship and the Civilizing Mission Never Went Away* (Oxford: Oxford University Press 2008).

Wilhelm, René-Jean, Le caractère des droits accordés à l'individu dans les Conventions de Genève, *Revue international de la Croix-Rouge* 32 (1950), 561–590.

Windscheid, Bernhard, *Die Actio des römischen Zivilrechts vom Standpunkte des heutigen Rechts* (Düsseldorf 1857; Neudruck Aalen: Scientia 1969).

Winter, Gerd/Jans, Jan H./Macrory, Richard/Krämer, Ludwig, Weighing up the EC Environmental Liability Directive, *Journal of Environmental Law* 20 (2008), 163–191.

Woedtke, Niclas von, *Die Verantwortlichkeit Deutschlands für seine Streitkräfte im Auslandseinsatz und die sich daraus ergebenen Schadensersatzansprüche von Einzelpersonen als Opfer deutscher Militärhandlungen* (Berlin: Duncker & Humblot 2010).

Wohlfahrt, Christian, Veränderungen des Lissabon-Vertrages im Hinblick auf die Doktrin der unmittelbaren Wirkung, *Zeitschrift für ausländisches öffentliches Recht und Völkerrecht* 70 (2010), 523–545.

Wong, Jarrod, Reconstructing the Responsibility to Protect in the Wake of Cyclones and Separatism, *Tulane Law Review* 84 (2009), 219–263.

Wuerth, Ingrid, The Supreme Court and the Alien Tort Statute: Kiobel v. Royal Dutch Petroleum Co., *American Journal of International Law* 107 (2013), 601–621.

Xue, Hanquin, Chinese Contemporary Perspectives on International Law: History, Culture and International Law, *Recueil des Cours: Collected Courses of The Hague Academy of International Law* 355 (2011), 41–233.

Xue, Hanquin, Comments on Hurrell, in: James Crawford/Sarah Nouwen (eds), *Select Proceedings of the European Society of International Law* 3 (Oxford: Hart 2012), 27–29.

Zegveld, Liesbeth, Remedies for Victims of Violations of International Humanitarian Law, *International Review of the Red Cross* 85 (2003), 497–527.

Zegveld, Liesbeth, *The Accountability of Armed Opposition Groups in International Law* (Cambridge: Cambridge University Press 2002).

Zemanek, Karl, Internationale Organisationen als Handlungseinheiten in der Völkerrechtsgemeinschaft, *Österreichische Zeitschrift für öffentliches Recht* 7 (1956), 335–372.

Zimmermann, Andreas/Dörschner, Jonas, Article 22, in: Andreas Zimmermann (ed.), *The 1951 Convention Relating to the Status of Refugees and Its 1967 Protocols* (Oxford: Oxford University Press 2011), 1019–1042.

Zorn, Albert, *Grundzüge des Völkerrechts* (2nd ed. Leipzig: Verlagsbuchhandlung von J. J. Weber 1903).

INDEX

CAMBRIDGE STUDIES IN INTERNATIONAL AND COMPARATIVE LAW

Books in the series

Beyond Human Rights: The Legal Status of the Individual in International Law Anne Peters

The Doctrine of Odious Debt in International Law: A Restatement Jeff King

Static and Evolutive Treaty Interpretation: A Functional Reconstruction Christian Djeffal

Civil Liability in Europe for Terrorism-Related Risk Lucas Bergkamp, Michael Faure, Monika Hinteregger and Niels Philipsen

Proportionality and Deference in Investor-State Arbitration: Balancing Investment Protection and Regulatory Autonomy Caroline Henckels

International Law and Governance of Natural Resources in Conflict and Post-Conflict Situations Daniëlla Dam-de Jong

Proof of Causation in Tort Law Sandy Steel

The Formation and Identification of Rules of Customary International Law in International Investment Law Patrick Dumberry

Religious Hatred and International Law: The Prohibition of Incitement to Violence or Discrimination Jeroen Temperman

Taking Economic, Social and Cultural Rights Seriously in International Criminal Law Evelyne Schmid

Climate Change Litigation: Regulatory Pathways to Cleaner Energy? Jacqueline Peel and Hari Osofsky

Mestizo International Law: A Global Intellectual History 1842–1933 Arnulf Becker Lorca

Sugar and the Making of International Trade Law Michael Fakhri

Strategically-created Treaty Conflicts and the Politics of International Law Surabhi Ranganathan

Investment Treaty Arbitration as Public International Law: Procedural Aspects and Implications Eric De Brabandere

The New Entrants Problem in International Fisheries Law Andrew Serdy

Substantive Protection under Investment Treaties: A Legal and Economic Analysis Jonathan Bonnitcha

Popular Governance of Post-Conflict Reconstruction: The Role of International Law Matthew Saul

Evolution of International Environmental Regimes: The Case of Climate Change Simone Schiele

Judges, Law and War: The Judicial Development of International Humanitarian Law Shane Darcy

Religious Offence and Human Rights: The Implications of Defamation of Religions Lorenz Langer

Forum Shopping in International Adjudication: The Role of Preliminary Objections Luiz Eduardo Ribeiro Salles

Domestic Politics and International Human Rights Tribunals: The Problem of Compliance Courtney Hillebrecht

International Law and the Arctic Michael Byers

Cooperation in the Law of Transboundary Water Resources Christina Leb

Underwater Cultural Heritage and International Law Sarah Dromgoole

State Responsibility: The General Part James Crawford

The Origins of International Investment Law Kate Miles

The Crime of Aggression under the Rome Statute of the International Criminal Court Carrie McDougall

Crimes against Peace and International Law Kirsten Sellars

The Non-Legal in International Law Fleur Johns

Armed Conflict and Displacement: The Protection of Refugees and Displaced Persons under International Humanitarian Law Mélanie Jacques

Foreign Investment and the Environment in International Law Jorge Viñuales

The Human Rights Treaty Obligations of Peacekeepers Kjetil Larsen

Cyberwarfare and the Laws of War Heather Harrison Dinniss

The Right to Reparation in International Law for Victims of Armed Conflict Christine Evans

Global Public Interest in International Investment Law Andreas Kulick

State Immunity in International Law Xiaodong Yang

Reparations and Victim Support in the International Criminal Court Conor McCarthy

Reducing Genocide to Law: Definition, Meaning, and the Ultimate Crime Payam Akhavan

Decolonizing International Law: Development, Economic Growth and the Politics of Universality Sundhya Pahuja

Complicity and the Law of State Responsibility Helmut Philipp Aust

State Control over Private Military and Security Companies in Armed Conflict Hannah Tonkin

'Fair and Equitable Treatment' in International Investment Law Roland Kläger

The UN and Human Rights: Who Guards the Guardians? Guglielmo Verdirame

Sovereign Defaults before International Courts and Tribunals Michael Waibel

Making the Law of the Sea: A Study in the Development of International Law James Harrison

Science and the Precautionary Principle in International Courts and Tribunals: Expert Evidence, Burden of Proof and Finality Caroline E. Foster

Transition from Illegal Regimes in International Law Yaël Ronen

Access to Asylum: International Refugee Law and the Globalisation of Migration Control Thomas Gammeltoft-Hansen

Trading Fish, Saving Fish: The Interaction between Regimes in International Law Margaret Young

The Individual in the International Legal System: Continuity and Change in International Law Kate Parlett

'Armed Attack' and Article 51 of the UN Charter: Evolutions in Customary Law and Practice Tom Ruys

Theatre of the Rule of Law: Transnational Legal Intervention in Theory and Practice Stephen Humphreys

Science and Risk Regulation in International Law Jacqueline Peel

The Participation of States in International Organisations: The Role of Human Rights and Democracy Alison Duxbury

Legal Personality in International Law Roland Portmann

Vicarious Liability in Tort: A Comparative Perspective Paula Giliker

The Public International Law Theory of Hans Kelsen: Believing in Universal Law Jochen von Bernstorff

Legitimacy and Legality in International Law: An Interactional Account Jutta Brunnée and Stephen J. Toope

The Concept of Non-International Armed Conflict in International Humanitarian Law Anthony Cullen

The Principle of Legality in International and Comparative Criminal Law Kenneth S. Gallant

The Challenge of Child Labour in International Law Franziska Humbert

Shipping Interdiction and the Law of the Sea Douglas Guilfoyle

International Courts and Environmental Protection Tim Stephens

Legal Principles in WTO Disputes Andrew D. Mitchell

War Crimes in Internal Armed Conflicts Eve La Haye

Humanitarian Occupation Gregory H. Fox

The International Law of Environmental Impact Assessment: Process, Substance and Integration Neil Craik

The Law and Practice of International Territorial Administration: Versailles to Iraq and Beyond Carsten Stahn

United Nations Sanctions and the Rule of Law Jeremy Farrall

National Law in WTO Law: Effectiveness and Good Governance in the World Trading System Sharif Bhuiyan

Cultural Products and the World Trade Organization Tania Voon

The Threat of Force in International Law Nikolas Stürchler

Indigenous Rights and United Nations Standards Alexandra Xanthaki

International Refugee Law and Socio-Economic Rights Michelle Foster

The Protection of Cultural Property in Armed Conflict Roger O'Keefe

Interpretation and Revision of International Boundary Decisions Kaiyan Homi Kaikobad

Multinationals and Corporate Social Responsibility: Limitations and Opportunities in International Law Jennifer A. Zerk

Judiciaries within Europe: A Comparative Review John Bell

Law in Times of Crisis: Emergency Powers in Theory and Practice Oren Gross and Fionnuala Ní Aoláin

Vessel-Source Marine Pollution: The Law and Politics of International Regulation Alan Tan

Enforcing Obligations Erga Omnes in International Law Christian J. Tams

Non-Governmental Organisations in International Law Anna-Karin Lindblom

Democracy, Minorities and International Law Steven Wheatley

Prosecuting International Crimes: Selectivity and the International Law Regime Robert Cryer

Compensation for Personal Injury in English, German and Italian Law: A Comparative Outline Basil Markesinis, Michael Coester, Guido Alpa, Augustus Ullstein

Dispute Settlement in the UN Convention on the Law of the Sea Natalie Klein

The International Protection of Internally Displaced Persons Catherine Phuong

Imperialism, Sovereignty and the Making of International Law Antony Anghie

Necessity, Proportionality and the Use of Force by States Judith Gardam

International Legal Argument in the Permanent Court of International Justice: The Rise of the International Judiciary Ole Spiermann

Great Powers and Outlaw States: Unequal Sovereigns in the International Legal Order Gerry Simpson

Local Remedies in International Law, Second Edition C. F. Amerasinghe

Reading Humanitarian Intervention: Human Rights and the Use of Force in International Law Anne Orford

Conflict of Norms in Public International Law: How WTO Law Relates to Other Rules of International Law Joost Pauwelyn

Transboundary Damage in International Law Hanqin Xue

European Criminal Procedures Edited by Mireille Delmas-Marty and John Spencer

The Accountability of Armed Opposition Groups in International Law Liesbeth Zegveld

Sharing Transboundary Resources: International Law and Optimal Resource Use Eyal Benvenisti

International Human Rights and Humanitarian Law René Provost

Remedies Against International Organisations Karel Wellens

Diversity and Self-Determination in International Law Karen Knop

The Law of Internal Armed Conflict Lindsay Moir

International Commercial Arbitration and African States: Practice, Participation and Institutional Development Amazu A. Asouzu

The Enforceability of Promises in European Contract Law James Gordley

International Law in Antiquity David J. Bederman

Money Laundering: A New International Law Enforcement Model Guy Stessens

Good Faith in European Contract Law Reinhard Zimmermann and Simon Whittaker

On Civil Procedure J. A. Jolowicz

Trusts: A Comparative Study Maurizio Lupoi

The Right to Property in Commonwealth Constitutions Tom Allen

International Organizations Before National Courts August Reinisch

The Changing International Law of High Seas Fisheries Francisco Orrego Vicuña

Trade and the Environment: A Comparative Study of EC and US Law Damien Geradin

Unjust Enrichment: A Study of Private Law and Public Values Hanoch Dagan

Religious Liberty and International Law in Europe Malcolm D. Evans

Ethics and Authority in International Law Alfred P. Rubin

Sovereignty Over Natural Resources: Balancing Rights and Duties Nico Schrijver

The Polar Regions and the Development of International Law Donald R. Rothwell

Fragmentation and the International Relations of Micro-States: Self-determination and Statehood Jorri Duursma

Principles of the Institutional Law of International Organizations C. F. Amerasinghe

Lightning Source UK Ltd.
Milton Keynes UK
UKHW02n0433070118
315668UK00009B/128/P

9 781107 164307